READING CRITICALLY, WRITING WELL

A Reader and Guide

FOURTH EDITION

READING CRITICALLY, WRITING WELL

A Reader and Guide

FOURTH EDITION

RISE B. AXELROD

*California State University,
San Bernardino*

CHARLES R. COOPER

*University of California,
San Diego*

ST. MARTIN'S PRESS
NEW YORK

SPONSORING EDITOR: Jimmy Fleming
DEVELOPMENT EDITOR: Kristin Bowen
EDITORIAL ASSISTANT: Griff Hansbury
MANAGER, PUBLISHING SERVICES: Emily Berleth
PUBLISHING SERVICES ASSISTANT: Meryl Perrin
PROJECT MANAGEMENT: Books By Design, Inc.
PRODUCTION SUPERVISOR: Dennis Para
TEXT DESIGN: Books By Design, Inc.
COVER DESIGN: Patricia McFadden
COVER PHOTO: Arnold Katz

Library of Congress Catalog Card Number: 95-67054

Manufactured in the United States of America.

0 9 8 7 6
f e d c b a

FOR INFORMATION, WRITE:
St. Martin's Press, Inc.
175 Fifth Avenue
New York, NY 10010

ISBN: 0-312-11525-3

ACKNOWLEDGMENTS
Acknowledgments and copyrights are continued at the back of the book on pages 503–505, which constitute an extension of the copyright page.

C O N T E N T S

CHAPTER 5

EXPLAINING CONCEPTS *159*

CHAPTER 8

PROPOSAL TO SOLVE A PROBLEM   *313*

PREFACE

Like previous editions, this fourth edition of *Reading Critically, Writing Well* is more than simply a collection of readings for a college writing course; our goal throughout continues to be to teach students practical strategies for critical reading, thereby enabling them to analyze thoughtfully the readings in this text and in their other college courses. We assume that as college students become better critical readers, they will also become more effective writers. To this instruction in reading, we add comprehensive guidance in writing, which helps students to understand and manage the composing process—from invention through planning and drafting to revision.

This book brings critical reading and writing together by teaching students two fundamental ways of reading: *Reading for Meaning* and *Reading like a Writer*. Students first read each selection for meaning. They annotate the text as they read, guided by suggestions that focus their attention on various aspects of the text and encourage them to bring their own knowledge and experience to bear on making meaning. They then use writing to explore and develop their understanding. Students may also extend meaning through conversation with other students. Next, they reread the essay, this time reading like a writer—annotating, analyzing, and writing about one or more of the essay's distinctive rhetorical features and strategies. Here we offer students specific guidance for analyzing the kind of essay they will be writing and criteria for evaluating its effectiveness. Based on these two critical reading strategies, students gain confidence in their ability to write an essay of their own in the same genre. While Reading for Meaning gives students insight into how other readers will understand their writing, Reading like a Writer teaches them how to construct texts rhetorically to influence their readers' understanding and response. The Guide to Writing that concludes each essay genre chapter helps students use what they have learned about reading critically to write well.

We believe that if students have specific strategies for reading and careful guidance with writing, they can study seriously and compose confidently the genres written by academics and professionals. Instead of exercises in the conventional modes of writing, this text offers real-world writing tasks; students read and write the genres they will encounter during college and on the job. They practice the forms of critical analysis, inquiry, and knowledge-making central to research and learning in college. In this way, the text introduces them to writing and learning across the college curriculum.

New to This Edition

This fourth edition of *Reading Critically, Writing Well* remains fundamentally the same book in its assumptions about students' learning and its attention to instruction in both reading and writing strategies. It is, nevertheless, a substantially revised book, as the following summary will suggest:

- Opportunities for small-group collaborative work have been expanded. Carried over from the previous edition is the occasion for practicing a genre orally and informally at the beginning of chapters 2 through 9. For example, in chapter 9 it is titled "Practicing Arguing a Position: A Collaborative Activity." New to this edition are three kinds of activities designed to deepen students' learning. The first, "Extending Meaning through Conversation," follows each reading in chapters 2 through 9. The second, "Learning More about Your Readers," occurs at an appropriate place in the Guide to Writing in chapters 2 through 9. Keeping in mind the writer's intended readers, partners speculate about readers' experience, knowledge, and values and try to suggest readers' likely questions. The third activity, "Reading a Draft Critically," toward the end of chapters 2 through 9, gives students comprehensive guidance in advising each other on improving their drafts.

- Two new activities allow students to reflect on their learning and achievement. One activity follows the readings in chapters 2 through 9 and enables students to review what they have learned about the genre. In chapter 9, for example, it is titled "Thinking about What Makes Position Papers Effective." The second activity concludes the Guide to Writing in chapters 2 through 9 and invites students to reflect on all they have achieved writing an essay. In chapter 9 it is titled "Reflecting on What You Have Learned about Writing Position Papers."

- Appendix 1, A Catalog of Critical Reading Strategies, has been revised and expanded. "Paraphrasing" has been added, and "Evaluating an Argument" has been divided into separate sections on evaluating the logic, emotional manipulation, and credibility of an argument.

- Appendix 2, Strategies for Research and Documentation, gains an extensive new section, "Using the Internet for Research." It offers guidance in searching the WorldWide Web, using special interest groups, and establishing e-mail contact with experts.

• A new design features expanded margins, leaving more room for students' annotations.

Noteworthy Features

Primary focus on fundamental critical reading strategies. The opening chapter of *Reading Critically, Writing Well* introduces the concept of critical reading through the example of a sample essay that has been annotated twice— first to explore its meaning (Reading for Meaning), then to analyze its key rhetorical features (Reading like a Writer)—followed in each instance by a written exploration of the annotations. A second essay in chapter 1 provides an opportunity for students to practice the same kinds of annotating and writing activities on their own.

Organization based on eight important genres. As in previous editions, chapters 2 through 9 focus on reading and writing particular genres: four personal and explanatory genres (autobiography, observation, reflection, and explanation of concepts) and four argumentative genres (evaluation, speculation about causes or effects, proposal to solve a problem, and taking a position on an issue). These eight chapters provide students with comprehensive support for striving toward the goals stated in our title: reading critically and writing well.

Detailed chapter introductions that guide students in reading each type of discourse closely and critically. Chapters 2 through 9 begin by introducing the rhetorical situation in which each genre is most commonly produced and read. To illustrate the importance of annotating in reading critically, a brief annotated excerpt from one of the chapter's reading selections is presented. Students are then guided through their own detailed annotations and written analyses of a brief representative essay. These analyses, based on the primary goals of reading for meaning and reading like a writer outlined in chapter 1, help students focus on particular ideas and issues raised in the essay and on basic rhetorical features and writing strategies, so they can learn to analyze, evaluate, and write the genre under discussion.

In addition to the more detailed guidance in annotation and critical reading are (1) an outline of three or four professional and academic *writing situations,* showing students how each particular genre is central to college writing assignments across the disciplines; and (2) *a collaborative exercise* that invites students to rehearse the assignment situation orally before they begin work in the chapter, with the goal of making the genre seem more understandable and approachable.

Provocative, illustrative readings. Next in chapters 2 through 9, five or six readings (including one written by a student) illustrate the range of writing situations and approaches typical to that kind of discourse, each preceded by headnotes that discuss the author and the context in which the selection was written and followed by ideas for students' own writing. Well over a third of these readings are new to the fourth edition, and our goal has been to choose new readings that—in terms of subject matter, rhetorical structure, and genre—are interesting and provocative and at the same time benefit from close, critical analysis.

Carefully focused apparatus that promotes critical reading. The apparatus following these readings reflects the more focused and streamlined goals of chapter 1: Instead of the usual list of questions, there are two clearly defined critical reading tasks. Under Reading for Meaning, students are invited to reread, annotate, and write at least a page about the selection, using suggestions based on current research into how readers make meaning for themselves from texts: bringing prior knowledge to bear, starting with what one understands best and then proceeding to what one may not yet understand, and responding to specific brief passages. Based on these suggestions, students decide for themselves how to engage the text through rereading, annotating, and writing. Consequently students see more in every essay than is possible after reading it once and answering a few perfunctory questions.

In addition, following at least one selection in chapters 2 through 9, a further critical strategy for reading for meaning is added. Described in detail in Appendix 1, A Catalog of Critical Reading Strategies, each of these offers an additional approach to analyzing a text. Students are introduced to these strategies as each is useful for analyzing a particular reading.

Next, the Reading like a Writer activity following each selection focuses on a single rhetorical feature or writing strategy that is different for each reading in the chapter. By considering a single rhetorical feature at a time, students are able to examine thoroughly how writers construct their texts in particular ways. They see the role convention plays in writing and the many imaginative ways writers may use—and may also resist—convention. As with the Reading for Meaning activity, once students have reread and annotated the selection, they are asked to write about what they have learned.

Comprehensive guide to writing each type of discourse. As in previous editions, chapters 2 through 9 conclude with a brief but comprehensive guide to writing that helps students through each stage of the writing process for that particular genre—from finding a topic to revising to reflecting on what they have learned.

Complete catalog of critical reading strategies. Appendix 1, A Catalog of Critical Reading Strategies, offers a variety of proven reading strategies including annotating, previewing, outlining, summarizing, paraphrasing, questioning to understand and remember, contextualizing, reflecting on challenges to your beliefs and values, exploring the significance of figurative language, looking for patterns of opposition, evaluating the logic of an argument, and comparing and contrasting related readings—along with two new separate strategies: recognizing emotional manipulation, and judging the writer's credibility. An excerpt from "Letter from Birmingham Jail" by Martin Luther King, Jr., is annotated and analyzed according to these strategies, and the full text of the letter concludes the appendix to allow further reading and analysis.

Brief guide to research and documentation. Appendix 2 discusses library and field research. It includes current MLA and APA guidelines for documenting sources.

Thorough instructor's manual. An *Instructor's Manual* outlines various course plans for using this text and offers suggestions for presenting each reading. It includes, as well, discussion of general teaching strategies that became central to our work as we taught previous editions and an annotated bibliography of recent research and theory on learning from text, sources that influenced our choice of critical reading strategies.

Acknowledgments

We first want to thank our students. Students in the Third College Writing Program at the University of California, San Diego, and at California State University, San Bernardino, have been generous and frank with their advice, and some of them contributed essays to this text. Their instructors also have had a major role in shaping the book. A special thanks to Kris Hawkinson for her excellent work on the *Instructor's Manual.*

We owe a debt of gratitude to the many reviewers and questionnaire respondents who made suggestions for the revision. They include Tom Albritton, High Point University; Sara M. Bates, University of Pittsburgh; Kathleen Bell, University of Central Florida; Marvin A. Bell, Kirkwood Community College; Arnold J. Berman, Rochester Institute of Technology; Barbara Bolz, Indiana University; Dianne Bruleigh, Syracuse University; B. Ayne Cantrell, Middle Tennessee State University; Virginia Schaefer Carroll, Kent State University—Stark; Anne L. Craft, Gettysburg College; Tricia L. Davis, Eastern Kentucky University; M. Anne Devane, SUNY Albany; Dallas E. Dillon, Merced College; Thane Doss, York College, CUNY; Carol Dudinetz, Middle Tennessee State University; Ann Forrester, Community College of Philadelphia; Paula Foster, California State University at Northridge; Jacquelyn George, Erie Community College; Theresia Hartz, University of Akron; Linda Lowes Hatchel, McLennan Community College; Clayton Glenn Holloway, Hampton University; Belinda Holman, Eastern Kentucky University; Katharine Ings, Indiana University; Chuck Jordan, Lake Michigan College; Mary Larson, Tulsa Junior College; Sean Lebovsky, Temple University; Deborah Loomis, Sacramento College; Carol A. Lowe, McLennan Community College; Wendy Hall Maloney, Brooklyn College; Joan Marcus, Syracuse University; J. L. McClure, Kirkwood Community College; Renée Ellen Olander, Old Dominion University; Roxanna Pisiak, SUNY Morrisville; Carol Posey, Virginia Wesleyan College; Jeanne Purdy, University of Minnesota, Morris; Steven Rayshick, Westmoreland County Community College; Paul Resnick, Illinois Central College; Susan Roberts, University of Connecticut; Elizabeth Rodacker, Merced College; Stuart Rosenberg, Cypress College; Margo Sampson, Syracuse University; Richard Sax, Madonna University; Walter Schlager, Butte College, Kathy O. Smith, Indiana University; Margaret Smith, University of Texas at El Paso; Mel Stagnaro, California State University, Sacramento; Linda Strahan, University of California, Riverside; Kip Strasma, Illinois Central College; Mary Torgoman, Des Moines Area Community College; Harriett S. Williams, University of South Carolina; and John Zoppi, Union County College.

To the crew at St. Martin's Press, we wish to convey our deepest appreciation. We are indebted to our editor, Jimmy Fleming, for his many contributions. We want to express our gratitude to Kristin Bowen for taking over at the eleventh hour and for giving so generously to our project her time, energy, and intelligence. Sincere thanks go especially to Nancy Benjamin and Emily Berleth for their smooth coordination, to Sandy Schecter for her work on the permissions, and to Griff Hansbury for her thoughtful assistance.

Finally, Charles dedicates this book to his daughter Laura, artist with recent shows in Los Angeles, New York, and Bruges, art teacher, gardener and specialist in gardening history, lively conversationalist, and instigator of a writing course for senior art majors at Pasadena College of Art and Design. Rise wishes to dedicate this book to her husband, Steven, for the loving care with which he so artfully cultivates their garden, and to Jeremiah, who blossoms more wondrously with each new year.

Rise B. Axelrod

Charles R. Cooper

READING CRITICALLY, WRITING WELL

A Reader and Guide

FOURTH EDITION

INTRODUCTION

Reading Critically, Writing Well helps prepare you for the special demands of learning in college, where all your reading should be critical reading—not only to understand what you have read but also to analyze and evaluate it.

When you read a text critically, you alternate between seeking to understand the text on its own terms and questioning the text's ideas and authority. Putting your questions aside even temporarily allows you to be open to new ideas and different points of view. But reading critically requires that eventually you examine every idea—your own as well as those of others—skeptically.

Learning to read critically helps you write well. Because writing in college often involves writing about what you are reading, the quality of your reading directly influences the quality of your writing. You may be called on to write explanations or reasoned arguments based on your reading. These kinds of writing require close critical reading to analyze, synthesize, and evaluate information derived from different sources. College writing also may require you to reflect on your own experience and learning. Critically examining what you know and how you came to know it leads to a deeper understanding of yourself and of the society that has helped shape your thinking. It also helps you recognize and appreciate diverse points of view.

Learning to read critically helps you write well in yet another important way: it enables you to read more like a writer by teaching you to anticipate what readers expect and the questions they will have. For example, if you know that readers expect arguments to acknowledge opposing points of view, you will take into consideration what your readers believe—explaining where you agree and disagree. Similarly, if you expect readers to question your ideas, you will back them up with facts and examples. Being able to anticipate how readers will respond to your writing does not mean, however, that as a writer you always seek to please readers. In fact, good writing often challenges readers. But to challenge readers' assumptions, you need to know what they expect.

You will learn from the activities in this book that reading critically and writing well are intellectually demanding and, therefore, take time and effort. Speed reading may be the best strategy when you need to get the gist of an article or sort through a pile of possible sources. But when you need to understand new ideas or to evaluate complex arguments, when you are reading to prepare for class discussion or to write an essay, then you need to read more slowly and thoughtfully, and probably to reread parts of the text.

The same principles apply to writing. Some kinds of writing can be dashed off in a single draft. The more practiced you are in a given kind of writing, the more efficient your writing process will be. If you write a lab report every week for a term, you should be able to write one rather quickly. If you know how to study for essay exams and have written them often, you should become quite adept. But when you need to do a kind of writing you have not mastered or to write about new and difficult material, then you will need more time to develop and organize your ideas.

Slowing down your reading and writing processes probably sounds like a bad idea to you right now, especially as you begin a new term and have just been told how much reading and writing you will have to do. *Reading Critically, Writing Well* offers practical and efficient ways to meet this challenge. We begin by introducing some basic strategies for reading critically, and then we introduce the guides to writing well.

REFLECTING ON YOUR PAST READING EXPERIENCE. Describe briefly the most difficult reading you have encountered in high school, in college, or at work. Why was it so difficult? How did you go about trying to understand it?

Also describe briefly the most challenging writing assignment you had in high school, in college, or at work. How did you attempt to meet this challenge, and what was the outcome?

Discuss your responses to these questions with two or three other students. Together, what can you conclude about what makes some reading and writing hard? What strategies would you recommend for dealing with difficult reading and writing?

READING CRITICALLY

This section introduces two basic strategies for reading critically: *reading for meaning* and *reading like a writer*. These strategies offer different but complementary ways of looking at a text.

When you read for meaning, you look at a text in terms of its ideas and information to understand and respond critically to what is being said. When you read like a writer, your focus shifts from meaning to rhetoric, from *what* is being communicated to *why* and *how* it is communicated. Although experienced readers sometimes combine these two ways of reading—simultaneously reading for meaning and reading like a writer—we separate them here to give you an opportunity to refine your critical reading skills.

In subsequent chapters, you will be asked to use these two ways of reading critically on a variety of reading selections. Additional strategies such as summarizing, outlining, and evaluating the logic of an argument will be introduced to extend and deepen your repertoire of critical reading skills. Appendix 1 presents a complete catalog of these strategies.

READING FOR MEANING

The first way of reading critically focuses on how you make meaning as you read. We use the expression *make meaning* to emphasize the active, even creative, role that readers play. As a reader, you are not a passive receptacle into which meaning is poured. Nor are you a decoder, deciphering the black marks on a page to discover the text's message. A better analogy for reading is *translating:* As you read, you transfer into your own words what you understand the words on the page to mean. Depending on what you already know and what you consider important, certain aspects of the text come to the foreground. Consequently, the meaning or interpretation you construct as you read is influenced by who you are as an individual—what you know, believe, value. It is also shaped by when and where you live—the historical and cultural contexts that inform your language and sense of identity.

Because reading for meaning depends on close analysis of the text, we recommend a two-step procedure: annotating, followed by writing to explore your understanding and response. Annotating as you read helps concentrate your attention on the text's language and leaves a record of the insights, reactions, and questions that occurred to you in the process of reading. Exploring your ideas by writing about them helps deepen your understanding and sharpen your critical response. You may be able to extend your understanding by adding a third step—conversing with other students who have also read the essay.

Annotating

Annotating can be defined simply as marking the page as you read. You note what you think is important, what you think it means, and what ideas and questions it raises for you. Annotating is easy to do. All it takes is a text you can write on and something to write with. Here are just a few ways to annotate a text:

- Highlight or underline key words and sentences.
- Bracket important passages.

- Connect related ideas with lines.
- Outline the main ideas in the margin.
- Circle words to be defined.
- Write brief comments and questions in the margin.

Some readers mark up the text extensively, while others mark only the parts they consider significant or problematic. What is important is not how you annotate or even how much you annotate, but *that* you annotate. The simple act of marking the page as you read makes it more likely that you will read closely and attentively.

When you read for meaning, your annotations should reflect your efforts to understand what you are reading, as well as your reactions to the text—including questions the reading raises, new ideas it suggests, and reactions you have to it.

There is no right or wrong way to annotate. Each reader has a different style. Following is an illustration of one student's annotations while reading for meaning. Notice, as you read the essay, what this reader marked in the text and wrote in the margin.

Katrina Foley and Sheila Moreland

THE DIRTY SECRET IN FRATERNITY DRINKING SONGS

This essay was written by two UCLA students for a campus publication and later published in the *Los Angeles Times* (March 15, 1992).

A fraternity book of drinking songs that glorifies necrophilia, rape and torture of women is no laughing matter. Consider the statistics. One in six college women will be raped before they earn their degrees. One in 12 college men admit to having committed, or having attempted to commit, rape, according to a National Institute of Mental Health study. Ninety percent of all rapes involve the use of alcohol.

amazing stats

Phi Kappa Psi President Chris Lee claims that his fraternity's "lyrics are a joke [and] are so exaggerated that it is fairly ridiculous to say these songs promote violence against women." But this defies research showing that such materials desensitize men to sexual violence.

make indifferent

To be sure, male bonding and its associated sexual pranks involve gender discrimination. The punch lines of their "dirty jokes" change from generation to generation but their underlying misogynistic message remains constant.

woman hating

fraternities /
sororities

Lee and his supporters refuse to recognize that sexual aggression 4
against women is perpetuated by such institutions as the Greek system. Indeed, victims' descriptions of sexual assault involving fraternity men resemble portrayals of female (degradation) found in such

humiliation

fraternity songs as "Push Her in a Corner."

Compare the lyrics of this Phi Psi song to a letter written to the 5
Daily Bruin by a woman who said she was raped by two UCLA fraternity men. (Lyrics italicized.)

He got
her drunk

The woman wrote that one brother told her that she needed to 6
relax as he kept filling her cup with "tasty pink punch." She soon
became "too sick to walk home alone," so he led her to the "safety"
of his room, where she could rest.

Just push her in a corner, and hold her tight like this. 7

then he
raped her

Mr. Considerate suddenly disappeared. 8
Just put your arms around her waist and on her lips a kiss. 9

Blames
her

He used words to "stun and shock her" into silence, and told her 10
it "was her fault, because she was pretty and he couldn't help himself." After he finished with her, he brought in his friend. Despite

Then his
friend
raped
her

her protests, the second round of rape began.
And if she starts to murmur, or if she starts to cry 11
Just tell her it's the sacred seal, of old Phi Kappa Psi. 12

What is
school's
responsibility?

The university, since it had nothing to do with the fraternity 13
party, refused to take a stand on the woman's case. She could either
press charges against the entire house or "represent her side of the
story to a group of fraternity brothers who would judge the case as
they saw fit." Either way, it would be one woman's story against a
system of brotherhood. No wonder only 1% of male students
accused of rape are prosecuted.

Why not
against
the rapists?

A fundamental mistake in the current approach to rape preven- 14
tion on campus is its emphasis on the potential victim. Sororities
"offer compulsory program nights that explore issues such as rape
and sexual harassment," according to Abbey Nelson, 13-sorority
Panhellenic Council president. Fraternity members, on the other
hand, are required to attend only one hour of rape "awareness"
workshop during their entire college careers. This is absurd.

Could this
be true?

According to researchers at the National Institute of Mental Health,
roughly three in 10 college men would sexually assault a female if
they were guaranteed of getting away with it.

Women students must learn effective self-defense measures, but 15
it is more important to educate men on the differences between
consensual sex and violence against women.

Winston Doby, UCLA's vice chancellor, claims that Phi Psi's 16
misogynistic songbook is protected speech. He is wrong. These

Against
the law?

"songs" constitute "sexual harassment," prohibited under the state
education code, because singing them creates "an intimidating, hostile or offensive . . . educational environment."

*Why
blame the
songs and
not the
singers?*

Rape, date rape and sexual harassment, feared or real, permeates   17
the experience of female college students <u>not because men are evil
and not because women ask for it.</u> <u>Oral traditions</u> created by men
and carried out in male-bonding rituals that deliberately exclude
women do not glorify "sex." They glorify sexism.

Writing

Writing after annotating is a powerful way of developing your understanding
of a reading. You will find that the very act of composing sentences leads you to
clarify and extend your ideas and to discover new insights about the reading.

Following is an illustration of exploratory writing by the student who annotated "The Dirty Secret in Fraternity Drinking Songs." She wrote a little more
than a page (roughly 300 words). Notice how she alternates between interpreting the essay (summarizing and quoting words and phrases) and commenting
(with her own feelings, questions, and ideas). Also notice that the writing does
not follow the annotations in any predictable way. This student uses writing to
go beyond her annotations, not to restate them.

It's clear that Foley and Moreland are angry about what happened   1
on their campus. I am too. They're angry at the rapists, but is it fair
to blame the fraternity songs? The essay basically argues that the
songbook should be banned because the songs are misogynist and
advocate rape. That makes it a censorship issue. Why don't they
focus instead on the university's refusal "to take a stand on the
woman's case" and punish the fraternity men and the fraternity itself
for allowing the rape to occur in their house (paragraph 13)?
Actions are a lot worse than words.

I wonder why they make such a big deal about the songs and say   2
so little about the woman's legal options. I find it strange that her
choices are either to "press charges against the entire house" or
have a group of fraternity brothers as judges (paragraph 13). Am I
missing something here?

I'm also surprised that they criticize dirty jokes (paragraph 3).   3
Dirty jokes seem so trivial compared to rape. And most people tell
or at least listen to dirty jokes. Maybe their point is that we're all
guilty in a way because making fun of others desensitizes everyone
(to use Foley and Moreland's word). We become insensitive to the
feelings of other people and treat them like objects instead of
human beings.

I think that's what they're saying in the last paragraph where they   4
blame the "oral traditions created by men" for glorifying sexism.
The frat songs would be in this tradition. What else? Some heavy
metal and rap songs. Comedians like Andrew Dice Clay. Movies like

Basic Instinct. Does that mean that they should all be censored? Preventing people from saying what they feel won't change their feelings. Are Foley and Moreland saying it could?

READING LIKE A WRITER

Reading like a writer, your focus shifts from interpreting the essay's ideas to analyzing and evaluating how they are presented. Reading like a writer, you study rhetoric—the ways in which writers try to make their ideas understandable and get readers to accept their point of view.

To analyze a text's rhetoric, first you need to identify its basic features and strategies. In analyzing "The Dirty Secret in Fraternity Drinking Songs," for example, you would look for the passages where Foley and Moreland state their position and support it with evidence. To evaluate the rhetoric, you need to gauge how well the text achieves its purpose for its readers. So, in evaluating Foley and Moreland's essay, you would decide which parts of their argument are likely to be most and least convincing to its original readers—other college students like you. Evaluating the rhetoric of the selections in this book will give you insights into the kinds of decisions writers typically make and the wisdom of those choices, insights that will help you make wiser choices in your own writing.

To read rhetorically, you need to think about writing in terms of its purpose, which is how we commonly classify types or genres of writing. For example, writing that aims primarily to tell about the writer's life and experience is called *autobiography.* Writing that tries to convince readers that something has or does not have value is an *evaluation.* Writing that tries to convince readers that the writer's opinion on a controversial issue ought to be adopted or at least taken seriously is called a *position paper.* "The Dirty Secret in Fraternity Drinking Songs" is a position paper.

When you read like a writer, you follow the same simple procedure as you do for reading for meaning: annotating, followed by writing.

Annotating

As we have suggested, the annotations you make as you read like a writer focus on the textual features and rhetorical strategies typical of the genre you are reading. Your aim is to use annotating as a way to begin analyzing the features and strategies in the particular text and also to begin evaluating how well they work.

Following is our sample essay, "The Dirty Secret in Fraternity Drinking Songs," reprinted with the original annotations for reading for meaning (written in the left-hand margin). In this version, a new set of annotations for reading like a writer appear in the right-hand margin. (We separate the two types of annotations here for purposes of illustration. Your own annotations may be mixed together.)

As you examine the annotations for reading like a writer in the right-hand margin, notice that the student labeled the basic features you would expect to find in any position paper: the issue, the writers' position (the essay's thesis), and the supporting argument, including counterargument of opposing positions. You will also find evaluative comments and questions.

A fraternity book of drinking songs that glorifies necrophilia, rape and torture of women is no laughing matter. Consider the statistics. One in six college women will be raped before they earn their degrees. One in 12 college men admit to having committed, or having attempted to commit, rape, according to a National Institute of Mental Health study. Ninety percent of all rapes involve the use of alcohol.

amazing stats

1 *Evidence links rape and drinking. Link to drinking songs?*

Phi Kappa Psi President Chris Lee claims that his fraternity's "lyrics are a joke [and] are so exaggerated that it is fairly ridiculous to say these songs promote violence against women." But this defies research showing that such materials (desensitize) men to sexual violence.

make indifferent

2 *Opposing position*

Counter-argument

To be sure, male bonding and its associated sexual pranks involve gender discrimination. The punch lines of their "dirty jokes" change from generation to generation but their underlying (misogynistic) message remains constant.

woman hating

3

Lee and his supporters refuse to recognize that sexual aggression against women is perpetuated by such institutions as the Greek system. Indeed, victims' descriptions of sexual assault involving fraternity men resemble portrayals of female (degradation) found in such fraternity songs as "Push Her in a Corner."

fraternities/ sororities

humiliation

4

Compare the lyrics of this Phi Psi song to a letter written to the *Daily Bruin* by a woman who said she was raped by two UCLA fraternity men. (Lyrics italicized.)

5 *Effective strategy— alternating song lyrics with a rape victim's account of the rape*

The woman wrote that one brother told her that she needed to relax as he kept filling her cup with "tasty pink punch." She soon became "too sick to walk home alone," so he led her to the "safety" of his room, where she could rest.

He got her drunk

6

Just push her in a corner, and hold her tight like this.

then he raped her

7

Mr. Considerate suddenly disappeared.

8

Just put your arms around her waist and on her lips a kiss.

9

He used words to "stun and shock her" into silence, and told her it "was her fault, because she was pretty and he couldn't help himself." After he finished with her, he brought in his friend. Despite her protests, the second round of rape began.

Blames her

Then his friend raped her

10

And if she starts to murmur, or if she starts to cry

11

Just tell her it's the sacred seal, of old Phi Kappa Psi.

12

The university, since it had nothing to do with the fraternity party, refused to take a stand on the woman's case. She could either press charges against the entire house or "represent her side of the story to a group of fraternity brothers who would judge the case as

What is school's responsibility?

Why not against the rapists?

13

they saw fit." Either way, it would be one woman's story against a system of brotherhood. No wonder only <u>1%</u> of male students accused of rape are prosecuted.

Statistic

14 *Secondary issue*

A <u>fundamental mistake</u> in the current <u>approach to rape preven-</u><u>tion on campus</u> is its emphasis on the potential victim. Sororities "offer compulsory program nights that explore issues such as rape and sexual harassment," according to Abbey Nelson, 13-sorority Panhellenic Council president. Fraternity members, on the other hand, are required to attend <u>only one hour of rape "awareness" workshop</u> during their entire college careers. This is absurd. According to researchers at the National Institute of Mental Health, roughly <u>three in 10</u> college men would sexually assault a female if they were guaranteed of getting away with it.

Could this be true?

Statistic

Women students must learn effective self-defense measures, but it is more <u>important to educate men</u> on the differences between consensual sex and violence against women.

15 *Main issue— clear position*

Against the law?

Winston Doby, <u>UCLA's</u> vice chancellor, claims that Phi Psi's <u>misogynistic songbook is protected speech.</u> <u>He is wrong.</u> These "songs" constitute "sexual harassment," prohibited under the <u>state</u> <u>education code,</u> because singing them creates "an intimidating, hostile or offensive . . . educational environment."

16 *Best reason to ban songbook But would it change any- thing?*

Why blame the songs and not the singers?

Rape, date rape and sexual harassment, feared or real, permeates the experience of female college students <u>not because men are evil</u> <u>and not because women ask for it.</u> <u>Oral traditions</u> created by men and carried out in male-bonding rituals that deliberately exclude women do not glorify "sex." They glorify sexism.

17

Writing

Identifying the textual features is just the first step in reading like a writer. You must also think about them in terms of how well they achieve the writer's purpose, which in the position paper is to convince readers to accept the writer's position or, at least, to take the argument seriously. Writing even a few sentences can help you develop your analysis and evaluation of an essay writer's strategies.

Here is a part of what the student wrote after annotating the rhetorical features and strategies of "The Dirty Secret in Fraternity Drinking Songs." Notice that she does not simply restate her annotations but tries to extend her thoughts as she writes.

Defining the Issue

Foley and Moreland apparently assume their readers already know something about the issue. I say this because they don't begin by filling in readers on what happened. Eventually, they do give some background information about the woman's charge of rape and the

1

university's refusal to support her. Since this essay originally followed newspaper reports, the authors' assumptions may be appropriate for their intended readers. But reading the essay in this book,
I wasn't certain what they're writing about.

It didn't become clear until halfway through the essay that Foley   2
and Moreland are taking issue not only with the fraternity for its
songbook but also with the university for not doing anything about
it. By calling the songbooks "protected speech," the university vice
chancellor defines the issue in terms of censorship. But, for the
authors, the issue centers on the right of women to be safe from
harassment and rape, and the university's responsibility to provide a
safe environment.

Asserting a Position

Foley and Moreland are clear on where they stand on the issue—   3
in opposition both to the fraternity and the university. The opening
sentence states their position on the drinking songs. In paragraph 4,
they blame fraternities, in general, for humiliating women and
encouraging violence toward them. Then, in paragraphs 14-16, they
claim the university was "wrong" in refusing to support the woman's
case against the fraternity. Finally, they blame the university for not
even trying to educate male students about violence towards
women.

Arguing Directly for the Position

It's easy to find where Foley and Moreland cite evidence like   4
statistics, song lyrics, and the girl's testimony of being raped. But I'm
not sure how to separate their reasons from their position. I guess
the reason they blame the fraternity is explained in paragraph 4
where they basically say that fraternity traditions like drinking songs
perpetuate sexual aggression against women. To prove this statement is true, they tell what happened to the girl who was raped at
the frat house, showing that the guys did what the song told them to
do. I thought it was really effective and dramatic. It got me angry. I
could see clearly the connection between the rape and the song.

The other thing they have to prove is that the university shares   5
the blame. They do this with statistics showing how ineffective the
one-hour rape awareness workshop is in changing college men's
attitudes and stopping rape. I also like the way they use the state
education code to argue against the vice chancellor's censorship
excuse.

PRACTICE IN READING CRITICALLY

Following is a second position paper for you to practice reading critically.
Read first for meaning—to understand the essay as fully as you can. As you

read, annotate anything that helps you interpret its meaning: key words you need to define, important ideas, your own comments and questions, whatever strikes you as important or intriguing. Later, we will help you practice reading this essay like a writer.

Robert C. Noble

THERE IS NO SAFE SEX

Robert C. Noble, a doctor and professor of medicine, wrote this essay for *Newsweek* (April 1991).

The other night on the evening news, there was a piece about condoms. Someone wanted to provide free condoms to high-school students. A perky, fresh-faced teenage girl interviewed said everyone her age was having sex, so what was the big deal about giving out condoms? Her principal replied that giving out condoms set a bad example. Then two experts commented. One was a lady who sat very straight in her chair, white hair in a tight perm, and, in a prudish voice, declared that condoms didn't work very well; teenagers shouldn't be having sex anyway. The other expert, a young, attractive woman, said that since teenagers were sexually active, they shouldn't be denied the protection that condoms afforded. I found myself agreeing with the prude.

What do I know about all this? I'm an infectious-diseases physician and an AIDS doctor to the poor. Passing out condoms to teenagers is like issuing them squirt guns for a four-alarm blaze. Condoms just don't hack it. We should stop kidding ourselves.

I'm taking care of a 21-year-old boy with AIDS. He could have been the model for Donatello's David, androgynous, deep blue eyes, long blond hair, as sweet and gentle as he can be. His mom's in shock. He called her the other day and gave her two messages. I'm gay. I've got AIDS. His lover looks like a fellow you'd see in Sunday school; he works in a bank. He's had sex with only one person, my patient (*his* second partner), and they've been together for more than a year. These fellows aren't dummies. They read newspapers. You think condoms would have saved them?

Smart people don't wear condoms. I read a study about the sexual habits of college women. In 1975, 12 percent of college women used condoms when they had sexual intercourse. In 1989, the percentage had risen to only 41 percent. Why don't college women and their partners use condoms? They know about herpes. They know about genital warts and cervical cancer. All the public-health messages of the past 15 years have been sent, and only 41 percent of the college women use condoms. Maybe your brain has to be working to use one. In the heat of passion, the brain shuts down. You have to use a condom every time. *Every time.* That's hard to do.

I can't say I'm comforted reading a government pamphlet called [5] "Condoms and Sexually Transmitted Diseases, Especially AIDS." "Condoms are not 100 percent safe," it says, "but if used properly will reduce the risk of sexually transmitted diseases, including AIDS." *Reduce* the risk of a disease that is 100 percent fatal! That's all that's available between us and death? How much do condoms reduce the risk? They don't say. So much for Safe Sex. Safe Sex was a dumb idea anyway. I've noticed that the catchword now is "Safer Sex." So much for truth in advertising. Other nuggets of advice: "If you know your partner is infected, the best rule is to avoid intercourse (including oral sex). If you do decide to have sex with an infected partner, you should *always* be sure a condom is used from start to finish, every time." Seems reasonable, but is it really helpful? Most folks don't know when their partner is infected. It's not as if their nose is purple. Lots of men and women with herpes and wart-virus infections are having sex right now lying their heads off to their sexual partners—that is, to those who ask. At our place we are taking care of a guy with AIDS who is back visiting the bars and having sex. "Well, did your partner use a condom?" I ask. "Did you tell him that you're infected with the virus?" "Oh, no, Dr. Noble," he replies, "it would have broken the mood." You bet it would have broken the mood. It's not only the mood that gets broken. "Condoms may be more likely to break during anal intercourse than during other types of sex. . . ." Condoms also break in heterosexual sex; one study shows a 4 percent breakage rate. "Government testing can *not* guarantee that condoms will always prevent the spread of sexually transmitted diseases." That's what the pamphlet says. Condoms are all we've got.

Nobody these days lobbies for abstinence, virginity or single life- [6] time sexual partners. That would be boring. *Abstinence and sexual intercourse with one mutually faithful uninfected partner are the only totally effective prevention strategies.* That's from another recently published government report. . . .

What am I going to tell my daughters? I'm going to tell them that [7] condoms give a false sense of security and that having sex is danger-ous. *Reducing* the risk is not the same as *eliminating* the risk. My message will fly in the face of all other media messages they receive. In the movie "The Tall Guy," a nurse goes to bed with the "Guy" character on their first date, boasting that she likes to get the sex thing out of the way at the beginning of the relationship. His roommate is a nymphomaniac who is always in bed with one or more men. This was supposed to be cute. "Pretty Woman" says you can find happi-ness with a prostitute. Who are the people that write this stuff? Have the '80s passed and everyone forgotten sexually transmitted diseases? Syphilis is on the rise. Gonorrhea is harder to treat and increasing among black teenagers and adults. Ectopic pregnancies and infertility from sexually transmitted diseases are mounting every year. Giving condoms to high-school kids isn't going to reverse all this.

    That prim little old lady on TV had it right. Unmarried people 8 shouldn't be having sex. Few people have the courage to say this publicly. In the context of our culture, they sound like cranks. Doctors can't fix most of the things you can catch out there. There's no cure for AIDS. There's no cure for herpes or genital warts. Gonorrhea and chlamydial infection can ruin your chances of ever getting pregnant and can harm your baby if you do. That afternoon in the motel may leave you with an infection that you'll have to explain to your spouse. Your doctor can't cover up for you. Your spouse's lawyer may sue him if he tries. There is no safe sex. Condoms aren't going to make a dent in the sexual epidemics that we are facing. If the condom breaks, you may die.

READING FOR MEANING

    Write at least a page about the meanings you find in "There Is No Safe Sex." Begin by stating Noble's position in your own words. Then discuss anything you think is important and interesting about his essay. Do not feel compelled to account for everything you annotated.

    If you need help to keep writing for at least a page, consider the following suggestions:

- Speculate about what is most important to Noble. What are his priorities? His values? How do you know?

- Relate your own position to Noble's. What concerns and values do you share? How are your interests or priorities different?

- Compare or contrast what Noble says with what others you have read say on the same subject.

- Explain the possible meaning or significance of "I found myself agreeing with the prude" (paragraph 1), "His lover looks like a fellow you'd see in Sunday school" (paragraph 3), "boasting that she likes to get the sex thing out of the way at the beginning of the relationship" (paragraph 7), or any other statement that catches your attention.

EXTENDING MEANING THROUGH CONVERSATION. It is important for you to make meaning on your own, but you may be able to extend your understanding of Noble's essay by conversing with other students. Get together with one or two classmates. Begin the conversation by pointing to one idea in the reading that interests, confuses, or challenges each of you.

    As you talk about the reading, you may find that you have somewhat different understandings of it. Your purpose is to develop the meaning you see and also to gain insight from other readers' perspectives on the essay. Your goal as a group is not necessarily to reach a consensus, but to help each other think critically about the reading. Keep your conversation focused on the essay by rereading and discussing parts of it together.

READING LIKE A WRITER

You have read "There Is No Safe Sex" to consider its meaning, and now you are ready to take the next step and look at the essay like a writer preparing to write an essay arguing a position of your own.

Reread the essay, using the following activities to help you identify, analyze, and evaluate the essay's basic features and argumentative strategies. First, you will annotate the text, labeling specific features—the issue, the writer's position, the supporting argument—along with any thoughts you have about their effectiveness. Then, you will write several sentences about each of the features, presenting what you have learned about the essay.

This partial list of the basic features of the position paper is intended to give you a taste of what reading like a writer involves. You will learn more about the position paper in Chapter 9.

Defining the Issue

Writers of position papers always devote some space to defining the controversial issue. They define it to inform readers, but also to set the stage for their argument. They try to impress on readers the importance of the issue by indicating what is at stake and for whom. Often, the terms writers use to define the issue sharply contrast the difference between how they see the issue and how people with opposing viewpoints see it. Foley and Moreland, for example, define the issue in terms of the university's responsibility to protect women and educate men on how to treat women in contrast to the university's view that the issue centers on the fraternity brothers' right to free speech.

ANALYZE. Reread Noble's essay and mark any passages where the issue is being defined. Note any information about why the issue is important, what is at stake, and for whom. Pay special attention to the terms used to classify the issue. What kind of issue is it for Noble? What kind of issue does he suggest it is for others with whom he disagrees?

WRITE. Write a few sentences reporting what you've discovered about the way Noble defines the issue. You also might comment briefly on how well his definition of the issue sets the stage for his argument.

Asserting a Position

Writers of position papers try to make clear to readers exactly where they stand on the issue, often asserting their position explicitly in a thesis statement.

Whether the position is stated explicitly or implied, what is important is that it comes across to readers as clear and consistent, and not as vague or waffling. The student who wrote about the Foley and Moreland essay, for example, had no trouble understanding the authors' position even though she could not find a single thesis statement that sums up the authors' two main points—that fraternities perpetuate violence against women and that the university should do something about it.

ANALYZE. Reread Noble's essay again to annotate the first place where Noble states his thesis explicitly. Then note any other places where he restates or implies his position. If you find any place in the essay where his position seems unclear or contradictory, mark it also.

WRITE. Write a few sentences identifying where the thesis is first stated or stated most clearly and emphatically. Point to any ambiguity or lack of clarity.

Arguing Directly for the Position

Writers of position papers know that if they want to convince readers to accept their position, they have to do more than merely assert it. They have to argue for it by giving reasons and evidence that clearly support the position. Foley and Moreland, for example, support their argument with several kinds of evidence, including facts, statistics, witness testimony, and quotations from sources like the fraternity songbook and the state education code. An argument's effectiveness depends on whether readers accept the evidence and also on whether the reasons and evidence lead them to accept the writer's position.

ANALYZE. Reread Noble's argument and mark the reasons and evidence he gives to support his position. Consider whether you can accept the evidence— perhaps because you know it to be correct or you respect its source. Then consider the larger question of whether the reasons and evidence lead you to accept the writer's position.

WRITE. Write a few sentences describing and assessing the argument. Specifically, what are the reasons and evidence? How well do you think they support the writer's position?

WRITING WELL

The writing you have done so far has all been brief writing about your reading—either writing about a text's meaning or its rhetorical features and strategies. This section introduces you to the essay-length writing you will be doing when you undertake the major assignments in *Reading Critically, Writing Well*. As you might have guessed, the briefer writings about the readings in each chapter prepare you for the essay writing.

Before previewing the essay assignments, pause to reflect on your own writing experience in high school, college, or on the job.

REFLECTING ON YOUR PAST WRITING EXPERIENCE. Think of the last time you wrote something fairly difficult, long, or complicated. Do not choose something written in class or under strict time limits. Describe the process you followed as fully as you can, beginning with several sentences explaining your purpose for writing and what assumptions you made about your readers' knowledge of the subject or their expectations about your writing.

Use the following questions to help you remember what you did, but do not feel you have to answer them all. Also, do not restrict yourself to these questions. Say whatever you want about how you went about writing the paper.

- How long did it take before you started putting your ideas on paper?
- What kind of plan did you have? How did your plan evolve as you worked?
- What did you change as you were writing? What changes, if any, did you make after completing your first draft?
- Did you discuss your ideas and plans or have someone read what you were writing?

THE WRITING ASSIGNMENTS

As you work through the assignments in this book, you will learn how to write the following kinds of essays:

Autobiography: writing about yourself or others who have been important in your life

Observation: writing about firsthand observations you make of places and activities

Reflection: exploring larger social implications in your personal experiences and observations

Explaining concepts: presenting established information about concepts—the ideas and principles that are fundamental to knowledge in academic disciplines and other human endeavors

Evaluation: justifying your judgment of a movie, book, performance, essay, noteworthy person, or other subject

Speculation about causes or effects: arguing for the plausibility of certain causes or effects to explain some event, trend, or phenomenon

Proposal to solve a problem: arguing for the feasibility of your proposed solution to a problem of concern in a group to which you belong

Position paper: arguing for the reasonableness of your position on a controversial issue

Each of these assignments identifies a kind or genre of writing done every day by countless writers. More than mere school writing exercises, they are real-world writing situations like those you will encounter in college and at work. Pause now to learn a bit more about these assignments.

PREVIEWING THE WRITING ASSIGNMENTS. Look at the kinds of writing, besides writing about reading, that are represented in this book. On the second or third page of each assignment chapter (chapters 2 through 9) is a set of brief Writing Situations. Read the situations in each chapter to get a quick sense of the genre. Then write several sentences responding to the following questions:

- Which of these kinds of essays have you already written?
- With which of these genres have you had the most experience? Where and when did you write this genre? What was most challenging about writing it?
- What other genre would you like to learn to write? Why does it interest you?

THE GUIDES TO WRITING

Following the readings in each assignment chapter is a Guide to Writing that will help you complete the assignment. These guides reflect the fact that writing is a special process, a process of discovery—one that makes discovery possible. As writers, we rarely if ever begin with a complete understanding of our subjects. We put together some information and ideas, start writing, and let the writing lead us to understanding. While writing helps us achieve greater understanding, it also raises questions and unexpected complexities, which, in turn, can lead to more writing and, nearly always, lead to further ideas and insights.

Experienced writers have learned to trust this fascinating discovery process because they know that writing is an unsurpassed thinking tool. Writing helps you discover, explore, develop, and refine your ideas in a way that cannot compare with "doing it in your head." Because writing leaves a record of your thinking, it reduces the burden of remembering and allows you to direct all your energy toward solving the immediate problem. By reading over what you have written, you can figure out where you became derailed or recall points that you forgot were important or see new possibilities you did not notice before.

In chapters 2 through 9, the Guide to Writing for each assignment leads and encourages you through the complex, creative process of discovery. Because writers usually approach the first draft of an essay with some notes and other brief writings in hand, the first brief writing activities you will do are called *invention,* a term used since classical Greek times to describe speakers' and writers' necessary attempts to discover what they know and might say about a subject. Because drafting can be more efficient and productive if you set goals to clarify your purpose and if you make even a tentative plan, the Guide to Writing offers you help with goal setting and planning. Because nearly any draft can be improved by advice from thoughtful readers, there are reminders to help you and your classmates read each other's drafts with a critical eye. And because revising gives you the opportunity to develop your ideas and to make your writing communicate clearly and effectively, each Guide to Writing includes suggestions for improving your draft.

Before reading about the resources offered to support your invention, drafting, critical reading, and revising, take this preview to a Guide to Writing.

PREVIEWING A GUIDE TO WRITING. Because you have been learning about strategies for reading critically essays that argue a position, turn to chapter 9, Position Paper. Following the readings, find the section (pp. 406–413) headed A Guide to Writing Position Papers and skim it, noticing the headings for each section and reading the first paragraph in each section to get an idea of what it offers.

Invention

Invention begins with finding a subject to write about. The Considering Ideas for Your Own Writing sections following each reading together with the suggestions in the Guide to Writing will help you list several possible subjects. This act of listing possibilities is itself inventive because one item suggests the next, and as the list grows you come to understand your options better and can therefore more confidently choose a subject. In each chapter, you will find suggestions that will help you make a good choice and understand the implications of developing the subject you choose. In chapter 9, Position Paper, for example, this initial invention activity is called Choosing an Arguable Issue. Following are the other invention activities in that chapter:

Analyzing Your Readers: identifying your readers and writing several sentences to explore their views and to search for common ground

Learning More about Your Readers: collaborating with two or three other students to learn what they think about the issue

Tentatively Stating Your Thesis: writing to figure out where you stand on the issue

Exploring Your Reasons: listing reasons you hold your position and considering readers' likely objections to them

Restating Your Thesis: drafting one or two sentences stating the position you will argue

Because each writing situation makes unique demands on writers, the invention activities in other chapters are different from these; you will discover these fundamental differences as you move from one assignment to the next. Pause here to look briefly at Invention in chapter 2, Autobiography (pages 61–63), and chapter 5, Explaining Concepts (pages 204–208), to see how the invention activities differ from one genre to the next.

The immediate advantage of this genre-specific invention is that it jump-starts your thinking process, getting you writing days before you begin drafting your essay. Although you will need no more than two hours to complete these invention activities, it is best to spread them over several days. As soon as you start writing the first few sentences about an issue, your mind goes to work on it, perhaps even offering ideas and insights when you are not consciously thinking about the issue. As you complete more invention writing, ideas will begin cascading. Your understanding of the issue will deepen and the possibilities for arguing your position will become more wide-ranging and subtle. An assignment that may have seemed daunting will become intellectually invigorating, and you will have pages of invention notes with which to launch your draft.

Drafting

After working on invention, you may be ready and eager to begin drafting your essay. If, however, you are having difficulty making the transition from jotting down invention notes to writing a first draft, the Guide to Writing in each chapter will show you how to construct achievable goals and devise a workable plan that will ease the process of drafting.

The Guide begins by recentering you in the genre you are writing and in your purpose for writing. You review the readings in the chapter to recall how they accomplished goals like the ones you have in mind. These goals give you direction as next you are invited to mine your invention writing for the purpose of creating a tentative plan for your draft. With suggestions reminding you of the various ways other writers organized their essays, you are encouraged to make a scratch outline designed for your particular goals and readers. Finally, the Guide to Writing helps you find a way to begin your essay—giving you a running start on writing a first draft, without further indecision or procrastination.

Reading a Draft Critically

Few writing situations require writers to produce and hand over writing so quickly that they do not have time to revise. Even newspaper writers, who usually must write for publication every day, find time to revise their writing. A reporter, for example, working from interview and research notes, may draft a brief story quickly but will then spend a few minutes looking it over, moving a phrase or clause, reducing unnecessary repetition, inserting additional information, even changing the order of paragraphs. Then a supervising editor reads the revision and may request further clarifications and additions. Finally, a copy editor checks the style, usage, and grammar. From the time the reporter sits down at the computer until the finished piece is ready to be formatted and printed, only an hour or two may pass. Yet the piece has gone through a full, intense process of invention, drafting, revision, and editing. An editorial writer—another kind of newspaper writer—takes a draft of an editorial to a daily meeting with other editorial writers who all read it and discuss ways it might be made more convincing. The writer makes revisions and electronically sends the revision to the editorial page editor, who suggests or even makes further revisions.

Fortunately, you and other writers at work every day—students, researchers, attorneys, engineers, academics, managers, screenwriters—do not face the necessary daily constraints and time pressures of newspaper writers. In this course, you will usually work for two or three weeks on an essay assignment. Other writers may work for months or years on a novel, biography, history, program evaluation, project proposal, or research report. What all writers gain as the days and weeks pass is time for the mind to work.

A mind can be stimulated to work in three principal ways: by the act of writing itself; by exchanging ideas with others; and by getting critical readings of drafts from readers who understand your project and genre. In a course using *Reading Critically, Writing Well,* invention and class discussion of the readings provide the first two kinds of stimulation, and the guides to Reading a Draft Critically provide the third.

Reading a Draft Critically enables you to give a classmate's draft an informed, comprehensive, collaborative reading. You become an ally of your classmate in that you seek responsibly to help him or her improve the draft and, presumably, this classmate or some other will return the favor. Your critical reading can be supportive and helpful because you will be giving the kind of advice writers in your situation most need—not which words are misspelled or where commas are missing but, in the case of revising a position paper, how to clarify your position, strengthen your argument, anticipate objections, tighten the logic, and so on. These are the essentials for arguing convincingly for a position on an issue. These basics require your classmate's attention and will give you a start in planning and carrying through a substantive revision of the draft.

Reading a Draft Critically invites you to make practical use of all you have learned about reading a genre. It invites you to deploy your newly acquired expertise, to take pride in demonstrating your achievement, even to show off a bit—while doing a classmate a big favor. Part of the favor you provide is the written record of your critical reading that you hand over to your classmate, a record the classmate can refer to the next day or next week when revising the essay. You do yourself a favor as well. Like your classmate, you too will be revising an essay in the same genre. As you read your classmate's essay critically, you will be reflecting intensely on your own just-completed draft. The more thoughtful and comprehensive your critical reading, the more likely you will be to discover ways to strengthen your own draft.

Revising

Revising requires the same patience and commitment as drafting or giving a critical reading. You need the right place, you need energy and alertness, and you need time. And, if you have composed on a computer, you will be glad you have done so.

The great opportunity revising offers is the chance to rethink what you have written given your purpose and your readers' expectations. Assume you will want to make bold changes and add substantial amounts of new material. Be prepared to cut sentences, move sentences, reorder paragraphs. You provide the brainpower, and the computer provides the technology to make reckless changes at least physically easy. The section on revising offers a range of suggestions for you to consider, along with advice you received from classmates and your instructor.

REFLECTING ON WHAT YOU HAVE LEARNED

You will find in each of the assignment chapters that you are learning a great deal about reading and writing a genre. Because this text includes so many occasions for you to demonstrate to yourself and others through writing that you are indeed learning—as you annotate and write about the meanings and rhetorical strategies you see in the reading selections; invent, draft, and revise essays; give critical readings of classmates' drafts—you will have accumulating evidence and, finally, an impressively large record of learning. We know from research on learning, however, that if learning is not reviewed, reflected on, and consolidated, it fades sooner and is therefore not available when occasions arise for using or applying or connecting it with new learning. Therefore, in each assignment chapter, we provide two occasions for you to pause and reflect on what you have learned.

Thinking about What Makes Essays Effective

The first occasion for reflecting on your learning comes at the end of the readings in each chapter. For example, in chapter 9, Position Paper, that section is titled Thinking about What Makes Position Papers Effective. You choose one reading that seemed to you a particularly good example of its genre, reread it critically in light of all you have learned about the genre, and then write a page or more justifying your choice. This activity enables you to review the characteristic features and rhetorical strategies of the genre you are about to write. Coming where it does before the Guide to Writing, this activity helps you complete the transition from thinking like a reader to thinking like a writer.

Reflecting on What You Have Learned about Writing Essays

This final occasion for reflection concludes the chapter by inviting you to describe what you are most pleased with in your revision and to explain what contributed to this achievement. It reminds you that there is much you have learned and much to learn about writing—from reading other writers, writing your own essays, and collaborating with other writers.

CHAPTER 2

AUTOBIOGRAPHY

Autobiography is a kind of writing important to both writers and readers. By telling their own stories, autobiographers get to represent themselves to the world, reinventing their own identities by deciding what is meaningful in their lives. Autobiography also helps writers locate themselves as part of a particular time, place, and culture.

Readers take pleasure in seeing their own experience reflected in another's writing as well as in recognizing otherness, seeing the many different ways people live and behave toward one another. Some autobiographies, in fact, challenge readers' certainties, surprising or even startling them. Reading autobiography reminds us of our commonalities *and* our differences.

Autobiography derives from a particular way of imagining the self as the product of experience, culture, and history. Relying on memory, autobiographers construct a representation of what happened at key points in their lives. But autobiographers also know how unreliable memory is, how much what we remember is influenced by the ways stories are told and retold in our society. As you read and write autobiography, you will become aware of these conventions of autobiographical storytelling. You will notice, for example, that many autobiographical stories depend on something happening that tests or changes the autobiographer or protagonist. The word *protagonist* derives from the Greek *agon,* meaning "struggle" or "contest." From our culture, then, we have come to see autobiography as a series of events—rituals or rites of passage—that challenge and change us, that affirm our sense of individuality, and, at the same time, make us feel a part of a larger community.

As you work through this chapter, you will learn more about autobiography by reading several different examples of it. You will see that some autobiographies tell a story about a single *event* that occurred over a brief period of time, while others relate what happened over an extended period of time, called a *phase*. Still others give a portrait of a *person* who played an important role in the autobiographer's life. Whether you decide to tell a story about an event or a phase, or to write a portrait of a person, your study of the selections in this chapter will suggest ideas about what to write and how to write it. As you read and write about the reading selections, keep in mind the following assignment, which sets out the goals for writing an autobiographical essay. To support your writing of this assignment, the chapter concludes with A Guide to Autobiographical Writing.

THE WRITING ASSIGNMENT

Autobiography

Write an autobiographical essay about a significant event, phase, or person in your life. Choose a topic with your readers in mind, one that you feel comfortable disclosing to others and that could lead them to reflect on their own lives.

Present your experience dramatically and vividly so readers can imagine what it was like for you. Through your choice of words and details, convey the meaning and importance—what we call the *autobiographical significance*—of this event, phase, or person in your life.

AUTOBIOGRAPHICAL WRITING SITUATIONS

You may think only famous people like scientists, novelists, politicians, and movie stars write their autobiographies. But autobiographical writing is actually much more widespread, as the following examples indicate:

- As part of her application to college, a high-school senior writes a brief autobiographical essay. In this essay, she recalls what happened when she did her first real scientific experiment studying the nutritional effects of different breakfast cereals on mice. As she writes about this experience, she conveys her reasons for wanting to study science and become a researcher.

- Asked to recall a significant early childhood memory as an assignment in a psychology class, a college student writes about a fishing trip he took when he was nine. He reflects that the trip was significant because it was the first he ever took alone with his father and because it began a new stage in their relationship.

- As part of a workshop on management skills, a business executive writes about a person who influenced his ideas about leadership. As he explores his memory and feelings, he realizes that he mistook fear for admiration. He recognizes that he has been emulating the wrong model, an autocratic leader who gets people to perform by intimidating them.

Practicing Autobiography
A COLLABORATIVE ACTIVITY

The preceding scenarios suggest some occasions for writing about events and people in one's life. This activity gives you a chance to rehearse writing about your own life and, with a group of peers, to play the dual roles of writer and reader.

PART 1. Assume that you are going to write about a significant childhood experience. Think of an event that shows a bit of what your childhood was like—perhaps something startling, amusing, sad, or joyous. The only requirements are for it to seem important to you now as you look back on it and for you to remember it well enough to tell what happened.

Then get together with two or three other students, and take turns briefly telling your stories to one another. After you have all told your stories, each student in the group should say one thing that each story communicated about its teller's experience. Listen carefully to see if everyone "hears" the same thing.

PART 2. Consider what you have learned about relating an important autobiographical event. Reflecting on the storytelling and responses of the group, discuss the following questions:

Why did you choose the event you did? How did your audience affect your choice?

What did you want others to learn about your experience from your story? Were you surprised by what they said they learned? What do you think led them to these conclusions?

What has this experience taught you about understanding others' autobiographical stories? What have you learned about telling your own story?

A GUIDE TO READING AUTOBIOGRAPHY

In this section, you will have the opportunity to read, annotate, and write about your understanding and responses to an autobiographical essay by the poet and autobiographer Audre Lorde. Then, guided by a list of basic features and strategies of autobiographical writing, you will reread the essay to examine the elements of strong autobiographical writing.

First, though, as a reminder of the many possibilities of annotating, here is a brief example of an annotated passage from another autobiographical essay, "A Chase" by Annie Dillard, which appears in its entirety later in this chapter.

It was cloudy but cold. The cars' tires laid behind them on the
snowy street a complex trail of beige chunks like crenellated castle   *battlements*
walls. I had stepped on some earlier; they squeaked. We could have   *war image*

wished for more traffic. When a car came, <u>we all</u> <u>popped</u> it one. In the intervals between cars <u>we</u> [reverted to the natural solitude of children.]

group "we" vs.
individual "I"

I started making an iceball—a <u>perfect</u> iceball, from <u>perfectly</u> white snow, <u>perfectly</u> spherical, and squeezed <u>perfectly</u> translucent so no snow remained all the way through. (The Fahey boys and I considered it <u>unfair</u> actually to throw an iceball at somebody, but it had been known to happen.)

Communal
standards

Why repeat
"perfectly"?
Proud?

I had just embarked on the iceball project when we heard tire chains come clanking from afar. A black Buick was moving toward us down the street. <u>We all</u> spread out, banged together some <u>regular</u> <u>snowballs</u>, took aim, and, when the Buick drew (nigh,) fired.

near

A <u>soft</u> snowball hit the driver's windshield right before the driver's face. It made a smashed star with a hump in the middle.

Emphasizes
fairness.
So why
does the man
chase them?
Different
rules?

Often, of course, we hit our target, but <u>this time</u>, <u>the only time in</u> all of life, the car pulled over and stopped. Its wide black door opened; a man got out of it, running. He didn't even close the car door.

Repetition
stresses
significance
like fairy tale
opening,
"Once upon a
time…"

Audre Lorde

THAT SUMMER I LEFT CHILDHOOD WAS WHITE

Audre Lorde (1934–1992) is probably best known for her poetry and for her autobiography, *Zami* (1982).

In this excerpt, Lorde recalls an incident that occurred in 1947, when she was thirteen. Before reading, consider what you know about the history of racism in the United States during and directly after World War II. Did you know, for example, that a million African American men and women served in the military during the war, but that the military was not integrated until 1948? Did you know that it did not become illegal to refuse service in a restaurant on the basis of race until the Civil Rights Act of 1964?

As you read, annotate anything that strikes you as interesting or especially effective in communicating Lorde's feelings about this particular experience. Mark on the text, and write comments in the margin.

The first time I went to Washington, D.C., was on the edge of the summer when I was supposed to stop being a child. At least that's what they said to us all at graduation from the eighth grade. My sister Phyllis graduated at the same time from high school. I don't know what she was supposed to stop being. But as graduation presents for us both, the whole family took a Fourth of July trip to Washington, D.C., the fabled and famous capital of our country.

It was the first time I'd ever been on a railroad train during the day. When I was little, and we used to go to the Connecticut shore, we always went at night on the milk train, because it was cheaper.

Preparations were in the air around our house before school was even over. We packed for a week. There were two very large suitcases that my father carried, and a box filled with food. In fact, my first trip to Washington was a mobile feast; I started eating as soon as we were comfortably ensconced in our seats, and did not stop until somewhere after Philadelphia. I remember it was Philadelphia because I was disappointed not to have passed by the Liberty Bell.

My mother had roasted two chickens and cut them up into dainty bite-size pieces. She packed slices of brown bread and butter and green pepper and carrot sticks. There were little violently yellow iced cakes with scalloped edges called "marigolds," that came from Cushman's Bakery. There was a spice bun and rock-cakes from Newton's, the West Indian bakery across Lenox Avenue from St. Mark's School, and iced tea in a wrapped mayonnaise jar. There were sweet pickles for us and dill pickles for my father, and peaches with the fuzz still on them, individually wrapped to keep them from bruising. And, for neatness, there were piles of napkins and a little tin box with a washcloth dampened with rosewater and glycerine for wiping sticky mouths.

I wanted to eat in the dining car because I had read all about them, but my mother reminded me for the umpteenth time that dining car food always cost too much money and besides, you never could tell whose hands had been playing all over that food, nor where those same hands had been just before. My mother never mentioned that Black people were not allowed into railroad dining cars headed south in 1947. As usual, whatever my mother did not like and could not change, she ignored. Perhaps it would go away, deprived of her attention.

I learned later that Phyllis's high school senior class trip had been to Washington, but the nuns had given her back her deposit in private, explaining to her that the class, all of whom were white, except Phyllis, would be staying in a hotel where Phyllis "would not be happy," meaning, Daddy explained to her, also in private, that they did not rent rooms to Negroes. "We will take you to Washington, ourselves," my father had avowed, "and not just for an overnight in some measly fleabag hotel."

American racism was a new and crushing reality that my parents had to deal with every day of their lives once they came to this country. They handled it as a private woe. My mother and father believed that they could best protect their children from the realities of race in america and the fact of american racism by never giving them name, much less discussing their nature. We were told we must never trust white people, but *why* was never explained, nor the nature of their ill will. Like so many other vital pieces of information in my childhood, I was supposed to know without being told. It always seemed like a very strange injunction coming from my mother, who looked so much like one of those people we were never supposed to trust. But something always warned me not to ask my mother why she wasn't white, and why Auntie Lillah and Auntie Etta weren't, even though they were all that same problematic color so different from my father and me, even from my sisters, who were somewhere in-between.

In Washington, D.C., we had one large room with two double   8
beds and an extra cot for me. It was a back-street hotel that belonged to a friend of my father's who was in real estate, and I spent the whole next day after Mass squinting up at the Lincoln Memorial where Marian Anderson had sung after the D.A.R.* refused to allow her to sing in their auditorium because she was Black. Or because she was "Colored," my father said as he told us the story. Except that what he probably said was "Negro," because for his times, my father was quite progressive.

I was squinting because I was in that silent agony that character-   9
ized all of my childhood summers, from the time school let out in June to the end of July, brought about by my dilated and vulnerable eyes exposed to the summer brightness.

I viewed Julys through an agonizing corolla of dazzling whiteness   10
and I always hate the Fourth of July, even before I came to realize the travesty such a celebration was for Black people in this country.

My parents did not approve of sunglasses, nor of their expense.   11

I spent the afternoon squinting up at monuments to freedom and   12
past presidencies and democracy, and wondering why the light and heat were both so much stronger in Washington, D.C., than back home in New York City. Even the pavement on the streets was a shade lighter in color than back home.

Late that Washington afternoon my family and I walked back   13
down Pennsylvania Avenue. We were a proper caravan, mother bright and father brown, the three of us girls step-standards in-between. Moved by our historical surroundings and the heat of the early evening, my father decreed yet another treat. He had a great sense of history, a flair for the quietly dramatic and the sense of specialness of an occasion and a trip.

"Shall we stop and have a little something to cool off, Lin?"   14

Two blocks away from our hotel, the family stopped for a dish of   15
vanilla ice cream at a Breyer's ice cream and soda fountain. Indoors, the soda fountain was dim and fan-cooled, deliciously relieving to my scorched eyes.

Corded and crisp and pinafored, the five of us seated ourselves   16

*D.A.R.: Daughters of the American Revolution. An organization of women descended from Americans who aided in the achievement of American independence (*Ed.*)

one by one at the counter. There was I between my mother and father, and my two sisters on the other side of my mother. We settled ourselves along the white mottled marble counter, and when the waitress spoke at first no one understood what she was saying, and so the five of us just sat there.

17

The waitress moved along the line of us closer to my father and spoke again. "I said I kin give you to take out, but you can't eat here. Sorry." Then she dropped her eyes looking very embarrassed, and suddenly we heard what it was she was saying all at the same time, loud and clear.

18

Straight-backed and indignant, one by one, my family and I got down from the counter stools and turned around and marched out of the store, quiet and outraged, as if we had never been Black before. No one would answer my emphatic questions with anything other than a guilty silence. "But we hadn't done anything!" This wasn't right or fair! Hadn't I written poems about Bataan and freedom and democracy for all?

19

My parents wouldn't speak of this injustice, not because they had contributed to it, but because they felt they should have anticipated it and avoided it. This made me even angrier. My fury was not going to be acknowledged by a like fury. Even my two sisters copied my parents' pretense that nothing unusual and anti-american had occurred. I was left to write my angry letter to the president of the united states all by myself, although my father did promise I could type it out on the office typewriter next week, after I showed it to him in my copybook diary.

20

The waitress was white, and the counter was white, and the ice cream I never ate in Washington, D.C., that summer I left childhood was white, and the white heat and the white pavement and the white stone monuments of my first Washington summer made me sick to my stomach for the whole rest of that trip and it wasn't much of a graduation present after all.

READING FOR MEANING

The activities that follow will help you to develop your understanding of "That Summer I Left Childhood Was White."

Write at least a page exploring Lorde's story. Begin by briefly explaining what you think is the significance of the event as Lorde has presented it. Then write about any other thoughts and reactions you have to the story.

As you write, it might help to review your annotations and to reread any passages that seemed important when you first read them. Do not be surprised if your understanding and response change as you write and reread. Pursue your ideas wherever they lead. Also, do not worry if your writing is a bit unorganized. Your aim now is simply to use writing to see what you think.

If you are having trouble getting started or continuing for at least a page, the following suggestions might stimulate your thinking:

- Mark the places where Lorde refers to vision. Apart from the literal meaning—that Lorde's vision was impaired—what other significance do you see in these references?

- Notice that Lorde responds differently from her parents. Why do you think they respond as they do and she responds as she does? Where in the story do you see any indication of how she feels about the difference between herself and her parents?

- Note that this event occurred in 1947, nearly fifty years ago. Could the same thing happen today? Why or why not? You may have recently seen signs in restaurants reserving the right to deny service to customers; often such signs specify persons not wearing shoes or a shirt, but sometimes the reasons are not specified. Do you think restaurant owners should have the right to deny service to customers? Or should customers have the right not to be discriminated against?

- Look back at paragraphs 7 and 19, where Lorde does not capitalize the proper nouns *America, American,* and *United States* (except at the beginning of the sentence). How do you explain this choice to break with convention?

- Explain the possible meaning or significance of "I was supposed to stop being a child" (paragraph 1), "They handled it as a private woe" (paragraph 7), "Hadn't I written poems about Bataan and freedom and democracy for all?" (paragraph 18), or any other statement that catches your attention.

READING LIKE A WRITER

This section leads you through an analysis of Lorde's autobiographical writing strategies: *telling the story, describing the scene, describing people,* and *conveying the autobiographical significance.* For each strategy you will be asked to reread and annotate part of Lorde's essay to see how she uses the strategy to accomplish her particular purpose. Although autobiographers' purposes are sometimes complex, they always try to give readers an impression of themselves as well as a sense of why their experience is important and meaningful.

As you study the selections later in this chapter, you will see how different autobiographers use these same strategies for different purposes. You will also see that the three types of autobiographical writing represented in this chapter—event, phase, and person—use these same strategies but foreground different ones. The Guide to Writing Autobiography at the end of the chapter suggests ways you can use these strategies in your own autobiographical writing.

Telling the Story

Autobiographical writing very often tells a story. Events are usually narrated like short stories, while phases covering a longer time span and portraits of people often include several brief stories as anecdotes. Although we think of a story as being about a single event, stories actually are a sequence of actions strung together. On the basis of the significance they want the story to bring out, autobiographers decide which actions to include, how to sequence them, and how much emphasis to give to each one. The story's significance usually centers on a conflict between the autobiographer and another person or within the autobiographer him- or herself.

Autobiographers try to shape the story's action dramatically around this central conflict. Good storytelling makes readers want to know what will happen, how the conflict will be resolved. But autobiographical stories seldom rush headlong from beginning to end. There are often side trips to fill in details about people and past events that put the central event into perspective. These side trips help readers to understand the story's significance, but they also tend to lessen the tension and drama. To instill tension, storytellers vary the pace of the action. They may take a leisurely pace when giving background information or describing the scene, but when the story gets to the main action, the pace usually intensifies. In the next story you will read, titled "A Chase," the narrative moves with breakneck speed toward the climax. In contrast, Lorde slows the pace to intensify the drama in a slow-motion close-up that pictures every movement and gesture Lorde and her family make as they leave the ice cream store.

In analyzing the way an autobiographer tells his or her story, consider what actions are included, how they are sequenced, and how they are paced to heighten the drama and the significance of the story.

ANALYZE. To get a sense of how Lorde's story is told, reread it and mark the climax. Notice the pacing—where the storytelling speeds up to cover a lot of time or slows down to give a close-up of the action—and its effect on you as a reader.

WRITE. Based on your analysis, write several sentences describing the story's shape and pacing. You might begin by saying how dramatic you find this story. Consider the following questions to help you develop your analysis: Around what conflict does the story revolve? How does the climax bring this conflict to a head? Describe the action preceding the climax.

Describing the Scene

Whether an autobiography centers on an event, phase, or person, it nearly always includes some description of the scene. Not only does the scenic description enable readers to picture what happened there, but it also reinforces the story's significance. Particularly evocative is language that describes sense impressions—what the place looked, smelled, and sounded like.

Another important aspect of the way the scene is described is point of view. *Point of view* refers to the vantage point from which the scene is described— whether the scene is viewed from a fixed position or as the narrator moves through it, whether it is observed close up or from a panoramic distance, or some combination of perspectives. While point of view indicates the speaker's physical location in relation to the scene, it also can imply the autobiographer's emotional attitude toward it. For example, when Lorde describes herself as "squinting up at the Lincoln Memorial" (paragraph 8), her physical distance from Lincoln underscores and symbolizes how out of reach the freedom and equality he promised still seem to her. Point of view, in this way, can give readers insight into the autobiographer's feelings and can contribute to the significance of the story.

ANALYZE. To analyze Lorde's description, notice that there are four different locations or scenes: the train (paragraphs 3–5), the hotel room (briefly in paragraph 8), the streets and monuments of Washington, D.C. (paragraphs 8–14 and 20), and the ice-cream parlor (paragraphs 15–18 and 20). Reread the description of each scene, noting which senses—sight, sound, smell, touch, and taste—are evoked as well as the physical point of view from which each scene is presented.

WRITE. Based on your analysis of the four scenes, write a few sentences about Lorde's description. Indicate which images stick in your mind and try to describe the feelings they evoke for you. You might also note how the physical point of view contributes to your impression of these scenes.

Describing People

The central figure in an autobiography is generally the autobiographer, but, depending on the purpose, autobiographers describe other people in varying detail. A few quick details about the way others look, dress, or act may be all an autobiographer gives. If a person's appearance is not significant, little or no physical description will be given. Even portraits, the type of autobiography that presents a person who played an important role in the autobiographer's life, tend to have less physical description than one might expect. A single gesture or expression can be more revealing than a catalog of visual details.

Autobiographers reveal other people's personalities by direct statement or by allowing readers to infer what people are like from what they say and do. In portraits, direct statements are usually accompanied by illustrative anecdotes that show readers what the person is like. Because portraits focus on important and often complicated relationships, autobiographers try to indicate their strong and sometimes conflicted feelings about the person. They may show how the relationship has changed over time or how they have come to terms with their own ambivalence about it.

ANALYZE. In her autobiographical writing, Lorde presents her parents and her sisters in some detail—by providing physical description, by revealing aspects of their personalities, and by suggesting the nature of their relationship to each other.

Scan Lorde's story (particularly paragraphs 7, 13, 16–18, and 20), marking any specific physical details describing the people—the way they look and dress, their movements and gestures. Note also places where Lorde tells readers about various people's beliefs and attitudes (for example, in paragraph 11 where she states that her parents "did not approve of sunglasses, nor of their expense") and by relating their actions and words. Look for and mark clues that suggest Lorde's relationship with the people she presents as well as her feelings toward them. (Paragraph 19, for example, suggests a great deal about the complexity of Lorde's relationship with her family.)

WRITE. Based on your annotations, write a few sentences explaining how Lorde characterizes another person in this story. What do you learn about this person's personality and the relationship with Lorde from the way he or she is portrayed? Cite one or two specific examples that give you insight into Lorde's relationship with the person.

Conveying the Autobiographical Significance

What makes autobiography so interesting for most readers is that it gives us some insight into what other people feel and think about important events and relationships in their lives. Autobiographers do not write about trivial events or unmemorable relationships, but instead choose significant events and people. For example, autobiographers might write about events that surprised or disappointed them, that led them to reevaluate or make a change, or that helped them bear or throw off a burden they have been carrying for some time.

Autobiographers convey the significance of the event, phase, or person in two ways: by *showing* that it was important and by *telling* what it meant. Most writers do both. As you analyzed how Lorde tells the story and describes the scene and people, you have seen how she *shows* the event's significance. Now turn your focus to what she *tells* readers.

Autobiographers may tell us what they thought and felt at the time, or what they think and feel now as they look back. Often writers do both. As a close reader, you want to notice any differences in how the writer understood the experience at the time and how the writer understands it now in retrospect. Thinking critically about the writer's experience on its own terms can lead you to better understand other people as well as yourself.

ANALYZE. Reread the essay, writing in the margin the word *past* to indicate where Lorde's remembered feelings and thoughts are expressed, and *present* to mark where her more recent reflections on the past are expressed. Note any differences between these two perspectives—for example, how her parents' attitudes influenced her understanding of the event when she was a child and what her attitudes are now that she is an adult. Consider also historical changes in what Lorde calls "american racism" from her parents' generation to Lorde's generation—and to your generation.

WRITE. Write a few sentences exploring your understanding of this event's significance.

_____

READINGS

Annie Dillard

_____

A CHASE

Annie Dillard (b. 1945) is a poet, reporter, essayist, and literary theo-
rist. Since 1974, when she won the Pulitzer Prize for *Pilgrim at Tinker
Creek,* she has been considered one of America's finest nonfiction writers. She has published a book of poems, *Tickets for the Prayer Wheel*
(1982); a book of literary theory, *Living by Fiction* (1982); an autobiography, *An American Childhood* (1987); and an account of her working
life as a writer, *The Writing Life* (1989). In 1992, Dillard published her
first novel, *The Living.*

This selection from Dillard's autobiography focuses on a single event
that occurred one snowy morning when she was seven and with a friend
was chased relentlessly by an adult stranger at whom they were throwing
snowballs. She admits that she was terrified, and yet she asserts that she
has "seldom been happier since." As you read, think about this paradox.

Some boys taught me to play football. This was fine sport. You   1
thought up a new strategy for every play and whispered it to the
others. You went out for a pass, fooling everyone. Best, you got to
throw yourself mightily at someone's running legs. Either you
brought him down or you hit the ground flat out on your chin, with
your arms empty before you. It was all or nothing. If you hesitated in
fear, you would miss and get hurt: you would take a hard fall while
the kid got away, or you would get kicked in the face while the kid
got away. But if you flung yourself wholeheartedly at the back of his
knees—if you gathered and joined body and soul and pointed them
diving fearlessly—then you likely wouldn't get hurt, and you'd stop
the ball. Your fate, and your team's score, depended on your concentration and courage. Nothing girls did could compare with it.

Boys welcomed me at baseball, too, for I had, through enthusias-   2
tic practice, what was weirdly known as a boy's arm. In winter, in
the snow, there was neither baseball nor football, so the boys and I
threw snowballs at passing cars. I got in trouble throwing snowballs,
and have seldom been happier since.

On one weekday morning after Christmas, six inches of new   3
snow had just fallen. We were standing up to our boot tops in snow
on a front yard on trafficked Reynolds Street, waiting for cars. The

cars traveled Reynolds Street slowly and evenly; they were targets all but wrapped in red ribbons, cream puffs. We couldn't miss.

I was seven; the boys were eight, nine, and ten. The oldest two Fahey boys were there—Mikey and Peter—polite blond boys who lived near me on Lloyd Street, and who already had four brothers and sisters. My parents approved Mikey and Peter Fahey. Chickie McBride was there, a tough kid, and Billy Paul and Mackie Kean too, from across Reynolds, where the boys grew up dark and furious, grew up skinny, knowing, and skilled. We had all drifted from our houses that morning looking for action, and had found it here on Reynolds Street.

It was cloudy but cold. The cars' tires laid behind them on the snowy street a complex trail of beige chunks like crenellated castle walls. I had stepped on some earlier; they squeaked. We could have wished for more traffic. When a car came, we all popped it one. In the intervals between cars we reverted to the natural solitude of children.

I started making an iceball—a perfect iceball, from perfectly white snow, perfectly spherical, and squeezed perfectly translucent so no snow remained all the way through. (The Fahey boys and I considered it unfair actually to throw an iceball at somebody, but it had been known to happen.)

I had just embarked on the iceball project when we heard tire chains come clanking from afar. A black Buick was moving toward us down the street. We all spread out, banged together some regular snowballs, took aim, and, when the Buick drew nigh, fired.

A soft snowball hit the driver's windshield right before the driver's face. It made a smashed star with a hump in the middle.

Often, of course, we hit our target, but this time, the only time in all of life, the car pulled over and stopped. Its wide black door opened; a man got out of it, running. He didn't even close the car door.

He ran after us, and we ran away from him, up the snowy Reynolds sidewalk. At the corner, I looked back; incredibly, he was still after us. He was in city clothes: a suit and tie, street shoes. Any normal adult would have quit, having sprung us into flight and made his point. This man was gaining on us. He was a thin man, all action. All of a sudden, we were running for our lives.

Wordless, we split up. We were on our turf; we could lose ourselves in the neighborhood backyards, everyone for himself. I paused and considered. Everyone had vanished except Mikey Fahey, who was just rounding the corner of a yellow brick house. Poor Mikey, I trailed him. The driver of the Buick sensibly picked the two of us to follow. The man apparently had all day.

He chased Mikey and me around the yellow house and up a back-yard path we knew by heart: under a low tree, up a bank, through a hedge, down some snowy steps, and across the grocery store's delivery driveway. We smashed through a gap in another hedge, entered a scruffy backyard and ran around its back porch and tight between houses to Edgerton Avenue; we ran across Edgerton to an alley and up our own sliding woodpile to the Halls' front yard; he kept coming. We ran up Lloyd Street and wound through mazy backyards toward the steep hilltop at Willard and Lang.

He chased us silently, block after block. He chased us silently   13
over picket fences, through thorny hedges, between houses, around garbage cans, and across streets. Every time I glanced back, choking for breath, I expected he would have quit. He must have been as breathless as we were. His jacket strained over his body. It was an immense discovery, pounding into my hot head with every sliding, joyous step, that this ordinary adult evidently knew what I thought only children who trained at football knew: that you have to fling yourself at what you're doing, you have to point yourself, forget yourself, aim, dive.

Mikey and I had nowhere to go, in our own neighborhood or out   14
of it, but away from this man who was chasing us. He impelled us forward; we compelled him to follow our route. The air was cold; every breath tore my throat. We kept running, block after block; we kept improvising, backyard after backyard, running a frantic course and choosing it simultaneously, failing always to find small places or hard places to slow him down, and discovering always, exhilarated, dismayed, that only bare speed could save us—for he would never give up, this man—and we were losing speed.

He chased us through the backyard labyrinths of ten blocks   15
before he caught us by our jackets. He caught us and we all stopped.

We three stood staggering, half blinded, coughing, in an obscure   16
hilltop backyard: a man in his twenties, a boy, a girl. He had released our jackets, our pursuer, our captor, our hero: he knew we weren't going anywhere. We all played by the rules. Mikey and I unzipped our jackets. I pulled off my sopping mittens. Our tracks multiplied in the backyard's new snow. We had been breaking new snow all morning. We didn't look at each other. I was cherishing my excitement. The man's lower pants legs were wet; his cuffs were full of snow, and there was a prow of snow beneath them on his shoes and socks. Some trees bordered the little flat backyard, some messy winter trees. There was no one around: a clearing in a grove, and we the only players.

It was a long time before he could speak. I had some difficulty at   17
first recalling why we were there. My lips felt swollen; I couldn't see out of the sides of my eyes; I kept coughing.

"You stupid kids," he began perfunctorily.   18

We listened perfunctorily indeed, if we listened at all, for the   19
chewing out was redundant, a mere formality, and beside the point. The point was that he had chased us passionately without giving up, and so he had caught us. Now he came down to earth. I wanted the glory to last forever.

But how could the glory have lasted forever? We could have run   20
through every backyard in North America until we got to Panama.
But when he trapped us at the lip of the Panama Canal, what precisely could he have done to prolong the drama of the chase and cap
its glory? I brooded about this for the next few years. He could only
have fried Mikey Fahey and me in boiling oil, say, or dismembered us
piecemeal, or staked us to anthills. None of which I really wanted,
and none of which any adult was likely to do, even in the spirit of
fun. He could only chew us out there in the Panamanian jungle, after
months or years of exalting pursuit. He could only begin, "You
stupid kids," and continue in his ordinary Pittsburgh accent with his
normal righteous anger and the usual common sense.

    If in that snowy backyard the driver of the black Buick had cut off   21
our heads, Mikey's and mine, I would have died happy, for nothing
has required so much of me since as being chased all over Pittsburgh
in the middle of winter—running terrified, exhausted—by this
sainted, skinny, furious redheaded man who wished to have a word
with us. I don't know how he found his way back to his car.

READING FOR MEANING

Write at least a page about the meanings you find in Dillard's story, beginning by briefly speculating about what you think Dillard wants readers to understand about the significance of this incident. Then write about anything else that
intrigues you or that you find memorable in her story. To write, you may need to
do some rereading.

Use the following suggestions to stimulate your thinking and writing:

- Look again at the opening two paragraphs where Dillard introduces the
  story. What do you see as the point of these paragraphs, and how do they
  relate to the story that follows?

- In this story, Dillard indicates she was the only girl in a group of boys.
  Some of these boys had been "approved" by her parents because they were
  "polite blond boys who lived near" (paragraph 4). What does Dillard's
  description of the other boys imply about them? Do you think her parents
  would have approved of them? Why or why not?

- Explain the possible meanings of "Nothing girls did could compare" (paragraph 1), "we reverted to the natural solitude of children" (paragraph 5),
  "We all played by the rules" (paragraph 16), or any other statement that
  catches your eye.

- As you read the story, were you surprised to see Dillard use words like
  "hero" (paragraph 16) and "sainted" (paragraph 21) to describe the man who
  chased her? Skim the story and underline other words used to describe the
  man and his behavior. From your analysis of her word choices, what do you
  think Dillard is trying to say about the man or about her perception of him?

- If the climax of the story occurs when the man catches Dillard and Mikey,
  what do you think the ending paragraphs say about the event's meaning and

importance? Reread paragraphs 18–21, noting anything that might help you answer this question. Note, in particular, what Dillard says about the way the man chews them out. For example, why do you think she uses the word "perfunctorily" to describe both the way he begins to talk and the way she and Mikey listen to him? Also, what do you think she means when she writes about Panama and anthills and all?

- The book-length autobiography from which this story comes is titled *An American Childhood.* Dillard's choice of the word "an" instead of "the" suggests that she doesn't assume her childhood is typical, just one particular person's childhood experience. But the word "American" in the title does suggest something about what childhood was like in the United States in the 1950s for Dillard. What image of childhood in the United States do you get from reading this story? How does it compare to Audre Lorde's or to your own experience of childhood?

EXTENDING MEANING THROUGH CONVERSATION. After you consider the story's meaning on your own, discussing the story with others who have also read and thought about it will help to develop your understanding. Work with one or two other students. Before getting together, reread what you wrote about Dillard's story. Begin your conversation by taking turns recalling something in the story that you found particularly curious or puzzling.

As your conversation proceeds, you may discover you have understood the reading differently. Reread parts of the story to clarify the meaning. But do not worry if you still see the story differently. Disagreement can help sharpen your insights while also alerting you to other interpretations.

READING LIKE A WRITER
TELLING A STORY DRAMATICALLY

The stories autobiographers tell are often full of action and drama. Dillard's "A Chase" is worth examining closely to see just how she uses words to create a vivid motion picture.

Verbs that show action make the writing vivid and can add to the drama and tension of the story. Action verbs give writing the effect of a motion picture rather than a still photograph. Instead of freezing people in time and space, action verbs allow us to imagine people running, shouting, or flailing their arms in the air.

ANALYZE. Begin by examining the way Dillard shows action. Underline each verb in paragraphs 12–15, including the *-ing* forms, putting a second line under the verbs that name an action. For example, there are two verbs in the following sentence—one names an action (double underline), the other does not (single underline): "The air was cold; every breath tore my throat" (paragraph 14).

Review the verbs you have underlined, looking for two or three places where you not only get an impression of action and movement but also get a sense of tension and drama. Single out two or three sentences and consider what the verbs contribute to the feeling you get as you read. Also note any words other than verbs that enable you to experience the drama of the chase. What do these words add?

WRITE. Write several sentences explaining what you have discovered about the way Dillard represents action and makes it dramatic.

CONSIDERING IDEAS FOR YOUR OWN WRITING

List several times when you were amused, frightened, or surprised by the way another person behaved toward you or toward another person in your presence. Choose one particularly significant event, and recall who was present and what happened. What would you emphasize to make the story dramatic? How could you convey the story's significance to your readers?

Russell Baker

SMOOTH AND EASY

Born in 1924, Russell Baker grew up in small towns in Virginia and in the cities of Newark and Baltimore. He began his career as a journalist with the *Baltimore Sun* and for many years covered the White House, Congress, and national politics for the *New York Times*. Since 1962, he has written his nationally syndicated "Observer" column. He was awarded the Pulitzer Prize for Distinguished Commentary in 1979, and won a second Pulitzer in 1983 for his autobiography *Growing Up.* His other books include *The Good Times* (1989), *There's a Country in My Cellar* (1990), and *Russell Baker's Book of American Humor* (1993). Recently, he has become a familiar face as host of the PBS program *Masterpiece Theater.*

In this selection from *Growing Up,* Baker recounts a turning point in his life, an event that occurred toward the end of World War II. The narrative focuses on the test he had to pass to qualify as a Navy pilot. As you read, notice how Baker uses humor to present himself in this difficult situation.

For the longest time . . . I flew and flew without ever being in control of any airplane. It was a constant struggle for power between the plane and me, and the plane usually won. I approached every flight like a tenderfoot sent to tame a wild horse. By the time I arrived at the Naval Air Station at Memphis, where Navy pilots took over the instruction, it was obvious my flying career would be soon ended. We flew open-cockpit biplanes—"Yellow Perils," the Navy called them—which forgave almost any mistake. Instructors sat in the front cockpit, students behind. But here the instructors did not ride the controls. These were courageous men. Many were back from the Pacific, and they put their destinies in my hands high over the Mississippi River and came back shaking their heads in sorrow.

"It's just like driving a car, Baker," a young ensign told me the day I nearly killed him trying to sideslip into a farm field where he wanted to land and take a smoke. "You know how it is when you let in the clutch? Real smooth and easy." 2

I knew nothing about letting in the clutch, but didn't dare say so. "Right," I said. "Smooth and easy." 3

I got as far as the acrobatic stage. Rolls, loops, Immelman turns. Clouds spinning zanily beneath me, earth and river whirling above. An earnest young Marine pilot took me aside after a typical day of disaster in the sky. "Baker," he said, "it's just like handling a girl's breast. You've got to be gentle." 4

I didn't dare tell him I'd never handled a girl's breast, either. 5

The inevitable catastrophe came on my check flight at the end of the acrobatic stage. It was supposed to last an hour, but after twenty minutes in the sky the check pilot said, "All right, let's go in," and gave me a "down," which meant "unfit to fly." I was doomed. I knew it, my buddies knew it. The Navy would forgive a "down" only if you could fly two successful check flights back-to-back with different check pilots. If you couldn't you were out. 6

I hadn't a prayer of surviving. On Saturday, looking at Monday's flight schedule, I saw that I was posted to fly the fatal reexamination with a grizzled pilot named T. L. Smith. It was like reading my own obituary. T. L. Smith was a celebrated perfectionist famous for washing out cadets for the slightest error in the air. His initials, T. L., were said to stand for "Total Loss," which was all anyone who had to fly for him could expect. Friends stopped by my bunk at the barracks to commiserate and tell me it wasn't so bad being kicked out of flying. I'd probably get soft desk duty in some nice Navy town where you could shack up a lot and sleep all day. Two of my best friends, wanting to cheer me up, took me to go into Memphis for a farewell weekend together. Well, it beat sitting on the base all weekend thinking about my Monday rendezvous with Total Loss. Why not a last binge for the condemned? 7

We took a room at the Peabody Hotel and bought three bottles of bourbon. I'd tasted whiskey only two or three times before and didn't much like it; but now in my gloom it brought a comfort I'd never known. I wanted more of that comfort. My dream was dying. I would plumb the depths of vice in these final hours. The weekend quickly turned into an incoherent jumble of dreamlike episodes. Afterwards I vaguely remembered threatening to punch a fat man in a restaurant, but couldn't remember why. At some point I was among a gang of sailors in a hotel corridor, and I was telling them to 8 stop spraying the hallway with a fire hose. At another I was sitting fully dressed on what seemed to be a piano bench in a hotel room—not at the Peabody—and a strange woman was smiling at me and taking off her brassiere.

This was startling, because no woman had ever taken her brassiere off in front of me before. But where had she come from? What were we doing in this alien room? "I'll bet I know what you want," she said.

"What?"

"This," she said, and stepped out of her panties and stretched out flat on her back on the bed. She beckoned. I stood up, then thought better of it and settled to the floor like a collapsing column of sand. I awoke hours later on the floor. She'd gone.

With the hangover I took back to the base Sunday night, I would have welcomed instant execution at the hands of Total Loss Smith, but when I awoke Monday morning the physical agony was over. In its place had come an unnatural, disembodied sensation of great calm. The world was moving much more slowly than its normal pace. In this eerie state of relaxation nothing seemed to matter much, not the terrible Total Loss Smith, not even the end of my flying days.

When we met at the flight line, Total Loss looked just as grim as everybody said he would. It was bitterly cold. We both wore heavy leather flight suits lined with wool, and his face looked tougher than the leather. He seemed old enough to be my father. Wrinkles creased around eyes that had never smiled. Lips as thin as a movie killer's. I introduced myself. His greeting was what I'd expected. "Let's get this over with," he said.

We walked down the flight line, parachutes bouncing against our rumps, not a word said. In the plane—Total Loss in the front seat, me in the back—I connected the speaking tube which enabled him to talk to me but didn't allow me to speak back. Still not a word while I taxied out to the mat, ran through the cockpit checks, and finished by testing the magnetos. If he was trying to petrify me before we got started he was wasting his efforts. In this new state of peace I didn't give a damn whether he talked to me or not.

"Take me up to 5,000 feet and show me some rolls," he growled as I started the takeoff.

The wheels were hardly off the mat before I experienced another eerie sensation. It was a feeling of power. For the first time since first stepping into an airplane I felt in complete mastery of the thing. I'd noticed it on takeoff. It had been an excellent takeoff. Without thinking about it, I'd automatically corrected a slight swerve just before becoming airborne. Now as we climbed I was flooded with a sense of confidence. The hangover's residue of relaxation had freed me of the tensions that had always defeated me before. Before, the plane had had a will of its own; now the plane seemed to be part of me, an extension of my hands and feet, obedient to my slightest

whim. I leveled it at exactly 5,000 feet and started a slow roll. First a
shallow dive to gain velocity, then push the stick slowly, firmly, all
the way over against the thigh, simultaneously putting in hard rudder, and there we are, hanging upside down over the earth and
now—keeping it rolling, don't let the nose drop—reverse the controls and feel it roll all the way through until—coming back to
straight-and-level now—catch it, wings level with the horizon, and
touch the throttle to maintain altitude precisely at 5,000 feet.

"Perfect," said Total Loss. "Do me another one."   17

It hadn't been a fluke. Somewhere between the weekend's bour-   18
bon and my arrival at the flight line that morning, I had become a
flyer. The second slow roll was as good as the first.

"Show me your snap rolls," Total Loss said.   19

I showed him snap rolls as fine as any instructor had ever shown   20
me.

"All right, give me a loop and then a split-S and recover your alti-   21
tude and show me an Immelman."

I looped him through a big graceful arc, leveled out and rolled   22
into the split-S, came out of it climbing, hit the altitude dead on at
5,000 feet, and showed him an Immelman that Eddie Rickenbacker
would have envied.

"What the hell did you do wrong on your check last week?" he   23
asked. Since I couldn't answer, I shrugged so he could see me in his
rearview mirror.

"Let me see you try a falling leaf," he said.   24

Even some instructors had trouble doing a falling leaf. The plane   25
had to be brought precisely to its stalling point, then dropped in a
series of sickening sideways skids, first to one side, then to the
other, like a leaf falling in a breeze, by delicate simultaneous manipu-
lations of stick, rudder pedals, and throttle. I seemed to have done
falling leaves all my life.

"All right, this is a waste of my time," Total Loss growled. "Let's   26
go in."

Back at the flight line, when I'd cut the ignition, he climbed out   27
and tramped back toward the ready room while I waited to sign the
plane in. When I got there he was standing at a distance talking to
my regular instructor. His talk was being illustrated with hand movements, as pilots' conversations always were, hands executing little
loops and rolls in the air. After he did the falling-leaf motion with his
hands, he pointed a finger at my instructor's chest, said something I
couldn't hear, and trudged off. My instructor, who had flown only
with the pre-hangover Baker, was slackjawed when he approached
me.

"Smith just said you gave him the best check flight he's ever had   28
in his life," he said. "What the hell did you do to him up there?"

"I guess I just suddenly learned to fly," I said. I didn't mention the 29
hangover. I didn't want him to know that bourbon was a better

teacher than he was. After that I saw T. L. Smith coming and going frequently through the ready room and thought him the finest, most manly looking fellow in the entire corps of instructors, as well as the wisest.

READING FOR MEANING

Write at least a page about your understanding of Baker's essay. Begin by telling what you think is the most important part of the story and why you think so. Then write about your responses to anything else in the reading, keeping in mind that your responses may change as you write. You will probably find it helpful to look back and annotate passages to quote or summarize.

If you have trouble continuing for at least a page, consider the following possibilities:

- Explain the event as a rite of passage, which, for men, often involves a test of physical prowess.
- Consider how Baker uses humor. In what ways do you think he makes fun of himself? What does this self-irony contribute to the story?
- Consider the implications of comparing flying to wild horses, cars, and women in paragraphs 1, 2, and 4. What is Baker saying about power and mastery?
- Speculate about how being a man or a woman influences your reading of this essay.
- Think of any personal experiences you have had that help you understand what happened to Baker. Explain what happened to you and how it relates to Baker's experience.

EXTENDING MEANING THROUGH CONVERSATION. You can enhance your own understanding of Baker's essay by discussing it with one or two classmates who have also thought about the story's meaning. Before getting together, reflect on your current understanding. Begin the conversation by pointing to one passage that seems especially significant to you.

As you share your insights, you may find that you see some things differently. Probe these differences by rereading problematic passages together and discussing your interpretations of them.

CONTEXTUALIZING. A further strategy for reading for meaning not covered in this chapter is *contextualizing,* or recognizing the differences between your values and attitudes and those represented in a text from another time or place.

As you read this essay, you bring to it certain attitudes and values typical of the 1990s. Baker's essay, however, evokes an earlier era—the 1940s. To conceptualize, you need to think about questions like these: What do you know about the 1940s? Where do your images and ideas of the World War II period come from? How does Baker's essay reinforce or contradict those images and ideas? How do your modern sensibilities lead you to react to the attitudes and stereotypes the essay represents?

Refer to the section on Contextualizing in Appendix 1, A Catalog of Reading Strategies, for instructions on using the strategy to enhance your understanding of Baker's autobiographical event.

READING LIKE A WRITER
DESCRIBING PEOPLE

Autobiographical stories sometimes feature several people other than the autobiographer. The physical description of most of these people is likely to be brief, but those who play a central role may be described in somewhat more detail. In addition to detailing a person's physical appearance, autobiographers often show the person's typical mannerisms, ways of talking, and personality traits.

ANALYZE. To locate descriptions of all the people in Baker's story, reread it carefully, annotating every passage where someone other than the young Baker appears or is mentioned. For each person, mark any language that describes who the person is as well as how he or she looks, acts, and thinks. Consider what you learn about the person from what he or she says and how it is said. Finally, note what you learn about how others, including the autobiographer, regard each person.

WRITE. Reflect on your annotations, and write a paragraph discussing what you have discovered about how Baker describes people in this story. Choose one or two people and say something about Baker's choice of descriptive detail. What impression do these details give you?

COMPARE. Look back at the Annie Dillard selection "A Chase." Skim paragraphs 4, 10, 13, 16, and 21 where people are described. Here, too, mark any language that describes how a person looks, acts, and thinks as well as what that person says and how it is said. Then write a few more sentences pointing out any similarities or differences you see in the kinds of details Baker and Dillard use to describe people in their autobiographical stories.

CONSIDERING IDEAS FOR YOUR OWN WRITING

Psychologists might say that the young Baker was paralyzed because he felt his self-worth was at stake. Think of one or more times when you felt that your self-worth was on the line, for example, when you were taking a test, applying for a job, going on a first date, attending a new school. Perhaps there was an occasion when you were unfairly criticized or singled out in front of other people. How did you react at the time, and how do you feel now looking back in retrospect?

Itabari Njeri

LAND OF THE DOO-WOPS

Itabari Njeri (b. 1952) is a professional singer, actress, reporter, art critic, essayist, and producer. She graduated from Boston University and the Columbia University Graduate School of Journalism. Her journalistic pieces have been featured on National Public Radio, and in the *Miami Herald* and the *Los Angeles Times*. She has received many fellowships and awards, including the American Book Award, the Associated Press Award for feature writing, and the National Endowment for Black Journalists Award.

This selection from her autobiography, *Every Good-Bye Ain't Gone* (1990), represents a phase in Njeri's life when she worked as a backup singer in a group called Brown Sugar. As you read, think about what you learn about Njeri from reading her story and what she learns about herself from writing it.

1   By the time I reached Bermuda, the act I was in had hit every region of the United States in a series of mostly one-night stands with a minor talent named Major Harris. You remember Major, once a member of the Delfonics, once high on the record charts as a soloist with the 1975 hit "Love Won't Let Me Wait." You can still get it in record stores or in a collection of Top 40 pop for lovers advertised on late-night TV and available through the mail with your VISA or MasterCard. The record was most notable for the orgasmic moaning of an anonymous background singer. It wasn't me.

2   The background singers on the record were replaced with the three members of a hastily thrown together group called Brown Sugar. I was the crystal on the left.

3   Brown Sugar had problems. Angela, a childhood friend, did too many drugs and was always hoarse. Candi, who was beautiful, had a tiny voice and hated singing heavy rhythm and blues—which really wasn't what we were doing, but what we did was still too gutbucket for her. And I hadn't been back in the real world long.

4   I had gone from opera to jazz to political theater with the Spirit House Movers, playwright Amiri Baraka's theater company, and Blakluv, a theater group I co-founded in Boston. I was unaccustomed to the world of commercial entertainment. And I definitely was not used to singing anything but lead.

5   "You take the next solo," Barry Manilow said. I launched into "Heat Wave" and blew away the competition at the audition—I thought. Manilow called me at home and gave me the nicest rejection I ever received as a performer. But I knew what the problem was before he opened his mouth. I was fine as a soloist. But background singing is an ensemble art, and one has to blend, not stand

out. When he listened to me with the other two singers, my vibrato could be heard above everyone else, he said.

But I was willing to bottle my voice and my ego as part of Brown   6
Sugar. I may have had the best pipes in the group, but doo-wop artistry was new to me, as well as the life-style that accompanied it. I was willing to look, listen and learn. I was also content to let Angela assume control of the group. She had been a touring backup singer for years, as she constantly reminded me. And her ears were better attuned to the collective art we were practicing. She could "help me" spot and squelch my occasional lapses into operatic style. She took delight in telling me this, now that I was performing on her turf. Angela had felt the need to compete with me since the day we met in high school.

We both attended Music and Art. I won the school's top vocal   7
music award the year I graduated. Angela flunked out and had to go to another high school. I made my debut at Carnegie recital hall when I was sixteen. I'd been named best new pop vocalist in the 1969 equivalent of *Star Search,* a talent show at the Brooklyn Academy of Music sponsored by M-G-M Records and Metromedia Television in New York.

A talent scout claiming to represent Motown came backstage   8
after the show and said he wanted me to cut a demo. Whether he was for real or not, I don't know, but in my youthful wisdom, I primly said: "No thank you. I intend to be an opera singer."

"Is Leontyne Price ready?" I heard Angela ask, as we prepared to   9
open for the Ohio Players and the Spinners. I was twenty-three and the one-night stands were killing my voice.

I could move well onstage, but had great difficulty following a set   10
pattern of steps. ("They're not going to ask you to dance, are they?" my own mother wanted to know when I got the job.) When Angela and Candi turned left, I swung to the right. When they were facing front, I was facing back.

One night, on the stage of a packed Shreveport, Louisiana, arena,   11
we stepped up to our microphones dressed in royal blue satin gowns, the backs cut to just above the derriere, a touch of pale blue ostrich feathers clinging to the plunging halter necklines. With our pelvises swirling and some fancy variations on the cha-cha, we finished the last "*Ooh ooh, loving you is mellow*" riff, a line from a nonhit Major Harris tune of the same name. Then came the opening strains of the song for which the audience had been clamoring, "Love Won't Let Me Wait."

"*The time is right, you hold me tight, and love's got me high,*" Major   12
sang. The young girls in the audience, barely past puberty, shrieked in ecstasy. "*Please tell me yes.*"

"*Yes,*" Brown Sugar whispered in response, after navigating a   13
choreographed turn that placed us in front of the microphone at the appropriate moment. I got there first. But I was in step that time;

Angela and Candi were behind the beat. The three of us eyed each other evilly in an attempt to escape blame.

As the tune arched toward a climax, Major sang, "*Now move a little close to me. You owe it to yourself. And I will selfishly take a little for myself. . . .*" Then Angela moaned in mock ecstasy while we vamped, "*Love won't let me wait,*" and Major crooned, "*Temperature's rising, 'cause you're so tantalizing. . . . Love won't let me way-ay-ait. . . .*" 14

Angela dropped her head slightly as she groaned and looked at me sideways for approval. I wouldn't moan onstage, but I'd been coaching her to take the girlish grin off her face, the whine out of her voice, and moan like a woman. I half rolled my eyes at her; she still didn't have it down. 15

In the middle of the next song, I heard a "pssst, pssst, pssst" from the wings. I couldn't figure out what the road manager was trying to say, but I could tell he was trying to say it to me. We did a quick turn and a chorus of deep-voiced "Yeahs" rose from the audience. The hook on the low back of my royal blue gown had come undone, exposing the major portion of my derriere. One of the Spinners came onstage and hooked me up while I smiled wide to the applause and kept misstepping. 16

Major's record producers checked out the show in Miami. They were not crazy about Brown Sugar's sound. We didn't do Major's big L.A. concert. But we joined him in Bermuda. He stayed in a big, fancy hotel. We stayed two steps up from a dump. 17

I was depressed. I went bike riding with the concert promoter. At every stop, he told the bartender I was one of the "girls" in the show. We were always called girls. Background singers who are fifty are called girls. I considered it sexist and demeaning and asked the men on the tour not to call me that, much to Angela's annoyance. "This is show business," she said. But "girls" and "show" were all the island bartenders had to hear to fill for free my half-empty glass before I knew it. 18

By the time I went on the stage of the Zodiac Club, I was seriously wopped. And when I sang my third or fourth doo and misstepped that night, I fell into football giant Roosevelt Grier's lap. He picked me up, put me back onstage and I kept going. 19

But it wasn't Brown Sugar's mismatched voices or my failure to master the simplest dance steps that did us in. 20

One of Major's producers had come with the show to Bermuda. He had the hots for Candi. She wasn't called Candi for nothing. He drove her to an isolated beach. He told his chauffeur to come back in the morning. They struggled on the beach. She kicked him in the groin. They had to walk back to Hamilton. It took all night, though I don't recall the beach being that far from town. I guess he limped most of the way. 21

We got canned the next day. We had plane tickets back to the States but no money. We hadn't been paid for several weeks. 22

I told Major I was broke. He gave me two hundred dollars cash   23
and said he liked me, liked my voice, liked the way I carried myself.
Look him up when I get back home.

I looked him up for the rest of my money. I went to the record   24
company in Philadelphia with the rest of Brown Sugar. I told Angela,
our designated manager, to get out of my face when she failed to get
our funds in Philly, then I took over.

Major was in Cherry Hill, New Jersey, we were told. We got a   25
lift with the band and Major's sleazy brother-in-law roadie.

In New Jersey, the sleaze tried to keep me from seeing Major and   26
started wagging his finger in my face. I jumped at him, pushed him
aside and dared him to lay a hand on me.

The guys in the band, their noses pressed against their car win-   27
dows, watched me with shocked expressions. I'd been the least
assertive member of Brown Sugar, but only because the road experience was new to me. The sleaze said he was going to talk to Major.
He came back a few minutes later and said the star would see me.
One of the band members rolled down the car window. "You can
represent me anytime," he said.

I saw Major and got our money.   28

At the end of the "Love Won't Let Me Wait" tour, I decided I   29
hadn't spent my life studying music to put up with the crap I'd experienced *and* sing music I didn't like. I wanted to sing jazz—that's
what I'd been doing in Boston during college—and I decided to
return to it. I put together material for an act and started perfecting
it in showcase performances at New York clubs.

At the same time, Angela—we were still talking—had arranged   30
to get studio work for us as background singers. Neither of us was
making enough money, though. She suggested we tour again. Out of
financial desperation, I told her I'd think about it.

I didn't have to sing for a living if I didn't want to, however. I'd   31
decided my second year in college to drop music as my major and
get my degree in communications—always have something to fall
back on, my mother told me. I had worked as a broadcast journalist
right after college. But I missed singing; it is the most immediate kind
of creative expression. I sang first and foremost just for the joy of it.
When all else seemed to fail me during a very troubled adolescence,
there was always music. It was my religion—an unrealistic perspective for an entertainer. In this country music is, above all else, a
business. And until one attains clout in that business, other people dictate what one sings and how one sings it. I considered that
messing with my religion. But this was the reality I had to confront
whether I was singing Top 40 or jazz.

I still hadn't decided what I was going to do professionally when   32
my agent called. I had an audition to join the road company of *Bubblin' Brown Sugar,* she said—oh no, I was wary of anything with
Brown Sugar in the name. I told her I'd think about it.

In the meantime, I had two other auditions set up, one with the   33
manager of an act I had met while touring with Major Harris, the
other with Luther Vandross.

The Vandross audition took place in his New York apartment a   34
few years before he became a stellar soul balladeer. He was very
friendly and down-to-earth. I'd brought my own accompanist,
Richard Cummings, a childhood friend who has been Harry Bela-
fonte's musical director for years. He is a sensitive pianist and
arranger, and I'd asked him to write a soulful, torchy arrangement of
"You and Me Against the World." Vandross loved it. But he wanted
me to come back for a final audition with the other singers. "I want
to hear how you blend," he said.

The next day I went to the manager of the group I'd met while   35
touring with Major. We talked for a few minutes in a large, empty
office in a midtown Manhattan skyscraper. I thought it a strange
place for an audition. "I've heard you, I know you can sing," he said.
"But we need more than a singer." He abruptly excused himself, said
he'd be back in a moment and went into an adjoining room. Well, if
he wants a singer who can dance, it's all over, I thought.

He called me from the other room. When I walked in, he was sit-   36
ting naked on the desk. "I'd like to make a film with you," he said,
standing now, smiling.

I really didn't think stuff this gross happened outside the movies.   37
He was a very short man.

I smiled back, moved toward him slowly, put my arms around his   38
neck and kneed him in the groin.

When Vandross called me for the second audition, I told him I   39
wasn't interested. When I called my agent, I told her to forget about
Bubblin' Brown Sugar. Then I put my application to Columbia University's School of Journalism in the mail.

I don't think I would have had much of a future as a background   40
singer in any case. I kept hearing rumors about me from people still
in the business: "That girl, she's got a real attitude problem."

READING FOR MEANING

Write at least a page about the significance of this phase in Njeri's life. Begin
by indicating in a sentence or two what you think she discovered about herself,
specifically about her abilities and aspirations. Then comment about anything
that intrigues you about her experience. To get you started, here are some
suggestions:

- What do you think Njeri means when she explains that one of Brown
  Sugar's problems was that she herself "hadn't been back in the real world
  long" (paragraph 3)? We often use the phrase "real world," but what do you
  think Njeri means by it in this context? What relation does the world she's
  describing bear to the "real world" that you know?

- Review paragraphs 4–8 where Njeri tells about her youthful accomplishments. Compare this self-representation with the way she describes herself in paragraphs 10–16. What strikes you most about the attitude of the older Njeri as she remembers and writes about her younger self?

- In paragraph 18, Njeri tells us she considered being called one of the girls "sexist and demeaning," but that Angela disagreed. Why do you think Njeri feels this way? What does Njeri tell us about Angela that might help us understand her point of view? With which of the two do you agree? Why?

- Njeri reports that people in the music business think "she's got a real attitude problem" (paragraph 40). What do you think the expression "attitude problem" means? How would you describe Njeri's "attitude"? For whom do you think it would present a problem? Why?

EXTENDING MEANING THROUGH CONVERSATION. After reading for meaning on your own, you may be able to increase your understanding by talking with other students who have also read and written about the selection. Before getting together, reread what you wrote. Begin the conversation by noting one passage you find especially significant.

As you talk about your different ways of understanding and responding to the reading, examine these differences by rereading parts of the essay together.

READING LIKE A WRITER
PRESENTING A PHASE THROUGH ANECDOTES

Autobiographers sometimes organize their writing into phases, distinct periods in their lives when something special happened or when they made an important discovery about themselves. In this phase, Njeri recalls the period of her life when she attempted a career as a background singer, first with Major Harris and later with Luther Vandross.

Although phases cover a substantial period of time, writers present just a few select incidents from the many events that occurred. These incidents are presented as brief, pointed narratives, arranged chronologically, often including dialogue and specific descriptive detail.

ANALYZE. Make an outline of the essay, identifying where each incident begins and ends. The first incident, for example, extends from paragraph 11 to paragraph 16. Its beginning is signaled by the introductory phrase "One night," and the place in which it occurs is specifically identified.

Then choose one incident you find particularly entertaining or significant to analyze closely. Annotate any especially vivid or memorable language— descriptive images, actions, bits of dialogue, or authorial comments.

WRITE. Write a few sentences explaining what you think this particular incident contributes to your understanding of this phase in Njeri's life.

CONSIDERING IDEAS FOR YOUR OWN WRITING

Recall a period in your life when you tried out some new activity—playing in a band or on a team, performing in a play, working at a job, studying computer programming or the Civil War. How long did the phase last? How did you get involved in the activity in the first place? Why did it come to an end? Who else was involved in this activity with you? List some anecdotes that occurred during this period. What do you think makes them memorable? Looking back, how do you feel about this phase in your life?

Laurie Abraham

DIVORCED FATHER

Laurie Abraham (b. 1965), a public health reporter, wrote this portrait of her father for a collection of autobiographical essays titled *Reinventing Home: Six Working Women Look at Their Home Lives.* As the title of this selection suggests, Abraham's essay is about her father after her parents were divorced. As you read and annotate the essay, note Abraham's feelings about how the divorce changed her father and affected her relationship with him.

I have seen tears in my father's eyes twice: during the premiere 1 of the Waltons' Christmas special and on the drive to his new apartment. If I had asked about the tears in his eyes the morning he left home, he probably would have blamed them on the sun. It was a too-bright day in June when my father left home, exactly eighteen years after my parents were married. He took his clothes, the old black-and-white TV, the popcorn popper, a pot and skillet, and a few other things. It took only two trips in the brown Pinto station wagon to move half of my father's life. Not that he couldn't have claimed his share of the tables, chairs, and pictures—but he chose to leave the fallout of two decades of acquiring with my mother.

From a house full of things, he went to an apartment of four 2 empty rooms carpeted in gold-and-white shag. Soon, though, a queen-sized bed jutted from the middle of his bedroom wall, a butcher-block table with four matching chairs sat in the dining room, and an L-shaped brown velvet sofa dwarfed the 19-inch TV. He never bought a picture, a coffee-table, a knickknack or anything that said, "Harold Abraham lives here." A few things that my dad had claimed from the divorce, however, definitely bore his mark: cocktail glasses printed with the Dow Jones Industrial Average; four plastic beer mugs (one with the Bud Man, another with "Michelob" tastefully printed in gold); a stoneware coffee mug with sailboats. But these weren't the possessions of a father of two with a master's degree and a CPA degree. These were pieces of "Abe," that hard-drinking wild boy who wore garlic around his neck for a week to gain admission to a fraternity that stole a cow for a pet, a fraternity that was banned from the campus the year after my father left.

Money certainly didn't prevent my father from decorating his 3 apartment. He usually had enough of it, and when he didn't, he spent it anyway. Surprisingly, the explanation for the starkness of his home came to me from people who have less in common with my father than my mother did: low-income teenagers who picked up trash and trimmed grass in a government jobs program.

"Where do you stay?" several of them asked me during the sum- 4 mer that I worked as their supervisor. At first I wondered about their word choice: I always asked new acquaintances where they lived, not where they stayed. But after listening to them all summer I understood why "stay" was the most appropriate word to describe their experiences. They were always moving, from their mother's apartment, to their grandmother's, to an aunt's. None of these places was necessarily bad, just temporary. These kids didn't live at East Seventy-fifth and Superior, they stayed there for a time. My father was doing that, too—staying. He had no intention of living in his apartment, or calling it home. It was a way station between his first wife and the one to come—except on Sundays. When his girls came to visit, my dad rushed to throw together a home.

I know little about my father's childhood, but I won't forget the 5 few memories that he's let slip over the years. He slept in a dresser drawer because his family could not afford a crib. His dad never said to him, "Harold, how was school today?" He went without many of the furnishings that make up a home, never mind the nurturing. Making a home for his children was important so that he could give us what he never got. He did his best—for us and for the boy whose parents never quite made it to his high school football games.

But since he had been deprived of the emotional sustenance that 6 makes a home a home, my father was never quite sure what to do with my sister and me once he had us. He relied on food—the most straightforward kind of nurturing—to turn his bachelor's apartment into a home. Breakfast was pancakes. In the beginning, when all three of us were trying to fight off sadness and before my sister and I grew to resent the Sunday morning call, "Your father's here," he flipped them. By high school, the pancakes didn't fly and I slumped in my chair, suffering from the six-pack I had downed the night before. By dinner I'd usually recovered enough to enjoy either spaghetti with Ragú sauce or Kentucky Fried Chicken—always carryout; the restaurant wasn't home. These dishes were hearty but deliciously junky, the kind of food men with few cooking skills and one chance a week to win their children's approval are apt to serve. Between meals, we'd eat some more: popcorn or pizza rolls while watching football on TV, or ice cream after an awkward, time-filling walk in the woods.

My father's homemaking hit full stride at Christmas, when the shortcomings we never could ignore became that much more obvious and sad. First, we'd pick the right tree with my mother. Then, another tree with Dad, if we could arrange a time that was "mutually convenient." To the scratchy strains of "Christmas in Killarney," a Ray Conniff album my parents bought when they were first married, we pushed the lights onto the prickly branches of a spruce or Scotch pine. (We never used garden gloves with my father, although my mother used them; he probably didn't own a pair anyway.) My father's half of the ornaments included a few of the "good" ones—the papier-mâché Santa, the Ohio State football helmet trimmed with holly—but he also had his share of the back-of-the-tree duds such as clear plastic teardrops, one for each of the twelve days of Christmas. Most years, decorating the tree with Dad was fun, but to my sister and me, it wasn't our *real* tree in our *real* home. It was what we put up with Dad so he wouldn't be lonely at Christmas. 7

Long after I began to consider the two times I saw my father almost cry, I realized that there might be a connection between the tears of moving day and those provoked by the Waltons' Christmas show. Its plot was this: Pa Walton was lost during a snowstorm on Christmas Eve. A man was cut off from his family. I doubt back then, watching that show, that Dad imagined one day he would be driving away from his wife and girls, but somehow he identified. And what my father missed the most when he left home was something the Waltons had plenty of—people. That's what my father was forced to give up: lots of people around, people he might not necessarily be close to (like my mom), but who were present. He didn't want to struggle to build a new family from scratch; he needed to be plopped down in the middle of one. And so he was, finally. His second wife comes from a large and raucous family, and my dad has three new stepchildren. Large Christmas Eve parties at his new wife's home have become something of a tradition for us. 8

For me, the parties are events. I wear red, or something that stands out in a crowd of relatives I see once a year. Yet although I always have a good time, I still feel that my real Christmas is the next day at treeside, in those more intense, heartfelt moments with my mother. Spending the day with my mother is what I want, but I do not think I could enjoy myself if my father were alone on Christmas. He would never ask my sister or me to spend part of the day with him; he is too proud. Instead, he would call us around eleven in the morning to wish us "Merry Christmas" in a loud voice. His conversation would be punctuated by laughs that seemed to end before they started. I knew from experience that when he wasn't talking, he was gritting his teeth slightly, tightening the line of his jaw. "Love you 9 big bunches," he would say rapidly, before hanging up. Then the phone would ring again right away. He had forgotten to tell me that I left my sweatshirt at his apartment. "Oh, thanks, Dad; I'll get it next time we come over," I would say.

"Okay, then. Merry Christmas."   10

"Merry Christmas, Dad."   11

I am grateful to my new stepfamily for sheltering my father and   12
me from this coldest cold. Without them, my father would get lost in the snow.

READING FOR MEANING

Write at least a page exploring your understanding and response to "Divorced Father." You might begin by stating your impression of Abraham's father and her relationship with him. Include specific details from the story to illustrate. Then point to anything in this selection that evokes a strong reaction in you or leads you to reflect on parent-child relationships or the effects of divorce.

To explore beyond your first impressions, you may need to reread certain passages and add to your annotations before writing. Use the following suggestions to develop your ideas and response:

- Abraham seems to feel she understands her father pretty well. Look back at paragraphs 3 and 4 where she explains how she gained insight into him from what some people said to her. Explain in your own words the point Abraham is making here.

- In the opening paragraph, Abraham says that had she asked her father "about the tears in his eyes the morning he left home, he probably would have blamed them on the sun." What does this observation tell you about Abraham's attitude toward and assumptions about her father?

- In paragraphs 1 and 2, Abraham names every possession her father took with him to his new apartment. But in paragraph 3, she notes the "starkness of his home." What do you think she's trying to say about her father in these paragraphs?

- Abraham juxtaposes two Christmas memories in paragraphs 7 and 8. Why do you think Abraham sets up this contrast? What does it add to your impression of her father or your understanding of Abraham's relationship with him?

EXTENDING MEANING THROUGH CONVERSATION. After you have considered this essay's meaning on your own, discussing it with others who have read and thought about it may help to develop your understanding. Work with one or two other students. Before getting together, reread what you wrote about Abraham's portrait of her father. Begin your conversation by taking turns recalling one aspect of the reading that you found especially significant.

READING LIKE A WRITER
DESCRIBING A PERSON THROUGH ANECDOTES
AND RECURRING ACTIVITIES

In describing a person, autobiographers usually have many experiences from which to choose. These experiences may be one-time occurrences that show something special about the person or the writer's relationship with that person. Or the experiences may be recurring activities, habits, or rituals the writer associates with the person. In Abraham's portrait of her father, we find both one-time anecdotes and recurring activities.

ANALYZE. Reread paragraphs 1 and 8, where Abraham tells brief anecdotes about what happened on the two occasions she saw tears in her father's eyes, and paragraphs 6 and 7, where she relates the recurring activities of eating at her father's apartment and celebrating Christmas with him. As you read, notice where instead of only making general statements such as "My father cried" or "We ate dinner," Abraham gives specific details; for example, it was a "too-bright day in June" or the kind of spaghetti sauce used. Underline the details that help you imagine what it was like during these occasions.

WRITE. Write a few sentences explaining what you learn about her father and about Abraham's feelings toward him from these anecdotes and recurring activities.

CONSIDERING IDEAS FOR YOUR OWN WRITING

Autobiographers often write about people with whom they have close relationships over a long period of time. In this selection, Abraham wrote about a particular phase in her relationship with her father. About whom would you choose to write and on which phase in your relationship would you focus? Like Abraham, you could write about a relative or friend with whom you have had a long-term relationship. You might choose someone who lives far away but with whom you have close ties. Or perhaps you would like to write about a relationship that changed at some point—suddenly or over a period of time.

What anecdotes or recurring activities do you think you might relate? What do you think those anecdotes or recurring activities suggest about the person and your relationship?

Brad Benioff

RICK

Brad Benioff was a freshman at the University of California, San Diego, when he wrote the following essay for his composition class.

Like the Abraham selection, Benioff's essay focuses on a memorable person. Benioff writes about his high-school water polo coach, Rick Rezinas. As you read, notice how Benioff uses dialogue to dramatize his relation to Rick and how he discloses Rick's significance in his life.

I walked through the dawn chill, shivering as much from nervous- 1
ness as from the cold. Steam curled up from the water in the pool and disappeared in the ocher morning light. Athletes spread themselves about on the deck, lazily stretching and whispering to each other as if the stillness were sacred. It was to be my first prac- tice with the high school water polo team. I knew nothing about the game, but a friend had pushed me to play, arguing, "It's the most fun of any sport. Trust me." He had awakened me that morning long before daylight, forced me into a bathing suit, and driven me to the pool.

"Relax," he said. "Rick is the greatest of coaches. You'll like him. 2
You'll have fun."

The mythical Rick. I had heard of him many times before. All the 3
older players knew him by his first name and always spoke of him as a friend rather than a coach. He was a math teacher at our school, and his classes were very popular. Whenever class schedules came out, everyone hoped to be placed in Mr. Rezinas's class. He had been known to throw parties for the team or take them on week- end excursions skiing or backpacking. To be Rick's friend was to be part of an exclusive club, and I was being invited to join. And so I looked forward with nervous anticipation to meeting this man.

My friend walked me out to the pool deck and steered me 4
toward a man standing beside the pool.

"Rick," announced my friend, "I'd like you to meet your newest 5
player."

Rick was not a friendly looking man. He wore only swim trunks, 6
and his short, powerful legs rose up to meet a bulging torso. His big belly was solid. His shoulders, as if to offset his front-heaviness, were thrown back, creating a deep crease of excess muscle from his sides around the small of his back, a crease like a huge frown. His arms were crossed, two medieval maces placed carefully on their racks, ready to be swung at any moment. His round cheeks and chin were darkened by traces of black whiskers. His hair was sparse. Huge, black, mirrored sunglasses replaced his eyes. Below his prominent nose was a thin, sinister mustache. I couldn't believe this menacing-looking man was the legendary jovial Rick.

He said nothing at first. In those moments of silence, I felt more 7
inadequate than ever before in my life. My reflection in his glasses stared back at me, accusing me of being too skinny, too young, too stupid, too weak to be on his team. Where did I get the nerve to approach him with such a ridiculous body and ask to play water

polo, a *man's* game? Finally, he broke the silence, having finished appraising my meager body. "We'll fatten him up," he growled.

Thus began a week of torture. For four hours a day, the coach stood beside the pool scowling down at me. I could do nothing right.

"No! No! No!" He shook his head in disgust. "Throw the damn ball with your whole arm! Get your goddamn elbow out of the water!"

Any failure on my part brought down his full wrath. He bellowed at my incompetence and punished me with push-ups and wind sprints. Even when I was close to utter exhaustion, I found no sympathy. "What the hell are you doing on the wall?" he would bellow. "Coach . . . my side, it's cramped."

"Swim on it! If you can't take a little pain, then you don't play!" With this, he would push me off the wall.

He seemed to enjoy playing me against the older, stronger players. "Goddamn it, Brad! If someone elbows or hits you, don't look out at me and cry, 'It's not fair.' Push back! Don't be so weak!" I got elbowed around until it seemed that none of my internal organs was unscathed. He worked me until my muscles wouldn't respond, and then he demanded more.

"You're not trying! Push it!"

"Would you move? You're too slow! Swim!"

"Damn it! Get out and give me twenty!"

It took little time for me to hate both the game and the man who ruled it.

I reacted by working as hard as I could. I decided to deprive him of the pleasure of finding fault with me. I learned quickly and started playing as flawlessly as possible. I dispensed with looking tired, showing pain, or complaining of cramps. I pushed, hit, and elbowed back at the biggest of players. No matter how flawless or aggressive my performance, though, he would find fault and let me know it. He was never critical of other players. He would laugh and joke with the other players; but whenever he saw me, he frowned.

I decided to quit.

After a particularly demanding practice, I walked up to this tyrant. I tried to hold his gaze, but the black glasses forced me to look down.

"Coach Rezinas," I blurted, "I've decided that I don't want to play water polo." His scowl deepened. Then after a moment he said, "You can't quit. Not until after the first game." And he walked away. The dictator had issued his command.

There was no rule to keep me from quitting. Anger flushed through me. Somehow I would get revenge on this awful man. After the first game? Okay. I would play. I would show him what a valuable player I was. He would miss my talents when I quit. I worked myself up before the first game by imagining the hated face: the black glasses, the thin mustache, the open, snarling mouth. I was not surprised that he placed me in the starting lineup because I was certain he would take me out soon. I played furiously. The ball, the goal, the opposition, even the water seemed to be extensions of Rick, his face glaring from every angle, his words echoing loudly in my ears. Time and time again I would get the ball and, thinking of his tortures, fire it toward the goal with a strength to kill. I forgot that he might take me out. No defender could stand up to me. I would swim by them or over them. Anger and the need for vengeance gave me energy. I didn't notice the time slipping by, the quarters ending.

Then, the game ended. My teammates rushed out to me, congratulating and cheering me. I had scored five goals, a school record for one game, and shut out the other team with several key defensive plays. Now I could get revenge. Now I could quit. I stepped out of the pool prepared with the words I would spit into his face: "I QUIT!" 22

As I approached him, I stopped dead. He was smiling at me, his glasses off. He reached out with his right hand and shook mine with exuberance. 23

"I knew you had it in you! I knew it!" he laughed. 24

Through his laughter, I gained a new understanding of the man. He had pushed me to my fullest potential, tapping into the talent I may never have found in myself. He was responsible for the way I played that day. My glory was his. He never hated me. On the contrary, I was his apprentice, his favored pupil. He had brought out my best. Could I really hate someone who had done that much for me? He had done what he had promised: he had fattened me up mentally as well as physically. All this hit me in a second and left me completely confused. I tried to speak, but only managed to croak, "Coach . . . uh . . . I, uh . . . " He cut me off with another burst of laughter. He still shook my hand. 25

"Call me Rick," he said. 26

READING FOR MEANING

Write at least a page exploring your understanding of the relationship between Benioff and Coach Rick Rezinas. Begin by considering how Benioff represents the relationship. Then write about anything else that strikes you as important or revealing, going back to reread and annotate specific passages that contribute to your understanding.

If you have trouble continuing for at least a page, consider these suggestions:

- Review paragraphs 1–7 to see what Benioff expected when he first met Rick and how Rick initially treated him.

- Evaluate Rick's coaching style.

- Tell what you learned about Benioff from his reactions to Rick. What did he do when Rick criticized him?

- Explain the likely meaning or significance of "To be Rick's friend was to be part of an exclusive club, and I was being invited to join" (paragraph 3); "My reflection in his glasses stared back at me, accusing me of being too skinny, too young, too stupid, too weak to be on his team" (paragraph 7); "I dispensed with looking tired, showing pain, or complaining of cramps" (paragraph 17); "Anger and the need for vengeance gave me energy" (paragraph 21); "He was responsible for the way I played that day. My glory was his" (paragraph 25); or any other statement that catches your attention.
- Explain how something in your own experience or reading helps you to understand Benioff's relationship with Rick.

EXTENDING MEANING THROUGH CONVERSATION. Discussing the story with others who have read and thought about it may help you to develop your understanding. Work with one or two other students. Begin your conversation by taking turns describing an aspect of the reading that you found especially significant.

READING LIKE A WRITER
DESCRIBING A PERSON THROUGH VISUAL DETAILS
AND DIALOGUE

Visual description and dialogue not only make a person come alive for readers but also tell a lot about how the person relates to others, particularly to the autobiographer. Detailing of facial features, for example, might show whether the person smiles or frowns, looks others directly in the eye, or looks down on others. Similarly, bits of dialogue indicate how the person addresses others as well as what that person actually says.

ANALYZE. To examine Benioff's visual description of Rick, reread paragraph 6 and underline the details that let you picture Rick. Note the physical features on which Benioff focuses and also how he characterizes them. For example, one feature Benioff points out is Rick's legs, which he characterizes as "short" and "powerful."

Then skim the selection, noting each time Rick says something. If the dialogue is accompanied by any visual description, underline the descriptive language.

WRITE. Write a few sentences explaining the impression you get of Rick from the visual description and dialogue. Quote examples to illustrate your points. Indicate which, if any, of the descriptive details or dialogue do not contribute to the overall impression or appear to contradict it.

COMPARE. Look back at Abraham's essay and underline visual details that let you see her father as well as dialogue that enables you to hear him. Write a few sentences comparing what you found in Abraham's use of visual description and dialogue with that in Benioff's.

CONSIDERING IDEAS FOR YOUR OWN WRITING

Consider coaches, teachers, employers, and other mentors who have influenced your life. Choose one of these people, and think about how you might describe what the individual taught you and how he or she went about it. How would you reveal what you learned about the person and about yourself? Or consider people with whom you have had continuing disagreements or conflicts. Choose one of these people and speculate about how you might describe your relationship with this person.

THINKING ABOUT WHAT MAKES AUTOBIOGRAPHY EFFECTIVE

In this chapter you have been learning how to read autobiography for meaning and how to read it like a writer. Before going on to write a piece of autobiography, pause here to review and consolidate what you have learned about what makes autobiographical writing successful.

ANALYZE. Choose one reading from this chapter that seems to you to be especially effective. Before rereading the selection, note one or two things that led you to remember it as an example of good autobiographical writing.

Reread your chosen selection, adding further annotations about what makes it particularly successful as a work of autobiography. To begin, consider the selection's purpose and how well it achieves that purpose for its readers. Then focus on how well the selection

- tells the story
- describes the scene
- describes people
- conveys the autobiographical significance

You can complete this activity on your own, or your instructor may ask you to work with a small group of students who have chosen the same reading. If you work with others, take time initially for everyone to reread the selection, adding to their annotations as suggested above. Then discuss what makes this particular autobiographical selection so effective. Take notes.

WRITE. Write at least a page explaining and justifying your choice of this reading as an example of effective autobiographical writing. Assume that your readers—your instructor and classmates—have read the selection but will not remember many details about it. They also may not remember it as an especially successful piece of autobiography. Therefore, you will want to use details and refer to specific parts of the reading as you explain how it works as autobiography and justify your evaluation of its effectiveness. You need *not* argue that it is the best reading in the chapter or that it is flawless, only that it is, in your view, a strong example of the genre.

A GUIDE TO AUTOBIOGRAPHICAL WRITING

From the autobiographical selections you have read and analyzed in this chapter, you have learned that autobiographical essays include engaging stories; vivid scenes; memorable people; and personal disclosure by the writer, indicating the significance of the event, phase, or person. Having learned to question, evaluate, and appreciate autobiography as a reader, you can now approach autobiography more confidently as a writer. You can more readily imagine the problems autobiographers must solve, the materials and possibilities they have to work with, the choices and decisions they must make. This section offers specific guidelines for writing autobiographical essays and suggestions to help you solve the special problems this kind of writing presents.

INVENTION

The following activities will help you find an autobiographical topic to write about, recall details of this topic, and explore its significance in your life. Completing these activities will produce a record of remembered details and thoughts that will be invaluable as you draft your essay.

Finding an Autobiographical Topic

The readings in this chapter illustrate many possible autobiographical topics, as do the ideas for your own writing that follow each reading. You might want to review them quickly before you begin.

It is more likely that you will find a promising topic if you have many diverse possibilities from which to choose. You might begin your search by listing potential subjects, using the three autobiographical categories illustrated in this chapter—event, phase, and person—as a starting point. List as many specific topics as you can under each of these categories. The growing list may suggest still further topics that might not have come to mind immediately.

For *events,* list especially memorable brief events lasting a few hours or, at most, a day. Think of the first time you did something; of accidents, surprises, victories, defeats; of elation or frustration, achievement or disappointment at school, home, or work.

For *phases,* list periods of several weeks or months when something important was happening in your life, when you were changing in a significant way. Perhaps participating in a particular group, class, or team challenged you in some way or changed your beliefs or ideas. Perhaps at work you were part of an especially productive or an ineffective team for a while. Or maybe as a parent or a spouse you went through a particularly rough or happy period. You may have moved to a new city or school and had to make a difficult adjustment, or you may have been ill for a long time. Maybe you learned something new or developed a new interest. Think of recent phases as well as ones much earlier in your life.

For *people,* list significant people in your life. Think of people who taught you something about yourself, who surprised or disappointed you, or who had authority over you. These could be people with whom you worked closely, such as another student, colleague, or parent.

This list-making process will almost certainly produce a number of possible topics for your autobiographical essay. The topic you ultimately choose should be one you truly care about, one that will give you the pleasure of recalling past experience and deciding what it means to you. Your topic should also be one that is likely to engage your readers, who will enjoy learning about someone else's life. Finally, and of the greatest importance, your topic should have autobiographical significance that you feel comfortable sharing with readers. Writing autobiography can be an occasion for self-exploration and discovery, but remember that it is public, not private, writing. Decide for yourself—as all autobiographers must—just how personal you want your autobiography to be.

Probing Your Topic

After you have selected a topic, probe your memory to recall details and feelings. You should explore your present perspective on this topic and attempt to establish its autobiographical significance. The following activities will guide you in probing your subject to produce a fuller, more focused draft. Each activity takes only a few minutes.

RECALLING FIRST IMPRESSIONS. Write for a few minutes about your very first thoughts and feelings about the event, phase, or person. What happened? Who was there? How did you react? What thoughts did you have? What feelings can you remember? What do your first impressions reveal about you as a person?

EXPLORING YOUR PRESENT PERSPECTIVE. Next, shift your focus from the past to the present. From your present perspective, what ideas do you have about the event, phase, or person? Write for a few minutes, trying to express your present thoughts and feelings. How have your feelings changed? What insights do you now have? What does your present perspective reveal about you as a person?

DISCOVERING AUTOBIOGRAPHICAL SIGNIFICANCE. Readers want not only to hear your story but also to know what it means to you, what you learned from it, how it changed you. Now that you have explored your first impressions and present perspective of the event, phase, or person, try writing two or three sentences that state its significance in your life. These sentences may eventually help you focus your draft, providing a purpose and a main point for your writing.

LEARNING MORE ABOUT YOUR READERS:
A COLLABORATIVE ACTIVITY

Get together with two or three other students at this point in your invention process. In turn, tell one another what you plan to write about and the autobiographical significance you want to convey to your readers. Then each student should tell what seems to be most significant about each other student's experience.

You can benefit greatly from hearing what others understand from your brief description. Listen to what they have to say. They may have insights you can use to deepen your own understanding of the significance. Their responses will also enable you to better anticipate what readers will be thinking when they read your autobiography and, therefore, can help you convey more effectively the significance of your experience.

DETAILING THE SCENE. To make the scene vivid and memorable for readers and to understand its significance for you, visualize it. List what you see in the scene—objects as well as people. Choose one or two items from your list, and write about each for a few minutes, detailing each object or person as fully as you can. Try to recall specific sensory details: size, appearance, dress, way of walking and gesturing, posture, and mannerisms of a person; size, shape, color, condition, and texture of an object. Imagine the object or person seen from the side, from behind, from a distance, and close up. Write what you see.

RECONSTRUCTING DIALOGUE. Reconstructed conversations are often important in modern autobiography. If another person plays a role in your topic—even a minor role—reconstruct what the two of you might have said to each other. Keep your dialogue as close to informal talk as you can, and use the following format:

[Your name]: [What you said]

[Other person's name]: [What the other person said]

[Continue alternating contributions down the page.]

RESTATING AUTOBIOGRAPHICAL SIGNIFICANCE. Now that you have explored your topic in several ways, write two or three sentences restating its significance in your life. Why is this event, phase, or person still important to you? What do you think you might learn about yourself as you write? What do you want to disclose about yourself to your readers?

This final restatement of autobiographical significance will help you focus your thoughts before you begin drafting. It will also guide you in selecting details to include in your essay.

DRAFTING

Before you begin drafting, review the invention writing you have completed. Reread your notes, searching for promising ideas and notable details; then jot down any further ideas and details your notes suggest to you.

You are now ready to proceed to your first draft. The following guidelines will help you set goals to focus your writing, make specific plans for your essay, and decide how to begin.

Setting Goals

Establishing specific goals before writing the first draft will enable you to draft more confidently. The following questions may help you to set goals for your draft and help you recall how the writers you have read tried to achieve similar goals.

How can I present my topic vividly and memorably to my readers? Like Baker and Benioff, should I rely on reconstructed conversation to dramatize the event, phase, or person? Can I use graphic details to describe the scene to reinforce the significance, as do Lorde, Njeri, and Abraham? Should I concentrate on action rather than dialogue, like Dillard?

How will I help readers understand why this event, phase, or person is important to me? For example, Benioff leaves us to infer how Coach Rick Rezinas has been a significant influence in his life, just as Dillard leaves us to infer why "A Chase" has remained so vivid in her memory. Lorde is more explicit, concluding her autobiographical essay with a direct explanation of the Washington incident's significance.

How can I avoid superficial or one-dimensional presentations of myself and my relations with others? Readers are turned off by predictable stories and people. Readers expect surprises, contradictions, paradoxes, ironies—signs that the writer is thinking deeply, freshly, and honestly, probing remembered experience in a way that may teach both the writer and the reader something. Recall the paradox in Dillard's feeling both terror and pleasure when she was chased by the man in the black Buick; the irony implicit in Baker's suggestion that after the flight, he found T. L. Smith the "most manly looking fellow in the entire corps of instructors"; the contradictions Lorde sets up in relating her parents' behavior and their beliefs.

Planning Your Draft

The particular goals you have established will determine the plan of your draft. Although this plan can unfold as you write, many writers find it helpful to sketch out a tentative plan before they begin drafting. If you will narrate a single event, for example, you could outline briefly what happens from beginning to end. If you will describe a person, you might plan the order in which major features of your description will appear. Reviewing plans of selections in this chapter will suggest possibilities. Be prepared to depart from your plan after you have started writing, because drafting nearly always produces unexpected discoveries that may make it necessary to change direction.

Beginning

A strong beginning will immediately engage readers' interest, so consider beginning your essay with dialogue, with an unusual detail of a person or scene, or with an action. You might also begin by presenting the context for your essay, orienting readers in a general way to the event, phase, or person.

For example, Abraham begins by remembering the two times she saw her father cry. Benioff begins with a specific scene, the school's swimming pool in the early morning light. Lorde begins with a pointed reference to the significance of the event, which will be developed fully only at the end. Dillard, Baker, and Njeri begin more conventionally, though no less successfully, by giving us a context for the stories they will tell.

You might have to try two or three different beginnings before finding a promising way to start, but do not agonize for too long over the first sentence. Try out any possible beginning and see what happens.

Choosing Relevant Details

If you have had a successful period of invention, you probably already have more particular details than you can use in one essay. Well-prepared writers must spend a great deal of time deciding which details and information to leave out. As you draft, remember to include enough details so readers can imagine the person or scene but only those details that support the autobiographical disclosure you are making.

READING A DRAFT CRITICALLY

Now that you have written a draft, getting one or more readers who know something about autobiographical writing to take a close look at what you have written could help you see how to improve your draft. This section will help your readers give you useful advice. Get a written response to your draft so that later when you sit down to revise, you will have specific criticisms and suggestions to follow.

You gain from receiving a critical reading, but you can also benefit from giving one to someone else. Not only do you learn more about the features and strategies that make autobiographical writing effective, but you also learn about the writing process—what kinds of problems other autobiographers typically encounter when they write and how they solve those problems.

Reading a draft critically means reading it more than once, first to get a general impression and then to analyze its basic features and strategies. Before you read, number the paragraphs so you can refer easily to specific parts of the draft.

Reading for a First Impression

Read quickly through the draft, and then write a couple of sentences indicating your general impressions. After you have finished reading, write down any immediate reaction. What did you find most striking and memorable about the event, phase, or person from your first, quick reading?

Reading to Analyze

Read the draft a second time to focus on the basic features and strategies of autobiography. Jot down your responses to the following features as you read.

TELLING THE STORY. For an autobiographical event or phase, look first at the overall shape and pace of the story and let the writer know what you find most engaging about the story. Indicate whether you cannot identify the climax, whether the central conflict is confusing, or whether the story seems to meander pointlessly. Mark any particular places where the tension slackens or where background information interrupts the drama.

Note which anecdotes seem especially effective as well as any that seem unnecessary or confusing. Identify any places where an additional anecdote might help you better imagine what happened or what a person was like. Suggest how an anecdote could be made more dramatic by intensifying the action or by revising the dialogue, for example.

DESCRIBING THE SCENE. Identify the most effective part of the description— an especially vivid detail, a striking image, or how well the details of the scene go together to form a dominant impression. Note any passages where you need more description as well as any where the description distracts from the action. Show the writer where you find the point of view confusing or where a shift in point of view (coming in for a close-up, for example) might enliven the description.

DESCRIBING PEOPLE. Identify one passage where a person comes across most vividly. Let the writer know where more specific, visual description—such as what the person looks like or how the person gestures when talking—could be added. Also point out any detail that seems inconsistent or contradictory. Focus on the dialogue, indicating where it could be made more dramatic or where it might be summarized rather than reconstructed word for word.

CONVEYING THE AUTOBIOGRAPHICAL SIGNIFICANCE. Tell the writer what you think is significant about this event, phase, or person. If the significance seems unclear to you, try to help the writer think more about it. Note any word choices—in the way people and scenes are described or in the way the story is told—that explicitly contradict or implicitly undercut the stated significance. Also indicate whether the significance strikes you as too pat or simplistic, such as whether a person is demonized or idealized, or whether a troubling event is shrugged off too lightly.

REVISING

This section provides suggestions for revising your draft, suggestions that will remind you what makes autobiographical writing meaningful both to the writer and to the readers. To revise effectively, you need to refocus on what is most important in your writing, what you want readers to know and feel about your life experience. Anything that blurs the focus or diverts attention away from what is important may need to be cut or rewritten.

The biggest mistake you can make in revising is to turn your attention away from the big picture and concern yourself too soon with correcting spelling errors or improving your style. At this point, you need to think about larger issues like how you can impress on readers the excitement you felt, convey your mixed feelings, or capture a dramatic turning point. Technically, if you can use a computer, revising has never been so easy or fast. But intellectually and emotionally, revising remains a challenge as well as possibly the most satisfying part of the writing process.

If your draft received a thoughtful critical reading by a classmate or two, you will have received some valuable help in deciding which parts of your draft need revising and what specific changes you could make. Before making a plan or starting to revise, you can reread your own draft analytically by following the guidelines for Reading a Draft Critically. As you revise, keep in mind the following suggestions.

Revising to Tell the Story

If the climax is hard to identify, try to increase the drama leading up to it or consider using a different part of the story as the high point.

If the central conflict is confusing, consider simplifying it or adding action or dialogue that would help explain it.

If the story seems to meander, tighten the narrative by cutting irrelevant action or detail.

Where the tension slackens, try using more active verbs, more dialogue, and staccato phrases and clauses.

Where background information interrupts the drama, consider presenting the information at another point in the story.

Describing the Scene

If the details of the scene do not go together well to form a dominant impression, cut the details that do not fit.

Where readers cannot imagine the scene, add more sensory detail.

Where the description distracts from the action, cut or move the description.

Where the point of view is confusing, consider simplifying it.

Describing a Person

Where more specific, visual description is needed, give physical details showing what the person looks like or how the person gestures.

If any detail seems inconsistent or contradictory, cut it.

If the dialogue seems vague or unnecessary, make it more dramatic or simply summarize it.

Conveying the Autobiographical Significance

If readers do not understand the significance of your remembered event, phase, or person, look for places where it could be conveyed more directly. Or consider giving readers more insight into your personal or cultural background.

If the significance seems too pat or simplistic, consider whether you have expressed the full range of your feelings, even if you are somewhat ambivalent.

REFLECTING ON WHAT YOU HAVE LEARNED ABOUT WRITING AUTOBIOGRAPHY

In this chapter, you have read critically several pieces of autobiography and have written one of your own. To remind yourself how much you have learned and to help you remember it, pause now to reflect on your reading and writing experiences while working through this chapter.

Write a page or so reflecting on your learning. Begin by describing what you are most pleased with in your autobiographical essay and explaining what contributed to your achievement. Be very specific about this contribution. If it was something you learned from the readings, indicate which readings and specifically what you learned from them. If it came from your invention writing, point out the section or sections that helped you most. If you got good advice from a critical reader, explain exactly how the person helped you—perhaps to understand a particular problem in your draft or to add a new dimension to your writing. Try to write about your achievement in terms of what you have learned about the genre of autobiography.

Then write about anything else that accounts for your learning this special kind of writing. Feel free at this point to add anything you have learned about the writing process—for example, how to use time efficiently before writing a draft to discover what you want to say about the subject or how to get constructive criticism and practical advice from other readers of your draft.

CHAPTER 3

—

OBSERVATION

————

Certain kinds of writing are based on fresh observation or direct investigation. Travel writers, for example, may write about a place they have visited; naturalists may describe phenomena they have observed. Investigative reporters or clinical psychologists may write about a person they have talked to many times, while cultural anthropologists may write ethnographies of groups or communities they have studied for several months or years.

Much of what we know about people and the world we learn from this kind of writing. Because it often deals with unfamiliar subjects, observational writing can be enormously interesting.

Writing up your own observations can offer special rewards and challenges. You can visit places and interview people you are interested in. In reporting what you have found, you translate your discoveries and perceptions about your subject into writing you can share with others. These activities of observing, note taking, and perceptive reporting form the basic strategies of research and knowledge making in many of the academic disciplines you will study as a college student.

An observational writer's primary purpose is to inform readers. Whether writing about people, places, or activities, the writer must satisfy the readers' desire for interesting material presented in a lively and engaging manner. Although readers might learn as much about a popular African American woman comic-strip artist from an entry in *Contemporary Authors* as from the essay on this same artist by Lisa Jones in this chapter, reading Jones's observations is sure to be more enjoyable.

Readers of observational essays expect to be surprised. When writing about your observations, you will have an immediate advantage if you choose a place, an activity, or a person that is likely to surprise and intrigue your readers. Even if the subject is familiar, you can still interest readers by presenting it in a way they have never before considered.

Observational writers try both to entertain and to inform readers. Not content with generalizations and summaries, they vividly present scenes and people to their readers. As readers, we can imagine specific details of a scene—objects, shapes, textures, colors, sounds, smells. We see people dressed a particular way. We see them moving and gesturing, and we hear them talk. All the details contribute to a dominant impression of the subject that conveys the writer's attitudes and ideas.

As you read, discuss, and write about the selections that follow in this chapter, you will learn a lot about observational writing. You should also get ideas for an observational essay of your own, based perhaps on the ideas for writing that follow each selection. As you work through the chapter, keep in mind the following assignment, which sets out the goals for writing an observational essay.

THE WRITING ASSIGNMENT

Observation

Write an observational essay about an intriguing person, place, or activity in your community. Your essay may be a brief profile of an individual based on one or two interviews; a description of a place or an activity observed once or twice; or a longer, more fully developed profile of a person, a place, or an activity based on a number of observational visits and interviews conducted over several weeks.

Observe your subject closely, and then present what you have learned in a way that both informs and engages readers.

OBSERVATIONAL WRITING SITUATIONS

Journalists often write articles (sometimes called *profiles*) based on their personal observations. College students frequently write observational articles. Following are examples of such articles:

- A journalist assigned to write about a Nobel Prize–winning scientist decides to profile a typical day in her life. He spends a couple of days observing her at home and at work, and interviews colleagues, students, and family, as well as the scientist herself. Her daily life, he learns, is very much like that of other working mothers—a constant effort to balance the demands of her career against the needs of her family. He conveys this impression in his essay by alternating details about the scientist's career with those about her home life.

- A student in an art-history class fulfills an assignment by writing about a local artist recently commissioned to paint outdoor murals for the city. The student visits the artist's studio and talks with him about the process of painting murals. The artist invites the student to spend the following day as a part of a team of local art students and neighborhood volunteers working on the mural under the artist's direction. This firsthand experience helps the student describe the process of collaboration involved in mural painting.

- A student studies a controversial urban renewal project for an end-of-semester project in a sociology class. After reading newspaper reports for the names of opponents and supporters of the project, she interviews several of them. Then she tours the site with the project manager. Her report alternates description of the project with analysis of the controversy.

PRACTICING OBSERVATION
A COLLABORATIVE ACTIVITY

Think of people, places, or activities on your campus or in your community that you could observe in detail and then write about. Consider subjects that interest you and that you would like to know more about. List as many of them as you can. Consider local personalities (an eccentric store owner, perhaps, or a distinguished teacher); places or activities on campus (the student health center or an experimental laboratory) or in the community (a computer-software company or a recycling center).

Then get together with two or three other students and read your lists of possible subjects to one another. Ask the others to tell you which item on your list is most interesting to them and to explain briefly why. Jot down their comments.

After you have all read your lists and received responses, consider the following questions:

Were you surprised by which item on your list the other members of the group found most interesting? Why?

Which of their reasons for being interested in your subject surprised you most? Why?

Given the group's reasons for being interested in your subject, how might you go about observing the subject to enhance this interest?

A GUIDE TO READING OBSERVATIONAL WRITING

To become familiar with the features and strategies of observational writing, read, annotate, and write about your responses to the brief selection that follows. Then, guided by a list of the basic features of observational writing, reread the selection to examine the particular elements of strong observational writing.

First, though, as a reminder of the many possibilities for annotating, here is an illustration of an annotated passage from another observational essay, by an unnamed *New Yorker* magazine writer, which appears in its entirety later in this chapter.

probably jabs his finger at his workers, too

"I am not prejudiced against color or religion," Mr. Yeganeh told us, and he jabbed an index finger at the flashing sign. "Whoever follows that I treat very well. My regular customers don't say anything. They are very intelligent and well educated. They know I'm just trying to move the line. The New York cop is very smart—he sees everything but says nothing. But the young girl who wants to stop and tell you how nice you look and hold everyone up—*yah!*"

off with her head?!

He made a guillotining motion with his hand. "I tell you, I hate to work with the public. They treat me like a slave. My philosophy is: The customer is always wrong and I'm always right. I raised my prices to try to get rid of some of these people, but it didn't work."

unpleasant person who still makes money

so high it seems out of place

The other day, Mr. Yeganeh was dressed in chefs' whites with orange smears across his chest, which may have been some of the carrot soup cooking in a huge pot on a little stove in one corner. A three-foot-long handheld mixer from France sat on the sink, looking like an overgrown gardening tool. Mr. Yeganeh spoke to two young

visual details— colors

helpers in a twisted Armenian-Spanish barrage, then said to us, "I have no overhead, no trained waitresses, and I have the cashier here." He pointed to himself theatrically. Beside the doorway, a glass case with fresh green celery, red and yellow peppers, and

lots of info about the business

purple eggplant was topped by five big gray soup urns. According to a piece of cardboard taped to the door, you can buy Mr. Yeganeh's soups in three sizes, costing from four to fifteen dollars. The order of any well-behaved customer is accompanied by little waxpaper packets of bread, fresh vegetables (such as scallions and radishes), fresh fruit (such as cherries or an orange), a chocolate mint, and a plastic spoon. No coffee, tea, or other drinks are served.

Tracy Kidder

TEACHING CELERY

This selection comes from Tracy Kidder's *Among Schoolchildren* (1989). Kidder's books include *The Soul of a New Machine* (1982), for which he won the Pulitzer Prize, *House* (1985), and *Old Friends* (1993). Kidder is noted for his careful observations of people at work.

In this selection, we see an episode in the fifth-grade classroom of teacher Chris Zajac, whom Kidder observed for an entire school year. Such a classroom is a familiar scene to all of Kidder's readers; and yet Kidder presents a math lesson unlike any we are likely to remember.

Read the essay, annotating anything that strikes you as interesting and likely to contribute to your understanding of what happens in Zajac's classroom. Mark on the text, and write comments or questions in the margin.

It was a Wednesday morning, the dead middle of a week in late fall. Bracing air came in the cracked-open casement behind Chris's desk, the sort of air that ought to make children frisky. The clock read a little past eight. She stood in front of her low math group. As planned, she had begun to go over last night's homework, but Felipe had no ideas how many pumpkins *in all* were bought if two people had bought fourteen pumpkins each; Horace said he'd forgotten his book; Manny and Henrietta admitted they hadn't done the homework; Robert just shrugged when she asked where his was; and Alan, of all people, a schoolteacher's son, had a note from his mother saying that he'd lost the assignment. "I think that you think your mother fell off the turnip cart yesterday, too," Chris said to Alan. Then she came to a dead stop.

The day was overcast. Jimmy's skin looked gray under fluorescent light. He lay with his head down on his desk, shifting his sticklike forearms around under his cheek as if rearranging a pillow. The usually high-spirited Manny gazed open-mouthed toward the window. Felipe had slid halfway down the back of his chair and scowled at his lap. "You can't make me do it. I'm not going to do anything unless you give me more attention," Felipe seemed to be saying to her. It would feel good and constructive to spank him, but that would have to wait for the pretext of his birthday. Robert was dismantling another pen. Soon he'd have ink all over his hands and his pants. His mother could worry about that. Horace was trying to do his homework now, by copying from Margaret's. At least he seemed awake. Jorge's eyes were shut, literally shut. Jorge was staying back. He had told his homeroom teacher, who had told the story in the Teachers' Room, that he'd get even by not doing any work this year, and she couldn't make him, because his mother didn't care. He wore the same set of clothes as on the first days of school.

Chris had seen progress in this group. They would start long division fairly soon. But today even the well-behaved ones, such as Margaret, looked sleepy. Bring back Clarence from the room next door. Clarence, at least, never looked sleepy.

Chris considered telling them she couldn't teach *celery,* but the eyes that were open and looking at her seemed to say that they didn't want to hear it all from her again: they'd need to know this if they wanted to move on to something new; if they didn't want to get cheated at the grocery store; if they wanted to learn how to design cars and rocket ships. They did not want to hear that Mrs. Zajac couldn't drill holes in their heads and pour in information, that they had to help, which meant, first of all, paying attention. Jimmy yawned. He didn't even bother to cover his mouth. A paper fell off a child's desk and floated down, gently arcing back and forth like a kite without a tail. She'd try something different. An old trick might work.

Chris turned and wrote on the board: 5

$$296$$
$$\times 78$$

"All right, Jimmy, you go to the board." 6

Jimmy arose slowly, twisting his mouth. He slouched up to the 7 green board and stared at the problem.

Chris sat down in Jimmy's seat. "I want you to pretend you're the 8 teacher, and you're going to show me how to multiply, and I don't know how." So saying, and in one abandoned movement, Chris collapsed on Jimmy's desk, one cheek landing flat on the pale brown plastic top and her arms hanging lifelessly over the sides.

A child giggled. 9

"Gonna get my attention first, Jimmy?" called Mrs. Zajac. 10

Several children giggled. Jorge's eyes opened, and he grinned. All 11 around the little room, heads lifted. Chris's mouth sagged open. Her tongue protruded. Her head lay on the desk top. Up at the board, Jimmy made a low, monotonic sound, which was his laugh.

Abruptly, Chris sat up. "Okay, Jimmy," she called. "I'm awake 12 now. What do I do first? Seven times six is . . ."

Jimmy was shaking his head. 13

"No? Why can't I multiply seven times six first?" she said, and she 14 pouted.

There was a lot more light in the room now. It came from smiles. 15 The top group had all lifted their eyes from their papers. Judith smiled at Mrs. Zajac from across the room.

Jimmy got through the first step, and Chris turned around in 16 Jimmy's chair and said to Manny, "You're next. You're a teacher, too."

"*Diablo!*" Manny looked up toward the ceiling. 17

Chris climbed into Manny's seat as he sauntered to the board. 18

"I'm gonna give you a hard time, like you give me," Chris called at 19 Manny's back. She looked around at the other children. They were all looking at her. "When you sit in this seat, see, you've got to sit like this." She let her shoulders and her jaw droop, and she stared at the window.

"Look out in space!" declared Felipe. 20

"Look out in space," she agreed. 21

The clock over the closets jumped and rested, jumped and 22 rested. The smell of pencil shavings was thick in the air. Giggles came from all sides.

"Boy, do I have a lot of friends helping me out! Now who wants   23
to teach Mrs. Zajac?"

"Me!" cried most of the class in unison.   24

Crying "No!" and "No way!" at Chris's wrong answers and   25
"Yes!" when the child at the board corrected her and she turned to
the others to ask if the correction was right, the low group found
their way to the end of the problem. Arising from the last child's
chair she had occupied, her black hair slightly infused with the new
redness in her cheeks, her skirt rustling, she turned back into Mrs.
Zajac. "Okay, thank you. Now that I know how to do it, I hope you
know how to do it. I'm going to put examples on the board," she
said. "You are going to work on them."

READING FOR MEANING

Write at least a page, exploring your ideas about Kidder's observations. You
might begin by conjecturing about why Kidder singled out this math lesson
from among the many lessons he observed and speculating about what Kidder
intends readers to think and feel about Mrs. Zajac and her students. Then write
about anything else in the selection that contributes to your understanding of
Kidder's observations.

As you write, you may want to reread the selection and annotate it further.
Consider quoting phrases or sentences that help explain how you understand the
selection. You may find your understanding changing as you write.

If you have trouble writing a full page, consider these suggestions:

- Describe Zajac's teaching strategy in this lesson, noticing what Kidder tells
  us Zajac *does not* do.

- Explain what new information you acquired about life "among schoolchildren." What was surprising or unexpected?

- Explain the possible meaning or significance of "couldn't teach *celery*"
  (paragraph 4), "one abandoned movement" (paragraph 8), and "a lot more
  light in the room" (paragraph 15), or any other statement that catches your
  attention.

- Consider Zajac's decision to have students learn by teaching. Recall an
  occasion when you learned more about something by teaching it, and connect your experience specifically to that of Zajac and her students.

READING LIKE A WRITER

This section guides you through an analysis of Kidder's observational writing
strategies: *detailing the scene and people, organizing the observations, engaging and informing readers,* and *conveying an impression of the subject.* In each
part, we describe one strategy briefly and then pose a critical reading and writing task for you.

Consider this a writer's introduction to observational writing. You will learn
even more from activities following other selections in this chapter, and the
Guide to Observational Writing at the end of the chapter will suggest how you
can use in your own observational essay what you have learned in this chapter.

Detailing the Scene and People

A vivid, detailed presentation of the subject is a recognizable feature of any
observational essay. Writers of observation detail both scene and people. They
rely primarily on visual details of the scene (what they *see*), but they do not overlook sounds or smells. They present people through concrete visual details as
well—how they look, how they dress, how they move, what they do. They also
show how people talk, often creating dialogues or paraphrasing what people
have said. They may even report what others have said about particular people.

ANALYZE. Reread "Teaching Celery," annotating the details Kidder uses to
characterize each named student in the low math group and their teacher. Look
for details of appearance, dress, posture, movement, and speech. Then annotate
the objects and features of the room itself that Kidder singles out to present the
scene of this math lesson.

WRITE. Write several sentences, explaining what you have discovered about
Kidder's use of details, using examples from your annotations. What kinds of
details does he single out? Which details seem most vivid and telling? How
strong an image do you have of the scene and the people?

Organizing the Observations

Observational writers usually present their subjects narratively—as a story.
Other ways of organizing are possible, and you will see some of them in this
chapter, but narrative offers certain advantages: It engages readers and pulls
them along, at its best providing the tension and drama of a good novel or
movie.

ANALYZE. Skim Kidder's essay to remind yourself of the story line. Then
mark in the margin places where the action seems slow and places where the
action seems fast. Think about the differences in these parts of Kidder's story.
Where does he rely on action and dialogue to move the story along?

WRITE. Write a few sentences about how Kidder's story unfolds. Does it
seem to you a full, comprehensive narrative, one that answers all your questions
about what happened? Explain your response by pointing out what was most
and least satisfying to you.

Engaging and Informing Readers

Along with presenting their subjects vividly, observational writers strive to
engage their readers and at the same time to inform them about the subject.

Readers expect to learn something new from observational writing, and they anticipate savoring and enjoying this learning. Here, we will consider how Kidder engages readers with his subject.

Readers who might tolerate a dull textbook or how-to manual have no patience for observational writing that is lifeless and dull. Observational writing strikes readers as lively and engaging when the subject is unusual or when it is familiar but seen in a new way. Writers try to engage readers by beginning in a surprising way, by presenting intriguing portraits of the scene and people, by introducing humor, by telling stories that have uncertain outcomes.

ANALYZE. Notice how Kidder begins his essay—not just where he begins the story but what he includes in the first paragraph. Then reread the selection, annotating places where you felt curious about what might happen, where you were intrigued by a particular individual, where you enjoyed something humorous.

WRITE. Write several sentences, explaining what Kidder does to engage and sustain your interest, to keep you reading. How successful was he in doing so for you? Point to specific features you enjoyed most and least.

Conveying an Impression of the Subject

Readers expect observational writers to convey a particular impression or interpretation of the subject. They want to know the writer's insights into the subject after having spent time observing the scene and talking to people. Indeed, this interpretation is what separates observational essays from mere exercises in description and narration.

To convey an impression, writers express an attitude toward the subject and offer an interpretation of it. The attitude a writer expresses toward the subject can usually be summed up in several words. For example, a writer may exhibit admiration, concern, detachment, fascination, skepticism, amusement—perhaps even two or three different feelings that complement or contradict one another.

The interpretation may be stated directly. It can be announced at the beginning, woven into the ongoing observations, or presented as a conclusion. Just as often, however, writers interpret by implication. Kidder, for example, does not state his interpretation directly but implies it through his attitude and choice of details.

As writers draft and revise to arrive at an interpretation of their subjects, they are continually selecting and rejecting details and putting details together to convey a particular impression. It is this orchestration of details that separates strong observational writing from writing that merely presents information.

ANALYZE. Think about how Kidder conveys a particular impression, and decide how you would describe his attitude toward Zajac and her students.

WRITE. Write a few sentences naming this attitude in a word or phrase and quoting from at least three or four places in the essay to support your inference that this is Kidder's attitude. Does it seem to you that all of the details of the scene and people are well orchestrated to express a consistent attitude and to convey a dominant impression?

READINGS

The New Yorker

SOUP

Written by an unidentified staff writer, this selection appeared in the "Goings On about Town" section of the *New Yorker* magazine (January 1989). The *New Yorker,* which brings together fiction, poetry, observational writing, and reviews, is known for the detailed clarity of its reporting and the grace and precision of its editorial style. "Goings On about Town" is a weekly compendium of brief, anonymous observations of New York places and people in action.

The author of this piece reports firsthand observations of a Manhattan takeout soup kitchen and its creative and demanding owner, Mr. Albert Yeganeh. As you read, you can readily imagine the reporter interviewing the owner, writing down soup names and menu items, observing people in line, and even standing in line as well for a bowl of soup. As you read this selection, notice that the writer relies on extended quotations from the interview to keep the focus on Mr. Yeganeh. Besides letting the owner speak for himself, what other strategies does the writer adopt for presenting the owner and his soup kitchen?

When Albert Yeganeh says "Soup is my lifeblood," he means it. And when he says "I am extremely hard to please," he means that, too. Working like a demon alchemist in a tiny storefront kitchen at 259-A West Fifty-fifth Street, Mr. Yeganeh creates anywhere from eight to seventeen soups every weekday. His concoctions are so popular that a wait of half an hour at the lunchtime peak is not uncommon, although there are strict rules for conduct in line. But more on that later.

"I am psychologically kind of a health freak," Mr. Yeganeh said the other day, in a lisping staccato of Armenian origin. "And I know that soup is the greatest meal in the world. It's very good for your digestive system. And I use only the best, the freshest ingredients. I am a perfectionist. When I make a clam soup, I use three different kinds of clams. Every other place uses canned clams. I'm called crazy. I am not crazy. People don't realize why I get so upset. It's because if the soup is not perfect and I'm still selling it, it's a torture. It's *my* soup, and that's why I'm so upset. First you clean and then you cook. I don't believe that ninety-nine per cent of the restaurants in New York know how to clean a tomato. I tell my crew to wash the parsley *eight* times. If they wash it five or six times, I scare them. I tell them they'll go to jail if there is sand in the parsley. One time, I found a mushroom on the floor, and I fired that guy who left it there." He spread his arms, and added, "This place is the only one like it in . . . in . . . the whole earth! One day, I hope to learn something from the other places, but so far I haven't. For example, the other day I went to a very fancy restaurant and had borscht. I had to send it back. It was *junk.* I could see all the chemicals in it. I never use chemicals. Last weekend, I had lobster bisque in Brooklyn, a very well-known place. It was *junk.* When I make a lobster bisque, I use a whole lobster. You know, I never advertise. I don't have to. All the big-shot chefs and the kings of the hotels come here to see what *I'm* doing."

As you approach Mr. Yeganeh's Soup Kitchen International from   3
a distance, the first thing you notice about it is the awning, which proclaims "Homemade Hot, Cold, Diet Soups." The second thing you notice is an aroma so delicious that it makes you want to take a bite out of the air. The third thing you notice, in front of the kitchen, is an electric signboard that flashes, saying, "Today's Soups . . . Chicken Vegetable . . . Mexican Beef Chili . . . Cream of Watercress . . . Italian Sausage . . . Clam Bisque . . . Beef Barley . . . Due to Cold Weather . . . For Most Efficient and Fastest Service the Line Must . . . Be Kept Moving . . . Please . . . Have Your Money . . . Ready . . . Pick the Soup of Your Choice . . . Move to Your Extreme . . . Left After Ordering."

"I am not prejudiced against color or religion," Mr. Yeganeh told   4
us, and he jabbed an index finger at the flashing sign. "Whoever follows that I treat very well. My regular customers don't say anything. They are very intelligent and well educated. They know I'm just trying to move the line. The New York cop is very smart—he sees everything but says nothing. But the young girl who wants to stop and tell you how nice you look and hold everyone up—*yah!*" He made a guillotining motion with his hand. "I tell you, I hate to work with the public. They treat me like a slave. My philosophy is: The customer is always wrong and I'm always right. I raised my prices to try to get rid of some of these people, but it didn't work."

The other day, Mr. Yeganeh was dressed in chefs' whites with   5
orange smears across his chest, which may have been some of the carrot soup cooking in a huge pot on a little stove in one corner. A three-foot-long handheld mixer from France sat on the sink, looking like an overgrown gardening tool. Mr. Yeganeh spoke to two young

helpers in a twisted Armenian-Spanish barrage, then said to us, "I have no overhead, no trained waitresses, and I have the cashier here." He pointed to himself theatrically. Beside the doorway, a glass case with fresh green celery, red and yellow peppers, and purple eggplant was topped by five big gray soup urns. According to a piece of cardboard taped to the door, you can buy Mr. Yeganeh's soups in three sizes, costing from four to fifteen dollars. The order of any well-behaved customer is accompanied by little waxpaper packets of bread, fresh vegetables (such as scallions and radishes), fresh fruit (such as cherries or an orange), a chocolate mint, and a plastic spoon. No coffee, tea, or other drinks are served.

"I get my recipes from books and theories and my own taste,"   6
Mr. Yeganeh said. "At home, I have several hundreds of books. When I do research, I find that I don't know anything. Like cabbage is a cancer fighter, and some fish is good for your heart but some is bad. Every day, I should have one sweet, one spicy, one cream, one vegetable soup—and they *must* change, they should always taste a little different." He added that he wasn't sure how extensive his repertoire was, but that it probably includes at least eighty soups, among them African peanut butter, Greek moussaka, hamburger, Reuben, B.L.T., asparagus and caviar, Japanese shrimp miso, chicken chili, Irish corned beef and cabbage, Swiss chocolate, French calf's brain, Korean beef ball, Italian shrimp and eggplant Parmesan, buffalo, ham and egg, short rib, Russian beef Stroganoff, turkey cacciatore, and Indian mulligatawny. "The chicken and the seafood are an addiction, and when I have French garlic soup I let people have only one small container each," he said. "The doctors and nurses love that one."

A lunch line of thirty people stretched down the block from Mr.   7
Yeganeh's doorway. Behind a construction worker was a man in expensive leather, who was in front of a woman in a fur hat. Few people spoke. Most had their money out and their orders ready.

At the front of the line, a woman in a brown coat couldn't decide   8
which soup to get and started to complain about the prices.

"You talk too much, dear," Mr. Yeganeh said, and motioned her   9
to move to the left. "Next!"

"Just don't talk. Do what he says," a man huddled in a blue parka   10
warned.

"He's downright rude," said a blond woman in a blue coat. "Even   11
abusive. But you can't deny it, his soup is the best."

READING FOR MEANING

Write at least a page, exploring your understanding of "Soup." You might begin by explaining why you think the writer singled out Mr. Yeganeh and his Soup Kitchen International. What seems to be the writer's attitude toward

Yeganeh, and what does the writer want us to know about him and to think about him? Then write about anything else in the essay that contributes to your understanding of the *New Yorker* writer's observations.

As you write, you may want to reread all or part of the essay, annotating material that may be useful in your writing. If you have difficulty continuing for at least a page, consider the following suggestions:

- Identify Yeganeh's personal qualities, and give an example of each quality.

- Explain the possible meaning or significance of "People don't realize why I get so upset" (paragraph 2), "This place is the only one like it in . . . in . . . the whole earth!" (paragraph 2), "The customer is always wrong and I'm always right" (paragraph 4), and "When I do research, I find that I don't know anything" (paragraph 6), or any other statement that catches your attention.

- Consider that an often-stated principle of business in a free-market economy is the importance of friendly service. Why do you think Yeganeh violates this principle? How does he do so and succeed? Consider possible differences between his fast-food place and others you know about where the service is friendly.

- Yeganeh seems obsessed with quality. Describe a time when you wanted to do something the best way possible or when you observed someone else doing that. Connect your experience specifically to Yeganeh's.

EXTENDING MEANING THROUGH CONVERSATION. It is important for you to make meaning on your own; however, you may be able to extend your understanding of the reading by conversing with other students about the *New Yorker* writer's observations.

Get together with one or two other students. Begin your conversation by identifying one idea in the essay that surprised, engaged, or informed each of you.

As you talk about the reading, you may find that each student has a somewhat different understanding of it. Your goal is not necessarily to agree on what is most surprising, engaging, or informative but rather to get a fuller view of the essay by considering other readers' perspectives. Keep your conversation focused on the essay by rereading and discussing parts of it together.

READING LIKE A WRITER

DETAILING THE SCENE AND PEOPLE

Observational writers succeed by presenting their subjects vividly and concretely. They focus on specific details of the physical scene and of the people there. Analyze how the *New Yorker* writer details the scene and people.

ANALYZE. Reread paragraphs 3 through 5 and 7 through 10 of "Soup," bracketing details the writer presents of the scene and of people, including the following:

- Physical details of the soup kitchen
- Details of what can be smelled or heard
- Details about what people are wearing and what they say

In the margin, make notes about what these details tell—or fail to tell—you about the soup kitchen, its owner, and its patrons.

WRITE. Using examples from your annotations, write several sentences, explaining how the *New Yorker* writer has presented the scene and people at Yeganeh's soup kitchen. Consider what seems most vivid and memorable among all the details, as well as why it stands out for you. Add a few final sentences, evaluating the presentation of the scene and people in this profile: Given the writer's likely purpose, do you find too many or too few details, irrelevant details, too much attention to certain features of the scene, or a satisfying balance? Point to specific examples.

CONSIDERING IDEAS FOR YOUR OWN WRITING

If you were to write about an unusual place on campus or in your community, what place might you choose? List as many places as you can think of, sort through your list, and concentrate on two or three possibilities. Whom would you interview for each? What might interest your readers about each place? What appeals to you personally?

Lisa Jones

GIRLS ON THE STRIP

Lisa Jones (b. 1961) lives in Brooklyn, New York, where she writes for the *Village Voice.* A graduate of Yale University and New York University's Graduate School of Film and Television, she is the author of radio and stage plays that have been produced nationally. She is perhaps best known for coauthoring three books with Spike Lee, the noted African American film director: *Uplift the Race: The Construction of School Days* (1988), *Do the Right Thing* (1989), and *Mo' Better Blues* (1990). In 1994, Jones published a collection of essays, *Bulletproof Diva,* most of them from her *Village Voice* column, in which she frequently explores "what it means to be black and female at the end of the twentieth century."

This selection comes from *Bulletproof Diva.* Like the *New Yorker* writer in the previous selection, Jones profiles a talented person in the context of that person's work, a common subject for observational writers. Relying on interviews and observations, Jones presents Barbara Brandon and her comic strip, "Where I'm Coming From." Unlike the *New Yorker* writer, however, Jones focuses more on the work than on the person, and she also draws more attention to herself as the observer and writer. As you read, notice this more personal role for the observer. Notice, too, Jones's efforts to engage her readers with language that is informal, lively, and direct. In the opening, Jones compares Brandon's comic strip to the "comic strip" of her own life and the "girls" in Brandon's comic strip to her own girlfriends.

The comic strip that is my life might be perfect material for Barbara Brandon's "Where I'm Coming From," if it weren't so, damn, excuse me, X-rated. Like Brandon's strip, mine has a dozen *dames de couleur** ("the girls," Brandon calls them) who run around with piled-high hairdos and argue all day, usually on the phone, about racism or sexism on the job, what a dog boyfriend has been this week, and whether Clarence Thomas** will suffer a nervous breakdown by the year 2000. Why my girls won't play well in the *Des Moines Register* is because, when it comes to boyfriend's p-size or beating the yeast monster, they find it hard to hold their tongues. I tell them, you girls won't play in Albuquerque until you wash your mouths with Lysol. But who listens to me?

Barbara Brandon, however, has been playing in Albuquerque, Harrisburg, Pennsylvania, and a dozen other cities. As of last November, Brandon became the first black woman cartoonist to be syndicated nationally so she's getting plenty of ink. *Glamour, People,* and *Time* have all descended on her little studio in Brooklyn's Fort Greene to have a peek.

Brandon has mixed feelings about being, in the nineties, a "first black something." Though with the prospect of seeing her characters on T-shirts, calendars, and greeting cards by fall, thrill is winning out. "Girl," she says, in stylish outer-borough girlfriendese: "Don't we just *need* greeting cards? I'm tired of coloring in those faces."

The girls have been making noise in Brandon's head since college. *Elan,* a black women's magazine, bought the strip in the eighties, only to fold soon after. Her next stop was *Essence,* where they needed a fashion writer more than a cartoonist. Brandon took the writing gig, as it beat dressing mannequins for JCPenney. Eventually she sold the strip to the *Detroit Free Press,* where it has appeared weekly in the life-style section since 1989. Getting by on seventy-five dollars a week from the strip and the odd freelance job, she left *Essence* to devote 24–7† to her girls.

Cutting a syndication deal,†† Brandon's next move, was no weekend at Virginia Beach. The strip was criticized by potential buyers for its Feiffer-style‡ talking heads. Put the girls in real

---

**dames de couleur:* "Women of color" (*Ed.*)

***Clarence Thomas:* African American Supreme Court Justice, whose controversial appointment was approved in 1991 (*Ed.*)

†24–7: Twenty-four hours a day, seven days a week (*Ed.*)

††*a syndication deal:* Syndicators distribute cartoon strips to newspapers and collect a fee for the artist (*Ed.*)

‡*Jules Feiffer:* Cartoonist, novelist, writer of stage and screen plays, Feiffer (b. 1929) won a Pulitzer Prize for editorial cartooning (*Ed.*)

environments, they said, draw some male characters, make it a daily. Brandon stood ground, and finally signed with Universal Press Syndicate, where she's in good company with "Doonesbury" and "The Far Side," and is encouraged to be as political as she can get away with.

Fifty papers have signed on so far, yet some, like the *Minneapolis Star Tribune,* may have done it to beat the local competition—they've yet to run the strip. "Where I'm Coming From" is as far north as Calgary, Alberta, and as south as Houston. New York City papers, though they serve a majority nonwhite population, are holdouts. Is it a question of space (an old cop-out) or are Big Apple dailies not ready for women who talk loud about pregnancy out of wedlock, affirmative action, and racial identity? 6

"I'm personally insulted," says Brandon, "if a paper is not interested in the strip because it only features black women. Does that mean my existence can't teach anything? Hey, I didn't grow up with a community of ducks, but I read 'Donald Duck.' And I don't live with a dog, but I read 'Marmaduke,' and I understand it too." 7

The girls of "Where I'm Coming From" are twenty- and thirty-something and have names like Lekesia, Nicole, and Alisha. Lydia, who owns a business, named her new baby Aretha. Judy wants to be a novelist. You won't see "cleavage or hot pants" here, says Brandon; the emphasis is on minds for once, not rumps. As single women, the girls are inevitably compared to "Cathy," queen of the coffee mug and greeting card set. With due respect to creator Cathy Guisewite, this is Brandon's comeback: "Buying a bathing suit and worrying about when we'll be size six again, we all trip like that, but I don't want to in my strip. I think I have more of a responsibility." Instead of one character being the repository of every stereotypically female neurosis, Brandon offers a balance. If a strip shows Nicole going on about boyfriend, then Lekesia is on the other end of the phone rolling her eyes. 8

Brandon's critique of hetero relationship-obsession is an ongoing theme. She takes digs at women who have blinders on when it comes to everything but their man. That men appear in the strip only as voices on the telephone speaks to their complicated presence and absence in the lives of black women of Lekesia and Nicole's generation. These male phone voices, disembodied and shown in blownup and cluttered type, remind me of the adults in "Peanuts," who are presented only as high-pitched garble. 9

Brandon is a walking library of black comic-strip history, having grown up putting in Letratone (the dots that suggest Negro skin) for her father, Brumsic Brandon, Jr.'s strip "Luther." In 1969, the year Barbara turned eleven, "Luther" became the third black feature to go national. Images of blacks in American comics have paralleled those in film: Step-in Fetchit* characters ruled until pioneer strips 10

Steppin Fetchit: Film name of Lincoln Perry (1902–1985), Hollywood's first African American star. In films made during the 1930s and 1940s Steppin Fetchit was lazy, a flirt, and inarticulate—a comic and stereotyped role for which Perry never apologized (*Ed.*)

by black artists, like Morrie Turner's "Wee Pals" and Ted Shearer's "Quincy," won syndication in the sixties. By the eighties, newspapers lost interest in efforts to integrate the comics. After fifteen years in newsprint, "Luther" was dropped. Brandon traces her lineage to Jackie Ohms, a black woman cartoonist whose character Torchy Brown, a girl reporter, ran in black newspapers like *The Chicago Defender* in the 1930s, ten years before the debut of "Brenda Starr." Torchy dealt with "sexism, racism, and her man," so Brandon preens, and was way ahead of her time.

A *Mad* magazine kid who didn't care much for the Archies, Brandon kept a Feiffer strip tacked above her bed in junior high. In a house that doubled as a gallery for her father's comic art, she was never at a loss for black images in the medium. I, on the other hand, remember combing newspaper strips, cartoon shows, and comic books for little black girls—and drawing a blank. It seemed we couldn't be imagined on screen as live characters or on paper as illustrated ones. I ask one of my foul-mouth friends to confirm this, and she comes up with "Josie and the Pussycats," a 1970s television cartoon that followed the escapades of a female rock group. Remember Val, she asks, the black girl who played drums? Didn't you feel liberated by Val? ¹¹

READING FOR MEANING

Write at least a page, exploring your understanding of "Girls on the Strip." You might begin by explaining why you think Jones was drawn to Brandon as a subject for a profile. Then write about any other ideas or observations in the essay that contribute to your understanding of Jones's observations.

As you write, you may want to reread and further annotate parts of the essay. Do not be surprised if your understanding changes as you write. If you have difficulty continuing for at least a page, consider the following suggestions:

- Summarize the personal history and work experiences that brought Brandon to the point where she could launch a successful comic strip.
- How would you describe Jones's attitude toward Brandon, and what do you believe she wants readers to think about Brandon and her work?
- Explain the significance of "first black something" (paragraph 3), "encouraged to be as political as she can get away with" (paragraph 5), "Does that mean my existence can't teach anything?" (paragraph 7), "the emphasis is on minds for once, not rumps" (paragraph 8), and "men appear in the strip only as voices on the telephone" (paragraph 9), or any other statement that catches your attention.
- Describe a time when something creative you did was misunderstood and devalued. Connect your experience specifically to that of Brandon.

EXTENDING MEANING THROUGH CONVERSATION. While it is important for you to make meaning of the ideas in the selection on your own, you may be able to extend your understanding by conversing with other students about Jones's essay.

Converse with one or two other students. Begin by identifying one thing in the essay that each of you finds particularly informative, engaging, or unexpected.

As you talk about the reading, you may find that you have somewhat different impressions of it. As a group, you may not necessarily see it the same way, but you may see more in it than each of you saw on your own. Keep your conversation focused on the essay by rereading and discussing parts of it together.

READING LIKE A WRITER
ENGAGING AND INFORMING READERS

Perhaps an observational writer's major challenge is to engage readers' interest through closely observed details and storytelling while informing them about the subject. Jones clearly makes an energetic effort to engage readers' interest in Brandon and in her comic strip. It is equally clear, even on the first reading, that she aims to inform readers about Brandon's history as a comic-strip artist, her struggles for recognition and syndication, and the features of her strip that make it truly new and controversial. To accomplish these intertwined goals of engaging and informing readers, Jones must locate information strategically and balance it with potentially more engaging material.

ANALYZE. The three major blocks of information, all of it coming from interviews with Brandon—probably a combination of in-person and phone interviews—are in paragraphs 4 through 6, paragraphs 8 and 9, and paragraph 10 and the first part of paragraph 11. Reread these blocks of information and make marginal notes about the type of information in each block. To learn about Jones's strategy for locating this information in the essay, notice what comes just before and after each block, and make notes about what you discover. Finally, notice how much space these information blocks occupy in relation to other material in the essay.

WRITE. Write several sentences, describing the types of information Jones includes. Also explain where that information has been placed in the essay, what kind of material surrounds it, and how it is located in relation to that material. Finally, add a few sentences evaluating how useful the information is and how successfully Jones integrates it into her other observations and comments. Is the information always clear and well organized? For you as one reader, is there too much of one kind of information? Too little? Does any block of information extend so far that you lose interest? In general, how successful do you find Jones's strategy for alternating information with other, more explicitly engaging material?

CONSIDERING IDEAS FOR YOUR OWN WRITING

Consider profiling someone who works alone or with a few others, relying on creativity or skill. There are many possibilities: stonemason, carpenter, gardener, artist, composer of music, musician, singer, architect, owner-chef of a small restaurant, specialty baker, home-care provider. These are examples of enterpreneurs or freelancers, rather than employees of a large company or institution. You would need to visit the person's place of work. You could ask about work in progress and about the difficulties and pleasures of such work. You would not want to ignore the market for the work; that is, how the person makes a living from the work. You would want to be able to describe the place of work and the appearance of the work.

Jane and Michael Stern

BULL RIDING SCHOOL

Jane and Michael Stern (b. 1946 and 1946) collaborate on magazine articles, screenplays, television scripts, and books. They specialize in travel, food, and the West. Their books include *Goodfood* (1983), *American Gourmet* (1991), *Roadfood* (1992), *Jane and Michael Stern's Encyclopedia of Pop Culture* (1992), and *Way Out West* (1993). Their column, "A Taste of America," is syndicated in over two hundred newspapers. The Sterns are contributing editors at *Gourmet* magazine.

This selection was published in the *New Yorker* magazine. It appeared in an occasional section, "A Reporter at Large," which has featured some of America's finest observational writers. The selection illustrates the advantage of unusual persons and activities as subjects for observational writing. The Sterns travel to a small town in California to observe a bull-riding school. Bull riding is a rodeo event requiring a rider to stay on a twisting, lurching, bucking bull for eight seconds to qualify for a prize. You will see that the students come with different degrees of experience and for different reasons, and you will meet the school's founder and teacher, a retired champion bull rider named Gary Leffew. As you read, notice how the Sterns present Leffew and his students.

In 1970, Gary Leffew won the world. Now he teaches others how to do it, at the Gary Leffew Bull Riding School. School is not where most bull riders learn their trade. Some pick it up as youngsters on a farm or ranch, by sneaking onto cattle when their fathers aren't looking, or, in town, by tethering a swinging barrel in the air between back-yard trees. But, for competitors who want an edge, school can be the place to get it. Gary Leffew has a reputation for turning neophytes into contenders, and ranked riders into champions; his alumni include Ted Nuce, the top bull rider of 1986, and dozens of men who have made it to the Finals in the last twenty years.

Leffew himself placed among the top fifteen riders seven times, starting in 1966, and in his championship year he performed the astonishing feat of going eight seconds on nine out of the ten bulls he drew in the Finals. Now forty-seven and retired from rough-stock events, he holds five week-long clinics a year at his ranch, in the town of Nipomo, California, fifty miles north of Santa Barbara, and others at various ranches around the West. When he isn't teaching the fine points of posting, arching, gripping, and mental conditioning, he makes his living by lending his name, face, and reputation to TV and print advertisements for such products as Bull's-Eye barbecue sauce, Tony Lama boots, Coca-Cola, Busch beer, Nissan trucks, and Right Guard deodorant. Another source of income is an enormous bull he once rode, which a taxidermist has immortalized in a dramatic pose, with his hind legs kicking high in the air, and which Leffew transports around the country to fairs and rodeos; for a small fee, you can climb on the bull's back, grip the rigging, wave your free hand in the air, and have your picture taken.

Thirty-eight aspiring bull riders signed up for school at Leffew's ranch in Nipomo this past May. Each of them paid three hundred dollars tuition, plus half the cost of a room—shared with a fellow-student—at a nearby motel. Most of them travelled at least two hundred miles; one came from New York State, and one from Australia. A few brought their wives; five or six, too young to drive, were chaperoned by parents. Except for two Native American sisters, who spat tobacco juice on the ground at regular intervals, all the aspirants were male. Some had ridden bulls before, in high school or in regional rodeos, but there were at least half a dozen who had never seen a bull in person.

Every day, before any bulls are brought out, Gary Leffew implants a positive mental attitude in his pupils. This process takes place at 9 A.M. in an outdoor lecture area. Instead of a podium, there is an empty metal heating oil drum, suspended in such a way that men on either side can grab long wooden handles and make it tilt and pivot. The oil drum represents the thick midsection of the bull. Students can climb on it and practice their leg locks and arm swings, and the teacher can analyze what they are doing. It is from this lofty perch that Gary Leffew, straddling the swinging can, holds forth each day for almost an hour; and it would be fair to say that, whatever his talents as a bull rider were, they could hardly have surpassed his talents as a teacher. His morning lessons combine technical instruction with a rousing pep talk about overcoming odds and the joy of winning. Spiced with tales of his own days on the rodeo circuit, the lectures build to a whooping intensity that makes him sound like a Bible Belt preacher for whom riding rank bulls is a sure way to Heaven.

Like many bull riders, Gary Leffew is a small man with a big ego. "A hundred and forty-five pounds of twisted steel and sex appeal" is

how, with a grin, he describes himself to the class, and it is an accurate description. He is cowboy handsome, bronzed from years of
outdoor living, and saved from prettiness by the kind of well-placed
crow's feet and laugh lines that have helped make Clint Eastwood a
movie star. He dresses in skintight Wranglers and a chest-hugging T-
shirt that shows off his pumped muscles and lean lines. On his head
he wears a four-hundred-dollar black 20X-beaver Resistol hat; his
feet are encased in sharp-toed boots made of the hide of some
endangered creature; and he looks out at his students from behind a
pair of aviator shades with amber lenses.

What the students come to hear is the story of how Gary Leffew   6
rose from being a nobody to win the world. For two decades, he has
been telling his tale, using himself as the best example of how anyone
with some talent and the right mental attitude can be a success. He
recalls his humble beginnings, in the mid-sixties: newly married and
with a pregnant wife, he had quit his job painting missile gantries to
rodeo full time, and had found himself being bucked off everything he
tried to ride. His luck changed, however, when he met up with a fellow bull rider who had found the secret of success. This cowboy had
suffered through his own slump not long before and was now walking away with all the money. He said he owed his change of fortune
to a hypnotist in Dallas who periodically reprogrammed his mind in
such a way that he automatically made all the right moves when he
got on a bull. That cowboy's winning streak ended when he got
rowdy and smacked his Svengali in the face with a rare steak at a
fancy Dallas restaurant. But Leffew soon discovered that the hypnotist had derived his techniques from a book—"Psycho-Cybernetics,"
a self-help manual, by Maxwell Maltz, that instructed readers how to
use mental conditioning to transform themselves from losers into
winners. Leffew got a copy and devoured every page. He went into
seclusion, during which he spent all his time imagining himself riding
the rankest bulls with the utmost authority. After two months of
resolutely thinking like a winner, Leffew declared himself a walking,
talking bull-riding machine. He came out of his retreat and executed
an eighty-nine-point ride on a whirling bull at the Denver rodeo. "It
worked!" Leffew exulted. And from nowhere in the standings in
1967 he rose to No. 2 in 1968. . . .

By this point in his sermon, Leffew's new students are misty-eyed   7
with the joy of rodeoing, imagining what bliss it must be to be Gary
Leffew, savoring the taste of victory he has given them—perhaps
even picturing themselves starring in a buddy movie, playing Gary or
Donny in that magnificent summer of '72. Now it is time for them to
ride a bull. Most of the bull-riding students have brought chaps,
spurs, and rope rigging with them, and also sheepskin knee pads to
wear under their jeans. Nearly everybody wears a cowboy hat and
boots. Some students look more likely born to ride than others.
Zane Page, a tough, wiry twenty-four-year-old, has been to other
bull-riding schools, and he rodeos in his spare time, when he isn't

working as a long-haul truck driver; he doesn't expect to win the world, but for him a few days of riding bulls in the company of an hombre like Gary Leffew is a little piece of paradise on earth. Jason Pluhar, on the other hand, is a novice, and he looks a little nervous. He is seventeen, with a chubby pink face, and he seems to puff from the exertion it takes to walk from the lecture area to the arena.

Michael Battles is about as green as a student gets. He has never   8
been near a bull, and recalls that the only four-legged animal he has ever ridden was a pony; he was in the third grade, and a teen-ager pulled the little animal along with a rope. Battles has just graduated from West Point, and a week at the Gary Leffew Bull Riding School was a present from his father. He has owned a Harley-Davidson, and after his summer vacation he is to join the Army's élite Rangers, but he can't imagine anything that could be quite as thrilling as riding a bull. "I would have paid three hundred dollars just to sit on the fence with these cowboys!" he exclaims, staring, enraptured, at the leathery-faced professional wranglers who are sitting above the bull chutes nearby. "This is a whole other life. The great thing about these cowboys is that they are all for one, one for all. I tell you, bull riders are the best, and Gary is the best bull rider. I mean, it's like if a guy out there is hurt, I would lay my life down to help him, and I know he would do it for me." When Michael was asked how long he had known Gary and the other men at the bull-riding school, he estimated that it was probably about three hours.

Shane Saulsbury was driven to school by his stepmother from   9
their home, near San Luis Obispo. He is fifteen and a real rodeo fan, who relishes the cowboy life and spends whatever time he can around the chutes with the pros. He tries to live his life as true to cowboy ways as possible, and, as he sees it, that involves eating as much meat as he can. "I guess I eat beef five times a week for dinner," he says, adding, "If you don't have beef in your diet, your heart will stop pumping." Saulsbury has made quick friends with Juan Holsbo, a shy, thin eighteen-year-old part-Diegueño Indian who lives on a reservation near San Diego. When Holsbo is asked why he came to rodeo school, he says, with no evident irony, "My heroes have always been cowboys."

Barry Baker is twenty-three, a lanky, tan blond from Huntington   10
Beach, California, and for the last nine years he has been a trophy-winning surfer. Recently, he grew weary of surfing, partly because of ocean pollution and partly because he came to feel that bull riding might afford a better kind of kick. He has already ridden a few bulls in amateur rodeos, and believes that the balance it takes to ride a gnarly wave is hardly different from the skill required to stay on a bucking bull. "You have to flow with the wave for surfing. Here you have to flow with the bull," he says. Baker's outfit is half cowboy, half beach boy: psychedelic T-shirt, cowboy boots that have been secured at the ankles with little leather straps, and well-worn jeans,

under which is a girdlelike pair of neoprene scuba pants for added protection.

Michael (Doc) Yager is a returning student. He is forty-six years old and is a physician's surgical assistant from Albany, New York. Doc rodeos in the First Frontier Circuit, which includes the entire Northeast, from Virginia to Maine, and which is notable for having never produced a national champion. Doc is a dude, and though a hurt wrist prevents him from mounting many bulls, he makes a glorious sight in custom-made chaps with flowing purple metallic fringe, and with leather gloves tucked into the waist; his shirt is a red-striped Wrangler Brush Popper, and he wears a tall white hat and has a custom-made rigging rope slung over his shoulder.

When it is time to ride, students hustle toward the arena—a dirt circle enclosed by a tall wooden fence. There is an announcer's booth set high enough for Gary to see all the action and videotape every ride for instant replay. From the booth, he calls instructions to his crew above the din of a country-music radio station playing over loudspeakers. There are bull chutes at opposite ends of the arena, and behind the chutes are holding pens for more cattle. Students and wranglers perch on top of the fence to watch the action—railbirds. . . .

The bulls to be ridden are not drawn at random but are chosen by Leffew and his twenty-four-year-old son, Brett, to match the riders' abilities, to instill confidence, and to rectify weaknesses. Rank bulls, for experienced students, are let out of chutes to the left of the announcer's booth; tamer ones buck from chutes to the right. Of all the bulls at the school, the fattest, named Tiny, is also the gentlest. Low, wide, and black, Tiny weighs fifteen hundred pounds. He is ten years old and is especially suitable for first-timers. Some of the experienced ranch hands like to jump three at a time on Tiny's back, or ride him backward; others kiss him between the ears to show how mild he is. Tiny stands calmly in the chute and bucks softly; sometimes he needs to hear the sound of the electric prod to keep him kicking for the whole eight seconds.

In addition to videotaping the action, Gary Leffew cheers riders on from his booth, using the colorful jargon of pro rodeo announcers. Sometimes, to break the tension or the monotony, he grows irreverent—especially when a very young or very bad rider goes out on a plodding old side of beef like Tiny and cannot stay aboard for eight seconds. "Hall of Fame ride!" Leffew calls out as a novice tilts sidewise and tries desperately to hold on. "One for the record books!" he cries as a rider loses his grip on the rigging and falls face first into the dirt. "Ninety points for sure! He's got the spectators on their feet!" The railbirds guffaw, Tiny lopes away, and the fallen rider spits dirt from his mouth as he struggles to his feet, perhaps considering a career in auto sales.

All the instant-replay critiques contain similar advice, because, although there are a thousand ways to be bucked off a bull, there is only one way to stay on: find what Leffew calls the comfort zone, in which you feel that you are so tuned in to the bull's rhythm that you use it instead of fighting it, and the ranker the bull, the better you ride. "Come on!" he cries out, watching a cowboy do it right. "Come on! Buck! The higher you jump is just a little too low for me!" Leffew stops the tape to show a rider how he hunches forward, giving the bull an edge. "Stick your chest out more," Leffew tells the student, not only because it will improve his balance but because it will make him feel proud on top of the bull; it will make him look—and ride—like a winner. "I don't see any daylight under your seat. . . . Move your free arm right up high. . . . Get up on those legs. . . . Find your center of balance." Whatever his critique, Leffew always fills it with compliments. As bull riding's grand master of positive thinking, he believes that it's his job to make even beginners feel that they have a shot at victory. It is also his job to assure them that the broken bones, pulled ligaments, and bloody noses are part of the game, too.

By the middle of the second day, some of the students' early wild   16
enthusiasm has begun to wane; bruised muscles are starting to hurt and swell, and once-spiffy cowboy outfits are torn and caked with muck. When Michael Battles was thrown by his first bull, he ripped his bluejeans from the ankle to the knee, and now he's using silver duct tape to secure the flapping fabric to his body. Doc is out of commission. Jason Pluhar comes back from a brutal ride limping with a pulled groin muscle. "Where does it hurt?" a veteran asks, and Jason whispers, "Everywhere."

READING FOR MEANING

Write at least a page, exploring your ideas about Jane and Michael Stern's observations of Gary Leffew and his bull-riding school. You might begin by giving your general impression of Leffew, the school, and the students. You might also comment on the Sterns's attitude toward their subject. Then write about anything else that contributes to your understanding of the Sterns's observations.

As you write, you may find that you need to reread the observations and annotate them further. Consider quoting phrases or sentences that illustrate the meaning you find. You may find your ideas changing as you reread and write.

If you have trouble sustaining your writing, consider these suggestions:

- Describe the basic activities at the bull-riding school.
- Summarize the generalizations about the students as a group in paragraphs 3 and 7 or contrast two quite different students as a way to understand better the diversity within the group.
- Explain the possible meaning or significance of "like a Bible Belt preacher for whom riding rank bulls is a sure way to Heaven" (paragraph 4), "reso-

lutely thinking like a winner" (paragraph 6), "bull riding's grand master of positive thinking" (paragraph 15), or any other statement that catches your attention.

- Describe a focused, brief period of voluntary training or schooling you undertook. What were your motives for signing up? Who was the teacher? What did you learn? How did you learn it? Connect your experience specifically to that of Leffew's students.

EXTENDING MEANING THROUGH CONVERSATION. While it is important for you to make meaning on your own, you may be able to enhance your understanding by conversing with other students about the Sterns's profile of Leffew and his bull-riding school.

Meet with one or two classmates. Begin your conversation by identifying one thing in the reading that seems particularly informative, engaging, or vivid to each of you.

As you talk about the reading, you may find that each person's impressions of it differ. Your goal is not necessarily to see it the same way but to see more in it than each of you originally saw on your own. Reread and discuss parts of the essay together to keep your conversation focused.

EXPLORING THE SIGNIFICANCE OF FIGURATIVE LANGUAGE. You can learn still more about the Sterns's attitudes toward Gary Leffew by looking closely at the figurative language they use to present him. Guidelines for this productive critical reading strategy are in Appendix 1 under Exploring the Significance of Figurative Language.

Because the figurative language used to present Leffew is widely scattered in the essay, the examples of it are listed for you here, completing step 1 of the activity. Beginning with this list and checking the context of each example, go on and complete steps 2 and 3.

Leffew won the world (paragraph 1)

Leffew implants a positive mental attitude (paragraph 4)

from this lofty perch (paragraph 4)

Spiced with tales (paragraph 4)

like a Bible Belt preacher (paragraph 4)

cowboy handsome (paragraph 5)

bronzed (paragraph 5)

Leffew. . . devoured every page (paragraph 6)

a walking, talking bull-riding machine (paragraph 6)

grand master of positive thinking (paragraph 15)

READING LIKE A WRITER

Writers of observations strive to give readers a strong image of people, especially those who are the center or focus of an activity, as is Gary Leffew in this essay. Writers have diverse resources for detailing a person: describing appearance, giving facts about background, noting current projects or activities, summarizing a story a person tells, noting interactions with other people, and capturing conversations with others. These resources come from interviews and observations, and the Sterns use all of them when they present the confident, optimistic, stylish bull-riding champion and master teacher, Gary Leffew. When you write your observational essay, you will want to use some, or even all, of these writers' resources or strategies.

ANALYZE. Reread paragraphs 2, 5, 6, 14, and 15, where the Sterns detail Leffew to present a clear, memorable image of him. In the margin, write a note identifying the most prominent *kind* of detail in each paragraph. If you read all the paragraphs together first, the contrasts among them will make it easier for you to label the kind of detail in each one.

WRITE. Write a page or so identifying the kind of detail in each of the five paragraphs. With each identification, include one or two examples from the paragraph to illustrate the category in which you have put it.

Then, in a few sentences, evaluate how successfully the Sterns deploy their writers' resources for detailing Leffew. Throughout, are the details telling and well orchestrated? Note any details that seem inconsistent with the impression you believe the Sterns want to convey about Leffew. Where do you think more details are needed to fill out the impression? Where might fewer details be appropriate? What for you is the most successful part of the detailing? The least successful?

COMPARE. If you wish—or your instructor requests—you can use the analysis of detailing people you have just completed as the basis for comparing how other writers detail people. Such a comparison would give you a fuller idea of the resources available to observational writers for presenting people, especially the central person in a profile; this knowledge would be very useful to you when you write your own observational essay. Recall that this reading and previous readings in this chapter all feature a single person: Tracy Kidder features a teacher, the *New Yorker* writer a soup chef, Lisa Jones a comic-strip artist, and Jane and Michael Stern a retired bull-riding champion and bull-riding instructor.

Skim each reading, making notes about the kinds of details the writer uses to present the central person. Do we get to know this person through description of appearance and dress, dialogue, interaction with other people, or other details? Is there a predominant kind of detail in each essay? You will, of course, notice similarities and differences among the four essays. Think about what might account for the differences. For example, two possible factors might be the writer's attitude toward the person or the person's line of work. Make notes about what might explain the different kinds of detailing you observe in the four essays.

CONSIDERING IDEAS FOR YOUR OWN WRITING

You might want to consider profiling a leisure or educational activity that brings people together briefly for special training. This kind of training is usually offered in scheduled classes that meet only a few times (one to five times is typical) on evenings or weekends. You may have taken such a class or know other people who have. The offerings reflect people's diverse interests and differ somewhat from community to community: dog training, motorcycle riding, dancing, cooking, decorating for a holiday, stress reduction, conflict resolution, training for new computer software, public speaking, introduction to political candidates, speed reading. You can find these classes advertised in newspapers and in your college's extension-course catalog. Ask for the instructor's permission to observe the class, and arrange to interview him or her for a few minutes before or after class. Be bold in approaching two or three students to discover why they are there and what they have to say about the class. Take careful notes about all that you can observe during at least one class meeting.

John McPhee

THE NEW YORK PICKPOCKET ACADEMY

John McPhee (b. 1931) lives in Princeton, New Jersey, where he occasionally teaches a writing workshop in the "Literature of Fact" at Princeton University. He is highly regarded as a writer of profiles—in-depth reporting about people, places, and activities—and is a shrewd observer and masterful interviewer. In his profiles, he ingeniously integrates information from observations, interviews, and research into engaging, readable prose. Readers marvel at the way he explains clearly such complex subjects as experimental aircraft or modern physics and captures interest in such ordinary subjects as bears or oranges. Among his books are *Oranges* (1967), *Coming into the Country* (1977), *Table of Contents* (1985), *The Control of Nature* (1989), *Looking for a Ship* (1990), *Assembling California* (1993), and *The Ransom of Russian Art* (1994).

This selection comes from *Giving Good Weight* (1979), a long profile of the New Jersey farmers who sell produce at a farmers' market in Brooklyn. McPhee spent several weeks working at Rich Hodgson's produce stand, gathering material for his essay. Among other things he observed pickpockets at work; from these observations came this profile of pickpocketing and other crimes, focusing on the criminals, their victims, and the reactions of the farmers.

Right away, as we begin reading, we meet two pickpockets and three farmers, Melissa Mousseau, Bob Lewis, and Rich Hodgson, who get the story—this "narrative of fact"—under way. The narrator of the story is McPhee himself, weighing and sacking produce, all the while looking beyond the zucchini and tomatoes for material that might interest readers.

As you read, notice the many details McPhee provides about the people and the scene: the vegetables and trucks and hats and colors and sounds of the market. Notice, too, the great variety of examples he presents of crime—and honesty. Do these diverse examples add up to anything special? What would you say McPhee's purpose is in sharing his observations with us?

Brooklyn, and the pickpocket in the burgundy jacket appears just   1
before noon. Melissa Mousseau recognizes him much as if he were an old customer and points him out to Bob Lewis, who follows him from truck to truck. Aware of Lewis, he leaves the market. By two, he will have made another run. A woman with deep-auburn hair and pale, nervous hands clumsily attracts the attention of a customer whose large white purse she is rifling. Until a moment ago, the customer was occupied with the choosing of apples and peppers, but now she shouts out, "Hey, what are you doing? Your hand is in my purse. What are you doing?" The auburn-haired woman not only has her hand in the purse but most of her arm as well. She withdraws it, and with intense absorption begins to finger the peppers. "How much are the peppers? Mister, give me some of these!" she says, looking up at me with a gypsy's dark, starburst eyes. "Three pounds for a dollar," I tell her, with a swift glance around for Lewis or a cop. When I look back, the pickpocket is gone. Other faces have filled in—people unconcernedly examining the fruit. The woman with the white purse has returned her attention to the apples. She merely seems annoyed. Lewis once sent word around from truck to truck that we should regularly announce in loud voices that pickpockets were present in the market, but none of the farmers complied. Hodgson shrugged and said, "Why distract the customers?" Possibly Fifty-ninth Street is the New York Pickpocket Academy. Half a dozen scores have been made there in a day. I once looked up and saw a well-dressed gentleman under a gray fedora being kicked and kicked again by a man in a green polo shirt. He kicked him in the calves. He kicked him in the thighs. He kicked him in the gluteal bulge. He kicked him from the middle of the market out to the edge, and he kicked him into the street. "Get your ass out of here!" shouted the booter, redundantly. Turning back toward the market, he addressed the curious. "Pickpocket," he explained. The dip did not press charges.

People switch shopping carts from time to time. They make off   2
with a loaded one and leave an empty cart behind. Crime on such levels is a part of the background here, something in the urban air, so many parts per million. The condition is accepted with a resignation that approaches nonchalance.

Most thievery is petty and is on the other side of the tables. As   3

Rich describes it, "Brooklyn, Fifty-ninth Street, people rip off stuff everywhere. You just expect it. An old man comes along and puts a dozen eggs in a bag. Women choosing peaches steal one for every one they buy—a peach for me, a peach for you. What can you do? You stand there and watch. When they take too many, you complain. I watched a guy one day taking nectarines. He would put one in a plastic bag, then one in a pocket, then one in a pile on the ground. After he did that half a dozen times, he had me weigh the bag."

"This isn't England," Barry Benepe informed us once, "and a lot of people are pretty dishonest."   4

Now, in Brooklyn, a heavyset woman well past the middle of life is sobbing pitifully, flailing her arms in despair. She is sitting on a bench in the middle of the market. She is wearing a print dress, a wide-brimmed straw hat. Between sobs, she presents in a heavy Russian accent the reason for her distress. She was buying green beans from Don Keller, and when she was about to pay him she discovered that someone had opened her handbag—even while it was on her arm, she said—and had removed several books of food stamps, a telephone bill, and eighty dollars in cash. Lewis, in his daypack, stands over her and tells her he is sorry. He says, "This sort of thing will happen wherever there's a crowd."   5

Another customer breaks in to scold Lewis, saying, "This is the biggest rip-off place in Brooklyn. Two of my friends were pickpocketed here last week and I had to give them carfare home."   6

Lewis puts a hand on his forehead and, after a pensive moment, says, "That was very kind of you."   7

The Russian woman is shrieking now. Lewis attends her like a working dentist. "It's all right. It will be O.K. It may not be as bad as you think." He remarks that he would call the police if he thought there was something they could do.   8

Jeffrey Mack, eight years old, has been listening to all this, and he now says, "I see a cop."   9

Jeffrey has an eye for cops that no one else seems to share. (A squad car came here for him one morning and took him off to face a truant officer. Seeing his fright, a Pacific Street prostitute got into the car and rode with him.)   10

"Where, Jeffrey?"   11

"There," Jeffrey lifts an arm and points.   12

"Where?"   13

"There." He points again—at trucks, farmers, a falafel man.   14

"I don't see a policeman," Lewis says to him. "If you see one, Jeffrey, go and get him."   15

Jeffrey goes, and comes back with an off-duty 78th Precinct cop who is wearing a white apron and has been selling fruits and vegetables in the market. The officer speaks sternly to the crying woman. "Your name?"   16

"Catherine Barta."   17

"Address?"   18

"Eighty-five Eastern Parkway."   19

Every Wednesday, she walks a mile or so to the Greenmarket.   20
She has lived in Brooklyn close to half her life, the rest of it in the
Ukraine. Heading back to his vegetables, the officer observes that
there is nothing he can do.

Out from behind her tables comes Joan Benack, the baker, of   21
Rocky Acres Farm, Milan, New York—a small woman with a high,
thin voice. Leaving her tropical carrot bread, her zucchini bread, her
anadama bread, her beer bread, she goes around with a borrowed
hat collecting money from the farmers for Catherine Barta. Bills
stuff the hat, size 7—the money of Alvina Frey and John Labanowski
and Cleather Slade and Rich Hodgson and Bob Engle, who has seen
it come and go. He was a broker for Merrill Lynch before the stock
market imploded, and now he is a blond-bearded farmer in a basketball shirt selling apples that he grows in Clintondale, New York. Don
Keller offers a dozen eggs, and one by one the farmers come out
from their trucks to fill Mrs. Barta's shopping cart with beans and
zucchini, apples, eggplants, tomatoes, peppers, and corn. As a result,
her wails and sobs grow louder.

A man who gave Rich Hodgson a ten-dollar bill for a ninety-five-   22
cent box of brown eggs asks Rich to give the ten back after Rich has
handed him nine dollars and five cents, explaining that he has some
smaller bills that he wants to exchange for a twenty. Rich hands him
the ten. Into Rich's palm he counts out five ones, a five, and the ten
for a twenty and goes away satisfied, as he has every reason to be,
having conned Rich out of nine dollars, five cents, and a box of
brown eggs. Rich smiles at his foolishness, shrugs, and sells some
cheese. If cash were equanimity, he would never lose a cent. One
day, a gang of kids began taking Don Keller's vegetables and throwing them at the Hodgson truck. Anders Thueson threw an apple at
the kids, who then picked up rocks. Thueson reached into the back
of the truck and came up with a machete. While Hodgson told him
to put it away, pant legs went up, switchblades came into view. Part
of the gang bombarded the truck with debris from a nearby roof.
Any indication of panic might have been disastrous. Hodgson packed
deliberately, and drove away.

Todd Jameson, who comes in with his brother Dan from Farm-   23
ingdale, New Jersey, weighed some squash one day, and put it in a
brown bag. He set the package down while he weighed something
else. Then, reaching for the squash, he picked up an identical bag
that happened to contain fifty dollars in rolled coins. He handed it to
the customer who had asked for the squash. Too late, Todd discovered the mistake. A couple of hours later, though, the customer—
"I'll never forget him as long as I live, the white hair, the glasses, the
ruddy face"—came back. He said, "Hey, this isn't squash. I didn't ask
for money, I asked for squash." Whenever that man comes to mar-

ket, the Jamesons give him a bag full of food. "You see, where I come from, that would never, never happen," Todd explains. "If I made a mistake like that in Farmingdale, no one—no one—would come back with fifty dollars' worth of change."

Dusk comes down without further crime in Brooklyn, and the   24 farmers are packing to go. John Labanowski—short, compact, with a beer in his hand—is expounding on his day. "The white people are educating the colored on the use of beet greens," he reports. "A colored woman was telling me today, 'Cut the tops off,' and a white woman spoke up and said, 'Hold it,' and told the colored woman, 'You're throwing the best part away.' They go on talking, and pretty soon the colored woman is saying, 'I'm seventy-three on Monday,' and the white says, 'I don't believe a word you say.' You want to know why I come in here? I come in here for fun. For profit, of course, but for relaxation, too. I like being here with these people. They say the city is a rat race, but they've got it backwards. The farm is what gets to be a rat race. You should come out and see what I—" He is interrupted by the reappearance in the market of Catherine Barta, who went home long ago and has now returned, her eyes hidden by her wide-brimmed hat, her shopping cart full beside her. On the kitchen table, at 85 Eastern Parkway, she found her telephone bill, her stamps, and her cash. She has come back to the farmers with their food and money.

READING FOR MEANING

Write at least a page, exploring your ideas about McPhee's observations. You might begin by describing your overall impression of the market, the people, and the people's activities. You could comment on McPhee's attitude toward his subject and on a possible reason for the observations. Include anything else that contributes to your understanding of the essay. Try to find quotations you can use to help explain your understanding. Expect the writing you do to lead you to new insights into McPhee's essay.

If you have difficulty continuing for at least a page, consider the following suggestions:

- List the types of crime McPhee observes, as described in paragraphs 1, 2, 3, 22, and 23.
- Single out two or three things you learned about urban farmers' markets and the typical crimes that take place there.
- Describe the attitude of people who work at the market toward the crimes. Give specific examples.
- Describe a theft you observed at a farmers' market, at a flea market, or on the street. Connect it to one of the crimes in McPhee's essay.

EXTENDING MEANING THROUGH CONVERSATION. After making meaning of the essay on your own, you may be able to extend your understanding of it by conversing with other students about McPhee's observations.

Meet with one or two classmates. Begin your conversation by taking turns identifying something in McPhee's essay that seems particularly informative, engaging, or vivid.

As you talk about the reading, you may find that you have somewhat different impressions of it. Your goal as a group is not necessarily to see it the same way but to see more in it than each of you saw on your own. Reread and discuss parts of the essay together to keep your conversation focused.

READING LIKE A WRITER
ORGANIZING THE OBSERVATIONS

Writers of observational essays generally organize either *narratively* (as a chronological story of their observations) or *topically* (according to particular points they wish to make about their subjects). The organizational plan a writer chooses depends on the subject, the purpose of the essay, and the writer's perspective on the subject. McPhee organizes his profile narratively, telling us part of the story of pickpockets and their victims during one day at the farmers' market. In the first paragraph, McPhee provides a beginning time marker: "just before noon." In the final paragraph, he tells us when the narrative ends: "dusk comes down." Although McPhee does much more than narrate events as the story moves along, the basic organization of the essay is narrative.

ANALYZE. Make a scratch outline of McPhee's organization. (For an illustration of scratch outlining see Appendix 1, A Catalog of Critical Reading Strategies.) Note each main event during the afternoon, sections of commentary, and events that happened sometime earlier. Using your outline as a reference, skim the essay, thinking about how McPhee allots the time from noon to dusk. Is the time apportioned evenly across the afternoon or focused on specific events that take a limited amount of time? Where are events of the afternoon interrupted by other material, and where do events that happened earlier intervene?

WRITE. Write several sentences explaining what you have learned from the essay. Comment on your scratch outline, making clear what you consider to be the main parts and their relations to each other. Did you find the overall plan easy to follow? If so, how, given that previous events intervene in the narration of the afternoon's events?

COMPARE. To understand the difference between narrative and topical organization in observational essays, compare McPhee's narrative plan with the topical plan in either "Soup" or "Bull Riding School." First, make a scratch outline of either topical essay. Then write several sentences speculating about why each writer chose the particular organizational plan. Given the subject and the writer's purpose, what advantages or disadvantages do you see in the organization chosen? Could McPhee have organized topically around the types of crime he had observed at the market, telling a story as an example of each type, instead of organizing around some of the events on one afternoon? Could the Sterns have organized narratively around a typical bull-riding lesson? Could the *New Yorker* writer have told the story of a typical day at the soup kitchen, weaving in the information he offers in the topical organization? If you think any of these alternatives is possible, then offer your ideas about why the writers might have chosen the plans they did. Do you think they chose wisely?

CONSIDERING IDEAS FOR YOUR OWN WRITING

Public scenes filled with people and action offer good material for observational essays. They also present problems, mainly their huge size and scope: So many people are present and so much is happening at once, the observer may not be able to decide where to focus. Notice how McPhee solves this problem by remaining in one location, the stall where he is selling vegetables. The action takes place in this one small area of a huge market. McPhee presents only a few people and events. You could likewise find such a focus in some large public scene. Here are examples to start you thinking about possibilities: the souvenir sellers or grounds keepers at a baseball game; the lifeguards (or one lifeguard) at a beach; an unusual store or the mall manager's office at a shopping mall; one stall at a flea market; a small group of riders from the same club at a Harley-Davidson motorcycle reunion; one section of your college library; an ice-skating rink at a city park; a musician, vendor, or guard in a subway station. You need not seek some unexpected activity, like the pickpockets at the Brooklyn farmers' market, but you could probably interest readers in the people and activities in one limited area of a large, amorphous public scene.

Craig Elsten

DEAD AIR

Craig Elsten wrote this essay about a campus radio station when he was a first-year student in 1991 at the University of California, San Diego.

Elsten uses a variety of observed detail, as well as information he learned from interviewing station personnel, to present a balanced, entertaining portrait of a slightly wacky alternative to the average broadcast organization. While his primary audience might be students at UCSD, notice how he provides enough background to make his profile understandable and appealing to a general readership.

KSDT, UCSD's campus radio station, keeps on playing.
The question is, does anyone listen?

"Thirty seconds!"   1
Studio A, the nerve center of radio station KSDT, is abuzz with   2

action. Student-DJ Shane Nesbitt frantically flips through a pile of records, looking for a song to put on the air. His partner, Nathan Wilson, frets at the control board, listening to the current song, "Chew Me, Chew Me," by a band called Intense Mutilation. The song is almost over, and Nesbitt and Wilson have nothing ready to go on afterwards.

A cry of triumph rings out as Nesbitt finds his record of choice,   3
the Pogues' "If I Should Fall from Grace with God." Quickly, the DJs scramble to cue up a song. Then, Wilson skillfully starts the Pogues' song at low volume, bringing it up as Intense Mutilation fades into the distance. The segue is complete; the crisis is over. Leaning back on his stool, Wilson smooths his hair and laughs.

"Whew!" he exclaims, "Business as usual. I just hope someone is   4
listening."

While student volunteers strive to bring alternative radio to   5
UCSD, most of the campus is unable to tune in. KSDT operates without an FCC license, so it is unable to broadcast over standard airwaves. The station instead sends its signal over "cable radio," which works similarly to cable television. The problem is, almost nobody has cable radio. On campus, the Revelle and Muir dormitories are able to pick up KSDT on carrier current at 540 AM, but even then reception is erratic at best.

The obvious question then is, why broadcast at all?   6

"For the fun of it," responds Nesbitt. "On cable radio, we can be   7
less careful and do more crazy things. We can play a crude rap song and then follow it with a jazz number, or, if we want, we can just talk for twenty minutes. On regular radio, we couldn't do that."

"Here there is no pressure," Wilson agrees. "If we screw up and   8
knock the needle off the record, or if we play a lousy song or say something rude, no one is going to call and complain." Then he adds, "It's kind of a bummer to think that throughout your whole show, there might not be anyone out there at all."

The lobby of KSDT is decorated in a fashion that befits alternative   9
radio. Posters and stickers, many of bands that have long since faded out of memory, decorate the walls. One message stands out from the lobby door, a bumper sticker reading, "Still Crazy after All These Beers." Nearby, a sticker for the band Elvis Christ is pasted on a file cabinet. There, the King does his pelvis thrusts on a crucifix.

There is an old couch in the lobby, one that looks like it has   10
rested many a posterior. Indeed, the sofa looks like it was purchased from a garage sale—in 1978. The woman at the lobby desk, when asked, said that she had no idea when the couch was last cleaned. She did, however, suggest not rolling on the cushions. "The cockroaches will wake up," she smiled.

A striking feature of KSDT is its vast collection of records. Over   11
fifteen thousand vinyls, at last count, were stored in the station library. With modern musical technology being the way it is, it seems

surprising that vinyl records are in use at all. According to DJ Scott Garrison, however, a lot of stuff they play is released by minor-label recording companies, which can't afford to produce CDs.

From a newcomer's standpoint, it seems curious that so few   12
steps have been taken to bring the station to the listeners. After all, KSDT has been in operation for over fifteen years.

One of the "key people" that keeps the station alive is general   13
manager Steve Branin. Branin remarks that one of KSDT's main problems is in its power structure. "The management has been so weak for so many years now that the DJs have taken over," Branin says. "Now, it seems that we can't get the DJs to follow any rules at all. We ask them to play promos [promotions of upcoming events], and they don't. We ask them to pay quarterly dues [five dollars], and most DJs don't. Our hands are tied."

With KSDT being primarily a volunteer effort (only the general   14
manager, assistant manager, and secretary are paid), enforcement of rules becomes difficult. "I've tried suspending a DJ's air privileges," Branin says, "but then the person will just quit. We have a hard enough time getting air time filled as it is. We need all the DJs we can get."

Branin has attempted this year to start the procedure to obtain   15
an FCC license, but he admits that the station is "at least five years away from going public."

Assistant manager Brad Darlow feels that the wait will be much   16
longer. "There is no way that KSDT will have an FCC license in the next five years," he says, "because people here are unwilling to give up any of their freedoms. If we got on public radio, DJs wouldn't be able to play whatever they wanted, or to skip their shows. The disorganization here is incredible, and it's not going to change."

Darlow recalls a weekend afternoon when he walked into the   17
station and found no one around. "Whoever the last DJ was had left, and the CD that he had going over the air was skipping, making this horrendous sound. It sounded sort of like a car engine trying to turn over, but louder. I turned it off, but who knows how long the station was putting that sound over the airwaves."

News director Dan Schuck, however, feels that too much is   18
being made of the station's problems. "Sure, a lot of stuff that could get done around here doesn't," Schuck says, "but remember, one of the main reasons this place is here is so people can learn something about radio."

This attitude is shared by several people at KSDT. While some   19
station members are concerned with increasing the profile of the station on campus, many are pleased just to be around KSDT's progressive atmosphere or to admire the station's impressive, if eclectic, record library.

"Did you know that we have nine Culture Club albums?" Wilson   20
says. "There are so many obscure albums here, I could spend years just trying to listen."

Along with the over eleven thousand records in the station's 21
main library, KSDT has a second room filled with over four thousand old, unpopular, or little-known albums. This collection is
known affectionately as "Dinosaur Rock."

"This place is a music lover's dream come true," Nesbitt says. 22
"One of the reasons I became a DJ was just so I could keep on top
of what's happening in the current music scene."

Indeed, one of the best-organized departments at the station is 23
the music department. Music director Vicky Kim receives albums
from across the country every day, sometimes before commercial
stations do. "It's funny to see a band go big on 91X [a San Diego
commercial station] that we have been playing here for a long time,"
Kim remarked. "The DJs there will say, 'Here's a brand new band,'
and I just have to laugh."

The situation at KSDT will soon come to a head. Earlier this year, 24
UCSD Associated Students president John Edson mentioned that if
KSDT could not become an FCC licensed station, it could be shut
down to avoid its high cost of operation. Other people in the campus administration have questioned the intelligence of spending the
$21,000 per year for a station that, for all intents and purposes, is
nothing but a training lab.

General manager Branin remains optimistic, however. "I think 25
that once everything gets settled, KSDT could be a real asset to the
campus, as well as to all of San Diego. It would bring a higher profile
to UCSD and would give the students something to identify with."

Schuck adds, "It would be great if UCSD students driving in to 26
the campus could tune into the station for campus news instead of
having to rely on the *Guardian*. That's my dream: the day will come
when the *Guardian* has to use *us* as a news source."

Finally, Shane Nesbitt adds, "I don't really care what happens in a 27
couple of years. I'm having fun doing a show right now."

The Pogues are done playing. Nathan Wilson talks about his 28
romantic problems, while Nesbitt goes off in search of an industrial
band called Sandy Duncan's Eye. The music continues, and the station continues, into the dead of the night.

READING FOR MEANING

Write at least a page, exploring your understanding of "Dead Air." You
might begin by describing what seems to be the impression Elsten wants to convey about this campus radio station. Then write about anything else in the essay
that contributes to your understanding of Elsten's observations, quoting to indicate the key sources of your understanding. Your understanding may change as
you write.

If you have difficulty continuing for at least a page, consider the following
suggestions:

- Explain briefly what you learned about the operations of KSDT.
- Observational writers want to engage readers, while informing and making a point. Describe what was most engaging for you in Elsten's essay.
- Speculate about Elsten's attitude toward what he is observing. Does he seem to favor one faction or another in the disputes about DJ's irresponsibility or KSDT's obtaining an FCC license?
- Describe a place you worked on or off campus where the ingredients for success were present but somehow things just couldn't seem to come together. What was it like, and what did you and others feel about it? Connect your work experience specifically to that at KSDT.

EXTENDING MEANING THROUGH CONVERSATION. You should make meaning of the essay on your own, then converse with other students about Elsten's essay to try to extend your understanding.

Get together with one or two other students. Begin your conversation by taking turns identifying one thing that seemed particularly informative, unexpected, or vivid.

As you talk about the reading, you may find that you have somewhat different impressions of it. By sharing your ideas, you may see more in it than you saw on your own. Keep your conversation focused on the essay by reading and discussing parts of it together.

READING LIKE A WRITER
CONVEYING AN IMPRESSION

In this chapter, we have reviewed various ways observational writers interpret and evaluate their subjects so readers will have the satisfaction of seeing the point of the observations. Kidder and the *New Yorker* writer convey an impression of their subjects by implication. By contrast, Jones states her interpretation explicitly: It is easy to find several sentences where she offers her own commentary on the scene and the action, telling us unmistakably what the point is. Elsten does the same.

ANALYZE. Reread Elsten's essay, marking any sentences in which the writer comments directly on the situation at KSDT, including the comment offered by the title and subtitle. Note any ways these comments help you recognize Elsten's interpretation or point.

WRITE. Write several sentences, stating your understanding of the point of Elsten's essay and illustrating the point by quoting key parts of the essay. How early does Elsten introduce the point you have identified? Where and how often does he reiterate it, if he does? Finally, add a few sentences, evaluating how successfully Elsten offers an interpretation. What more, if anything, might he have done? Might he have done less, leaving more for you to infer? Does he succeed in providing the interpretation—through events, dialogue, and details of the scene—as well as asserting it? Explain briefly.

CONSIDERING IDEAS FOR YOUR OWN WRITING

If you were to write about a student-run organization on your campus, which one might you choose? Make a list of campus organizations, with the help of other students. Using a published list of student organizations, choose two or three to consider carefully as possible subjects for an observational essay. What would you expect to learn at these organizations? What might interest your readers about each one? What would you want to learn in a preliminary visit to each organization to decide about which one to write?

THINKING ABOUT WHAT YOU HAVE LEARNED
ABOUT OBSERVATIONAL ESSAYS

In this chapter, you have been learning about reading observational essays—reading them for meaning and reading them like a writer. Before moving on to write an observational essay, you should pause here to review and consolidate what you have learned about what makes observational writing successful.

Choose one reading in this chapter that seems to you especially effective. Before rereading the essay, write down one or two reasons that you remember it as an example of effective observational writing.

Then reread the essay, annotating the features that make it so effective. As a starting point, consider the essay's purpose and how well it achieves that purpose for its intended readers. Then focus on how well the essay

- Details the scene and people
- Organizes the observations
- Engages and informs readers
- Conveys an impression of its subject

You can complete this activity on your own, or your instructor may ask you to collaborate with a small group of other students who have chosen the same essay. If you work with others, take time initially for everyone to read the essay thoughtfully, annotating as suggested above. Then discuss what makes the essay so effective. Take notes. One member of your group can then report to the class what you have learned about this effective essay, or you can individually write up what you have learned.

Write at least a page justifying your choice of this essay as the most effective observational essay among the chapter's readings. Assume that your readers—your instructor and classmates—have read the essay but will not remember the details of how the essay works or what makes it so effective. You need not argue that the essay is the best in the chapter, only that it is in your view a particularly effective observational essay.

A GUIDE TO OBSERVATIONAL WRITING

From the readings in this chapter, you have learned that observational writers try both to engage and to inform readers. Not content with generalizations and summaries, they vividly present scenes and people to their readers. We can imagine specific details of a scene—objects, shapes, textures, colors, sounds, even smells. We see people dressed a particular way. We see them moving and gesturing, and we hear them talk. All the details contribute to a single dominant impression of the subject.

Observational writing presents special challenges. Writers necessarily collect large amounts of original and diverse material from visits and interviews, which must be sorted, organized, and integrated into a readable draft. The guide to invention, drafting, and revising that follows is designed to assist you in solving the special problems you encounter in this kind of writing.

INVENTION

The following activities can help you choose a subject, plan and carry through your observations, decide on an impression you mean to convey, and analyze your readers. If you complete each activity before you write your first draft, you will have collected all, or nearly all, the information you will need—and you will then be free to focus on your actual writing.

Choosing a Subject

Finding just the right subject is critical. A good way to begin is by listing a wide variety of subjects. Give your list time to grow—at least a day or two. Ask others for suggestions. Add more items as they come to mind. After a while, your list should be long enough to ensure that you have not overlooked a possible subject. Listing and reviewing your ideas will help you choose a subject.

For an essay based on personal observation and interviews, your subject should be a person or a place. Each type of essay is illustrated by a reading in this chapter.

You might begin by listing possible subjects in each category. For a *person,* list people doing work that appeals to you, people with unusual jobs or hobbies, people recognized for service or achievement, local or campus personalities. For a *place,* list places you are curious about and would be able to visit and study. If you can think of unusual places, fine, but consider also places from everyday life—a computer center, a weight-reduction clinic, a small-claims court, a nursery school. Some students find that they are unable to list subjects in both of these categories; if this happens to you, just concentrate on the ideas that do come to mind.

After reflecting on your lists, choose a subject about which you are genuinely curious. Select one you can visit several times, observing closely and in detail.

Most important, choose a subject that interests you—and that you think might appeal to your readers.

Probing Your Subject

Before you observe your subject, jot down everything you presently know and feel about it. You may discover that you know more than you think you do.

Start by writing for several minutes without stopping, putting down everything you know about your subject. Include personal memories, facts, anecdotes, statistics, visual details—anything that comes to mind. How would you define or describe this subject? What is its purpose or function?

Next, state something about your attitude toward your subject. What feelings do you have about it? Do you feel neutral, anxious, eager? Why does it interest you? What preconceptions do you have about it? How do other people feel about it?

Continue with your expectations. What do you expect to discover? Do you anticipate being surprised, amused, shocked? What kind of profile or report would you really like to write about this subject? What readers do you want to address?

This initial probing of your subject will probably help you decide whether you are interested enough to continue with it.

Investigating Your Subject

Observational writing requires that you gather original information. To guarantee that you complete the information gathering within the time available, take time now to plan. Decide what times you have open within the next few days, then make phone calls to schedule visits. When you write down your appointments, be sure to include names, addresses, phone numbers, dates and times, and any special arrangements you have made for a visit. Appendix 2, Strategies for Research and Documentation, provides helpful guidelines for observing, interviewing, and taking notes.

VISITING A PLACE. If you profile a place or a person engaged in an activity at a particular place, you will need to make one or more visits to the place to gather information. Appendix 2 provides useful guidelines for observing a place, taking notes on the spot, supplementing your notes later, and reflecting on what you have seen.

INTERVIEWING A PERSON. If your profile requires that you interview someone, you will find the guidelines for interviewing in Appendix 2 to be invaluable. These guidelines will help you plan and set up an interview, take notes during an interview, supplement your notes immediately after an interview, and reflect on what you have learned.

GATHERING PUBLISHED INFORMATION. If you are profiling a person or place, you may be able to pick up appropriate fliers, brochures, or reports, and you may want to do background reading on a particular kind of work or activity. Take careful notes from your reading, and keep accurate records of sources.

Deciding on the Impression You Mean to Convey

Find a focus in the material you have collected and then decide on exactly what you want to say about it. Review all your notes and impressions with the following kinds of questions in mind: What is the single most important thing you learned? What surprises or contradictions did you encounter? What larger social or personal implications do you see in your material? What do you most want readers to know about your subject? What will be your purpose in writing about this subject? What are your feelings about the subject? From your reflections on these questions, you should be able to write a few sentences that identify the impression you mean to convey about the subject. When you begin drafting, however, you may find that a different impression emerges.

Analyzing Your Readers

Before you begin drafting, you will find it helpful for planning and selecting material to analyze your readers carefully—who they are will influence your writing. You could try to write for several minutes about your readers, just to see what turns up. What do they know about your subject? What preconceptions are they likely to have? Why would they want to read about it? How can you interest them in it? What parts of your material might especially interest them?

LEARNING MORE ABOUT YOUR READERS: A COLLABORATIVE ACTIVITY

Get together with two or three other students to learn more about the preconceptions, knowledge, and questions readers will bring to your essay. If you are writing for a general readership, other students in your class are probably much like the readers you have in mind. However, if you are writing for a specialized readership—the elderly, young children, bicycling enthusiasts, experienced rodeo participants—let your partners know so they can try to put themselves in the place of these readers.

Take turns identifying the subject of your observations and describing it briefly; give no more detail than is required for your partners to know the who-what-where of your subject. Then your partners will tell you what they know about the subject, their attitudes toward it, their preconceptions about it, and the kinds of questions they would expect to have answered by your essay. You need not answer or explain; rather, take careful notes about what your partners have to say. You may need to draw them out with questions that will keep them talking for a few minutes.

From this activity, you will get a fuller understanding of what your readers will be thinking about your subject. Consequently, as you draft and revise, you will be able to select details that will help your readers imagine your subject and learn more about it. You will have sound ideas about how to interest your readers and how to focus your observations.

DRAFTING

When you have completed the invention activities, you will probably have made many discoveries about your subject and, with your substantial notes in hand, will be ready to proceed to a first draft. The following discussion describes how to set goals for drafting, plan your draft, and decide how to begin.

Setting Goals

Establish specific goals with your readers and purpose in mind. Consider how much your readers already know about the subject. If they are familiar with it, you will need to find an engaging angle from which to present it. If they are likely to be unfamiliar with the subject, you may need to define special terms or describe fully unusual procedures or activities. Considering how you will enable them to visualize the subject for themselves should lead you to determine a larger strategy for engaging and holding their interest throughout your essay. Notice, for instance, how Kidder chooses a particularly unusual lesson to engage readers' interest in the familiar subject of a grade-school classroom; how the Sterns appeal to our curiosity about bull riding and the people who want to learn how to do it; how McPhee emphasizes the dramatic interactions among vendors, customers, and pickpockets in the farmers' market. Each focuses on the unfamiliar to sustain reader interest.

Not only should you keep your readers' expectations in mind as you draft, but you should also include everything that serves your own purposes of presentation. McPhee, for example, chose from a wealth of sights and sounds just those details that serve his purpose: telling about crime at the farmers' market. Similarly, Jones and Elsten concentrate on those details that help support the dominant impression of their subjects they wish to convey.

Planning Your Draft

If you are profiling a person or place, you will have several choices of plans. Much observational writing is organized narratively. Sometimes, as in the piece by Kidder, the narrative is a straightforward, chronological presentation of activities observed over a limited period. Writers may also punctuate their main narrative with additional stories observed on other occasions: McPhee, for example, tells about what happened over a few hours at a Brooklyn farmers' market but also weaves in other stories about the market that took place at different times.

You might also choose to organize your observations around features of your subject or by grouping together related examples. "Soup" is organized around Mr. Yeganeh's values and attitudes; the Sterns's profile of Gary Leffew and his bull-riding school alternates information about Leffew and the students with activities at the school; Elsten groups related quotations from different sources to develop each of his points about radio station KSDT.

Beginning

It is sometimes difficult to know how to lead the reader into an observational essay. As you begin to draft, you can start with any part of the material, but it is usually best to start with an easy part—something you know you want to include or information you understand particularly well. Eventually you will want to open with something that will capture the readers' attention, but there is no reason you must write it first. Jones opens her essay with a comparison of herself and her friends to her subject's comic-strip characters, and the Sterns open with an introduction to their subject. The other writers in this chapter begin with specific scenes or actions: "Soup" opens with pithy quotations from its subject; McPhee focuses immediately on two pickpockets at work; Elsten places us in Studio A of radio station KSDT.

READING A DRAFT CRITICALLY

Now that you have a first draft, you need one or more readers who know something about observational writing to take a close look at what you have done and to advise you about what you might want to do to improve your draft. The guidelines in this section will ensure that you can get an in-depth analysis of your draft. You can use them to give someone else useful advice.

It is important to make or get a written record of specific suggestions for revising from a critical reading of a draft because a revision is usually done some time after a critical reading.

Just as you gain from receiving a critical reading, you also benefit greatly from giving one. You learn more about the features of observational writing when you can put this learning to use in your own writing. You also take on the role of reader, and that role enables you to imagine more easily what your readers will be expecting from your essay.

Reading a draft critically means reading it more than once, first to get a general impression and then to analyze its basic features. Before you read, number the paragraphs so you can refer easily to specific parts of the essay.

Reading for a First Impression

Read quickly through the draft to get an overall impression. After you have finished reading, jot down your immediate reaction. What do you consider most informative or entertaining in the essay? What seems to be the writer's attitude toward the subject and the point in writing about it? Did the essay hold your interest?

Reading to Analyze

Read now to focus on the basic features of a profile. Read to discover what the writer has achieved, given the resources available to observational writers, and what the writer might do to produce a more informative, engaging essay.

DETAILING THE SCENE AND PEOPLE. Analyze how well the draft presents the scene and people through specific, revealing, memorable details. Look closely at each place in the essay where some part of a physical scene or setting is identified or where a person appears or is referred to. How are these scenes and people detailed? What more might readers need to know to have strong visual images? Are there places where the detailing seems excessive or exaggerated?

Point out effective detailing, and advise the writer on strengthening details elsewhere. (Remember from your work with the readings in this chapter the diverse resources available to observational writers.)

ORGANIZING THE OBSERVATIONS. The essay should engage readers immediately and lead them smoothly, without frustrations or puzzlements, to the end. If the essay is organized narratively, look for places where you need further narration to understand what is happening or where the narrative seems needlessly slow. Look for gaps or jumps. Suggest specific material or cues to close the gaps—time markers or time sequence (initially, then, afterwards) or orientation in the scene or toward others (alongside, toward the front). Does the narrative move toward a high point or does it just wander? Tell the writer where the narrative is working well and where it needs improvement.

If the essay is organized topically, consider whether any sections could be placed earlier or later. What about balance among the parts, given the subject and the impression the writer seems to want to convey? Do some topics get too much attention and some too little? Are connections and transitions between topics clear?

ENGAGING AND INFORMING READERS. Does the essay succeed in engaging, or even intriguing, readers? Does it offer new and interesting information about the subject, especially if the subject is one with which most readers will be familiar? If the opening seems flat, advise the writer about how to make it more engaging. Are there long blocks of information that may try readers' patience? How might they be broken up? Although readers cannot learn everything about a subject in one essay, does the information offered seem adequate to inform the reader about the subject?

CONVEYING AN IMPRESSION. The draft should do more than describe or inform or narrate: It should convey the writer's impression or interpretation of the subject. Writers can announce their impression directly; or they can imply it through details, especially through careful orchestration or arrangement of details, and through their attitude toward the subject.

Show the writer where you believe the impression of the subject is stated; or, if it is only implied, try to state in your own words what that impression is. Point out any details that seem extraneous. Suggest ways to strengthen or clarify the impression.

REVISING

The suggestions in this section for revising your draft by now may be merely reminders of the possibilities for developing an engaging, informative observational essay. Although you have been working on this assignment for some time, you need to gather one more burst of energy for thoughtful revising. Revising means re-envisioning your draft, trying to see it in a new way, given your purpose and readers, to make your observations more vivid, pointed, and memorable.

The biggest mistake you can make in revising is to focus initially on words or sentences. Instead, you want to see your draft as a whole to assess its likely impact on your readers. You want to think imaginatively and boldly about cutting bland or obvious material, adding new material, and moving material around. Your computer will make the most drastic revisions easy to accomplish.

You may have received help with the challenge of revising from classmates who have read your draft critically. If not, you can read your own draft critically, following the guidelines in Reading a Draft Critically.

Keeping in mind any advice you have received from your instructor or classmates about revising your draft, reread it carefully, making a list of major problems you want to solve or new dimensions you want to add. As you make plans to revise, keep the following suggestions in mind.

Revising to Detail the Scene and People

Readers want to imagine the people, places, and activities in observational writing. Consider carefully how you might make your scene and people more imagineable by adding concrete details, particularly visual details like the physical appearance of things and people, and dialogue. Be certain, however, that any details you add contribute to the impression you want to convey about your subject. If people's interactions were an important part of what you observed, then readers also want to see people moving and gesturing and hear them talk to one another. Remember that we take our cues about people as much from what they say and how they say it as how they dress or gesture.

Revising to Organize the Observations

One of the biggest challenges of observational writing is to bring your diverse observations together into a readable pattern. Your basic decision is to organize either narratively or topically; but even after you have made that decision, there remain countless decisions about how to arrange details, information, and commentary.

To evaluate your organization, it helps if you can see your draft "cold," after several hours or a day has passed. Try to see it like another reader seeing it for the first time. Note where you pause or stumble or have to reread or where there seem to be gaps. Do not stop to repair stumbles or gaps. Mark them and keep reading to simulate another reader's experience of moving straight through your essay from beginning to end. As you start to revise, if you find that you are struggling to smooth out the flow, reconsider your basic organization. Consider whether your material might lend itself better to narrative than to organization by topics or vice versa.

Revising to Engage and Inform Readers

From the beginning, you want to engage your readers, to draw them into your essay. If you drafted your beginning first, before drafting the other parts of your essay—which is not unusual—you should reconsider that beginning seriously because only now are you in a good position to decide whether it is the best possible beginning, given how you have developed your essay and what impression you want to convey of your subject. Do not hesitate to draft an alternative beginning.

Engaging your reader comes primarily from novelty. Consider deleting details and information that may seem obvious to your readers. If your subject is familiar to your readers, present information and details in such a way to let your readers see the familiar in a new way. Do not overwhelm your readers with information, but give them enough so they feel satisfied they have learned something.

Revising to Convey an Impression of the Subject

Although your essay presents many details and considerable information about your subject, all of it must convey a single dominant impression that you want readers to take away. They get this impression from details, from what they sense is your attitude toward the subject, and from your interpretation of the observations. You can state your interpretation directly or let the details imply it, but everything in your essay must contribute to the interpretation and to the overall impression of the subject you mean to convey.

Be clear about your attitude and interpretation. Then look for details and information that may contradict your intentions. Revise or delete details and information that do not support your attitude and interpretation.

REFLECTING ON WHAT YOU HAVE LEARNED
ABOUT OBSERVATIONAL WRITING

In this chapter, you have read critically several observational essays and have written one of your own. To remind yourself how much you have learned and to help you remember it, pause now to reflect on your reading and writing experiences while working through this chapter.

Write a page or so reflecting on your learning. Begin by describing what you are most pleased with in your essay and explaining what contributed to your achievement. Be very specific about this contribution. If it was something you learned from the readings, indicate which readings and specifically what you learned from them. If it came from your interviews or observations, point out what helped you most. If you got good advice from a critical reader, explain exactly how the person helped you—perhaps by helping you to understand a particular problem in your draft or by suggesting a new dimension to your writing. Try to write about your achievement in terms of what you have learned about the genre of observational writing.

Then write about anything else that accounts for your learning this special kind of writing. Discuss what you have learned about the writing process; for example, how to use time efficiently before writing a draft to discover what you want to say about the subject or how to get constructive criticism and practical advice from other readers of your draft.

C H A P T E R   4

REFLECTION

Reflective writing, like autobiography and observation, comes out of experience. In autobiography and observation, the central aim is to show specific incidents, people, and places—not to tell readers what to think or to draw larger generalizations. Autobiographers and observational writers often suggest larger meanings in what they show, but they seldom explore such meanings directly and in detail. In reflection, however, the focus shifts from showing to telling. Writers present something they did, saw, overheard, or read to tell us what they think it suggests about people and society.

The range of topics for reflection is wide. One writer in this chapter reflects on her reluctance to tell people that she is deaf. Another comments on the fear of "the other"—the person marked by racial, gender, or class difference. Many reflective essays explore ideas on social customs and problems (such as those related to dating and child rearing); virtues and vices (such as pride, jealousy, and compassion); hopes and fears (such as the desire for intimacy and the fear of it).

These subjects may seem far reaching, but writers of reflection have relatively modest goals. They do not attempt to exhaust their subjects, nor do they set themselves up as experts. They simply try out their ideas. One early meaning of the word *essay* was "to try out." From the very first reflective essays by Montaigne in 1580, the essay has been regarded as an exercise in the art of inquiry—short, informal, tentative, exploratory, inconclusive.

What makes reflective writing so enjoyable to write and so interesting to read is its inventiveness. Successful reflective writing enables us, as readers and writers, to see even the most familiar things in new ways. Avoiding the obvious, resisting the impulse to moralize, revealing a contradiction, finding fresh language to revitalize old truths, taking a critical view of what we typically accept as true—these are some of the characteristics of the best reflective essays.

The writer of the reflective essay typically addresses readers directly and openly. It is as if the writer were sitting across from the reader, talking about what happened and what it might mean. The conversational tone characterizes the reflective essay and can be quite seductive.

As you read, discuss, and write about the essays in this chapter, you will learn a good deal about reflective writing. You should also get ideas for a reflective essay of your own, based perhaps on the suggestions for writing that follow each reading. As you work through the selections in this chapter, keep in mind the following assignment, which sets out the goals for writing a reflective essay.

THE WRITING ASSIGNMENT

Reflection

Write a reflective essay based on something you experienced or observed. Describe it vividly so readers can understand what happened and will care about what you have to say. In reflecting on what the particular occasion suggests, explore your own and society's attitudes and values. Reflective writing is like a conversation—you are writing not just for yourself but to share your thoughts with others, to stimulate their thinking as well as your own.

REFLECTIVE WRITING SITUATIONS

Reflective essays are written on all kinds of subjects and in many different contexts. Following are a few examples to suggest this variety of topics and situations:

- A former football player writes a reflective essay based on his experience playing professional sports. He recalls a specific occasion when he sustained a serious injury but continued to play because he knew that playing with pain was regarded as a badge of honor, a sign of manliness and dedication. He recalls that he had played many times before with minor injuries, but that this time he feared he might be doing irreparable damage to himself. As he reflects on what happened, he considers whose interests were really being served by this cult of heroism.

- Writing for a political science course, a student reflects on her first experience voting in a presidential election. She recalls a conversation she had had with friends that led her to reflect on the ways people choose candidates. Instead of making choices on the basis of record, character, or even campaign promises, most people she talked to made choices for trivial, even bizarre, reasons. For example, she notes that one person's choice was based on the fact that a candidate reminded her of a relative, while another person voted against a candidate because he didn't like the way the candidate dressed. The writer reflects on the humorous as well as the serious implications.

- A first-year college student in a composition course reflects on a performance of his high school chorus that far surpassed their best previous performance. He describes their trip to the statewide competition and their anxious rehearsals before the performance. Their teacher-conductor seemed tense; the student and his close friends talked about their fears that the chorus had come further than it deserved; they complained that their teacher had chosen unnecessarily difficult music. Then he describes their unexpected feelings of confidence as the performance began and their flawless precision and control along with exuberant expressiveness during the performance. He contrasts this memorable occasion with examples of another chorus performance and other personal experiences that turned out worse than expected, trying to discover the secret of the unexpected success. He tries out the possibility that luck, fear of embarrassment, affection for their teacher, or the excitement of a trip to the state capital led to their success. Then he acknowledges the possibility that they did so well simply because they had rehearsed especially attentively for weeks because the music was so challenging. Finally, he gives up trying to establish a reason for their success and instead makes a few general statements about the special pleasures of success in groups like choruses, orchestras, soccer teams, and drama groups, where cooperation and precise timing are essential.

PRACTICING REFLECTION
A COLLABORATIVE ACTIVITY

As the preceding examples show, the most important part of writing a reflective essay is being inventive, thinking of interesting things to say about the subject suggested by the particular occasion. This activity invites you to practice reflecting by talking with others in a small group.

PART 1. With two or three other students, choose one of the following occasions as the basis for a thoughtful conversation. (Your group may wish to think of an occasion of its own.)

- During an important exam you are taking, you notice that someone or several people are cheating.
- In a crowded restaurant, you see a parent hitting a young child and notice how the onlookers (including yourself) react.
- You visit with family or friends after being away for some time and notice how predictably (or unpredictably) everyone, including yourself, behaves.
- You find yourself a stranger among a group of friends, or a stranger enters your group of friends.
- In a class, one student dominates the discussion, talking most of the time or controlling the direction and content of what others say.

Now take turns talking to each other about the occasion and what it implies. Try to stimulate one another's thinking by asking questions and responding to each other's ideas. Keep the conversation going for at least fifteen minutes. You might begin by asking one another how you would feel and what you would do, if anything. Discuss your different responses to the occasion. What seems important to each of you about it? What does it say about such things as your social values, individual beliefs and attitudes, and how people relate to one another?

PART 2. When you have finished your discussion or simply run out of time, consider the following questions about reflective discourse:

- When the discussion began, what seemed important to imagine about the particular occasion? How often did it come up again in the conversation? Were other specific incidents or examples brought up? If so, what role did they play?

- When conversation faltered, what got it going again? List the strategies (such as asking questions and giving examples) that members of the group used to keep the discussion going.

- What did you find most interesting or surprising about what was said? What would you have wanted to hear more about?

A GUIDE TO READING REFLECTIVE WRITING

As an introduction to the reflective essay, first read, annotate, and write about your understanding and response to the brief essay that follows. Then, guided by a list of basic features and strategies of reflective writing, reread the essay to examine the particular elements of strong reflective writing.

First, though, as a reminder of the many possibilities for annotating, here is an illustration of an annotated passage from a reflective essay by Brent Staples, which appears in its entirety later in the chapter.

Startling way to open

My first victim was a woman—white, well dressed, probably in her late twenties. I came upon her late one evening on a deserted street in Hyde Park, a relatively affluent neighborhood in an otherwise mean, impoverished section of Chicago. As I swung onto the avenue behind her, there seemed to be a discreet, uninflammatory distance between us. Not so. She cast back a worried glance. To

Describes himself as she saw him

her, the youngish black man—a broad six feet two inches with a beard and billowing hair, both hands shoved into the pockets of a bulky military jacket—seemed menacingly close. After a few more quick glimpses, she picked up her pace and was soon running in earnest. Within seconds she disappeared into a cross street.

What the incident made him recognize

That was more than a decade ago. I was twenty-two years old, a graduate (student) newly arrived at the University of Chicago. It was in the echo of that terrified woman's footfalls that I first began to know the unwieldy inheritance I'd come into—the ability to alter public space in ugly ways. It was clear that she thought herself the quarry of a (mugger,) a (rapist,) or worse. Suffering a bout of insomnia, however, I was stalking sleep, not defenseless wayfarers. As a (softy) who is scarcely able to take a knife to a raw chicken—let alone hold

How it made him feel

one to a person's throat—I was surprised, embarrassed, and dismayed all at once. Her flight made me feel like an (accomplice) in tyranny. It also made it clear that I was indistinguishable from the muggers who occasionally seeped into the area from the surround-

What it meant

ing ghetto. That first encounter, and those that followed, signified that a vast, unnerving gulf lay between nighttime pedestrians—particularly women—and me. And I soon gathered that being perceived

Ironic— threat to him, not to her

as dangerous is a hazard in itself. I only needed to turn a corner into a dicey situation, or crowd some frightened, armed person in a foyer somewhere, or make an errant move after being pulled over by a policeman. Where fear and weapons meet—and they often do in urban America—there is always the possibility of death.

Nicollette Toussaint

HEARING THE SWEETEST SONGS

This reflective essay was published in 1994 in *Newsweek* magazine. In this essay, Toussaint writes about her deafness, relations with family and friends, and thoughts about disabilities. As you read, annotate anything that strikes you as interesting or effective in Toussaint's reflections. Mark on the text, and write comments in the margin.

Every year when I was a child, a man brought a big, black, squeaking machine to school. When he discovered I couldn't hear all his peeps and squeaks, he would get very excited. The nurse would draw a chart with a deep canyon in it. Then I would listen to the squeaks two or three times, while the adults—who were all acting very, very nice—would watch me raise my hand. Sometimes I couldn't tell whether I heard the squeaks or just imagined them, but I liked being the center of attention.

My parents said I lost my hearing to pneumonia as a baby; but I knew I hadn't *lost* anything. None of my parts had dropped off. Nothing had changed: if I wanted to listen to Beethoven, I could put my head between the speakers and turn the dial up to 7. I could hear jets at the airport a block away. I could hear my mom when she was in the same room—if I wanted to. I could even hear my cat purr if I put my good ear right on top of him.

I wasn't aware of *not* hearing until I began to wear a hearing aid at the age of 30. It shattered my peace: shoes creaking, papers crackling, pencils tapping, phones ringing, refrigerators humming, people cracking knuckles, clearing throats and blowing noses! Cars, bikes, dogs, cats, kids all seemed to appear from nowhere and fly right at me.   3

I was constantly startled, unnerved, agitated—exhausted. I felt as though inquisitorial Nazis in an old World War II film were burning the side of my head with a merciless white spotlight. Under that onslaught, I had to break down and confess: I couldn't hear. Suddenly, I began to discover many things I couldn't do.   4

I couldn't identify sounds. One afternoon, while lying on my side watching a football game on TV, I kept hearing a noise that sounded like my cat playing with a flexible-spring doorstop. I checked, but the cat was asleep. Finally, I happened to lift my head as the noise occurred. Heard through my good ear, the metallic buzz turned out to be the referee's whistle.   5

I couldn't tell where sounds came from. I couldn't find my phone under the blizzard of papers on my desk. The more it rang, the deeper I dug. I shoveled mounds of paper onto the floor and finally had to track it down by following the cord from the wall. . . .   6

For the first time, I felt unequal, disadvantaged and disabled. Now that I had something to compare, I knew that I *had* lost something: not just my hearing, but my independence and my sense of wholeness. I had always hated to be seen as inferior, so I never mentioned my lack of hearing. Unlike a wheelchair or a white cane, my disability doesn't announce itself. For most of my life, I chose to pass as abled, and I thought I did it quite well.   7

But after I got the hearing aid, a business friend said, "You know, Nicolette, you think you get away with not hearing, but you don't. Sometimes in meetings you answer the wrong question. People don't know you can't hear, so they think you're daydreaming, eccentric, stupid—or just plain rude. It would be better to just tell them."   8

I wondered about that then, and I still do. If I tell, I risk being seen as *un*able rather than *dis*abled. Sometimes, when I say I can't hear, the waiter will turn to my companion and say, "What does she want?" as though I have lost my power of speech.   9

If I tell, people may see *only* my disability. Once someone is labeled "deaf," "crippled," "mute" or "aged," that's too often all they are. I'm a writer, a painter a slapdash housekeeper, a gardener who grows wondrous roses; my hearing is just part of the whole. It's a tender part, and you should handle it with care. But like most people with a disability, I don't mind if you ask about it.   10

In fact, you should ask, because it's an important part of me, something my friends see as part of my character. My friend Anne   11 always rests a hand on my elbow in parking lots, since several times, drivers who assume that I hear them have nearly run me over. When I hold my head at a certain angle, my husband, Mason, will say, "It's a plane" or "It's a siren." And my mother loves to laugh about the things I *thought* I heard: last week I was told that "the Minotaurs in the garden are getting out of hand." I imagined capering bullmen and I was disappointed to learn that all we had in the garden were overgrown "baby tears."

Not hearing can be funny, or frustrating. And once in a while, it   12
can be the cause of something truly transcendent. One morning at the shore I was listening to the ocean when Mason said, "Hear the bird?" What bird? I listened hard until I heard a faint, unbirdlike, croaking sound. If he hadn't mentioned it, I would never have noticed it. As I listened, slowly I began to hear—or perhaps imagine—a distant song. Did I *really* hear it? Or just hear in my heart what he shared with me? I don't care. Songs imagined are as sweet as songs heard, and songs shared are sweeter still.

That sharing is what I want for all of us. We're all just tempo-   13
rarily abled, and every one of us, if we live long enough, will become disabled in some way. Those of us who have gotten there first can tell you how to cope with phones and alarm clocks. About ways of holding a book, opening a door and leaning on a crutch all at the same time. And what it's like to give up in despair on Thursday, then begin all over again on Friday, because there's no other choice—and because the roses are beginning to bud in the garden.

These are conversations we all should have, and it's not that hard   14
to begin. Just let me see your lips when you speak. Stay in the same room. Don't shout. And ask what you want to know.

READING FOR MEANING

Explore your understanding and response to "Hearing the Sweetest Songs" by writing at least a page about it. You might begin by identifying two or three of the ideas or insights in Toussaint's reflections. Consider what she is trying to say about the abled and the disabled and about their relations to each other.

As you write, you will want to reread parts of the essay and to annotate significant passages. Your ideas may change as you think and write about your understanding of the essay. Consider occasionally quoting brief phrases or sentences to help support your ideas. If you have difficulty continuing for at least a page, consider the following suggestions:

- Toussaint says that not hearing can be funny, frustrating, or transcendent. For each of these, summarize briefly the examples she offers.

- If you have a disability, compare your experience with that of Toussaint's. If you do not have a disability, comment on Toussaint's comparison of the disabled with the abled.

- Do you think Toussaint feels sorry for herself? If not, how do you think she feels about her disability? Point to specific evidence in the text to support your answer.

- Explain the possible meaning or significance of "I knew I hadn't *lost* anything. None of my parts had dropped off" (paragraph 2); "I wasn't aware of *not* hearing until I began to wear a hearing aid at the age of 30" (paragraph 3); "If I tell, people may see *only* my disability" (paragraph 10); or any other statement that catches your attention.

READING LIKE A WRITER

This activity leads you through an analysis of Toussaint's reflective writing strategies: *presenting the particular occasion, developing the reflections, maintaining topical coherence,* and *engaging readers.* Each strategy is described briefly and followed by a critical reading and writing task to help you see how Toussaint uses that particular strategy in her essay.

Consider this activity a writer's introduction to reflective writing. You will learn more about how different writers use the reflective writing strategies from the activities following the selections in this chapter. The Guide to Reflective Writing at the end of the chapter also suggests how you can use these strategies in writing your own reflective essay.

Presenting the Particular Occasion

The particular occasion is the experience that originally got the writer thinking. Writers may describe the occasion at length, or they might just give a quick sketch to help readers grasp the point. The key is to present the occasion in such a vivid and suggestive way that readers are eager to see what the writer thinks about it. To succeed, writers rely on the same strategies you may have practiced in Chapter 2 (Autobiography) and Chapter 3 (Observation), strategies of describing the scene and people through visual details, movement and gesture, and dialogue, as well as strategies of narrating a well-shaped and carefully paced incident.

In analyzing the presentation of the particular occasion, consider first how the writer narrates the occasion and then how well the occasion introduces the subject and anticipates the rejections that arise from it.

Toussaint's essay opens with two specific occasions, separated by many years: The first is an early recollection of school hearing tests (paragraph 1); the second focuses on what happened when Toussaint began wearing a hearing aid (paragraphs 3 through 6). While neither of these occasions offers an extended narrative of a particular incident, there is the recurring event of the hearing tests and the briefly sketched incidents about the football referee's whistle and the search for the telephone. Moreover, the two occasions for reflection offer vivid visual and aural details.

ANALYZE. Reread the two occasions, annotating any words and phrases that name or suggest sounds. Consider the variety and types of sounds Toussaint identifies.

WRITE. Write several sentences explaining how Toussaint helps readers imagine the sounds she hears. Comment on the effect these sounds have on you at the beginning of the essay (in paragraphs 1 through 6), specifically how well they prepare you for the reflections to follow.

Developing the Reflections

An occasion introduces a subject, and reflections explore the subject. What does it mean to explore a subject by developing the reflections about it? It means simply to examine the subject inventively in every possible way that illuminates it. Although this illumination takes place in the mind of the reader, the writer decides how to bring it about through strategies used for centuries by reflective writers; for example, asserting ideas, giving examples, posing questions, comparing and contrasting. In addition, the writer of a reflective essay might examine an idea by placing it in a surprising context, saying what it is not, associating it with other ideas, speculating about where it came from, trying to apply it, taking it seriously or taking it lightly. To avoid the obvious, the writer must resist easy moralizing, rise above talk-show psychology, and face life's complexities. Reflective writers must think creatively about a subject or idea and present it in a new way.

Look closely at the way Toussaint offers ideas and gives examples to illustrate them. We are interested mainly in her ideas not just about herself but about people in general. For example, in paragraph 10 she asserts, "Once someone is labeled 'deaf,' 'crippled,' 'mute' or 'aged,' that's too often all they are." Then, using herself as an example, she says, "I'm a writer, a painter, a slapdash housekeeper, a gardener who grows wondrous roses; my hearing is just part of the whole." In addition, in paragraphs 5 and 6, Toussaint uses longer examples to support her recollections about the effects of the hearing aid on her hearing.

ANALYZE. Paragraphs 12 and 13 open with a two-sentence statement of an idea about deafness or its implications. Each idea is followed by examples that develop it. Reread these two paragraphs, noting the opening ideas and the kinds of examples that follow.

WRITE. First write a few sentences evaluating these two ideas. Do they seem obvious or overly simple? Do they illustrate Toussaint's experience? Has she prepared the reader for them through the occasions and the reflections that precede these ideas?

Then write several sentences describing the example that illustrates each idea. Do these examples seem appropriate and interesting? Are they detailed enough to make their point? Do they ring true? From these two idea-and-example pairs, what can you conclude about the connection between ideas and examples in reflective writing?

Maintaining Topical Coherence

Because reflective essays explore ideas on a topic by turning them this way and that, examining them first from one perspective and then from another, and sometimes piling up examples to illustrate the ideas, such essays usually seem rambling, with one idea or example added to another in a casual way. It is not always clear where the essay is going, and it may not seem to arrive anywhere conclusive at the end. This apparently casual plan or organization is deceptive, however, because in fact the writer has arranged the parts carefully to give the appearance of a mind playfully at work on an idea. Whatever the plan and no matter how casual it may appear, it must seem coherent to the reader. This special kind of coherence in reflective essays is *topical coherence. Topical* refers to the topic or subject of the essay and *coherence* to a reader's sense that all the parts of an essay seem relevant to the topic and related to it; while each new idea or example in the reflective essay may be unexpected or may turn the essay in a new direction, it will seem somehow connected to what has gone before and will seem to lead without a gap or break to the next idea or example.

ANALYZE. Reread paragraphs 7 through 14, where the reflections are concentrated. As you read, be alert to places where it seems that coherence breaks down—where there seems to be a gap or you feel uncertain about the relation of one part to the next or you have to stop and reread to proceed. If you find any such places, mark them in the margin. Then go back and look closely at the first sentence in each paragraph, beginning with paragraph 8, to discover whether these sentences provide explicit cues about the connection between what came before and what follows. Underline any cues you find.

WRITE. Now write several sentences evaluating the topical coherence in Toussaint's reflections. Describe how she tries to maintain coherence through cues at paragraph boundaries and through any other strategies. Indicate any places where it seemed to you coherence was broken. As you work, keep in mind the topic of her reflections: disability, particularly deafness, and the relations between those who are disabled and those who are not disabled.

Engaging Readers

Readers of reflective essays, like readers of autobiography and observational writing, expect to feel personally engaged. They expect more than mere entertainment; they want to reflect and question and do not object to having their beliefs and values challenged or their minds stretched.

Reflective writers may attempt to engage their readers in several ways. They may attempt to present the occasion in a way that makes it seem of interest or personal significance to readers, even though the occasion may be foreign to readers' experience. They may strive to present unexpected ideas about a familiar topic. They will make an effort to discover surprisingly apt examples or comparisons and contrasts. They may take risks they would not ordinarily take in their writing because they know they are simply trying out some ideas on the topic without coming to any particular conclusion. In addition, they avoid the impression that they have borrowed the ideas from someone else. Using "I," they claim the ideas as their own, saying to the reader without coyness, self-effacement, or apology, "Here's my mind at work on a topic that should be of interest to you."

ANALYZE. Review Toussaint's essay, thinking about what engaged you—

interested you or seemed of personal significance to you or struck you as having larger social significance—when you first read the essay. Mark those places in the margin. Then, in the reflective paragraphs (7 through 14), underline two or three ideas that seem to you surprising and insightful, now that you have had time to analyze the essay and to think about it. Finally, underline a few examples of language—words, phrases, sentences—that seem to you particularly fresh and effective. You may find that you can identify few if any ideas or examples of fresh language, or you may find that you can readily identify several.

WRITE. Write several sentences about your personal engagement with Toussaint's essay. Then consider whether you find her ideas surprising and inventive. Do you believe the ideas came out of deeply felt personal experience? Does she take risks by pushing beyond the usual talk-show banter about disabilities? Support your answers with examples from the essay.

READINGS

Brent Staples

BLACK MEN AND PUBLIC SPACE

Brent Staples (b. 1951) earned his Ph.D. in psychology from the University of Chicago and went on to become a journalist, writing for several magazines and newspapers, including the *Chicago Sun-Times.* In 1985, he became first assistant metropolitan editor of the *New York Times* and is now a member of the editorial board. His book, *Parallel Times: Growing Up in Black and White,* was published in 1994.

The particular occasion for Staples's reflections is an incident that occurred for the first time in the mid-1970s when he discovered that his mere presence on the street late at night was enough to frighten a young white woman. Recalling this incident leads him to reflect on issues of race, gender, and class in the United States.

Staples originally published this essay in *Ms.* magazine in 1986 under the title "Just Walk on By." He revised it slightly and published it in *Harper's* a year later under the present title. As you read, conjecture about why he chose the new title, "Black Men and Public Space."

My first victim was a woman—white, well dressed, probably in   ı
her late twenties. I came upon her late one evening on a deserted
street in Hyde Park, a relatively affluent neighborhood in an otherwise mean, impoverished section of Chicago. As I swung onto the

avenue behind her, there seemed to be a discreet, uninflammatory distance between us. Not so. She cast back a worried glance. To her, the youngish black man—a broad six feet two inches with a beard and billowing hair, both hands shoved into the pockets of a bulky military jacket—seemed menacingly close. After a few more quick glimpses, she picked up her pace and was soon running in earnest. Within seconds she disappeared into a cross street.

That was more than a decade ago. I was twenty-two years old, a graduate student newly arrived at the University of Chicago. It was in the echo of that terrified women's footfalls that I first began to know the unwieldy inheritance I'd come into—the ability to alter public space in ugly ways. It was clear that she thought herself the quarry of a mugger, a rapist, or worse. Suffering a bout of insomnia, however, I was stalking sleep, not defenseless wayfarers. As a softy who is scarcely able to take a knife to a raw chicken—let alone hold one to a person's throat—I was surprised, embarrassed, and dismayed all at once. Her flight made me feel like an accomplice in tyranny. It also made it clear that I was indistinguishable from the muggers who occasionally seeped into the area from the surrounding ghetto. That first encounter, and those that followed, signified that a vast, unnerving gulf lay between nighttime pedestrians—particularly women—and me. And I soon gathered that being perceived as dangerous is a hazard in itself. I only needed to turn a corner into a dicey situation, or crowd some frightened, armed person in a foyer somewhere, or make an errant move after being pulled over by a policeman. Where fear and weapons meet—and they often do in urban America—there is always the possibility of death.

In that first year, my first away from my hometown, I was to become thoroughly familiar with the language of fear. At dark, shadowy intersections, I could cross in front of a car stopped at a traffic light and elicit the *thunk, thunk, thunk, thunk* of the driver—black, white, male, or female—hammering down the door locks. On less traveled streets after dark, I grew accustomed to but never comfortable with people crossing to the other side of the street rather than pass me. Then there were the standard unpleasantries with policemen, doormen, bouncers, cabdrivers, and others whose business it is to screen out troublesome individuals *before* there is any nastiness.

I moved to New York nearly two years ago and I have remained an avid night walker. In central Manhattan, the near-constant crowd cover minimizes tense one-on-one street encounters. Elsewhere—in SoHo, for example, where sidewalks are narrow and tightly spaced buildings shut out the sky—things can get very taut indeed.

After dark, on the warrenlike streets of Brooklyn where I live, I often see women who fear the worst from me. They seem to have set their faces on neutral, and with their purse straps strung across their chests bandolier-style, they forge ahead as though bracing themselves against being tackled. I understand, of course, that the danger they perceive is not a hallucination. Women are particularly vulnerable to street violence, and young black males are drastically overrepresented among the perpetrators of that violence. Yet these truths are no solace against the kind of alienation that comes of being ever the suspect, a fearsome entity with whom pedestrians avoid making eye contact.

Over the years, I learned to smother the rage I felt at so often 6 being taken for a criminal. Not to do so would surely have led to madness. I now take precautions to make myself less threatening. I move about with care, particularly late in the evening. I give a wide berth to nervous people on subway platforms during the wee hours, particularly when I have exchanged business clothes for jeans. If I happen to be entering a building behind some people who appear skittish, I may walk by, letting them clear the lobby before I return, so as not to seem to be following them. I have been calm and extremely congenial on those rare occasions when I've been pulled over by the police.

And on late-evening constitutionals I employ what has proved to 7 be an excellent tension-reducing measure: I whistle melodies from Beethoven and Vivaldi and the more popular classical composers. Even steely New Yorkers hunching toward nighttime destinations seem to relax, and occasionally they even join in the tune. Virtually everybody seems to sense that a mugger wouldn't be warbling bright, sunny selections from Vivaldi's *Four Seasons*. It is my equivalent of the cowbell that hikers wear when they know they are in bear country.

READING FOR MEANING

Write at least a page, exploring your understanding and response to Staples's essay. You decide what to focus on, but you could begin by expressing your initial understanding of Staples's difficulty and his reaction to it. As you write, you may find it useful to reread parts of the essay and quote selected passages. Do not be surprised if your ideas change as you write.

Consider the following suggestions if you need help getting ideas:

- List the ways Staples tries to reduce people's fear of him and speculate about why he feels responsible for alleviating others' fear.

- Although writing about something he first experienced years ago, Staples suggests that not much has changed since then. Based on your personal experience, observation, or reading, do you think that the situation Staples describes still exists? If so, give one or two examples and comment on them.

- Notice that Staples was only twenty-two and away from home for the first time when the initial incident occurred. What words does he use to describe his feelings? How do you think you would have felt in his place?

- How would you feel in the position of the woman Staples describes in the opening paragraph? How well do you think he understands her feelings?

EXTENDING MEANING THROUGH CONVERSATION. While it is important for you to make meaning on your own, you may be able to extend your understanding by conversing with classmates about Staples's essay. Before getting together, reflect on your own understanding by reviewing your annotations and writing. Begin your conversation by identifying one idea in Staples's reflections that especially interested each of you.

As you converse about the meanings you have found, you may discover that you have somewhat different understandings of the essay. You need not strive to reach agreement, however. Instead, help each other think critically about the essay by seeing it in new ways. As you explore your understandings, reread and discuss parts of the essay together.

LOOKING FOR PATTERNS OF OPPOSITION. A further strategy for reading for meaning not covered in this chapter is looking for patterns of opposition. The situation Staples reflects on has implications about how society is fragmented by race and gender. A good way to examine how Staples represents these and other divisions in our society is to analyze the system of oppositions in the essay. If you are unfamiliar with this critical reading strategy, look at the illustration Looking for Patterns of Opposition in Appendix 1, A Catalog of Critical Reading Strategies.

Begin by making a list of all the opposites you find in the essay. For example, in the title and the first paragraph, Staples sets up the following pairs of oppositions:

public space	private
woman	man
white	black
well dressed	bulky military jacket
affluent neighborhood	impoverished section
distant	close
uninflammatory	menacing

Start your list with these oppositions, and then add to it other pairs you find in the essay. After you have identified the oppositions, explore their implications by following steps 2 through 4 as demonstrated in Appendix 1.

READING LIKE A WRITER
PRESENTING THE PARTICULAR OCCASION

Reflective writing generally grows out of a particular occasion—a specific incident or experience that sets the writer's thoughts in motion.

ANALYZE. Reread paragraph 1, where Staples presents the incident that serves as the particular occasion for his reflections. Examine carefully how Staples presents the incident. Annotate details like the following:

- The words Staples uses to describe the woman and those he uses to describe himself as the woman saw him (for example, his choice of the word *shoved* to describe his hands in his pockets)
- His description of the scene—time, place, social setting
- How he tells the story, the specific verbs he uses, the quick shifts from what he did to what the woman did in reaction

WRITE. Based on your annotations, write several sentences explaining what you have learned about how Staples creates a vivid incident. Illustrate with details from the incident. How do Staples's descriptive and narrative choices highlight a sense of drama? Of danger? How might he have decided what was and was not relevant? How successfully does the incident introduce the subject and anticipate the reflections that follow?

COMPARE. To learn still more about how writers of reflective essays launch their reflections from a particular occasion, look closely at the opening occasions in the other readings in this chapter.

CONSIDERING IDEAS FOR YOUR OWN WRITING

Staples is writing about what happens in "public space." List any incidents you can recall in which you or others reacted peculiarly or surprisingly in public. Consider different kinds of public space—on the highway, in the classroom, at a concert, at a mall. Also list incidents from your own experience that suggest how people interact privately under different situations—for example, during a first date or at a family gathering.

Staples is writing about a situation that shows how society is fragmented by race and gender. As you think of incidents in public and private realms, consider what they might imply about our ways of relating to other people.

Barbara Ehrenreich

ARE FAMILIES DANGEROUS?

Barbara Ehrenreich (b. 1941) is the author of seven books, including a critique of the 1980s, *The Worst Years of Our Lives: Irreverent Notes from a Decade of Greed* (1990), and a study of the middle class, *Fear of Falling* (1989). Her essays appear regularly in journals and magazines like the *American Scholar,* the *Atlantic Monthly,* the *New Republic,* and *Time.*

This essay was published in *Time* magazine in 1994. The occasion for Ehrenreich's reflections is three well-publicized cases of family violence: Erik and Lyle Menendez have been accused of murdering their parents, claiming their parents abused them; Lorena Bobbitt cut off her husband's penis because he abused her; and O. J. Simpson abused his wife, Nicole, but was found not guilty of murdering her. As you read, notice how Ehrenreich weaves these cases in and out of her reflections about how dangerous, even deadly, families can be. You will find yourself drawn into intense reflection about your own family and into evaluation of Ehrenreich's ideas.

A disturbing subtext runs through our recent media fixations.   1
Parents abuse sons—allegedly at least, in the Menendez case—who in turn rise up and kill them. A husband torments a wife, who retaliates with a kitchen knife. Love turns into obsession, between the Simpsons anyway, and then perhaps into murderous rage: the family, in other words, becomes personal hell.

This accounts for at least part of our fascination with the Bob-   2
bitts and the Simpsons and the rest of them. We live in a culture that fetishes the family as the ideal unit of human community, the perfect container for our lusts and loves. Politicians of both parties are aggressively "pro-family," even abortion-rights bumper stickers proudly link "pro-family" and "pro-choice." Only with the occasional celebrity crime do we allow ourselves to think the nearly unthinkable: that the family may not be the ideal and perfect living arrangement after all—that it can be a nest of pathology and a cradle of gruesome violence.

It's a scary thought, because the family is at the same time our   3
"haven in a heartless world." Theoretically, and sometimes actually, the family nurtures warm, loving feelings, uncontaminated by greed or power hunger. Within the family, and often only within the family, individuals are loved "for themselves," whether or not they are infirm, incontinent, infantile or eccentric. The strong (adults and especially males) lie down peaceably with the small and weak.

But consider the matter of wife battery. We managed to dodge it   4
in the Bobbitt case and downplay it as a force in Tonya Harding's life. Thanks to O. J., though, we're caught up now in a mass consciousness-raising session, grimly absorbing the fact that in some areas domestic violence sends as many women to emergency rooms as any other form of illness, injury or assault.

Still, we shrink from the obvious inference: for a woman, home   5
is, statistically speaking, the most dangerous place to be. Her worst enemies and potential killers are not strangers but lovers, husbands and those who claimed to love her once. Similarly, for every child like Polly Klaas who is killed by a deranged criminal on parole, dozens are abused and murdered by their own relatives. Home is all too often where the small and weak fear to lie down and shut their eyes.

At some deep, queasy, Freudian level, we all know this. Even in the ostensibly "functional," nonviolent family, where no one is killed or maimed, feelings are routinely bruised and often twisted out of shape. There is the slap or put-down that violates a child's shaky sense of self, the cold, distracted stare that drives a spouse to tears, the little digs and rivalries. At best, the family teaches the finest things human beings can learn from one another—generosity and love. But it is also, all too often, where we learn nasty things like hate and rage and shame.

Americans act out their ambivalence about the family without ever owning up to it. Millions adhere to creeds that are militantly "pro-family." But at the same time millions flock to therapy groups that offer to heal the "inner child" from damage inflicted by family life. Legions of women band together to revive the self-esteem they lost in supposedly loving relationships and to learn to love a little less. We are all, it is often said, "in recovery." And from what? Our families, in most cases.

There is a long and honorable tradition of "anti-family" thought. The French philosopher Charles Fourier taught that the family was a barrier to human progress; early feminists saw a degrading parallel between marriage and prostitution. More recently, the renowned British anthropologist Edmund Leach stated that "far from being the basis of the good society, the family, with its narrow privacy and tawdry secrets, is the source of all discontents."

Communes proved harder to sustain than plain old couples, and the conservatism of the '80s crushed the last vestiges of life-style experimentation. Today even gays and lesbians are eager to get married and take up family life. Feminists have learned to couch their concerns as "family issues," and public figures would sooner advocate free cocaine on demand than criticize the family. Hence our unseemly interest in O. J. and Erik, Lyle and Lorena: they allow us, however gingerly, to break the silence on the hellish side of family life.

But the discussion needs to become a lot more open and forthright. We may be stuck with the family—at least until someone invents a sustainable alternative—but the family, with its deep, impacted tensions and longings, can hardly be expected to be the moral foundation of everything else. In fact, many families could use a lot more outside interference in the form of counseling and policing, and some are so dangerously dysfunctional that they ought to be encouraged to disband right away. Even healthy families need outside sources of moral guidance to keep the internal tensions from imploding—and this means, at the very least, a public philosophy of gender equality and concern for child welfare. When, instead, the larger culture aggrandizes wife beaters, degrades women or nods approvingly at child slappers, the family gets a little more dangerous for everyone, and so, inevitably, does the larger world.

READING FOR MEANING

Write at least a page, exploring your understanding of Ehrenreich's essay. Although you will decide what aspect of the article to focus on, you might begin by listing the dangers in families, according to Ehrenreich. Then write about anything else in the essay that contributes to your understanding of Ehrenreich's reflections.

As you write, you may find that you need to reread and further annotate parts of the essay. You may also find that your understanding changes. If you have difficulty writing at least a page, try one of the following suggestions:

- Explain what you think to be Ehrenreich's primary purpose in these reflections on the family.

- Speculate about what reaction she expects to get from her readers and what attitude she has toward them. Include quotations from the essay that might support your speculations.

- Explain the possible significance of "the family may not be the ideal and perfect living arrangement after all" (paragraph 2), "sometimes actually, the family nurtures warm, loving feelings" (paragraph 3), "for a woman, home is, statistically speaking, the most dangerous place to be" (paragraph 5), "Even healthy families need outside sources of moral guidance . . . at the very least, a public philosophy of gender equality and concern for child welfare" (paragraph 10), or any other statement that catches your attention.

- Does your experience with your own family (birth or adoptive or both) or with families you know about tend to support or challenge Ehrenreich's ideas about families? Try to connect your experience directly to one or more of Ehrenreich's ideas.

EXTENDING MEANING THROUGH CONVERSATION. The understanding you have developed of Ehrenreich's essay on your own may be enhanced by discussing it with one or two classmates who have also thought about the essay's meanings. Before getting together, reflect on your current understanding by reviewing your annotations and writing. Begin your conversation by taking turns pointing to the one insight in the reflections that was most surprising for each of you.

As you converse about the reading, you may find that each person has a different understanding of it. Explore these differences by rereading and discussing parts of the text together. You need not reach consensus about the meanings you find, but you do want to deepen your understanding by considering different meanings.

READING LIKE A WRITER
MAINTAINING TOPICAL COHERENCE

Because writers of reflective essays are merely trying out some ideas on their readers and not necessarily attempting to reach any definitive conclusions, their essays may appear organized by the first-I-had-this-idea-and-then-I-had-another-idea principle. The essay may seem rambling and loosely organized, and yet readers will find it coherent; that is, the essay can be read straight through without the reader encountering any gaps or breaks or becoming confused. The coherence results from the writer staying on topic and providing minimal cues about the movement from one idea or example to the next. This kind of coherence in reflective writing is called *topical coherence.*

ANALYZE. Reread Ehrenreich's essay, looking for and underlining the cues in the first sentence of each paragraph that link it to the previous paragraph. Then choose any paragraph—it does not matter which one—that seems coherent to you and underline the cues in each sentence that keep you on track. These cues may be, for example, key words repeated, pronouns referring back to something, sentence patterns repeated, or phrases that make a connection.

WRITE. Write several sentences reporting what you have learned about topical coherence in Ehrenreich's essay. Give examples of several cues. Categorize the cues if you notice similarities among them. Then write a few more sentences evaluating the coherence. Did you find helpful cues at every paragraph boundary? Did some cues seem more helpful than others? Are there any breaks in coherence between paragraphs or within the paragraph you analyzed? What can you conclude about the pattern of coherence cues in Ehrenreich's essay?

CONSIDERING IDEAS FOR YOUR OWN WRITING

Ehrenreich reflects on a topic—violence in families—that she claims most people prefer to ignore. Think of other topics that people are reluctant to discuss openly. They need not be dangerous or negative topics, just topics that remain underground. Examples are reluctance to take credit for one's successes, fear of success, sexually transmitted diseases, death, one's place in the economic scheme, excessive drinking, an interest in pornography, anxieties about speaking in public or about writing. You will think of others.

Ishmael Reed

WHAT'S AMERICAN ABOUT AMERICA?

Ishmael Reed (b. 1938) has written many essays, as well as novels and poems. His publications include the novels *Mumbo Jumbo* (1978), *Reckless Eyeballing* (1986), and *The Terrible Threes* (1991), and the essay collections *Shrovetide in Old New Orleans* (1979), *Writin' Is Fightin'* (1988), and *Airing Dirty Laundry* (1993). In addition, Reed has produced a video soap opera and founded a publishing company devoted to the work of unknown ethnic artists. He currently teaches at the University of California, Berkeley.

This essay was published in the March–April 1989 *Utne Reader,* and a longer version appears in *Writin' Is Fightin'.* As the next to the last paragraph suggests, Reed wrote the essay partly in response to those who do not seem to recognize that people of many different ethnic groups live in America. As you read the essay, think of examples of ethnic diversity with which you are familiar.

An item from the *New York Times*, June 23, 1983: "At the annual   1
Lower East Side Jewish Festival yesterday, a Chinese woman ate a pizza slice in front of Ty Thuan Duc's Vietnamese grocery store. Beside her a Spanish-speaking family patronized a cart with two signs: 'Italian Ices' and 'Kosher by Rabbi Alper.' And after the pastrami ran out, everybody ate knishes."

On the day before Memorial Day, 1983, a poet called me to   2
describe a city he had just visited. He said that one section included mosques, built by the Islamic people who dwelled there. Attending his reading, he said, were large numbers of Hispanic people, 40,000 of whom lived in the same city. He was not talking about a fabled city located in some mysterious region of the world. The city he'd visited was Detroit.

A few months before, as I was visiting Texas, I heard the taped   3
voice used to guide passengers to their connections at the Dallas Airport announcing items in both Spanish and English. This trend is likely to continue; after all, for some southwestern states like Texas, where the largest minority is now Mexican-American, Spanish was the first written language and the Spanish style lives on in the western way of life.

Shortly after my Texas trip, I sat in a campus auditorium at the   4
University of Wisconsin at Milwaukee as a Yale professor—whose original work on the influence of African cultures upon those of the Americas has led to his ostracism from some intellectual circles— walked up and down the aisle like an old-time Southern evangelist, dancing and drumming the top of the lectern, illustrating his points before some Afro-American intellectuals and artists who cheered and applauded his performance. The professor was "white." After his lecture, he conversed with a group of Milwaukeeans—all who spoke Yoruban, though only the professor had ever traveled to Africa.

One of the artists there told me that his paintings, which included   5
African and Afro-American mythological symbols and imagery, were hanging in the local McDonald's restaurant. The next day I went to McDonald's and snapped pictures of smiling youngsters eating hamburgers below paintings that could grace the walls of any of the country's leading museums. The manager of the local McDonald's said, "I don't know what you boys are doing, but I like it," as he commissioned the local painters to exhibit in his restaurant.

Such blurring of cultural styles occurs in everyday life in the   6
United States to a greater extent than anyone can imagine. The result is what the above-mentioned Yale professor, Robert

Thompson, referred to as a cultural bouillabaisse.[*] Yet members of the nation's present educational and cultural elect still cling to the notion that the United States belongs to some vaguely defined entity they refer to as "Western civilization," by which they mean, presumably, a civilization created by people of Europe, as if Europe can even be viewed in monolithic terms. Is Beethoven's Ninth Symphony, which includes Turkish marches, a part of Western civilization? Or the late-nineteenth- and twentieth-century French paintings, whose creators were influenced by Japanese art? And what of the cubists, through whom the influence of African art changed modern painting? Or the surrealists, who were so impressed with the art of the Pacific Northwest Indians that, in their map of North America, Alaska dwarfs the lower forty-eight states in size?

Are the Russians, who are often criticized for their adoption of "Western" ways by Tsarist dissidents in exile, members of Western civilization? And what of the millions of Europeans who have black African and Asian ancestry, black Africans having occupied several European countries for hundreds of years? Are these "Europeans" a part of Western civilization? Or the Hungarians, who originated across the Urals in a place called Greater Hungary? Or the Irish, who came from the Iberian Peninsula? 7

Even the notion that North America is part of Western civilization because our "system of government" is derived from Europe is being challenged by Native American historians who say that the founding fathers, Benjamin Franklin especially, were actually influenced by the system of government that had been adopted by the Iroquois hundreds of years prior to the arrival of Europeans. 8

Western civilization, then, becomes another confusing category—like Third World, or Judeo-Christian culture—as humanity attempts to impose its small-screen view of political and cultural reality upon a complex world. Our most publicized novelist recently said that Western civilization was the greatest achievement of mankind—an attitude that flourishes on the street level as scribbles in public restrooms: "White Power," "Niggers and Spics Suck," or "Hitler was a prophet." Where did such an attitude, which has caused so much misery and depression in our national life, which has tainted even our noblest achievements, begin? An attitude that caused the incarceration of Japanese-American citizens during World War II, the persecution of Chicanos and Chinese Americans, the near-extermination of the Indians, and the murder and lynchings of thousands of Afro-Americans. 9

The Puritans of New England are idealized in our schoolbooks as the first Americans, "a hardy band" of no-nonsense patriarchs whose discipline razed the forest and brought order to the New World (a term that annoys Native American historians). Indus- 10

*bouillabaisse: a stew made with several kinds of fish (Ed.)

trious, responsible, it was their "Yankee ingenuity" and practicality that created the work ethic.

The Puritans, however, had a mean streak. They hated the theater and banned Christmas. They punished people in a cruel and inhuman manner. They killed children who disobeyed their parents. They exterminated the Indians, who had taught them how to survive in a world unknown to them. And their encounter with calypso culture, in the form of a servant from Barbados working in a Salem minister's household, resulted in the witchcraft hysteria.   11

The Puritan legacy of hard work and meticulous accounting led to the establishment of a great industrial society, but there was the other side—the strange and paranoid attitudes of that society toward those different from the elect.   12

The cultural attitudes of that early elect continue to be voiced in everyday life in the United States; the president of a distinguished university, writing a letter to the *Times,* belittling the study of African civilization; the television network that promoted its show on the Vatican art with the boast that this art represented "the finest achievements of the human spirit."   13

When I heard a schoolteacher warn the other night about the invasion of the American educational system by foreign curricula, I wanted to yell at the television set, "Lady, they're already here." It has already begun because the world is here. The world has been arriving at these shores for at least 10,000 years from Europe, Africa, and Asia. In the late nineteenth and early twentieth centuries, large numbers of Europeans arrived, adding their cultures to those of the European, African, and Asian settlers who were already here, and recently millions have been entering the country from South America and the Caribbean, making Robert Thompson's bouillabaisse richer and thicker.   14

North America deserves a more exciting destiny than as a repository of "Western civilization." We can become a place where the cultures of the world crisscross. This is possible because the United States and Canada are unique in the world: The world is here.   15

READING FOR MEANING

Reed is reflecting on the ethnic or cultural diversity of American society. Much has been said and written about this topic. Starting with some reflection on what you already know and think about the topic, write at least a page, exploring your understanding and response to Reed's essay.

You might find some of the following suggestions helpful in getting started or sustaining your writing:

• Reed opens his essay with five examples indicating the surprising diversity of American life. Think of other examples based on your personal experience, observation, reading, and conversation. Explain how your examples relate to those of Reed.

- List four or five words Reed uses in this essay that you need to look up in a dictionary or an encyclopedia. Why do you think Reed uses so many unfamiliar words and makes so many references requiring historical and geographical knowledge?

- In the past, it was common to refer to the United States as a *melting pot,* whereas Reed calls it a *bouillabaisse.* Which of the two terms do you prefer? If you find neither of these terms appropriate, what would you propose? What advantages do you see in your preferred term?

- Reed sets up a contrast in paragraph 6 between "cultural bouillabaisse" and "Western civilization." What different attitudes, beliefs, or values are associated with each? Would Reed say we have to choose between them? Would you?

EXTENDING MEANING THROUGH CONVERSATION. It is important for you to interpret the essay on your own, but you may be able to extend your understanding by conversing with one or two classmates about Reed's essay. Before getting together, review your annotations and writing and reflect on your own understanding. Take turns identifying one idea in Reed's reflections that especially interested each of you.

As you converse about the meanings you have found, you may discover that you have somewhat different understandings of the essay, which will help each of you to think critically about the essay by seeing it in new ways. As you explore your understandings, reread and discuss parts of the essay together.

READING LIKE A WRITER

DEVELOPING THE REFLECTIONS BY PILING UP EXAMPLES

The reflections of most of the writers in this chapter grow out of a single particular occasion—a personal or observed experience that serves as an initial example of the larger subject the writer wishes to explore. Reed, however, opens with five paragraphs relating five separate particular occasions that serve as the basis for his reflections about the diversity of American culture. More than most of the other writers in this chapter, Reed continues his essay by piling up example after example.

ANALYZE. Skim Reed's essay. Number in the margin each example of American diversity Reed describes, and underline or write in the margin a key word or phrase that summarizes the example. Then read through Reed's examples, making notes about any of the following:

- How many examples do you find altogether in the essay?

- What similarities and differences do you find among the examples? Can any be grouped according to the general ideas they illustrate?

- What is the effect of some examples taking the form of questions?

- Why do you think Reed devotes more attention to some examples than to others, particularly the Puritans (paragraphs 10 through 12)?

WRITE. Write several sentences describing Reed's use of examples. Consider how well the examples, individually and together, justify Reed's generalizations in the essay.

CONSIDERING IDEAS FOR YOUR OWN WRITING

Reed cites numerous examples of the great cultural mix in the United States. He favors Thompson's word *bouillabaisse* over the traditional term *melting pot* to describe this cultural mix. Whereas each component in a melting pot loses whatever originally made it distinctive, each component in a bouillabaisse retains its individuality.

Based on your own experience and observation, how might you reflect on this idea of cultural difference? What are some specific differences you see among people? What benefits arise from these differences? What problems do the differences create? What specific occasion from your own experience would you choose to anchor your reflections?

Diana Trilling

ON SEXUAL SEPARATISM

Since 1949, Diana Trilling (b. 1905) has been an influential freelance writer and critic. She regularly contributes essays and reviews to many diverse magazines and journals, and she is a member of the Editorial Board of the journal *American Scholar*. Recognition of the importance of her work has come in her election to the American Academy of Arts and Sciences and nomination for a Pulitzer Prize for her 1981 book, *Mrs. Harris: The Death of the Scarsdale Diet Doctor*.

This essay was published in *Newsweek* magazine in 1994. The occasion for Trilling's reflections is a brief story about her mother. Her reflections include two somewhat surprising ideas: that women's concerns about sexual harassment have created "sexual separatism" (notice that she names and defines her own topic) and that sexual separatism is comparable to racial separatism. As you read, you will want to evaluate these two ideas. Also think about a distinction she makes between sexual nuisance and sexual harassment. A nuisance is something annoying and unpleasant, whereas harassment is something repeatedly, persistently annoying and unpleasant.

I find it difficult to think about the issue of sexual harassment without recalling my mother's account of her first job in America. At 18 she had come to this country alone, from Poland. With no knowledge of English, but a good figure, she had become a model in the New York City garment district. But she soon wearied of having to fend off the advances of the male buyers. She gave up modeling to become a milliner's apprentice.

There was no note of insult or injury in my mother's report of this experience. She even seemed to have been mildly flattered by the overtures that had been made to her. But she had found them a nuisance to handle.

The distinction between sexual nuisance and harassment is a crucial one, but it has all but disappeared in a feminist culture which appears to be bent upon raising always-new and higher barriers between men and women. While there are many forms of male behavior which legitimately call for censure and even for the intervention of law—they include not only any imposition of physical force but the kind of indignity which our female naval officers at Tailhook were made to suffer—the legitimate effort to guard women against gender-initiated mistreatment now reaches the point where the most casual expression of male interest in women, whistling at a woman on the street or remarking on her dress, is taken to be an infringement of her "personhood." She has been made into a mere "object."

Yet one wonders what enterprise there is in our society to which women are more universally and urgently dedicated than to being the objects of male notice and desire. A first imperative of our society is that women make themselves attractive to men. Our cosmetic and clothing industries are driven by it; our newly thriving fitness industry depends upon it. Indeed, sex has come to displace sport as our national obsession. Slyly or overtly, it riddles our fiction, our television and movies, our advertising.

In the past, because of our country's background in Puritanism, Americans were often accused of sexual hypocrisy. Today, we are less guilty of sexual hypocrisy than of sexual paradox and disingenuousness. Even while our college campuses ring with the cry of date rape, our female students cheerily invite male students to all-night study sessions in their rooms. In a culture which demands that women have equal access with men to positions of authority and power in business and the professions, we encourage women to feel that they need the protection of society against a man who tells them a dirty joke.

We recall, for instance, Anita Hill's remarkable appearance before the Senate Judiciary Committee at the hearings for Clarence Thomas and her account of Judge Thomas's pursuit of her with dirty stories. Charming in speech and manner, backed by parents of incontestable respectability, Miss Hill was the very image of maidenly modesty. Yet the forthrightness with which she repeated to the Committee and to an audience of untold millions of television listeners Judge Thomas's dirty jokes in all their tasteless detail would have done credit to a truck driver.

A half century ago, the gifted humorist James Thurber created a   7
cartoon series "The War Between Men and Women" in which he
satirized the often-bizarre marital struggle between the sexes. We
have only to compare Thurber's bloodless war with the death-deal-
ing spirit which animates the sexual manual which was recently
drafted by the students of Antioch College to recognize the dangerous distance we have traveled in the relation of men and women.
According to the Antioch rules, verbal permission must be re-
quested and received before one's sexual partner may proceed from
one "level" (their word) to the next in sexual intimacy. Although the
manual is at pains to address itself to men as well as women, it does
a poor job of disguising its basic assumption that men are natural
predators and that women are at one and the same time sacred vessels, shatterable at a touch, and the traffic managers of love.

This is scarcely a useful axiom to disseminate in our society, but   8
for several years now it has been establishing itself in our sexual culture, and it accounts, of course, for the increase in charges now
being brought by women against men, the most recent and unpleasant of them the charge of sexual harassment brought by Paula Jones
against President Clinton. A woman who doesn't flinch at alleging
that the president of the United States attempted to seduce her
by letting down his pants demands legal and financial recompense
for the damage which this is supposed to have done to her delicate
sensibility!

We live in a world which runs with the blood of hostility between   9
racial and religious groups, between ethnic and national groups. To
these lamentable separations among people, we now add another
division, a separatism of the sexes. Where it used to be that the act
of love (as it was then called) was regarded as an aspect, and even a
celebration, of our shared humanity, it now becomes a dehumanized
exercise and a new arena for conflict.

Black separatism came into existence in this country in the late   10
'60s as an effort of prideful self-assertion. In claiming its separate
identity, the black minority undertook to assert its equality with the
white majority. At the time, the program may perhaps have had its
symbolic use, but with the passage of the years we see its sorry consequences. Far from contributing to racial harmony, it has produced
only a spiraling racial antagonism. Is this what we are aiming for in
the relation of men and women: a spiraling discord?

It is still possible for this trend to be reversed in our society if   11
feminism will take warning from all the other separatisms which
now divide our world. Surely nothing is gained for society, nothing is
gained for either men or women, by fostering the idea that men are
ruthless aggressors against women and that women need to keep
themselves in cautionary command of any relation which they have
with men. Ours is not a moment in history in which to widen the
divisions among people.

READING FOR MEANING

Write at least a page, exploring your understanding of "On Sexual Separatism." Begin by stating what you think Trilling hopes to accomplish with this essay. Then write about any aspect of the essay that contributes to your understanding of Trilling's reflections.

As you write, reread parts of the essay to clarify your understanding and to find material to include in your writing. If you have difficulty continuing for at least a page, use one of the following ideas:

- State two or three of Trilling's ideas in your own words and respond to them.

- Summarize the Antioch College rules (paragraph 7), explain why you support or question them, and evaluate Trilling's response to them.

- Explain your understanding of the key comparison in Trilling's essay, that of racial separatism to sexual separatism in paragraphs 9 through 11. Specifically, what is being compared? Does the comparison make sense to you personally? Do any parts of it make sense?

- Explain the possible significance of "feminist culture . . . appears to be bent upon raising always-new and higher barriers between men and women" (paragraph 3), "A first imperative of our society is that women make themselves attractive to men" (paragraph 4), "Today, we are less guilty of sexual hypocrisy than of sexual paradox and disingenuousness" (paragraph 5), "women are at one and the same time sacred vessels, shatterable at a touch, and the traffic managers of love" (paragraph 7), or any other statement that catches your attention.

EXTENDING MEANING THROUGH CONVERSATION. Your understanding of Trilling's essay may be enhanced by discussing it with one or two classmates who have also thought about the essay's meanings. Before getting together, review your annotations and writing and reflect on your current understanding. Then begin the conversation by taking turns presenting the one idea that each of you found most surprising or controversial.

As you share your insights, you may find that you have interpreted the essay differently. Explore these differences by rereading the text together and discussing the ideas.

READING LIKE A WRITER
DEVELOPING THE REFLECTIONS THROUGH
COMPARISON AND CONTRAST

Reflective writing succeeds if it can offer readers some interesting, even surprising, ideas. We have seen how Trilling offers many ideas about the relations between men and women, ideas that will please some readers and irritate others, ideas that show Trilling's independence of mind and willingness to risk irritating some readers. Ideas are crucial; yet the writer cannot merely list ideas, regardless of how fresh and daring they may be. Instead, the writer must work inventively to develop these ideas, to explain and elaborate them, to turn them one way and then another. One well-established way to do this is through comparison and contrast.

ANALYZE. Closely examine each of the following comparisons or contrasts:

- Nuisance and harassment (paragraph 3)
- The cry of date rape and male-female all-night study sessions (paragraph 5)
- Anita Hill's respectable appearance and her public retelling of dirty jokes (paragraph 6)
- Thurber's cartoon series and Antioch College's rules (paragraph 7)
- Racial separatism and sexual separatism (paragraph 10)

WRITE. Write several sentences summarizing each of these comparisons and contrasts and evaluating each in terms of how well it supports Trilling's purpose and develops her ideas. Point out which comparisons and contrasts seem most and least successful, as well as most and least complete. Then add a few sentences in which you evaluate Trilling's strategy of relying mainly on comparisons and contrasts to develop her ideas. Why do you think she relies on them to such a great extent?

CONSIDERING IDEAS FOR YOUR OWN WRITING

Trilling writes about sexual relations. Consider writing about other relations between the sexes: jealousy, cooperation, competition, parenting, conversational styles. Or write about relations between women or between men. If a specific relation interests you particularly, think of an occasion—something you experienced or observed—that would launch your reflections. You do not need specialized knowledge nor do you need to feel pressured to come up with any conclusions. You need only to explore confidently your own ideas, relying on examples from your own experience.

Katherine Haines

WHOSE BODY IS THIS?

Katherine Haines wrote this essay in 1987 for a freshman composition course at the University of California, San Diego.

As the title suggests, this essay expresses the writer's dismay and anger about our society's obsession with the perfect body—especially the perfect female body. Note, as you read, the many kinds of details Haines uses to develop her general reflections.

"Hey Rox, what's up? Do you wanna go down to the pool with me? It's a   ¹ gorgeous day."

"No thanks, you go ahead without me."   2

"What? Why don't you want to go? You've got the day off work, and what   3
else are you going to do?"

"Well, I've got a bunch of stuff to do around the house . . . pay the bills,   4
clean the bathroom, you know. Besides, I don't want to have to see myself in a
bathing suit—I'm so fat."

Why do so many women seem obsessed with their weight and   5
body shape? Are they really that unhappy and dissatisfied with themselves? Or are these women continually hearing from other people
that their bodies are not acceptable?

In today's society, the expectations for women and their bodies   6
are all too evident. Fashion, magazines, talk shows, "lite" and fat-free
food in stores and restaurants, and diet centers are all daily
reminders of these expectations. For instance, the latest fashions for
women reveal more and more skin: shorts have become shorter, to
the point of being scarcely larger than a pair of underpants, and the
bustier, which covers only a little more skin than a bra, is making a
comeback. These styles are only flattering on the slimmest of bodies, and many women who were previously happy with their bodies
may emerge from the dressing room after a run-in with these styles
and decide that it must be diet time again. Instead of coming to the
realization that these clothes are unflattering for most women, how
many women will simply look for different and more flattering
styles, and how many women will end up heading for the gym to
burn off some more calories or to the bookstore to buy the latest
diet book?

When I was in junior high, about two-thirds of the girls I knew   7
were on diets. Everyone was obsessed with fitting into the smallest
size miniskirt possible. One of my friends would eat a carrot stick, a
celery stick, and two rice cakes for lunch. Junior high (and the onset
of adolescence) seemed to be the beginning of the pressure for
most women. It is at this age that appearance suddenly becomes
important. Especially for those girls who want to be "popular" and
those who are cheerleaders or on the drill team. The pressure is
intense; some girls believe no one will like them or accept them if
they are "overweight," even by a pound or two. The measures these
girls will take to attain the body that they think will make them
acceptable are often debilitating and life threatening.

My sister was on the drill team in junior high. My sister wanted to   8
fit in with the right crowd—and my sister drove herself to the edge
of becoming anorexic. I watched as she came home from school,
having eaten nothing for breakfast and at lunch only a bag of pretzels
and an apple (and she didn't always finish that), and began pacing the
oriental carpet that was in our living room. Around and around and

around, without a break, from four o'clock until dinnertime, which was usually at six or seven o'clock. And then at dinner, she would take minute portions and only pick at her food. After several months of this, she became much paler and thinner, but not in any sort of attractive sense. Finally, after catching a cold and having to stay in bed for three days because she was so weak, she was forced to go to the doctor. The doctor said she was suffering from malnourishment and was to stay in bed until she regained some of her strength. He advised her to eat lots of fruits and vegetables until the bruises all over her body had healed (these were a result of vitamin deficiency). Although my sister did not develop anorexia, it was frightening to see what she had done to herself. She had little strength, and the bruises she had made her look like an abused child.

This mania to lose weight and have the "ideal" body is not easily   9
avoided in our society. It is created by television and magazines as they flaunt their models and latest diet crazes in front of our faces. And then there are the Nutri-System and Jenny Craig commercials, which show hideous "before" pictures and glamorous "after" pictures and have smiling, happy people dancing around and talking about how their lives have been transformed simply because they have lost weight. This propaganda that happiness is in a large part based on having the "perfect" body shape is a message that the media constantly sends to the public. No one seems to be able to escape it.

My mother and father were even sucked in by this idea. One   10
evening, when I was in the fifth grade, I heard Mom and Dad calling me into the kitchen. Oh no, what had I done now? It was never good news when you got summoned into the kitchen alone. As I walked into the kitchen, Mom looked up at me with an anxious expression; Dad was sitting at the head of the table with a pen in hand and a yellow legal pad in front of him. They informed me that I was going on a diet. A diet!? I wanted to scream at them, "I'm only ten years old, why do I have to be on a diet?" I was so embarrassed, and I felt so guilty. Was I really fat? I guess so, I thought, otherwise why would my parents do this to me?

It seems that this obsession with the perfect body and a woman's   11
appearance has grown to monumental heights. It is ironic, however, that now many people feel that this problem is disappearing. People have begun to assume that women want to be thin because they just want to be "healthy." But what has happened is that the sickness slips in under the guise of wanting a "healthy" body. The demand for thin bodies is anything but "healthy." How many anorexics or bulimics have you seen that are healthy?

It is strange that women do not come out and object to society's   12
pressure to become thin. Or maybe women feel that they really do want to be thin, and so go on dieting endlessly (they call it "eating sensibly"), thinking this is what they really want. I think if these

women carefully examined their reasons for wanting to lose weight—and were not allowed to include reasons that relate to society's demands, such as a weight chart, a questionnaire in a magazine, a certain size in a pair of shorts, or even a scale—they would find that they are being ruled by what society wants, not what they want. So why do women not break free from these standards? Why do they not demand an end to being judged in such a demeaning and senseless way?

Self-esteem plays a large part in determining whether women succumb to the will of society or whether they are independent and self-assured enough to make their own decisions. Lack of self-esteem is one of the things the women's movement has had to fight the hardest against. If women didn't think they were worthy, then how could they even begin to fight for their own rights? The same is true with the issue of body size. If women do not feel their body is worthy, then how can they believe that it is okay to just let it stay that way? Without self-esteem, women will be swayed by society and will continue to make themselves unhappy by trying to maintain whatever weight or body shape society is dictating for them. It is ironic that many of the popular women's magazines—*Cosmopolitan, Mademoiselle, Glamour*—often feature articles on self-esteem and how essential it is and how to improve it, and then in the same issue give the latest diet tips. This mixed message will never give women the power they deserve over their bodies and will never enable them to make their own decisions about what type of body they want. 13

"Rox, why do you think you're fat? You work out all the time, and you just bought that new suit. Why don't you just come down to the pool for a little while?" 14

"No, I really don't want to. I feel so self-conscious with all those people around. It makes me want to run and put on a big, baggy dress so no one can tell what size I am!" 15

"Ah, Rox, that's really sad. You have to learn to believe in yourself and your own judgment, not other people's." 16

READING FOR MEANING

Write at least a page, exploring your understanding of and response to Haines's essay. Begin by considering how you feel about your own weight and body shape. How do these personal feelings affect your interest in this essay?

If you need help thinking of something more to say, use any of the following suggestions:

- In paragraph 7, Haines suggests that the preoccupation with body image begins for many women at the onset of adolescence. Why do you think this might be so? Connect your speculations specifically to Haines's statements.

- When people think of body-image disorders, they usually think about women, not men. How do you account for this disparity? Do men also have an ideal body image? If so, how would you describe it? Where does it come from?

- Haines asserts in paragraph 9 that "[t]his mania to lose weight and have the 'ideal' body . . . is created by television and magazines." How would you argue for or against this idea?

- Explain the possible meaning or significance of "the sickness slips in under the guise of wanting a 'healthy' body" (paragraph 11); "if these women carefully examined their reasons for wanting to lose weight . . . they would find that they are being ruled by what society wants, not what they want" (paragraph 12); "It is ironic that many of the popular women's magazines . . . often feature articles on self-esteem and how essential it is and how to improve it, and then in the same issue give the latest diet tips" (paragraph 13); or any other statement that catches your attention.

EXTENDING MEANING THROUGH CONVERSATION. After you make meaning on your own, you may be able to extend your understanding by conversing with classmates about Haines's essay. Before getting together, reflect on your own understanding by reviewing your annotations and writing. Begin your conversation by identifying one idea in Haines's reflections that especially interested each of you.

As you converse about the meanings you have found, you may discover that you have somewhat different understandings of the essay. You need not strive to reach agreement, however. Instead, help each other think critically about the essay by seeing it in new ways. As you explore your understandings, reread and discuss parts of the essay together.

READING LIKE A WRITER
ENGAGING READERS

Writers of reflection attempt to engage readers in the subject by making a special effort to interest readers in the topic, by drawing them into the reflections from the beginning, and by showing an awareness of what readers may be thinking as the reflections unfold. Although reflective writing is highly personal, it is nevertheless public writing—writing to be read and enjoyed and reflected on in turn. It has an obligation to its readers primarily to show them new ways of thinking about a topic but also to pointedly engage them in the topic and the reflections on it.

Haines attempts to engage her readers in several ways. For example, she creates a brief dialogue to open her essay. In addition to introducing her topic effectively, this dialogue might also draw readers into her essay.

ANALYZE. Skim the essay annotating Haines's attempts to engage readers and to hold their interest. Look for specific references likely to be recognized immediately by readers, questions for readers to ponder, especially surprising ideas, unusual or dramatic personal experiences, humor—or anything that shows Haines thinking about her readers and trying to engage them in her reflections.

WRITE. Write several sentences describing how Haines attempts to engage her readers and hold their interest. You may find few or several attempts. Then write a few sentences evaluating how successfully she engages her readers. (If you are a man, you may want to decide first whether she assumes men to be among her readers.)

COMPARE. Now that you have some ideas about how Haines attempts to engage her readers, you are in a good position to learn more about this strategy by comparing Haines's attempts with those of Ehrenreich, Reed, or Trilling. Choose any one of these essays and annotate it carefully for its attempts to engage its readers. Then write a page or so about what you learn about engaging readers from the essay you have chosen as well as a comparison of its attempts to engage readers with those of Haines. What seems most successful to you in each essay?

CONSIDERING IDEAS FOR YOUR OWN WRITING

Haines is concerned in this essay with the ways society influences how we think about and judge ourselves. Haines focuses on how we perceive our own bodies. You could explore this question from another angle: for example, our cultural ideals of masculine and feminine beauty. You might think about beauty in terms of different ethnic and racial groups. You might think about it historically in terms of the painting and sculpture that have influenced our sense of the beautiful.

You could explore also our cultural ideas about success. The Horatio Alger rags-to-riches story is the prototypical expression of the American Dream. But we all know that success does not have to be measured in terms of money. In what other ways do we measure success?

THINKING ABOUT WHAT MAKES REFLECTIVE WRITING EFFECTIVE

In this chapter, you have been learning how to read reflective writing for meaning and how to read it like a writer. Before going on to write a reflective essay, pause here to review and consolidate what you have learned about what makes reflective writing successful.

ANALYZE. Choose one reading from this chapter that seems to you to be especially effective. Before reading the selection again, write down one or two reasons you remember it as an example of good reflective writing.

Reread your chosen selection, adding further annotations about what makes it particularly successful as a reflective essay. Consider the selection's purpose and how well it achieves that purpose for its intended readers. (You can make an informed guess about readership by noting the publication source of the essay and inferring some of the writer's assumptions about what readers know and believe.) Then focus on how well the essay

- Narrates the occasion or occasions for the reflections
- Develops the reflections, paying particular attention to the variety of development strategies the writer uses
- Engages readers

You can review all of these basic features in Reading like a Writer following the Toussaint essay in the Guide to Reading Reflective Writing at the beginning of this chapter.

You can complete this activity on your own or your instructor may ask you to work with a small group of other students who have chosen the same essay. If you work with others, take time initially for everyone to reread the selection, adding to their annotations as suggested above. Then discuss what makes this particular reflective essay so effective. Take notes. One person in your group should present a report to the class about what you have learned about reflective writing, or you can write individually.

WRITE. Write at least a page explaining and justifying your choice of this reading as an example of effective reflective writing. Assume that your readers—your instructor and classmates—have read the selection but will not remember many details. They also may not remember it as an especially successful reflective essay. Therefore, you will want to use details and refer to specific parts of the essay as you explain how it works as reflective writing and seek to justify your evaluation of its effectiveness. You need not argue that it is the best essay in the chapter, only that it is, in your view, a strong example of the genre.

A GUIDE TO REFLECTIVE WRITING

As the selections in this chapter suggest, reflective essays can be engaging reading. They are interesting, lively, insightful—like good conversation—and at the same time focus on basic human and social issues that concern us all. Writers of reflection, while never pretentious or preachy, are not reluctant to say what they think or to express their most personal observations.

Because reflective essays attempt to broaden personal experience into exploration of larger issues, they can be particularly challenging to write. This section guides you through the various decisions you will need to make as you plan, draft, and revise a reflective essay.

INVENTION

The following activities should spur your thinking. They will help you to find a particular occasion and general subject, develop your subject, and identify your main point. Taking some time now to consider a wide range of possibilities will pay off later when you draft your essay because it will give you confidence in your choice of subject and in your ability to develop it effectively.

Finding a Particular Occasion and General Subject

As the selections in this chapter illustrate, writers usually center their essays on one (or more) particular event or occasion that provides a base for their reflections on a general subject. In the process of invention, however, the particular occasion does not always come before the general subject. Sometimes writers set out to reflect on a general subject such as envy or friendship and must search for just the right image or anecdote with which to particularize it.

To help you find an occasion and subject for your essay, make a chart like the one that follows by matching particular occasions to general subjects. In the left-hand column, list particular occasions—a conversation you have had or overheard, a scene you have observed, something memorable you have read or seen in movies or on television, an incident in your own or someone else's life—that might lead you to reflect more generally. In the right-hand column, list general subjects—human qualities like compassion, vanity, jealousy, faithfulness; social customs and mores for dating, eating, working; abstract notions like fate, free will, the imagination—suggested by the particular occasions in the left-hand column.

Move from left to right and also from right to left, making your lists as long as you can. You will find that a single occasion might suggest several subjects and that a subject might be particularized by a variety of occasions. Each entry will surely suggest other possibilities for you to consider. If you are having trouble getting started, review your notes for Practicing Reflection: A Collaborative Activity in the beginning of this chapter and the Considering Ideas for Your Own Writing following each reading in this chapter. Your chart of possibilities is likely to become quite messy, but do not let that concern you. A full and rich exploration of topics will give you confidence that the one you finally choose is the most promising.

Particular Occasions	General Subjects
Saw junior high girls wearing makeup as thick as clown's	Makeup; makeover, mask the real self; ideas of beauty
Punk styles of the '90s	New fashions: conformity or rebellion?
Rumor about Diane and Tom spread by a friend of theirs	Malicious like gossip? How do they start? stop?
Saw film called *Betrayal*	Friendship & betrayal
TV story about a 15-year-old who killed a woman to get her car	Violence in our society. Why are teenage men so violent? Danger in cities.
Buying clothes, I couldn't decide and let the salesperson pressure me	Decisions & indecisiveness; bowing to outside pressure; low self-esteem; can't or won't think of self—conformity again!
Take friends to help me make a decision	

As further occasions and subjects occur to you over the next two or three days, add them to your chart.

Choosing a Subject

Review your chart, and select an occasion and subject you now think looks promising.

To test whether this selection will work, write for fifteen minutes, exploring your thoughts on it. Do not make any special demands on yourself to be profound or even to be coherent. Just put your ideas on paper as they come, letting one idea suggest another. Your aim is to determine whether you have anything to say and whether the topic holds your interest. If you discover that you do not have very much to say or that you quickly lose interest in the subject, choose another one and try again. It might take you a few preliminary explorations to find the right subject.

Developing the Particular Occasion

The following activities will help you recall details about the occasion for your reflection that will make your narrative of it vivid and dramatic.

Write for five minutes, narrating what happened during the event or, if your reflections are based on something you have read or viewed in the media, restating the particulars of that subject. Include as many details as you can recall.

For an event, write about the people involved, their appearance and behavior (including snippets of dialogue, if appropriate), and the setting. For something you have read or viewed in the media, recall as much as you can that may be pertinent to your reflections.

LEARNING MORE ABOUT YOUR READERS:
A COLLABORATIVE ACTIVITY

Your instructor may ask you to get together with two or three other students at this point in your invention process. In turn, tell one another what your subject is and describe the occasion or occasions that will launch your essay. Then the other students in your group will tell you about their personal experience of your occasion and subject.

You can benefit greatly from hearing what others know about your subject because they can enhance your thinking about your subject and suggest specific ways you might develop your reflections. Their responses will also enable you to better anticipate what readers will be thinking when they read your reflections and, therefore, can help you develop your reflections in ways that readers will find insightful and even surprising.

Developing Your Reflections on the Subject

To explore your ideas about the subject, try the invention activity called *cubing*. Based on the six sides of a cube, this activity leads you to turn over your subject as you would a cube, looking at it in six different ways. Complete the following activities in any order, writing for five minutes on each. Your goal is to invent new ways of considering your subject.

GENERALIZE ABOUT IT. Consider what you learn from the experience that will be the occasion for your reflections/ideas. What does it suggest to you? What does it suggest about people in general or about the society in which you live?

GIVE EXAMPLES OF IT. Illustrate your subject with specific examples. Think of what would help your classmates understand the ideas you have about it.

COMPARE AND CONTRAST IT. Think of a subject that compares with yours. Explore the similarities and the differences.

EXTEND IT. Take your subject to its logical limits. Speculate about its implications. Where does it lead?

ANALYZE IT. Take apart your subject. What is it made of? How are the parts related to one another? Are they all of equal importance?

APPLY IT. Think about your subject in practical terms. How can you use it or act on it? What difference would it make to you and to others?

DRAFTING

After completing the invention activities, you should feel confident in your choice of a particular occasion, knowing that it suggests a subject that you can develop in interesting ways. The following suggestions for setting goals, planning, and deciding how to begin your essay prepare you to write your first full draft.

Setting Goals

Writers need to set goals—specific (or local) goals as well as general (or global) ones—to guide them as they draft their essays. These goals ought to be determined based on who will be reading the essay and what the writer wants to get across to these readers.

Before establishing specific goals, consider what the general goals should be. Ask yourself what your purpose is: What do you want your readers to think about? Ask yourself how you want your readers to view you.

If, for example, you think your readers have already thought seriously about your subject, you might try to give your essay a surprising turn, as Trilling does in paragraphs 9 and 10 when she compares sexual separatism to racial separatism.

If you expect readers to have overly simple answers to your questions, you might push them to probe your subject more deeply, as Reed does when he asks, in paragraph 7, whether Russians, Europeans of black African ancestry, Hungarians, or the Irish can be considered "Westerners."

If you assume readers are satisfied with their own understanding of your subject, you might approach your subject from a unique angle, as Toussaint does when she details in paragraphs 3 through 6 how her new hearing aid "shattered my peace" and in specific ways made it harder for her to "hear."

Planning Your Draft

Your invention writings will probably have given you many ideas. In fact, you might feel overwhelmed by the amount of material in your invention writing. Use *clustering* to sort through your ideas and find ways of grouping them. In this process, you will need to refer repeatedly to what you have written thus far, and you may also need to generate more material to fill out some points.

First, decide on a single word or phrase that summarizes your subject (such as "Families can be dangerous"). Put it in the center of a page, and circle it. Second, skim your invention writings to find key ideas or questions. Label and circle these, and place them at various points around the central idea, connecting them with a line to the center. Third, look again at your invention writing to find material—questions, facts, examples—relating to each of these subordinate points. Cluster these around the relevant point.

This one-page graphic provides a visual representation of your initial, tentative ideas about your subject and possible examples that will help you present your ideas to your readers. Use it only as a starting point for drafting your essay and to reassure yourself that you do have some workable material. It is not an outline. You will still need to decide which idea or example to start with, which one to present next, and so on.

Beginning

Most reflective essays begin with the particular occasion, but they present it in a variety of ways. For example, Staples opens with a dramatic anecdote, whereas Reed piles up five different kinds of particular occasions. Ehrenreich opens with brief references to events of the times and with generalizations, whereas Trilling narrates a brief anecdote about her mother to make a distinction between sexual nuisance and sexual harassment.

READING A DRAFT CRITICALLY

With a completed draft of your essay in hand, you can benefit from having one or more readers who know something about reflective writing take a close look at what you have done and advise you about what you might want to do to improve your draft. The guidelines in this section will ensure that you can get an insightful critical reading of your draft. You, too, can use them to give someone else useful advice.

Make or get a written record from a critical reading of a draft. The written record provides the writer one important advantage: With a written record, criticism or suggestions that might otherwise have been forgotten between the time of the critical reading and of the revision are retained and available for reference.

While you obviously gain from receiving a critical reading, you also benefit greatly from giving one. When you complete a careful analysis of someone's draft, you learn more about the possibilities of reflective writing at just the time when you can put the learning to use in your own writing. Taking on the role of critical reader enables you to imagine more easily what your readers will be expecting from your essay.

Reading a draft critically means reading it more than once, first to get a general impression and then to analyze its basic features. Before you read, number the paragraphs so you can refer easily to specific parts of the essay.

Reading for a First Impression

Read quickly through the draft to get an overall impression. After you have finished reading, write down your immediate reaction. What seems most interesting and insightful to you about this essay?

Reading to Analyze

Read now to focus on the basic features of a reflective essay. Read to discover what the writer has achieved, given the resources available to reflective writers, and what the writer might do to produce a more thought-provoking essay.

PRESENTING THE PARTICULAR OCCASION. Identify the occasion or occasions that launch the reflections. The writer may return to the occasion later in the essay. Notice first how the writer has presented the occasion. Is there a set of general statements, a specific scene, an incident involving other people, or reference to a book or movie?

Then evaluate how successfully the writer has presented the occasion. Does it set up an adequate context for the whole essay? Is it engaging, drawing the reader immediately into the essay? Does it suggest the significance or importance of the subject? Does the occasion dominate the essay, or is it so slight that it needs further development or further occasions to complement it? If it focuses on a particular incident and scene, does it provide enough concrete details so the reader can easily imagine what happened? Tell the writer what you see and make specific suggestions for strengthening the occasion. What is working well and what needs rethinking?

DEVELOPING THE REFLECTIONS. Most of the essay should present and develop ideas about the subject. You can be particularly helpful if you see possibilities the writer has overlooked for thinking about the subject in creative, unexpected ways. Look first for ideas that strike you as especially interesting, insightful, or surprising. Point out two or three, and explain to the writer what interests you about them. Then offer the writer perhaps the most helpful advice you will give in your critical reading: Suggest specific ways to take these ideas further. Free your imagination. Take some risks. List examples, questions, new perspectives, complexities, implications, or associations that might help the writer develop these ideas.

Next, identify ideas you do not find interesting. Focus on one or two and explain to the writer why you find the ideas uninteresting or obvious or predictable. Your explanation may help the writer decide how to rework the ideas.

Now look for ideas that are merely mentioned, not developed, or for ideas that could possibly be developed further. Start with any one of these. (It will be more helpful if you thoroughly, creatively examine one or two ideas than if you skim across several.) What more might be done to explore this idea? Suggest specific examples, contrasts, comparisons, connections to other ideas, questions to pose, applications of the idea, or anything else that will help the writer see more possibilities in the idea.

MAINTAINING TOPICAL COHERENCE. Although reflective essays may seem rambling, exploratory, and digressive, they must nevertheless be coherent. Readers must be able to move through them smoothly, without having to leap across any chasms or even small gaps.

As you have been analyzing the essay, you may have been aware of breakdowns in coherence. Now skim the essay, looking for these gaps, and mark any that you find. Look particularly at connections between paragraphs. Consider also that coherence can be disrupted by irrelevant material. Do you find anything that seems irrelevant or unnecessary?

In some drafts, overall coherence can be strengthened by rearranging blocks of material. Consider whether the writer's reflections would be easier to follow if ideas were sequenced differently or if examples were reordered. Give suggestions.

ENGAGING READERS. Writers of reflective essays can engage their readers in several ways. They can immediately draw readers into the essay through the human interest or social significance of the opening occasion. They can show a personal commitment to the subject. Their ideas and reflections seem to come from deeply felt personal experiences. They inspire readers to think, reflect, and question. They may even challenge readers' attitudes and values.

Tell the writer about your level of engagement with the essay. Point to any aspects of the essay that engaged you. Suggest ways the writer might further engage readers, keeping them reading until the end, ensuring that they will think it was worthwhile when they get there.

REVISING

Even the most promising first draft will need revision, sometimes substantial revision, especially with reflective writing, in which engaging and insightful ideas need time to emerge. A first draft can only be the starting point. When revising reflective writing, you will want to be particularly concerned with the appropriateness and concreteness of your opening occasion, the extension and development of your reflections, the coherence of your plan for sequencing your ideas, and the engagement and ability to hold a reader's interest.

You will benefit greatly from having others read your draft and give you suggestions for revising. You will, of course, be reading your own draft critically as you decide how to revise it. To give it a careful, systematic critical reading, follow the guidelines in Reading a Draft Critically. Begin your revision with the following suggestions in mind.

Revising to Enliven the Particular Occasion

Because the occasion for your reflections opens your essay, it must successfully identify your subject and declare or imply its significance. If you tell about a specific incident, it should present enough details to enable readers to imagine what happened. The occasion should draw readers into your essay and make them want to know what ideas you have about it. Review the occasions that open the readings in this chapter for ideas about revising your own. Perhaps you have thought of a more appropriate occasion for launching your reflections. If so, substitute it. Or perhaps you could add it to the one with which you now open.

Revising to Develop Your Reflections

Focus both on coming up with more ideas about your subject and on developing further the ideas in your draft. Think of examples that will illustrate an idea for readers. These examples can come from your experience, observations, reading, or movie going. Think about ways to contrast your subject with other subjects. Your goal is to lead your reader to think about your subject in new ways.

Revising to Ensure Coherence

All of the parts of your essay must be in an ideal and obvious relation to one another and their sequence must seem meaningful. The reader will expect to be able to move smoothly from one sentence to the next without encountering gaps. First, consider your draft as a whole to decide whether any of the material— occasions, ideas, examples—should be rearranged. Imagine the reader moving through your essay from beginning to end, and decide whether each part is in the ideal order for the reader to encounter it. (If you are composing on a computer, you can easily move large blocks of material.) After you have done any necessary rearranging, read your draft again slowly, looking for gaps between sentences. Pay particular attention to your transitions at paragraph boundaries to ensure that they lead the reader confidently from one part to the next. Repair any gaps by revising sentences to ensure coherence.

Revising to Engage and Hold Your Readers' Interest

All of the revisions suggested so far will make your essay more engaging and interesting to your readers. In addition, consider whether your reflections are likely to be surprising and even challenging for your readers. Readers will lose interest unless they begin to see early in your essay new ways of thinking about your subject. Continue thinking imaginatively about ways to heighten the drama and significance of your presentation of the occasion and to develop your reflections.

REFLECTING ON WHAT YOU HAVE LEARNED ABOUT WRITING REFLECTION

In this chapter, you have read critically several reflective essays and have written one of your own. Pause now to reflect on your reading and writing activities while working through this chapter to remind yourself how much you have learned and to help you remember it.

Write a page or so reflecting on what you learned. Describe what you are most pleased with in your essay and explain what contributed to your achievement. Be very specific about this contribution. If it was something you learned from the readings, indicate which readings and specifically what you learned from them. If it came from your invention writing, indicate the section or sections that helped you most. If you got good advice from a critical reader, explain exactly how the person helped you—perhaps by helping you understand a particular problem in your draft or by suggesting a new dimension to your writing. Try to write about your achievement in terms of what you have learned about the genre of reflection.

Then write about anything else that helped you to learn this special kind of writing. Feel free to include anything you have learned about the writing process; for example, how to use time efficiently before writing a draft to discover what you want to say about the subject or how to get constructive criticism and practical advice from other readers of your draft.

CHAPTER 5

EXPLAINING CONCEPTS

Explanatory writing has a limited but important purpose: to inform readers. It does not feature its writers' experiences and feelings as autobiography does, or reveal its writers' exploration of a subject as reflection does. Instead, explanatory writing confidently and efficiently presents information. It is, in fact, the writing job required most frequently of professionals in every field. Explanation may be based on firsthand observation, but it always moves beyond description of specific objects and scenes to general concepts and ideas. Because it deals almost exclusively with established information, explanatory writing does not need to give reasons why readers should accept the information it offers. Explanatory writing does not aspire to be more than it is: a way for readers to find out how to do something or to learn more about a particular subject. This is the writing we find in newspapers and magazines, encyclopedias, instruction manuals, reference books and textbooks, memos and research reports.

This chapter focuses on one important kind of explanatory writing: explaining a concept to readers to increase their understanding of the concept and its application and consequences. The selections you will be analyzing all explain a single concept, such as *parthenogenesis* is biology or *markedness* in linguistics. The explanatory essay that you write will explain a concept that you choose from your current studies or special interests.

This focus on explaining concepts has several advantages for you as a college student: It gives you strategies for reading critically the textbooks and other concept-centered explanatory material in your college courses; it enables you to learn to write confidently a common type of essay examination question and paper assignment; and it acquaints you with the basic strategies—definition, classification or division, comparison and contrast, process narration, illustration, causal explanation—common to all types of explanatory writing, not just explanation of concepts.

A *concept* is a major idea or principle. Every field of study has its concepts: physics has quark, subatomic, the Heisenberg principle; psychiatry has neurosis, schizophrenia, bipolar; composition has invention, heuristics, recursiveness; business management has corporate culture; sailing has tacking; music has harmony; and mathematics has probability. Concepts include abstract ideas, phenomena, and processes. Concepts are central to the understanding of virtually every subject. Indeed, much of human knowledge is made possible by concepts. Our brains evolved to do conceptual work—to create concepts, name them, communicate them, and think with them.

Although it need not affect you much when you choose a concept to write about, you should know that concepts exist at different levels of abstraction; that is, certain concepts in a field are "larger," or more inclusive, than others. For example, in physics, *atom* is more abstract than *electron,* which is an element of atoms; in filmmaking, *editing* is more abstract than *jump cut,* which is one strategy of film editing. The level of abstraction of the concept you choose to write about will depend on your interest and knowledge and your readers' current understanding of your subject.

Keep in mind as you work through this chapter that we learn by connecting what we are presently learning to what we have previously learned. Good explanatory writing, therefore, must be incremental, adding bit by bit to the reader's knowledge base. Explanatory writing goes wrong when the flow of new information is either too fast or too slow for the particular reader, when the information is too difficult or too simple, or when the writing is too abstract or just plain dull, lacking in vividness and energy.

Reading the essays in this chapter will help you see what makes explanatory writing interesting and informative. You will also get ideas for writing your own essay about a concept, perhaps from the ideas for writing that follow each selection. As you analyze the selections, keep in mind the following assignment that sets out the goals for writing about a concept.

THE WRITING ASSIGNMENT

Explaining Concepts

Write an essay that explains a concept. Choose a concept that interests you and that you want to study further. Consider carefully what your readers already know about the concept and how your essay might add to what they know.

WRITING SITUATIONS FOR EXPLAINING CONCEPTS

Writing that explains concepts is familiar in college and professional life, as these examples show:

- For a presentation at the annual convention of the American Medical Association, an anesthesiologist writes a report on the concept of *awareness during surgery*. He presents evidence that patients under anesthesia, as in hypnosis, can hear; and he also reviews research demonstrating that they can perceive and carry out instructions that speed their recovery. He describes briefly how he applies the concept in his own work: how he prepares patients before surgery, what he tells them while they are under anesthesia, and how their recovery goes.

- A business reporter for a newspaper writes an article about *virtual reality*. She describes the lifelike, three-dimensional experience created by wearing gloves and video goggles wired to a computer. To help readers understand this new concept, she contrasts it with television. For investors, she describes which corporations have shown an interest in the commercial possibilities of virtual reality.

- As part of a group assignment, a college student at a summer biology camp in the Sierra Nevada mountains reads about the condition of mammals at birth. She discovers the distinction between infant mammals that are *altricial* (born nude and helpless within a protective nest) and those that are *precocial* (born well formed with eyes open and ears erect). In her part of a group report, she develops this contrast point by point, giving many examples of specific mammals but focusing in detail on altricial mice and precocial porcupines. Domestic cats, she points out, are an intermediate example—born with some fur but with eyes and ears closed.

- For a final exam in a literature course, a student writes an essay on *scapegoat figures* in literature. He begins by defining the scapegoat concept, emphasizing its origins in psychological studies of social conflict. Then he applies it to one novel and one film, identifying a scapegoated character in each work and using the scapegoat concept to explain how and why each character is blamed unfairly for other characters' troubles.

PRACTICING EXPLAINING CONCEPTS
A COLLABORATIVE ACTIVITY

PART 1. Identify a familiar concept you would like to explain to two or three other students. Some possible concepts are the following:

socialization	osmosis	interval training
representative government	male bonding	federalism
romantic love	photosynthesis	ethnicity
genre	work ethic	role model
hypertext	body image	collaborative learning

After you have chosen a concept, think about what others in the group are likely to know about it and how you can inform them about it in two or three minutes. Consider how you will define the concept and what other strategies you might use—giving examples, comparing it to a better-known concept, and so on—to explain it in an interesting, memorable way.

Then take turns explaining your concepts to one another. After each explanation, the other members should tell the speaker one or two things they learned about the concept and ask questions they still have about it.

PART 2. When you have all explained your concepts, discuss as a group what you learned from the process of explaining.

- How successfully did you estimate listeners' prior knowledge of your concepts?
- What surprised you in listeners' responses to your concept explanation? If you were to repeat your explanation for similar listeners, what would you add, subtract, or change?
- What strategies did you find yourselves using to present your concepts?

A GUIDE TO READING ESSAYS EXPLAINING CONCEPTS

Here you will have the opportunity to read, annotate, and write about your understanding of the concept explanation that follows. Then, guided by a list of explanatory writing strategies, you will reread the essay to examine the particular elements of strong explanatory writing.

First, though, as a reminder of the many possibilities for annotating, here is an illustration of an annotated passage from another explanatory essay, by Deborah Tannen, which appears later in this chapter.

hard to understand

The term "marked" is a (staple) of linguistic theory. It refers to the way language alters the base meaning of a word by adding a linguistic particle that has no meaning on its own. The unmarked form of a word carries the meaning that goes without saying—what you think of when you're not thinking anything special.

9 *necessary*

makes it clearer

Is "base meaning" same as "unmarked form"?

These examples make it even clearer

The unmarked tense of verbs in English is the present—for example, *visit*. To indicate past, you mark the verb by adding *ed* to yield *visited*. For future, you add a word: *will visit*. Nouns are presumed to be singular until marked for plural, typically by adding *s* or *es*, so *visit* becomes *visits* and *dish* becomes *dishes*.

10

Social, not just linguistic

The unmarked forms of most English words also convey "male." Being male is the unmarked (case.) Endings like *ess* and *ette* mark words as "female." Unfortunately, they also tend to mark them for frivolousness. Would you feel safe entrusting your life to a doctorette? Alfre Woodard, who was an Oscar nominee for best supporting actress, says she identifies herself as an actor because "actresses worry about eyelashes and cellulite, and women who are

11 *grammatica term*

Curious authority Not a linguist

another illustration

erfect example of
ow adding "ette"
iminishes the
hing

actors worry about the characters we are playing." Gender markers
pick up extra meanings that reflect common associations with the
female gender: not quite serious, often sexual.

meaning
stereotypes

David Quammen

IS SEX NECESSARY? VIRGIN BIRTH AND OPPORTUNISM IN THE GARDEN

The following selection comes from David Quammen's *Natural Acts: A Sidelong View of Science and Nature* (1985), a collection of his essays, mainly from *Outside,* a magazine for which he has been natural-science columnist. The readers of *Outside* have special interests in nature, outdoor recreation, and the environment, but few have advanced training in ecology or biology. Quammen's books include three novels and another collection of essays, *The Flight of the Iguana* (1988). In this selection, we get a nonscientist's introduction to parthenogenesis: not only to the facts of it but also to its significance in nature.

Read the essay, annotating anything that strikes you as interesting and likely to contribute to your understanding of parthenogenesis. Notice Quammen's attempts to amuse as well as inform, and think about how his playfulness might help readers understand the concept or how it might get in the way. Mark on the text, and write comments or questions in the margins.

Birds do it, bees do it, goes the tune. But the songsters, as usual, would mislead us with drastic oversimplifications. The full truth happens to be more eccentrically nonlibidinous: Sometimes they *don't* do it, those very creatures, and get the same results anyway. Bees of all species, for instance, are notable to geneticists precisely for their ability to produce offspring while doing *without.* Likewise at least one variety of bird—the Beltsville Small White turkey, a domestic dinnertable model out of Beltsville, Maryland—has achieved scientific renown for a similar feat. What we are talking about here is celibate motherhood, procreation without copulation, a phenomenon that goes by the technical name *parthenogenesis.* Translated from the Greek roots: virgin birth.

And you don't have to be Catholic to believe in this one.

Miraculous as it may seem, parthenogenesis is actually rather common throughout nature, practiced regularly or intermittently by at least some species within almost every group of animals except (for reasons still unknown) dragonflies and mammals. Reproduction

1

2

3

by virgin females has been discovered among reptiles, birds, fishes, amphibians, crustaceans, mollusks, ticks, the jellyfish clan, flatworms, roundworms, segmented worms; and among insects (notwithstanding those unrelentingly sexy dragonflies) it is especially favored. The order *Hymenoptera,* including all bees and wasps, is uniformly parthenogenetic in the manner by which males are produced: Every male honeybee is born without any genetic contribution from a father. Among the beetles, there are thirty-five different forms of parthenogenetic weevil. The African weaver ant employs parthenogenesis, as do twenty-three species of fruit fly and at least one kind of roach. The gall midge *Miastor* is notorious for the exceptionally bizarre and grisly scenario that allows its fatherless young to see daylight: *Miastor* daughters cannibalize the mother from inside, with ruthless impatience, until her hollowed-out skin splits open like the door of an overcrowded nursery. But the foremost practitioners of virgin birth—their elaborate and versatile proficiency unmatched in the animal kingdom—are undoubtedly the aphids.

Now no sensible reader of even this can be expected, I realize, to care faintly about aphid biology *qua* aphid biology. That's just asking too much. But there's a larger rationale for dragging you aphidward. The life cycle of these little nebbishy sap-sucking insects, the very same that infest rose bushes and house plants, not only exemplifies *how* parthenogenetic reproduction is done; it also very clearly shows *why*.

First the biographical facts. A typical aphid, which feeds entirely on plant juices tapped off from the vascular system of young leaves, spends winter dormant and protected, as an egg. The egg is attached near a bud site on the new growth of a poplar tree. In March, when the tree sap has begun to rise and the buds have begun to burgeon, an aphid hatchling appears, plugging its sharp snout (like a mosquito's) into the tree's tenderest plumbing. This solitary individual aphid will be, necessarily, a wingless female. If she is lucky, she will become sole founder of a vast aphid population. Having sucked enough poplar sap to reach maturity, she produces—by *live birth* now, and without benefit of a mate—daughters identical to herself. These wingless daughters also plug into the tree's flow of sap, and they also produce further wingless daughters, until sometime in late May, when that particular branch of that particular tree can support no more thirsty aphids. Suddenly there is a change: The next generation of daughters are born with wings. They fly off in search of a better situation.

One such aviatrix lands on an herbaceous plant—say a young climbing bean in some human's garden—and the pattern repeats. She plugs into the sap ducts on the underside of a new leaf, commences feasting destructively, and delivers by parthenogenesis a great brood of wingless daughters. The daughters beget more daughters, those daughters beget still more, and so on, until the poor bean plant is encrusted with a solid mob of these fat little elbowing greedy sisters. Then again, neatly triggered by the crowded conditions, a generation of daughters are born with wings. Away they fly, looking for prospects, and one of them lights on, say, a sugar beet. (The switch from bean to beet is fine, because our species of typical aphid is not inordinately choosy.) The sugar beet before long is covered, sucked upon mercilessly, victimized by a horde of mothers and nieces and granddaughters. Still not a single male aphid has appeared anywhere in the chain.

The lurching from one plant to another continues; the alternation between wingless and winged daughters continues. But in September, with fresh tender plant growth increasingly hard to find, there is another change.

Flying daughters are born who have a different destiny: They wing back to the poplar tree, where they give birth to a crop of wingless females that are unlike any so far. These latest girls know the meaning of sex! Meanwhile, at long last, the starving survivors back on that final bedraggled sugar beet have brought forth a generation of males. The males have wings. They take to the air in quest of poplar trees and first love. *Et voilá.* The mated females lay eggs that will wait out the winter near bud sites on that poplar tree, and the circle is thus completed. One single aphid hatching—call her the *fundatrix*—in this way can give rise in the course of a year, from her own ovaries exclusively, to roughly a zillion aphids.

Well and good, you say. A zillion aphids. But what is the point of it?

The point, for aphids as for most other parthenogenetic animals, is (1) exceptionally fast reproduction that allows (2) maximal exploitation of temporary resource abundance and unstable environmental conditions, while (3) facilitating the successful colonization of unfamiliar habitats. In other words the aphid, like the gall midge and the weaver ant and the rest of their fellow parthenogens, is by its evolved character a galloping opportunist.

This is a term of science, not of abuse. Population ecologists make an illuminating distinction between what they label *equilibrium* and *opportunistic* species. According to William Birky and John Gilbert, from a paper in the journal *American Zoologist:* "Equilibrium species, exemplified by many vertebrates, maintain relatively constant population sizes, in part by being adapted to reproduce, at least slowly, in most of the environmental conditions which they meet. Opportunistic species, on the other hand, show extreme population fluctuations; they are adapted to reproduce only in a relatively narrow range of conditions, but make up for this by reproducing extremely rapidly in favorable circumstances. At least in some cases, opportunistic organisms can also be categorized as colonizing organisms." Birky and Gilbert also emphasize that "The potential for rapid reproduction is the essential evolutionary ticket for entry into the opportunistic lifestyle."

And parthenogenesis, in turn, is the greatest time-saving gimmick   12
in the history of animal reproduction. No hours or days are wasted
while a female looks for a mate; no minutes lost to the act of mating
itself. The female aphid attains sexual maturity and, bang, she
becomes automatically pregnant. No waiting, no courtship, no fooling around. She delivers her brood of daughters, they grow to
puberty and, zap, another generation immediately. If humans
worked as fast, Jane Fonda today would be a great-grandmother.
The time saved to parthenogenetic species may seem trivial, but it is
not. It adds up dizzyingly: In the same time taken by a sexually
reproducing insect to complete three generations for a total of
1,200 offspring, an aphid (assuming the *same* time required for each
female to mature, and the *same* number of progeny in each litter),
squandering no time on courtship or sex, will progress through six
generations for an extended family of 318,000,000.

Even this isn't speedy enough for some restless opportunists.   13
That matricidal gall midge *Miastor,* whose larvae feed on fleeting
eruptions of fungus under the bark of trees, has developed a
startling way to cut further time from the cycle of procreation. Far
from waiting for a mate, *Miastor* does not even wait for maturity.
When food is abundant, it is the *larva,* not the adult female fly, who
is eaten alive from inside by her own daughters. And as those vora-
cious daughters burst free of the husk that was their mother, each
of them already contains further larval daughters taking shape omi-
nously within its own ovaries. While the food lasts, while opportunity endures, no *Miastor* female can live to adulthood without dying
of motherhood.

The implicit principle behind all this nonsexual reproduction, all   14
this hurry, is simple: Don't argue with success. Don't tamper with a
genetic blueprint that works. Unmated female aphids, and gall
midges, pass on their own gene patterns virtually unaltered (except
for the occasional mutation) to their daughters. Sexual reproduction
on the other hand, constitutes, by its essence, genetic tampering.
The whole purpose of joining sperm with egg is to shuffle the genes
of both parents and come up with a new combination that might
perhaps be more advantageous. Give the kid something neither
Mom nor Pop ever had. Parthenogenetic species, during their hur-
ried phases at least, dispense with this genetic shuffle. They stick
stubbornly to the gene pattern that seems to be working. They produce (with certain complicated exceptions) natural clones of themselves.

But what they gain thereby in reproductive rate, in great explo-   15
sions of population, they give up in flexibility. They minimize their
genetic options. They lessen their chances of adapting to unforeseen
changes of circumstance.

Which is why more than one biologist has drawn the same con-   16
clusion as M. J. D. White: "Parthenogenetic forms seem to be

frequently successful in the particular ecological niche which they occupy, but sooner or later the inherent disadvantages of their genetic system must be expected to lead to a lack of adaptability, followed by eventual extinction, or perhaps in some cases by a return to sexuality."

So it *is* necessary, at least intermittently (once a year, for the aphids, whether they need it or not), this thing called sex. As of course you and I knew it must be. Otherwise surely, by now, we mammals and dragonflies would have come up with something more dignified. [17]

READING FOR MEANING

Write at least a page about your understanding of Quammen's essay. Begin by writing a few sentences, stating the main facts that seem to you essential for a basic understanding of parthenogenesis.

Then write about whatever interests you in Quammen's explanation of parthenogenesis. As you write, you may find you need to reread parts of the essay and annotate it further so you can quote phrases or sentences. Don't be surprised if your understanding changes somewhat as you write.

If you have trouble sustaining your writing, consider the following suggestions:

- Comment on Quammen's suggestion that sex is undignified (paragraph 17) or that sexual reproduction involves "genetic tampering" (paragraph 14) or any other idea that intrigues you in this essay.

- At the end of paragraph 10, Quammen says the aphid "is by its evolved character a galloping opportunist." Why does he call it an "opportunist" and why does he refer to its character as "evolved"?

- If the fact that parthenogenesis is so widespread in nature suggests anything to you about human sexual behaviors, explore some of your thoughts about that. Show how your ideas relate to Quammen's ideas.

READING LIKE A WRITER

This section guides you through an analysis of Quammen's writing strategies: *devising a readable plan, using appropriate explanatory strategies, using sources responsibly,* and *engaging readers' interest.* In each part, we describe one strategy briefly and then pose a critical reading and writing task to help you see how Quammen uses that particular strategy to explain the concept of parthenogenesis.

Consider this a writer's introduction to explanatory writing. You will learn even more from the Reading like a Writer activities following other selections in this chapter, and the Guide to Writing Essays Explaining Concepts at the end of this chapter will suggest how you can use these same strategies in your own concept essay.

Devising a Readable Plan

Experienced writers of explanation know that readers have a hard time making their way through new and difficult material. Writers who want readers to understand an explanation and not give up in frustration construct a reader-friendly plan by dividing the information into clearly distinguishable topics. They also give readers a map and road signs to guide them through the explanation. Writers provide a forecasting statement that lets readers know in advance what the topical divisions are going to be; they also provide cues like topic sentences to announce each topic as it comes up, transitions to relate what is coming to what came before, and summaries to remind readers what has been explained already.

ANALYZE. To see how reader friendly the plan of Quammen's essay is, reread the essay and make a topical outline on the text itself. (You can find help in Outlining in Appendix 1, A Catalog of Critical Reading Strategies.) Then skim the text again, underlining the forecasting statement, topic sentences, transitions, and summaries. (Topic sentences may include transitional words as well as a brief summary.)

WRITE. Write several sentences explaining and evaluating Quammen's use of cues to make his explanation readable. Note how well the forecasting statement introduces the topics discussed in the essay. Look at the transitions to see how well they announce the logical relationship between sentences. For example, beginning the second sentence with *but* signals a contrast is being made to the information in the first sentence.

Using Appropriate Explanatory Strategies

When writers organize and present information, they rely on several strategies—the building blocks—of explanatory essays: defining, classifying or dividing, comparing and contrasting, narrating a process, illustrating, and reporting causes or effects. The strategies a writer chooses are determined by the topical divisions and the kinds of information available with which to work. Following are brief descriptions of the writing strategies that are particularly useful in explaining concepts:

Defining: Briefly stating the meaning of the concept or any other word likely to be unfamiliar to readers

Classifying or dividing: Grouping related information about a concept into two or more discrete groups and labeling each group, or dividing a concept into its constituent parts to consider the elements of each part separately

Comparing and contrasting: Pointing out how the concept is similar to and how it is different from another related concept

Narrating a process: Presenting procedures or a sequence of steps as they unfold over time to show the concept in practice

Illustrating: Giving examples, relating anecdotes, listing facts and details, and quoting sources to help readers understand a concept

Reporting causes or effects: Identifying the known causes or effects related to a concept

ANALYZE. Quammen makes good use of all these fundamentally important explanatory strategies: *defining* in paragraphs 1, 8, 11; *classifying* in paragraphs 10 and 11; *comparing and contrasting* in paragraphs 11 through 14 (as well as the analogy between asexual insects and sexual humans that runs through the essay); *narrating a process* in paragraphs 5 through 8; *illustrating* in paragraph 3; and *reporting known effects* in paragraphs 12 through 14. Review Quammen's use of each strategy, and select one to analyze more closely.

WRITE. Write a few sentences, describing how the strategy works. Exactly how does this particular comparison, definition, or whatever help readers understand the concept?

Using Sources Responsibly

Explaining concepts nearly always draws on information from many different sources. Writers often draw on their own experiences and observation, but they almost always do additional research into what others have said about their subject. Referring to sources, particularly to expert ones, always lends authority to an explanation.

How writers treat sources depends on the writing situation. Certain formal situations, such as college assignments or scholarly publications, have prescribed rules for citing and documenting sources. Students and scholars are expected to cite their sources formally because their writing will be judged in part by what they have read and how they have used their reading. For more informal writing occasions—newspaper and magazine articles, for example—readers do not expect writers to include page references or publication information, but they do expect writers to identify their sources.

Experienced writers make judicious decisions about when to summarize, paraphrase, or quote their sources. (Summary reduces the original source to its main ideas: paraphrase retains all the information in the original source but in different words. See Appendix 1 for advice on summarizing and paraphrasing.) They take special care to integrate quotations smoothly into their own texts, deliberately varying the way they do it.

ANALYZE. Quammen quotes sources directly in paragraphs 11 and 16. Nearly all of the information elsewhere in the essay came from published sources, as well. Look closely at the two instances where Quammen quotes sources directly, and try to decide what they contribute to the essay. What advantages might Quammen have seen in quoting these sources, rather than presenting the information in his own words? (Notice particularly how Quammen sets up his own sentence to incorporate the quoted material.)

WRITE. Write a sentence or two, reporting what you learn about Quammen's use of sources.

Engaging Readers' Interest

Most people read explanations of concepts for work or study. Consequently, they do not expect the writing to entertain, but simply to inform them. However, explanations that make clear the concept's importance or that keep readers awake with lively writing are usually appreciated. Writers explaining concepts may engage readers' interest in a variety of ways. For example, they may remind readers of what they very likely know already about the concept. They may assert that they can show readers a new way of using a familiar concept or declare that the concept has greater importance or significance than readers may realize. They can connect the concept, sometimes through metaphor or analogy, to common human experiences. They may present the concept in a humorous way to convince readers that learning about a concept can be painless, or even pleasurable.

Quammen relies on many of these strategies to engage his readers' interest. Keep in mind that his original readers could either read or skip his column. Those who enjoyed and learned from previous Quammen columns would be more likely to try out the first few paragraphs of this one, but Quammen could not count on their having any special interest in parthenogenesis. He has to try to generate that interest—and rather quickly in the first few sentences.

ANALYZE. Reread the essay, annotating ways in which Quammen seeks to engage and hold readers' interest in parthenogenesis. Examine particularly paragraphs 1, 4, 10, and 12. Notice also the analogy to human sexuality and families running through the essay.

WRITE. Write several sentences that describe what you have learned about how Quammen attempts to engage and hold readers' interest in parthenogenesis. What parts seemed most effective? Why?

READINGS

Perry Nodelman

READING AGAINST TEXTS

Perry Nodelman (b. 1942) is a professor of English at the University of Winnipeg, Manitoba, Canada, where he specializes in literary theory and children's literature. Since completing his Ph.D. at Yale, he has published over fifty articles and two books, *Words about Pictures: The Narrative Art of Children's Picture Books* (1988) and *The Pleasures of Children's Literature* (1992).

This selection comes from Nodelman's *The Pleasures of Children's Literature,* a book written for teachers and parents. In one section of the book, Nodelman tries to demonstrate how concepts from contemporary literary theory can suggest new ways for both children and adults to read literature. Here, he introduces the concept of *reading against a text.* To *read against a text* involves paying close attention to its assumptions about social hierarchies, gender, and race, rather than accepting such assumptions unquestioningly.

Before you read, recall a recent novel, television show, or movie that represented politicians, young people, women, recent immigrants, southerners, suburban families, business executives, or some other group. Reflect on how the group was characterized or caricatured—not the surface depiction of a group, but something hidden, unwritten, or unspoken, an assumption the author made.

As you read, annotate details that will contribute to your understanding of what it means to read against a text. Nodelman mentions several classics of children's literature, some of which you may remember from your childhood or have read to your own children.

We can focus on the ways in which books express the values of specific historical periods and cultures only if we remain at some distance from them and allow ourselves to think about how the views they present differ from our own. In other words, we must become conscious of what are sometimes called a text's *absences,* the ideas or assumptions it takes for granted and therefore does not actually assert. Our awareness of absences allows both children and adults to enjoy stories written in different times without assuming that sexist or racist or just plain old-fashioned values in the stories are ones we should share.

In order to *surface* absences—that is, bring them to our consciousness—we must first understand that they are in fact merely assumptions. . . . [H]uman beings have generally taken it for granted that the specific values which define their own ideals—their own ideologies—are in fact absolutely and universally true. In *The Tale of Mr. Jeremy Fisher,* for instance, [Beatrix] Potter simply assumes the universality of the social hierarchy underlying her characters' motivations and responses. The book does not assert that there is a social scale which places water beetles lower than frogs, but takes for granted that there is such a social scale and that everyone knows it. Because writers assume that their specific view of reality is universal, texts act as a subtle kind of propaganda, and tend to manipulate unwary readers into an unconscious acceptance of their values.

But if we notice the absences in a text and define the ideology they imply, we can protect ourselves from unconscious persuasion. Rather than allowing ourselves to become immersed in a text to the point of accepting its description of reality as the only true one, we can define its values and so arrive at a better understanding of our own. In other words, instead of going along with the values a text implies, we can read *against* it.

Surfacing Political Assumptions

The most obvious way of reading against a text is to approach it   4
from a point of view that questions its political and social assumptions. We do not necessarily have to share the values or the point of view we use in this way; we can merely use it as a device to allow us some distance from our assumptions in order to discover the writer's assumptions.

If we don't share [Kenneth] Grahame's assumptions about social   5
hierarchy, for instance, it is not difficult to see how Grahame's *Wind in the Willows* asks readers to take its social hierarchy for granted: the book never questions the assumption of the gentlemanly riverbank animals that the creatures who live in the wild woods are their social and moral inferiors. It would be revealing to think about the events the book describes from the point of view of these citizens of the Wild Woods; in fact, Jan Needle has done just that in his novel *Wild Wood,* which describes how the poverty of the woodland creatures, caused in part by the thoughtlessness of the wealthy Mr. Toad, drives them to rebellion against their supposed superiors; they are not so much thieves and rascals as they are oppressed and deprived. Needle's novel cleverly fills in the absences of Grahame's.

The closer the values of a text come to our own ideologies, the   6
harder it is to read its absences. In some cases it may be impossible. But even then the attempt to do so is worthwhile. We can ask ourselves *why* it is that certain books strike us as being convincingly realistic, and we can help children better understand themselves by encouraging them to do so also.

Surfacing Assumptions about Gender

Another way of reading against a text is to notice its assumptions   7
about gender. . . . As has often been pointed out, gender bias has been so deeply rooted in our culture that words like "he" and "him" traditionally referred to both males and females, but words like "she" and "her" referred only to females. In other words, while a "he" was supposed to be merely a genderless human being, a "she" was specifically female, set apart by gender from the typical state of being human.

Traditionally, writers have assumed that their audience consists   8
of "he's": that is, of either males or females who, while they read, are conscious only of that aspect of their being which is not specifically female—of their basic genderless humanity. But, of course, the

"he's" implied as the audience of literature are no more genderless than the "he's" of traditional grammar. In equating the male with the typically human, both literature and grammar suggest that women are less than human, and that femininity is a sign of inferiority.

The extent to which implications of male superiority color litera- 9 ture becomes apparent to anybody who stops reading as a "typical" human being, without consciousness of gender—as a traditional "he"—and tries to read with a consciousness of gender—as a traditional "she." A girl or a woman can read without ignoring her femaleness, as many feminist literary critics do; a boy or a man can read without ignoring the extent to which his responses are governed by the specific limitations of his maleness.

To read in this way is to become conscious of the absences of lit- 10 erary texts that relate specifically to gender. We can see how Anne Shirley's rebellion and ambition in *Anne of Green Gables* are controlled by the need for her to remain acceptably feminine, a good mother and homemaker. Or we can realize how much *Charlotte's Web* asks us to admire the undemanding, selfless, maternal love that Charlotte offers Wilbur: Charlotte devotes herself to Wilbur at the expense of her own needs in a way many people would find less admirable if she were a male and he a female.

If it is possible to read like a woman, then it should be equally pos- 11 sible to write like one. Feminist literary critics have explored books by women to see if they differ significantly from books by men.

Some critics pursue these investigations from the conviction that 12 women are essentially and inherently different from men, that biological differences create differences in attitude. Others believe that the possibility of differences in attitudes means only that the different experiences society offers women and men have led them to think differently of themselves and of others.

In any case, feminist critics have discovered that women tend not 13 only to write about different aspects of experience—as an obvious example, domestic events rather than adventures in the big world away from home—but also to do so in different ways. For instance, it seems that the way we usually describe the plot of a story or a novel—as a single, unified action that rises toward a climax and then quickly comes to an end—accurately describes the action of many books written by men (and also, of course, of many written by women who have accepted the conventional ideal). But that definition of plot would suggest that the more episodic events of books like *Anne of Green Gables* are amateurish and unexciting. *Anne* has many less intense climaxes rather than one central one, and there's not much unity in its action. Nevertheless, *Anne of Green Gables* is a pleasurable book, even though the pleasure is different from that offered in suspenseful books like *Treasure Island*. Furthermore, many other enjoyable books for both children and adults are similarly episodic—and a large proportion of them are by women. Apparently some women prefer a different kind of pattern of events from the one conventionally assumed to be desirable.

Robert Scholes has likened the pleasure in narrative to that of sexuality. He has suggested that the "archetype of all fiction is the sexual act . . . the fundamental orgastic rhythm of tumescence and detumescence, of tension and resolution, of intensification to the point of climax and consummation" (26). But psychological studies suggest that what Scholes is describing here is typical *male* sexuality—and that female sexuality might just as typically express itself in rhythmic patterns like those of *Anne of Green Gables*. As Beatrice Faust suggests, "Female sexuality can include both intense arousal, which seeks release in orgasm, and a pleasant drift on the plateau level of arousal, which may continue indefinitely" (59). 14

Furthermore, the fact that the care and education of children have traditionally been the domain of women has meant that a large proportion of the writers and editors of texts for children have been (and continue to be) women. Women have largely been responsible for the development of children's literature, so if this literature has distinct traits, they might well be those that can be identified in women's writing in general. If so, then even male writers who try to satisfy the generic characteristics of children's literature would be writing as women. 15

In fact, many children's books by males do have an episodic series of minor climaxes rather than one major one. Perhaps children's literature as a whole is a sort of women's literature. That may explain why so many of the children who are ardent readers are females. 16

But even if we assume that one sort of plot is inherently male and the other inherently female, we should not conclude that only men can enjoy the more conventional plot, and only women the episodic ones—or that if children's literature is a form of women's writing, only girls should enjoy it. For centuries, women have learned to take pleasure in the kinds of plots that seem to be inherently male. There is no reason why men cannot learn to take pleasure from the kinds of plots that seem to be inherently female—and, thus, if these *are* female plots, to develop some insight into the nature of femininity. A world in which both boys and girls had escaped conventional gender assumptions enough to enjoy, equally, *Anne of Green Gables* and *Treasure Island* would be a healthy one. 17

Surfacing Assumptions about Race

Just as the texts of a male-dominated society inevitably express a male view as if it were a universal one, and, thus, ask women readers to think like men, the texts of a white-dominated society inevitably express a white view as if it were a universal one—and, thus, ask black or native American readers to think like whites. Consequently, another way of reading against a text is to surface its 18 assumptions about race. To what degree does the behavior of the characters represent racial stereotypes?

As with traditional statements of praise for the nobility of a [19] woman's sacrifice of her own goals in the service of others, racial stereotypes sometimes mask their disdain under apparent praise. Many texts depict nobly innocent natives or blissfully ingenuous blacks whose lack of sophistication prevents them from taking part in white corruption. The apparent nobility is just a polite way of asserting a belittling deviation from white normalcy.

Furthermore, a sense of racial otherness is sometimes so uncon- [20] scious that it expresses itself in highly subtle ways. A possible example is Paula Fox's award-winning *The Slave Dancer,* a beautifully written book about life on a slave ship, which I had greatly admired. Recently in a children's literature class, however, I was surprised and then convinced by a student's claim that this book expresses a subtle racism. The author has chosen to tell the story of the suffering of captured black slaves from the point of view of a white adolescent who has himself been shanghaied onto the ship, and there seems to be an assumption that young readers of this book would probably identify with such a point of view—not with the blacks who are being so cruelly mistreated, but instead with a white outsider who learns to feel sympathy for their plight. Presumably, then, the audience is white—and perhaps, also, those blacks willing to think about the history of their people from the point of view of a white person.

It is certainly true that the point of view makes the white protag- [21] onist's emotional upset at having to observe suffering seem more important than the physical pain he observes. And if we think about the book in this way, we realize that the blacks in the book are left without a voice, and with no way to speak of their own suffering or tell their own story. We are told of only three words spoken by a black; and one of these is mispronounced.

Works Cited

Faust, Beatrice. *Women, Sex, and Pornography.* Harmondsworth, Middlesex: Penguin, 1981.
Scholes, Robert. *Fabulation and Metafiction.* Urbana: U of Illinois P, 1979.

READING FOR MEANING

Write at least a page, explaining your understanding of the concept of *reading against a text.* Begin by defining some of the other concepts—*absence, surfacing,* and *ideology*—that Nodelman introduces in paragraphs 1 through 3. Then write about anything else in the essay that contributes to your understanding of how readers can read against a text.

If you have difficulty writing a page, consider the following suggestions:

- Write about an occasion when you encountered these ideas in a high-school or college course. What was the occasion, and what was the text? What did you learn? Explain how Nodelman challenges or adds to what you learned.

- Speculate about what use you can make of the reading-against concept. Does Nodelman give you enough information to read this way on your own? If not, what seems incomplete or unclear?

- See again a favorite movie or video, and practice reading against it. Explain what you learn.

- Nodelman asserts certain special advantages for reading against, but consider what you might discover if you read *against* Nodelman's text, questioning *his* assumptions and values.

EXTENDING MEANING THROUGH CONVERSATION. You can learn even more about the concept of *reading against a text* by discussing Nodelman's explanation with other students who have also read the essay. You could begin your conversation by rereading together and discussing a passage you did not understand fully to see how others in the group understood it. Do not be surprised if members of the group understand particular passages differently. Discussing such differences can lead to a better appreciation of how readers' own experience and attitudes influence their interpretations.

You also might try reading against Nodelman's essay or some other text together to see how reading against works as a critical reading strategy. If you have had classroom or other experience reading against—particularly trying to discover hidden assumptions about politics or ideology, gender, and race—you might begin the discussion by sharing your experience with the others in your group. You might then explore the possible value of this way of reading. Discuss whether you agree with Nodelman that "we must become conscious of . . . the ideas or assumptions [texts take] for granted" (paragraph 1).

QUESTIONING TO UNDERSTAND AND REMEMBER. Questioning to understand and remember, a further strategy for reading for meaning, can help you to grasp the meaning of the new information contained in Nodelman's explanation of *reading against a text.* This strategy is explained and illustrated in Appendix 1, A Catalog of Critical Reading Strategies.

READING LIKE A WRITER
DEVISING A READABLE PLAN

Writers of concept explanations know that when something new is being explained, readers may have a hard time understanding it. If readers are not highly motivated, convinced that the concept is important to them and worth the effort required to understand it, they can become frustrated and may stop trying to understand it. Consequently, most writers try to make their explanations readable by the way they organize the information and provide cues to help readers follow from one point to the next.

ANALYZE. Skim the essay to remember how Nodelman organizes his explanation of the concept of reading against a text's assumptions. He divides the concept into main topics and he uses headings to announce each topic in turn. Headings are an easy and graphic way to help readers see how the explanation is organized. In addition to headings, Nodelman uses two other cueing devices to keep readers on track: an introductory forecast of the main topics and topic sentences introducing each topic.

To see how Nodelman forecasts the main topics, search the opening paragraphs for references to the main topics. Underline each main topic the first time it is named. Then look at the beginning of each section of the essay, following the headings. Although the headings announce the main topics, Nodelman begins each section with a topic sentence. Find and underline the topic sentence of each section.

WRITE. Write a few sentences, explaining how the headings and topic sentences in Nodelman's essay helped you as a reader. Explain why, if the headings make it impossible for readers to miss the topics, Nodelman would bother to forecast the topics in the introductory paragraphs and introduce each topic with a topic sentence.

CONSIDERING IDEAS FOR YOUR OWN WRITING

Your instructor, who probably has advanced training in literature, could suggest key concepts in literary study. You might recall concepts from high-school literature classes, or you might want to learn more about concepts like the following: *the gaze, antihero, archetype, picaresque, the absurd, pastoral, realism, New Historicism, reader response, formalism, Harlem Renaissance, carnivalesque.*

You might also be interested in learning about concepts in composition studies or rhetoric. Possibilities include *invention, ethos, freewriting, collaborative writing, cohesion, periodic/cumulative sentences, counterargument, genre, writer's block, logical fallacies, heuristics.*

Choose a concept that intrigues you, and make notes about how you could make your essay readable. For example, consider how you could divide the concept into topics and in what order you might present those topics.

Deborah Tannen

MARKED WOMEN

Deborah Tannen (b. 1945) holds the prestigious title of University Professor in Linguistics at Georgetown University in Washington, D.C.

She has written more than a dozen books and scores of articles. Although most of her writing is addressed to other linguists, Tannen occasionally writes for a more general audience. Some of her research focuses on the ways that a language reflects the society in which it develops, particularly the society's attitudes about gender. Both her 1986 book, *That's Not What I Meant!: How Conversational Style Makes or Breaks Your Relations with Others,* and her 1990 book, *You Just Don't Understand: Women and Men in Conversation,* were best-sellers. This selection comes from an article that was originally published in the *New York Times Magazine* in 1993.

In this essay, Tannen explains the linguistic concept of *markedness,* a concept she calls a "staple of linguistic theory." Linguistic theory is concerned with the form of different languages as well as how they function in society. Although linguistics began with the study of spoken and written language, it now includes the study of any kind of communication as long as it carries meaning. For example, a linguist might study the meaning of body language such as crossing your arms in front of you, cultural icons like Elvis, advertising images like sports car ads featuring sexy women. These are visual rather than verbal, but they are signs that convey meaning to those who know how to read them.

As you read the opening paragraphs of this essay in which Tannen describes what various conference participants are wearing, note anything about their appearance that you find meaningful. What image or images do you think they are hoping to project to the other conference participants?

Some years ago I was at a small working conference of four women and eight men. Instead of concentrating on the discussion I found myself looking at the three other women at the table, thinking how each had a different style and how each style was coherent. 1

One woman had dark brown hair in a classic style, a cross between Cleopatra and Plain Jane. The severity of her straight hair was softened by wavy bangs and ends that turned under. Because she was beautiful, the effect was more Cleopatra than plain. 2

The second woman was older, full of dignity and composure. Her hair was cut in a fashionable style that left her with only one eye, thanks to a side part that let a curtain of hair fall across half her face. As she looked down to read her prepared paper, the hair robbed her of bifocal vision and created a barrier between her and the listeners. 3

The third woman's hair was wild, a frosted blond avalanche falling over and beyond her shoulders. When she spoke she frequently tossed her head, calling attention to her hair and away from her lecture. 4

Then there was makeup. The first woman wore facial cover that made her skin smooth and pale, a black line under each eye and 5 mascara that darkened already dark lashes. The second wore only a light gloss on her lips and a hint of shadow on her eyes. The third had blue bands under her eyes, dark blue shadow, mascara, bright red lipstick and rouge; her fingernails flashed red.

I considered the clothes each woman had worn during the three days of the conference: In the first case, man-tailored suits in primary colors with solid-color blouses. In the second, casual but stylish black T-shirts, a floppy collarless jacket and baggy slacks or a skirt in neutral colors. The third wore a sexy jump suit; tight sleeveless jersey and tight yellow slacks; a dress with gaping armholes and an indulged tendency to fall off one shoulder. 6

Shoes? No. 1 wore string sandals with medium heels; No. 2, sensible, comfortable walking shoes; No. 3, pumps with spike heels. You can fill in the jewelry, scarves, shawls, sweaters—or lack of them. 7

As I amused myself finding coherence in these styles, I suddenly wondered why I was scrutinizing only the women. I scanned the eight men at the table. And then I knew why I wasn't studying them. The men's styles were unmarked. 8

The term "marked" is a staple of linguistic theory. It refers to the way language alters the base meaning of a word by adding a linguistic particle that has no meaning on its own. The unmarked form of a word carries the meaning that goes without saying—what you think of when you're not thinking anything special. 9

The unmarked tense of verbs in English is the present—for example, *visit*. To indicate past, you mark the verb by adding *ed* to yield *visited*. For future, you add a word: *will visit*. Nouns are presumed to be singular until marked for plural, typically by adding *s* or *es*, so *visit* becomes *visits* and *dish* becomes *dishes*. 10

The unmarked forms of most English words also convey "male." Being male is the unmarked case. Endings like *ess* and *ette* mark words as "female." Unfortunately, they also tend to mark them for frivolousness. Would you feel safe entrusting your life to a doctorette? Alfre Woodard, who was an Oscar nominee for best supporting actress, says she identifies herself as an actor because "actresses worry about eyelashes and cellulite, and women who are actors worry about the characters we are playing." Gender markers pick up extra meanings that reflect common associations with the female gender: not quite serious, often sexual. 11

Each of the women at the conference had to make decisions about hair, clothing, makeup and accessories, and each decision carried meaning. Every style available to us was marked. The men in our group had made decisions, too, but the range from which they chose was incomparably narrower. Men can choose styles that are marked, but they don't have to, and in this group none did. Unlike the women, they had the option of being unmarked. 12

Take the men's hair styles. There was no marine crew cut or oily   13
longish hair falling into eyes, no asymmetrical, two-tiered construction to swirl over a bald top. One man was unabashedly bald; the
others had hair of standard length, parted on one side, in natural
shades of brown or gray or graying. Their hair obstructed no views,
left little to toss or push back or run fingers through and, consequently, needed and attracted no attention. A few men had beards.
In a business setting, beards might be marked. In this academic gathering, they weren't.

There could have been a cowboy shirt with string tie or a three-   14
piece suit or a necklaced hippie in jeans. But there wasn't. All eight
men wore brown or blue slacks and nondescript shirts of light colors. No man wore sandals or boots; their shoes were dark, closed,
comfortable, and flat. In short, unmarked.

Although no man wore makeup, you couldn't say the men didn't   15
wear makeup in the sense that you could say a woman didn't wear
makeup. For men, no makeup is unmarked.

I asked myself what style we women could have adopted that   16
would have been unmarked, like the men's. The answer was none.
There is no unmarked woman.

There is no woman's hair style that can be called standard, that   17
says nothing about her. The range of women's hair styles is staggering, but a woman whose hair has no particular style is perceived as
not caring about how she looks, which can disqualify her from many
positions, and will subtly diminish her as a person in the eyes of
some.

Women must choose between attractive shoes and comfortable   18
shoes. When our group made an unexpected trek, the woman who
wore flat, laced shoes arrived first. Last to arrive was the woman in
spike heels, shoes in hand and a handful of men around her.

If a woman's clothing is tight or revealing (in other words, sexy),   19
it sends a message—an intended one of wanting to be attractive, but
also a possibly unintended one of availability. If her clothes are not
sexy, that too sends a message, lent meaning by the knowledge that
they could have been. There are thousands of cosmetic products
from which women can choose and myriad ways of applying them.
Yet no makeup at all is anything but unmarked. Some men see it as a
hostile refusal to please them.

Women can't even fill out a form without telling stories about   20
themselves. Most forms give four titles to choose from. "Mr." carries no meaning other than that the respondent is male. But a
woman who checks "Mrs." or "Miss" communicates not only
whether she has been married but also whether she has conservative tastes in forms of address—and probably other conservative
values as well. Checking "Ms." declines to let on about marriage
(checking "Mr." declines nothing since nothing was asked), but it
also marks her as either liberated or rebellious, depending on the
observer's attitudes and assumptions.

I sometimes try to duck these variously marked choices by giving   21
my title as "Dr."—and in so doing risk marking myself as either
uppity (hence sarcastic responses like "Excuse *me!*") or an over-
achiever (hence reactions of congratulatory surprise like "Good for
you!").

All married women's surnames are marked. If a woman takes her   22
husband's name, she announces to the world that she is married and
has traditional values. To some it will indicate that she is less herself,
more identified by her husband's identity. If she does not take her
husband's name, this too is marked, seen as worthy of comment:
She has *done* something; she has "kept her own name." A man is
never said to have "kept his own name" because it never occurs to
anyone that he might have given it up. For him using his own name is
unmarked.

A married woman who wants to have her cake and eat it too   23
may use her surname plus his, with or without a hyphen. But this
too announces her marital status and often results in a tongue-tying
string. In a list (Harvey O'Donovan, Jonathan Feldman, Stephanie
Woodbury McGillicutty), the woman's multiple name stands out. It
is marked.

I have never been inclined toward biological explanations of gen-   24
der differences in language, but I was intrigued to see Ralph Fasold
bring biological phenomena to bear on the question of linguistic
marking in his book *The Sociolinguistics of Language.* Fasold stresses
that language and culture are particularly unfair in treating women as
the marked case because biologically it is the male that is marked.
While two X chromosomes make a female, two Y chromosomes
make nothing. Like the linguistic markers *s, es,* or *ess,* the Y chromosome doesn't "mean" anything unless it is attached to a root form—
an X chromosome.

Developing this idea elsewhere Fasold points out that girls are   25
born with full female bodies, while boys are born with modified
female bodies. He invites men who doubt this to lift up their shirts
and contemplate why they have nipples.

In his book, Fasold notes "a wide range of facts which demon-   26
strates that female is the unmarked sex." For example, he observes
that there are a few species that produce only females, like the
whiptail lizard. Thanks to parthenogenesis, they have no trouble
having as many daughters as they like. There are no species, however, that produce only males. This is no surprise, since any such
species would become extinct in its first generation.

Fasold is also intrigued by species that produce individuals not   27
involved in reproduction, like honeybees and leaf-cutter ants.
Reproduction is handled by the queen and a relatively few males; the
workers are sterile females. "Since they do not reproduce," Fasold
said, "there is no reason for them to be one sex or the other, so
they default, so to speak, to female."

Fasold ends his discussion of these matters by pointing out that if   28
language reflected biology, grammar books would direct us to use
"she" to include males and females and "he" only for specifically
male referents. But they don't. They tell us that "he" means "he or
she," and that "she" is used only if the referent is specifically female.
This use of "he" as the sex-indefinite pronoun is an innovation introduced into English by grammarians in the eighteenth and nineteenth
centuries, according to Peter Mühlhäusler and Rom Harré in *Pronouns and People.* From at least about 1500, the correct sex-indefinite pronoun was "they," as it still is in casual spoken English. In
other words, the female was declared by grammarians to be the
marked case.

Writing this article may mark me not as a writer, not as a linguist,   29
not as an analyst of human behavior, but as a feminist—which will
have positive or negative, but in any case powerful, connotations for
readers. Yet I doubt that anyone reading Ralph Fasold's book would
put that label on him.

I discovered the markedness inherent in the very topic of gender   30
after writing a book on differences in conversational style based on
geographical region, ethnicity, class, age, and gender. When I was
interviewed, the vast majority of journalists wanted to talk about
the differences between women and men. While I thought I was
simply describing what I observed—something I had learned to do
as a researcher—merely mentioning women and men marked me as
a feminist for some.

When I wrote a book devoted to gender differences in ways of   31
speaking, I sent the manuscript to five male colleagues, asking them
to alert me to any interpretation, phrasing, or wording that might
seem unfairly negative toward men. Even so, when the book came
out, I encountered responses like that of the television talk show
host who, after interviewing me, turned to the audience and asked if
they thought I was male-bashing.

Leaping upon a poor fellow who affably nodded in agreement, she   32
made him stand and asked, "Did what she said accurately describe
you?" "Oh, yes," he answered. "That's me exactly." "And what she
said about women—does that sound like your wife?" "Oh, yes," he
responded. "That's her exactly." "Then why do you think she's
male-bashing?" He answered, with disarming honesty, "Because
she's a woman and she's saying things about men."

To say anything about women and men without marking oneself   33
as either feminist or anti-feminist, male-basher or apologist for men
seems as impossible for a woman as trying to get dressed in the
morning without inviting interpretations of her character.

Sitting at the conference table musing on these matters, I felt sad   34
to think that we women didn't have the freedom to be unmarked
that the men sitting next to us had. Some days you just want to get
dressed and go about your business. But if you're a woman, you
can't, because there is no unmarked woman.

TANNEN / MARKED WOMEN   **183**

READING FOR MEANING

Write at least a page, discussing your understanding of this essay. Begin writing by explaining in your own words what Tannen means by "marked." Then write about anything else in the essay that intrigues you. Before you write, reread all or part of the essay, adding to your annotations any new insights or questions. To help you continue for at least a page, consider the following suggestions:

- In paragraph 11, Tannen explains that word endings like *ess* and *ette* are "gender markers" that "pick up extra meanings that reflect common associations with the female gender: not quite serious, often sexual." Interestingly, words with the *ess* ending like *actress* and *hostess* are still used, whereas words with the *ette* ending like *bachelorette* and *suffragette* are rarely used. Although both endings mark the female gender, the *ette* ending also connotes an imitation (such as *leatherette* for fake leather) or a diminutive (such as *cigarette* for a much smaller cigar). Consider what these additional connotations might suggest about the linguistic marking of the female gender with the *ette* ending.

- Tannen uses the word *style* repeatedly in this essay. In paragraphs 17 and 19, she suggests that clothing and hairstyles, for women at least, always send a message. What message or messages do you think are being sent by the styles of the women attending the conference? What about the men's styles? What relation, if any, do you see between the concepts of style and markedness?

- The word *parthenogenesis* appears in paragraph 26. If you have read the essay at the beginning of this chapter by David Quammen, you should be familiar with the concept of parthenogenesis. Use what you learned from reading Quammen's essay to explain Ralph Fasold's ideas about biology and the linguistic marking of women.

- Explain the possible meaning or significance of "no makeup at all is anything but unmarked. Some men see it as a hostile refusal to please them" (paragraph 19); "Writing this article may mark me not as a writer, not as a linguist, not as an analyst of human behavior, but as a feminist—which will have positive or negative, but in any case powerful, connotations for readers" (paragraph 29); or any other statement that catches your eye.

EXTENDING MEANING THROUGH CONVERSATION. While it is important for you to develop an understanding of the essay on your own, your understanding may grow in surprising ways when you discuss the essay with other students who have also read and thought about it.

You might begin the discussion by pointing to anything you did not understand. Or you might begin by talking about how well Tannen's examples illustrate her assertions about gender and marking.

As you exchange views, you may find that you do not all share the same interpretation or evaluation of the concept. Probe your differences by rereading problematic passages together and discussing how each of you understands them.

READING LIKE A WRITER
EXPLAINING THROUGH ILLUSTRATION

Because concepts are abstractions, they tend to be hard to grasp. One way to explain an abstract concept is through illustration. Illustrations such as examples, anecdotes, descriptive detail, and specific facts and figures provide concrete images readers use to help them grasp abstract concepts.

ANALYZE. To examine Tannen's use of illustration to explain the linguistic concept of markedness, reread paragraphs 1 through 8 and paragraphs 12 through 19. As you read, notice the illustrations Tannen uses and also what she says about these illustrations, how she generalizes first about the women and then about the men. Then look closely at the first two sentences in paragraph 19 to see how she connects the illustrations to the concept of markedness. Finally, consider how Tannen's making the connection explicit, rather than letting you make the connection yourself, helps or hinders you as a reader.

WRITE. In a few sentences, explain what you have learned about how Tannen uses illustration as a strategy for explaining an abstract concept.

CONSIDERING IDEAS FOR YOUR OWN WRITING

If you are interested in studying language and society, you might want to learn about and then explain another linguistic concept such as *semantics, language acquisition, connotation,* or *discourse community,* or a semiotic concept like *signification, code, iconography,* or *popular culture.* Related fields with interesting concepts to learn and write about are gender studies and sociology. Gender studies is concerned with concepts like *femininity, masculinity, objectification,* and *construction of desire.* Sociology uses concepts such as *socialization,* the *family, role model, community,* and *status.*

Choose a concept that you already know well and want to share with others or a concept that you are just learning about.

Philip Elmer-DeWitt

WELCOME TO CYBERSPACE

Philip Elmer-DeWitt (b. 1949) is a *Time* magazine senior editor specializing in computer-related topics, including everything from reviewing video games to explaining basic concepts and new technologies.

This selection is excerpted from an article introducing a special Spring 1995 issue of *Time* magazine on the future uses of cyberspace and its potential impact on the economy and politics.

Elmer-DeWitt's essay introduces and explains the basic concept of *cyberspace*, a concept you may understand quite well. As you read and annotate the essay, think about what Elmer-DeWitt is assuming his readers already know about computers and cyberspace. Mark any places where you think he might be assuming too much or too little prior knowledge on the part of his readers.

It started, as the big ideas in technology often do, with a science-fiction writer. William Gibson, a young expatriate American living in Canada, was wandering past the video arcades on Vancouver's Granville Street in the early 1980s when something about the way the players were hunched over their glowing screens struck him as odd. "I could see in the physical intensity of their postures how *rapt* the kids were," he says. "It was like a feedback loop, with photons coming off the screens into the kids' eyes, neurons moving through their bodies and electrons moving through the video game. These kids clearly *believed* in the space the games projected."

That image haunted Gibson. He didn't know much about video games or computers—he wrote his breakthrough novel *Neuromancer* (1984) on an ancient manual typewriter—but he knew people who did. And as near as he could tell, everybody who worked much with the machines eventually came to accept, almost as an article of faith, the reality of that imaginary realm. "They develop a belief that there's some kind of *actual space* behind the screen," he says. "Some place that you can't see but you know is there."

Gibson called that place "cyberspace," and used it as the setting for his early novels and short stories. In his fiction, cyberspace is a computer-generated landscape that characters enter by "jacking in"—sometimes by plugging electrodes directly into sockets implanted in the brain. What they see when they get there is a three-dimensional representation of all the information stored in "every computer in the human system"—great warehouses and skyscrapers of data. He describes it in a key passage in *Neuromancer* as a place of "unthinkable complexity," with "lines of light ranged in the nonspace of the mind, clusters and constellations of data. Like city lights, receding . . ."

In the years since, there have been other names given to that shadowy space where our computer data reside: the Net, the Web, the Cloud, the Matrix, the Metaverse, the Datasphere, the Electronic Frontier, the information superhighway. But Gibson's coinage may prove the most enduring. By 1989 it had been borrowed by the online community to describe not some science-fiction fantasy but today's increasingly interconnected computer systems—especially the millions of computers jacked into the Internet.

Now hardly a day goes by without some newspaper article, some   5
political speech, some corporate press release invoking Gibson's
imaginary world. Suddenly, it seems, everybody has an E-mail
address, from Hollywood moguls to the Holy See. Billy Graham has
preached on American Online; Vice President Al Gore has held
forth on CompuServe; thousands chose to celebrate New Year's
this year with an online get-together called first Night in
Cyberspace. . . .

Corporations, smelling a land rush of another sort, are scram-   6
bling to stake out their own claims in cyberspace. Every computer
company, nearly every publisher, most communications firms, banks,
insurance companies and hundreds of mail-order and retail firms are
registering their Internet domains and setting up sites on the World
Wide Web. They sense that cyberspace will be one of the driving
forces—if not the primary one—for economic growth in the 21st
century.

All this is being breathlessly reported in the press, which has   7
seized on cyberspace as an all-purpose buzz word that can add
sparkle to the most humdrum development or assignment. For
working reporters, many of whom have just discovered the pleasures of going online, cyber has become the prefix of the day, and
they are spawning neologisms as fast as they can type: cyberphilia,
cyberphobia, cyberwonk, cybersex, cyberslut. A Nexis search of
newspapers, magazines, and television transcripts turned up 1,205
mentions of cyber in the month of January, up from 464 the previous January and 167 in January 1993.

One result of this drum roll is a growing public appetite for a   8
place most people haven't been to and are often hard-pressed to
define. In a *Time*/CNN poll of 800 Americans conducted in January by
Yankelovich Partners, 57% didn't know what cyberspace meant, yet
85% were certain that information technology had made their life
better. They may not know where it is, but they want desperately to
get there. The rush to get online, to avoid being "left behind" in the
information revolution, is intense. Those who find fulfillment in
cyberspace often have the religious fervor of the recently converted.

These sentiments have been captured brilliantly in an IBM ad on   9
TV showing a phalanx of Czech nuns discussing—of all things—the
latest operating system from Microsoft. As they walk briskly
through a convent, a young novice mentions IBM's competing system, called Warp. "I just read about it in *Wired*," she gushes. "You
get true multitasking . . . easy access to the Internet." An older sister
glances up with obvious interest; the camera cuts to the mother
superior, who wistfully confesses, "I'm dying to surf the Net." Fade
as the pager tucked under her habit starts to beep.

Cybernuns.   10

What is cyberspace? According to John Perry Barlow, a rock-'n'-   11
roll lyricist turned computer activist, it can be defined most suc-

cinctly as "that place you are in when you are talking on the telephone." That's as good a place to start as any. The telephone system, after all, is really a vast, global computer network with a distinctive, audible presence (crackling static against an almost inaudible background hum). By Barlow's definition, just about everybody has already been to cyberspace. It's marked by the feeling that the person you're talking to is "in the same room." Most people take the spatial dimension of a phone conversation for granted—until they get a really bad connection or a glitchy overseas call. Then they start raising their voice, as if by sheer volume they could propel it to the outer reaches of cyberspace.

12   Cyberspace, of course, is bigger than a telephone call. It encompasses the millions of personal computers connected by modems—via the telephone system—to commercial online services, as well as the millions more with high-speed links to local area networks, office E-mail systems and the Internet. It includes the rapidly expanding wireless services: microwave towers that carry great quantities of cellular phone and data traffic; communications satellites strung like beads in geosynchronous orbit; low-flying satellites that will soon crisscross the globe like angry bees, connecting folks too far-flung or too much on the go to be tethered by wires. Someday even our television sets may be part of cyberspace, transformed into interactive "teleputers" by so-called full-service networks like the ones several cable-TV companies (including Time Warner) are building along the old cable lines, using fiber optics and high-speed switches.

13   But these wires and cables and microwaves are not really cyberspace. They are the means of conveyance, not the destination: the information superhighway, not the bright city lights at the end of the road. Cyberspace, in the sense of being "in the same room," is an experience, not a wiring system. It is about people using the new technology to do what they are genetically programmed to do: communicate with one another. It can be found in electronic mail exchanged by lovers who have never met. It emerges from the endless debates on mailing lists and message boards. It's that bond that knits together regulars in electronic chat rooms and newsgroups. It is, like Plato's plane of ideal forms, a metaphorical space, a virtual reality.

14   But it is no less real for being so. We live in the age of information, as Nicholas Negroponte, director of M.I.T.'s Media Lab, is fond of pointing out, in which the fundamental particle is not the atom but the bit—the binary digit, a unit of data usually represented as a 0 or 1. Information may still be delivered in magazines and newspapers (atoms), but the real value is in the contents (bits). We pay for our goods and services with cash (atoms), but the ebb and flow of capital around the world is carried out—to the tune of several trillion dollars a day—in electronic funds transfers (bits).

Bits are different from atoms and obey different laws. They are   15
weightless. They are easily (and flawlessly) reproduced. There is an
infinite supply. And they can be shipped at nearly the speed of light.
When you are in the business of moving bits around, barriers of
time and space disappear. For information providers—publishers,
for example—cyberspace offers a medium in which distribution
costs shrink to zero. Buyers and sellers can find each other in
cyberspace without the benefit (or the expense) of a marketing
campaign. No wonder so many businessmen are convinced it will
become a powerful engine of economic growth.

At this point, however, cyberspace is less about commerce than   16
about community. The technology has unleashed a great rush of
direct, person-to-person communications, organized not in the top-
down, one-to-many structure of traditional media but in a many-to-
many model that may—just may—be a vehicle for revolutionary
change. In a world already too divided against itself—rich against
poor, producer against consumer—cyberspace offers the nearest
thing to a level playing field.

Take, for example, the Internet. Until something better comes   17
along to replace it, the Internet *is* cyberspace. It may not reach
every computer in the human system, as Gibson imagined, but it
comes very close. And as anyone who has spent much time there
can attest, it is in many ways even stranger than fiction.

Begun more than 20 years ago as a Defense Department experi-   18
ment, the Internet escaped from the Pentagon in 1984 and spread
like kudzu during the personal-computer boom, nearly doubling
every year from the mid-1980s on. Today 30 million to 40 million
people in more than 160 countries have at least E-mail access to the
Internet; in Japan, New Zealand and parts of Europe the number of
Net users has grown more than 1,000% during the past three years.

One factor fueling the Internet's remarkable growth is its reso-   19
lutely grass-roots structure. Most conventional computer systems
are hierarchical and proprietary; they run on copyright software in a
pyramid structure that gives dictatorial powers to the system operators who sit on top. The Internet, by contrast, is open (nonproprietary) and rabidly democratic. No one owns it. No single
organization controls it. It is run like a commune with 4.8 million
fiercely independent members (called hosts). It crosses national
boundaries and answers to no sovereign. It is literally lawless.

Although graphics, photos, and even videos have started to show   20
up, cyberspace, as it exists on the Internet, is still primarily a text
medium. People communicate by and large through words, typed
and displayed on a screen. Yet cyberspace assumes an astonishing
array of forms, from the utilitarian mailing list (a sort of junk E-mail
list to which anyone can contribute) to the rococo MUDs, or Multi-
User Dungeons (elaborate fictional gathering places that users create one "room" at a time). All these "spaces" have one thing in

common: they are egalitarian to a fault. Anybody can play (provided he or she has the requisite equipment and access), and everybody is afforded the same level of respect (which is to say, little or none). Stripped of the external trappings of wealth, power, beauty and social status, people tend to be judged in the cyberspace of the Internet only by their ideas and their ability to get them across in terse, vigorous prose. On the Internet, as the famous New Yorker cartoon put it, nobody knows you're a dog.

READING FOR MEANING

Write at least a page, exploring your understanding of the concept of cyberspace as it is explained in this essay. Begin by defining the concept briefly in your own words. Then respond to anything in the essay that interests you.

As you reread and your understanding of the essay develops, add your new insights and questions to your annotations. To expand your understanding even further, consider the following suggestions:

- Skim the essay, underlining any words the meaning of which is unclear to you. You might begin with *feedback loop, photons, moguls, the Holy See, nonproprietary.* Look up the words on your list in a recently revised college dictionary, and add to your annotations the dictionary definition that seems most appropriate.

- In paragraph 3, Elmer-DeWitt relates William Gibson's idea that people playing video games "eventually came to accept, almost as an article of faith, the reality of that imaginary realm" behind the screen. Words like *article of faith* and *belief* suggest that video game playing or Internet surfing is comparable in some way to a religious experience. What do you think Gibson is saying about this comparison? If you have any experience playing video games or surfing the Internet, consider how Gibson's description relates to your experience.

- In paragraph 6, Elmer-DeWitt talks about cyberspace as a "vehicle for revolutionary change." Skim the essay looking for anything that indicates the kinds of change he thinks cyberspace could help bring about. Why do you think he associates cyberspace with these changes?

- Explain the possible meaning or significance of "Cyberspace . . . is about people using the new technology to do what they are genetically programmed to do: communicate with one another" (paragraph 13); "Anybody can play (provided he or she has the requisite equipment and access), and everybody is afforded the same level of respect (which is to say, little or none)" (paragraph 20); or any other statement that catches your attention.

- If you have had any firsthand experiences with cyberspace, relate what you have experienced to the concept of cyberspace that Elmer-DeWitt presents in this essay.

EXTENDING MEANING THROUGH CONVERSATION. Discussing Elmer-DeWitt's explanation of cyberspace with other students who have also read the essay may lead you to understand more than you understood on your own. You could begin the conversation by pointing to a specific sentence or passage that you did not understand to learn how the others interpreted it. Or you could tell the others what you wrote, perhaps in response to one of the suggestions listed above, to see what they think. Or you could begin a discussion by taking turns saying how your experiences in cyberspace either support or contradict what Elmer-DeWitt says about it.

After the conversation has begun, try not to stray too far from Elmer-DeWitt's essay. Refocus on the essay by finding a specific statement that relates to what your group has been saying or that you think needs to be clarified, extended, or questioned.

READING LIKE A WRITER
EXPLAINING THROUGH COMPARISON AND CONTRAST

One of the best ways of explaining something new is to relate it—through comparison or contrast—to something that is already known. A comparison points out similarities between what is already known and what is being explained; a contrast points out differences. Sometimes writers use both comparison and contrast; sometimes they use only one.

ANALYZE. Reread paragraphs 11 through 15, noting Elmer-DeWitt's comparison between cyberspace and the telephone as well as the contrast between bits and atoms. Look at the comparison and the contrast closely and consider what role each plays in explaining the concept of cyberspace.

WRITE. Write a few sentences, reporting what you have found.

COMPARE. Look at any other essay in this chapter that uses comparison or contrast to see the role it plays in explaining that essay's concept. For example, look at paragraphs 1 through 8 and 12 through 20 in Deborah Tannen's explanation of *marked forms,* or look at paragraphs 1, 7, 9, 10, and 14 through 16 in Csikszentmilhalyi's explanation of the *autotelic self.*

Write another sentence or two explaining how the comparison or contrast contributes to your understanding of the concept explained in that essay.

CONSIDERING IDEAS FOR YOUR OWN WRITING

If you know something about computers and cyberspace, you might consider writing about one of the concepts Elmer-DeWitt mentions but does not explain in any detail, such as *jacking in, information superhighway,* or *virtual reality.* Or you could explain some other computer-related concept like *interactivity, virtual community,* or *Usenet.* An alternative to these concepts from the fields of computer science and communications might be a concept from business or some other engineering or technological area such as *automotive design.* Some business concepts you might consider explaining are *biotechnology, junk bonds, portfolio, progressive tax, management style, contingent worker,* and *escrow.* In automotive design, you might consider *ergonomics, torque, aerodynamic,* or *fuel injection.* To find information about concepts that are new, you would need to look at current newspapers, books, and magazines in the field.

Choose a concept and write down some questions you would try to answer for your readers to help them understand the concept. Also think of some comparisons or contrasts you could use to help explain the concept.

Mihaly Csikszentmilhalyi

THE AUTOTELIC SELF

Mihaly Csikszentmilhalyi has enjoyed a distinguished career at the University of Chicago, where he is professor and former chairperson of the Department of Psychology. His special interest has been the psychology of creativity. His scholarly publications include *Beyond Boredom and Anxiety* (1977) and *The Creative Vision* (1976). In addition, he has regularly written for newspapers and magazines and has appeared on television in the United States (notably on the *Nova* series), England, and Italy.

This selection comes from Csikszentmilhalyi's most recent book, *Flow: The Psychology of Optimal Experience* (1990), a national bestseller. As Csikszentmilhalyi describes it, the book presents to nonspecialist readers "decades of research on the positive aspects of human experience—joy, creativity, the process of total involvement I call *flow.*" This section focuses not on the concept of *flow* but on the related concept of the *autotelic self,* a set of personal characteristics that both enable flow and benefit from it. Csikszentmilhalyi's term for this concept comes from two Greek roots—*auto* meaning "self" and *telos* meaning "goal"—and he defines the autotelic self as "the self that has self-contained goals."

Before you read, reflect on one or two special moments in your life when you confidently took on some challenge not imposed by someone else, never lost sight of your goal, and became completely, unself-consciously immersed in what you were doing. How did this moment come about? How did you feel during and after? What did you accomplish? As you read, annotate any characteristics of the autotelic self that you find interesting or striking or that you have trouble understanding.

A person who is never bored, seldom anxious, involved with what goes on . . . most of the time may be said to have an autotelic self. The term literally means "a self that has self-contained goals," and it reflects the idea that such an individual has relatively few goals that do not originate from within the self. For most people, goals are shaped directly by biological needs and social conventions, and therefore their origin is outside the self. For an autotelic person, the primary goals emerge from experience evaluated in consciousness, and therefore from the self proper.

    . . . [T]he rules for developing such a self are simple. . . . Briefly, they can be summarized as follows:

    1. *Setting goals.* . . . [O]ne must have clear goals to strive for. A person with an autotelic self learns to make choices—ranging from lifelong commitments, such as getting married and settling on a vocation, to trivial decisions like what to do on the weekend or how to spend the time waiting in the dentist's office—without much fuss and the minimum of panic.

    Selecting a goal is related to the recognition of challenges. If I decide to learn tennis, it follows that I will have to learn to serve, to use my backhand and forehand, to develop my endurance and my reflexes. Or the causal sequence may be reversed: because I enjoyed hitting the ball over the net, I may develop the goal of learning how to play tennis. In any case goals and challenges imply each other.

    As soon as the goals and challenges define a system of action, they in turn suggest the skills necessary to operate within it. If I decide to quit my job and become a resort operator, it follows that I should learn about hotel management, financing, commercial locations, and so on. Of course, the sequence may also start in reverse order: what I perceive my skills to be could lead to the development of a particular goal that builds on those strengths—I may decide to become a resort operator because I see myself as having the right qualifications for it.

    And to develop skills, one needs to pay attention to the results of one's actions—to monitor the feedback. To become a good resort operator, I have to interpret correctly what the bankers who might lend me money think about my business proposal. I need to know what features of the operation are attractive to customers and what features they dislike. Without constant attention to feedback I would soon become detached from the system of action, cease to develop skills, and become less effective.

    One of the basic differences between a person with an autotelic self and one without it is that the former knows that it is she who has chosen whatever goal she is pursuing. What she does is not random, nor is it the result of outside determining forces. This fact results in two seemingly opposite outcomes. On the one hand, having a feeling of ownership of her decisions, the person is more strongly dedicated to her goals. Her actions are reliable and internally controlled. On the other hand, knowing them to be her own, she can more easily modify her goals whenever the reasons for preserving them no longer make sense. In that respect, an autotelic person's behavior is both more consistent and more flexible.

2. *Becoming immersed in the activity.* After choosing a system of action, a person with an autotelic personality grows deeply involved with whatever he is doing. Whether flying a plane nonstop around the world or washing dishes after dinner, he invests attention in the task at hand. 8

To do so successfully one must learn to balance the opportunities for action with the skills one possesses. Some people begin with unrealistic expectations, such as trying to save the world or to become millionaires before the age of twenty. When their hopes are dashed, most become despondent, and their selves wither from the loss of psychic energy expended in fruitless attempts. At the other extreme, many people stagnate because they do not trust their own potential. They choose the safety of trivial goals, and arrest the growth of complexity at the lowest level available. To achieve involvement, . . . one must find a relatively close mesh between the demands of the environment and one's capacity to act. 9

Involvement is greatly facilitated by the ability to concentrate. People who suffer from attentional disorders, who cannot keep their minds from wandering, always feel left out of the flow of life. They are at the mercy of whatever stray stimulus happens to flash by. To be distracted against one's will is the surest sign that one is not in control. Yet it is amazing how little effort most people make to improve control of their attention. If reading a book seems too difficult, instead of sharpening concentration we tend to set it aside and instead turn on the television, which not only requires minimal attention, but in fact tends to diffuse what little it commands with choppy editing, commercial interruptions, and generally inane content. 10

3. *Paying attention to what is happening.* Concentration leads to involvement, which can only be maintained by constant inputs of attention. Athletes are aware that in a race even a momentary lapse can spell complete defeat. A heavyweight champion may be knocked out if he does not see his opponent's uppercut coming. The basketball player will miss the net if he allows himself to be distracted by the roaring of the crowd. The same pitfalls threaten anyone who participates in a complex system: to stay in it, he must keep investing psychic energy. The parent who does not listen closely to his child undermines the interaction, the lawyer whose attention lapses may forfeit the case, and the surgeon whose mind wanders may lose the patient. 11

Having an autotelic self implies the ability to sustain involvement. Self-consciousness, which is the most common source of distraction, is not a problem for such a person. Instead of worrying about how he is doing, how he looks from the outside, he is wholeheartedly committed to his goals. In some cases it is the depth of involvement that pushes self-consciousness out of awareness, while 12 sometimes it is the other way around: it is the very lack of self-consciousness that makes deep involvement possible. The elements of the autotelic personality are related to one another by links of mutual causation. It does not matter where one starts—whether one chooses goals first, develops skills, cultivates the ability to concentrate, or gets rid of self-consciousness. One can start anywhere, because once the flow experience is in motion the other elements will be much easier to attain.

A person who pays attention to an interaction instead of worrying about the self obtains a paradoxical result. She no longer feels like a separate individual, yet her self becomes stronger. The autotelic individual grows beyond the limits of individuality by investing psychic energy in a system in which she is included. Because of this union of the person and the system, the self emerges at a higher level of complexity. This is why 'tis better to have loved and lost than never to have loved at all. 13

The self of a person who regards everything from an egocentric perspective may be more secure, but it is certain to be an impoverished one relative to that of a person who is willing to be committed, to be involved, and who is willing to pay attention to what is happening for the sake of the interaction rather than purely out of self-interest. 14

During the ceremony celebrating the unveiling of Chicago's huge outdoor Picasso sculpture in the plaza across from City Hall, I happened to be standing next to a personal-injury lawyer with whom I was acquainted. As the inaugural speech droned on, I noticed a look of intense concentration on his face, and that his lips were moving. Asked what he was thinking, he answered that he was trying to estimate the amount of money the city was going to have to pay to settle suits involving children who got hurt climbing the sculpture. 15

Was this lawyer lucky, because he could transform everything he saw into a professional problem his skills could master, and thus live in constant flow? Or was he depriving himself of an opportunity to grow by paying attention only to what he was already familiar with, and ignoring the aesthetic, civic, and social dimensions of the event? Perhaps both interpretations are accurate. In the long run, however, looking at the world exclusively from the little window that one's self affords is always limiting. Even the most highly respected physicist, artist, or politician becomes a hollow bore and ceases to enjoy life if all he can interest himself in is his limited role in the universe. 16

READING FOR MEANING

Write at least a page about anything in the essay that contributes to your understanding of the autotelic self. Begin by noting what was for you the single most important or unexpected characteristic of the autotelic self. As you write, you may need to reread all or part of this selection. Annotate material that may be useful in your writing, and quote some of this material if it helps you develop your ideas.

If you have difficulty continuing for at least a page, consider these suggestions:

- Reread the anecdote about the lawyer in paragraphs 15 and 16. Do you think Csikszentmilhalyi is saying that the lawyer does or does not have an autotelic self? Specifically, what characteristics of the autotelic self does the lawyer appear to possess or to lack? Based on this example, do you think an autotelic self is a good thing to have? Why or why not?

- Briefly relate an incident when you or another person you know displayed an autotelic self, explaining what specifically exemplifies an autotelic self.

- Apply the concept of the autotelic self to one of the autobiographical essays you read in chapter 2. Indicate whether the person has an autotelic self, and what makes you think so.

- Near the end of the first paragraph, Csikszentmilhalyi asserts that people get their goals either from "outside the self" through "biological needs and social conventions" or from "the self proper" through "experience evaluated in consciousness." Why do you suppose he thinks of "biological needs and social conventions" as coming from outside the self? Explain whether you think it's desirable or even possible to escape one's own biological needs or to go one's own way, rather than the way of the society in which one lives?

- Speculate about the conditions for becoming an autotelic self. Is it easier for a man than for a woman? Is it more likely if you have money, leisure time, or a certain kind of education? Can it be achieved in a small, isolated community? Connect your speculations to details in the selection.

EXTENDING MEANING THROUGH CONVERSATION. You might be able to improve your understanding of the concept of the autotelic self by discussing Csikszentmilhalyi's explanation with one or two other students. If there is something specific you do not understand, reread the passage together and then discuss its meaning. Or you could begin by seeing what everyone thinks of the paradox Csikszentmilhalyi describes in paragraph 13.

Another way to start the conversation might be to find out if everyone in the group agrees with Csikszentmilhalyi on the value of having an autotelic self or agrees in their interpretation of the concluding anecdote about the lawyer. If you do not agree, discussing your differences could be illuminating.

SUMMARIZING. Summarizing, a further strategy for reading for meaning, helps the reader to better understand a writer's explanation of a concept by distilling the important details in an essay. To write a summary of "The Autotelic Self," follow the guidelines on Summarizing in Appendix 1, A Catalog of Critical Reading Strategies.

READING LIKE A WRITER
EXPLAINING THROUGH NARRATING A PROCESS

To explain certain concepts, writers may need to describe what happens over a period of time. For example, Quammen (in paragraphs 5 through 8) outlines the stages in the aphid reproductive cycle from a single aphid hatching in March from an egg that has been dormant all winter, through a series of generations of females produced by parthenogenetic reproduction, to the birth in September of a generation of males who mate with females who then lay eggs that wait dormant during the winter for the March hatchling that starts the cycle all over again. To understand precisely what parthenogenesis is, readers need this kind of overview of the process.

Whereas Quammen devotes a few paragraphs to explaining the cycle of parthenogenesis, Csikszentmilhalyi uses the strategy of narrating a process as the organizing strategy for his entire explanation. He could have explained the concept of the autotelic self in some other way, but showing how it is developed enables him to explain each element that makes up the autotelic self, and to show how these elements relate to one another. In addition, explaining the process of developing an autotelic self might anticipate readers' most likely question: How can I get one?

ANALYZE. Reread the essay, labeling in the margin each new stage in the process as it is introduced. Annotate anyplace where you find the narration confusing, where you need more information to bridge a gap, where you are given too much information, or where you have any other problem following the process. Also note any sections that are especially easy for you to follow and that give you the most helpful information.

WRITE. Write several sentences, reporting what you discovered about what writers can do in explanatory essays to help readers understand a process.

CONSIDERING IDEAS FOR YOUR OWN WRITING

The work of psychologists and psychological counselors has produced countless concepts that name stages of cognitive development, personality types, strategies of thinking and problem solving, aspects of memory, and types of mental disorder. Some examples are *hypochondriasis, mood disorders, autism, Hawthorne effect, short-term memory, tip-of-the-tongue phenomenon, social cognition, assimilation/accommodation.* Textbooks and handbooks or encyclopedias used by psychologists and counselors offer many possibilities. For example, in your college library you could scan the *Encyclopedia of Psychology* and *DSM-V (Diagnostic and Statistical Manual of Mental Disorders).*

Melissa McCool

REINCARNATION

Melissa McCool wrote this essay in her first-year composition course.

Reincarnation is a defining belief of several major Asian religions, notably Buddhism and Hinduism. Although it is not part of the Western Judeo-Christian tradition, interest in it has always been present in the United States. Several major writers have written about reincarnation or advocated it since the eighteenth century. Since late in the nineteenth century, the American Theosophical Society has nourished the concept; and, more recently, the New Age movement has embraced it.

Before you read, recall what you know, if anything, about reincarnation. With whom do you associate this belief? As you read, annotate details of the essay that contribute to your understanding of reincarnation and its twin concept of *karma.*

Recently, actor and New Age author Shirley MacLaine was a guest on the David Letterman show. As she discussed some of her experiences, Letterman jokingly asked, "Now, was that in your fourth or fifth life?" The audience roared with laughter, as MacLaine stared at Letterman, visibly annoyed. Readers of her books know that reincarnation is one of her most cherished beliefs, and it certainly must have upset her to have Letterman dismiss this ancient belief as a trivial joke in front of millions of viewers. Many Americans, unfortunately, have misconceptions about reincarnation because it is not a familiar concept in Judeo-Christian society. It is often looked on as a passing New Age fad. In fact, however, reincarnation has a rich history and hundreds of millions of present-day believers worldwide, including, surprisingly, millions of Americans.

In simplest terms, reincarnation is the belief that the soul passes from one body to another through a series of different lives. Some believe that the soul is reincarnated in a new body immediately after death, while others believe that it is reincarnated after some time has passed, perhaps while the soul rests somewhere else in the universe (Kelly 384). This immortal soul-self is neither body, nor mind, nor rationality, nor ego, but rather an invisible "subjective center of human personality" (Sharma 68). In effect, the soul is three dimensional: past, present, and future (Sharma 100). Ultimately, each soul has the same potential to attain spiritual perfection, but some will reach this end sooner than others. The freedom of will granted to individuals influences the choice of speed, hesitation, or even retreat on the path to spiritual perfection. Therefore, reincarnationists insist that at the very core of our nature we possess the right and responsibility to choose the path we will take.

Within the context of choice, reincarnation can be better under- 3
stood. The entire blueprint of our development and rebirth is determined by the choices that we make. Every action has a reaction, and
every decision has consequences—either positive, neutral, or negative. This is the moral law of cause and effect, or *karma*. This law of
just retribution extends over a soul's various incarnations: the soul
may reap in one lifetime what it has sown in another (Humphreys
15). For instance, someone who is generous with his or her money
by giving it to needy people in one lifetime may in a following life win
the lottery. Or, a person who performs acts of senseless violence in
one lifetime may be the victim of similar crimes in the next life. In
this way, karma can explain the inequalities in life that otherwise
seem unfair.

It is difficult for many Westerners to take reincarnation seri- 4
ously because it seems so foreign to the Judeo-Christian tradition.
However, reincarnation is not in itself at odds with Christian,
Jewish, or any other ideology. Rather, reincarnation is a philosophy
that can be integrated into many different religious beliefs: one
may be a reincarnationist and also a Christian, a Hindu, a Buddhist, a
Jew.

In fact, belief in a concept related to reincarnation was widespread 5
among early Christians. To attract converts after Christianity separated from Judaism in the first century A.D., Christians began preach-
ing that when true believers died, their souls lived on in heaven. St.
Paul, for example, preached "Brethren, be not deceived. God is not
mocked, for whatever a man sows that shall he reap" (quoted in
Humphreys 16). There is no evidence, however, that the early Christians ever believed in reincarnation as it had come to be defined by
Eastern religions (Kelly 386). At the Council of Constantinople in
A.D. 551, the Christian church leaders declared the concept of reincarnation as heresy. They reasoned that people had to be personally
responsible for their sins. They believed that baptism, an important
Christian practice, washed away all sins and relieved the person of
any guilt or punishment. They decided that "each soul had to be created fresh for each person and only had one lifetime on earth" (Kelly
387). Regardless of the decision made in A.D. 551, it may be pointed
out that in Christianity (and other religions that officially reject reincarnation) the goal is spiritual perfection in a believer's lifetime. Reincarnation simply allows the individual more than one lifetime to
achieve spiritual perfection.

In other religious traditions, such as Buddhism and Hinduism, the 6
principle of reincarnation is an accepted reality. Some groups of people, such as the Tibetans and Indians, structure their entire social systems around belief in reincarnation. For example, Tibetans believe
that the Dalai Lama, the spiritual and temporal leader of the six million Tibetan people, chose to be reborn for the purpose of serving
other human beings. The current Dalai Lama, Tenzin Gyato, was rec-

ognized at the age of two as the reincarnation of his predecessor, the thirteenth Dalai Lama. As the leader of the Tibetan people, Gyato is recognized by most of the world as a great political and spiritual leader. In 1989, he was awarded the Nobel Peace Prize for leading Tibet's passive struggle against the Chinese. When the fourteenth Dalai Lama dies, the Tibetan government will not seek to appoint a successor, but rather to discover a child in whom the Dalai Lama has been reincarnated.

Many great Western thinkers throughout history have pondered the idea of the immortal soul, regardless of religious tradition. As early as the sixth century B.C., Greek and Roman philosophers and intellectuals pondered the idea of the immortal soul. In fact, the most influential philosophers of ancient Greece, Socrates and Plato, discussed reincarnation quite openly. As reported by Plato in the *Phaedo,* a dialogue from the last day of Socrates' life, Socrates commented, "I am confident that there truly is such a thing as living again, and that the living spring from the dead, and that the souls of the dead are in existence, and that the good souls have a better portion than the evil" (quoted in Head and Cranston 211). Plato explained his belief in the immortal soul in terms of motion: "Every soul is immortal—for whatever is in perpetual motion is immortal" (quoted in Head and Cranston 214). The teachings of Socrates and Plato have greatly influenced the modern fields of philosophy, sociology, and theology.

The Renaissance and Reformation produced a rebirth of progressive ideals and the abstract search for truth, a search that led to a revival of Western interest in reincarnation. The Italian painter and sculptor Leonardo da Vinci accepted the idea of the preexistence of the soul. During the Enlightenment, Voltaire, David Hume, and Immanuel Kant alluded to and wrote about reincarnation. Hence, history is saturated with references to reincarnation by many of the most enlightened people in Europe, and similar references can be found in the writings of American authors.

Most Americans are probably unaware of how many of their fellow citizens take reincarnation seriously and how influential the concept has been during the course of the history of our country. David Letterman would probably be surprised to know that several opinion polls in the 1980s "revealed that more than 20 percent of the American public believe in some form of reincarnation" (Kelly 384). In addition, several American religious leaders and other intellectuals have expressed their interest or belief in reincarnation. A group of psychologists has developed a counseling approach called post-life therapy that explores "traumatic events believed to have occurred in a patient's previous incarnations" (Kelly 384).

From a book that collects statements of belief in some form of reincarnation by Western thinkers over the centuries (Head and Cranston), I have selected several statements by famous American

intellectuals and leaders. These statements show how seriously reincarnation has been taken by some Americans almost from the beginning of the United States. This selection may make the 20-percent
figure less surprising and make Shirley MacLaine seem less of a New
Age weirdo.

Benjamin Franklin (1706–1790), statesman, scientist, and philoso-   11
pher: "Thus, finding myself to exist in the world, I believe I shall, in
some shape or other, always exist; and, with all the inconveniences
human life is liable to, I shall not object to a new edition of mine,
hoping, however, that the *errata* of the last may be corrected."

Ralph Waldo Emerson (1803–1882), author: "As far back as I can   12
remember I have unconsciously referred to the experiences of a previous state of existence."

Emily Dickinson (1830–1886), poet: "Afraid? Of whom am I   13
afraid? Not death; for who is he? . . . /Twere odd I fear a thing / That
comprehendeth me / In one or more existences / At Deity's decree."

Henry Ford (1863–1947), inventor and businessperson: "I   14
adopted the theory of Reincarnation when I was twenty-six. . . .
Religion offered nothing to the point. . . . Even work could not give
me complete satisfaction. Work is futile if we cannot utilize the
experience we collect in one life in the next. When I discovered
Reincarnation it was as if I had found a universal plan. I realized that
there was a chance to work out my ideas. Time was no longer limited. I was no longer a slave to the hands of the clock. . . . The discovery of Reincarnation put my mind at ease. . . . If you preserve a
record of this conversation, write it so that it puts men's minds at
ease. I would like to communicate to others the calmness that the
long view of life gives to us."

Robert Frost (1874–1963), poet: "I'd like to get away from earth   15
awhile / And then come back to it and begin over. / May no fate will-
fully misunderstand me / and half grant what I wish and snatch me
away / Not to return."

Norman Mailer (b. 1923), author, has this to say in a biography of   16
Marilyn Monroe: "Yet if we are to understand Monroe, and no one
has . . . why not assume that [she] may have been born with a des-
perate imperative formed out of all those previous debts and failures of her whole family of souls. . . . To explain her at all, let us
hold to that karmic notion as one more idea to support in our mind
while trying to follow the involuted pathways of her life."

Reincarnation, it seems, is not so much a religion as it is a concept   17
that has been fundamental in some religions and easily accommo-
dated by others. It has had a surprisingly persistent appeal to American thinkers over the last three hundred years. The 1980s surveys
and the popularity of Shirley MacLaine's books show that the appeal
of reincarnation to Americans may be increasing. If so, the explanation could lie in Americans' growing interest in Asian religions since
the 1950s (Long 269) and the increase in Asian immigrants to this
country since the mid-1960s. The concept, with its twin concept of

karma, is easy to understand and seems to provide some people the reassurance Henry Ford experienced. Perhaps that fact, more than anything else, explains its appeal to so many Americans.

Works Cited

Head, Joseph, and S. L. Cranston, eds. *Reincarnation.* New York: Julian-Crown, 1977.

Humphreys, Christmas. *Karma and Rebirth.* London: Curzon, 1983.

Kelly, Aidan A. "Reincarnation and Karma." *New Age Encyclopedia.* Ed. J. Gordon Melton. New York: Gale Research, 1990.

Long, J. Bruce. "Reincarnation." *The Encyclopedia of Religion.* Ed. Mircea Eliade. 16 vols. New York: Macmillan, 1987.

Sharma, Ishwar Chandra. *Cayce, Karma, and Reincarnation.* New York: Harper, 1975.

READING FOR MEANING

Write at least a page, exploring your understanding of reincarnation. Begin by briefly summarizing McCool's explanation. Then write about anything else in the essay or in your own experience that contributes to your understanding of reincarnation. As you write, you may need to reread all or part of McCool's essay. Annotate material that may be useful in your writing. Quote some of this material if it helps you develop your understanding.

If you have difficulty continuing for at least a page, think about the following suggestions:

- Explain briefly the concept of karma, and describe the relation between it and reincarnation.

- Describe what you knew about reincarnation before reading McCool's essay. Point to particular places in the essay where your prior knowledge was confirmed or contested.

- Explore any connections between reincarnation and your religious beliefs. Does it remind you of any aspect of your beliefs, or does it seem wholly foreign?

- Explain the possible meaning or significance of "This immortal soul-self is neither body, nor mind, nor rationality, nor ego, but rather an invisible subjective center of human personality'" (paragraph 2); "every decision has consequences—either positive, neutral, or negative" (paragraph 3); or "The Renaissance and Reformation produced a rebirth of progressive ideals and the abstract search for truth" (paragraph 8); or any other passage that you find intriguing.

EXTENDING MEANING THROUGH CONVERSATION. To expand your understanding of McCool's essay, discuss it with two or three other students in the class. You might begin by taking turns telling the others what you found most interesting or surprising about McCool's explanation. Or you could discuss one of the suggestions listed above. Another way to begin might be to see whether reincarnation is a tenet of the religious beliefs of anyone in your group. If not, you might see whether you all agree with McCool's assertion that "reincarnation is a philosophy that can be integrated into many different religious beliefs" (paragraph 4).

READING LIKE A WRITER
USING SOURCES

Writers explaining concepts rely on published sources. Because you will want to search out established information in published sources and integrate these sources smoothly into your essay, you may find it helpful to evaluate McCool's use of sources. McCool follows the documentation style of the Modern Language Association. You can find directions for this style in Appendix 2, Strategies for Research and Documentation.

ANALYZE. Begin by reviewing the sources in the works-cited list at the end of McCool's essay. What can you tell about them from their authors, titles, publishers, and dates? Do they seem similar or diverse? Then annotate each use of these sources in the essay. Note the frequency of citations in relation to McCool's own words. Consider the contribution each quotation makes to the essay. What, specifically, does each quotation add to the explanation of reincarnation and to illustrating its significance to American readers? Note, also, that McCool sometimes cites sources without quoting from them. To what effect?

WRITE. Write several sentences, reporting what you learn about McCool's use of sources in her essay.

CONSIDERING IDEAS FOR YOUR OWN WRITING

Religious studies, world religions, and philosophy offer many possible concepts. If reincarnation interests you, you might want to follow up on McCool's essay by writing about *karma*. Or you could skim the two encyclopedias in her list of works cited or a text you are using in one of your classes, looking for a concept that interests you. Some possibilities are *animism, ancestor worship, pantheism, polytheism, mysticism, free will, Platonic forms, Jungian archetypes, halakah, Calvinism, fundamentalism*.

THINKING ABOUT WHAT MAKES ESSAYS
EXPLAINING CONCEPTS EFFECTIVE

In this chapter, you have been learning how to read essays explaining concepts—reading for meaning and reading like a writer. Before writing in this genre yourself, review what you have learned about what makes concept explanations successful.

ANALYZE. Choose one reading from this chapter that you think works especially well as an example of good explanatory writing. Reread the selection, adding annotations about what makes this essay work well as an explanation. To begin, consider the selection's purpose and how well it achieves that purpose for its particular readers. Then focus on how well the selection

- devises a readable plan
- uses appropriate explanatory writing strategies
- uses sources responsibly
- engages readers' interest

You can complete this activity on your own, or your instructor may ask you to work collaboratively with a small group of other students who have chosen the same reading. If you work with others, take time initially for everyone to reread the selection thoughtfully, adding to their annotations as suggested above. Then discuss your reasons for thinking that this concept explanation works well. Although you may all agree that the essay is good, do not be surprised if you do not agree on the specifics. Take notes on what in the essay you think works well and what the group is divided about.

WRITE. Write at least a page explaining and justifying your choice of this reading as an example of effective explanatory writing. Assume that your readers—your instructor and classmates—have read the selection but will not remember many details. They also may not remember it as an especially successful concept explanation. Therefore, you will want to use details and refer to specific parts of the reading as you explain how it works well as a concept explanation and seek to justify your evaluation of its effectiveness. You need *not* argue that it is the best reading in the chapter or that it is flawless, only that it is, in your view, an excellent example of the genre.

A GUIDE TO WRITING ESSAYS EXPLAINING CONCEPTS

As the selections you have read in this chapter suggest, essays explaining concepts help us understand unfamiliar ideas or learn more about ideas with which we may already be familiar. Writers of explanation avoid entering into controversy or asserting arguable points of their own; their purpose is to present information that is generally accepted by most authorities in the field. Because they are trying to present new information, writers have to think about their readers—anticipating what they are likely to know already and what may be confusing to them. The guide to writing that follows will help you at every stage in the process of composing an essay explaining a concept—from choosing a concept and organizing your explanatory strategies to evaluating and revising your draft.

INVENTION

The following activities can help you get started gathering the information you will need to explain a concept. The more deliberately you work through these preliminary stages of invention, the closer your first draft will come to satisfying your own and your readers' needs and expectations. Beginning with choosing a concept, these activities will help you explore what you already know, consider what your readers need to know, gather and sort through your information, and decide on which explanatory strategies to use in presenting your information.

Listing Possible Concepts

Unless you have been assigned a concept, you will need to choose one. Review the Considering Ideas for Your Own Writing sections that follow each reading selection in this chapter and also recall the concepts you and your classmates tried during the collaborative activity when you began work on this chapter. Make a list of possible concepts you could explain, including concepts you already know about as well as those you would like to learn about.

Your courses provide many concepts you will want to consider. Following are typical concepts from several academic and other subjects. Your class notes or textbooks will suggest many others.

Literature: representation, figurative language, canon, post colonialism, modernism, subject position

Philosophy: existentialism, nihilism, logical positivism, determinism

Business management: autonomous work group, quality circle, cybernetic control system, management by objectives, zero-based budgeting, benchmarking

Psychology: intimacy, phobia, narcissism, object relation, fetish, intelligence, divergent/convergent thinking, operant conditioning

Government: one person/one vote, minority rights, federalism, popular consent, exclusionary rule, political machine, interest group, political action committee

Biology: photosynthesis, morphogenesis, ecosystem, electron transport, plasmolysis, phagocytosis, homozygosity, diffusion

Art: cubism, composition, Dadaism, surrealism, expressionism

Math: Mobius transformation, boundedness, null space, eigenvalue, complex numbers, integral exponent, rational exponent, polynomial, factoring, Rolle's theorem, continuity, derivative, indefinite integral

Physical sciences: gravity, mass, weight, energy, atomic theory, law of definite proportions, osmotic pressure, first law of thermodynamics, entropy, free energy

Public health: alcoholism, epidemic, vaccination, drug abuse, contraception, prenatal care

Environmental studies: acid rain, recycling, ozone depletion, sewage treatment, toxic waste, endangered species

Sports psychology: Ringelman effect, leadership, cohesiveness, competitiveness, anxiety management, aggression, visualization

Law: arbitration, strike, minimum wage, liability, reasonable doubt, sexual harassment

Physical geography: jet stream, hydrologic cycle, El Niño, Coriolis effect, Chinook/Foehn/Santa Ana wind, standard time system

Nutrition and health: vegetarianism, bulimia, diabetes, food allergy, aerobic exercise, obesity, Maillard reaction

Choosing a Concept

Choose a concept from your list. To discover what you already know about this concept, write down everything you know about it and why you find it interesting and worth learning more about.

Analyzing Your Readers

Consider who might be interested in learning about this concept and write a few sentences describing them. (Even if you are writing only for your instructor, you must be aware of his or her knowledge of your concept.) For example, in what kind of publication would these readers be likely to read an explanation of this concept? (This question may be productive for you to consider even if you have no intention of publishing your essay.) What would these particular readers be likely to know already about this concept, or about the academic or other field in which it is used? Why might they want to learn about this concept?

Finding Out More about Your Concept

Even if you know quite a bit about the concept, you may want to do additional library research or consult an expert. Before you begin, check with your instructor to discover whether there are any special requirements such as that you turn in photocopies of all your written sources or use a particular documentation style.

FINDING INFORMATION AT THE LIBRARY OR ON THE INTERNET. The best place to start your research is your college library. Appendix 2, Strategies for Research and Documentation, provides detailed guidance for finding information at a library and on the Internet.

CONSULTING AN EXPERT. Is there someone very knowledgeable about your subject who might be helpful? If you are writing about a concept from another college course, for example, you might consult the teaching assistant or professor. Not only could such a person answer questions, but also he or she might direct you to important or influential articles or books. (See the section on interviews in Appendix 2.)

FOCUSING YOUR RESEARCH. Skim and take notes from several obvious sources to see how you might limit and focus your essay. For example, if you were writing about schizophrenia, you might focus on the history of its description and treatment, its symptoms, its effects on families, the current debate about its causes, or current preferred methods of treatment. If you were writing a book, you might want to cover all these aspects of the concept. In an essay, however, you may refer to two or three of these aspects, but you would want to focus on only one. In this initial stage, you will usually find far more information than you can possibly use in a relatively brief essay. This first step will take from two to four hours, but it will save you time when you return to the library to complete your research.

AN EXAMPLE: MELISSA MCCOOL'S RESEARCH PROCESS. This section provides one example of how a writer might begin the research process and develop a focus for the research. You may use this example as a guide for beginning your essay.

Melissa McCool, whose essay appears in this chapter, began her library research by looking up *Reincarnation* in *The Encyclopedia of Religion.* The reference librarian had directed her to this authoritative encyclopedia as the best possible starting point. On the shelves nearby were several other encyclopedias and dictionaries of religion and philosophy. She selected the most recently published dictionary, the *Dictionary of Religion and Philosophy,* and looked up *reincarnation,* which led her to *karma* in the same dictionary. Knowing that the concept of reincarnation was important to New Age religious groups, she was drawn to another nearby book, *New Age Encyclopedia,* where she was pleased to find an entry titled "Reincarnation and Karma." Because she assumed that all of these relatively brief, concise entries might become central to her research, she photocopied them. The longest was only six pages.

McCool then went to the catalog to look up *reincarnation.* Here things became more complicated: There were about twenty books listed, and she found fourteen on the shelves. Skimming these books, she discovered that she could divide them into groups: those concerned with either supporting or rejecting reincarnation and those either describing and evaluating it or collecting various statement about it from different historical periods. She wrote down the authors, titles, and library call numbers of the books in these two categories; but she did not take extended notes or photocopy any pages because she was not yet sure of her focus. In just over two hours, she had found much more information than she could possibly use, even if she only lightly sampled all of her sources.

After discussing these options with her instructor and other students, she decided to avoid the debate and to focus on defining reincarnation and reviewing its history. She returned to the library to collect sources relevant to this focus. After she was well into her draft, she decided that the worldwide historical perspective was too sprawling for her to manage. Because she had noticed that her materials contained many references to American sources, she decided to focus on the history of the reception of reincarnation in the United States, knowing that this focus would be especially appropriate for her American readers. While her essay refers briefly to believers in reincarnation from many periods and Western countries, she focuses on (and gives most space to) American believers.

Deciding Which Explanatory Strategies to Use

Now that you have some idea of what your readers need to know about the concept and have considered ways to focus your explanation, you need to decide which information to include and how to present it to readers. The following questions correspond to the explanatory strategies (listed in parentheses). Answer these questions by writing a sentence or two on each. Answering them not only will help you determine which strategies to use but also will highlight any areas of information you might consider researching further.

- What term or terms are used to name the concept, and what do they mean? (defining)
- With what other concepts does it belong, and how can it be broken down into subclasses? (classifying and dividing)
- How is it like and unlike related concepts? (comparing and contrasting)
- What is a particular example or instance of it? (illustrating)
- How does it happen, or how do you do it? (narrating the process)
- What are its known causes or effects? (reporting causes or effects)

Beginning

Consider how you might open your essay. Writers explaining concepts often try to interest readers, as Quammen does by quoting popular song lyrics and as Tannen does by describing the people attending a conference. Elmer-DeWitt begins by telling a story about the origins of his concept and McCool recalls what was jokingly said on a television show. Sometimes, though, writers begin with a definition, as Csikszentmilhalyi does, or by providing a context for the concept, as Nodelman does.

LEARNING MORE ABOUT YOUR READERS:
A COLLABORATIVE ACTIVITY

You have done a good deal of thinking about the concept and are about to plan and draft your essay. Before you begin, your instructor may invite you to use class time to get together with one or two other students to try out your ideas and get some feedback.

Taking turns, each person in the group should explain his or her concept, using one or two explanatory strategies. The others in the group should listen carefully and, afterwards, tell the speaker what they found interesting about the concept, what else they would like to know about it, and what, if any, they found confusing in the explanation.

Explaining the concept to your classmates will not be the same as explaining it to your intended readers, but the rehearsal may help you think about what your actual readers need to know. Probably the most important benefits of this activity are the questions and suggestions the members of your group may be able to provide. At this point, do not try to answer the questions; simply write them down for later. If any of the questions surprises or baffles you, you might discuss the question with the questioner to make sure that you understand what is motivating it.

DRAFTING

Before you begin drafting, pause to review what you have written in response to the invention activities. Mark anything you think is especially interesting in your notes, anything you think will help readers understand the concept and appreciate its importance. Look for specifics—examples, anecdotes, facts, comparisons—that you could use to clarify the concept for readers. From your research materials, note any quotations that are particularly apt for your discussion. Make a list of any additional information you think you might need. As you plan and draft the essay, you may find that you can do without this additional information or that it really is essential. In drafting, you will be making all kinds of decisions; the following guidelines are designed to help you begin by setting goals and planning the draft of your essay.

Setting Goals

Setting goals involves considering carefully what you want to accomplish in the essay and deciding on how you might achieve these goals. You will find that keeping your goals in mind as you plan and draft will make the writing go easier and faster. Here are some questions to consider.

What do my readers know about the concept? How do I present information that will be new to them? For example, McCool seems to assume that reincarnation will be an unfamiliar—or even a distasteful—concept to readers, and therefore she stresses the serious attention it has received over the centuries from major American authors. Both Nodelman and Csikszentmilhalyi divide their basic information into three well-marked sections so readers can grasp it more easily.

How do I begin? What kind of opening is likely to capture my readers' attention? Quammen uses a witty title and song lyrics to capture readers' attention. Tannen begins by telling what she noticed about other participants at a conference. Elmer-DeWitt tells how William Gibson got the idea of cyberspace. Csikszentmilhalyi begins by describing the kind of person he assumes most readers would like to be. McCool opens with a brief anecdote about Shirley MacLaine's appearance on a well-known television show.

How can I orient readers so they do not get confused or bogged down? Three of the most common orienting devices are forecasting statements, topic sentences, and transitions. Good examples of forecasting can be found in the selections by Nodelman and McCool. Transitions appear in every essay. Quammen uses rhetorical questions and summary statements to help readers clarify their understanding.

How do I conclude the explanation? Quammen reminds readers of what parthenogenesis is and why it is important, but he manages to end as he began, on a humorous note. Tannen frames her essay by mentioning the conference she began with. Csikszentmilhalyi ends by stressing the importance of his concept.

Planning Your Draft

The goals you have set should help you decide what explanatory strategies you want to use and how to sequence them. You might want to try out different plans, but do not feel committed to any of them because drafting can itself lead you in new directions.

Having set specific goals, you are ready to plan the draft of your essay. Begin by making a tentative outline of the strategies you now think you will use, considering carefully the order of these strategies given what your readers are likely to know about the concept.

You could plan your essay around a series of implicit or explicit questions as Quammen does, interweave definition and explanation with a single extended example as Tannen does, organize around different aspects of the concept as Nodelman does, or narrate the stages in a process as Csikszentmilhalyi does.

READING A DRAFT CRITICALLY

Now that you have a draft of your essay, you can benefit from having one or more readers read it carefully to let you know how well it explains the concept and to indicate where it might be improved. The activities in this section will guide readers to give specific advice that will help you revise the draft. The advice will be most useful to you if it is put in writing so you can have it with you when you revise.

Reading a draft critically involves reading it completely to get a preliminary understanding of the concept and then rereading parts of it more closely to see how and where it might be improved.

Reading for a First Impression

Read quickly through the draft to get a sense of how the concept is explained. After you have finished reading and without looking back at the draft, write down in your own words several sentences stating what you have learned about the concept from reading this explanation.

Reading to Analyze

Reread the essay now more slowly and methodically to focus on its basic features and strategies. Read to discover where the explanation succeeds and where it could be improved.

USING APPROPRIATE EXPLANATORY STRATEGIES. Concept explanations may use several explanatory strategies or rely on only one. Skim the essay, noting in the margin each time one of the following strategies is used: defining terms, classifying and dividing, comparing and contrasting, narrating a process, illustrating, reporting known causes or effects.

Then take each strategy in turn and evaluate how well it works to help you, as one reader, to better understand the concept. Point out anything about the strategy that seems confusing or unhelpful. For example, note any terms that the writer could define or that you do not think need to be defined, if you do not get the point of a comparison, or if the steps in a process seem vague. Offer the writer specific suggestions about how particular strategies could be more effective or how different strategies might be added.

MAKING THE DRAFT READABLE. Review the draft to see how it is organized. Evaluate how well the opening section prepares the reader for what follows. Indicate if a forecasting statement, topic sentences, or transitions could be added or improved. Point to any place where you become confused or do not know how something relates to what went before. Comment also on whether the conclusion gives a sense of closure or leaves you hanging.

USING SOURCES RESPONSIBLY. If the writer relies on sources, notice how smoothly they are integrated into the writer's own sentences and whether the sources are acknowledged correctly. Indicate any quotations that seem especially appropriate as well as any that could have been put in the writer's own words just as effectively. If you can, suggest other sources the writer might consult.

ENGAGING READERS. If you are not one of the readers the writer had in mind, the best you may be able to do is let the writer know how well the draft engaged your interest. But, if possible, try to help the writer anticipate the intended readers' needs and expectations. Point to any passages that you found especially interesting, as well as any that allowed your mind to wander. Finally, tell the writer what questions still have not been answered.

REVISING

Experienced writers expect to revise their first draft of a concept explanation because they know that concepts inherently are abstract and hard to explain in a way that most readers will understand. Getting other readers' responses to your draft can help you see it as they do. But you will undoubtedly also want to give the draft a systematic critical reading yourself using the guidelines offered in the preceding section.

Do not try to revise everything at once. Focus first on one part and then on another. You may find the following suggestions helpful. If you cannot figure out how to solve a particular problem, review some of the concept explanation essays in this chapter to see what other writers chose to do in a similar situation.

As you reread your draft, list the two or three major problems you need to solve. At this point, focus only on the basic features of concept explanation, not on punctuation or other sentence-level editing issues. Although it is essential to edit carefully, you will probably change your draft substantially as you revise— reorganizing, rewriting, adding, and cutting. For now, focus on revising the draft so it explains the concept as fully and clearly as possible.

Revising to Improve the Plan

If readers have difficulty following the essay, improve the forecasting at the beginning of the essay by listing the topics in the order they will appear.

If there are places in a paragraph where the topic gets blurred or is changed from one sentence to the next, make the connections between the sentences clearer.

If there is a place where the essay digresses, perhaps to present an extended example, end the digression by making the point explicit.

If the essay seems to lose steam rather than come to a conclusion, consider again what you want readers to learn from your essay.

Revising the Explanatory Strategies

If the content seems thin, consider whether you could add any other explanatory strategies or develop the ones you are using already.

If some of the words you use are new to most readers, take more time defining them—perhaps explaining how they relate to more familiar terms or adding analogy and example to make them less abstract.

If the way you have divided or categorized the information is unusual or unclear, write a sentence or two making explicit what you are doing and why.

If the concept seems vague to readers, consider how you might compare it to something they are likely to know or how you could describe the process of applying the concept.

Revising the Use of Sources

If your essay quotes too much, examine each quotation to see what purpose quoting serves and whether anything would be lost if you put the idea into your own words while acknowledging the source.

If you rely on only one source, bolster the source's credibility by establishing the source's credentials and position among other experts.

If all source material is introduced the same way, consider how you might vary your presentation—perhaps by using different vocabulary or sentence structure.

Revising to Engage Readers

If you think your readers will find parts of your explanation irrelevant or digressive, make clearer your purpose in presenting that information or, if you cannot, consider cutting it.

If you think readers are likely to be uninterested in the concept, give them a reason to want to learn about it.

If your intended readers think they already know all there is to know about the concept, show that you are aware of what they already know and then tell them something new or surprising about the concept.

REFLECTING ON WHAT YOU HAVE LEARNED ABOUT WRITING CONCEPT EXPLANATIONS

In this chapter, you have read critically several essays explaining concepts and have written one of your own. To remind yourself how much you have learned and to help you remember it, pause now to reflect on your reading and writing experiences while working on this chapter.

Write a page or so reflecting on your learning. Begin by describing what you are most pleased with in your essay and explaining what contributed to your achievement. If the contribution came from something in the readings, indicate which readings and specifically what you learned from them. If it came from your invention writing, point out the section or sections that helped you most. If you got good advice from a critical reader, explain exactly how the person helped you—perhaps by helping you to understand a particular problem in your draft or by suggesting a new dimension to your writing. Try to write about your achievement in terms of what you have learned about the genre of explanation.

Then write about anything else that accounts for your learning this special kind of writing. Include anything you have learned about the writing process; for example, how to use time efficiently before writing a draft to discover what you want to say about the subject or how to get constructive criticism and practical advice from other readers of your draft.

CHAPTER 6

EVALUATION

We make evaluations every day, stating judgments about such things as food, clothes, books, classes, teachers, political candidates, television programs, performers, and films. Most of our everyday judgments simply express our personal preference—"I liked it" or "I didn't like it." But as soon as someone asks us "Why?" we realize that evaluation goes beyond individual taste.

If you want others to take your judgment seriously, you have to give reasons for it. Instead of merely asserting that "*Batman Returns* was fantastic," for example, you must explain your reasons for thinking so: the excellence of the acting, for example, or the haunting musical score by Oingo Boingo's Danny Elfman or the fascinating story of Catwoman's rebirth as a kind of radical-feminist avenger.

For readers to respect your judgment, not only do you have to give them reasons, your reasons must also be recognized as appropriate for evaluating that particular kind of subject. An inappropriate reason for the judgment "*Batman Returns* was fantastic," for instance, would be that the seats in the theater were comfortable. The comfort of the seats may contribute to your enjoyment of a film (and, indeed, would be an appropriate reason for judging the quality of a movie theater), but such a reason has nothing to do with the quality of a particular film.

For reasons to be considered appropriate, they must reflect the values or standards typically used in evaluating a certain kind of thing, such as a film or a car. The standards you would use for evaluating a film obviously differ from those you would use for evaluating a car. Acting, musical score, and story are common standards for judging films. Handling, safety, and styling are some of the standards used for judging cars.

In addition to reasons based on accepted standards, readers also expect writers of evaluations to provide supporting evidence. If one of your reasons for liking the Dodge Stealth sports car is its quick acceleration, you could cite the *Consumer Reports* road-test results (0 to 60 mph in 6.3 seconds) as evidence. (Statistical evidence like this, of course, makes sense only when it is compared with the acceleration rates of other cars.) Similarly, if one of your reasons for liking *Batman Returns* is the excellent acting, you could give examples from the film to show where you think the acting is particularly effective. You might discuss the scenes in which Michelle Pfeiffer transforms into Catwoman, pointing out how she alters her voice, facial expression, and body language as examples of good acting. Evidence is important because it deals in specifics, showing exactly what value terms like *quick* and *excellent* mean to you.

As you can see, evaluation of the kind you will read and write in this chapter is intellectually rigorous. In college, you will have many opportunities to write evaluations. You may be asked to critique a book or a journal article, judge a scientific hypothesis against the results of an experiment, assess the value of conflicting interpretations of a historical event or a short story, or evaluate a class you have taken. You will also undoubtedly read evaluative writing in your courses and be tested on what you have read.

Written evaluations will almost certainly play an important part in your work life, as well. On the job, you will probably be evaluated periodically and may have to evaluate people whom you supervise. It is also likely that you will be asked your opinion of various plans or proposals under consideration, and your ability to make fair and reasonable evaluations will affect your chances for promotion.

Examining others' evaluative arguments and developing your own also will help you understand how fundamental values and beliefs influence judgment. Evaluative arguments are basically about values, about what each of us thinks is important. Reading and writing evaluations will help you understand your own values, as well as those of others. You will learn that when basic values are in conflict, it may be impossible to convince others to accept a judgment different from their own. In such cases, you will know how to bridge the difference with mutual respect and shared concern.

As you read, discuss, and write about the essays in this chapter, you will learn a good deal about evaluative writing. You should also get ideas for an

---

THE WRITING ASSIGNMENT

Evaluation

Write an essay, evaluating a particular subject. State your judgment clearly, and back it up with reasons and evidence. Describe the subject for readers unfamiliar with it, and give them a context for understanding it. Your principal aim is to convince readers that your judgment is informed and your reasons are based on generally accepted standards for judging this kind of subject.

evaluative essay of your own, based perhaps on the ideas for writing that follow each selection. As you work through the selections in this chapter, keep in mind the preceding assignment that sets out the goals for writing an evaluative essay.

EVALUATIVE WRITING SITUATIONS

Following are a few examples to suggest the range of situations that may call for evaluative writing. These include academic and work-related writing situations.

- For a political science course, a student writes a term paper evaluating the election campaigns run by several Senate candidates. She argues that all of the candidates rely too much on television ads and not enough on grass-roots campaigning. Consequently, the candidates are not made to spell out anything in detail or to answer probing questions. She also points out that because much of the advertising is negative attack and counterattack, the electorate ends up without respect for either the candidates or the process itself.

- A supervisor writes an evaluation report on a probationary employee. She judges the employee's performance as being adequate overall but still needing improvement in several key areas, particularly completing projects on time and communicating clearly with others. To back up her judgment, she gives examples of several problems that the employee has had over the six-month probation period.

- A college junior writes a letter to his younger brother, a high-school senior who is trying to decide which college to attend. Because the older brother attends one of the colleges being considered and has friends at another, he feels competent to offer advice. He centers his letter on the question of what standards to use in evaluating colleges. He argues that if playing football is the primary goal, then college number one is the clear choice. But if having the opportunity to work in an award-winning scientist's genetics lab is more important, then the second college is the better choice.

PRACTICING EVALUATION
A COLLABORATIVE ACTIVITY

PART 1. Assume that you have been asked to review some form of popular entertainment. Get together with two or three other students, and choose a type of entertainment you all know fairly well: country-western music, horror movies, music videos, magic acts. Then discuss what standards for judgment you normally use in judging this type of entertainment. For example, the standards for a movie review might include the movie's entertainment value (if it is a comedy, is it funny?), the quality of its ideas (if it is about relationships, is it insightful?), and its technical qualities (how effective are its acting, direction, cinematography?). Try to agree on the two or three most important standards you would apply in evaluating the type of entertainment you have chosen.

PART 2. Finally, use these questions to reflect on what you have learned about making evaluations:

Which standards did you agree about readily, and which created disagreement in the group?

How can you account for these differences?

Where do you suppose your standards came from?

A GUIDE TO READING EVALUATIVE WRITING

To introduce evaluative writing, we first ask you to read, annotate, and write about your understanding and response to the brief essay that follows. Then, guided by a list of basic features and strategies, reread the essay to analyze and evaluate the elements of strong evaluative writing.

First, to remind you of the many possibilities for annotating, here is an illustration of an annotated passage from another evaluative essay, by Roger Angell, which appears in its entirety later in the chapter.

Transition from Reason #1: excesses to Reason #2: heroes

Statistics

This Series, for all its excesses, fulfilled a classic function by producing at its end a pair of heroes who had previously failed to win the full measure of attention that their distinguished careers deserved. Joe Carter's Series-winning homer was described by him in the postgame tumult as a dream and a miracle, but it was entirely in character. Carter is agreeable, calm, intelligent, durable, and effective—the consummate major-leaguer. In ten seasons, he has hit more than thirty home runs five times, and has driven in more than a hundred runs seven times; he leads all hitters, in both leagues, in these categories over the past nine years. It would not do to think of him as a machine, however, since he has hit three homers in a single game on five different occasions—an American League record, which means better than Reggie, better than Gehrig, better than the Babe. (Johnny Mize, with five National League and one American League three-homer games, leads all comers here.) Now, like Mazeroski and Bobby Thomson, he has a baseball feat that will always bear his name: the Carter homer. . . .

1st hero: Carter C's own words show he's not egotistical

Personal & professional qualities

Better than these all-time heroes

But still not the best

Special achievement

Amitai Etzioni

WORKING AT MCDONALD'S

This evaluation was written by sociology professor Amitai Etzioni (b. 1929). He has written numerous articles and books, including *The Spirit of Community: Rights, Responsibilities, and the Communitarian Agenda* (1993).

This essay was originally published in 1986 in the *Miami Herald.* The original headnote identifies Etzioni as the father of five sons, including three teenagers, and points out that his son Dari helped Etzioni write this essay—although it does not say what Dari contributed. As you read the essay, consider how this information—both about Etzioni's career and family and about his son's assistance—influences your willingness to accept his judgment. As you read the essay for the first time, annotate any point with which you disagree or agree.

McDonald's is bad for your kids. I do not mean the flat patties and the white-flour buns; I refer to the jobs teen-agers undertake, mass-producing these choice items. [1]

As many as two-thirds of America's high school juniors and seniors now hold down part-time paying jobs, according to studies. Many of these are in fast-food chains, of which McDonald's is the pioneer, trend-setter and symbol. [2]

At first, such jobs may seem right out of the Founding Fathers' educational manual for how to bring up self-reliant, work-ethic-driven, productive youngsters. But in fact, these jobs undermine school attendance and involvement, impart few skills that will be useful in later life, and simultaneously skew the values of teen-agers—especially their ideas about the worth of a dollar. [3]

It has been a longstanding American tradition that youngsters ought to get paying jobs. In folklore, few pursuits are more deeply revered than the newspaper route and the sidewalk lemonade stand. Here the youngsters are to learn how sweet are the fruits of labor and self-discipline (papers are delivered early in the morning, rain or shine), and the ways of trade (if you price your lemonade too high or too low . . .). [4]

Roy Rogers, Baskin Robbins, Kentucky Fried Chicken, *et al.,* may at first seem nothing but a vast extension of the lemonade stand. They provide very large numbers of teen jobs, provide regular employment, pay quite well compared to many other teen jobs and, in the modern equivalent of toiling over a hot stove, test one's stamina. [5]

Closer examination, however, finds the McDonald's kind of job highly uneducational in several ways. Far from providing opportunities for entrepreneurship (the lemonade stand) or self-discipline, self-supervision and self-scheduling (the paper route), most teen jobs these days are highly structured—what social scientists call "highly routinized." [6]

True, you still have to have the gumption to get yourself over to the hamburger stand, but once you don the prescribed uniform, your task is spelled out in minute detail. The franchise prescribes [7] the shape of the coffee cups; the weight, size, shape, and color of the patties; and the texture of the napkins (if any). Fresh coffee is to be made every eight minutes. And so on. There is no room for initiative, creativity, or even elementary rearrangements. These are breeding grounds for robots working for yesterday's assembly lines, not tomorrow's high-tech posts.

There are very few studies of the matter. One of the few is a 1984 study by Ivan Charper and Bryan Shore Fraser. The study relies mainly on what teen-agers write in response to questionnaires rather than actual observations of fast-food jobs. The authors argue that the employees develop many skills such as how to operate a food-preparation machine and a cash register. However, little attention is paid to how long it takes to acquire such a skill, or what its significance is.   8

What does it matter if you spend 20 minutes to learn to use a cash register, and then—"operate" it? What "skill" have you acquired? It is a long way from learning to work with a lathe or carpenter tools in the olden days or to program computers in the modern age.   9

A 1980 study by A. V. Harrell and P. W. Wirtz found that, among those students who worked at least 25 hours per week while in school, their unemployment rate four years later was half of that of seniors who did not work. This is an impressive statistic. It must be seen, though, together with the finding that many who begin as part-time employees in fast-food chains drop out of high school and are gobbled up in the world of low-skill jobs.   10

Some say that while these jobs are rather unsuited for college-bound, white, middle-class youngsters, they are "ideal" for lower-class, "non-academic," minority youngsters. Indeed, minorities are "over-represented" in these jobs (21 percent of fast-food employees). While it is true that these places provide income, work and even some training to such youngsters, they also tend to perpetuate their disadvantaged status. They provide no career ladders, few marketable skills, and undermine school attendance and involvement.   11

The hours are often long. Among those 14 to 17, a third of fast-food employees (including some school dropouts) labor more than 30 hours per week, according to the Charper-Fraser study. Only 20 percent work 15 hours or less. The rest: between 15 to 30 hours.   12

Often the stores close late, and after closing one must clean up and tally up. In affluent Montgomery County, Md., where child labor would not seem to be a widespread economic necessity, 24 percent of the seniors at one high school in 1985 worked as much as five to seven days a week; 27 percent, three to five. There is just no way such amounts of work will not interfere with school work, especially homework. In an informal survey published in the most recent yearbook of the high school, 58 percent of the seniors acknowledged that their jobs interfere with their school work.   13

The Charper-Fraser study sees merit in learning teamwork and 14
working under supervision. The authors have a point here. However, it must be noted that such learning is not automatically educational or wholesome. For example, much of the supervision in
fast-food places leans toward teaching one the wrong kinds of com-
pliance: blind obedience, or shared alienation with the "boss."

Supervision is often both tight and woefully inappropriate. Today, 15
fast-food chains and other such places of work (record shops, bowling alleys) keep costs down by having teens supervise teens with
often no adult on the premises.

There is no father or mother figure with which to identify, to 16
emulate, to provide a role model and guidance. The work-culture
varies from one place to another: Sometimes it is a tightly run shop
(must keep the cash registers ringing); sometimes a rather loose pot
party interrupted by customers. However, only rarely is there a
master to learn from, or much worth learning. Indeed, far from
being places where solid adult work values are being transmitted,
these are places where all too often delinquent teen values dominate. Typically, when my son Oren was dishing out ice cream for
Baskin Robbins in upper Manhattan, his fellow teen-workers considered him a sucker for not helping himself to the till. Most youngsters
felt they were entitled to $50 severance "pay" on their last day on
the job.

The pay, oddly, is the part of the teen work-world that is most 17
difficult to evaluate. The lemonade stand or paper route money was
for your allowance. In the old days, apprentices learning a trade
from a master contributed most, if not all of their income to their
parents' household. Today, the teen pay may be low by adult standards, but it is often, especially in the middle class, spent largely or
wholly by the teens. That is, the youngsters live free at home, ("after
all, they are high school kids") and are left with very substantial sums
of money.

Where this money goes is not quite clear. Some use it to support 18
themselves, especially among the poor. More middle-class kids set
some money aside to help pay for college, or save it for a major purchase—often a car. But large amounts seem to flow to pay for an
early introduction into the most trite aspects of American con-
sumerism: Flimsy punk clothes, trinkets and whatever else is the last
fast-moving teen craze.

One may say that this is only fair and square; they are being good 19
American consumers and spend their money on what turns them
on. At least, a cynic might add, these funds do not go into illicit
drugs and booze. On the other hand, an educator might bemoan
that these young, yet unformed individuals, so early in life are driven
to buy objects of no intrinsic educational, cultural or social merit,
learn so quickly the dubious merit of keeping up with the Joneses in
ever-changing fads, promoted by mass merchandising.

Many teens find the instant reward of money, and the youth sta-   20
tus symbols it buys, much more alluring than credits in calculus
courses, European history or foreign languages. No wonder quite a
few would rather skip school—and certainly homework—and
instead work longer at a Burger King. Thus, most teen work these
days is not providing early lessons in work ethic; it fosters escape
from school and responsibilities, quick gratification and a short cut
to the consumeristic aspects of adult life.

Thus, parents should look at teen employment not as automati-   21
cally educational. It is an activity—like sports—that can be turned
into an educational opportunity. But it can also easily be abused.
Youngsters must learn to balance the quest for income with the
needs to keep growing and pursue other endeavors that do not pay
off instantly—above all education.

Go back to school.   22

READING FOR MEANING

Explore your understanding and response to "Working at McDonald's" by
writing at least a page. Begin by saying in your own words what Etzioni's judgment is and why he makes this judgment. Then comment on anything in the
essay or in your experience that contributes to your understanding of Etzioni's
essay.

Reread and annotate pertinent parts of the essay that are unclear or to which
your response is particularly strong, and refer to these as you write. If you have
difficulty writing for at least a page, use any of the following suggestions:

- Examine the meaning or significance of "these jobs . . . skew the values of
  teen-agers—especially their ideas about the worth of a dollar" (paragraph
  3); these jobs "also tend to perpetuate [minority youngsters'] disadvantaged
  status" (paragraph 11); or any other statement that you find intriguing.

- Comment on the equation Etzioni makes between "being good American
  consumers" and spending money on "what turns [you] on" and "the dubious merit of keeping up with the Joneses in ever-changing fads, promoted
  by mass merchandising" (paragraph 19).

- In paragraphs 3 and 4, Etzioni brings up some basic American values such
  as self-reliance, the work ethic, and self-discipline. Choose one of these
  values or any other value that you consider important, perhaps one that
  Etzioni left out. Reflect on why the value you have chosen is important and
  how it is best learned.

- Reflect on your own high-school or college part-time work experience (or
  that of your friends or family). What were you required to do? What skills
  did you learn, if any? Why did you work while you were going to school?
  Explain how your experience supports or contradicts Etzioni's argument
  about the value of working while going to school.

READING LIKE A WRITER

This section leads you through an analysis of Etzioni's evaluative writing strategies: *presenting the subject, asserting an overall judgment, giving reasons and supporting evidence,* and *establishing credibility.* Each strategy is described briefly and followed by a critical reading and writing activity to help you see how Etzioni uses that particular strategy in his essay.

Consider this section a writer's introduction to evaluative writing. You will learn more about how different writers use these strategies from the Reading like a Writer activities following other selections in this chapter. The Guide to Writing an Evaluation at the end of the chapter suggests how you can use these same strategies in writing your own evaluative essay.

Presenting the Subject

Writers must present the subject so readers know what is being judged. This can be done simply by naming the subject, but usually writers describe it in some detail. A film reviewer, for example, might identify the actors, describe the characters they play, and tell some of the plot. As a critical reader, you will note that the language used to present the subject also may serve to evaluate it. Therefore, you should look closely at how the subject is presented. Note the use of evaluative words, where the writer's information about the subject comes from and its reliability, and whether anything important has been left out.

ANALYZE. Reread Etzioni's essay, underlining and annotating the factual details that describe who works at fast-food restaurants and what they do. Ask yourself the following questions as you analyze how Etzioni presents the subject. Where does he seem to get his information—from firsthand observation, conversation with others, reading published research? Based on your own knowledge of fast-food jobs, point to those details you accept and those you think are inaccurate or only partially true. Also, consider what he leaves out, and why—is it because he assumes readers already know it, because it is not important, or because it would not support his judgment? Given what he does and does not tell readers, to whom do you think Etzioni is writing primarily? What makes you think so?

WRITE. Write a couple of sentences, discussing how Etzioni presents the subject to his expected readers. Evaluate the presentation of the subject according to the criteria of accuracy and completeness.

Asserting an Overall Judgment

The writer's overall judgment is the thesis or main point of the evaluation—asserting that the subject is good or bad or better or worse than something comparable. Although readers expect a definitive judgment, they also appreciate a balanced one that acknowledges both good and bad qualities of the subject.

Evaluations usually explicitly state the judgment up front and may restate it in different ways throughout the essay.

ANALYZE. Etzioni flatly states his overall judgment in the opening sentence. Skim the essay, putting a check in the margin next to any restatement of the judgment. Note whether Etzioni modifies his judgment at any point—for example, suggesting that working at places like McDonald's might not be so bad under certain conditions or that it has its good qualities, as well as its bad.

WRITE. Write a few sentences, describing and evaluating the way Etzioni presents his overall judgment.

Giving Reasons and Supporting Evidence

Evaluative arguments must explain and justify the writer's judgment. To be convincing, reasons must be recognized by readers as appropriate for evaluating the type of subject under consideration. That is, the reasons must reflect the values or standards of judgment people typically use in similar situations.

Furthermore, reasons must be supported with evidence such as examples, quotations, facts, statistics, and personal anecdotes. Evidence may come from the writer's own knowledge and experience or from that of others (such as witnesses or authorities).

ANALYZE. Etzioni gives several reasons for his judgment. List the reasons and then choose one reason to analyze. Using the following questions, consider the appropriateness of the reason, given Etzioni's intended readers. Why do you think they would or would not be likely to accept this reason as appropriate for evaluating part-time jobs for teenagers? On what values or standard of judgment is it based? What objections, if any, might a critical reader have to this kind of reasoning? Why do you, as one reader, accept or reject the reason, based on the evidence? How clearly and strongly does the evidence support the reason?

WRITE. Write several sentences analyzing the reason you chose. Begin by summarizing the reason and the evidence given to support it.

Establishing Credibility

The success of an evaluation depends to a large extent on readers' confidence in the writer's judgment. Evaluative writers usually try to establish their credibility by showing they know a lot about the subject and by attempting to convince readers that their judgment is based on values and standards that readers recognize as valid.

Biographical information can provide facts about the writer's educational and professional accomplishments that readers can use in judging the writer's authority. It is the essay itself, however, that usually tells readers what the writer knows about the subject and from where that knowledge comes. The values or standards underlying the writer's judgment are usually easy to detect regardless of whether they are stated explicitly because they are implied in the kinds of reasons the writer uses. Occasionally, writers of evaluation justify their values and juxtapose them to other's values, inviting readers to choose sides.

ANALYZE. Evaluate how well Etzioni establishes his credibility on the subject of after-school work for teenagers. How, for example, does it help that he refers to one son's experience working at Baskin Robbins (paragraph 16) and credits another son with helping him write the essay (see the headnote)? How do his professional credentials—as sociologist, professor, former head of a Center for Policy Research, and author of several books—contribute to his authority? How does his claim that he has read the research help establish his credibility? Notice specifically his use of statistics from these studies and the fact that he disagrees with the Charper-Fraser study's conclusions about the merit of learning to work under supervision (paragraph 14).

WRITE. Based on your evaluation of Etzioni's credibility, write a few sentences on how credible his evaluation is. Indicate which of his judgments you found the most valid.

READINGS

David Ansen

WHEN AMERICA LOST ITS INNOCENCE— MAYBE

David Ansen is a film reviewer for Newsweek magazine.

This essay reviews the 1994 film *Quiz Show,* which was nominated for four Academy Awards, including best picture. *Quiz Show* is based on a true story, a 1959 scandal that shocked the nation when some of the contestants on a very popular television program called "Twenty-One" were given answers ahead of time. The film, like the original scandal, has inspired heated debate about television ethics and the power of money and fame to corrupt.

If you have not seen *Quiz Show,* you may want to rent the video so you can make your own evaluation. However, even without seeing the film, you will be able to understand and judge the effectiveness of Ansen's evaluative argument.

The fall season gets off to an auspicious, Oscar-contending start with *Quiz Show,* Robert Redford's savvy, snappy account of the TV quiz-show scandals of the late '50s. Its arrival has already provoked a favorite American question: when did we as a nation lose our innocence? It's an absurd question, of course, that assumes a homogeneous "we." (Ask a Native American that, and you'll get a very early citing.) Absurd too because, since this is a nation with no historical memory, every generation has its own answer. But it's a vital question nonetheless, for no country has been so obsessed with the myth of its innocence as ours. It's the clean slate from which we are able continually to reinvent ourselves, the source of what has been best in our optimistic, idealistic culture and what has kept us childish, close-minded and brutally provincial.

No era was more invested in the myth than the boom years of the 1950s, when television arrived to beam back at us gift-wrapped images of our cheery, wide-eyed selves, laugh track included. But it was through television and the print media that the cracks began to show. The demagoguery of Joe McCarthy was exposed on live TV. The U-2 spy-plane scandal: imagine, the United States spied on the Soviets, and had lied about it! Sherman Adams and his vicuña coat: we were shocked, shocked that a politician might take a gift!

Neck high in '90s cynicism, it's hard to believe the tremors these scandals provoked. What's a vicuña coat next to Iran-contra? Except by then the country was so blasé about governmental deception it could barely rouse itself to outrage. In the '50s, Ingrid Bergman was blacklisted from Hollywood for having a baby out of wedlock. Today, Oliver North makes hash of the Constitution and it jumpstarts his political career. What used to ruin your life gets you invited on "Oprah" and a fat book deal. Shame is for losers; public confession and a 12-step program can turn you into a role model.

In 1959 Charles Van Doren, who had become a national hero as a contestant on the NBC quiz show "Twenty-One," fell from grace when he admitted before a congressional hearing that he'd been fed the answers. A patrician intellectual, the son of Pulitzer Prize–winning poet Mark Van Doren, this Columbia University instructor had been hailed as the exemplary American "egghead." He was the great white hope of higher education, the man who made the cerebral sexy. After the revelations—the American public's rude awakening to television's capacity for mendacity—he lost his teaching post, got dumped from the "Today" show and slid into self-imposed obscurity working for the Encyclopedia Britannica.

Why should we care about a man who sold his soul for $129,000 more than 35 years ago? Redford and screenwriter Paul Attanasio, who wasn't even born when Van Doren entered his soundproof booth to vanquish his competitor Herbert Stempel, must have worried that old Faustian bargains would seem small potatoes in an era when celebrity scandals involve charges of child molestation and murder. But *Quiz Show* is about more than a bygone media frenzy or some questionable notion of lost American innocence. Its true subjects owe little to nostalgia. It's about where the power and the profits lie, about institutions and their scapegoats, and about how class and ethnicity color our view of the world in our supposedly classless society.

Redford approaches the story from three angles. There's Van Doren (Ralph Fiennes), wearing his privilege diffidently, who strolls into the wolf's den of showbiz and allows himself to be convinced that his ethical lapse is justified by all the good it will do the cause of education. Then there's Herbert Stempel (John Turturro). A Jew from Queens, seething with resentment that he had to take a fall for the glamour boy Van Doren, he's the first to spill the beans about the fraud, but he's so volatile, so transparently resentful—and so *unattractive* compared to Van Doren—that no one wants to believe him. The third figure is the movie's designated sleuth, Richard Goodwin (Rob Morrow), the hotshot Harvard law grad working for a congressional committee investigating game-show rigging. A Jew with a Harvard accent as thick as JFK's (for whom he would later write speeches), he wants to go after the networks themselves—not Van Doren, whose charm and lineage beguile him.

Attanasio's dense, smart screenplay takes some liberties with the facts: the chronology is toyed with, and Goodwin's role as a detective is fanciful—the grand-jury files that are denied him in the movie were in fact readily handed over, as he recounts in his book "Remembering America." Fortunately, the point is not to portray Goodwin as some shining, crusading hero. What's intriguing is his divided loyalties—his eagerness to be part of the patrician world of the man he may destroy. Stempel, played with broad brilliance by Turturro as a near-stereotypical pushy, neurotic Jew, tells Goodwin that the show "always follows a Jew with a Gentile—and the Gentile wins more." Goodwin doesn't want to believe Van Doren's crooked any more than the TV audience wanted to; he goes out of his way to protect him, causing his wife to call him the "Uncle Tom of the Jews." *Quiz Show* reveals how the tyranny of image was already in place in the '50s. There's a wonderfully double-edged scene when Van Doren makes his eloquent *mea culpa* at the hearing, and the lawmakers, cowed by class, fall over themselves to praise the cheater's candor. These are social observations Hollywood movies rarely think to explore.

Quiz Show is superbly shot (by Michael Ballhaus), and the acting ensemble could hardly be better. Morrow, once you get over his Saul Rubinek eyebrows and ostentatious accent, gives a finely reactive performance. Fiennes is magnetic in just the right understated way, a portrait of easy charm with a guilty conscience. All down the line there are rich turns: David Paymer and Hank Azaria as the show's producer and his assistant, Paul Scofield as Mark Van Doren, Allan Rich as the tough NBC honcho Robert Kintner, Martin Scorsese wickedly sly as the head of Geritol, "Twenty-One's" sponsor. If there are villains in the piece, these last two men qualify—they're the

ones who really called the shots. But we see how the power structure is rigged so that the truly guilty are untouchable. *Quiz Show* is
witty enough never to need to get on a soapbox to make its points.

Robert Redford may have become a more complacent movie star
in the last decade, but he has become a more daring and accom-   9
plished filmmaker. *Quiz Show* is his best movie since *Ordinary People,*
and it confirms him as one of our most astute cinematic chroniclers
and critics of WASP mores. He has kept his eye on the ball of
power, and in this shrewd and highly entertaining look back, shows
us some of the bounces that got us where we are today.

READING FOR MEANING

Write at least a page, exploring your understanding of "When America Lost
Its Innocence—Maybe." Begin by listing the main reasons Ansen gives to support his evaluation. Then respond to anything in the essay that contributes to
your understanding.

As you write, you will need to reread and further annotate parts of the essay.
If you have difficulty thinking of what to write, use any of the following suggestions:

- Skim the essay, circling any words whose meaning is unclear to you. You
  might begin with *auspicious, homogeneous, provincial, demagoguery,
  patrician.* In a college dictionary, look up the words you have circled and
  add the definition to your marginal annotations.

- In contrast to the innocence of the 1950s, Ansen says Americans today are
  cynical. How do you think people would respond today if it were revealed
  that television quiz-show contestants (for example, on "Jeopardy" or
  "Wheel of Fortune") were given the answers ahead of time?

- Reflect on your own assumptions, if you have any, about America in the
  1950s. Where do you suppose your assumptions came from? How do they
  influence your judgment of the events and people portrayed in *Quiz Show?*

- As a reader trying to understand this essay, how important is it that you
  know what each of the following refers to: Joe McCarthy, the U-2 spy-
  plane scandal, Sherman Adams, Iran-contra, Ingrid Bergman, Oliver North,
  "Oprah," and 12-step programs? When you're reading and encounter references with which you're unfamiliar, what if anything do you do? What else
  could you do?

- Explain the possible meanings or significance of "since this is a nation with
  no historical memory, every generation has its own answer" (paragraph 1);
  "What used to ruin your life gets you invited on 'Oprah'" (paragraph 3);
  "*Quiz Show* is about . . . where the power and the profits lie, about institutions and their scapegoats, and about how class and ethnicity color our view
  of the world in our supposedly classless society" (paragraph 5); or any
  other statement in the essay that catches your attention.

EXTENDING MEANING THROUGH CONVERSATION. After reading for meaning on your own, you might be able to expand your understanding of Ansen's review of *Quiz Show* by discussing it with two or three other students who also have read and written about the essay. You can begin a conversation in many different ways. If there is a particular passage you do not understand, you could ask the others to reread it and discuss it together. If one of you has seen the film, that person could comment on Ansen's description and evaluation of the film. If you were intrigued by one of the topic suggestions listed above, you could ask the others what they thought of it.

You may find that you interpret or evaluate the essay differently. Examine the differences closely; perhaps they will stimulate new ideas.

READING LIKE A WRITER
PRESENTING THE SUBJECT

Because many people read reviews to help them decide whether to see a film, most reviews serve a dual purpose: to describe the film for those who have not seen it and to convince them that the film is or is not worth seeing. Sometimes, however, it is hard to distinguish between these two purposes because information used to describe the film may also support the reviewer's judgment of it.

ANALYZE. Reread the essay, and mark the passages that you think primarily inform readers about the film. Underline any language in these passages that you think also asserts or supports Ansen's judgment of the film. Also consider whether the reasons Ansen gives for his judgment depend on anything said in these passages. Note which parts, if any, of the primarily presentational passages also play a role in Ansen's evaluative argument.

Then put yourself in the place of Ansen's editor and pretend that you knew that everyone who would read his review had already seen the film. How would you revise Ansen's essay to accommodate this special audience? Put brackets ([]) around anything you would advise him to leave out.

WRITE. Based on your analysis of Ansen's review and your general experience as a reader of film reviews, write several sentences explaining what you have learned about the way film reviews like this one handle the two purposes of informing readers about a film they have not seen and trying to convince readers that the film is or is not worth seeing.

CONSIDERING IDEAS FOR YOUR OWN WRITING

Think of a film or television show you have already seen that you would like to review. What would you choose? In addition to your judgment and the reasons for it, what do you think you would need to tell readers about the film or television show?

Roger Angell

OH, WHAT A LOVELY WAR

Roger Angell (b. 1920) is a *New Yorker* magazine writer and editor, following in the footsteps of his mother, Katherine Angell White, and his stepfather, E. B. White. Angell is probably best known for his essays on baseball, many of which have been reprinted in book-length collections, beginning with *The Summer Game* (1972) and, most recently, *Once More Around the Park* (1992).

In a July 1994 article, Angell describes a process of collaboration between editor and writer that should remind you of the kind of critical reading you are learning to give drafts. Two or three editors read each selection that is submitted and fill out an "opinion sheet," in which, as Angell puts it, "the editor should not feel much compunction about asking the writer the same questions he would put to himself about a swatch of his own prose: Is it clear? Does it say what I wanted it to say? Is it too long? Does it *sound* right—does it carry the tone that I want the reader to pick up right here? Is it, just possibly, too short? And so on." As is the case with your own drafts, "often the process turns up some structural flaws, and the work is shipped back to its creator for minor or major repairs."

In this excerpt from the November 1993 *New Yorker,* Angell evaluates the 1993 World Series between the Toronto Blue Jays and the Philadelphia Phillies. The seven-game Series decides the World Championship in baseball. Some readers may be baseball fans or even remember this particular Series. Consider, as you read, how your prior knowledge (or lack of it) affects your understanding and response to the essay.

The ball, catching a late flight, soared briefly and perhaps eagerly westward and disappeared over the blue left-field fence—the last excessive act in an excessive and astounding World Series, unless we count the deportment of the batter turned base runner, Joe Carter, who now imitated an Olympic hop-step-and-jump competitor, then a mid-veldt springbok, then a manic May Day solidarity demonstrator as he circled the bases and threw himself at last into the arms of his clustered and joyful teammates back at home plate. His fireworks-igniting ninth-inning three-run Game Six homer, which defeated the Phillies, 8–6, and captured the World Championship for the Blue Jays for a second consecutive year, was only the second Series-ending round-tripper in the long history of the classic; its predecessor, Bill Mazeroski's 1960 clout at Forbes Field, brought the Pirates an unexpected Game Seven victory over the Yankees in a Series also replete with swollen innings, high scores, and horrified pitchers. This one was *more* replete. Carter's blow, for one thing, brought his team from behind in the game (the Phillies were up, 6–5, with one out), while the Mazeroski poke settled a 9–9 tie. The Blue Jays' final three-run cluster at the SkyDome perfectly typified a week of thrilling and ghastly ball, during which the two clubs had demonstrated a shared propensity for blown leads; grisly or glorious bat-around innings; huge (in both senses of the word) homers or multiple, scary extra-base hits; games that dragged and drooped and then blew hot and breathless; and some pitching that one watched with horrid anticipation or else, hiding one's head in a towel, dared not watch at all. There were two games that, for good reason or bad, we just might remember forever.

Game Four, played at Philadelphia's Veterans Stadium in a relentless rain and won at last by the Blue Jays, 15–14, after their six-run rally in the eighth, proved to be (let us hope) like no other, establishing several genuine, if not previously coveted, Series records—most runs, most runs by a losing team, and longest nine-inning game (four hours, fourteen minutes)—along with a hatful of records tied, including the teams' combined thirty-two hits and the four first-inning bases on balls given up by the Blue Jays starter, Todd Stottlemyre. During one of the mid-inning truces for a change of pitchers, the Toronto outfielders Rickey Henderson, Devon White, and Joe Carter gathered in a murmurous confab out in center, like witnesses at a neighborhood street accident. "We were saying, 'Man, I never saw anything like *this* before,'" Henderson explained later. Carter, for his part, said, "You can't put it in words, you can't describe it—it's baseball."

This Series will linger in mind not just for its immoderate events but for its panoply of featured players and character actors—a double touring company seemingly assembled by Hogarth or Fellini. The Phillies, as we kept hearing, took pride in their raunchy looks and reputation ("We're a bunch of gypsies, tramps, and thieves," Mitch Williams pronounced during the summer), though in truth their clubhouse, when visited, felt about as threatening as a boys' tree house next door. But the Phils' hulk and hair, their tics and twitches, and all that mouthing and chomping and spitting were a trip and a half. We won't soon forget the amazingly bulked-up Lenny Dykstra in the batter's box, settling his helmet with a delicate touch of his inside wrist, twiddling his white-gloved fingers on the bat (I think he twiddled more when he was a Met), or, between pitches, executing that stalking little half knee bend, like an arthritic bullfrog. Or John Kruk—his mild eyes almost subverting the whole grungy-helmet, biker's-beard, bad-body getup—with his vertical, high-held bat sometimes making him look like a surveyor's assistant just up the highway. Or Mitch Williams apparently *gnawing* the ball behind his upraised shoulder before his next sprawling, unaccountable delivery. Or Curt Schilling peeping over the top of his outthrust mitt for the sign; the dusty and towering Darren Daulton wearily extending a tree-limb arm to pick up his scarlet helmet; Jim Eisenreich squinching his nose. And so on.

We knew the Blue Jays better. Because they were here in the   4
finals as defending champions and long-term October principals (this was their fourth matriculation into the post-season in the past five years), their decorous looks and ways felt more ominous than the Phillies' sideshow, and we studied them with apprehension: Rickey Henderson's anxiety-squeezed face and his tilted, sweeping stroke, which makes you think he is attacking the pitch from below; Robby Alomar's detached, stillwater gaze, suggesting a private time clock nothing like our own; Dave Stewart's glare of pure ill will exuding from under that cowling-like cap brim; and the hat-rack Olerud unfurling from nowhere his oiled and elegant swing. (The SkyDome has become a lively gallery for fan-banners, and my favorite this year, up on the first-base side, was a black-on-white "JOHN: .363"—not a Biblical verse this time but Olerud's league-leading final batting average.) All this and of course the presiding Cito Gaston, massively inert on the bench, with only his restless eyes to tell us how much was going on inside the manager and inside the game.

This Series, for all its excesses, fulfilled a classic function by pro-   5
ducing at its end a pair of heroes who had previously failed to win the full measure of attention that their distinguished careers deserved. Joe Carter's Series-winning homer was described by him in the post-game tumult as a dream and a miracle, but it was entirely in character. Carter is agreeable, calm, intelligent, durable, and effective—the consummate major-leaguer. In ten seasons, he has hit more than thirty home runs five times, and has driven in more than a hundred runs seven times; he leads all hitters, in both leagues, in these categories over the past nine years. It would not do to think of him as a machine, however, since he has hit three homers in a single game on five different occasions—an American League record, which means better than Reggie, better than Gehrig, better than the Babe. (Johnny Mize, with five National League and one American League three-homer games, leads all comers here.) Now, like Mazeroski and Bobby Thomson, he has a baseball feat that will always bear his name: the Carter homer.

The Blue Jays lost eight players to free agency after attaining their   6
championship last year, and it's worth noticing that their general manager, Pat Gillick, while allowing the likes of Dave Winfield, David Cone, and bullpen ace Tom Henke to slip away, made it a point to re-ink Joe Carter (at a salary of five million for three years, plus a ten-million-dollar signing bonus) on December 8, 1992, and on the same day to sign Paul Molitor (thirteen million, over three years), who had reluctantly taken his leave from the Milwaukee Brewers after fifteen seasons. Molitor, although six times voted into the All-Star Game, had always played a little in the shadow of Robin Yount,

and this summer, at thirty-seven, he flourished up across the border, batting .332 as the Jays' designated hitter and establishing career-high totals for games played, home runs, and runs batted in. To my way of thinking, it was his presence down there in the Toronto batting order—he batted sixth against right-handers and third against lefties—that made that lineup such a daunting, no-hope prospectus for opposing pitchers late this season. "With that bunch, you can't *breathe* between pitches," White Sox shortstop Ozzie Guillen said during the A.L. playoffs.

Molitor batted at a .391 clip against the Sox in those games, and then surpassed himself in the Series with a .500, twelve-for-twenty-four outburst, which featured two doubles, two triples, two homers, and eight runs driven home. He simply killed the ball, and, after rocketing line drives throughout the week (including some line-drive outs), delivered at the end the telling little ninth-inning, one-out single to center that turned Joe Carter's ensuing at-bat into such an intolerable muddle for Mitch Williams. During the mid-Series games, down in Philadelphia, he had stayed calm through the vast media fuss about which infield position he would occupy when the local no-d.h. rule deprived him of his normal spot in the lineup; he took over first base for a game, then third for two more, and came through without incident. Molitor, who is thin and pale, with a body that looks metallic beneath the skin, is matter-of-fact in the workplace, and his tearful embrace with Cito Gaston after the last game and then his dazed and damp acceptance of his Most Valuable Player award were a fresh reminder that it is pride and the need to win that drive the pro in the end, sometimes taking him a distance that he has almost stopped imagining as the years and seasons run down.

All this profligate hitting and high scoring (what Tony La Russa calls "crooked numbers") by the two teams had its other side, and I suspect that even the happiest Toronto fans might agree now that the frightful pitching we saw in the Series should keep it from ranking at the topmost level of these championships. Something is absent from the occasion when both starting pitchers are gone from a game after the third inning, having surrendered thirteen runs between them (as happened in Game Four); something feels amiss when the arrival of an ace bullpen closer is greeted by cheers and happy applause from the other team's fans (as happened at the SkyDome when Wild Thing Mitch Williams was announced in the last game); and something like pity is not quite the emotion one wants when watching the departure and arrival of further exhausted and clearly overmatched midgame relievers (as happened repeatedly when the Phillies were out there). It could be argued that the Phillies' 7.57 earned-run average and the Blue Jays' 5.77 were just further proof that this had been a tough year for pitchers right along.

The bull market in offense that so altered the look of things in   9
both leagues this season (there were almost a thousand more home
runs than in 1992, and better than thirty-five hundred more runs
scored, not to mention 1,428 additional bases on balls) was sometimes attributed to the attrition of pitching staffs brought about by
the draft that stocked the expansionist Florida Marlins and Colorado Rockies in the National League, but, like other cynics, I also
suspect that the ball was juiced. This can be debated, but what we
may be sure of is that worn-down and ineffective pitching will be a
commonplace in the World Series from now on, thanks to the addition of a third tier of post-season games next year.

READING FOR MEANING

Write at least a page, exploring your understanding of "Oh, What a Lovely
War." Begin by commenting on one thing you find confusing or surprising in
Angell's evaluation of the Series, and then respond to anything else in the essay
that interests you. If you have difficulty finding ideas to write about, consider
the following:

- Reread paragraphs 3 and 4, where Angell contrasts the two teams. What
  impressions of the teams do you get from these paragraphs? Single out a
  few specific details that contribute to your impression.

- In paragraph 5, Angell asserts that the Series "fulfilled a classic function by
  producing at its end a pair of heroes." Based on your own experience of
  baseball or sports in general, why do you think Angell makes this statement? What qualities, in your opinion, does a sports hero need? How do
  Angell's two heroes match your expectations?

- Skim the essay, underlining any words whose meaning is unclear to you.
  You might begin with *deportment, mid-veldt sprinkbok, replete, panoply.*
  After looking up the words you have underlined, add the definition to your
  marginal annotations. Then reflect on your assumptions about sports writ-
  ing. Did you expect to encounter the kind of vocabulary Angell uses here?
  Why or why not?

- Explain the possible meanings or significance of "it is pride and the need to
  win that drive the pro in the end" (paragraph 7); "the ball was juiced" (paragraph 9); or any other statement in the essay that catches your attention.

EXTENDING MEANING THROUGH CONVERSATION. Discuss your understanding
of Angell's evaluation of the 1993 World Series with two or three other students
who have also read and written about this essay. If some in the group know a lot
about baseball, get them to answer any questions the others may have. You
could begin your conversation by discussing Angell's title. Why do you think he
calls it a "war," and why add the word "lovely"? Or you might focus on another
aspect of the essay that seems curious, such as whether Angell's use of the word
"excessive" in the opening paragraph suggests praise or criticism, and why.

Talking about sports could lure the sports enthusiasts in the group away from
the essay. Try to keep the focus on what Angell is saying about this particular
Series and about sports in general.

READING LIKE A WRITER
ASSERTING AN OVERALL JUDGMENT

Evaluative writing must make clear to readers the writer's overall judgment of whatever is being evaluated. Writers often announce their judgment in one or more straightforward sentences early in the essay. Etzioni, for example, opens his essay with this paragraph: "McDonald's is **bad** for your kids. I do not mean the flat patties and the white-flour buns; I refer to the jobs teen-agers undertake, mass-producing these choice items." Similarly, Ansen begins his film review with this sentence: "The fall season gets off to an **auspicious, Oscar-contending** start with *Quiz Show*, Robert Redford's **savvy, snappy** account of the TV quiz-show scandals of the late '50s." Notice the words set in bold: bad, auspicious, Oscar-contending, savvy, and snappy. These are *value terms,* words that assert judgment.

ANALYZE. Reread Angell's essay, looking for the sentence or sentences that state Angell's overall judgment of the Series—the thesis of his evaluative essay. As you read the essay, underline the value terms you find. Notice where these terms appear; for example, in the opening sentences, scattered throughout the essay, at the end. Do you find them only where Angell states his overall judgment or where he makes a number of more specific judgments?

WRITE. Write a few sentences, reporting what you have found about the way Angell uses value terms to assert his judgment.

COMPARE. Compare the way Angell uses value terms with the way Etzioni, Ansen, or any other writer in this chapter uses them. Write another sentence or two explaining what your comparison reveals.

CONSIDERING IDEAS FOR YOUR OWN WRITING

Consider evaluating a sports event (a particular game or Series), a sports team (possibly comparing two teams), or a sports figure (national or local). To do such an evaluation, you would need to attend one or more games or view videotapes to collect concrete evidence to support your judgment. What event, team, or sports figure might you choose? On what basis would you make your judgment? What standards do you think your readers would apply when evaluating a game, a team, a player, or a coach?

Martha C. Nussbaum

DIVIDED WE STAND

Martha C. Nussbaum is a philosophy professor at Brown University who has written extensively about classical Greek philosophy, morality, and literature. In addition to several scholarly studies of Aristotle, her books include *The Fragility of Goodness: Luck and Ethics in Greek Tragedy and Philosophy* (1986) and *The Therapy of Desire: Theory and Practice in Hellenistic Ethics* (1994).

"Divided We Stand" evaluates William J. Bennett's popular collection of children's literature, *The Book of Virtues: A Treasury of Great Moral Stories*. Bennett chose the literature and wrote a general introduction as well as commentaries. A well-known political conservative, Bennett served under President Reagan as Secretary of Education as well as Chair of the National Endowment for the Humanities, and under President Bush as the Director of the Office of National Drug Control Policy. For a time, Bennett edited the *National Review,* the conservative counterpart to the liberal *New Republic,* the newsmagazine in which Nussbaum's review was originally published in January 1994. As you read the review, you will want to pay special attention to the way Nussbaum anticipates her readers' political concerns.

To understand Nussbaum's review, you need to know something about Bennett's objectives. In the Introduction, he explains that the book is "intended to aid in the time-honored task of the moral education of the young." He defines moral education as "the training of heart and mind toward good," which he says "involves rules and precepts—the *dos* and *don'ts* of life with others." "The purpose" of *The Book of Virtues* "is to show parents, teachers, students, and children what the virtues look like, what they are in practice, how to recognize them, and how they work." Stories provide the "stock of examples illustrating what we see to be right and wrong, good and bad." Each chapter is devoted to a different virtue: Self-Discipline, Compassion, Responsibility, Friendship, Work, Courage, Perseverance, Honesty, Loyalty, and Faith. Before reading Nussbaum's review, you might pause to recall how you learned these virtues when you were a child.

How do we learn good character? Aristotle argued that we must begin with good "habits," meaning not mindless behavioral conditioning, but patterns of increasingly intelligent choice guided by attachment and love. A child is initiated into good choices, in the first place, through the love and the gratitude of family attachments. But as age brings greater independence and the need for greater critical discernment, a central role will be played by paradigmatic examples of virtue, and those examples will be given in poems, stories and dramas. Reflecting on these examples, often in the company of the parent, the child becomes increasingly adept at identifying real life situations that call for courage or friendliness or justice or generosity. And the fact that the child learns to associate these examples with intense love for the parent lends them a radiance that exercises, in later life, a special power.

William Bennett thinks that Aristotle is correct. He also believes
that the project of forming good character can and should be undertaken in a democracy independently of political debate about the
issues that divide us. Despite the many vexing issues that separate us,
he argues, we can agree in a general way about the traits of character
that distinguish a good person and a good citizen; and it should not
be greatly controversial to say that these traits ought to include compassion, self-discipline, courage, honesty, perseverance, responsibility, the capacity for friendship, some sort of faith in goodness. And if
we focus on the cultivation of these common traits, we will do better
at the deliberative resolution of the divisive questions—better, for
example, than if moral instruction is left entirely to religious or ethnic
traditions that seem to differ about the fundamentals of morality.

In order to form character in this democratically shared way,
Bennett continues, we must recover paradigms that we once shared
as a nation, before the triviality of television absorbed most of our
children's attention, and before a prevailing cynicism made virtue
seem laughable. And for this we need to think Aristotelian thoughts
about stories and poems, building a conception of "moral literacy"
for citizenship by gathering for parents the inspiring and character-
building exempla on which earlier generations of Americans cut
their moral teeth. This anthology of poetry, fiction and philosophy is
intended for parents to read with their children, selecting materials
suited to the child's age and understanding.

Bennett's book comes wrapped up in a package that suggests a
narrow ideological focus: a sentimental Norman Rockwellish cover,
blurbs on the back from Margaret Thatcher (intelligent), Rush Limbaugh (abysmal), Roger Staubach. And of course Bennett's name will
at once call to mind his bullying public manner and his unsubtle
touch with many subtle issues. The reader may expect, therefore,
crude moralism, and open the text eager to have a few laughs at
Bennett's expense. This, it turns out, would be a big mistake. There
is some awful stuff here, and there is some simplistic flag-waving
stuff. But the project as a whole compels respect; and Bennett is
revealed to be more complicated, and more passionately justice-
driven, than many people will have understood him to be.

Let me put my cards on the table. I had an upbringing like the one
that Bennett envisages. My father had many of Bennett's tastes in
moral stories. He did not share, I hasten to add, the treacly Hallmark Card side of Bennett's pedagogy, but he certainly did share
Bennett's emphasis on fortitude and sacrifice. To this day the smell
of the sea is inexorably linked, for me, with an image of my father
carrying me out to swim beyond the breakers, and both of these
memories are bound up with William Ernest Henley's "Invictus" (a
poem inexplicably omitted here). "Out of the night that covers
me/Black as the pit from pole to pole": that severe pounding call to
virtue, that joyful praise of the "unconquerable soul," is now forever

mingled in my mind with the intense joy of those moments of love and adventure. So I agree with Bennett that these are the things that make one's responses to adversity. And if we let such lines be replaced by "Beavis and Butthead"—or, at a more elite level, by an aesthetic preference for ironic distancing—we will quickly become a nation impoverished in citizenship.

Anyone who remembers Bennett as an arch-foe of "multicultur-   6 alism" will be surprised to discover that this is a fairly multicultural book. To be sure, its heart is firmly in the Western tradition, and in the American tradition above all; but there are also African and Native American folktales, Hindu, Buddhist and Chinese texts, and very many works by, and about, women. The history of slavery and the history of race relations in the United States play a central role in the entire project. This material is scattered, and doesn't really succeed in conveying to children a sense of the world as a complex whole consisting of societies with richly different traditions. And yet there is the basic acknowledgment that "moral literacy" involves an acquaintance with the present and the past of other nations, and with the minorities within one's own nation. The reader experiences some astonishment, since the capacity to learn from his opponents never seemed to be one of Bennett's most salient traits. But there are even greater surprises in store as we proceed.

To illustrate the book's organization, which proceeds from the   7 simple to the complex within each virtue, let me describe the section on compassion; it is among the best in the book, and a model of how such a project should be done. Bennett's introduction, in clear and simple language, presents the basic idea that compassion "is a virtue that takes seriously the reality of other persons, their inner lives, their emotions, as well as their external circumstances." Drawing deftly on Rousseau, Hume and Josiah Royce, Bennett argues that the power of compassion to put oneself in the place of another lies at "the very heart of moral awareness," and inspires the desire to relieve want and suffering. He concludes by pointing out that the major obstacles to compassion are the forces of "animosity and prejudice," including "the divisive 'isms'. . . : racism, sexism chauvinism and the rest." Is this really the Bennett that liberals love to hate?

The section ends with a remarkable extract from Tocqueville,   8 which argues that compassion will not flourish where institutions do not work against hierarchy. For if people are not made equal by laws and institutions, how will they come to see themselves in one another, or view themselves and their fellow citizens as vulnerable to misfortune in similar ways? Thus American democracy, with its leveling of distinctions, offers the fairest hope for the virtue of compassion, for "the more equal social conditions become, the more do men display this reciprocal disposition to oblige each other."

Bennett's preface to the passage concludes: ". . . we are forced to   9 ask ourselves: How does modern America measure up to the portrait he painted more than a century and a half ago?" The child who gets to this thought—by a path that has led her through the Civil War and the anti-slavery cause and the ethnic migrations of the early twentieth century—will have a lot of questions here. (And not only the questions about race and ethnicity that Bennett repeatedly raises, but also questions about gender that he raises less frequently, questions about poverty and class that he raises only indirectly, and questions about sexual orientation about which he is completely silent.) How indeed have our institutions promoted, or failed to promote, the kind of equality that makes compassionate citizenship possible?

This sort of questioning is evidently what Bennett, in his Aris- 10
totelian mode, means by virtue. This is a conception of civic virtue that may seem to some readers difficult to square with the politics of Rush Limbaugh and Margaret Thatcher. But his book is not always this interesting. There is the problem, for a start, of Bennett's uneven judgment about poetry. There are many fine things, from Donne and Shakespeare to Blake and Emily Brontë and Emily Dickinson and Tennyson and Walt Whitman to Yeats and Frost. And Bennett is right to feel that some lesser classics, such as Emerson's "Concord Hymn" and Emma Lazarus's "The New Colossus," are still morally powerful. Let us grant him, too, his decision to stick to the past. (He cites the staggeringly high fees charged to reprint recent verse. Could this be the vice of stinginess?) But, even granting Bennett his premises, there is entirely too much poetry of the sentimental school—sometimes by reputable figures (Longfellow's "The Children's Hour") and sometimes by writers of doggerel such as Ella Wheeler Wilcox ("Laugh, and the world laughs with you"), the deservedly obscure Laura E. Richards ("To the Little Girl Who Wriggles") and above all the rebarbative Edgar Guest ("Only a dad with a tired face, / Coming home from the daily race").

But the large amount of *Reader's Digest* material is not just an 11
accident. I have so far described Bennett's project as Aristotelian. This is true, but not the whole story. Bennett has another side. It would be too imprecise, and too flattering, to call this other side Tolstoyan, but Tolstoy's argument in *What Is Art?* comes to mind. This other side of Bennett is exercised less by the ideal of an education aimed at reflective habits of choice and passion, and more by a conviction of moral simplicity, by a view of art as a force that unites people across divisions of race, gender, religion and class through the simple power of basic moral sentiments. This side of Bennett is closer to the populist, demagogic, eternal-verities sort of conservatism by which he made his name.

And so Bennett is divided against himself. The complicating Aris- 12
totelian ideal and the simplifying populist ideal are deadly rivals, and Bennett, complicated character that he turns out to be, is pulled this way and that between them. In *The Book of Virtues,* one comes upon

a kind of vulgar Tolstoyanism for Americans, according to which
virtue entails a rejection of the complex and formally exacting in art
and in ethics, a rejection of all that cannot be readily grasped by a
child's simple faith.

READING FOR MEANING

Write at least one page, exploring your understanding of "Divided We Stand."
Begin by summarizing Nussbaum's judgment and then respond to anything in
the essay, using the following suggestions to help you develop your understanding:

- Skim the essay, circling any words with which you are unfamiliar. You
  might begin with the following: *behavioral conditioning, discernment,
  paradigmatic, virtue, vexing, rebarbative, perseverance, divisive.* In a college dictionary, look up the words you have circled and use the context in
  which the word appears in the essay to help you define the word.

- Nussbaum recalls that when she was a child, her father told her moral stories and recited poems like "Invictus" that emphasize "fortitude and sacrifice" (paragraph 5). What kinds of stories or poems, if any, were you told as
  a child or, if you are a parent, what kind do you tell your children? What
  role, if any, do you think these stories and poems played in your own moral
  development or play in that of your children?

- Explain the possible meanings or significance of "we must recover [moral
  values] that we once shared as a nation, before the triviality of television
  absorbed most of our children's attention, and before a prevailing cynicism
  made virtue seem laughable" (paragraph 3); "This is a conception of civic
  virtue that may seem to some readers difficult to square with the politics of
  Rush Limbaugh" (paragraph 10); or any other statement in the essay that
  catches your attention.

- Nussbaum claims, in the last paragraph, that "Bennett is divided against
  himself. The complicating Aristotelian ideal and the simplifying [Tolstoy-
  an] populist ideal are deadly rivals, and Bennett, complicated character that
  he turns out to be, is pulled this way and that between them." Reread paragraphs 1 through 3, where Bennett discusses the Aristotelian idea of moral
  complexity and the need for children to learn to ask critical questions. Also
  reread paragraphs 4 and 11–12, where Bennett introduces the Tolstoyan
  idea that moral questions are really quite simple if children are taught
  properly. Explore these two points of view. With which do you agree?

EXTENDING MEANING THROUGH CONVERSATION. You might begin your conversation by asking the others in your group whether they found this essay difficult and, if so, what made it so difficult. Reread and discuss any part of the essay
you find confusing or obscure.

CONTEXTUALIZING. Contextualizing, a further strategy for reading for meaning, is a useful way to read critically, to recognize the differences between your values and attitudes and those represented in the text. To contextualize "Divided We Stand," follow the guidelines on Contextualizing in Appendix 1, A Catalog of Critical Reading Strategies.

READING LIKE A WRITER
ESTABLISHING CREDIBILITY

All writers present themselves to readers in a particular way. Writers of evaluation tend to be especially concerned about how they are viewed by readers because they know that if readers question their credibility, readers are unlikely to accept their judgment. Readers of evaluation want evaluators to be knowledgeable and fair. Among the ways writers can establish their authority is by demonstrating how much they know about the subject, including knowing what other authorities have said. Writers usually demonstrate fairness by showing that their judgment is balanced, that they take into consideration both the good and the bad qualities of what they are evaluating.

In addition, reviewers often try to show readers that the standards on which they base their judgment are reasonable and appropriate—in fact, the same standards readers themselves would apply. Occasionally, a reviewer will attempt to establish a bond with readers by adopting an intimate tone or relating something personal with which readers could identify.

ANALYZE. Reread the essay, noting places where you get an impression of Nussbaum. Mark any passages you find where she displays her knowledge and education, where she demonstrates her fairness (or unfairness), where she adopts a personal or intimate tone. Consider also the standards or values she uses in judging Bennett's book and whether they seem to you to be appropriate, the kind of standards you would apply.

WRITE. Write a few sentences, explaining what you have discovered about Nussbaum's attempts to establish her credibility in this essay. Indicate how credible you find her, and why.

COMPARE. Compare Nussbaum's essay with any other essay you have read in this chapter and write another sentence or two reporting what you have concluded about how writers of evaluation establish their credibility.

CONSIDERING IDEAS FOR YOUR OWN WRITING

Consider evaluating one of the stories or poems Bennett includes in his book or evaluating some other imaginative work. Would you, like Bennett, evaluate the work on the basis of its moral teaching or on some other basis?

Scorpia

BEWARE OF THE UNDER DROW

Scorpia is the pseudonym of a contributing editor of *Computer Gaming World* who reviews computer adventure or role-playing games. *Computer Gaming World* is a highly specialized magazine. In addition to reviews, it includes feature articles, editorials, letters and e-mail, and advertisements of computer games.

In this February 1995 essay, Scorpia reviews a new computer role-playing game called Menzoberranzan, published by Strategic Simulations, Inc. Although the review appears in a magazine addressed to computer-game enthusiasts, you do not need to know much about computer role-playing games in general or Menzoberranzan in particular to understand Scorpia's evaluation of it. But it might help to know that Menzoberranzan, like one of the earliest and most popular role-playing games, Dungeons and Dragons, is a story about elves and dwarves who cast magic spells and engage in dramatic battles.

It might also help to understand some of the technical terminology Scorpia uses. In paragraph 3, for example, she explains the way a player moves from screen to screen by using "step mode" or "free-scrolling mode." In paragraph 4, she refers to the "auto-mapping system," the system by which a player can save or print out maps of places the characters have successfully navigated. In addition to this technical detail, the opening paragraphs refer to a novel on which the game is based and two comparable computer games with which some readers may be familiar.

As you read this review, consider the difficulty of writing reviews that may be read by people who are less knowledgeable than your intended readers. Depending on your own knowledge of computer role-playing games, what do you think makes this review easy or hard to understand?

Menzoberranzan, for those unfamiliar with R. A. Salvatore's novel   1
The Legacy, is the underground capital city of Dark Elves, the Drow. Although normally comfortable in their dank and damp realm of Underdark, the Drow are rampaging on the surface of the Forgotten Realms, looking for a traitor to their cause. You see, Drizzt, the traitor, is an anomaly in the Dark Elf world, a black sheep, an outcast. He's a good guy.

Not able to find Drizzt the good Dark Elf, the Drow make off   2
instead with a selection of human villagers, hauling them to the underground city for slavery or worse. Your job, if you choose to dive into SSI's[*] MENZOBERRANZAN role-playing game, is to penetrate to the nethermost reaches of the Underdark, infiltrate the city of Menzoberranzan, and rescue the captives.

SSI: Strategic Simulations, Inc. (*Ed.*)

Those who've played SSI's earlier RAVENLOFT game will find much   3
that is familiar in MENZOBERRANZAN. While the party has room for four
characters, you create only two of your own; the remaining slots are
filled by other characters you meet along the way and invite to join
the group. The basic game mechanics are similar to RAVENLOFT, which
in turn came by way of EYE OF THE BEHOLDER. The view is 3D and the
party moves as a whole. Movement can be either in step mode or
free-scrolling mode. Step mode is just that: one click is one step forward, with turns of 90 degrees. Free mode is the full 360 degree
range, as in ULTIMA UNDERWORLD. If that sort of thing makes you dizzy,
stick with step mode. There are some places where free mode is necessary, but they are few and brief and not likely to upset anyone. . . .

MENZO features a very nice auto-mapping system. You can call it   4
up anywhere, anytime. Among other things, it shows where the
party has been, where it is now, nearby monsters (but only those
that are close), illusionary walls (once you know about them), locations of nearby non-hostile characters, and perhaps most importantly, locations of items to be picked up.

The maps are scrollable, and you can always look at maps of pre-   5
vious places the party has been, in that dungeon or another. In addition, you can write your own notes on this map, and even print it off
on a printer. Maps can also be saved to a separate file for viewing in
any word processor. . . .

Moving items from character to character is easy and simple: just   6
pick something up from one slot and put it in another. Happily, if
you dismiss one party member in favor of a new one, the departing
member hands over all items not his own to the newcomer. If the
joining character doesn't have enough room for everything, the
excess is placed on the ground for redistribution. This is a good system, and one I hope other designers will keep in mind for games
with similar add/dismiss-character features.

Moving to the game itself, unfortunately the best that can be said   7
about MENZO is that it is mediocre. Much of your time is spent on
getting to the city, plodding through caves and tunnels that follow
each other in dreary succession.

When you finally arrive, everything that follows is laid out for you   8
in a neat, linear path. The party is carefully directed from point to
point, event to event, like you're riding on a sightseeing tram at Disneyland. Go here, see him, get this, do that; after a while, you begin
to wonder whether you're playing a computer game or connect-
the-dots.

This is a shame, because so much could have been done with the   9
material at hand. Here we have three major Drow houses scheming
with and against each other, jockeying for power and possession of a
potent artifact, teetering on the edge of all-out war. Into this mael-
strom of chicanery, double-dealing, and assassination comes the
party, all unknowing.

What an opportunity for a well-developed, involving story—and 10
what a dismal hash was made of it. We could have had an exciting,
nerve-wracking excursion into the murky waters of Drow politics,
with treachery and surprise at every turn, and interesting choices to
be made. Instead, we end up with a ho-hum, "just follow the plan"
express railroad route to the endgame and inevitable showdown
with Foozle.

The dialogue doesn't help matters. It's grandiose, overblown, 11
melodramatic in the extreme. People don't so much speak as declaim everything they say, giving an unintended farcical overtone to
the game.

MENZO runs relatively clean, but does have some programming 12
problems. Most are trivial, such as some magical figurines that don't
work. . . . One that isn't so trivial is the "monsters in the wall" problem. You can see monsters stuck in the walls on the automap, and if
you stand in front of the wall and swing away, you can kill whatever
is in there.

Where this becomes a very nasty problem is in the endgame. 13
Here you break in on Matron Malice, in the middle of a sacrifice.
Naturally not pleased, she attacks, along with a Drow priestess and
several monsters. Killing her and the priestess initiates the endgame
sequence of congratulations and "once again, great heroes, you have
saved the day, etc."

You must kill Malice and friend to get that sequence, and it is 14
entirely possible for your party to walk into that room and she
won't be there. The monsters are there, but no Malice, no priestess.
You can kill off everything in sight, but the game doesn't end.

Current thought at SSI is that the game is placing Malice halfway 15
in the wall or altar. When a monster is stuck in that fashion, the
game "kills it off" to avoid problems (apparently fully in a wall isn't a
problem). So the software gets rid of her for you, but that doesn't
trigger the ending animations.

Unfortunately, there is absolutely no way of knowing if this will 16
happen until the party enters the room. This is one of those "tran-
sient" bugs that doesn't happen to everyone, just some players.
More bizarre, it could occur and not occur in separate games.

I had three teams altogether that went through to the finale. The 17
first two did not see Malice when they entered the altar room, no
matter how many times they tried it. However, the third team
walked in, and there she was, standing behind the altar! I was so
startled, the monsters got in a few hits before I recovered from the
amazement.

So you could have one game that will never end, and another 18
where a different party goes through properly all the way. SSI is
working on a patch, and it will likely be available by the time you
read this. In the meantime, it's the luck of the draw as to whether
Malice will be around or not when you get to her.

Overall, MENZOBERRANZAN is a disappointment. It has some nice   19
features, but nice features must be supported by a strong story.
Sadly, what could have been a superior entry in the CRPG[*] field
comes off as just another hack-n-slash product, suitable mainly as a
time-filler when nothing better is available.

READING FOR MEANING

Write at least a page, exploring your understanding of "Beware of the Under
Drow." Begin by explaining in your own words Scorpia's judgment of Menzoberranzan. Then write about anything in the essay that intrigues or confuses you.

As you look more closely at the essay and annotate it further, expect your
understanding to develop. If you have difficulty writing at least a page, consider
the following suggestions:

- In the opening paragraphs, Scorpia mentions R. A. Salvatore's novel *The
  Legacy,* on which Menzoberranzan is based, and three related SSI games,
  Ravenloft, Eye of The Beholder, and Ultima Underworld. If you are familiar with any of these references, how do they help you to understand this
  essay? If you are not familiar with the references, what effect if any do they
  have on you as a reader?

- Scorpia uses analogy twice in paragraph 8 when she compares playing
  Menzoberranzan to "riding on a sightseeing tram at Disneyland" and playing "connect-the-dots." How do these comparisons contribute to your
  understanding of her review?

- Notice the words Scorpia uses in paragraph 11 to describe the game's dialogue: *grandiose, overblown, melodramatic, declaim, farcical.* Look up in
  a college dictionary the definition of any word the meaning of which is
  vague to you. Then, in your own words, explain what you think Scorpia
  is saying in this paragraph.

- If you have ever played a role-playing game, computerized or not, briefly
  explain why being able to transfer items from one character to another is a
  "good system," as Scorpia claims in paragraph 6, or why a storyline that is
  "laid out for you in a neat, linear path" is bad, as she claims in paragraphs 7
  through 10.

EXTENDING MEANING THROUGH CONVERSATION. To further develop your
understanding of Scorpia's review, discuss the essay with a couple of classmates. You could start your conversation by asking if anyone in the group has
played a role-playing game like Menzoberranzan and, if so, how that experience
can help you understand the game and Scorpia's evaluation of it. Some readers
have difficulty with computer-game lingo like "step mode or free-scrolling
mode" (paragraph 3) and "auto-mapping system" and "illusionary walls" (paragraph 4). If anyone in your group has difficulty with the language, you might try

*CRPG: Computer Role-Playing Game (*Ed.*)

to define some of the terms. Or perhaps you could speculate about why Scorpia uses language only certain people will understand.

READING LIKE A WRITER

GIVING REASONS

In evaluations, writers express their judgment of the subject, as Scorpia does in her essay's final paragraph: "Overall, MENZOBERRANZAN is a disappointment." The reasons writers give often are themselves judgments, assertions about the subject's good or bad qualities. These assertions also may need to be explained and justified by more specific reasons.

Scorpia begins paragraph 4, for example, by praising the game's "very nice auto-mapping system." She then lists her many reasons for calling the system "very nice":

- "you can call it up anytime, anywhere"
- "it shows where the party has been, where it is now, . . . most importantly, locations of items to be picked up"
- "the maps are scrollable"
- "you can write your own notes . . . print . . . [save] to a separate file"
- "moving items from character to character is easy and simple"

Because they are so specific, these reasons can help readers understand precisely why Scorpia thinks the auto-mapping system is "very nice."

ANALYZE. In addition to her praise of the auto-mapping system, Scorpia points out two flaws in Menzoberranzan. Reread the rest of the essay, looking for the sentences asserting these two major flaws. Then, choose one of these assertions and list the reasons Scorpia gives to explain or justify the assertion.

How do you make sense of the fact that even though she praises its auto-mapping system, Scorpia still concludes that the game is a "disappointment"? Consider also the appropriateness of the reasons Scorpia gives in the light of your own experience with role-playing or computer games together with Scorpia's justifications and explanations of why these particular aspects of the subject deserve praise or criticism.

WRITE. Write a few sentences explaining what you have discovered about Scorpia's reasoning. Indicate how convincing you find her reasons and why.

CONSIDERING IDEAS FOR YOUR OWN WRITING

If you were to evaluate a computer game, word-processing program, or other software, what do you think you would choose to evaluate? What other computer-related item would you consider evaluating (a Bulletin Board you contribute to regularly on the Internet, a reference work on CD-ROM, or a new piece of hardware, for example)?

Ilene Wolf

BUZZWORM: THE SUPERIOR MAGAZINE

Ilene Wolf wrote this essay in a composition course at the University of California, San Diego.

The subject of this essay is a magazine, which was new at the time the essay was written. If you have seen *Buzzworm,* consider how accurately Wolf describes it and whether you agree with her judgment. If you have not seen the magazine, ask yourself whether Wolf gives you enough information to determine whether her judgment is sound.

Many people today exist within their environment without really knowing anything about it. If this ignorance continues, we will undoubtedly destroy the world in which we live. Only by gaining a better understanding of our planet will we be able to preserve our fragile environment from pollution, hazardous waste, endangerment of species, and ravaging of the land. A new magazine is dedicated to enlightening the general public about these important issues. It is called *Buzzworm.*

What makes *Buzzworm* superior to other magazines dealing with the same subject is that it not only fully explores all of the aspects of the environment but does so in an objective manner. *Buzzworm* effectively tackles the controversial question of how best to protect our planet and conveys the information in a way that all audiences can understand. In fact, the term *buzzworm,* borrowed from the Old West, refers to a rattlesnake. The rattlesnake represents an effective form of communication, for when it rattles or buzzes it causes an immediate reaction in those who are near. Thus the purpose of *Buzzworm* is to create a reaction in its readers regarding the conservation and preservation of the environment.

One of *Buzzworm'*s most striking features is its visual appeal. Excellent photographs complement the articles. Contrasted with the photography in *Sierra,* another environmental magazine, the superb photographs in *Buzzworm* only seem more striking. The Summer 1989 issue of *Buzzworm* features a dramatic full-page color picture of the grey wolf, which catches the reader's eye and draws attention to the article concerning the endangerment of the grey wolf's habitat. The current issue of *Sierra* also has a picture of the

grey wolf, yet it is not only smaller but the colors are not as clear—
resulting in a less effective picture. Whereas both photographs of
the animal pertain to their corresponding articles, it is the one in
Buzzworm that makes the reader stop and discover the plight of the
grey wolf.

Not only must a photograph be of excellent quality but it also   4
must be placed correctly in the layout to enhance the article. The
reader should be able to look at the picture and receive some information about the article it corresponds to. *Buzzworm*'s pictures of
the East African Masai convey specific information about the tribe.
Startling photographs depict the Masai in their traditional dress,
focusing on the elaborate beadwork done by the women and the
exquisite headdresses worn by the warriors. Looking at one picture
of a young warrior wearing a lion's mane headdress, the reader gets
a sense of the importance of the ritual and of the great respect that
is earned by becoming a warrior. Another picture depicts a mother
intently watching her daughter as she learns the art of beading. The
look on the woman's face displays the care that goes into the beadwork, which has been an important part of their heritage for many
generations. Thus, even before reading the article about the Masai,
readers have some understanding of the Masai culture and traditions.

Another functional and informative aspect of *Buzzworm*'s layout   5
is the use of subfeatures within an article. A subfeature functions in
two ways, first by breaking up the monotony of a solid page of print,
and second by giving the curious reader additional information. An
article entitled "Double Jeopardy" in the current issue gives the
reader an option of learning more about the subject through two
subfeatures. The article itself describes the detrimental effects that
excessive whale-watching and research are believed to have on the
humpback whale. To find further information about what might be
contributing to the already low numbers of the humpback whale,
one can read the subfeature "Humpback Whale Survival." Furthermore, for the reader who is not familiar with the subject, there is a
second subfeature, entitled "Natural History," which gives general
information about the humpback whale. No such subfeatures can be
found anywhere in *Sierra*.

In addition to being an effective way of adding pertinent informa-   6
tion to the article, the subfeatures also add to the unity of the magazine. The subfeatures in *Buzzworm* all share a common gray
background color, adding to the continuity in layout from one article to the next. This produces a cleaner, more polished, and visually
appealing magazine.

Once again, *Buzzworm* shows superior layout design in keeping   7
the articles from being overrun by advertisements. I realize that
ads do generate necessary revenue for the magazine, but nothing
is more annoying than an article constantly interrupted by ads.

Buzzworm's few ads are all in the back of the magazine. In fact, not once does an ad interrupt an article. On the other hand, *Sierra* is filled with advertisements that are allowed to interrupt articles, which only frustrates the reader and detracts from the article.

Buzzworm is unique in that it focuses on more than just one 8 aspect of the environment. In contrast, *Sierra* devoted its entire September/October issue to one subject, the preservation of the public lands in the United States. Although it is a topic worthy of such discussion, readers prefer more variety to choose from. The content of *Buzzworm* ranges from the humpback whale to the culture of the Masai to a profile of three leading conservationists. The great variety of issues covered in *Buzzworm* makes it more likely to keep the reader's attention than *Sierra*.

Buzzworm's ability to inform the reader is not limited to the 9 information in its articles. Captions also play a large part. Readers who are too lazy to read an entire article most often will look at the pictures and read the captions. Thus *Buzzworm*'s long and detailed captions are like miniature paragraphs, giving out more details than the terse captions in *Sierra,* which usually consist of only a few words. The difference in the amount of information in the two magazines is obvious from a look at a typical caption in *Buzzworm,* "Finding relaxation of a different kind, Earthwatch participants spend a vacation patrolling beaches and assisting female turtles in finding a secluded nesting area" compared to one in *Sierra*, "Joshua tree with Clark Mountain in background." Both captions give a description of their corresponding pictures, but only the caption found in *Buzzworm* gives any indication of what the article is about. The captions in *Buzzworm* supplement the articles, whereas the captions in *Sierra* only give brief descriptions of the pictures.

Finally, *Buzzworm* is objective, a rare quality in environmental 10 magazines. An article on tourism versus environmental responsibility focuses on both the environmental and economic aspects of tourism, stating that while tourism generates income, it often destroys places of natural beauty that are so often visited. In contrast to this point of view, the article also cites examples where tourism has actually helped to preserve the environment. For every argument presented in *Buzzworm,* the counterargument is also presented. This balance is important, for readers must have all of the facts to be able to make well-informed judgments about controversial issues.

Despite all of its wonderful aspects, *Buzzworm* does have its 11 flaws. Some of its graphics pale next to the color photographs. Also, the photograph sizes should be varied more to create a visually more appealing layout. Except for these minor flaws, *Buzzworm* achieves its goal of appealing to its readers. In informing the general public about conservation and protection of our environment, *Buzzworm* is far more effective than *Sierra*.

READING FOR MEANING

Write at least a page, exploring your understanding and response to the essay. Begin by listing the reasons for Wolf's judgment of *Buzzworm*. Then focus on whatever you like as you reread the essay and add to your annotations. For additional ideas to stimulate your writing, consider these suggestions:

- Why do you think Wolf emphasizes the quality of the photographs in *Buzzworm?*

- In paragraph 4, Wolf refers to an article about the Masai. Is this the kind of subject you thought would be covered in this magazine as it is described in the opening paragraphs? Why might enhancing readers' "understanding of the Masai culture and traditions" be an important part of teaching readers to preserve the environment?

- Wolf praises *Buzzworm*'s subfeatures because they allow the reader to learn more about the subject (paragraphs 5 and 6). Yet she criticizes *Sierra* because each issue treats a single subject in depth. Consider whether she is being inconsistent here.

- Explain the meaning or significance of "Only by gaining a better understanding of our planet will we be able to preserve our fragile environment" (paragraph 1); "balance is important, for readers must have all of the facts to be able to make well-informed judgments about controversial issues (paragraph 10); or any other statement that you find interesting.

- If you have ever read *Buzzworm* or *Sierra,* what is your judgment of the magazine? How do you react to Wolf's judgment?

EXTENDING MEANING THROUGH CONVERSATION. Get together with a few other students who have read Wolf's review of *Buzzworm* and discuss the essay's meaning. To develop your understanding, you might begin by sharing what you have written already about the essay or by exploring together one of the suggestions listed above.

You might also discuss some of Wolf's assumptions. Some examples from the first two paragraphs are that many of us are ignorant about the environment; the environment is fragile and in danger; magazines like *Buzzworm* can enlighten the general public, but at the same time it is important for a good magazine to be objective.

READING LIKE A WRITER
SUPPORTING REASONS WITH EXAMPLES

Reasons need supporting evidence, and examples are one of the most pervasive kinds of evidence used in evaluating written texts such as magazines, essays, and books. Often the effectiveness of an evaluative essay depends on the specificity and concreteness of the examples. That is especially true when the writer cannot assume readers will be familiar with the subject, as in this essay.

Wolf could have included copies of photographs to illustrate her points, but she still would have had to point out to readers what she wants them to notice about the photographs.

ANALYZE. Reread paragraphs 3 through 6, annotating the reasons and examples. Underline the details that you find most helpful and interesting. Put parentheses around any details that seem unnecessary or uninteresting. What additional information would you, as one reader, have wanted her to supply? Note how well Wolf connects each example to a reason.

Also note how Wolf interweaves the comparison and contrast between *Buzzworm* and *Sierra* magazines. How well do illustration with examples and comparison and contrast work together as strategies?

WRITE. Write a few sentences indicating what you have learned about Wolf's use of examples, and comparison and contrast.

CONSIDERING IDEAS FOR YOUR OWN WRITING

If you were to evaluate a magazine, newspaper, or textbook, which would you choose? On what basis do you think you would make your judgment? With what other work could you compare it so your readers, who might not be familiar with the work you are evaluating, would be able to understand your reasons for liking or not liking it?

THINKING ABOUT WHAT MAKES AN EVALUATION EFFECTIVE

You have been learning in this chapter how to read evaluative essays by reading for meaning and reading like a writer. Before writing an evaluation of your own, take a few minutes to think about what makes evaluative writing effective.

ANALYZE. Choose one reading from this chapter that you think works especially well as an example of good evaluative writing. Reread your chosen selection, adding to your original annotations further annotations about what makes this essay work so well as an evaluation. To begin, consider the selection's purpose and how well it achieves that purpose for its particular readers. Then focus on how well the selection

- presents the subject
- asserts a judgment
- gives reasons and supporting evidence
- establishes credibility

You can complete this activity on your own, or your instructor may ask you to work collaboratively with a small group of other students who have chosen the same reading as an example of good evaluative writing. If you work with others, take time initially for everyone to reread the selection thoughtfully, adding to their annotations. Then discuss your reasons for thinking that this evaluation works well. Although you all agree that the essay is good, do not be surprised if you do not agree on the specifics. Take notes on what in the essay the group agrees works well and what the group is divided about.

WRITE. Write at least a page explaining and justifying your choice of this reading as an example of effective evaluative writing. Assume that your readers— your instructor and classmates—have read the selection but will not remember many details. They also may not remember it as an especially successful evaluation. Therefore, you will want to use details and refer to specific parts of the reading as you explain how it works as an evaluation and seek to justify your view of its effectiveness. You need *not* argue that it is the best reading in the chapter or that it is flawless, only that it is, in your view, an excellent example of the genre.

A GUIDE TO WRITING AN EVALUATION

Although all evaluations argue for a judgment, they vary in how they present the subject and how they make their argument. For example, there may be wide variation in how much information about the subject is imparted to readers; writers may describe their subjects in detail, or they may assume that readers are already familiar with the subject.

As the selections in this chapter suggest, evaluations may also differ on how they support their reasons. An argument may be constructed around several reasons with specific evidence provided for each reason, or it may be centered on a single reason.

However you finally decide to present your subject and argue for your judgment, you will need to do some thoughtful planning. The following brief guide suggests some things to consider as you plan, draft, and revise your own evaluative essay.

INVENTION

Writing is a process of discovery—of learning what you already know about a subject and what you still need to know, of trying out ideas and arguments to see which are most effective, and of finding evidence that makes your judgment credible to readers. The following invention activities will help you make these discoveries in a systematic way.

Choosing a Subject

The selections in this chapter suggest several different types of subjects you could write about: particular jobs; films; recordings or music videos; books, magazines, or other publications. There are also countless other possibilities: public figures (in politics, sports, and so on); works of art or artists; restaurants and other businesses; groups in your community; educational programs; particular types of mechanisms or equipment (cars, stereos, sports gear, word-processing programs).

To find a subject, list specific examples in several of the following categories. Although you may be inclined to pick the first idea that comes to mind, try to make your list as long as you can. This will ensure that you have a variety of subjects from which to choose and also encourage you to think of unique subjects.

a film or group of films by the same director

a musical recording

a live or videotaped concert or theatrical performance

a magazine or newspaper

a book (perhaps a work—either fiction or nonfiction—that you have recently read for one of your classes)

a club or organized activity that people participate in—Little League, Girl Scouts, college sports programs, a particular educational curriculum (You might, like Etzioni, consider a subject generally viewed positively that your experience leads you to evaluate more negatively or, alternatively, a subject generally viewed negatively that your experience leads you to evaluate more positively.)

a contemporary political movement (Consider evaluating any such movement's methods as well as its goals and achievements.)

a proposed or existing law

a noteworthy person—either someone in the news or a local professional, such as a teacher, doctor, social worker, auto mechanic, or minister (Personal experience with at least two such local figures will enable comparison to strengthen your evaluation.)

an artist or writer, or his or her works

a local business

particular brands of machines or equipment with which you are familiar (Consider comparing a "superior" to an "inferior" brand to make your evaluation more authoritative.)

one of the essays in this text (arguing that it is a strong or weak example of its type) or two essays (arguing that one is better)

After you have a list of possibilities, consider the following questions as you make your final selection:

- Do I already know enough about this subject, or can I get the information I need in time? If, for instance, you decide to review a film, you should be able to see it soon. If you choose to evaluate a brand of machine or equipment, you should already be somewhat expert with it or have time to learn enough about it to be able to write with some authority.

- Do I already have strong feelings and a firm judgment about this subject? It is always easier to write about subjects on which you have formed opinions, although it is conceivable that you could change your mind as you write. If you choose a subject that leaves you cold, your readers will probably have the same reaction. The more sure you are of your judgment, the more persuasive you are likely to be.

Exploring Your Subject

Before you can go much further, you must ascertain what you already know about the subject and what additional information you may need. To do this, list everything you now know about the subject and all the questions you still have, or write about the subject for ten or fifteen minutes without stopping, putting down anything that enters your mind. If you discover that you need to gather more information, find out where you can get it and whether you have enough time for research.

Analyzing Your Readers

To decide how much information about the subject to include in your essay, you will need to estimate how much your readers know about the subject and how much they need to know to accept your judgment. In planning your argument, you must also anticipate readers' attitudes and opinions. Take some time to think about the readers you will be addressing, what they might already know about the subject and what you will need to tell them, and according to what standards they are likely to judge your subject.

LEARNING MORE ABOUT YOUR READERS:
A COLLABORATIVE ACTIVITY

The aim of this activity is twofold: to help you understand how much information about the subject your readers will need and to suggest how you can make your argument convincing to readers by basing it on shared values and standards of judgment.

Get together with two or three other students. Take turns telling one another about your subjects. Tell them the kind of subject you chose (a film, a computer program, an HMO) and any details that would help your classmates think about the basis on which they would evaluate such a subject. Do not discuss your judgment of the subject.

Then your classmates will tell you what else they need to know about the subject and what standards they would use to judge a subject of the kind you are evaluating. Listen carefully to what they have to say and take careful notes. Ask questions to get the members of your group to explain why they would base their own evaluations on these particular standards. Specifically, what qualities do they look for in a subject of this kind? Which of these qualities do they consider most important?

Considering Your Judgment

Although your opinion of the subject may change as you continue to think and write about it, state as directly as you can what your overall judgment of the subject is right now. Do not make an argument for your judgment at this time. But to figure out what you think, you may need to write for a few minutes, weighing the subject's good against its bad qualities. When you have finished with the balance sheet, reassert your overall judgment clearly and emphatically.

Listing Reasons

Consider all the reasons you might give in your essay, both those that support your overall judgment and those that show you have a balanced view of the subject. If you have difficulty identifying your reasons, try completing the following sentence:

[*The subject*] is a good or bad [*name the kind of thing it is*] because [*identify your reason*].

Write down all the reasons you can think of and then look over your list to consider which reasons you feel are the most important and which would be most convincing to your readers given your understanding of the standards on which they ordinarily base their evaluations of subjects of this kind.

Finding Evidence to Support Your Reasons

Before deciding which reasons to use in the essay, determine what kinds of evidence will support your most promising reasons. Evidence may take many different forms—facts, quotations from experts, statistics, personal experience—but most evaluations rely largely on details and examples from the subject itself. For that reason, you will have to reexamine the subject closely even if you know it quite well by now.

If you are evaluating a film, for example, it is best if you can see it on video so you can revisit certain scenes to transcribe some of the dialogue or note specific details. The amount of evidence you use to support your reasons will vary. Some reasons may need a lot of evidence, while others may seem more self-evident. The credibility of your argument will depend to a large extent on your citing specific examples and other kinds of evidence accurately and fairly without taking them out of context or distorting them.

Drawing Comparisons

Comparing and contrasting your subject with other subjects of the same kind can add an important dimension to your evaluation and also help you develop your thinking about the subject. Do some exploratory writing about one or more subjects you could compare with your subject. Try to pick subjects that your readers may know. Compare the good and bad qualities of each and note your own as well as other people's evaluations of these comparable subjects.

DRAFTING

After you have made a fairly detailed chart of your argument, you are probably ready to set your goals, plan the draft of your essay, and decide how to begin.

Setting Goals

The decisions you make about what to include in your evaluation and how to order your ideas should be guided by some specific goals that reflect your purpose and your understanding of the readers' needs and expectations. Considering the following questions may help you clarify your goals: What do I want to accomplish with this particular evaluation? Is my primary purpose to make a recommendation as Ansen and Wolf do? Do I want to celebrate my subject like Angell does, expose its flaws like Etzioni, or weigh its good and bad qualities as Scorpia and Nussbaum do?

How much experience evaluating a subject of this kind can I expect my readers to have? Will they share my standards, or will I have to explain them?

How much information about the subject do my readers need to understand my evaluation? Obviously, reviews of new books, films, and recordings should assume little or no familiarity on the part of readers.

Planning Your Draft

After you have decided how much your readers know and need to know, what reasons and evidence you will use, and how best to present them, plan the organization of your draft to best reflect these decisions. Like Wolf, you might offer an evaluative comparison of two subjects point by point; or you might begin with a comparison, then go on to treat your subject in detail.

Beginning

How you decide to begin your essay will depend on how familiar your readers are with your subject. If you are writing about something that is entirely new and unfamiliar, you will want to begin with a description or summary of the subject as Scorpia and Wolf do. If you expect your readers to have certain expectations about the subject, you may, like Nussbaum, begin by referring to these expectations. Or, like Etzioni, Ansen, and Angell, you may start off with a strong statement of your overall judgment.

Avoiding Logical Fallacies

Evaluative writing is particularly susceptible to certain kinds of faulty logic. To avoid these logical fallacies, ask yourself the following questions as you plan and draft your essay:

- Am I basing my argument on personal *taste* instead of on standards of judgment generally accepted as appropriate (praising a story, for example, because it reminds me of my own experience)?

- Am I basing my argument on *trivial reasons* and ignoring important ones (condemning a film because it has subtitles, for example)?
- Am I making *weak or misleading comparisons* (failing to acknowledge weaknesses of subjects I praise and strengths of those I criticize)?
- Am I accepting the *burden of proof* (giving reasons and backing instead of merely asserting my opinions)?
- Am I guilty of *either/or thinking* (seeing only the good or only the bad in my subject)?

READING A DRAFT CRITICALLY

With a draft in hand, you need someone to read critically what you have written and to advise you on how to improve your draft. The suggestions in this section will ensure that you get helpful advice, advice that is specific to the kind of evaluation you are writing. Get a written record of your reader's comments so that later, when you sit down to revise, you will have specific suggestions to consider.

Reading a draft critically means reading it more than once, first to get a general impression and then to analyze its basic features and strategies. Before you begin reading, number the paragraphs so you can refer easily to specific parts of the draft.

Reading for a First Impression

Read quickly through the draft to get a sense of the evaluative argument. Then write a few sentences describing your general impression. How clear is the writer's overall judgment? What in the argument seems most and least convincing?

Reading to Analyze

Read the draft a second time to focus on the basic features and strategies of evaluations.

PRESENTATION OF THE SUBJECT. Locate where in the draft the subject is described. It may be discussed in several places, serving both to explain the subject and to provide evidence supporting the argument. Point to any places where you do not understand what is being said about the subject or where you need more detail or explanation. Ask questions. If you are surprised by the way the writer has presented the subject, briefly explain how you usually think of this particular subject or subjects of this kind. Also indicate if any of the information about the subject seems to you to be unnecessary. Finally and most importantly, let the writer know if any of the information seems inaccurate or only partially true.

STATEMENT OF THE OVERALL JUDGMENT. Find the clearest statement of the overall judgment and underline it. If you cannot find a clear thesis, let the writer know. If there are several restatements of the thesis, examine them closely for consistency. Look specifically at the value terms that are being used to see if they are unclear or waffling. Remember that even though many evaluative essays point out the good as well as the bad qualities of the subject, they also make an explicit overall judgment that takes the good and bad into consideration. If the writer's overall judgment seems fuzzy or inconsistent, suggest how it might be made clearer or qualified to account for the subject's strengths and weaknesses.

SUPPORTING REASONS AND EVIDENCE. Highlight the reasons in the essay. Reasons in an evaluation may take the form of judgments of the subject's various qualities, judgments that in turn need to be explained and supported with evidence. Look closely at the reasons that seem most problematic and briefly explain what bothers you; for example, that the reason does not seem appropriate for judging this kind of subject, that you do not fully understand the reason or how it applies to this particular subject, why the connection between a particular reason and its supporting evidence is not clear or convincing for you. Be as specific and constructive as you can, not only pointing out what does not work but also suggesting what the writer might do to solve the problem. For example, if a reason seems inappropriate, explain why and indicate what kinds of reasons you expect people to use when evaluating a subject like this.

Also look for faulty reasoning. Note if the writer is basing the argument on personal taste rather than on generally accepted standards of judgment. Indicate if the writer has failed to accept the burden of proof and simply asserted a judgment rather than giving reasons and evidence to support it. Tell the writer if you detect either/or reasoning (seeing only the good or only the bad qualities) or if comparisons seem weak or misleading.

CREDIBILITY. Whether or not you agree with the writer's ultimate judgment, point to any place in the essay where you do not trust the writer; for example, where the writer does not seem sufficiently knowledgeable or the facts seem distorted. If you sense the writer is being unfair, perhaps criticizing something minor as though it were major or emphasizing something beyond the control of the subject's producers. Also let the writer know if you think the judgment is based on idiosyncratic, trivial, or simply the wrong standards of judgment.

REVISING

To revise effectively, refocus on what you want readers to understand about the subject and your evaluation of it. Anything that diverts attention away from your argument may need to be cut or rewritten.

Do not divert your attention by trying to correct spelling errors or improve your writing style. At this point, you need to think about big issues like how well you have described the subject, how clearly and emphatically you have stated your overall judgment, and how convincing your argument is. If you can use a computer, the technical part of revising is easy and fast. But intellectually, revising remains a challenge.

If your draft received a thoughtful critical reading by a classmate or two, you will have gotten some valuable help in deciding which parts of your draft need revising and what changes you could make. Before making a plan or starting to revise, reread your own draft analytically by following the guidelines for Reading a Draft Critically. As you revise, keep in mind the following suggestions.

Revising to Present the Subject

If more specific information about the subject is needed, review your invention writing to see if you have left out of the draft details you could now add. Or do some further invention to generate new information you could add.

If readers have asked specific questions, consider whether you need to answer them in your revision.

If you have included information readers regard as unnecessary or redundant, consider cutting it.

If any of the information strikes readers as inaccurate or only partially true, reconsider its accuracy and completeness and then make any necessary changes to reassure readers.

Revising to Clarify the Overall Judgment

If your overall judgment is not stated explicitly or clearly, make the thesis more obvious.

If readers think your restatements of the thesis are contradictory, reread them with a critical eye and, if you agree, make them more consistent.

If readers think your judgment is unemphatic or waffling, reconsider the value terms you use.

If your essay discusses both the good and the bad qualities of the subject, be sure that while the thesis statement asserts your overall judgment it also acknowledges what you have said in the essay.

Most important, if you have not fully supported your reasons with ample evidence from your subject, reread or reexamine it closely to collect further evidence.

Revising to Strengthen the Reasons and Evidence

If any of the reasons seem inappropriate to readers, consider how you might convince them the reason is appropriate—for example, that it is used often by others or that it is based on widely shared and valid standards of judgment.

If your readers do not fully understand how a particular reason applies to the subject, make your thinking more explicit.

If the connection between a reason and its supporting evidence seems vague or weak, explain why you think the evidence is relevant.

If readers think your essay does not carry the burden of proof, try making clearer the reasons and evidence on which you base your judgment.

Revising to Enhance Credibility

If readers question your knowledge of the subject or authority to evaluate it, reassure them by the way you discuss the subject and compare it to other subjects of the same kind. You could also add quotations from other recognized experts to bolster your credibility.

If your facts do not seem reliable, cite supporting evidence and respected sources.

If the qualities you choose to emphasize seem minor, explain why you think they are important.

If readers think your essay is too one-sided, consider if there is any quality of the subject you could either praise or criticize.

REFLECTING ON WHAT YOU HAVE LEARNED ABOUT WRITING EVALUATION

In this chapter, you have read critically several pieces of evaluation and have written one of your own. To remind yourself how much you have learned and to help you remember it in the future, pause now to reflect on your reading and writing experiences while working on this chapter.

Write a page or so reflecting on your learning. Begin by describing what you are most pleased with in your essay and explaining what contributed to your achievement. Be specific about this contribution. If it was something you learned from the readings, indicate which readings and specifically what you learned from them. If it came from your invention writing, point out the section or sections that helped you most. If you received good advice from a critical reader, explain exactly how the person helped you—perhaps to understand a particular problem in your draft or to add a new dimension to your writing. Try to write about your achievement in terms of what you have learned about the genre of evaluation.

Then write about anything else that accounts for your learning this special kind of writing. Add anything you have learned about the writing process; for example, how to use time efficiently before writing a draft to discover what you want to say about the subject, or how to get constructive criticism and practical advice from other readers of your draft.

CHAPTER 7

———

SPECULATION ABOUT CAUSES OR EFFECTS

———

When something surprising occurs, we automatically look to the past and ask, "Why did that happen?" Whether we want simply to understand it, to make it happen again, or to find a way to prevent it from happening again, we need to analyze what caused it.

Or our focus may shift from cause to effect, from "Why did that happen?" to "What is going to happen?" Anticipating effects can be useful in planning and decision making.

In many cases, questions about causes and effects are relatively easy to answer. Through personal experience or scientific experimentation, we know what causes some things to happen and what effects they will have. For example, scientists have discovered the virus that causes AIDS, and we all know its potential deadly effects. We cannot be completely certain, however, of the many factors that encourage the spread of the virus in particular individuals or of the long-term effects of AIDS on our society. In these situations, the best we can do is make educated guesses. In this chapter, you will be reading and writing speculative essays about causes and effects that cannot be known for certain.

We encounter this kind of speculative cause or effect writing every day. A political analyst conjectures about the cause of a surprising election defeat. An economist suggests reasons for an increase in the trade deficit with Japan. A sportswriter theorizes about why the Pacific Ten nearly always defeats the Big Ten in the Rose Bowl.

Causal argument also plays an important role in government, business, and education. To give credit where it is due, a mayor asks the police commission to report on why complaints of police brutality against African Americans and

Latinos have decreased recently. A salesperson writes a memo to the district sales manager explaining how a particular policy adversely affects sales. Before proposing changes in the math curriculum, a school principal appoints a committee to investigate the causes for falling math test scores at the school.

Speculation about causes or effects is equally important in college study. For example, you might read a history essay in which a noted scholar evaluates other scholars' proposed causes of the Civil War to argue for a never-before-considered cause. (If the essay merely summarized other scholars' proposed causes, the historian would be reporting established information, not speculating about new possibilities.) You might also encounter a sociological report conjecturing about the recent increase in marriages among the elderly; the writer could have no way of knowing for certain why more and more older people choose to marry for the first time or remarry but could only conjecture about the causes—and then argue with relevant facts, statistics, or anecdotes to support the conjectures.

Writing your own essay speculating about causes or effects will engage you in some of the most challenging problem-solving and decision-making situations a writer can experience. You will be able to test your powers of reasoning and creativity as you search out hidden, underlying causes or speculate about results that are surprising yet still plausible. You will continue to develop your sensitivity to your readers' knowledge and attitudes, anticipating their objections and discovering ways to communicate your ideas more effectively.

Reading the essays in this chapter will help you see what makes arguments about causes or effects convincing. You will also get suggestions for writing your own essay about causes or effects, perhaps from the ideas for writing that follow each selection. Keep the following goals for speculating about causes or effects in mind as you evaluate the essays in this chapter and plan to write one of your own.

THE WRITING ASSIGNMENT

Speculating about Causes or Effects

Choose a subject that invites you to speculate about its causes or effects—why it might have happened or what its effects may be. Write an essay, arguing for your proposed causes or effects. Essays about causes look to the past to ponder why something happened, whereas essays about effects guess what is likely to happen in the future. Whether you are writing an essay about causes or effects, you need to do two things: (1) establish the existence and significance of the subject (an event, a phenomenon, or a trend) and (2) convince readers that the causes or effects you propose are plausible.

CAUSE OR EFFECT WRITING SITUATIONS

In addition to some of the circumstances already indicated in which cause or effect essays are written, following are a few additional examples with some details to suggest the kinds of argument writers typically make.

- A science writer notes that relatively few women get advanced degrees in science and conjectures that social conditioning may be the major cause. To support her causal argument, she cites research on the way boys and girls are treated differently in early childhood. She also gives examples to attempt to show that the social pressure to conform to female role expectations may discourage junior-high-school girls from doing well in math and science. She acknowledges that other as-yet-unrecognized causes may contribute.

- A student writes in the school newspaper about the rising number of pregnancies among high-school students. Interviews with the pregnant students lead her to argue that the chief cause of the trend is the new requirement that parents must give written consent for minors to get birth-control devices at the local clinic. She explains that many of the students failed to get birth-control information, let alone devices, because of this regulation. She reports that her interviews fail to support alternative explanations that young women have babies to give meaning to their lives, gain status among their peers, or live on their own supported by welfare.

- A psychology student writes about the effects—positive and negative—of extensive video-game playing among preteens. Based on his own experience and observation, he suggests that children's hand-eye coordination might improve, as well as their ability to concentrate on a single task. He speculates that, on the negative side, some children's grades might suffer because they spend so much time playing video games.

PRACTICING SPECULATION ABOUT CAUSES OR EFFECTS

A COLLABORATIVE ACTIVITY

PART 1. With your instructor and classmates, make a list of some surprising or important events or trends on your campus or in your community. Has a losing team, for example, suddenly begun to win? Has a valued student service or benefit been reduced or canceled? Has there been a decrease in the popularity of business majors or an increase in political activism? In your community, are fewer summer and part-time jobs available, more movie theaters showing the same films?

Get together with two or three other students. Choose one subject you are all interested in understanding better, and discuss its likely causes or effects for ten to fifteen minutes. First, list all of the causes or effects you can come up with in two or three minutes. Then select three or four of the most convincing and make brief notes about how you would convince others that these are the most likely causes or effects.

PART 2. When you have finished, take another five or ten minutes to discuss the process of speculating about causes or effects. Use the following questions as points of discussion:

From where did your most convincing causes or effects come: reading, television, school, your own imagination, anywhere else?

On what basis did you decide which causes or effects to include and which to leave out?

How did you decide what arguments might convince others that your proposed causes or effects are plausible?

How would you learn more about the event or trend? What would you want to know?

A GUIDE TO READING SPECULATION ABOUT CAUSES OR EFFECTS

To introduce essays speculating about causes or effects, first you will have the opportunity to read, annotate, and write about your understanding of the brief causal-analysis essay that follows. Then, guided by a list of basic features and strategies, you will reread the essay to discover and evaluate what makes cause or effect arguments effective.

Here is an illustration of an annotated passage from another essay, by Natalie Angier, which appears in its entirety later in the chapter. In the following excerpt, Angier speculates about the causes of a new intolerance of boyish behavior.

Cause 3

quote authority

all boys aggressive?

boyishness + guns = violence

Cause 4

here only 1 of 3 suggests violence or aggression

scientific explanation: more energy = more likelihood for violence

Perhaps part of the reason why boyish behavior is suspect these days is Americans' obsessive fear of crime. "We're all really terrified of violence," said Dr. Edward Hallowell, a child psychiatrist at Harvard. "Groups of people who have trouble containing aggression come under suspicion." And what group has more trouble containing aggression than males under the age of 21? Such suspiciousness is not helped by the fact that the rate of violent crime has climbed most steeply among the young, and that everybody seems to own a gun or know where to steal one. Sure, it's perfectly natural for boys to roll around in the dirt fighting and punching and kicking; but toss a firearm into the equation, and suddenly no level of aggression looks healthy.

Another cause for the intolerance of boyish behavior is the current school system. It is more group-oriented than ever before, leaving little room for the jokester, the tough, the tortured individualist. American children are said to be excessively coddled and undisciplined, yet in fact they spend less time than their European or Japanese counterparts at recess, where kids can burn off the manic energy they've stored up while trapped in the classroom. Because boys have a somewhat higher average metabolism than do girls, they are likely to become more fidgety when forced to sit still and study.

Stephen King

WHY WE CRAVE HORROR MOVIES

The following causal-analysis essay was written by Stephen King (b. 1947), the preeminent writer of horror novels and films. Among his best-known works are *Misery, Four Past Midnight, Needful Things,* and *Nightmares and Dreamscapes.* The essay was originally published in *Playboy* magazine in 1981. As the title indicates, "Why We Crave Horror Movies" attempts to explain the causes for a common phenomenon.

I think that we're all mentally ill; those of us outside the asylums only hide it a little better—and maybe not all that much better, after all. We've all known people who talk to themselves, people who sometimes squinch their faces into horrible grimaces when they believe no one is watching, people who have some hysterical fear—of snakes, the dark, the tight place, the long drop . . . and, of course, those final worms and grubs that are waiting so patiently underground. [1]

When we pay our four or five bucks and seat ourselves at tenth-row center in a theater showing a horror movie, we are daring the nightmare. [2]

Why? Some of the reasons are simple and obvious. To show that we can, that we are not afraid, that we can ride this roller coaster. Which is not to say that a really good horror movie may not surprise a scream out of us at some point, the way we may scream when the roller coaster twists through a complete 360 or plows through a lake at the bottom of the drop. And horror movies, like roller coasters, have always been the special province of the young; by the time one turns 40 or 50, one's appetite for double twists or 360-degree loops may be considerably depleted. [3]

We also go to re-establish our feelings of essential normality; the horror movie is innately conservative, even reactionary. Freda Jackson as the horrible melting woman in *Die, Monster, Die!* confirms for us that no matter how far we may be removed from the beauty of a Robert Redford or a Diana Ross, we are still light-years from true ugliness. [4]

And we go to have fun. [5]

Ah, but this is where the ground starts to slope away, isn't it? Because this is a very peculiar sort of fun, indeed. The fun comes from seeing others menaced—sometimes killed. One critic has suggested that if pro football has become the voyeur's version of combat, then the horror film has become the modern version of the public lynching. [6]

It is true that the mythic, "fairy-tale" horror film intends to take away the shades of gray. . . . It urges us to put away our more [7] civilized and adult penchant for analysis and to become children again, seeing things in pure blacks and whites. It may be that horror movies provide psychic relief on this level because this invitation to lapse into simplicity, irrationality and even outright madness is extended so rarely. We are told we may allow our emotions a free rein . . . or no rein at all.

If we are all insane, then sanity becomes a matter of degree. If   8
your insanity leads you to carve up women like Jack the Ripper or the Cleveland Torso Murderer, we clap you away in the funny farm (but neither of those two amateur-night surgeons was ever caught, heh-heh-heh); if, on the other hand, your insanity leads you only to talk to yourself when you're under stress or to pick your nose on your morning bus, then you are left alone to go about your business . . . though it is doubtful that you will ever be invited to the best parties.

The potential lyncher is in almost all of us (excluding saints, past   9
and present; but then, most saints have been crazy in their own ways), and every now and then, he has to be let loose to scream and roll around in the grass. Our emotions and our fears form their own body, and we recognize that it demands its own exercise to maintain proper muscle tone. Certain of these emotional muscles are ac-cepted—even exalted—in civilized society; they are, of course, the emotions that tend to maintain the status quo of civilization itself. Love, friendship, loyalty, kindness—these are all the emotions that we applaud, emotions that have been immortalized in the couplets of Hallmark cards and in the verses (I don't dare call it poetry) of Leonard Nimoy.

When we exhibit these emotions, society showers us with posi-   10
tive reinforcement; we learn this even before we get out of diapers. When, as children, we hug our rotten little puke of a sister and give her a kiss, all the aunts and uncles smile and twit and cry, "Isn't he the sweetest little thing?" Such coveted treats as chocolate-covered graham crackers often follow. But if we deliberately slam the rotten little puke of a sister's fingers in the door, sanctions follow—angry remonstrance from parents, aunts and uncles; instead of a choco-late-covered graham cracker, a spanking.

But anticivilization emotions don't go away, and they demand   11
periodic exercise. We have such "sick" jokes as, "What's the differ-ence between a truckload of bowling balls and a truckload of dead babies?" (You can't unload a truckload of bowling balls with a pitch-fork . . . a joke, by the way, that I heard originally from a ten-year-old). Such a joke may surprise a laugh or a grin out of us even as we recoil, a possibility that confirms the thesis: If we share a brother-hood of man, then we also share an insanity of man. None of which is intended as a defense of either the sick joke or insanity but merely as an explanation of why the best horror films, like the best fairy tales, manage to be reactionary, anarchistic, and revolutionary all at the same time.

The mythic horror movie, like the sick joke, has a dirty job to do.   12
It deliberately appeals to all that is worst in us. It is morbidity
unchained, our most base instincts let free, our nastiest fantasies
realized . . . and it all happens, fittingly enough, in the dark. For those
reasons, good liberals often shy away from horror films. For myself,
I like to see the most aggressive of them—*Dawn of the Dead,* for
instance—as lifting a trap door in the civilized forebrain and throwing a basket of raw meat to the hungry alligators swimming around
in that subterranean river beneath.

Why bother? Because it keeps them from getting out, man. It   13
keeps them down there and me up here. It was Lennon and
McCartney who said that all you need is love, and I would agree
with that.

As long as you keep the gators fed.   14

READING FOR MEANING

Write at least a page, exploring your understanding of "Why We Crave Horror Movies." Begin by considering how King's original audience for this
essay—*Playboy* readers, predominantly men in their twenties and thirties—may
have influenced his argument. Do you think King assumed that many of his
readers were horror-movie fans? Which of King's ideas do you think would
have most surprised these readers? Which surprise you most?

As you explore your understanding, you may need to reread the essay and
annotate it further. Consider occasionally quoting brief phrases or sentences to
help you present your understanding. You also may change your mind as you
reread the essay and write about it. If you have difficulty sustaining your writing
for at least a page, use any of the following suggestions that stimulate your
thinking:

- In the last few paragraphs, King categorizes emotions either as pro- or anticivilization. Explain, in your own words, the differences between these two
  kinds of emotion and the roles they play in society. Then indicate whether
  these categories make sense to you, and why.

- Explain the possible meaning or significance of "we're all mentally ill;
  those of us outside the asylums only hide it a little better—and maybe not
  all that much better, after all" (paragraph 1); "horror movies, like roller
  coasters, have always been the special province of the young" (paragraph
  3); "The fun comes from seeing others menaced" (paragraph 6); or any
  other statement that catches your attention.

- King mentions the fact that women often are the objects of violence in horror films, but he does not discuss specifically why this might be so. What
  reasons would you offer? Try to connect your ideas to King's argument.

- King seems to be saying that horror films perform a social function by
  allowing us to exercise (or possibly exorcise) our "anticivilization emotions" (paragraph 11). Whereas King argues that horror films provide an
  outlet for feelings that already exist, others might argue that horror films

actually create these feelings. What do you think of these ideas? Compare your ideas with King's ideas on this issue.

READING LIKE A WRITER

This activity leads you through an analysis of King's causal-writing strategies: *presenting the subject, making a cause or effect argument, handling objections and alternative causes or effects,* and *establishing credibility.* Each strategy is described briefly and followed by a critical reading and writing task to help you see how King uses that particular strategy in his essay.

Consider this activity a writer's introduction to causal argument. You will learn more about how different writers use these strategies from the activities following other selections in this chapter. You will also learn about the strategies for speculating about effects from the Kozol and Waldman selections later in the chapter. The Guide to Writing Speculations about Causes or Effects at the end of the chapter suggests how you can use these same strategies in writing your own essay speculating about causes or effects.

Presenting the Subject

In trying to explain why something happened or what its effects may be, writers must be sure that readers understand what happened. In some writing situations, a writer can safely assume that readers already know a great deal about the subject; then the writer can simply identify the subject and immediately begin the speculations about causes or effects. In many cases, however, writers must present an unfamiliar subject in enough detail so readers will understand it fully. On occasion, writers may even need to convince readers that the subject is important and worth speculating about.

How much space you need to devote to presenting the subject depends on how knowledgeable you can expect your readers to be about it. If the subject is a recent and well-known *event,* such as an election or a widely viewed football game, readers may not need a lot of information. If, however, the event occurred in the more distant past or is less well known, you need to provide more information. For an ongoing *phenomenon*—the relative lack of power of women in government, for example, or the astronomical salaries paid to professional ball players—readers may well need authoritative evidence regarding how widespread and significant the phenomenon is. Similarly, if what is being explained is a *trend*—a marked increase or decrease over a period of time in the number of women elected to public office or in the number of serious, career-threatening injuries among professional ball players—then readers definitely will want to see reliable evidence indicating that the change has been significant before they are ready to consider what might have caused such a change to occur or what its effects might be.

When writers decide they need to prove that the trend or phenomenon they are writing about exists, they may describe it in specific detail, give examples, offer factual evidence, cite statistics, or quote statements by authorities. To establish the significance of the subject, writers may show that it involves a large number of people or has great importance to certain people.

ANALYZE. How does King make the subject clear to readers? Skim the essay to see what horror movies are actually mentioned. In the original *Playboy* magazine article, several paragraphs in the beginning referred to horror movies that were popular at the time. These references were cut because contemporary readers would be unlikely to recognize them. How do you think examples help readers? Are the few examples left in the essay sufficient? Do you think readers need to know the movies mentioned to get the point? What horror movies do you think of as examples, and how do they help you understand King's subject?

Also consider how King establishes the significance of the subject. Underline one or two things King says to make you feel curious about why people crave horror movies. How does he make you feel that this subject is worth thinking about? What else might he have said to convince you?

WRITE. Write a page or so explaining how King presents his subject.

Making a Cause or Effect Argument

At the heart of an essay speculating about causes or effects is the causal argument. The argument is made up of at least two parts: the proposed causes or effects, and the reasoning and evidence supporting each cause or effect. In addition, the writer may acknowledge some objections readers might have while refuting others, strategies we take up in the next section.

In analyzing King's argument, we will look at some of the causes he proposes and how he supports them.

Writers speculating about causes or effects rarely consider only one possibility. They know that most things have multiple possible causes and many potential effects. However, they also know that it would be foolish to try to identify every possible cause or effect. The best essays avoid the obvious. They offer imaginative, new ways of thinking—either proposing new possibilities or arguing for familiar ideas in new ways.

Writers support their arguments with various kinds of evidence: facts, statistical correlations, personal anecdotes, testimony of authorities, examples, analogies.

ANALYZE. Reread King's essay, marking in the margin where each new cause is introduced. Then examine how King supports his argument. You will notice that King argues by analogy at several points in the essay. In arguing by analogy, the writer reasons that if two situations are alike, their causes will also be similar. Reread, for example, paragraph 3 where King asserts that people watch horror films for the same reason they ride roller coasters: "To show that [they] can, that [they] are not afraid." The strength of this argument, as in all attempts to argue by analogy, depends on how well the comparison holds up.

WRITE. Write a page or so identifying the causes King proposes to explain why people like horror movies. Then evaluate these causes. If any of them seems to you to be either too obvious or too improbable, explain why you think so. Note which causes, if any, seem most important to King's argument and why you think so. King presents his causes as alternative possibilities, but consider as well how they are interrelated—as links in a chain or as sections of a web.

Continuing your analysis, describe and evaluate King's support-by-analogy in paragraph 3. To do this, you need to fill out the picture by identifying relevant similarities between viewing horror films and riding roller coasters. Are these experiences frightening in the same way and for the same reasons?

Then find one other analogy in the essay (see, for example, paragraph 6, 11, or 12), and write a few sentences describing and evaluating it. Ask yourself both *how* the analogy works and *how well* it works to advance King's causal argument.

Handling Objections and Alternative Causes or Effects

When causes or effects cannot be known for certain, there is bound to be disagreement. Writers try to anticipate possible objections and alternative causes or effects readers might put forward. Simply acknowledging different points of view may not be enough, however; writers usually either refute (argue against) them or find a way to accommodate them in the argument.

ANALYZE. King anticipates a possible objection when he poses the rhetorical question "Why bother?" (paragraph 13). Reread the last few paragraphs, including paragraph 13, to identify the objection and evaluate King's handling of it.

WRITE. Write a few sentences, explaining whether you think the objection is sensible and whether you are satisfied with King's response. Also, you may have thought of another objection or question—one that King has not anticipated. Write a few more sentences, presenting your idea and indicating how you would have expected King to respond to it.

Establishing Credibility

Because analyzing causes or effects is highly speculative, much depends on whether readers trust the writer. Readers sometimes use information about the writer's professional and personal accomplishments in forming their judgment. The most important information, however, comes from the writing itself, specifically how writers argue for their own proposed causes or effects, as well as how they handle readers' objections and alternative causes or effects.

Writers seek to establish credibility with readers by making their reasoning clear and logical, their evidence relevant and trustworthy, and their handling of objections fair. They try to be authoritative (knowledgeable) without appearing authoritarian (opinionated and dogmatic).

ANALYZE. Most people who read this essay already know something about Stephen King. What do you know about him? Explain in a few sentences how this knowledge influences your willingness to accept what he says in this essay. Then, putting aside this extrinsic knowledge, focus on the essay itself.

WRITE. Write several sentences, describing the impression you have of the author from reading the essay. What makes you trust or distrust what he is saying? Notice, for example, that King uses plural pronouns (*we* and *us*) to establish a bond with readers. What else does he try to do to make you trust him, and how do you, as one reader, respond to these rhetorical strategies?

READINGS

Natalie Angier

INTOLERANCE OF BOYISH BEHAVIOR

One of America's preeminent science writers, Natalie Angier (b. 1958) won a Pulitzer Prize in 1991 for reports on various scientific topics in the *New York Times,* where she has worked as a reporter since 1990. Her specialties are biology and medicine. She began her journalism career in 1980 after graduating magna cum laude from Barnard College with a degree in English and physics. As both a staff writer and freelancer she has published articles in several magazines, including *Discovery, Time,* and *The Atlantic.* Her 1988 book, *Natural Obsessions: The Search for the Oncogene,* won the Lewis Thomas Award for excellence in writing about the life sciences. She is also a 1990 recipient of the International Biomedical Journalism Prize for outstanding media coverage of cancer.

In this selection, which appeared in the *New York Times* in 1994, Angier seeks to explain the increasing intolerance by teachers, parents, counselors, and therapists of certain kinds of behavior that has been labeled *boyish.* Angier speculates not about the causes of a phenomenon but about the causes of a *trend*—an increase or decrease in something over time. Unexpected or alarming social trends—like increasing medication of boys for behavior that was previously tolerated or overlooked—especially seem to invite causal speculation. You will notice that Angier is careful to demonstrate that there is in fact an increasing intolerance of boyish behavior.

As you read, think about your own experience as a sibling, friend of other young children, and student in elementary school. Does Angier convince you that most boys are more rambunctious than most girls? Do you believe that many teachers and parents now see this as a big problem? Consider also how plausible you find Angier's proposed causes for intolerance of boyish behavior.

Until quite recently, the plain-spun tautology "boys will be boys"   1
summed up everything parents needed to know about their Y-chro-
mosome bundles. Boys will be very noisy and obnoxious. Boys will
tear around the house and break heirlooms. They will transform any
object longer than it is wide into a laser weapon with eight settings
from stun to vaporize. They will swagger and brag and fib and not do
their homework and leave their dirty underwear on the bathroom
floor.

But they will also be . . . boys. They will be adventurous and   2
brave. When they fall down, they'll get up, give a cavalier spit to the
side, and try again. Tom Sawyer may have been a slob, a truant and a
hedonist; he may have picked fights with strangers for no apparent
reason; but he was also resourceful, spirited and deliciously clever.
Huckleberry Finn was an illiterate outcast, but as a long-term rafting
companion he had no peer.

Today, the world is no longer safe for boys. A boy being a shade   3
too boyish risks finding himself under the scrutiny of parents, teachers, guidance counselors, child therapists—all of them on watch for
the early glimmerings of a medical syndrome, a bona fide behavioral
disorder. Does the boy disregard authority, make snide comments
in class, push other kids around and play hooky? Maybe he has a
conduct disorder. Is he fidgety, impulsive, disruptive, easily bored?
Perhaps he is suffering from attention-deficit hyperactivity disorder,
or ADHD, the disease of the hour and the most frequently diagnosed behavioral disorder of childhood. Does he prefer computer
games and goofing off to homework? He might have dyslexia or
another learning disorder.

"There is now an attempt to pathologize what was once consid-   4
ered the normal range of behavior of boys," said Melvin Konner of
the departments of anthropology and psychiatry at Emory University in Atlanta. "Today, Tom Sawyer and Huckleberry Finn surely
would have been diagnosed with both conduct disorder and
ADHD." And both, perhaps, would have been put on Ritalin, the
drug of choice for treating attention-deficit disorder.

To be fair, many children do have genuine medical problems like   5
ADHD, and they benefit enormously from the proper treatment.
Psychiatrists insist that they work very carefully to distinguish
between the merely rambunctious child, and the kid who has a serious, organic disorder that is disrupting his life and putting him at risk
for all the demons of adulthood: drug addiction, shiftlessness, under-
employment, criminality and the like.

At the same time, some doctors and social critics cannot help but   6
notice that so many of the childhood syndromes now being diagnosed in record numbers affect far more boys than girls. Attention-
deficit disorder, said to afflict 5 percent of all children, is thought to
be about three to four times more common in boys than girls.
Dyslexia is thought to be about four times more prevalent in boys

than girls; and boys practically have the patent on conduct disorders. What is more, most of the traits that brand a child as a potential syndromeur just happen to be traits associated with young males: aggression, rowdiness, restlessness, loud-mouthedness, rebellious-ness. None of these characteristics is exclusive to the male sex, of course—for the ultimate display of aggressive intensity, try watching a group of city girls engaged in a serious game of jump-rope—but boys more often will make a spectacle of themselves. And these days, the audience isn't smiling at the show.

"People are more sensitized to certain extremes of boyishness," said Dr. John Ratey, a psychiatrist at Harvard Medical School. "It's not as acceptable to be the class clown. You can't cut up. You won't be given slack anymore." Woe to the boy who combines misconduct with rotten grades; he is the likeliest of all to fall under professional observation. "If rowdiness and lack of performance go together, you see the button being pushed much quicker than ever before," he said, particularly in schools where high academic performance is demanded.

Lest males of all ages feel unfairly picked upon, researchers point out that boys may be diagnosed with behavioral syndromes and disorders more often than girls for a very good reason: their brains may be more vulnerable. As a boy is developing in the womb, the male hormones released by his tiny testes accelerate the maturation of his brain, locking a lot of the wiring in place early on; a girl's hormonal bath keeps her brain supple far longer. The result is that the infant male brain is a bit less flexible, less able to repair itself after slight injury that might come, for example, during the arduous trek down the birth canal. Hence, boys may well suffer disproportionately from behavioral disorders for reasons unrelated to cultural expectations.

However, biological insights can only go so far in explaining why American boyhood is coming to be seen as a state of protodisease. After all, the brains of boys in other countries also were exposed to testosterone in utero, yet non-American doctors are highly unlikely to diagnose a wild boy as having a conduct disorder or ADHD.

"British psychiatrists require a very severe form of hyperactivity before they'll see it as a problem," said Dr. Paul R. McHugh, chairman and director of psychiatry at the Johns Hopkins School of Medicine in Baltimore. "Unless a child is so clearly disturbed that he goes at it until he falls asleep in an inappropriate place like a wastebasket or a drawer, and then wakes up and starts it all over again, he won't be put on medication." Partly as a result of this sharp difference in attitudes, the use of Ritalin-like medications has remained fairly stable in Britain, while pharmaceutical companies here have bumped up production by 250 percent since 1991.

Perhaps part of the reason why boyish behavior is suspect these days is Americans' obsessive fear of crime. "We're all really terrified of violence," said Dr. Edward Hallowell, a child psychiatrist at Harvard. "Groups of people who have trouble containing aggression come under suspicion." And what group has more trouble containing aggression than males under the age of 21? Such suspiciousness is not helped by the fact that the rate of violent crime has climbed most steeply among the young, and that everybody seems to own a gun or know where to steal one. Sure, it's perfectly natural for boys to roll around in the dirt fighting and punching and kicking; but toss a firearm into the equation, and suddenly no level of aggression looks healthy.

Another cause for the intolerance of boyish behavior is the current school system. It is more group-oriented than ever before, leaving little room for the jokester, the tough, the tortured individualist. American children are said to be excessively coddled and undisciplined, yet in fact they spend less time than their European or Japanese counterparts at recess, where kids can burn off the manic energy they've stored up while trapped in the classroom. Because boys have a somewhat higher average metabolism than do girls, they are likely to become more fidgety when forced to sit still and study.

The climate is not likely to improve for the world's Sawyers or Finns or James Deans or any other excessively colorful and unruly specimens of boyhood. Charlotte Tomaino, a clinical neuropsychologist in White Plains, notes that the road to success in this life has gotten increasingly narrow in recent years. "The person who used to have greater latitude in doing one thing and moving onto another suddenly is the person who can't hold a job," she said. "We define success as what you produce, how well you compete, how well you keep up with the tremendous cognitive and technical demands put upon you." The person who will thrive is not the restless version of a human tectonic plate, but the one who can sit still, concentrate and do his job for the 10, 12, 14 hours a day required.

A generation or two ago, a guy with a learning disability—or an ornery temperament—could drop out of school, pick up a trade and become, say, the best bridge builder in town. Now, if a guy cannot at the very least manage to finish college, the surging, roaring, indifferent Mississippi of the world's economy is likely to take his little raft, and break it into bits.

READING FOR MEANING

Write at least a page, exploring your understanding of "Intolerance of Boyish Behavior." Begin by listing a few of the basic facts about the trend about which Angier speculates. (She presents the trend mainly in paragraphs 1 through 6.) Then write about anything else in the essay that contributes to your understanding of Angier's speculations.

Expect your understanding to grow as you reread and annotate further. If you have difficulty writing at least a page, consider the following suggestions:

- Identify, in your own words, the causes Angier proposes to explain intolerance of boyish behavior. (You will find a major cause introduced in paragraphs 7, 8, 11, 12, and 13.) Then identify one of these causes that you find most and one that you find least plausible and explain your judgment.

- If you have read Mark Twain's novels *Tom Sawyer* and *Huckleberry Finn,* annotate the essay for every reference to these novels. Then explain what use Angier makes of the novels and how the references contribute to your understanding.

- In paragraph 11, Angier asserts that it is "perfectly natural" for boys to fight, punch, and kick. Do you agree? Examine your opinion about this question. Consider also what else Angier claims to be natural behavior and what evidence she offers to support her claims.

- Describe one or more personal experiences relevant to intolerance of boyish behavior, to its likely causes, or to its current treatment. Connect your experience to ideas or examples in Angier's essay.

EXTENDING MEANING THROUGH CONVERSATION. It is important for you to make meaning on your own; however, you may be able to extend your understanding by conversing with other students about Angier's essay.

Get together with one or two other students. Begin your conversation by identifying one idea that still interests, confuses, or challenges each one of you.

As you talk about the reading, you may find that each student has a somewhat different understanding of it. Your goal as a group is not necessarily to reach a consensus but to help each other think critically about the reading. You want to develop the meaning you see and also to gain insight from other readers' perspectives on the essay. Keep your conversation focused on the essay by rereading and discussing parts of it together.

READING LIKE A WRITER
HANDLING OBJECTIONS

A writer speculating about causes must work imaginatively and persistently to support the proposed causes, using all the relevant resources available, such as quoting authorities, statistics, research findings, comparisons and contrasts, rhetorical questions, literary allusions, and metaphor, among others. (Angier uses all of the resources in this list.) In addition to supporting their proposed causes, writers usually do more. Because they are trying to convince particular readers of the plausibility of their causal argument, writers remain keenly aware at every point in the argument that their readers will have questions. A writer knows that there will be some readers who share the writer's understanding of a trend and who find all the proposed causes plausible but who, nevertheless, will question details and emphasis. Moreover, a writer knows that at least some readers—in some situations, most or all readers—will have little understanding of a trend or a different understanding of it. Readers may even have a serious *mis*understanding of a trend. Some readers may resist or reject the proposed causes, or they may believe that other causes better explain the trend. Experienced writers anticipate these predictable concerns. Just as imaginatively as they argue for their proposed causes, writers attempt to answer readers' questions, react to their objections, and evaluate their preferred causes. When you write your essay, anticipating and responding to your readers' concerns will be one of the most challenging and interesting parts of your work.

ANALYZE. Angier anticipates readers' objections or questions in at least three places in her causal argument: paragraphs 5, 6, and 9 and 10. Reread these paragraphs to identify the objection or question Angier anticipates and to examine how she handles it.

WRITE. Write several sentences reporting what you have learned about how Angier anticipates her readers' concerns. Specifically, in each case, how does she support her response to readers? How appropriate do you find her response? How convincing do you find it? Try to think of one or two likely objections or questions she overlooked.

CONSIDERING IDEAS FOR YOUR OWN WRITING

Are you aware of any increases or decreases in group characteristics or behavior? For example, does it seem to you that girls or women are increasingly interested in math and science or in participating in team sports? If you have been working for a few years, have you noticed that employees are more docile and more eager to please management? If you have young children, does it seem to you that day-care people are increasingly professional? Think about other groups or categories of people you have the opportunity to observe, and try to identify increases or decreases in their behavior.

Select one group whose behavior is changing and consider how you would convince readers that it is in fact changing—increasing or decreasing over time. Can you offer any evidence beyond your personal impressions? What causes can you suggest to explain this trend?

Andrew M. Greeley

WHY DO CATHOLICS STAY IN THE CHURCH? BECAUSE OF THE STORIES

An ordained Roman Catholic priest and for ten years a parish priest, Andrew M. Greeley is now a leading American authority on the sociology of religion, with academic appointments at both the University of Arizona and the University of Chicago. He has published hundreds of articles and dozens of books. American universities have awarded him five honorary degrees in recognition of the importance of his scholarly work. As critical of the Catholic church as devoted to it, he has been a controversial figure within the church. He has published novels, religious books, and sociological studies. Recent novels are *Fall from Grace* (1993) and *Wages of Sin* (1992). Religious books include *The Book of Irish American Prayers and Blessings* (1991) and *Love Affair: A Prayer Journal* (1992). His best-regarded sociological studies may be *The Making of the Popes, 1978: The Politics of Intrigue in the Vatican* (1979) and *The Irish Americans: The Rise to Money and Power* (1980).

This essay was published in 1994 in the *New York Times Magazine,* a supplement to the Sunday editions of the *Times.* Though most of the *Times'* readers live in and around New York City, the *Times* also circulates nationwide. As a result, it has become an important national newspaper. (Many college bookstores sell the daily *Times.*) These facts are essential to your understanding of Greeley's argumentative strategies. Greeley knew that many of his readers would be fellow Catholics, and he probably assumed that nearly all of them would be eager to know why he thought they remained Catholics. Greeley also knew, however, that most of his readers would either belong to some other religious faith or never or only rarely attend church. He knew, in short, that he was writing for a diverse, national audience. And he knew, as well, that a high percentage of Americans goes to church and therefore might be interested in an argument about the appeal of religious faith, even one different from their own. (Twenty-three percent of Americans are Catholic, 52 percent Protestant, 19 percent nonreligious.)

In this essay, Greeley speculates about a phenomenon. He wants to try out some ideas about why Catholics remain Catholic. If you are not Catholic or not a church-goer, think about how Greeley attempts to engage your interest and hold it. Whatever your religious beliefs, notice as you read how carefully and fully Greeley supports the one cause he announces in his title for why Catholics remain faithful.

You can make a persuasive case against Catholicism if you want. The Church is resolutely authoritarian and often seems to be proud of the fact that it "is not a democracy." It discriminates against women and homosexuals. It tries to regulate the bedroom behavior of married men and women. It tries to impose the Catholic position regarding abortion on everyone. It represses dissent and even disagreement. The Vatican seems obsessed with sex. The Pope preaches against birth control in countries with rapidly expanding populations. Catholics often cringe when the local bishop or cardinal pontificates on social policy issues. Bishops and priests are authoritarian and insensitive. Lay people have no control of how their contributions are spent. Priests are unhappy, and many of them leave the priesthood as soon as they can to marry. The Church has covered up sexual abuse by priests for decades. Now it is paying millions of dollars to do penance for the sexual amuse-ments of supposedly celibate priests while it seeks to minimize, if not eliminate altogether, the sexual pleasures of married lay people.

One might contend with such arguments. Research indicates that   2
priests are among the happiest men in America. The Church was orga-nized in a democratic structure for the first thousand years and could be so organized again. But let the charges stand for the sake of the argument. They represent the way many of those who are not Catholic see the Catholic Church, and with some nuances and qualifications the way many of those inside the church see the Catholic institution. Nonetheless this case against Catholicism simply does not compute for most Catholics when they decide whether to leave or stay.

Do they in fact remain? Are not Catholics leaving the church in   3
droves? Prof. Michael Hout of the Survey Research Center at the University of California at Berkeley has demonstrated that the Catholic defection rate has remained constant over 30 years. It was 15 percent in 1960 and it is 15 percent today. Half of those who leave the Church do so when they marry a non-Catholic with stronger religious commitment. The other half leave for reasons of anger, authority and sex—the reasons cited above.

How can this be, the outsider wonders. For one thing, as the   4
general population has increased, the number of Catholics has increased proportionately. Still, how can 85 percent of those who are born Catholic remain, one way or another, in the church? Has Catholicism so brainwashed them that they are unable to leave?

The answer is that Catholics like being Catholic. For the last 30   5
years the hierarchy and the clergy have done just about everything they could to drive the laity out of the church and have not suc-ceeded. It seems unlikely that they will ever drive the stubborn lay folk out of the Church because the lay folk like being Catholic.

But why do they like being Catholic?   6

First, it must be noted that Americans show remarkable loyalty   7
to their religious heritages. As difficult as it is for members of the academic and media elites to comprehend the fact, religion is impor-tant to most Americans. There is no sign that this importance has declined in the last half century (as measured by survey data from the 1940's). Skepticism, agnosticism, atheism are not increasing in America, as disturbing as this truth might be to the denizens of mid-town Manhattan.

Moreover, while institutional authority, doctrinal propositions and   8
ethical norms* are components of a religious heritage—and important components—they do not exhaust the heritage. Religion is experi-ence, image and story before it is anything else and after it is every-thing else. Catholics like their heritage because it has great stories.

If one considers that for much of Christian history the population   9
was illiterate and the clergy semiliterate and that authority was far

---

*doctrinal propositions: statements about the basic beliefs of a religion; ethical norms: widely shared beliefs about good and bad behavior (Ed.)

away, one begins to understand that the heritage for most people most of the time was almost entirely story, ritual, ceremony and eventually art. So it has been for most of human history. So it is, I suggest (and my data back me up), even today.

Roger C. Schank, a professor of psychology at Northwestern   10 University who specializes in the study of artificial intelligence, argues in his book *Tell Me a Story* that stories are the way humans explain reality to themselves. The more and better our stories, Schank says, the better our intelligence.

Catholicism has great stories because at the center of its heritage   11 is "sacramentalism," the conviction that God discloses Himself in the objects and events and persons of ordinary life. Hence Catholicism is willing to risk stories about angels and saints and souls in purgatory and Mary the Mother of Jesus and stained-glass windows and statues and stations of the cross and rosaries and medals and the whole panoply of images and devotions that were so offensive to the austere leaders of the Reformation.[*] Moreover, the Catholic heritage also has the elaborate ceremonial rituals that mark the passing of the year—Midnight Mass, the Easter Vigil, First Communion, May Crowning, Lent, Advent, grammar-school graduation and the festivals of the saints.

Catholicism has also embraced the whole of the human life cycle   12 in Sacraments (with a capital S), which provide rich ceremonial settings, even when indifferently administered for the critical landmarks of life. The Sacrament of Reconciliation (confession that was) and the Sacrament of the Anointing of the Sick (extreme unction that was) embed in ritual and mystery the deeply held Catholic story of second chances.

The "sacramentalism" of the Catholic heritage has also led it to   13 absorb as much as it thinks it can from what it finds to be good, true and beautiful in pagan religions: Brigid is converted from the pagan goddess to the Christian patron of spring, poetry and new life in Ireland; Guadalupe is first a pagan and then a Christian shrine in Spain and then our Lady of Guadalupe becomes the patron of poor Mexicans. This "baptism" of pagan metaphors (sometimes done more wisely than at other times) adds yet another overlay of stories to the Catholic heritage.

The sometimes inaccurate dictum "once a Catholic, always a   14 Catholic," is based on the fact that the religious images of Catholicism are acquired early in life and are tenacious. You may break with the institution, you may reject the propositions, but you cannot escape the images.

The Eucharist (as purists insist we must now call the Mass) is a   15 particularly powerful and appealing Catholic ritual, even when it is done badly (as it often is) and especially when it is done well (which

Reformation: a religious movement that swept Western Europe during the sixteenth century, beginning as a reform movement within the Roman Catholic Church and eventuating in the establishment of Protestant churches dissenting from papal authority (*Ed.*)

it sometimes is). In the Mass we join a community meal of celebration with our neighbors, our family, our friends, those we love. Such an awareness may not be explicitly on the minds of Catholics when they go to Church on Saturday afternoon or Sunday morning, but is the nature of metaphor that those who are influenced by it need not be consciously aware of the influence. In a *New York Times*–CBS News Poll last April, 69 percent of Catholics responding said they attend Mass for reasons of meaning rather than obligation.

Another important Catholic story is that of the neighborhood parish. Because of the tradition of village parishes with which Catholics came to America, the dense concentration of Catholics in many cities and the small geographical size of the parish, parishes can and often do become intense communities for many Catholics. They actuate what a University of Chicago sociologist, James S. Coleman, calls "social capital," the extra resources of energy, commitment and intelligence that overlapping structures produce. This social capital, this story of a sacred place in the heart of urban America, becomes even stronger when the parish contains that brilliant American Catholic innovation—the parochial school. 16

Perhaps the Catholic religious sensibility all begins with the Christmas crib. A mother shows her child (perhaps age 3) the crib scene. The child loves it (of course) because it has everything she likes—a mommy, a daddy, a baby, animals, shepherds, shepherd children, angels and men in funny clothes—and with token integration! Who is the baby? the little girl asks. That's Jesus. Who's Jesus? The mother hesitates, not sure of exactly how you explain the communication of idioms to a 3-year-old. Jesus is God. That doesn't bother the little girl at all. Everyone was a baby once. Why not God? Who's the lady holding Jesus? That's Mary. Oh! Who's Mary? The mother throws theological caution to the winds. She's God's mommy. Again the kid has no problem. Everyone has a mommy, why not God? 17

It's a hard story to beat. Later in life the little girl may come to understand that God loves us so much that He takes on human form to be able to walk with us even into the valley of death and that God also loves us the way a mother loves a newborn babe—which is the function of the Mary metaphor in the Catholic tradition. 18

It may seem that I am reducing religion to childishness—to stories and images and rituals and communities. In fact, it is in the poetic, the metaphorical, the experiential dimension of the personality that religion finds both its origins and raw power. Because we are reflective creatures we must also reflect on our religious experiences and stories; it is in the (lifelong) interlude of reflection that propositional religion and religious authority become important, indeed indispensable. But then the religiously mature person returns to the imagery, having criticized it, analyzed it, questioned it, to commit the self once more in sophisticated and reflective maturity to the story. . . . 19

When I was in grammar school in the mid-1930's, the nuns told a   20
story that sums up why people stay Catholic. One day Jesus went on
a tour of the heavenly city and noted that there were certain new
residents who ought not to be there, not until they had put in a long
time in purgatory and some of them only on a last-minute appeal.
He stormed out to the gate where Peter was checking the day's
intake on his Compaq 486DX Deskpro computer (I have edited the
nuns' story)—next to which, on his work station, was a fishing pole
and a papal crown.

"You've failed again, Simon Peter," said the Lord.   21

"What have I done now?"   22

"You let a lot of people in that don't belong."   23

"I didn't do it."   24

"Well, who did?"   25

"You won't like it."   26

"Tell me anyway."   27

"I turn them away from the front gate and then they go around   28
to the back door and your mother lets them in!"

It is the religious sensibility behind that fanciful story that explains   29
why Catholics remain Catholic. It might not be your religious sensibility. But if you want to understand Catholics—and if Catholics
want to understand themselves—the starting point is to comprehend the enormous appeal of that sensibility. It's the stories.

READING FOR MEANING

Write at least a page, exploring your ideas about Greeley's argument for why
Catholics stay in the Church. Begin by explaining what you think to be Greeley's purpose in this essay, given his diverse national audience. Support your
explanation with details from the essay. Also identify your own religious affiliation and mention two or three ideas in the essay you found to be especially surprising, interesting, or controversial. Then write about anything else that
contributes to your understanding of Greeley's argument.

As you write, you may find that you need to reread the essay and annotate it
further. Consider quoting phrases or sentences that illustrate the meaning you
find. Your ideas may change as you reread and write. If you encounter difficulty
sustaining your writing for at least a page, consider the following ideas:

- Comment on Greeley's criticism of the Church in paragraphs 1 through 5,
  keeping in mind that Greeley is a Catholic priest.

- In paragraphs 11 through 18, Greeley gives examples of the kinds of stories
  that keep Catholics in the Church. List these stories and then choose one
  story and speculate about why it has such a powerful appeal.

- If you consider yourself a member of a non-Catholic religious faith, explain
  why you stay in your church. Compare or contrast why you stay with why
  (Greeley claims) Catholics stay. Or list criticisms you have of your faith
  and compare or contrast them to the criticisms Greeley has of Catholicism.

- Explain the possible meaning or significance of "Skepticism, agnosticism, atheism are not increasing in America" (paragraph 7); "Religion is experience, image, and story before it is anything else" (paragraph 8); and "The more and better our stories . . . the better our intelligence" (paragraph 10), or any other statement that catches your attention.

EXTENDING MEANING THROUGH CONVERSATION. Although it is important for you to make meaning on your own, you may be able to increase your understanding by conversing with other students about Greeley's essay.

Get together with one or two other students. Take turns identifying one thing about the essay that still interests, confuses, or challenges you.

As you talk about the reading, you may find that the group has somewhat different understandings of it. Try to help each other think critically about the reading to develop the meaning further by gaining insight from other readers' perspectives. Keep your conversation focused on the essay by reading and discussing parts of it together.

RECOGNIZING THE EMOTIONAL APPEAL OF AN ARGUMENT. A further strategy for reading for meaning, which is not described in this chapter, is recognizing emotional manipulation. Arguments appeal to readers' logic and to their emotions. Thoughtful readers usually do not resist appeals to their feelings of sympathy or concern or idealism, but they resent feeling emotionally manipulated by appeals to sentimentality, fear, or prejudice. You can learn something about this important aspect of argument by identifying and evaluating emotional appeals in "Why Do Catholics Stay in the Church? Because of the Stories."

For guidelines and an illustration of this strategy turn to the part titled Recognizing Emotional Manipulation in Appendix 1, A Catalog of Critical Reading Strategies.

READING LIKE A WRITER
MAKING A CAUSAL ARGUMENT THROUGH EXAMPLES

When writers argue for or support their causes, as Greeley does for his claim that stories keep Catholics coming back for more, they have many resources available to them. For example, they may use statistics, quote authorities, evoke history, create dialogue, tell a story. Greeley deploys all of these resources in paragraphs 8 through 29, where he attempts to convince readers that there is indeed one principal cause for Catholics' loyalty. However, he relies primarily on examples to support his argument. Because Greeley knew that many of his readers would have little familiarity with the Catholic stories he claims have such power, he names, describes, or tells many of these stories. These are his examples and they give his argument whatever plausibility it may have with his readers.

ANALYZE. Carefully reread paragraphs 8 through 29, annotating every story Greeley mentions. Notice, as you read, that Greeley uses the concept of "story" broadly, to include narratives with a beginning and an end, as well as institutions, events, and rituals.

In addition to naming, describing, and telling stories in these paragraphs, Greeley provides commentary of several different kinds. Review again paragraphs 9, 10, 16, 19, and 29. Try to describe, in a phrase, what kind of commentary Greeley is making in each instance. For example, you might say that the commentary in paragraph 9 is historical. What is the relation of the commentary in these paragraphs to the stories, and what role do the commentaries play in the essay? What do they add to the information we get about the stories?

WRITE. Write a page or so reporting what you have learned about Greeley's use of stories and commentary to support his argument. Describe how he presents some of the stories, and explain the various ways he attempts in the commentaries to help readers see why the stories are important. Then add a few sentences evaluating how successfully Greeley uses examples. Which examples were especially clear and convincing to you? Which were thin or puzzling? Which commentary was most revealing?

CONSIDERING IDEAS FOR YOUR OWN WRITING

Greeley's essay may suggest to you several ideas for writing in a category we can call "what might cause a group of people to do something." Some examples are why people stay in or drop out of college, devote themselves to strenuous exercise programs, abuse their spouses, join cults or gangs, become vegetarians, or listen to talk radio. You will think of other examples.

Like Greeley, you might speculate about why people stay in your religious faith or at your particular church. Or you might speculate about why people leave your faith or church. Because you would be writing for readers of other faiths and those who are nonbelievers, you would need to assume that they might initially consider your faith unusual, if not strange. For your speculations to be convincing, you would want to show a certain detachment or distance from your own beliefs so readers could trust your judgment. You would want to avoid seeming to recruit others to your faith or attacking other faiths. A successful essay would lead your readers to reflect on why they stay in their own faiths or leave them.

Jonathan Kozol

THE HUMAN COST OF AN ILLITERATE SOCIETY

A well-known critic of American schools, Jonathan Kozol (b. 1936) was in the forefront of educational reformers during the 1970s and 1980s. He has taught in the Boston and Newton, Massachusetts, public schools, as well as at Yale University and the University of

Massachusetts at Amherst. To support his writing and research, he has been awarded numerous prestigious fellowships from the Guggenheim, Ford, and Rockefeller Foundations. Kozol's books include *Death at an Early Age* (1967), for which he won the National Book Award, *Free Schools* (1972), *Children of the Revolution* (1978), *On Being a Teacher* (1981), *Illiterate America* (1985), *Savage Inequalities: Children in America's Schools* (1991), and *Blueprint for a Democratic Education* (1992).

This selection comes from Kozol's *Illiterate America,* a comprehensive study of the nature, causes, and consequences of illiteracy. In this chapter, Kozol speculates about the human consequences of illiteracy, outlining the limitations and dangers in the lives of adults who cannot read or write. Elsewhere in the book, Kozol conjectures about the causes of illiteracy, but here he concentrates on the effects of the phenomenon, speculating about what life is like for illiterates. He adopts this strategy to argue that the human costs of the problem pose a moral dilemma for our country.

PRECAUTIONS. READ BEFORE USING.
Poison: Contains sodium hydroxide (caustic soda-lye).
Corrosive: Causes severe eye and skin damage, may cause blindness.
Harmful or fatal if swallowed.
If swallowed, give large quantities of milk or water.
Do not induce vomiting.
Important: Keep water out of can at all times to
prevent contents from violently erupting . . .

WARNING ON A CAN OF DRANO

Questions of literacy, in Socrates' belief, must at length be judged   1
as matters of morality. Socrates could not have had in mind the moral compromise peculiar to a nation like our own. Some of our Founding Fathers did, however, have this question in their minds. One of the wisest of those Founding Fathers [James Madison] recognized the special dangers that illiteracy would pose to basic equity in the political construction that he helped to shape:

> A people who mean to be their own governors must arm   2
> themselves with the power knowledge gives. A popular government without popular information or the means of acquiring it, is but a prologue to a farce or a tragedy, or perhaps both.

Tragedy looms larger than farce in the United States today. Illiterate   3
citizens seldom vote. Those who do are forced to cast a vote of questionable worth. They cannot make informed decisions based on serious print information. Sometimes they can be alerted to their interests by aggressive voter education. More frequently, they vote for a face, a smile, or a style, not for a mind or character or body of beliefs.

The number of illiterate adults exceeds by 16 million the entire   4
vote cast for the winner in the 1980 presidential contest. If even one
third of all illiterates could vote, and read enough and do sufficient
math to vote in their self-interest, Ronald Reagan would not likely
have been chosen president. There is, of course, no way to know for
sure. We do know this: Democracy is a mendacious term when used
by those who are prepared to countenance the forced exclusion of
one third of our electorate. So long as 60 million people are denied
significant participation, the government is neither of, nor for, nor
by, the people. It is a government, at best, of those two thirds whose
wealth, skin color, or parental privilege allows them opportunity to
profit from the provocation and instruction of the written word.

The undermining of democracy in the United States is one   5
"expense" that sensitive Americans can easily deplore because it
represents a contradiction that endangers citizens of all political
positions. The human price is not so obvious at first.

Illiterates cannot read the menu in a restaurant.   6

They cannot read the cost of items on the menu in the *window* of   7
the restaurant before they enter.

Illiterates cannot read the letters that their children bring home   8
from their teachers. They cannot study school department circulars
that tell them of the courses that their children must be taking if
they hope to pass the SAT exams. They cannot help with homework. They cannot write a letter to the teacher. They are afraid to
visit in the classroom. They do not want to humiliate their child or
themselves.

Illiterates cannot read instructions on a bottle of prescription   9
medicine. They cannot find out when a medicine is past the year of
safe consumption; nor can they read of allergenic risks, warnings to
diabetics, or the potential sedative effect of certain kinds of nonpre-
scription pills. They cannot observe preventive health care admoni-
tions. They cannot read about "the seven warning signs of cancer"
or the indications of blood-sugar fluctuations or the risks of eating
certain foods that aggravate the likelihood of cardiac arrest.

Illiterates live, in more than literal ways, an uninsured existence.   10
They cannot understand the written details on a health insurance
form. They cannot read the waivers that they sign preceding surgical
procedures. Several women I have known in Boston have entered a
slum hospital with the intention of obtaining a tubal ligation and have
emerged a few days later after having been subjected to a hysterec-
tomy. Unaware of their rights, incognizant of jargon, intimidated by
the unfamiliar air of fear and atmosphere of ether that so many of us
find oppressive in the confines even of the most attractive and
expensive medical facilities, they have signed their names to documents they could not read and which nobody, in the hectic situation
that prevails so often in those overcrowded hospitals that serve the
urban poor, had even bothered to explain.

Even the roof above one's head, the gas or other fuel for heating   11
that protects the residents of northern city slums against the threat
of illness in the winter months become uncertain guarantees. Illiterates cannot read the lease that they must sign to live in an apartment which, too often, they cannot afford. They cannot manage
check accounts and therefore seldom pay for anything by mail.
Hours and entire days of difficult travel (and the cost of bus or
other public transit) must be added to the real cost of whatever
they consume. Loss of interest on the check accounts they do not
have, and could not manage if they did, must be regarded as another
of the excess costs paid by the citizen who is excluded from the
common instruments of commerce in a numerate society.

"I couldn't understand the bills," a woman in Washington, D.C.,   12
reports, "and then I couldn't write the checks to pay them. We
signed things we didn't know what they were."

Illiterates cannot read the notices that they receive from welfare   13
offices or from the IRS. They must depend on word-of-mouth
instruction from the welfare worker—or from other persons whom
they have good reason to mistrust. They do not know what rights
they have, what deadlines and requirements they face, what options
they might choose to exercise. They are half-citizens. Their rights
exist in print but not in fact.

Illiterates cannot look up numbers in a telephone directory. Even   14
if they can find the names of friends, few possess the sorting skills to
make use of the yellow pages; categories are bewildering and trade
names are beyond decoding capabilities for millions of nonreaders.
Even the emergency numbers listed on the first page of the phone
book—"Ambulance," "Police," and "Fire"—are too frequently beyond the recognition of nonreaders.

Many illiterates cannot read the admonition on a pack of   15
cigarettes. Neither the Surgeon General's warning nor its reproduction on the package can alert them to the risks. Although most people learn by word of mouth that smoking is related to a number of
grave physical disorders, they do not get the chance to read the
detailed stories which can document this danger with the vividness
that turns concern into determination to resist. They can see the
handsome cowboy or the slim Virginia lady lighting up a filter
cigarette; they cannot heed the words that tell them that this product is (not "may be") dangerous to their health. Sixty million men
and women are condemned to be the unalerted, high-risk candidates for cancer.

Illiterates do not buy "no-name" products in the supermarkets.   16
They must depend on photographs or the familiar logos that are
printed on the packages of brand-name groceries. The poorest people, therefore, are denied the benefits of the least costly products.

Illiterates depend almost entirely upon label recognition. Many   17
labels, however, are not easy to distinguish. Dozens of different

kinds of Campbell's soup appear identical to the nonreader. The purchaser who cannot read and does not dare to ask for help, out of the fear of being stigmatized (a fear which is unfortunately realistic), frequently comes homes with something which she never wanted and her family never tasted.

Illiterates cannot read instructions on a pack of frozen food. [18] Packages sometimes provide an illustration to explain the cooking preparations; but illustrations are of little help to someone who must "boil water, drop the food—*within* its plastic wrapper—in the boiling water, wait for it to simmer, instantly remove."

Even when labels are seemingly clear, they may be easily mis- [19] taken. A woman in Detroit brought home a gallon of Crisco for her children's dinner. She thought that she had bought the chicken that was pictured on the label. She had enough Crisco now to last a year—but no more money to go back and buy the food for dinner.

Illiterates cannot travel freely. When they attempt to do so, they [20] encounter risks that few of us can dream of. They cannot read traffic signs and, while they often learn to recognize and to decipher symbols, they cannot manage street names which they haven't seen before. The same is true for bus and subway stops. While ingenuity can sometimes help a man or woman to discern directions from familiar landmarks, buildings, cemeteries, churches, and the like, most illiterates are virtually immobilized. They seldom wander past the streets and neighborhoods they know. Geographical paralysis becomes a bitter metaphor for their entire existence. They are immobilized in almost every sense we can imagine. They can't move up. They can't move out. They cannot see beyond. Illiterates may take an oral test for drivers' permits in most sections of America. It is a questionable concession. Where will they go? How will they get there? How will they get home? Could it be that some of us might like it better if they stayed where they belong?

Travel is only one of many instances of circumscribed existence. [21] Choice, in almost all its facets, is diminished in the life of an illiterate adult. Even the printed TV schedule, which provides most people with the luxury of preselection, does not belong within the arsenal of options in illiterate existence. One consequence is that the viewer watches only what appears at moments when he happens to have time to turn the switch. Another consequence, a lot more common, is that the TV set remains in operation night and day. Whatever the program offered at the hour when he walks into the room will be the nutriment that he accepts and swallows. Thus, to passivity, is added frequency—indeed, almost uninterrupted continuity. Freedom to select is no more possible here than in the choice of home or surgery or food.

"You don't choose," said one illiterate woman. "You take your [22] wishes from somebody else." Whether in perusal of a menu, selection of highways, purchase of groceries, or determination of affordable enjoyment, illiterate Americans must trust somebody else: a friend, a relative, a stranger on the street, a grocery clerk, a TV copywriter.

Billing agencies harass poor people for the payment of the bills 23 for purchases that might have taken place six months before. Utility companies offer an agreement for a staggered payment schedule on a bill past due. "You have to trust them," one man said. Precisely for this reason, you end up by trusting no one and suspecting everyone of possible deceit. A submerged sense of distrust becomes the corollary to a constant need to trust. "They are cheating me . . . I have been tricked . . . I do not know . . . "

Not knowing: This is a familiar theme. Not knowing the right word 24 for the right thing at the right time is one form of subjugation. Not knowing the world that lies concealed behind those words is a more terrifying feeling. The longitude and latitude of one's existence are beyond all easy apprehension. Even the hard, cold stars within the firmament above one's head begin to mock the possibilities for self-location. Where am I? Where did I come from? Where will I go?

"I've lost a lot of jobs," one man explains. "Today, even if you're 25 a janitor, there's still reading and writing . . . They leave a note saying, 'Go to room so-and-so . . . ' You can't do it. You can't read it. You don't know."

"Reading directions, I suffer with. I work with chemicals . . . 26 That's scary to begin with . . . "

"You sit down. They throw the menu in front of you. Where do 27 you go from there? Nine times out of ten you say, 'Go ahead. Pick out something for the both of us.' I've eaten some weird things, let me tell you!"

A landlord tells a woman that her lease allows him to evict her if 28 her baby cries and causes inconvenience to her neighbors. The consequence of challenging his words conveys a danger which appears, unlikely as it seems, even more alarming than the danger of eviction. Once she admits that she can't read, in the desire to maneuver for the time in which to call a friend, she will have defined herself in terms of an explicit importance that she cannot endure. Capitulation in this case is preferable to self-humiliation. Resisting the definition of oneself in terms of what one cannot do, what others take for granted, represents a need so great that other imperatives (even one so urgent as the need to keep one's home in winter's cold) evaporate and fall away in face of fear. Even the loss of home and shelter, in this case, is not so terrifying as the loss of self.

Another illiterate, looking back, believes she was not worthy of 29 her teacher's time. She believes that it was wrong of her to take up space within her school. She believes that it was right to leave in order that somebody more deserving could receive her place.

People eat what others order, know what others tell them, 30 struggle not to see themselves as they believe the world perceives them. A man in California spoke about his own loss of identity, of self-location, definition:

"I stood at the bottom of the ramp. My car had broke down on the freeway. There was a phone. I asked for the police. They was nice. They said to tell them where I was. I looked up at the signs. There was one that I had seen before. I read it to them: ONE WAY STREET. They thought it was a joke. I told them I couldn't read. There was other signs above the ramp. They told me to try. I looked around for somebody to help. All the cars was going by real fast. I couldn't make them understand that I was lost. The cop was nice. He told me: 'Try once more.' I did my best. I couldn't read. I only knew the sign above my head. The cop was trying to be nice. He knew that I was trapped. 'I can't send out a car to you if you can't tell me where you are.' I felt afraid. I nearly cried. I'm forty-eight years old. I only said: 'I'm on a one-way street . . . '"   31

Perhaps we might slow down a moment here and look at the realities described above. This is the nation that we live in. This is a society that most of us did not create but which our President and other leaders have been willing to sustain by virtue of malign neglect. Do we possess the character and courage to address a problem which so many nations, poorer than our own, have found it natural to correct?   32

The answers to these questions represent a reasonable test of our belief in the democracy to which we have been asked in public school to swear allegiance.   33

READING FOR MEANING

Write at least a page, exploring your understanding of "The Human Cost of an Illiterate Society." Begin by conjecturing about why Kozol gives so many examples of what it is like to be an adult who cannot read. Which example do you think is most powerful? Why?

If you have difficulty writing at least a page, consider the following ideas:

- Kozol quotes James Madison as writing "A people who mean to be their own governors must arm themselves with the power knowledge gives" (paragraph 1). Think of one way in which knowledge can be said to give a person power.
- Explain the meaning or significance of "Questions of literacy . . . must at length be judged as matters of morality" (paragraph 1); illiterates "do not know what rights they have, what deadlines and requirements they face, what options they might choose to exercise. They are half-citizens. Their rights exist in print but not in fact" (paragraph 12); "the fear of being stigmatized (a fear which is unfortunately realistic)" (paragraph 16); or any other statement that catches your eye.
- Kozol argues that illiterates cannot make informed voting decisions because they cannot read "serious print information" (paragraph 2). Polls

show, however, that fewer Americans (especially below the age of twenty-five) read the newspapers and newsmagazines today than in the past. They rely mainly on television to tell them what they want to know. What effect do you think this fact has on the persuasiveness of Kozol's argument about the importance of literacy?

EXTENDING MEANING THROUGH CONVERSATION. After you have made meaning on your own, you may be able to extend your understanding by conversing with other students about Kozol's essay.

Get together with one or two other students. Begin your conversation by identifying an idea that still interests, confuses, or challenges each one of you.

As you discuss the reading, you may find that you have somewhat different understandings of it. You need not necessarily reach a consensus, but try to help each other think critically about the reading to develop the meaning you see and also to gain insight from other readers' perspectives. Keep your conversation focused on the essay by rereading and discussing parts of it together.

READING LIKE A WRITER

MAKING AN EFFECTS ARGUMENT BY ORGANIZING AND SEQUENCING EFFECTS

When writers speculate about effects, they nearly always propose more than one possibility. As soon as they offer two, they must decide how to sequence them to create the most convincing argument. If they offer three or more, as writers usually do, they must consider, as well, how those effects might best be grouped or related to each other. For example, in speculating about possible effects of some social problem, a writer might want to propose economic, political, and psychological effects. If so, the writer would probably present each group of effects together, sequencing the groups and the effects within groups to have the greatest impact on readers. The writer would be striving for a logical, rather than apparently random, sequencing, hoping that readers would see that one effect follows logically from the previous one and be impressed by such careful step-by-step sequencing. When you plan your own essay, you will have important decisions to make about grouping and sequencing your proposed causes or effects.

ANALYZE. To determine what decisions Kozol made and to understand how he organizes his essay, reread the essay, writing in the margin a word or phrase to identify each effect as it is introduced. If an effect reappears, indicate this by putting brackets around your identifying word. Also consider the way Kozol has ordered these effects. Can any be grouped together? Does he sequence the effects according to their importance? Does he move from the most general or widespread effect to the most individual (or vice versa)? Do the effects form a causal chain, with one effect being the cause of the next? Do you see some other pattern or no pattern at all?

WRITE. Write a page, evaluating Kozol's presentation of possible effects. Begin by describing how Kozol has grouped and sequenced the effects; be sure to refer to specific paragraphs. Then evaluate how successfully Kozol has grouped and sequenced the effects. What do you admire most about what he has done? Try to imagine different groupings or alternate sequences that would have more of an impact on readers. Try to think of one or two possible effects of illiteracy that Kozol does not mention. If you can think of one, where would you locate it in his sequence or in your alternate sequence? Do you find his presentation persuasive, or do you think he has offered too many or too few possible effects?

CONSIDERING IDEAS FOR YOUR OWN WRITING

Consider speculating, like Kozol, about the effects of a significant social problem. List some of the major social problems (local or national) that concern you. Your list might include the high pregnancy rate among unmarried teenagers, high dropout rates from schools, or high costs of a college education; unsafe working conditions or high employee turnover at your job; poor academic advising at your college or too many required courses; congested traffic or uncontrolled development in your community; or lack of good bookstores in your area or limited access to local news because there is only one daily newspaper. Choose one problem, and consider how you might go about speculating about its effects. What effects might you argue for? How could you convince your readers to consider your proposed effects plausible? Would you need to research the problem to write about it more authoritatively? You need not propose a solution to this problem, but only speculate about its possible effects.

Alternatively, recall recent controversial decisions by college or community leaders. Perhaps there have been controversial decisions about campus life (convenience, safety, recreation, tutoring, or other special services) or about the future of your community (growth, transportation, safety). List specific decisions, and choose one you might write about. Consider how you would write a letter to your college or community newspaper speculating about the effects or consequences of the decision. What short-term and long-term consequences would you propose? How would you convince readers to take your ideas seriously?

Steven Waldman

THE TYRANNY OF CHOICE

Steven Waldman is a Washington correspondent for *Newsweek* and writes frequently for other newsmagazines such as the *New Republic*, from which this selection is taken. His first book is *The Bill* (1995), a study of national service legislation in Congress.

In this half-serious, half-humorous essay, Waldman conjectures about a fundamental change in our society: the proliferation of choice. He explains in the opening paragraphs that he first became aware of this dis-concerting trend on a simple shopping expedition. His essay explores the effects of having to face so many choices in our daily lives.

Before reading the essay, stop to consider the wide range of choices you make every day. For you personally, what are the advantages and disadvantages of having so many choices to make? Do you find this range of choice frustrating or exhilarating?

Why did I nearly start crying the last time I went to buy socks? I'd stopped in a store called Sox Appeal, the perfect place, one might imagine, to spend a pleasant few minutes acquiring a pair of white athletic socks. After a brief visit to the men's dress sock depart-ment—dallying with more than 300 varieties, among them products embroidered with bikini-clad women, neckties, flowers, Rocky and Bullwinkle, and elegant logos such as "The Gold Bullion Collection: Imported" and "D'zin Pour Homme"—I finally made it into the ath-letics section. Here, the product-option high was even headier. Past the "Hypercolor" socks that change hue, combination "sport-and-dress" white socks, and "EarthCare" environmentally safe socks (which, unfortunately, boast of decomposing easily) were hosiery for every sport: racquetball, running, walking, cycling, hiking, basket-ball, and aerobics. I needed help.

"What if I play racquetball occasionally and run occasionally and walk sometimes, but don't want to get a different sock for each one?" I asked the saleswoman. She wrinkled her nose: "It's really a matter of personal preference." Did she have any standard-issue white tube socks? The nosewrinkle again. "Well, yeah, you *could* get those, but . . . " I started reading the backs of the boxes, elaborately illustrated with architects' renderings of the stress points in the "Cushion-Engineered (TM) Zone Defense." After briefly contem-plating the implications of the Cross-Training Sock—"Shock-Woven elastic arch brace contours to arch, providing additional support and normal articulation of the bones in the foot, while keeping sock migration minimal"—I spent another five minutes studying shapes (anklet, crew, or quarter) and manufacturers, and grabbed a Cross Trainer, two walkers, and, in an environmental guilt-spasm, one pair of the EarthCare.

Since that day, the sock metaphor has crept constantly into my mind—and not just when I'm buying consumer products. At work I pick through dozens of options on my cafeteria insurance benefits plan. At the doctor's I'm offered several possible treatments for a neck problem and no real way to decide. At the video rental store I end up renting four movies even though I'll watch only one. Choices proliferate everywhere. My mental "tilt" light flashes continuously. I keep thinking that the more choices there are, the more wrong choices there are—and the higher the odds I'll make a mistake.

Think it over. A typical supermarket in 1976 had 9,000 products;   4
today it has more than 30,000. The average produce section in 1975
carried sixty-five items; this summer it carried 285. (Kiwi has hit the
top 20 list.) A Cosmetic Center outside Washington carries about
1,500 types and sizes of hair care products. The median household
got six TV stations in 1975. Thanks to deregulation of the cable TV
industry, that family now has more than thirty channels. The number
of FM radio stations has doubled since 1970. A new religious denom-
ination forms every week. (The 1980s brought us major additions
such as the Evangelical Presbyterian Church and smaller groups such
as the Semjase Silver Star Center, which follows the Twelve Bids
from Patule that were given by extraterrestrial Space Brothers to
Edmund "Billy" Meier.) In 1955 only 4 percent of the adult population had left the faith of their childhood. By 1985 one-third had. In
1980, 564 mutual funds existed. This year there are 3,347.

There has been a sharp rise in the number of people choosing   5
new faces. More than twice as many cosmetic surgery operations
were performed in the 1980s than in the 1970s, estimates the
American Academy of Cosmetic Surgery. In the past decade a new
periodical was born every day. Some have perished, but the survivors include: *Elvis International Forum, Smart Kids* (recent cover
headline: "Should Babies Learn to Read?"), *American Handgunner,
Triathlete, Harley Women, Log Home Living, Musclecar Classics,* and (my
favorite) *Contemporary Urology.*

The growth of variety predates this recession, will continue after   6
it, and, to a large extent, has persisted during it. *New Product News*
reports that despite the depressed economy 21 percent more new
products were introduced in supermarkets and drug stores in 1991
than the year before. Obvious benefits abound, of course, and not
just for people with money. Telephone deregulation has made it
cheaper to stay in touch with faraway friends; periodical proliferation meant I had *Fantasy Baseball* magazine to help me prepare for
Rotisserie draft day; increased social tolerance has allowed more
people (including me) to marry outside their faith or ethnic group;
low sodium orange juice means people with high blood pressure can
drink it (and it has increased juice sales); more cosmetics mean black
women have shades that match their complexions. And so on. And
in the words of Morris Cohen, a professor at the Wharton Business
School: "If you're overwhelmed by the sock store, don't go there
anymore." The beauty of the free market, he explains, is that each
individual can select which options to exploit and which to ignore.

But Cohen's rational approach fails to account for how the mind   7
actually processes all this variety. In fact, choice can be profoundly
debilitating. It forces us to squander our time, weakens our connections to people and places, and can even poison our sense of con-
tentedness. What follows is a simple checklist—take your pick—of
the drawbacks of our new way of choosing.

Choice Erodes Commitment. The same psychological dynamic that   8
has led to a decline in brand loyalty can operate on more important
decisions. The more options we have, the more tenuous our commitment becomes to each one. The compulsion to take inventory of
one's wants and continually upgrade to a better deal can help explain
everything from the rise of the pathological channel switcher who
can never watch one TV show straight through to staggering divorce
rates and employer-employee disloyalty. Baseball players have never
had as many career options as they do now. As a result, sportswriter Thomas Boswell notes, the slightest sign of trouble leads the
player or team to try someplace or someone better, producing
many "insincere love affairs and very few committed marriages."
Sound familiar? Yes, even the infamous male commitment problem
results in part from the same thinking. I recently married a wonderful woman, but only after several years of embarrassingly tortured
contemplation of what kind of "options" I might be foreclosing.
There are, after all, 9,538,000 unmarried females aged 24–39, each
with the potential to be more "perfect" than the one before.

Choice Leads to Inept Consumption. The more choice available, the   9
more information a consumer must have to make a sensible selection. When overload occurs, many simply abandon the posture of
rational Super-Consumer. Warning labels on products have become
so common that many shoppers simply ignore them all, including the
important ones. Several friends have confessed that the selection of
car models—591 and rising—has become so dizzying that they
tossed aside *Consumer Reports* and relied entirely on the recommendation of a friend. Some become so paralyzed by the quest for the
better deal that they postpone decisions indefinitely, while others
become so preoccupied with absorbing the new features touted by
a manufacturer that they forget to consider the basics. After all the
fretting over the migration patterns of the socks, I took them home
and found them to be quite fluffy and supportive, but the wrong size.

Consumers may be better informed than they were two decades   10
ago, but salespeople have more tools with which to fight back. I
spent three days studying up for a trip to Circuit City to buy a CD
player. Despite having read several magazine and newspaper articles,
I was, within minutes, putty in the salesman's hands. When I asked
for a particular model, he rolled his eyes and laughed, "You must
have gotten that from *Consumer Reports.*" With a simple well-timed
chuckle he made me doubt my entire research regimen. He then
battered me with a flurry of technoterms and finally moved in for
the kill by giving me an audio comparison test between two different
systems that sounded exactly alike. My resistance was exhausted, so
I bought the system he suggested, which, of course, cost more than I
had intended to spend.

Choice Causes Political Alienation. Voters don't necessarily have   11
more choices than they used to—an increase in primaries and refer-

enda having been offset by the influence of incumbency and money—but the *way* voters choose has changed dramatically. As a result of the weakening of political parties, voting behavior now closely resembles the consumption of products. The biggest political group is not Democrats or Republicans, but "independents," shopper-equivalents who've dropped brand loyalty in favor of product-by-product analysis. Last century two-thirds of voters went straight party line; in 1980 two-thirds split tickets. In theory, this means voters carefully weigh the candidate's policies, character, and history. In reality, it's nearly impossible to sort through a candidate's "stands" on the "issues" from a blizzard of untrustworthy ads, a newspaper editorial, or a blip on the TV news. Was he the one who wants a revolving loan fund for worker retraining or the one who gives flag burners early parole? No wonder voters, like shoppers, act impulsively or vote according to the wisdom of their favorite interest group. Many who vote for ballot initiatives or lower offices simply follow the recommendation of the local newspaper, which is like buying a car on the word of the local auto columnist. When I was voting absentee in New York I selected judicial candidates on the basis of gender and race since I knew little else about them. The ultimate political choice overload came in California in 1990, when voters received a 222-page ballot pamphlet to help them decide among twenty-eight initiatives.

Candidates have responded to the rise of the consumer-voter by   12
turning to marketing professionals who've only made the voters' dilemma worse. In the 1950s political consultants were advertising men who selected a candidate attribute and then sold it, the way an automaker might remind consumers of a large car's natural advantages, like spaciousness and safety. Political consulting has evolved, though. Candidates now rely heavily on market researchers—i.e., the pollsters—trying less to determine what part of their essence they should highlight than what they should become to match voters' desires. Sometimes that means candidates become more responsive to public thinking, but more often it means politicians forget to consult (or have) their own core beliefs. Witness the breathtaking spectacle of pro-life pols who once assailed the supreme immorality of baby-killing quickly becoming pro-choice because of the supreme importance of polls. This "politics as consumption" (in the phrase of University of Rochester professor Robert Westbrook) seems to produce more gelatinous politicians—precisely the sort that voters have the hardest time judging.

Choice Erodes the Self. In theory, choice enables an individual to   13
select the car, money market fund, or spouse that expresses herself most precisely. But if choice is self-definition, more choices mean more possible definitions. Kenneth Gergen, a professor of psychology at Swarthmore, argues in his new book, *The Saturated Self,* that the postmodern personality becomes "populated" with growing

numbers of "selves" as it's bombarded by an ever increasing number of potential relationships from TV, travel, telephones, faxes, computers, etc. From an insecure sense of self, you then spiral toward what Gergen calls "multiphrenia," in which the besieged, populated self frantically flails about trying to take advantage of the sea of choices. This condition may never merit its own telethon, but as choices increase so do the odds that multiphrenia will strike, leaving the scars of perpetual self-doubt. It's why the people who work hardest to improve their appearance never seem to feel much better than before they sampled the offerings of the Self-Perfection Industry (exercise videos, customized makeup, cosmetic surgery, health food). They become like politicians with their own private pollsters; the quest to recreate virtually supplants whatever person was once there.

Choice Reduces Social Bonding. The proliferation of choice helps 14 cause, and results from, another trend—social fragmentation. Together they ensure that Americans share fewer and fewer common experiences. A yuppie diet bears less and less resemblance to that of a lower-income family. I don't even know who's on the Wheaties box anymore because my cereal is located about ninety feet down the aisle. As marketers divide us into increasingly narrow segments, we inevitably see ourselves that way too. When there was one movie theater in a neighborhood, everyone sat under the same roof and watched the same film. Video rental stores enable you to be a movie junkie without ever having to sit next to another human being. Three decades ago, even when everyone was sitting in their own homes they were at least all watching "Gunsmoke." Today's viewing public scatters to its particular demographic niche on the cable dial.

Dealing with an abundance of choices mostly requires a mental 15 reorientation. Choice overload helped me finally understand what was so offensive about the stereotypical yuppie obsession with "quality," of which I have often been guilty. It's not that some coffee beans aren't, in fact, more flavorful than others, it's that people who spend so much of their lives thinking about small differences become small people.

Imagine instead a world in which we used our choice brain lobes 16 for the most important decisions and acted more arbitrarily on the rest. Perhaps you might select a brand name and buy all its products for the next four years, scheduling Choice Day during non-presidential election years. Or you might embrace the liberating powers of TV commercials. As everyone knows, ads brainwash us into choosing products through insidious appeals to sex or other animal urges. But sometimes it feels good to let an ad take us by the hand. A few years ago I had an epiphany while deciding what to eat for dinner. I looked in the refrigerator, thought about nearby restaurants and markets, and grew puzzled. Just then an ad came on the TV for

Burger King, featuring a luscious Whopper with fake charcoal stripes painted with perfect symmetry across the juicy meat. I put on my coat and immediately walked, zombielike, to the nearby Burger King and ordered a Whopper. I found it exhilarating, because I knew it wasn't the behavior of a rational economic player, and that it didn't matter.

READING FOR MEANING

Write at least a page, exploring your understanding of "The Tyranny of Choice." Begin by selecting at least two consequences of choice that seem to you especially appealing or convincing. Summarize, in your own words, what Waldman says about these consequences. Then write about anything else in the essay that contributes to your understanding of Waldman's speculations.

As you write, you will need to reread and annotate. You may find that your understanding of the essay changes as you write.

The following suggestions offer additional avenues you might explore in your writing:

- Waldman suggests that there is a connection between the abundance of choice and "the stereotypical yuppie obsession with 'quality'" (paragraph 15). What's a "yuppie"? Why do you suppose Waldman considers making choices on the basis of quality a bad thing? What do you think?

- Recall a time recently when you were overwhelmed by choices in one of the categories on which Waldman focuses; for example, commitment, inept consumption, and so on. Write about what happened. What choices did you face? Were you on your own, or were others involved? What was the outcome? Connect your experience directly to relevant speculations in Waldman's essay.

- Explain the meaning or significance of "the more choices there are, the more wrong choices there are" (paragraph 3); "The more options we have, the more tenuous our commitment becomes to each one" (paragraph 8); "voting behavior now closely resembles the consumption of products" (paragraph 11); or any other statement that you find provocative.

- In paragraph 16, Waldman writes about the power of advertising to influence our choices: "As everyone knows, ads brainwash us into choosing products through insidious appeals to sex or other animal urges." Select a television commercial or a magazine or newspaper advertisement that makes such an appeal, and explain how you think it works. Connect what you discover to Waldman's essay.

EXTENDING MEANING THROUGH CONVERSATION. After you have had a chance to make meaning on your own, you may be able to extend your understanding by conversing with other students about Waldman's essay. Get together with one or two classmates. Begin your conversation by taking turns identifying one idea in Waldman's essay that interests, confuses, or challenges each of you.

As you talk about the reading, you may find that you each understand it differently. Your goal as a group is not necessarily to reach a consensus, but to help each other think critically about the reading. Develop the meaning you see while you gain insight from other readers' perspectives on the essay. Keep your conversation focused on the essay by reading and discussing parts of it together.

READING LIKE A WRITER
PRESENTING THE SUBJECT BY ESTABLISHING THE TREND

When speculating about the causes or effects of a trend, writers need to demonstrate that the trend exists. This requires showing a significant increase or decrease over a particular period of time. It may also involve arguing that the subject is in fact a trend—a marked change that has lasted for some time—as opposed to a fad—a short-term, superficial change. A new form of exercise or type of music, for example, might become a fad if it is popular for a few months. But such fads are not trends, although they may be representative of some more significant, lasting change—such as an increase in health consciousness among a certain group of people or the increasing popularity of certain types of ethnic music among general audiences.

In establishing a trend, writers usually provide statistical information. When did it start? Is still continuing, or has it ended? How rapidly has it increased or decreased? Has it changed steadily over time, or have there been noticeable stages? A thorough presentation of the trend may have to answer all of these questions. As a critical reader, you should consider whether the essay answers all of the relevant questions and whether the answers are reliable. Their reliability depends in part on your confidence in the writer's credibility and in part on the sources used.

ANALYZE. Reread paragraphs 1 through 5, where Waldman presents the subject and establishes the trend. Annotate as you read, noting anything that contributes to your understanding of the trend and convinces you that it is indeed a trend and not a fad.

WRITE. Write a few sentences, explaining how the personal anecdote in paragraphs 1 through 3 helps establish the trend. Refer to specific details you annotated to illustrate your ideas. Then write several sentences discussing Waldman's use of statistics in paragraph 4. How does he use them to establish the trend? How reliable do they seem to you to be? On what basis can you decide? Note also that Waldman concludes the section with a quote by someone he identifies as a professor from Wharton Business School. Why do you think he bothers to give all this information rather than just giving the person's name?

CONSIDERING IDEAS FOR YOUR OWN WRITING

Waldman's essay raises a number of topics that lend themselves to further cause-and-effect analysis. For example, Waldman speculates on how choice contributes to the erosion of commitment. You could write about what causes us to develop a sense of commitment in the first place. Or you could focus on the possible effects of having or losing a sense of commitment. Similarly, whereas Waldman speculates about the role of choice in increasing political alienation, you could speculate about other possible causes of political alienation or its potential effects for our democracy.

Choose a subject you would be interested in thinking more about, and propose one or more possible causes or effects.

On your own or with classmates, rely on Waldman's "the tyranny of" title to think of more essay topics. For example, you might think of the tyranny of leisure time, working while in college, commuting, ambition, television, living at home, poverty, workplace rules, both parents working, or gun control. You will readily think of others. As you think of each tyranny, try to come up with two or three possible effects of it, as a way of testing quickly whether it might have promise as an essay topic.

Reese Mason

BASKETBALL AND THE URBAN POOR

Reese Mason wrote this essay in 1990 for a freshman composition course at the University of California, Riverside.

This essay was occasioned by the untimely death of college basketball star Hank Gathers. The death was sudden but not entirely surprising because Gathers had collapsed during a game only three months earlier. Mason tries in this essay to understand why Gathers risked his life by continuing to play basketball.

For a while there, Gathers had beaten the system, the cycle that traps so many black youths in frustration and poverty.

ART SPANDER

On the evening of March 4, 1990, much like any other night, I sat in my living room fixed to the television as ESPN's Sport Center broadcast the day's sporting news. The lead story was about last year's national leader in rebounding and scoring in collegiate basketball, Loyola Marymount's Hank Gathers. It was not unusual for Gathers to be in the news, given his many fantastic performances and displays of great character. He had become much more than a premier basketball player since achieving athletic stardom. Hank Gathers had become an inspiration to all those who, like himself, had the misfortune of being born poor. This story, however, was not about a new scoring record or a buzzer-beating shot. Nor was it a commentary on how Gathers had not forgotten what community he hailed from, and how he intended to move his mother and son out of poverty when he made it to the "Show" (Almond). This news story was about a twenty-three-year-old basketball player collapsing and dying on the court.

In utter dismay, I immediately demanded some reason for the unbelievable events. After an incident some three months earlier, Gathers had been tested and found to have cardiomyopathy (a type of arrhythmia). How in the world could the doctors have allowed him to continue playing? With such a heart defect, how could he allow himself to continue playing? How could the game of basketball have become more important to Hank Gathers than life itself? The night of March 4 was a sleepless one for this sports fan. I lay awake in restless wonder at what could have compelled a man of my age to risk his life for a game.

The answers came to me the next day in a follow-up story about the tragic death. The piece was a tribute to the life of Hank Gathers. Appropriately, the story began where Gathers's life began, and suddenly, with one shot of the camera, I understood. I understood what drove him to greatness on the basketball court. I understood what compelled Gathers to continue playing even after he knew he had a heart defect. Like most middle-class sports fanatics, I was well aware that many African-American athletes come from the inner city. I was even aware that Gathers had risen out of a Philadelphia ghetto to achieve greatness in college basketball. Never, though, had I really sat down and considered why growing up in the ghetto might make the game of basketball seem so important—and in Gathers's case, as valuable as life itself.

Basketball is popular among the urban poor because it is virtually the only way for young African-American men to make it, to become idolized superstars. Unlike football or baseball, basketball requires little money or formal organization to play. All that is needed is a few dollars for a ball and access to a hoop, found at any school or playground. Additionally, it can be practiced and all but perfected without the need for coaches, expensive facilities, or even many other players.

The examples of basketball stars like Magic Johnson and Michael Jordan probably inspired Gathers, as they have thousands of others who cling to the game of basketball as their ticket out of the ghetto. There aren't many alternatives. The unemployment rate for African-American teenagers is over 40 percent, and what jobs they can find are mostly low-paying, dead-end work. Many inner-city youth resort to drugs and crime, and, not surprisingly, about a quarter of all African-American men between twenty and twenty-nine wind up in jail, on parole, or on probation (*Statistical Abstract*).

Our society offers those who can play basketball well an education that might not otherwise be obtained. Education is a limited and insufficient resource to the urban poor. There are no easy answers, I admit, but the facts are indisputable. In order to get a quality education, the poor have to win scholarships. Because of its popularity in America, and its college connection, basketball has become one avenue to a higher education. Even when college basketball players are unable to continue playing in the pros, their university degrees may lead to other good jobs and thus to economic success.

Yet, education is not the motivating factor behind the success 7 stories of the poor any more than it is among the success stories of the middle class; money is. After all, money is what you are judged on here in America, along with popular recognition. Basketball provides an avenue from the urban ghetto to the highest echelons in America via money and popularity. Gathers was honest about what was important to him when he said, "I'm in college to play basketball. The degree is important to me, but not that important" (Hudson and Almond). Gathers understood that basketball was the vehicle that would take him where he wanted to go. It offered him money (multimillions, in fact), education, and popularity—the three components of the American Dream.

We recognize Hank Gathers because of his tragic death, but only 8 because he was a fantastic basketball player. It is hard for us to admit, but who would have taken time out for Gathers and his family had he died of a heart defect while playing ball in the Rowand Rosen housing project where his family still lives? Those who were close to him, assuredly, but not the nation. This is why basketball was so important to Gathers, and it may be why he continued playing despite the risk of dying on the court. Hank Gathers's story helps us see why basketball is so popular among, and dominated by, the urban poor. Basketball is an E-Ticket* out of the ghetto, one of the best available means of getting nationwide recognition and providing for their family.

Works Cited

Almond, Elliot. "Gathers, Pepperdine's Lewis Had Special Bond." *Los Angeles Times* 7 Mar. 1990: C8.

Hudson, Maryann, and Elliot Almond. "Gathers Suit Asks for $32.5 Million." *Los Angeles Times* 21 Apr. 1990: C1, C20.

Spander, Art. "Who's to Blame for Gathers' Tragic Death?" *Sporting News* 19 Mar. 1990: 5.

Statistical Abstract of the United States 1989, U.S. Bureau of Census, 109th ed. Washington, DC: GPO, 1989.

READING FOR MEANING

Write for at least a page, exploring your understanding of "Basketball and the Urban Poor." Begin by summarizing the causes Mason proposes to explain Gathers's death. Then write about anything else in the essay that contributes to your understanding of Mason's speculations.

*E-Ticket: a reference to the old system of ticketing at Disneyland, when an E-Ticket was needed for the best, most exciting rides (*Ed.*)

If you are having difficulty writing at least a page, consider the following ideas:

- "I'm in college to play basketball," Mason quotes Gathers as saying. "The degree is important to me, but not that important" (paragraph 7). Reflect on why you are in college. What is important to you? Compare your reasons for going to college with what you understand to be Gathers's reasons.

- Compare Mason's attitudes toward college basketball with your own attitudes toward college sports.

- Explain the meaning or significance of "Gathers had beaten the system, the cycle that traps so many black youths in frustration and poverty" (epigraph); "In order to get a quality education, the poor have to win scholarships" (paragraph 6); "money is what you are judged on here in America" (paragraph 7); or any other statement that catches your eye.

- For Mason, "the three components of the American Dream" are money, education, and popularity (paragraph 7). Think of your own notion of the American Dream and how well it corresponds to Mason's. Would you include these same components? Why or why not?

EXTENDING MEANING THROUGH CONVERSATION. You may be able to extend your understanding of this essay by conversing with other students about it. Get together with one or two other students. Begin your conversation by taking turns identifying one idea in Mason's essay that interests, confuses, or challenges each of you.

As you talk about the reading, you may find that you have somewhat different understandings of it. By helping each other think critically about the reading, each member of the group may further develop his or her own understanding of the essay through other readers' perspectives on the essay. Keep your conversation focused on the essay by reading and discussing parts of it together.

READING LIKE A WRITER
ESTABLISHING CREDIBILITY

To be credible is to be believable. When you write an essay speculating about the causes or effects of something, readers will find you believable if they sense that you are able to see the complexities of your subject. You do not oversimplify, trivialize, or stereotype your subject. You do not overlook possible alternative causes or effects that occur to readers easily while reading your essay. You convey more than casual knowledge of your subject and show that you have thought about it deeply and seriously.

Before you attempt your own essay speculating about causes or effects, it will be helpful for you to consider carefully how Mason attempts to establish his credibility to speculate about Gathers's death and to evaluate how well he succeeds. After you have described and evaluated Mason's attempts at credibility, you will have the opportunity to compare Mason's attempts with those of another author in this chapter.

ANALYZE. Reread this brief essay, annotating it for evidence of credibility or lack of it. (Because you cannot know Mason personally, you must look closely at the words and ideas of his essay to decide whether he has constructed a credible argument about the causes of Gathers's death.) Consider whether Mason has ignored or slighted likely causes of Gathers's death. If you think that he may have done so, consider whether it seems justified, given his knowledge of the event and of Gathers. Consider that expressions of feeling and concern may or may not contribute to credibility. Consider also whether Mason stereotypes Gathers or overgeneralizes about African Americans or about college sports or whether he credibly relies on Gathers as a typical college athlete raised poor in a big city. (That Mason does not know Gathers personally, that he may not be African American, and that he may not play on a college sports team does not necessarily disqualify him from speculating about all three.) As you reread, reflect on how Mason presents himself in paragraphs 1 through 3, where he refers to himself as "I." Throughout, reflect on the likely sources of Mason's knowledge and speculations.

WRITE. Write several sentences presenting evidence of Mason's attempts to establish his credibility. Then evaluate how credible his essay is to you as one reader. To explain your judgment, point to parts of the essay and also comment on the influence of your own attitudes and experience.

COMPARE. To expand your understanding of how speculative writers attempt to establish their credibility with readers, select another essay in this chapter with which you are already familiar. Reread it carefully, annotating the writer's attempts to establish credibility and evaluating the writer's success with you as one reader. Write several sentences presenting your insights, providing support with details from the essay. Then write several more sentences generalizing about how writers who speculate about causes or effects attempt to establish their credibility.

CONSIDERING IDEAS FOR YOUR OWN WRITING

Think of a phenomenon, an event, or a trend in sports you might consider writing about. For example, you might speculate about why a particular team has done well (or poorly) this season. You might be interested in conjecturing about the increasing popularity of women's sports or why some high schools and colleges fail to support women's teams on a parity with men's teams. You might want to focus on changes in management or playing style. You could also consider effects, for example, how the trend in higher salaries affects a particular sport, or how the 1994–1995 baseball strike influenced fans' perception of the sport.

Mason speculates about the causes of Gathers's intense motivation to play basketball. Similarly, you could speculate about what motivates people to do something: sacrifice for their children or, conversely, neglect or even abuse their children; cheat on exams; choose a college major in a particular discipline; choose a particular kind of work or career; become vegetarian; decline to

become vegetarian; smoke cigarettes; work for a cigarette company; stop working for a cigarette company; become active in student government; persist in
sexist or racist behavior; persist in dangerous sexual practices; choose abstinence; kill wild animals with guns; kill wild animals only with bow and arrows;
refuse to kill wild animals; fail to vote in local, state, or national elections; be
optimistic about the future; be pessimistic about the future; donate time or
money or both to improve the lives of others. Consider what you would need to
know to describe the kind of motivation you want to speculate about so readers
would accept your authority to speculate about it. What causes would you propose to explain the motivation? Could you argue convincingly for each cause
relying solely on your personal knowledge and experience, or might you need to
do some library research?

THINKING ABOUT WHAT MAKES SPECULATION ABOUT CAUSES OR EFFECTS EFFECTIVE

In this chapter you have been learning about reading cause or effect argument—reading it for meaning and reading it like a writer. Before moving on to
write this kind of argument genre yourself, pause here to review and consolidate
what you have learned about what makes cause or effect essays successful.

Choose one reading in this chapter that seems to you to be especially effective as speculative writing. Before rereading the essay, jot down one or two
things that led you to remember it as an example of effective cause or effect
writing.

Then reread your chosen essay, adding to your annotations notes about what
made it so effective. As a starting point, consider the essay's purpose and how
well it achieves that purpose for its intended readers. Then focus on how well
the essay

- presents the subject, trend, or phenomenon
- makes a logical, step-by-step cause or effect argument
- handles likely objections to its own speculations
- handles alternative causes or effects its readers may prefer to the ones for
  which the essay argues
- convinces you of its credibility

You can complete this activity on your own, or your instructor may ask you
to collaborate with a small group of other students who have chosen the same
essay. If you work with others, take time initially for everyone to read the essay
thoughtfully, annotating as suggested above. Then discuss what makes it so
effective. Take notes. Someone in your group can then report to the class what
you have learned about this effective essay, or you can individually write up
what you have learned.

Write at least a page, justifying your choice of this essay as the most effective
cause or effect argument among the chapter's readings. Assume that your readers—

your instructor and classmates—have read the essay but will not remember the details of how the essay does its work or what made it so effective. Therefore, refer to details of the essay as you explain how it works and seek to justify your choice of it as particularly effective. You need not argue that it is the best essay in the chapter, only that it is, in your view, a particularly effective cause or effect argument.

A Guide to Writing Speculations about Causes or Effects

The readings in this chapter have helped you learn a great deal about writing that analyzes causes or effects, and you are in a good position to understand the problems and possibilities of this kind of writing. This section offers guidance for writing an essay of this type. You will find activities to help you identify a topic and discover what to say about it, organize your ideas and draft the essay, and revise your draft to strengthen your argument and improve readability.

INVENTION

The following activities can help get you started and enable you to explore your subject fully. A few minutes spent completing each of these writing activities will improve your chances of producing a detailed and convincing first draft. You can decide on a subject for your essay, explore what you presently know about it and gather additional information, conjecture about possible causes or effects, and develop a plausible argument.

Choosing a Subject

The subject of an essay analyzing causes or effects may be a trend, an event, or a phenomenon, all of which are illustrated by the selections in this chapter. Before considering a subject for your essay, you might want to review the Considering Ideas for Your Own Writing sections that follow each selection. These varied possibilities for analyzing causes or effects may suggest a subject you would like to write about.

After reviewing the ideas for writing, you may still need to find an appropriate subject for your essay. You might begin by listing as many possibilities as you can. Making a list generates ideas: as soon as you start a list, you will think of possibilities you cannot imagine now.

Even if you feel confident that you already have a subject, listing other possibilities will help you to test your choice. Make separate lists for *trends, events, or phenomena.* List specific subjects suggested by the possibilities included here for each category.

For *trends,* consider the following possibilities:

changes in men's or women's roles and opportunities in marriage, education, or work

changing patterns in leisure, entertainment, life-style, religious life, health, technology

completed artistic or historical trends (various art movements or historical changes)

long-term changes in economic conditions or political behavior

For *events,* these ideas might help you start your own list:

a recent college, community, national, or international event about which there is puzzlement or controversy

a recent surprising event at your college like the closing of a tutorial or health service, cancellation of popular classes, changes in library hours or dormitory regulations, the loss of a game by a favored team, or some violent act by one student against another

a recent puzzling or controversial event in your community like the abrupt resignation of a public official, a public protest by an activist group, a change in traffic laws, a zoning decision, or the banning of a book from school libraries

a historical event about which there is still some dispute as to its causes or effects

For *phenomena,* there are many possibilities:

social problems like discrimination, homelessness, child abuse, illiteracy, rising high-school dropout rates, youth suicides, teenage pregnancy

various aspects of college life like libraries too noisy to study in, classes too large, lack of financial aid, difficulties in scheduling the classes you want, shortcomings in student health services, unavailability of housing (in this essay you will not need to solve these problems, but only to analyze their causes or effects)

human traits like anxiety, selfishness, fear of success, fear of failure, leadership, jealousy, lack of confidence, envy, opportunism, curiosity, openness, health or fitness

After you have completed your lists, reflect on the possibilities you have compiled. Because an authoritative essay analyzing causes or effects requires sustained thinking, drafting, revising, and possibly even research, you will want to choose a subject to which you can commit yourself enthusiastically for a week or two. Choose a subject that interests you, even if you feel uncertain about how to approach it. Then consider carefully whether you are more interested in the causes or in the effects of the event, trend, or phenomenon. Consider, as well, whether the subject in which you are interested invites speculation about either its causes or effects or perhaps even precludes speculation about one or the other. For example, you could speculate about the causes for increasing membership in your church, whereas the effects (results, consequences) of the increase might for now be so uncertain as to discourage plausible speculation. Some subjects invite speculation about both their causes and effects. For this assignment, however, you need not do both.

The writing and research activities that follow will enable you to test your subject choice and to discover what you have to say about it.

Exploring Your Subject

You may discover that you know more about your subject than you suspected if you write about it for a few minutes without stopping. This brief sustained writing stimulates memory search, helps you probe your interest in the subject, and enables you to test your subject choice. As you write, consider the following questions: What interests me in this subject? What is there about it that might interest readers? What do I already know about it? Why do we not already have an accepted explanation for this subject? What causes or effects have people already suggested for this subject? How can I learn more about it?

Considering Causes or Effects

Before you research your subject (should you need to), you will want to discover which causes or effects you can already imagine. Make a list of possible causes or effects. For causes, consider underlying or background causes, immediate or instigating causes, and ongoing causes; for effects, consider both short-term and long-term consequences, as well as how one effect may lead to another in a kind of chain. Try to think not only of obvious causes or effects but also of ones that are likely to be overlooked in a superficial analysis of your subject.

Identify the most convincing causes or effects on your list. Do you have enough to make a strong argument? Imagine how you might convince readers of the plausibility of some of these causes or effects.

Researching Your Subject

When developing an essay analyzing causes or effects, you can often gain great advantage by researching your subject. (See Appendix 2, Strategies for Research and Documentation.) You can gain a greater understanding of the event, trend, or phenomenon; and you can review and evaluate others' proposed causes or effects in case you want to present any of these alternatives in your own essay. Reviewing others' causes or effects may suggest to you plausible causes or effects you have overlooked. You may also find evidence and arguments to use in your own counterarguments to readers' objections.

Analyzing Your Readers

Your purpose is to convince readers that your proposed causes or effects are plausible. To succeed, you will need to choose causes or effects, evidence, and arguments that will convince your readers. You will want to anticipate objections these readers may have to any of your proposed causes or effects and to identify alternatives they may favor.

To analyze your readers, write for a few minutes, identifying who the readers are, what they know about the subject, and how they can be convinced by your proposed causes or effects.

Meet with two or three other students. In turn, tell each other about your subjects and whether you will be speculating about the causes or effects, but do not tell them *which* causes or effects you intend to argue for.

Then each member of your group will tell you what causes or effects come to mind when they think about your subject. Take careful notes about each cause or effect that is mentioned. Do not get involved in the conversation yourself. Instead, keep them talking. Your goal is to exhaust the possibilities for causes or effects they can think of. You can ask for clarification, of course.

From this activity each of you will get a much fuller understanding of what your readers will be thinking about your subject. Consequently, you can be very effective in anticipating what causes or effects they might initially think are more plausible than the ones for which you will be arguing.

Rehearsing Your Argument

The heart of your essay will be the argument you make for the plausibility of your proposed causes or effects. Like a ballet dancer or baseball pitcher warming up for a performance, you can prepare for your first draft by rehearsing part of the argument you will make. Select one of your causes or effects and write several sentences about it, trying out an argument for your readers. How will you convince them to take seriously this cause or effect? This writing activity will focus your thinking and encourage you to keep discovering new arguments until you start drafting. It may also lead you to search for additional evidence to support your arguments.

DRAFTING

Review the lists, writings, and notes you produced in the preceding invention activities. Note the most promising material. You may realize that you need further information, a deeper analysis, or a better understanding of your readers. If you have the time, stop now to fill in these gaps. If you feel reasonably confident about your material, however, you may be ready to begin drafting. Remember that you will solve some problems and make further discoveries as you draft. The following guidelines will help you set goals for your draft and plan your draft.

Setting Goals

If you establish goals for your draft before you begin writing, you will be able to move ahead more quickly. With general goals in mind, you can make particular writing decisions more confidently. Consider the following questions now, and keep them in mind as you draft so you can maintain your focus.

How will I convince my readers that my proposed causes or effects are plausible? Shall I marshal statistical evidence like Waldman, give many examples like Greeley, quote authorities and published research like Angier, include personal anecdotes and cases like Kozol, or introduce analogies like King and Angier?

How should I anticipate readers' objections to my argument? What should I do about alternative causes or effects? Shall I anticipate readers' objections and questions like Angier or answer readers' likely questions like Greeley? Shall I dismiss alternative causes like Mason?

How much will my readers need to know about my subject? Will I need to describe my subject in some detail in the way that Waldman establishes the plethora of choices we face, Greeley describes Catholicism for non-Catholics, and Mason describes the history of Hank Gathers? Or can I assume that my readers have personal experience with my subject? If my subject is a trend, how can I demonstrate that the trend exists?

How can I begin engagingly and end conclusively? Shall I begin by emphasizing the importance or timeliness of my subject like Angier? Might I begin with a personal anecdote like Waldman and Mason, or with an unusual statement like King's?

How will I establish my authority to argue the causes or effects of my subject? Shall I do this by citing personal experience and presenting a carefully researched consideration of the trend like Waldman, by showing a comprehensive understanding of the effects of the phenomenon like Kozol, or by relying on what I have learned through research and interviews like Angier?

Planning Your Draft

With goals in mind and invention notes at hand, you are ready to make a tentative outline of your draft. The sequence of proposed causes or effects will be at the center of your outline, but you may also want to plan where you will consider alternatives or counterargue objections. Notice that some writers who conjecture about causes consider alternative causes—evaluating, refuting, or accepting them—before they present their own. Much of an essay analyzing causes may be devoted to considering alternatives. Both writers who conjecture about causes and writers who speculate about effects usually consider readers' possible objections to their causes or effects along with the argument for each cause or effect. If you must provide readers with a great deal of information about your subject as context for your argument, you may want to outline this information carefully. For your essay, this part of the outline may be a major consideration. Your plan should make the information readily accessible to your readers. This outline is tentative; you may decide to change it when you start drafting.

Avoiding Logical Fallacies

Speculating about trends, phenomena, and events poses special challenges. Reasons and evidence must be thoughtfully selected, and certain common errors in causal reasoning must be avoided. To avoid making errors in your reasoning, ask yourself the following questions as you plan and draft your essay:

- How can I avoid the *post hoc, ergo propter hoc* (Latin for "after this, therefore because of this") fallacy? Have I mistakenly assumed that something that occurred prior to the beginning of the phenomenon or trend was therefore a cause?

- How can I be sure not to *confuse causes with effects?* Sometimes effects can be sustaining causes of a trend, but, if that is so, I should acknowledge it as such. Are any of my causes also results? Are any of my causes actually results and not causes at all?

- How can I show readers that I have *accepted the burden of proof?* I must offer proof for all my assertions and not *shift the burden of proof* to my readers by assuming they will automatically understand certain assertions.

- How can I refute counterarguments without committing the *ad hominem* (Latin for "to the man") fallacy? Can I argue against readers' objections without ridiculing the readers themselves?

- How can I consider and reject alternative causes without committing the *straw man* fallacy? (A straw man is easy to push over.)

- Can I argue for one cause only without being accused of the *either/or* fallacy? Should I not argue for several related causes? Might readers find my argument more convincing if I acknowledge alternative causes?

READING A DRAFT CRITICALLY

Now that you have a draft of your essay in hand, you can benefit from having someone else read your draft critically to describe what you have accomplished and give you advice on possible improvements. Your instructor might do this, or another student might do it. Your instructor might ask you to do the same for a classmate. The following guidelines, which will bring together everything you have learned about speculating about causes or effects, will ensure that these critical readings are focused.

It is important to get or give a written record of a critical reading. Because you are unlikely to start revising your draft immediately after having it read critically, you need a written record to remind you later of all the observations, insights, and advice about your draft.

Before the critical reading, number the paragraphs of your essay so you and the critical reader can refer efficiently to parts of the draft.

Reading a draft with a critical eye means reading it more than once, first to get a general impression and then to analyze its basic features.

Reading for a First Impression

Read the essay straight through, without stopping to comment or advise. Then write a few sentences giving your first impression. What most surprised you? What did you like best? Could you easily follow the argument step by step to its conclusion? Did you find the argument convincing?

Reading to Analyze

Now read to focus on the basic features of an essay speculating about causes or effects.

PRESENTING THE SUBJECT. Focus first on how well the draft presents the event, trend, or phenomenon. Tell the writer what you found most interesting and useful and try to point out one or more places where a reader unfamiliar with the subject might need more information. Suggest ways the writer could make the subject seem more interesting.

If the subject is a trend, look closely at how the writer demonstrates that the subject is increasing or decreasing over time. Explain what you understand to be the increase or decrease and let the writer know whether you think further evidence is required to demonstrate conclusively that the subject is indeed a trend.

MAKING A CAUSE OR EFFECT ARGUMENT. Begin by making your own list of the causes or effects proposed in the draft. If you find this difficult, tell the writer so and try to identify what may be the problem. For example, the writer may not have signaled clearly where each cause or effect appears or maybe the draft merely discusses the subject rather than speculate about its causes or effects. Identify any that seem perhaps too obvious and not likely to interest readers. Suggest additional causes or effects that would strengthen the writer's argument.

Next, look critically at the writer's argument for each proposed cause or effect. Focus on the support or evidence the writer offers for each one to convince readers to consider it seriously. Point out which causes or effects seem convincingly argued and, most important, suggest ways the writer can strengthen the argument for others. Might personal experience anecdotes, statistics, facts, examples, retold stories, analogies, comparisons or contrasts, quoting authorities, literary or cinematic allusions, or metaphors—all the kinds of support that you have seen in the readings in this chapter—be helpful?

HANDLING OBJECTIONS AND ALTERNATIVE CAUSES OR EFFECTS. Identify places where the writer has anticipated readers' likely objections or questions. The writer may merely mention objections and questions, assimilate them into his or her own argument, or refute them. Describe what the writer has done in each case and advise the writer on strengthening the handling of objections and questions. You can be particularly helpful to the writer if you can think of objections or questions not anticipated.

Now identify any alternative causes or effects the writer mentions. These are causes or effects readers may prefer over those for which the writer argues. Again, the writer may merely mention, accommodate, or refute these causes or effects. Help the writer improve this important part of the argument. Refutation of readers' preferred causes or effects must seem convincing to them without seeming to ridicule them for preferring those alternatives. Equally important, try to think of alternative causes or effects readers are likely to be thinking about.

Having identified all of the draft's proposed causes or effects and anticipations of readers' objections, questions, and preferred alternative causes or effects, step back from the details to consider the overall plan or sequence of the argument. First, outline the argument, identifying in a brief phrase each cause or effect, readers' objection or question, and mention of readers' preferred alternative causes or effects. These various fundamental parts of the argument can be sequenced in many different ways. The writer's goal should be a convincing, logical, step-by-step argument with causes or effects sequenced for maximum effect on the reader with the readers' objections, questions, and preferred causes or effects handled at appropriate moments as the argument moves along. Help the writer reach this goal by commenting on what is effective in the present sequence, how the argument can be more convincing by resequencing some parts, and where new material you may have suggested earlier might best be inserted.

ESTABLISHING CREDIBILITY. Comment on the credibility of the essay, on how believable and authoritative the writing seems. Let the writer know where the writing seems most credible. Point to at least one specific place or feature and explain briefly what makes it seem credible. Indicate other places or features where credibility seems weak or lacking. Try to suggest specific strategies for improvement. Readers are continuously assessing credibility, perhaps word for word and certainly sentence by sentence. A readers' judgment that an essay is credible comes from countless small impressions of every aspect of the essay.

REVISING

This section provides suggestions for revising your draft, suggestions that by now will be merely reminders to you of the possibilities for developing a plausible cause or effect argument. Although you have been working on this assignment for some time, you need to revise one more time. Revising means reenvisioning your draft, trying to see it in a new way, given your purpose and readers, to strengthen your cause or effect argument.

The biggest mistake you can make in revising is to focus initially on words or sentences. Instead, first try to see your draft as a whole to assess its likely impact on your readers. Think imaginatively and boldly about cutting out unconvincing material, adding new material, and moving material around. Your computer makes even drastic revisions easy, but you make the effort and decisions that will improve your draft.

You may have received help with this challenge from classmates who have given your draft a critical reading. If not, you can read your own draft critically, following the guidelines in Reading a Draft Critically.

As you prepare to revise, keep the following suggestions in mind.

Revising to Improve the Presentation of Your Subject

If you can be certain your subject is very familiar to your readers, you may not need to present it in any detail, although even readers familiar with a subject will want to see that you understand it well.

If your readers are unfamiliar with your subject, present it to them fully. In this case, you might need to devote one third to one half of your essay to present the subject, without slighting your argument for its causes or effects, of course. Particularly in the case of speculating about the causes or effects of a trend, you must carefully demonstrate that it is in fact a trend—that it has been increasing or decreasing over time.

Revising to Strengthen Your Cause or Effect Argument

Your goal is to convince readers your speculations are plausible. Consider your proposed causes or effects. Should you drop one or more implausible or weakly argued causes or effects? Should you add new causes or effects to your essay? Do some of your causes or effects go beyond what readers would think of by just knowing your subject but before reading your essay?

Evaluate how successfully you have argued for each cause or effect. What further support can you present to make each cause or effect seem plausible to your readers? Consider adding personal experience, statistics, examples, facts, quotations from authorities, analogies—anything relevant that will make your argument more convincing.

Ensure that your causes or effects are sequenced logically step-by-step, with one leading naturally to the next in what is sometimes called a *chain of reasoning*.

Revising to Improve Your Handling of Objections and Alternative Causes or Effects

Consider carefully whether you have anticipated the major objections readers may have about your argument as well as any alternative causes or effects they may think more plausible than those you have proposed. Remember that you can accommodate or refute objections; that is, you can acknowledge some wisdom in the objection and perhaps incorporate it into your own argument, or you can argue that it is mistaken or misinformed. You must do more than dismiss an objection; you must argue against it without seeming to personally attack its likely proponents.

Alternative causes or effects require careful handling. If they pose a serious challenge to your argument, you should attempt to refute them decisively. You should at least acknowledge that you are aware of certain alternative causes or effects you suspect readers may be thinking of as they read your essay.

Revising to Enhance Your Credibility

If you have strengthened your argument and handled readers' objections effectively, you will have gone a long way toward establishing your credibility—your plausibility, believability, or authority. If you suspect lapses in credibility anywhere in your essay, work to overcome them by modifying your language, supporting your argument, and showing your readers that you take seriously their objections even though you must refute them. You want to convince your readers sentence by sentence that you are a writer they can trust to speculate on your chosen subject.

REFLECTING ON WHAT YOU HAVE LEARNED ABOUT WRITING ESSAYS SPECULATING ABOUT CAUSES OR EFFECTS

In this chapter, you have read critically several essays speculating about causes or effects and written one of your own. To remind yourself how much you have learned and to consolidate this learning so you can use it later, pause now to reflect on your reading and writing experiences.

Write a page or so reflecting on your learning. Begin by describing what you are most pleased with in your essay and explaining why. Describe in detail what contributed to your achievement. Was it something you observed in one of the readings? Did it come from your invention writing? Did you get good advice from someone? Try to write about your achievement in terms of the special requirements of essays speculating about causes or effects.

Then write about anything else that accounts for your learning about this special kind of writing.

PROPOSAL TO SOLVE A PROBLEM

Proposals are written every day in the workplace. A team of engineers and technical writers in an engineering firm, for example, might write a proposal to compete for a contract to build an intraurban rail system. The business manager of a trucking company might write a memo to a company executive proposing an upgrading of the computer system to include electronic mail and networking. Seeking funding to support her research on the American poet Walt Whitman, a university professor might write a proposal to the National Endowment for the Humanities.

Other proposals address social problems and attempt to influence the direction of public policy. A special United Nations task force recommends ways to eliminate acid rain worldwide. The College Entrance Examination Board commissions a report proposing strategies for reversing the decline in Scholastic Assessment Test (SAT) scores. A specialist in children's television writes a book in which he proposes that the federal government support several years' work to develop new educational programming for preschool and elementary school students.

Still other proposals are written by individuals who want to solve problems involving groups or communities to which they belong. A college student irritated by long waits to see a nurse at the campus health clinic writes the clinic director, proposing a more efficient way to schedule and accommodate students. After funding for dance classes has been cut by their school board, students and parents interested in dance write a proposal to the school principal, asking her help in arranging after-school classes taught by a popular high-school teacher who would be paid with community funds. The board of directors of a historical society in a small ranching community proposes to the county board of supervisors that it donate an unused county building to the society so it can organize and display historical records, photographs, and artifacts.

Proposals to solve problems are a familiar genre of writing, and they also involve a way of thinking that is fundamental to much of the world's work. In most disciplines and professions, problem solving is a basic way of thinking. For example, scientists use the scientific method, a systematic form of problem solving; political scientists and sociologists propose solutions to troubling political and social problems; engineers regularly use problem-solving techniques to build bridges, automobiles, or computers; attorneys find legal precedents to solve their clients' problems; teachers continually make decisions about how to help students with specific learning problems; counselors devote themselves to helping clients solve personal problems; business owners or managers define themselves as problem solvers; auto-assembly teams in newer plants study problems that reduce their efficiency to propose a solution. Problem solving depends on a questioning attitude, called *critical thinking*. In addition, it demands imagination and creativity. To solve a problem, you need to see it anew, to look at it from new angles and in new contexts. The essay you write for this chapter will fully engage you in this special and important way of thinking.

Because a proposal tries to convince readers that its way of defining and solving the problem makes sense, proposal writers must be sensitive to readers' needs and expectations. As you plan and draft a proposal, you will want to determine whether your readers know about the problem and whether they are aware of its seriousness. In addition, you will want to consider what your readers might think of other possible solutions. Knowing what your readers know, what their assumptions and biases are, and what kinds of arguments will be appealing to them is central to proposal writing, as it is to all good argumentative writing.

As you read the essays in this chapter, you will discover why proposals are so important and how they work. You will also get many ideas for writing a proposal to solve a problem that you care about. Keep the following goals for writing a proposal in mind as you analyze the essays and think about writing one of your own. Following the readings is a Guide to Writing Proposals to Solve Problems, which will support your writing of this assignment.

THE WRITING ASSIGNMENT

Proposal to Solve a Problem

Write an essay, proposing a solution to a clearly defined problem affecting a group or community to which you belong. Your task is to establish that the problem exists, to offer a solution that can reasonably be implemented, to lay out the particulars by which your proposal would be put into effect, and to consider objections and alternative solutions.

WRITING SITUATIONS FOR PROPOSING SOLUTIONS TO PROBLEMS

Writing that proposes solutions to problems plays a significant role in college and professional life, as the following examples show:

- The business manager of a large hospital writes a proposal to the board of directors requesting the purchase of a new word-processing and billing system that she recently saw demonstrated at a convention. She argues that the new system would both improve efficiency and save money. In support of her proposal, she reminds the board of the limitations of the present system and points out the advantages of the new one.

- A newspaper columnist writes about the problem of controlling the spread of AIDS. Because symptoms may take years to appear, he notes, people infected with HIV, the virus that causes AIDS, unwittingly pass it on to their sexual partners. He discusses three solutions that have been proposed: having only one sexual partner, engaging in safer sexual practices, or notifying and testing the sexual partners of those found to have the disease. He argues that the first solution would solve the problem but may not be feasible and that the second would not work because safer sexual practices are not absolutely reliable. In support of the third solution—tracing sexual partners—he argues that tracing has worked to control the spread of other diseases and that it should also help control the spread of AIDS.

- For a political science class, a college student analyzes the question of presidential terms of office. Citing examples from recent history, she argues that presidents spend the first year of each term getting organized and the fourth year either running for reelection or weakened by their status as a lame duck. Consequently, they are fully productive for only half of their four-year terms.

  She proposes limiting presidents to one six-year term, claiming that this change would remedy the problem by giving presidents four or five years to put their programs into effect. She acknowledges that it could make presidents less responsive to the public will, but insists that the system of legislative checks and balances would make that problem unlikely.

- For an economics class, a student looks into the many problems arising from *maquiladoras,* new industries in Mexico near the border with the United States that provide foreign exchange for the Mexican government, low-paying jobs for Mexican workers, and profits for American manufacturers. He discovers that in Mexico there are problems of inadequate housing, health care, injuries on the job, and environmental damage. His instructor encourages him to select one of the problems, research it more thoroughly, and propose a solution. Taking the problem of injuries on the job as most immediately within the control of American manufacturers, he proposes that they observe standards established by the U.S. federal Occupational Safety and Health Administration.

PRACTICING PROPOSING SOLUTIONS
TO PROBLEMS
A COLLABORATIVE ACTIVITY

You can readily experience the complexities and possibilities involved in proposing solutions by thinking through a specific problem and trying to come up with a feasible proposal.

PART 1. Form a group with two or three other students, and select someone to take notes during your discussion. List several problems within your college or community, and choose one that everyone in your group knows something about.

Then consider possible solutions to this problem, and identify one that you can all support. Decide on an individual or group who could take action on your proposed solution, and figure out how you would convince this audience that the problem is serious and must be solved and that your proposed solution is feasible and should have their support. Consider carefully what questions readers might ask about your solution and what objections they might have to it.

PART 2. With the group, reflect on your efforts at proposing a solution to a problem.

What approach did you take in attempting to convince the audience that the problem is serious and should be solved? How did you appeal to this audience?

How did you go about attempting to convince the audience that your proposed solution is feasible? What specific ideas did you come up with?

What was most difficult in devising a convincing argument for your proposed solution? What seemed easiest and most satisfying? In making this special kind of argument, what seemed familiar and unfamiliar to you?

A GUIDE TO READING A PROPOSAL
TO SOLVE A PROBLEM

To introduce the features and strategies of writing to propose solutions to problems, read, annotate, and write about your understanding of the brief essay that follows. Then, following the guidelines for writing a proposal, reread the essay to examine the particular features of strong proposal writing.

First, though, as a reminder of the many possibilities for annotating, here is an illustration of an annotated passage from another proposal essay, by Edward J. Loughran, which appears in its entirety later in the chapter.

The problem explained by:
1. rise in serious crime
2. more young first-time offenders

Two primary factors explain the growing numbers of juvenile offenders. First, there is indeed a rise in serious crime among young people, fueled by the steady stream of drugs and weapons into their hands. These dangerous offenders are committed—legitimately—to juvenile-correction agencies for long-term custody or treatment.

But a second, larger group is also contributing to the increase. It consists of 11-, 12-, and 13-year-old first-time offenders who have failed at home, failed in school, and fallen through the cracks of state and community social-service agencies. These are not serious offenders, or even typical delinquents. But they are coming into the correctional system because we have ignored the warning signs among them.

reasons for number 2

Each year in Massachusetts, roughly 20,000 youths become involved with the justice system. Although many of them will not receive probation or commitment to the department, each is signaling a need for help. Studies indicate that youths at risk to offend will begin to show signs as early as 2nd or 3rd grade. School failure, child abuse and neglect, drug abuse, and teenage pregnancy may all be indicators of a future involving crime.

Problem is obvious, but it's being ignored

solution— how to pay for this?

Waiting for "problem children" to outgrow negative behavior is a mistake—in most cases, they don't. Unless intensive community supports are developed to improve their school experiences and the quality of life in their families and neighborhoods, as many as one in four American young people—some 7 million youths—are in danger of destroying their opportunities in life.

significance of problem

Robert J. Samuelson

REFORMING SCHOOLS THROUGH A FEDERAL TEST FOR COLLEGE AID

Robert Samuelson (b. 1945) began his journalism career at the *Washington Post.* For many years, he has been a free-lance writer, producing a biweekly column on socioeconomic issues that appears in *Newsweek,* the *Washington Post,* the *Los Angeles Times,* the *Boston Globe,* and other newspapers. He is the author of *The Good Life and Its Discontents: The American Dream and the Age of Entitlement 1945–1995* (1996). This selection, which appeared in *Newsweek* in May 1991, offers a solution to the problem, as Samuelson sees it, with American high schools.

Read the essay, annotating anything that helps you understand Samuelson's view of the problem and his proposal for solving it. Mark on the text, and write comments and questions in the margin. Because you are a high-school graduate, you are among his intended readers. React to his argument on the basis of your experience in high school.

We are not yet serious about school reform. The latest plan 1
from the Bush administration mixes lofty rhetoric (a pledge to
"invent new schools") with vague proposals to rate our schools with
national tests. It doesn't address the most dreary—and important—
fact about American education: our students don't work very hard.
The typical high-school senior does less than an hour of homework
an evening. No school reform can succeed unless this changes.
What's depressing is that we could change it, but probably won't.

We could require students receiving federal college aid to pass a 2
qualifying test. This is a huge potential lever. Nearly two-thirds of
high-school graduates go to college (including community colleges
and vocational schools), and roughly two-fifths—6 million students—
get federal aid. In fiscal 1991, government grants and guaranteed loans
totaled $18.1 billion. As a practical matter any federal test would also
affect many unaided students; most colleges couldn't easily maintain a
lower entrance requirement for the rich. The message would be: anyone wanting to go to college can't glide through high school.

Just how well our schools perform depends heavily on student 3
attitudes. This is one reason why the Bush plan, which proposes
tests to evaluate schools, is so empty. The tests hold no practical
consequences for students and, therefore, lack the power to moti-
vate them. When students aren't motivated, they don't treat school
seriously. Without serious students, it's hard to attract good people
into teaching no matter how much we pay them. And bad teachers
ensure educational failure. This is the vicious circle we must break.

Unfortunately, we don't now expect much of our students. For 4
most high-school students, it doesn't pay to work hard. Their goal is
college, and almost anyone can go to some college. There are perhaps
50 truly selective colleges and universities in the country, Chester
Finn Jr., professor of education at Vanderbilt University, writes in his
new book, "We Must Take Charge: Our Schools and Our Future."
To survive, the other 3,400 institutions of "higher learning" eagerly
recruit students. Entrance requirements are meager and financial
assistance from states and the federal government is abundant.

"Coast and get into college and have the same opportunities as 5
someone who worked hard," says one senior quoted by Finn. "That
is the system." It's this sort of silly rationalization that hurts American students, precisely because they can't always make up what
they've missed in the past. Opportunities go only to those who have
real skills—not paper credentials or many years spent on campus.
The college dropout rate is staggering. After six years, less than half
of students at four-year colleges have earned a degree. The graduation rate is even lower for community colleges.

Every other advanced society does it differently. "The United 6
States is the only industrial country that doesn't have some (testing)
system external to the schools to assess educational achievement,"
says Max Eckstein, an expert on international education. Their tests,

unlike ours, typically determine whether students can continue in school. As the lone holdout, we can compare our system with everyone else's. Well, we rank near the bottom on most international comparisons.

In the media, the school "crisis" is often pictured as mainly a problem of providing a better education for the poor and minorities. Stories focus on immigrants and inner-city schools. Almost everyone else is (by omission) presumed to be getting an adequate education. Forget it. In fact, the test scores of our poorest students, though still abysmally low, have improved. Likewise, high-school dropout rates have declined. What we minimize is the slippage of our average schools.

Common Sense

When mediocrity is the norm, even good students suffer. In international comparisons, our top students often fare poorly against other countries' top students, notes economist John Bishop of Cornell University. Grade inflation is widespread. In 1990 1.1 million high-school students took the college board exams. These are the best students: 28 percent had A averages, 53 percent B's and the rest C's. Yet, two-fifths of these students scored less than 390 on the verbal SAT.

The idea that college-bound students should be required (by test) to demonstrate the ability to do college-level work is common sense. It's hard to see how anyone could object, especially with so much public money at stake. But almost no educators or political leaders advocate it. The American belief in "equality" and "fairness" makes it hard for us to create barriers that block some students. Our approach is more indirect and dishonest: first, we give them meaningless high-school degrees; then we let them drop out of college.

The same spirit of self-deception pervades much of the school debate. We skirt the obvious—students will work if there's a good reason—and pursue painless and largely fictitious cures. There's a constant search for new teaching methods and technologies that will, somehow, miraculously mesmerize students and automatically educate them. Computers are a continuing fad. Liberals blame educational failure on inadequate spending; conservatives lambast public schools as rigid bureaucracies. These familiar critiques are largely irrelevant.

Low spending isn't the main problem. Between 1970 and 1990, "real" (inflation adjusted) spending per student in public schools rose 63 percent. In 1989, U.S. educational spending totaled 6.9 percent of gross national product, which equals or exceeds most nations'. As for "vouchers" and "choice"—conservatives' current cure—the experiment has already been tried in higher education. It failed. Government loans and grants are vouchers that allow students choice. The perverse result is that colleges compete by reducing entrance requirements in order to increase enrollments and maximize revenues.

A test for college aid would stem this corrosive process. The   12 number of college freshmen would decline, but not—given the high dropout rates—the number of college graduates. Because high-school standards are so lax, the passing grade of any meaningful test would flunk many of today's seniors. Tests are available, because a few state college systems, such as New Jersey's and Tennessee's, give them to freshmen. Failing students must take remedial courses. In 1990, 37 percent of New Jersey freshmen flunked a verbal-skills test and 58 percent an algebra test.

An Uproar

Who would be hurt? Not students who can pass the test today: 13 that's perhaps 40 to 60 percent of college freshmen. Not students who might pass the test with more study: that's another big fraction. (In New Jersey and Tennessee, most students pass remedial courses. If they can do it at 18 or 19, they can do it at 17.) Some students who now go to college wouldn't. Often, these students drop out after saddling themselves with a hefty student loan. Would they be worse off? On college loans, default rates range as high as 25 percent.

But let's be candid. None of this is about to happen soon. Requir-   14 ing tests for college aid would cause an uproar. There would be charges of elitism, maybe racism. Colleges and universities would resist. They depend on the current open-ended flow of students and, without it, some would have to shut down. This wouldn't be bad for the country, because we now overinvest in higher education. With one-fifth the students, colleges and universities account for two-fifths of all educational spending. But today's waste has spawned a huge constituency.

Little wonder that President Bush—and all politicians—steer   15 clear of this sort of reform. It's too direct. It wouldn't cure all our educational problems, but it would make a start. It would jolt students, parents and teachers. It would foster a climate that rewards effort. It would create pressures for real achievement, not just inflated grades. It would force schools to pay more attention to non-college-bound students, rather than assuming everyone can go somewhere. It would strip away our illusions, which, sadly, are precisely what we cherish most.

READING FOR MEANING

Write at least a page, exploring your understanding of Samuelson's proposal. Begin by writing a few sentences about Samuelson's approach to his readers, college students or college graduates with at least a casual interest in the state of American education. What does he seem to assume about your experience of high school? How would you describe his attitude toward his readers? What does he want you to do, if anything? Indicate two or three places in the text that support your understanding.

Then write about anything else that helps you develop your ideas about Samuelson's analysis of the problem and his proposed solution for it. As you write, you may find you need to reread the essay and annotate it further. Consider quoting phrases and sentences that explain your ideas and reactions. You may find your ideas changing as you write.

If you have trouble sustaining your writing, consider the following ideas:

- In paragraphs 3 through 9, Samuelson argues that students' lack of effort really is the basic problem with high schools. Summarize his main points, and then state what you find most and least convincing, based on your own educational experiences.

- List the beneficial results Samuelson claims for his proposed solution. Which results do you find most likely? Which do you question? Can you think of any results Samuelson has not foreseen?

- React to any of Samuelson's assertions that especially please, challenge, or irritate you.

- Many states have a three-tier system of higher education: community colleges, state colleges, universities. SAT or American College Test scores and high-school records determine where students matriculate. What difficulties might a three-tier system present for Samuelson's proposal?

READING LIKE A WRITER

This section guides you through an analysis of Samuelson's argumentative strategies: *introducing the problem, presenting the solution,* and *convincing readers to accept the solution.* In each part, we describe one strategy briefly and then pose a critical reading and writing task for you.

Consider this activity a writer's introduction to proposal writing. You will learn even more from a similar activity following each selection in this chapter.

Introducing the Problem

Every proposal begins with a problem. Writers must define or describe this problem. Writers may go well beyond simply identifying it and telling readers how to recognize it. Depending on what their readers know, writers may, for example, explain how the problem came to be or what attempts have been made to solve it. In addition, if they think their readers may require it, writers will argue for the importance of the problem and the consequences of failing to solve it.

Sometimes, readers are already aware of a problem, especially if it affects them directly. In such cases, a writer can merely identify the problem and move directly to presenting a solution. At other times, many readers may be unaware a problem exists or may have difficulty imagining the problem. In these situations, writers may have to describe the problem in detail, helping readers recognize it and understand fully what it involves. Writers may also believe that readers misunderstand the problem, failing to recognize it for what it really is. They may then decide that their first task is to redefine the problem and help readers see it in a different way.

While describing the problem requires information about it, convincing readers of its significance requires argument. Here is where Samuelson concentrates his efforts.

Samuelson recognizes that many people, including the former president, would like to see improvements in American schools, but he apparently believes their reform efforts are doomed because they fail to recognize the real problem. His opening effort must be, then, to redefine the problem.

ANALYZE. Reread paragraphs 3 through 6, making notes about Samuelson's strategy for convincing readers that the problem of student motivation is indeed the most serious issue. Does he point to causes of the problem and to its consequences? Does he rely on comparisons? Indicate in the margins the kinds of evidence on which he draws.

WRITE. Write several sentences, explaining Samuelson's strategy and evaluating how convincing he is. What do you think he gains or loses by neglecting to describe the problem and concentrating instead on its significance? Are you convinced by his redefinition of the problem? Do you see ways he could have made his argument more convincing?

Presenting the Solution

The proposed solution is the heart of a proposal essay because the writer's primary purpose is to convince readers to accept the wisdom of that solution and even to take action on it. Readers can more readily make this decision if they can imagine the solution and envision just how it would be implemented.

A proposed solution to a highly technical engineering problem might require many pages, but a tentative proposal to encourage greater student preparedness for college, such as Samuelson's, could be brief.

Some proposals have little chance of success unless every small step of implementing them is detailed for readers. Proposals like Samuelson's, however, refer to implementation without detailing it, perhaps deferring to specialists who could step in later to work out the details. Also, when a writer initially floats a highly speculative proposal, details of implementation may be premature; the real purpose may be to invite readers' reactions before committing the time required to work out all the details. Given his space limitations and readers' expectations of a weekly newsmagazine, Samuelson has limited opportunity to detail the implementation of a massive and complex national testing program involving some six million high-school graduates in America.

ANALYZE. Reread paragraphs 2 and 12, underlining the few details Samuelson gives about his proposed solution. Make marginal notes of any ideas you have about who would need to be involved in solving the problem and what they would have to do to borrow or devise and then administer a test to every high school graduate who hopes for a federal grant or loan.

WRITE. Summarize the few details Samuelson gives about his solution and then write several sentences speculating about how the solution might be implemented. Finally, add a few sentences evaluating whether Samuelson gives enough details so that a high-school graduate or first-year college student like you could imagine how the solution might be implemented even though it is not spelled out. Keeping in mind his space constraints in a magazine essay, list two or three key details Samuelson might have included to help his readers more easily imagine how the solution would look.

Convincing Readers to Accept the Solution

Whatever else proposal writers do they must argue energetically, imaginatively, and sensitively for their proposed solutions. A proposal is not a proposal without some argument supporting the solution. It may describe a problem well or complain with great feeling about a problem; if it goes no further, however, it cannot be a proposal.

Writers must argue in support of their proposed solutions to convince readers the solution is feasible, cost-effective, and more promising than alternative solutions. Although Samuelson describes his solution only briefly and says nothing about how it might be implemented, he does argue energetically for it, relying on a variety of strategies.

In arguing for solutions, writers rely on three interrelated strategies: arguing directly for the solution, counterarguing readers' likely objections and questions about the argument, and evaluating alternative solutions.

Writers argue for solutions by giving reasons why the solution may feasibly solve the problem and presenting evidence to support these reasons. Such evidence may include personal experience, hypothetical cases and scenarios, statistics, facts, and quotations from authorities. The most convincing evidence surprises readers: They see it and think, "I never thought of it that way."

As they argue for their solutions, experienced writers are continually aware of readers' objections to the argument or questions about it. As they write, they may *acknowledge* readers' objections and questions by simply mentioning them, letting readers know they are aware of the objections and questions without evaluating or refuting them. Writers may also *accommodate* readers' likely objections and questions into their own arguments. What better way to disarm a skeptical or antagonistic reader! Finally, writers may *refute* readers' objections and questions; that is, try to show them to be groundless or just plain wrong. Experienced arguers bring their readers' questions and objections right into their arguments. They do not ignore their readers or pretend that readers are not reading the argument critically.

Experienced proposal writers quite often mention other solutions readers may be thinking about or may even strongly favor over the writer's solution. If a writer knows or suspects readers may have alternative solutions in mind, it is better to discuss them directly in the argument. Had Samuelson failed to acknowledge obvious alternative solutions, readers would think he was not well informed about the problem. As in counterarguing, a writer may merely mention another solution, integrate all or part of it into his or her own solution, or dismiss it as unworkable.

ANALYZE. Samuelson argues directly for his solution in paragraphs 8, 9, 12, 13, and 15. Reread these paragraphs carefully, annotating each one for the kinds of evidence Samuelson presents. Consider especially the range and variety of evidence.

WRITE. Write several sentences, describing Samuelson's argument in these paragraphs. What kinds of evidence does he use? What appeals does he make to readers' experience and values? Comment on anything else you notice. Conclude with a few sentences that evaluate the effectiveness of Samuelson's argument. What did you find most and least convincing? Indicate any evidence that seemed surprising or imaginative and any that might strike you as irrelevant or misleading.

Also write a few sentences evaluating Samuelson's counterarguments in paragraphs 7 and 14 and his consideration of alternative solutions in paragraphs 10 and 11. How successfully do you think he handles readers' likely objections to his argument? How do you think advocates of the alternative solutions Samuelson evaluates would respond to his evaluation?

READINGS

Mark Kleiman

CONFER COLLEGE DEGREES BY EXAMINATION

Mark A. R. Kleiman (b. 1951) is an associate professor of public policy and a research fellow with the Program in Criminal Justice Policy and Management at the John F. Kennedy School of Government, Harvard University. Kleiman is the author of *Marijuana: Costs of Abuse, Costs of Control* (1989), *Against Excess: Drug Policy for Results* (1992), and *The Drugs/Crime Connections* (1997). Kleiman advises local governments on drug policy.

This selection was published in the *Wall Street Journal,* an influential daily national newspaper primarily for business managers and investors. Kleiman proposes that because some people have great difficulty finding the time and money to get a degree by attending college for four years, they should have the opportunity to get one by taking a comprehensive

examination for which they have carefully prepared. Because this proposal has never been adopted by a college in the United States, you
might predict that Kleiman would need to devise an imaginative, convincing argument if he is to be taken seriously. He addresses the proposal to business managers, so he uses language associated with business.

Before you read, reflect on why Kleiman might have directed his proposal to business managers, most of whom are college graduates, rather
than to college professors and administrators. Also, consider how you
might go about studying for a college degree on your own. What kind of
guidance and materials might you require? As you read, annotate any
parts of the selection that help you understand Kleiman's argument for
his unorthodox proposal.

1   Colleges and universities offer their undergraduate students two
distinct commodities: an education (or rather the opportunity for
one) and a degree. The offer is what antitrust lawyers call a "tie sale":
They won't sell you the diploma unless you buy the whole package.

2   As fall approaches and parents dig into their pockets (or apply to
their banks) for the $15,000 a year it now costs to send a child to a
"prestige" institution such as the one where I work, it's time to ask
why the education-and-degree package shouldn't be unbundled. If a
student can achieve on his own, and demonstrate to the faculty,
knowledge and competence higher than, say, the median of a
school's graduating class, why shouldn't he be able to buy a certificate testifying as much?

3   Such a certificate—a B.A. by examination—would qualify its hold-
er for employment, or for graduate or professional study, without
costing him four years of forgone earnings plus the cash price of a
small house. . . .

4   There are three arguments for such a proposal.

5   First, it would save resources.

6   Second, it would make a valuable credential available to some who
cannot now afford it, thus contributing to social mobility. (In addition
to those earning their first degrees in this way, B.A.-by-exam programs at high-prestige schools might attract students who feel, often
correctly, that their obscure sheepskins are holding them back.)

7   Third, and more speculatively, it might free high-powered but
unconventional high-school graduates to pursue a self-education
more useful to them than any prepackaged education, without shut-
ting themselves out of jobs and advanced-degree programs.

8   There are two obvious objections. Those who took their B.A.s
by examination might miss out on the opportunities college provides for social interaction and other forms of personal and intellectual development. It might also be said that, since no examination
could capture the richness of an undergraduate education, B.A.s
by exam would have incentives to become, and would in fact be,

narrower and shallower than their eight-semesters-in-residence counterparts.

The first objection is probably true but not conclusive. Some who would choose the exam route over the regular undergraduate course would probably be wise not to buy the nonacademic attributes of college for four years' income plus $60,000; others will not, in fact, choose the more expensive option, even if it is the only one offered.

To the second objection there are two solutions: high standards and resource-intensive examinations. A process lasting a month and costing $3,000 to administer and score, testing both general knowledge and competence in a major field, and involving written, oral and practical components and the preparation of a thesis or the equivalent, should suffice to evaluate breadth and depth at least as well as the current system does. The interests of the group running an examination program would run parallel with those of the rest of the institution in keeping standards high, and the social and moral pressure to award degrees in borderline cases ought to be much less for exam students than for ordinary undergraduates. By setting standards for examination B.A.s above the median of the eight-semester graduates, an institution could ensure that the exam program raised the average education level of its degree-holders.

The price to candidates could reflect fully loaded cost plus a substantial contribution to overhead and still look like a bargain. To deal with the unwillingness of potential candidates to gamble several thousand dollars on their chances of success, it might make sense to administer a fairly cheap ($200) screening test and give anyone who passed a money-back guarantee on the more thorough (and expensive) degree exam. The failure rate could be built into the price, or some insurance company might be willing to administer the screening test and sell failure insurance.

This proposal should not be confused with college credit for "life experience," "urban semesters" or other moves to substitute the pragmatic for the scholarly in undergraduate education. The point is to tie the degree more rather than less tightly to specific academic competence, to certify the result—an educated person—rather than the *process* leading to that result.

If this idea required a consensus in order to be tried out, it would never stand a chance. Fortunately, no such consensus is needed. All it takes is one undeniably first-rate institution willing to break the credential cartel.

READING FOR MEANING

Write at least a page, exploring your understanding of Kleiman's proposal. Begin by explaining in your own words the problem Kleiman proposes to solve.

Then write about anything else that helps you develop your ideas about Kleiman's definition of the problem and his proposed solution.

As you write, you may find you need to reread the proposal and annotate it further. Consider quoting phrases or sentences that support your ideas and reaction. You may find your ideas changing as you write.

If you have trouble sustaining your writing, consider these possibilities:

- Speculate about why Kleiman risks arguing for such an unorthodox, never-before-implemented solution. After all, readers might laugh at him and publishers might refuse to publish him again.

- List the key points in Kleiman's proposed solution (see paragraphs 3, 10, 11, 12).

- Demonstrate that you understand the solution, then explain why you think the solution is or is not workable.

- Comment on what so far in your college experience leads you to agree or disagree with Kleiman's dismissal of the importance of the college experience itself.

EXTENDING MEANING THROUGH CONVERSATION. After you make meaning on your own, discuss Kleiman's proposal with others who have also read and thought about it to help further develop your understanding. Work with one or two other students. Before getting together, reread what you wrote about Kleiman's proposal. Begin your conversation by taking turns explaining what seems likely to be most convincing to the business managers Kleiman hopes to influence.

In your conversation, you may find that you have understood the reading differently from your classmates. Because your goal is to work together to understand the problem as Kleiman presents it and the solution he offers, you will want to reread parts of the essay together to see what additional meanings you find.

You will also want to share your evaluations of how successfully Kleiman presents his proposal for his intended readers. Here you may disagree, but disagreement will help each of you see more clearly where Kleiman succeeds and fails.

READING LIKE A WRITER

CONVINCING READERS TO ACCEPT THE SOLUTION
BY COUNTERARGUING OBJECTIONS

Kleiman devotes approximately a third of his proposal to counterarguing two presumed objections. By doing so, he hopes to gain the respect of readers who might otherwise dismiss his proposal. He also hopes to enhance his authority to propose this solution by seeming thoughtful about what is involved in granting college degrees by examination.

ANALYZE. Reread paragraphs 8 through 10, noting the two objections in paragraph 8 and the counterarguments to both in paragraphs 9 and 10. Notice the difference in the amount of attention Kleiman gives to each counterargument. What strategy does he use in each?

WRITE. Write several sentences, explaining how Kleiman counterargues the two objections. What do you think he means by "not conclusive" in paragraph 9? How would you describe his strategy or approach in each counterargument? Finally, add a few sentences evaluating the two counterarguments. Which do you think is likely to be more convincing to business managers and investors? Explain briefly. What one argument might be added to strengthen the weaker one? Kleiman says there are "two obvious objections." Might there be three? If you think so, identify a third possible objection to his proposal.

CONSIDERING IDEAS FOR YOUR OWN WRITING

Without substantial time for research, you would not want to take on a national or statewide problem in higher education, but you could write a proposal to solve a local problem on your own campus. If you have been on campus long enough to recognize a problem that needs solving, you can research it by interviewing students, faculty, or administrators; and you can find out precisely the group or person to whom to direct your proposal. With these advantages, you may be able to write an authoritative, convincing proposal.

Consider general campus problems, as well as problems within any campus group, community, team, committee, or course in which you have participated. You need not limit yourself to such predictable problems as noise in the dorms, bad food in the cafeteria, or lack of parking. Some of the more interesting problems on campus may include a poorly edited student newspaper, lack of facilities for handicapped students, inaccessible computer facilities, inefficient use of time in a work-study assignment, alienation of commuting students, too few current magazines and books and too many T-shirts and sports banners in the bookstore, and a shortage of practice rooms in the music building.

Edward J. Loughran

PREVENTION OF DELINQUENCY

Edward J. Loughran (b. 1939) served as commissioner of the Massachusetts Department of Youth Services from 1985 to 1993. He is now director of the National Juvenile Justice Project for the Robert F. Kennedy Memorial in Boston.

A frequent lecturer and writer on topics of juvenile justice, Loughran has taught graduate-level courses in juvenile justice and has served as a consultant to a variety of juvenile-justice agencies throughout the country. A book, *Balancing Juvenile Justice,* coauthored with Susan Gorino-Ghezzi, was published in 1995.

This proposal was published in *Education Week in* 1990, a newspaper read by public- and private-school administrators, school-board members, and state and federal education policymakers. For Loughran, a specialist in youth services, the problem is the increasing number of young people who are jailed (or, as he says, incarcerated or institutionalized) each year. He has in mind a solution that requires early attention to troubled eight- to twelve-year-olds in their homes, schools, and neighborhoods. You will be interested to see the range of specific programs he recommends, one of them involving college students as paid tutors and mentors.

Loughran begins by contrasting two responses to teenage delinquents: putting them in jail and assigning them to community-based programs. Before you read, recall a sentenced delinquent you know about or remember reading about. What was the crime? What happened to this person? Also, reflect for a moment on this question: How would you explain the increase in juvenile delinquency since the mid-eighties?

As you read, pay close attention in the early paragraphs to the way Loughran presents the problem, describing it and arguing for its seriousness.

The National Council on Crime and Delinquency recently reported that the number of young people incarcerated in the United States reached 53,000 last year—the highest number in the nation's history, despite a decline over the last decade in the juvenile population.

Many of these youths are placed in large, overcrowded facilities, where physical and sexual abuse and substandard correctional practices are on the rise. Educational and clinical programs in these settings are often ineffective.

The study found that young people treated in such institutions had a significantly higher rate of recidivism* than those in community-based, rehabilitative programs. In a comparison between California's institutional system and Massachusetts' community-based program, the council determined that 62 percent of the former state's sample, as opposed to only 23 percent in Massachusetts, were re-incarcerated after leaving a facility.

Most states continue to operate large institutions as their primary response to juvenile crime. But many are now examining the community-based approach as an alternative, for reasons of cost as well as rehabilitation. The shift in focus from correction to prevention that underlies such changes is essential if we are to help those children most likely to become delinquents.

Today's juvenile offenders, reflecting a growing underclass, have a complex profile. They typically are poor and virtually illiterate. Chronic truants or dropouts, they possess no marketable job skills.

*recidivism: a return to delinquent behavior (*Ed.*)

Many are children of teenage parents, and nearly 50 percent of them have already repeated that cycle. Though years below the legal drinking age, most have serious drug and alcohol problems.

Like most states, Massachusetts has seen a dramatic increase in the number of young people coming into its youth-services system. Since 1982, the number of juveniles detained with the youth-services department while awaiting trial has doubled, from 1,500 to 3,044 in 1989. In addition, there were 835 new commitments to the department in 1989—121 more than in the preceding year. Yet these increases come at a time when the juvenile population in the state and in the nation is shrinking. In 1990, there are fewer than 500,000 juveniles in Massachusetts; in 1970, there were 750,000. Even more perplexing, juvenile arraignments on delinquency charges have also dropped significantly in the state, from 25,943 in 1980 to 18,902 in 1989.

These numbers show that something is wrong with the way that juvenile-justice systems, courts, schools, and social-service agencies are addressing the problem of delinquency.

Two primary factors explain the growing numbers of juvenile offenders. First, there is indeed a rise in serious crime among young people; fueled by the steady stream of drugs and weapons into their hands. These dangerous offenders are committed—legitimately—to juvenile-correction agencies for long-term custody or treatment.

But a second, larger group is also contributing to the increase. It consists of 11-, 12-, and 13-year-old first-time offenders who have failed at home, failed in school, and fallen through the cracks of state and community social-service agencies. These are not serious offenders, or even typical delinquents. But they are coming into the correctional system because we have ignored the warning signs among them.

Each year in Massachusetts, roughly 20,000 youths become involved with the justice system. Although many of them will not receive probation or commitment to the department, each is signaling a need for help. Studies indicate that youths at risk to offend will begin to show signs as early as 2nd or 3rd grade. School failure, child abuse and neglect, drug abuse, and teenage pregnancy may all be indicators of a future involving crime.

Waiting for "problem children" to outgrow negative behavior is a mistake—in most cases, they don't. Unless intensive community supports are developed to improve their school experiences and the quality of life in their families and neighborhoods, as many as one in four American young people—some 7 million youths—are in danger of destroying their opportunities in life.

If we want to interrupt criminal paths and reduce the number of juveniles launching criminal careers, a shift in our priorities is necessary. States must invest their money in delinquency-prevention programs—at the front end rather than the back end of problems. These efforts should be targeted at elementary-school students from poor, high-crime neighborhoods, where traditional avenues to success are blocked.

For youths appearing in court on petty larceny or trespassing charges, we should develop restitution programs or innovative alternatives to costly lockups. Young people will learn something positive from a work assignment in the community, but not from 15 days' incarceration spent rubbing shoulders with more sophisticated offenders. And—at a time when correction resources are scarce— states will spend less money, gaining a greater return on investment.

Our department spends an average of $60,000 a year on each of its most serious offenders; much needs to be done in a short period of time to change behavior reinforced over many years. Less serious offenders are placed in group homes, at half the cost of secure facilities. For the least serious offenders, we operate day-treatment and outreach and tracking programs, which annually cost between $9,000 and $15,000 per youth. All of these programs include intensive educational and clinical components tailored to the individual.

The cost of constructing a 30-bed secure facility for juvenile offenders in Massachusetts is approximately $6 million dollars; annual operating expenses are $1.8 million. A delinquency-prevention program costs about $10,000 per year.

The efforts of youth-services departments must necessarily remain accountable for public safety. But the juvenile-justice system should join together with local schools and social-service and religious organizations to implement prevention and intervention strategies such as the following:

- *Home-builders:* Dispatch workers to the homes of children who have been abused, neglected, or recently released from a juvenile-detention program. Keep workers in homes at times of high stress: early in the morning, when the children might resist leaving for school, and after school, to supervise homework and nightly curfews. The annual cost for 1 worker to supervise 1 family is $4,000, with each worker responsible for 4 to 5 families.

- *Mentors:* Assign a teaching assistant or college student to work with youths who are beginning to fail in school. Mentors would serve as adult companions, helping children with homework and supervising them during after-school hours. The annual cost of 1 mentor working with 4 youngsters is $8,500. Public schools should employ students from local colleges or citizens in the community as part-time mentors.

- *Restitution:* Establish a plan whereby youths are assigned a community service or job to reimburse their victims, as well as serve justice and instill a sense of accountability in the offenders. A restitution program would also introduce a young offender to the world of work.

- *Streetworkers:* More and more 8- to 12-year-olds are being swept   20
  up in the excitement and status that accompany gang membership
  and urban violence. To counter the influence of gang leaders and
  reduce incidents of violence among these youngsters, hire full-
  time "streetworkers"—residents of the target areas who are
  street savvy and who want change in their neighborhood. Estimated cost is $8,000 per youth.
- *After-school employment:* Arrange for local businesses to hire high-   21
  school students as paid interns to work with a designated professional and learn a particular aspect of business. This would not
  only expose youths to professional opportunities but also provide
  positive role models. These private-public ventures could be
  overseen by community and state agencies, and by the larger businesses.

   There are many other possibilities. The important thing is to   22
begin reaching kids sooner. We must refocus our efforts from correcting the problem after the crime to creating alternatives that prevent the crime—not only in the interest of dollars but also for the
sake of lives.

READING FOR MEANING

Write a page or more about your understanding of Loughran's proposal.
Begin by stating in your own words Loughran's proposed solution, and then
explain briefly how he goes about arguing for it in paragraphs 12 through 16.
Then write about anything else that helps you develop your ideas about
Loughran's presentation of the problem and his proposed solution.

If you have trouble continuing your writing for a page or more, consider the
following ideas:

- Speculate about some of the "many other possibilities" Loughran suggests
  may be available to reduce delinquency and recidivism. Try to come up
  with two or three, and explain how they would complement Loughran's list
  of activities in paragraphs 17 through 21.

- Write about unstated assumptions in Loughran's argument. One assumption seems to be that the state is responsible for preventing delinquency.
  Can you think of others? How does awareness of these assumptions influence your response to the proposal?

- Select the one activity among those outlined in paragraphs 17 through 21
  that you would most like to work in, and explain why it appeals to you.

- Describe a personal experience (or that of a friend or family member) with
  the juvenile-justice system. Evaluate the experience in the light of
  Loughran's recommendations.

EXTENDING MEANING THROUGH CONVERSATION. Although it is important for
you to make meaning on your own, you can further develop your understanding

by discussing Loughran's proposal with others who have also read and thought about it. Work with one or two classmates. Before getting together, reread what you wrote about Loughran's proposal. Begin your conversation by taking turns explaining what seems likely to be most convincing to the educators Loughran hopes will take action on his proposed solution.

You may find that you and your classmates have understood the reading differently. Your goal is to work together to understand the problem as Loughran presents it and the solution he offers; you will want to reread parts of the essay together to see what further meanings you find.

You will also want to share your evaluations of how successfully Loughran presents his proposal to educators. You may disagree about how successful he is, but disagreement may help each of you understand more fully where Loughran succeeds and fails.

JUDGING THE WRITER'S CREDIBILITY. A further strategy of reading for meaning, which is not dealt with extensively in this chapter, is judging the writer's credibility or the ability to win and hold readers' confidence. Proposal writers who seem credible demonstrate their knowledge of the problem, establish common ground with readers, and respond fairly to objections and alternative solutions.

To analyze and evaluate Loughran's credibility, follow the guidelines in Judging the Writer's Credibility in Appendix 1, A Catalog of Critical Reading Strategies.

READING LIKE A WRITER
INTRODUCING THE PROBLEM

To introduce the problem, writers may define or describe it as well as argue for its seriousness. They may also present its history and speculate about its causes. Depending on their purpose and their readers, writers may identify the problem briefly (as Samuelson and Kleiman do), or they may introduce it at some length. Loughran devotes a relatively large portion of his proposal to introducing the problem.

ANALYZE. Reread paragraphs 5 through 11, where Loughran defines "juvenile offenders," describes the problem they pose, and argues for the importance or significance of the problem. To orient yourself to his strategies for introducing the problem, annotate each paragraph with a phrase or two identifying its topic or purpose.

WRITE. Write several sentences, describing how Loughran presents the problem and emphasizes its importance in these paragraphs. What strategies and kinds of evidence does he use? Conclude with a few sentences that evaluate Loughran's presentation of the problem. Given his purpose and readers, how successful do you think he is? What seems to you most and least convincing about what he does? Is he able to devise a logical, step-by-step progression in these paragraphs? Explain briefly.

CONSIDERING IDEAS FOR YOUR OWN WRITING

What immediate, local, troublesome social problems might you write about authoritatively? There may be social problems about which you are aware—homelessness, for example; but unless you have talked to homeless people or could interview several of them and also schedule time to talk to local authorities working with homeless people, you could not write authoritatively about this problem. Should you want to pursue it nevertheless through interviews and observation, you would want to focus on some special *local* problem that homeless people encounter or that they pose for the community.

Another possibility might be the lack of accessible, affordable child care for children of college students or working mothers. Although this problem is national in scope, it can only be solved locally—campus by campus, business by business, neighborhood by neighborhood. You would want to start by talking to others who have the same problem to enlarge your understanding. Then you might talk to two or three people who presently have adequate child care. They can help you think about alternative solutions. You might address your proposal to the campus president, the chief executive officer of a business, or a neighborhood minister with an underutilized church building.

With these two examples in mind—homelessness and lack of child care—talk with your instructor and other students about social problems that have unique local aspects or that can only be solved locally.

Samuelson's essay, which opens this chapter, reminds us that a familiar national problem with a concrete local manifestation is the widely perceived "failure" of American high schools to provide their students a rigorous education. What problems did you experience in your own high school? You need not focus on its general failure, even if you do consider it so. You could focus instead on some specific problem of administration, counseling, curriculum, facilities, or climate for learning. (Avoid focusing on one teacher or student.) Again, you would need to talk to others who had experienced the problem and especially, if at all possible, to students now at the school who are aware of the problem. You could address your proposal to the principal, a department head, the president of the school board or parent-teacher organization, or the editor of the local newspaper. Do not take this as an opportunity to air a complaint or grudge, however. Your goal should be to write an informed, thoughtful—even considerate—proposal. You intend to bring about change.

John Beilenson

GIVING THE YOUNG A VOICE IN NATIONAL SERVICE PROGRAMS

John Beilenson (b. 1962) is a communications consultant and writer who produces public relations materials and develops communications strategies for various organizations. He is founder and director of the

Chapel Hill, North Carolina, Youth Voice Project, which seeks to give young people a greater role in decision making in organizations set up to serve them. His books include *Sukarno: Indonesia's Revolutionary* (1989), *Educating the Whole Child* (1993), and *The Book of Coffee* (1995).

Beilenson's proposal appeared in 1993 in the journal *Social Policy,* read by academic social scientists and by federal and state policymakers who look to social science for ideas about current social problems. Presidential candidate Clinton's platform included a volunteer national service program for young people that would be the domestic version of the popular international Peace Corps program launched by President Kennedy. Beilenson proposes to give the volunteers in Clinton's program a more important role in planning, administering, and evaluating local projects and also in setting national policy.

Before reading, reflect for a moment on any volunteer work you may have done. How big was the organization for which you worked, and what were its goals? Who was in charge? What role, if any, did you and other volunteers have in the operation of the program and in monitoring its success?

As you read, notice the ways Beilenson attempts to convince his readers, national and local adult administrators of the National Service Corporation, the name of Clinton's program at the time, to take his proposal seriously.

Where are the young people?

This is the question I find myself asking as I make my way around the offices of national and community service programs in Washington and across the country. I have worked in and for youth service and youth serving organizations since 1985, so I have few illusions. Offices are for adults. If you want to find the youth in youth service, you generally have to get out to project sites—schools and playgrounds and parks—where young people are actually doing service.

Some of the offices of the top programs around the country, however, have a significantly more youthful ambiance. Young people are in the office for training sessions and meetings. They are helping with the administrative work or waiting to travel with staff to a funding or press meeting. It is not your typical work environment. It is noisier, more dynamic. You can almost hear what many call "youth voice"—young people involved in planning the fundamentals of community service programs. . . .

Ways to Include Youth Voice

In the rush to make application deadlines, it is easy to consult only the people who are in the office. Programs and planners must resist this expediency and make deliberate and ongoing efforts to listen to young people—their ideas, their hopes and fears, and their expert knowledge of their peers. It's not always easy, but it is far from an insurmountable goal. Here are some basic ways to do it.

1. *Put young people on the team.* The easiest way to get youth voice 5 heard on the national level is to include young people in all upper-level planning meetings and groups for the burgeoning National Service Corporation.* The over-30 crowd, wary of letting inexperienced young people into the process, need not worry. Groups of young people—many with their own programs—are well-versed and well-prepared to present some of the best thinking in the field. One need only look as far as Young People for National Service, Youth Service America's Youth Action Council, the Points of Light Foundation's Youth Engaged in Service (YES) Ambassadors,** or the Participant Council developed during Summer of Service to find fistfuls of qualified young advisers.

2. *Bring young people on the board.* The National Service Corpora- 6 tion should also appoint a significant number of young people (ages 16 to 25)—as many as four—to its planned 14-member board. This will ensure that young people have a meaningful role in the broad decision-making that will take place in the coming months and years. Again, these need not be "token" appointments. Some recent college graduates involved in service have almost a decade of experience in the field. Young people's presence on this highly visible national board, as well as on state commissions on national and community service, sends an important message to young people that their concerns are important and, through their representatives, their issues can be raised.

3. *Get out of the office.* National, state and local planners should 7 also get out into the field to hear what community service program participants are saying and suggesting. PennSERVE, Pennsylvania's state office of volunteerism, has developed "speakouts," where administrators and board members travel to different communities to listen to what young people and adults in the field have to say. These "hearings" are informal and interactive and create a "safe" environment for young people to talk frankly with adults. Young people might well be hired to do this research themselves.

4. *Create youth forums.* Another way planners can get the feed- 8 back required to ensure their ideas meet the needs and inspire the hopes of young people is to fund and create national, state and local youth advisory councils. Many states—including Michigan, California, Maryland, and Ohio—have already formed these 15- to 25-member

*National Service Corporation: an initiative of the Clinton administration begun in 1994, now called the Corporation for National and Community Service or AmeriCorps (*Ed.*)
**Young People for National Service: a lobbying group that pushed for passage of the National Service Act of 1993; *Youth Service America* was founded in 1985 by the Ford Foundation to advocate a variety of youth service programs; *Youth Engaged in Service* was one of the Points of Light, volunteer organizations recognized by the Bush administration to promote community service (*Ed.*)

bodies that meet quarterly. Some point to the danger of marginaliz-
ing youth voice by locating it simply in these groups. Real decision-
makers, the argument goes, can then more easily ignore youth input.
From what I've seen, these councils are widely effective. They provide sound advice for service planners, but also train young people to
participate in other local, state, and national forums around service—
including state commissions and non-profit boards of directors.

The strength of youth advisory councils is that they create a 9
sanctioned space for talented young people to think and act together, to gain a sense of their own power. Once involved on this
kind of a state platform, they become savvy political players and
articulate spokespeople.

5. *Let young people decide.* Finally, the Corporation, as well as 10
state and local groups planning service initiatives, can ask young people to read and review grant and other proposals. The success of
numerous mini-grant programs run entirely by young people (such
as the scores now operating in Michigan under the aegis of the
Michigan Council of Foundations) speaks to young people's proven
seriousness and fiscal responsibility. Unused to throwing money at
problems, young people gravitate to practical, low-cost alternatives
that nevertheless meet their needs.

How Youth Voice Helps

Serious inclusion of youth voice in the national and community 11
service initiatives will go a long way toward improving service programs. The stress and routine of young people's lives are largely
known only by young people themselves. Even team leaders, teachers, and community service staffers are a step removed. One junior
high school program in Washington state, for example, foundered
until *the students* pointed out that few could participate because
after-school buses were not available. When City Year in Boston
changed its year-round program to a nine-month one, adult planners
intended to start the program in January and end in September, until
a young corps member argued that it would be far better to coordi-
nate with the school year, to start in September and end in June.
Teach for America built in more training and support mechanisms
for its teachers after listening to its first year of recruits, who found
their teaching environments much tougher than expected. Aspects
of day-to-day life that escape over-30 planners in a central office
may seem obvious to young people, and can make all the difference
in whether a program works. How can we succeed in providing
meaningful service experiences for young people—and good services to the community—if we are not continually asking young people, "Does this make sense to you? Will this work?"

Making sure youth voice is heard at the policy level has a double 12
benefit. On the one hand, it helps insure getting better programs.

On the other, it gives young people an opportunity to take on leadership roles they otherwise have few opportunities to attain. At its
best, national service can be a rite of passage in a society with few
constructive routes into adulthood. Service, however, can only play
this role if young people are challenged in work that builds skills and
offers increasing amounts of responsibility. Though menial tasks may
be part of the package when it is necessary to get a job done,
national service should not be menial. Asking young people—working in a corps team, for example—to plan out their work each day,
to take turns serving as a site leader, and to spend time investigating
the impact their service is having on the community—distinguishes
the service experience from entry-level jobs that demand little
responsibility and allow no autonomy.

To reach its transformative potential, service must ultimately give   13
young people an opportunity to act on their own ideas. Throughout
our society and our educational system, young people are expected
to follow along, to sit passively while a teacher or perhaps even
Beavis and Butt-head inform them about how the world works. Service gets young people off the couch, but may unwittingly reinstanti-
ate societal codes that expect young people simply to follow orders.
National service, of course, can do much better.

There are models of good, individual placement programs—like   14
Southern Community Partners, for example—that allow young people to propose, start, and then run their own community initiative.
Some may argue that this kind of fellowship is suitable only for an
elite few, but even individual placements set in community agencies
(like those proposed as a national service option) could well provide
an analogous opportunity, where a young person might spend his or
her second six months working on a self-designed project. When
young people get this kind of a chance, they take responsibility for
their successes and failures, and learn about the complexities decision-making involves. In short, they learn a little of what it's like to
be an adult in our culture today.

Seeking out young people's ideas and involving them in the plan-   15
ning and decision-making of national service should be part of a
larger process of seeking out and valuing important information and
informants that mainstream culture and government planners often
ignore. While adult society generally disregards young people, we
must ask for their ideas on national service because young people
know young people best. . . .

John Bell at YouthBuild USA* has described extensively the   16
"adultism" in American society—adults' systematic mistreatment of
young people simply because of their age. In YouthBuild's *Leadership
Development* handbook, Bell argues that with the exception of pris-
oners, "young people's lives are more controlled than any other

*YouthBuild USA: a Boston organization that helps low-income youth learn carpentry
and other skills to rehabilitate housing, noted for its strong leadership development
program (*Ed.*)

group in society." Adults tell young people when to eat, go to bed, go to school, and talk. They "reserve the right to punish, threaten, hit, take away 'privileges,' and ostracize young people," says Bell, all in the name of "discipline." Institutions, in particular school, reinforce this mistreatment, enabling young people to accept others evaluating their work, performance, thinking, and ultimately themselves. From "adultism," young people learn two important lessons—first, that it is all right to be disrespected, and second, that it is all right to disrespect others.

Of course, not all adults are "adultist." But all young people, Bell   17
argues, are disrespected in some form or another. I highlight this analysis because it suggests an important role for the service initiatives. National and community service programs that encourage respectful youth-adult partnerships, that encourage youth voice, can help to combat "adultism." Service programs can be safe places where young people are listened to, where their ideas are respected and acted upon, where decisions about them are made with them.

Creating these kinds of programs is not easy. It is not as simple as   18
adults simply handing over all responsibility to young people. Nor is it simply using a young person on a board as "window dressing" to demonstrate a commitment to young people. Rather, it involves finding a middle ground. Adults must make the space for young people to take an active and engaged role in their service experience; in turn, young people must respect adults' skills and resources. Adults must provide enough support that young people have a chance to succeed, but not so much that their freedom to test out their ideas is too constrained or even too safe. Young people, in turn, must take their work seriously and commit to the ongoing effort success demands. Building youth voice into national and community service programs is a process that takes time and an unyielding belief in the potential of young people. It is worth the effort.

READING FOR MEANING

Write at least a page, exploring your understanding of Beilenson's proposal. Begin by summarizing in your own words the solution Beilenson outlines in paragraphs 4 through 10. For each numbered aspect of the solution, refer to at least one example. Then write about anything else that helps you develop your understanding of the argument Beilenson is making to adult administrators of the National Service Corporation.

As you write, you will want to reread parts of the proposal and annotate them further. You may want to quote phrases or sentences that support your understanding. Do not be surprised if your understanding changes as you reread and write.

If you find it difficult to sustain your writing for at least a page, consider the following possibilities:

• List the main arguments Beilenson offers in paragraphs 11 through 17 to support his proposal.

- Explain the concept of "adultism" (paragraphs 15 and 16) in your own words and comment on Beilenson's use of it in his conclusion.

- Writing in his mid-thirties and no longer a youth himself, Beilenson may not fully understand the attitudes and motivations of youth in their late teens and early twenties who now volunteer for community and national service programs. If you are in this volunteer age bracket, comment on any ways that Beilenson seems to be out of touch. If he seems to you to be *in* touch, point to some evidence of that in the proposal.

- If you have participated in a school, college, community, or national volunteer service program (anything from tutoring to rehabilitating housing), describe the leadership roles of volunteers and the extent of "adultism." Relate your experience directly to Beilenson's proposal.

EXTENDING MEANING THROUGH CONVERSATION. Discussing Beilenson's proposal with others who have also read and thought about it may help to refine and enlarge your understanding. Work with one or two classmates. Before getting together, reread what you wrote about Beilenson's proposal. Begin your conversation by taking turns explaining what seems likely to be most convincing to the National Service Corporation managers Beilenson hopes will take action on his proposed solution.

As your conversation proceeds, you may find that you have understood the reading differently. Because your goal is to work together to understand the solution Beilenson outlines and the argument he makes to support it, you will want to reread parts of the essay together to see what further meanings you find.

You will also want to share your evaluations of how successfully Beilenson presents his proposal to adult managers of the National Service Corporation. You may disagree about how successful he is, but disagreement may help each of you understand more fully the strengths and weaknesses of Beilenson's proposal.

READING LIKE A WRITER
PRESENTING THE SOLUTION

Convincing managers of any organization—including youth programs—to make fundamental changes in their policies or practices is a daunting task for a proposal writer. Presenting the solution so it is understandable and seems feasible is one key to success. Managers must understand how the solution would be implemented. They need to imagine how life would be different for themselves and all others in the organization after the solution is in place. Their predictable fears and anxieties must be allayed. Because Beilenson devotes considerable space to presenting the solution (and almost as much space arguing to support it), it will be worthwhile analyzing how he manages the presentation.

ANALYZE. Reread paragraphs 4 through 10, annotating evidence of how the solution could be implemented, what resources may be needed, what is to be gained, what models or examples may be instructive. Note also any places where Beilenson anticipates adults' likely resistance or anxiety.

WRITE. Write a page or so explaining how Beilenson presents the solution. Include specific examples from the essay. Also evaluate Beilenson's success in presenting the solution to National Service Corporation managers. Because you have observed so many adult managers—teachers, coaches, school administrators, ministers or rabbis, youth-group leaders, bosses at work—you can confidently assess what would be convincing to them. (You may even have managed younger people.) Where does Beilenson seem most successful? Least successful?

CONSIDERING IDEAS FOR YOUR OWN WRITING

Beilenson's proposal suggests a type of proposal you might want to consider for your essay—the proposal to improve the functioning of a goal-directed organization like a business, public institution (small-claims court, traffic offenders' school, welfare office, recreation center, school), sports team, or cooperative (nursery school, condominium owners association). You could propose a solution to a problem in an organization or institution in which you participated or one in which you had only a single disappointing experience. Your goal is not to ridicule or complain, however, but to attempt to bring about change that would make the organization more humane, efficient, productive, or successful in fulfilling its goals. Do not limit yourself to your own experience with the organization. Seek out former and current members or people who experienced problems like yours. They can help you understand the problem in a deeper way and refine your presentation of a solution and your argument for it.

Beilenson's proposal also suggests a wide range of problems that involve misunderstandings or lack of communication or wide gaps in experience between groups—leaders and led, workers and bosses, novices and professionals, full timers and part timers, educated and uneducated, powerful and powerless, insiders and outsiders, native speakers and second-language learners, experienced and inexperienced, instructors and learners, administrators and administrated to, managers and managed. Your proposal could be aimed at either half of one of these pairs. Avoid simply complaining or expressing resentment. You want to make a reasoned argument for a solution that promises to bring about significant, lasting change.

Toby Haynsworth and Gerald Perselay

A U.S. YOUTH APPRENTICESHIP PROGRAM

Toby Haynsworth (b. 1933) and Gerald Perselay (b. 1927), professors in the School of Business Administration at Winthrop University in Rock Hill, South Carolina, currently specialize in the development and implementation of school-to-work programs at regional and national levels. Since 1993, they have collaborated on several studies and reports on this topic. School-to-work programs are often referred to as *apprentice-ship programs.* They enable high-school students to earn credit toward graduation and a small amount of money by working under the supervision of someone in business or industry while continuing to attend school part time.

This report appeared in 1994 in the *Journal of Education for Business,* an academic journal read by professors who teach college courses in business education and by business managers and government policymakers concerned with the way schools prepare students for the world of work. Now that you have read one or more proposals, you will be able to watch this one unfold in a predictable way: introduction of the problem; brief consideration of other peoples' proposed solutions, including a lengthy evaluation of one alternative solution; and presentation of the proposed solution and argument for it.

As you read, pay particular attention to the way the authors present and evaluate one alternative or competing model: the German apprentice-ship program, which enrolls about 70 percent of German secondary-school students. For any proposed solution to which there is a well-known and well-regarded competing solution, responsible authors must present the competing solution fairly and argue carefully that it is not so appropriate as their own. Consider whether Haynsworth and Perselay do so.

The U.S. educational system is failing to adequately prepare its [1] young people to earn a decent living. The Secretary of Labor's Commission on Achieving Necessary Skills put it this way: "More than half our young people leave school without the knowledge or foundation required to find and hold a good job" (Arays, 1992, p. 110). Ten years ago, *A Nation at Risk: The Imperative for Educational Reform,* a report by the National Commission on Excellence in Education, documented the fact that U.S. public schools were not giving their students sufficient knowledge and skills in language, mathematics, science, and citizenship to qualify them for the higher paying jobs available in industry (National Commission on Excellence in Education, 1983). And the nation's 30% dropout rate is compounding the problem (Lee & Wallbaum, 1991). The result, according to Professor Steven F. Hamilton of Cornell University, is that "work-bound American youths (are) the products of the worst school-to-work system in the Western World" (McKenna, 1992, p. 15).

Many researchers have suggested that one solution to the prob- [2] lem of poor student preparation for work is simply to increase the requirements for academic courses and to make those courses longer and more rigorous (Hamilton, 1990). Other solutions that have been suggested include increasing teacher salaries, lowering the student/teacher ratio, and implementing various innovative programs. An example of this last idea is Tech Prep, a curriculum that would place a greater emphasis on independent study, problem solving, and academic rigor than has traditionally been incorporated into the high school courses offered to non-college-bound students.

Though each of these efforts is worthy of support, each fails to address a number of major problems associated with classroom-based preparation for the world of work. Professor John Bishop of the New York School of Industrial and Labor Relations at Cornell University has given seven reasons that appear to support a thesis that employer-provided training is generally more effective than school-based training (Bishop, 1991):

1. Most young people who obtain training in a school do not end up in jobs that use the occupation they studied in school.

2. The fact that the on-the-job training (OJT) is virtually certain to be used in the job's successful accomplishment is an excellent motivator to learning.

3. OJT is usually tutorial (i.e., one-on-one) in nature, which makes it a highly effective teaching method.

4. Because the training is done by the student's supervisor or co-workers, feedback as to how well or how poorly the student is able to apply the lessons of the OJT is easily accomplished and is a natural consequence of the work setting.

5. The equipment and materials needed to accomplish the training are readily available at the OJT work sites, whereas the equipment in a school may be quite different from equipment that will actually be used on the job.

6. The trainer on the job is held directly accountable for the success of the training given because the training is designed to increase the productivity of the work group to which the trainee belongs.

7. The time of both the trainer and the trainee tends to be more efficiently used in the workplace than in the classroom because the employer is paying for the time that both the trainer and the trainee spend in the teaching/learning process.

Insofar as certain subject matter is concerned, however, the classroom offers advantages over OJT. Basic skills such as reading, writing, science, social studies, and mathematics do not depend upon a work setting for teaching/learning efficiency. In fact, economies of scale can be achieved by having a single teacher who is a specialist in one academic area work with a group of students together in a classroom setting. And the experience that teachers gain as specialists presumably improves their skills in imparting special kinds of knowledge to groups of students.

It is therefore the conclusion of the authors that a program of learning that evolves from a purely classroom-oriented curriculum to a primarily job-related training program by way of a period of mixed classroom and OJT learning activities would be the one that would provide the best school-to-work transition. In addition to improving the productive potential of the graduates of such a program, it would likely be much more attractive to that 25% to 50% of young people who currently drop out of school, either literally or figuratively, before they receive their high school diplomas. In other words, it would result not only in a better entry level worker, but more of these better workers as well. We therefore recommend that an extensive program of youth apprenticeships that exploit the best of classroom instruction in combination with OJT be introduced into the high school curricula of the U.S. public school system.

The German Model

A "youth apprentice" is a high school student learning a craft or   6
occupation by working at a job under the direct guidance of a mentor or master craftsman while attending school part time.

Probably the best-known program for youth apprenticeships is the   7
one found in Germany. There, at about 11 years of age, students are guided into one of three kinds of schools. Those that are deemed capable of succeeding at the university level are enrolled in a *Gymnasium*. Those with above average academic aptitude, but who are more interested in the "practical" occupations, enter a *Realschule,* whereas those who have demonstrated only modest academic skills are directed to a *Hauptschule.* Whereas the graduates of a Gymnasium usually enter a university and graduate into such professions as medicine or the law, the typical graduate of Realschule or Hauptschule (i.e., about 70% of all German youth [Schares, 1992]) enters an apprenticeship in one of literally hundreds of occupations. At the same time that they are working in these apprenticeships, it is usual for them to be attending, as well, a vocational-type school called *Berufsschule* at least 1 day a week. In Figure 1, we represent this multitrack system graphically. The curricula of the postsecondary vocational schools are designed to complement the OJT that the apprentices receive. This leads to a naturally synergistic effect between the relatively abstract or theoretical instruction received in the classroom and the application of that knowledge on the job. The young apprentices learn more quickly at the workplace than they would without the knowledge acquired in school, and they apply themselves to their classwork with greater enthusiasm because they know that it will improve their on-the-job performance as apprentices.

A very important incentive for young people to successfully complete their apprenticeship programs is the journeyman certification   8
awarded to those who succeed in their efforts to do so. They are granted this transportable credential only after passing certain written and practical examinations that are uniform nationwide. These tests are prepared by committees composed of representatives of

employers, trade unions, vocational school teachers, and government education officials. Apprentices are allowed to take these examinations as many as three times, and as a result, less than 10% ultimately fail to receive certification.

German youth apprentices are considered to be students first and workers second. They are paid a "training allowance" of about 25% of the salary earned by a skilled worker in the trade for which they are training (Lee & Wallbaum, 1991). Even at this relatively low wage, however, it is estimated that the value of the productive work accomplished by the typical apprentice is only about 40% of the total costs of training incurred by the employer. German businesses are willing to absorb a significant portion of the costs associated with the training of youth apprentices, however, because they are looked upon as long-term investments in human capital and as effective tools for the recruitment of skilled workers. One longitudinal study has shown that 81% of those youngsters who completed their apprenticeships in the period of 1979 to 1980 received offers for permanent employment; and only 5% of those who wanted to obtain permanent employment with the company that trained them failed to receive an offer to do so (Casey, 1986).

A very important factor in the success of youth apprenticeships in Germany, and in such other countries as Denmark, Holland, and Switzerland, for that matter, is the strong support the programs receive from government at both the state and federal levels. For example, the states provide subsidies that cover about one third of the cost of apprenticeships (Lee & Wallbaum, 1991). In addition, the federal government acts as a coordinator for, and regulator of, the programs. Federally funded employment offices serve as clearinghouses for available apprenticeships and as career counselors to aspiring apprentices. The government runs the vocational schools and makes sure that they support the programs provided by participating businesses. And, more importantly, government acts as a promoter of training activities within the business community across a broad spectrum of occupations (Hamilton, 1990).

Difficulties in Applying the German Model in the United States

The German model for youth apprenticeship training cannot be transplanted into the U.S. educational system without modification. Some of the laws regulating the work that young people can do are very restrictive. As a practical matter, it would be impossible to have an effective apprenticeship program for those under 16 years of age without major changes to the child labor laws, and there would likely be a great deal of political opposition to such changes.

Because a significant part of the knowledge acquired by youth apprentices takes place outside of a school setting, changes to existing requirements for high school graduation will be necessary.

FIGURE 1. The West German Educational System (Hamilton, 1990)

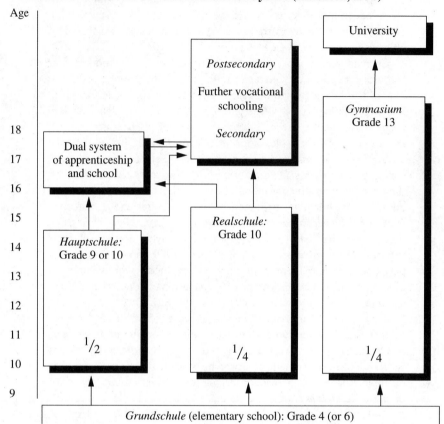

The costs of hiring and training relatively unproductive teenagers   13
are not likely to be trivial. For example, there is not only the fact
that the value of the output of an apprentice is likely to be less than
the wages and costs of benefits paid to the individual, but there is
the cost in lost productivity of the apprentice's mentor/trainer to be
considered. Given the extent of competition that exists today in the
worldwide marketplace, U.S. businesses would be very reluctant to
assume the total burden of these expenses by themselves.

There are societal factors that make the German model impracti-   14
cal here. Americans would be very unlikely to support an educational system that determined at an age of 14 or under whether or
not a young person could pursue a college degree. The democratic
ideal of giving all citizens the chance to go to college is deeply
ingrained in the American concept of an appropriate educational
system. It is very unlikely that the public would be willing to accept
any program that would inhibit this opportunity.

Another factor to consider is the strong desire of American   15
teenagers to be part of a group of their peers. Focus-group discussions held in Arkansas as part of that state's planning for the imple-

mentation of youth apprenticeships there made it very clear that there was a very great reluctance among the young people to enter any kind of school-connected program that made it difficult to routinely interact with their schoolmates or to participate in the school system's extracurricular activities (Jobs for the Future, Inc., 1991).

Though these difficulties are very real, they do not preclude the development of acceptable youth apprenticeship programs here in the United States. States can change the requirements for graduation from high school by granting credit for knowledge acquired from mentors and as a result of OJT. This credit would be made contingent upon the passing of tests jointly prepared and administered by representatives of business and the educational establishment. These tests could be used both for certification of journeyman status and to qualify for receipt of a high school diploma.

16

Because the business community will be assuming the responsibility for a portion of the education of the state's youth, some subsidies or tax relief to cover at least some of the costs of these efforts would be justifiable. This would make a company's investments in youth apprenticeship training less onerous and therefore more practical in a purely business sense.

17

The courses taught by the high schools could be designed to both meet the immediate job-related needs of the young apprentices and the admission requirements of institutions of higher education. In fact, the synergism of linking classroom theory to on-the-job application of such subjects as science and social studies may well result in a better preparation for college than is possible under the current practice of learning only in a classroom/lecture-centered process.

18

High school and college class schedules could be designed to facilitate a combination of work and school schedules. Many state-supported and private technical schools have long since discarded the 8:00 AM-to-3:30 PM Monday-through-Friday program. Evening, weekend, and summer classes coordinated with work schedules are a fact of life in many such educational institutions. Businesses might be agreeable to adjustments in work schedules so as to permit their apprentices to participate in such common high school programs as sports and club activities. All that is needed is good will and determination on the part of the parties concerned, and a uniquely American youth apprenticeship model becomes possible.

19

A Proposed U.S. Model

There are virtually an infinite variety of ways to blend classroom coursework with on-the-job learning. The model we propose in this article is in no way intended to be the definitive one. It is presented only as an example of what could be done.

20

Career counseling would begin early. It could start in elementary school by discussion of the many varied jobs held by students, parents, relatives, or family friends. Reading assignments could be given

21

that further inform students about the world of work that awaits them when they finish school, regardless of whether that will be at 18 or 25 years of age. More specific counseling tailored to the individual needs of students could be given starting in middle or junior high school so that by the ninth grade the young people would be able to begin thinking about what career options they would like to create for themselves in high school.

At this point a tentative program of study would be developed for the student in such a way as to provide her or him with a reasonable amount of flexibility to make changes to that program as time passes and goals change. A very important component of this development process is the determination of which occupational field is the one that is most likely to fit the needs of the student. Though there are currently over 830 occupations ranging from accordian maker to x-ray equipment tester currently registered with the U.S. Department of Labor (Bureau of Labor Statistics, 1992), there is no need for students to limit their long-term goals to a choice from among occupations that have traditionally used craft apprenticeships as a primary source of entry-level workers (Del Valle, 1993). For example, a young person with ambitions to become a civil engineer could be apprenticed to a construction firm while taking college preparatory courses in math and physics in high school. Those whose goal is to become a physician could fill such apprentice positions in the health care industries as laboratory technician or nurse assistant while studying chemistry and biology in school. The most important considerations, as they have always been in advising and career counseling, are the needs, skills, and desires of the student. Therefore, the decision as to whether or not to apply for entry into a youth apprenticeship program should be one jointly arrived at by the student and his or her advisor. In Table I, we provide an example of such a program. 22

Though the above program addresses only the high school components of a young person's education, the specific courses included in it could be those that would also prepare the student for continuing the education process either in an associate degree program at a community/technical college or in a baccalaureate degree program at a university. Again, the talents and needs of the individual student should dictate the specifics of his or her particular course of study. 23

TABLE 1   **A Model for the U.S. Youth Apprentice**

9th grade :	English, Math, Social Studies, Health, Science, and History
10th grade:	English, Math, Social Studies, Science, OJT for 16 hours per week
11th grade:	English, Math, Language, OJT for 24 hours per week
12th grade:	English, Language, OJT for 32 hours per week

Conclusion

There is little doubt that at the highest levels the U.S. educational   24
system is outstanding. It may even be the best in the world in serving that small percentage of students who are able to avail themselves of these superlative programs. It is doing very poorly for the
majority of students, however. In recent years, and in spite of the
dire warnings contained in *A Nation at Risk,* our education, political,
and business leaders have only nibbled at the edges of the system in
their attempts to put things right. It is our opinion that the time has
come for admitting the patient for major surgery. Our prescription
is the adoption of a broad-based youth apprenticeship program that
makes better use of the resources now being invested in high school
education and the state-supported technical schools, colleges, and
universities, as well as the experience, equipment, and knowledge
that already exist within the business community. . . .

The youth of our great nation deserve the best educational sys-   25
tem in the world. Given that Americans are spending more per
capita on our current system than any other country, we should
be able to accomplish that objective without having to spend more.
We only need to spend more wisely.

References

Arays, B. K. (1992). Apprenticeships demand a second look. *Graphic Arts
Monthly,* March, p. 110.

Bishop, J. (1991). *A program of research on the role of employer training in ame-
liorating skill shortages and enhancing productivity and competitiveness.*
Philadelphia: National Center on the Educational Quality of the
Workforce.

Bureau of Labor Statistics. (1991–1992). *Occupational Outlook Quarterly,*
Winter, pp. 27–40.

Casey, B. (1986, March 1). The dual apprenticeship system and the recruitment and retention of young persons in West Germany. *British Journal of Industrial Relations,* pp. 63–81.

Del Valle, C. (1993, April 26). From high schools to high skills. *Business
Week,* pp. 110–112.

Hamilton, S. F. (1990). *Apprenticeship for adulthood: Preparing youth for the
future.* New York: The Free Press.

Jobs for the Future, Inc. (1991). *Voices from school and home, Arkansas parents and students talk about preparing for the world of work and the
potential for youth apprenticeships.* Somerville, MA: Author.

Lee, J. A., & Wallbaum, N. (1991). Apprenticeship training: The U.S. versus
West Germany. *Operations Management Review,* 83, 4), 19–25.

McKenna, J. F. (1992, January 20). Apprenticeships. Something old, something new, something needed. *Industry Week,* pp. 14–20.

National Commission on Excellence in Education. (1983). *A nation at risk:
The imperative for educational reform.* Washington, DC: U.S. Government Printing Office.

Schares, G. E. (1992). Experts in overalls. *Business Week, Special Issue Reinventing America,* p. 90.

READING FOR MEANING

Write at least a page, exploring your understanding of Haynsworth and Perselay's proposal. Begin by summarizing in your own words the solution Haynsworth and Perselay outline in paragraphs 3 through 5 and 20 through 23. Then write about anything else that helps you develop your understanding of the argument they are making to business educators and other educational policymakers.

As you write, you will want to reread parts of the proposal and annotate them further. You may want to quote phrases or sentences that support your understanding. Do not be surprised if your understanding changes as you reread and write.

If you encounter difficulty sustaining your writing for at least a page, consider these ideas:

- List the key features of the German model of apprenticeship training.

- Comment on one of the authors' assumptions. For example, they seem to assume that high schools should prepare students for work, that there are highly skilled jobs available for high-school graduates, that available jobs will all require a four-year internship, and that a close relationship can be found between any job and academic courses. You may see other assumptions.

- If you have held any kind of job, you probably received on-the-job training; and you may have participated in a high-school or private apprenticeship program. Given your experience, evaluate the claims made in paragraph 3 and in the description of the German model for the benefits of on-the-job training. Connect your experience directly to one or more of the claims.

- Eventually everyone—high-school or college or graduate and professional-school student—experiences on-the-job training. Explain what you personally believe to be the relation of academic course work to on-the-job training.

EXTENDING MEANING THROUGH CONVERSATION. Discussing Haynsworth and Perselay's proposal with others who have also read and thought about it may help to increase your understanding. Work with one or two other students. Before beginning your conversation, reread what you wrote about the proposal. Then take turns explaining what seems likely to be most convincing to the business educators and policymakers Haynsworth and Perselay hope to influence.

As your conversation proceeds, you may find that you have understood the reading differently. Because your goal is to work together to understand the solution the two business-education experts outline and the argument they make to support it, you will want to reread parts of the essay together to find further meanings.

You will also want to share your evaluations of how successfully Haynsworth and Perselay present their proposal to business educators and educational policymakers. You may disagree about how successful they are, but disagreement may help each of you understand more fully the strengths and weaknesses of their proposal.

READING LIKE A WRITER
CONVINCING READERS TO ACCEPT THE SOLUTION BY EVALUATING ALTERNATIVE SOLUTIONS

Because there is rarely a proposal-writing situation in which readers are not already aware of alternative solutions or do not think of one or two while reading the proposal, writers inevitably find themselves drawn into evaluating alternative or competing proposals. The most experienced, astute members of an organization—just the people the writer hopes will support the proposed solution—are likely to have the most alternatives in mind and be most skeptical of the solution being proposed. Through talking to their audience's members or researching the problem or thinking creatively, writers try to think of likely key alternative solutions. They then evaluate each one carefully, deciding either to borrow the best features of some, if that is possible, or to reject them as unfeasible.

ANALYZE. Haynsworth and Perselay evaluate six alternative solutions, five briefly (paragraphs 2 through 4) and one at length (paragraphs 6 through 19). Annotate these paragraphs to identify each alternative solution, to decide whether the authors borrow any of their best features or reject them, and to discover how the authors present the German alternative and go about evaluating it.

WRITE. Write a page or so reporting what you learn. Identify each alternative and its fate in the hands of the authors. Describe briefly the kinds of information or data the authors present on the German apprenticeship model. Explain how the authors' evaluation of the German alternative influences the authors' own solution. Then write a few sentences evaluating the authors' success in presenting their proposal to American educational policymakers. Keep in mind that even if business educators everywhere enthusiastically supported this proposal, they would have to convince the rest of the educational establishment to support it and to take action to change high-school programs and to work out relations with mentors in business and industry. Keep in mind also that because state and federal governments would be providing part of the financing, legislation would have to be written and passed. Does it seem to you that the authors' handling of alternative solutions would be convincing to educators and legislators? Think about what the authors might have overlooked, misjudged, ignored, or oversimplified. Point to specific strengths and weaknesses in their handling of alternative solutions.

CONSIDERING IDEAS FOR YOUR OWN WRITING

Consider writing a proposal to solve a problem in one group or organization to which you presently belong, a problem that everyone in the group seems to believe can best be solved by adopting a solution devised by a similar group for a similar problem. Nearly everyone in your group knows about this solution and talks about it uncritically, assuming it to be the obvious solution to your group's problem. You have a different solution in mind, however, which may or may not incorporate features of the favored solution. Write a proposal in which you attempt to convince members of your group that your proposed solution is superior and more feasible. Include a detailed evaluation of the currently preferred solution.

The Haynsworth and Perselay proposal, like the Samuelson and Loughran proposals, suggests the possibility of proposing a solution to some problem in your high-school or college curriculum. You could focus on a schoolwide or campuswide program like school-to-work apprenticeships. Possibilities include sports, tutoring, second languages, writing, humanities, math and science, computer literacy, at-home learning, health education, part-time work on campus, vocational education, student health clinic, or academic support. (See the discussion in Considering Ideas for Your Own Writing following the Loughran essay for suggestions on learning more about a school or college problem and developing a feasible solution.)

Will Scarvie

PROPOSAL TO INCREASE EFFICIENCY IN THE COMPUTER SECTION

Will Scarvie wrote this proposal in 1989 for a freshman composition course at the University of California, San Diego.

Like many students, Will Scarvie worked while he was attending college. He was a computer operator at a small firm of certified public accountants. Although he wrote this proposal for his composition course, he eventually sent it to the company president and, with some modification, the proposal was implemented. As you will see from skimming it, this proposal is written in the form of an interoffice memo.

As you might imagine, Scarvie found himself in a delicate rhetorical situation as he wrote this proposal. As you read, put yourself in Scarvie's place and consider these questions: How would you present your proposal without appearing to be telling the president how to run the company? How would you avoid appearing to be currying favor? How would you avoid placing blame on people with whom you must continue to work, even if you think they are responsible for the problem?

To: Rubin L. Gorewitz, President
From: Will Scarvie, Computer Operator
Subject: Proposal to Increase Efficiency in the Computer Section
As you may know, Rubin L. Gorewitz & Co. CPA has had an inordinate number of projects backlogged in the computer section.

Although some of us in the section have been blamed, we are not the cause. The problem stems from the increase in workload given us by the accountants, each of whom now handles more than seventy clients in the course of a year. I feel confident we could manage the increased workload efficiently if we had a priority system in place.

Every day, accountants give us projects that must be finished "right away." We have no criteria to help us decide which of these projects to do first. The accountants have equal authority and seem always to be in a rush. Their need is undoubtedly real, since I am sure that meeting with a client without the promised document could lead the client to question the firm's reliability. To remedy this problem, we need to improve communication between the accountants and the computer section, and to make clear to the computer operators which jobs have priority over the others.

I propose that we design a chart, which would be posted near the door of the computer section, that would let operators know what jobs need to be done and when. The sheet would consist of six columns. The first, titled "Client/Accountant," would contain the names of the client and accountant so that routing would be clear and we would know who to get in touch with if there were a problem. The next, "Job Type," would indicate precisely what needs to be done. At the same time that we make up this form, we also might take the opportunity to update the list of job types and have a meeting of the computer section staff and the accountants to make sure that we're all using the same language.

The third column, "Date and Time Needed," would identify clearly the deadline for the project. The fourth, "Job Notes," would be used by accountants to notify the computer operators of any special changes or additions to the standard job type. The fifth, "Number of Checks," would help the computer operator estimate how long the project will actually take. It is a crucial bit of information that we do not currently get. The final column, "Operator/Time In-Out," would indicate which computer operator (or operators in cases where two or more people work on a project) is doing the project, as well as when the project began and ended. Accountants needing to update instructions would be able simply to check the chart to see who to talk to. The in/out time could be used for a study of the time it takes to complete different types of projects; such a study would help us make more realistic estimates for future projects.

I would urge one further change in the current system: Assign one computer operator the job of coordinating the work of the computer section. The coordinator would be responsible for ranking projects in order of priority and seeing that the operators team up when a large project needs immediate action. Important criteria for the job of coordinator obviously would include experience dealing with a wide range of job types and problems. The person chosen for the job should also have good people skills, since he or she will need to negotiate with accountants to resolve conflicts about whose project has priority. Since this job involves more responsibility than the normal computer operator has, I would think it should be a somewhat higher-paid position.

One of the accountants offered an alternative solution you might   6
consider. She recommended that the company purchase additional computers and hire more computer operators to work them. She didn't specify how many new computers and operators should be added. Although this solution may become necessary as the company continues to expand and the workload increases, I do not think we are at the point yet where an expenditure of this kind is required. I believe that the problem we are having lies not in staffing but in organization. As it is, we are able to finish most projects on time. Centralizing the management of the workload and improving communication would, I think, enable us to get all projects done on time.

You may object that my solution is cumbersome and would take   7
too long to institute, but I think that all it would take is a brief meeting between the accountants and computer operators to explain the procedure. The chart itself would require little time to prepare and photocopy. Of course, you would have to select a coordinator, and that might take some time and money. I'd recommend that we have at least a one-week trial period to make sure that we all understand how the new system works and to make whatever revisions become necessary.

The chief difficulty I foresee is in estimating the time projects   8
take, but that is a problem we have with the current system as well. If we conduct the study I mentioned earlier, I am sure our ability to estimate will eventually improve. As we become more efficient, I also think the accountants will become more confident in our ability to do the job and therefore will be more realistic in prioritizing their projects. Given these benefits and the minimal costs, I respectfully urge you to give this proposal your immediate consideration.

READING FOR MEANING

Write a page or more about your understanding of Scarvie's proposal. Begin by explaining briefly what Scarvie hoped to accomplish. Then write about anything else that helps you develop your ideas about Scarvie's proposal.

As you write, you may find that you need to reread the proposal and annotate it further. Consider quoting phrases or sentences that support your ideas and reactions. Do not be surprised if your ideas change as you reread and write.

If you encounter difficulty sustaining your writing for a page or more, you may find these suggestions helpful:

• Summarize briefly the two parts to Scarvie's proposed solution.

- Speculate about Scarvie's situation. What do you learn from his approach and the facts as he presents them about his work environment? How do you think environment has affected his approach?
- Reflect on a problem you wanted to solve in a job you once held. Did you do or say anything about the problem? How was your job situation like or different from Scarvie's?
- In the last three paragraphs, Scarvie takes up an alternative solution, an objection, and a difficulty. Explain what he may gain and lose by doing so.

EXTENDING MEANING THROUGH CONVERSATION. Discussing Scarvie's proposal with others who have also read and thought about it may help to refine and enlarge your understanding. Work with one or two classmates. Before getting together, reread what you wrote about the proposal. Begin your conversation by taking turns explaining what seems likely to be most convincing to the company president, who Scarvie hopes will take action on his proposal.

As your conversation proceeds, you may find that you have understood the reading differently. Because your goal is to work together to understand the solution that Scarvie outlines and the argument he makes to support it, you will want to reread parts of the essay together to see what further meanings you find.

You will also want to share your evaluations of how successfully Scarvie presents his proposal to the company president. You may disagree about how successful he is, but disagreement may help each of you understand more fully the strengths and weaknesses of his proposal.

READING LIKE A WRITER

CONVINCING READERS TO ACCEPT THE SOLUTION

Writers must assemble all the parts of a proposal to create a logical step-by-step argument. The goal is to devise a plan that readers will find accessible and convincing.

ANALYZE. Reread Scarvie's proposal, annotating briefly the purpose of each paragraph.

WRITE. Write several sentences, presenting Scarvie's plan. Then evaluate the success of the plan. Try to imagine the parts in some different arrangement that would be an improvement on the present plan. Speculate about how compelling the company president would find the essay as he moves through it part by part. Also comment on how well Scarvie cues the reader to each new part.

CONSIDERING IDEAS FOR YOUR OWN WRITING

If you presently hold a part- or full-time job on or off campus, consider proposing a solution to solve a problem in your job. Write the proposal as a memo to someone in a position to take action on your solution. You might want to talk to other employees to discover whether they perceive the problem as you do. Find out whether other solutions have already been proposed. Try out your proposal on a few employees you trust to give you good advice.

THINKING ABOUT WHAT MAKES PROPOSALS EFFECTIVE

In this chapter, you have been learning how to read proposals for meaning and how to read them like a writer. Before writing a proposal essay, pause here to review and consolidate what you have learned about what makes proposal writing successful.

ANALYZE. Choose one reading from this chapter that seems to you to be especially effective. Before reading the selection, write down what makes you remember it as an example of good proposal writing.

Reread your chosen selection, adding further annotations about what makes it particularly successful as a proposal to solve a problem. To begin, consider the selection's purpose and how well it achieves that purpose for its intended readers. (The headnotes to each reading in this chapter inform you of the intended readers. You can always make an informed guess about readership by noting the publication source of the essay and inferring some of the writer's assumptions about what readers know and believe.) Then focus on how well the essay

- introduces the problem
- presents the solution
- convinces readers to accept the solution

You can review all of these basic features in Reading like a Writer following the Samuelson essay at the beginning of this chapter.

You can complete this activity on your own, or your instructor may ask you to work with a small group of other students who have chosen the same essay. If you work with others, take time initially for everyone to reread the selection, adding to your annotations. Then discuss what makes this particular proposal essay so effective. Take notes. Someone in your group should prepare a report to the class about what you have learned about proposals to solve problems, or you can write individually.

WRITE. Write at least a page explaining and justifying your choice of this reading as an example of an effective proposal. Assume that your readers—your instructor and classmates—have read the selection but will not remember many details about it. They also may not remember it as an especially successful proposal. Therefore, you will want to use details and refer to specific parts of the essay as you explain how it works as a proposal and seek to justify your evaluation of its effectiveness. You need not argue that it is the best essay in the chapter, only that it is, in your view, a strong example of proposal writing.

A GUIDE TO WRITING PROPOSALS TO SOLVE PROBLEMS

As the proposals in this chapter illustrate, a proposal has two basic features: the problem and the solution. To establish that the problem exists and is serious, the proposal writer may offer a detailed analysis of the problem, including facts, examples, and statistics. To convince readers to accept the solution offered, the writer presents an argument, often anticipating possible objections, evaluating alternative solutions, and demonstrating how the proposed solution can be easily implemented.

Proposal writing requires careful planning. The writer must not only determine exactly what the problem is and how to solve it but also consider how readers will respond to the argument. The following guide to invention, drafting, reading critically, and revising divides this complex writing task into smaller, more manageable parts and leads you systematically through each stage of the process.

INVENTION

Invention is the process of discovery and planning by which you generate something to say. The following invention activities will help you choose a problem to write about, analyze the problem and identify a solution, consider your readers, develop an argument for your proposed solution, and research your proposal.

Choosing a Problem

Begin the selection process by listing several groups to which you presently belong—for instance, your neighborhood, film society, dormitory, sports team, biology class, church group. For each group, list as many problems facing it as you can. If you cannot think of any problems for a particular organization, consult with other members. Then reflect on your list of problems, and choose the one for which you would most like to find a solution. It can be a problem that everyone already knows about or one about which only you are aware.

Proposing to solve a problem in a group or community to which you belong gives you one inestimably important advantage: You can write as an expert, an insider. You know about the history of the problem, have felt the urgency to solve it, and perhaps have already thought of possible solutions. Equally important, you will know precisely to whom to send the proposal, and you can interview others in the group to get their views of the problem and to understand how they might resist your solution. You will be in a position of knowledge and authority—from which comes confident, convincing writing.

The published writers in this chapter take on large national social problems—poor achievement in high schools, the need for an alternative to attending college, the high rate of delinquency among teenagers, the need to give young volunteers a say in the programs in which they work, and the lack of an effective work apprenticeship program in high schools. These proposals require wide-ranging knowledge of the problem and its social context. Unless you have time to learn about the often-extensive history of current social problems, you will learn more about proposal writing and produce a strong piece of writing that can actually bring about change if you write about a local problem in a group or community to which you presently belong. Doing so puts you in the same authoritative position as the published writers, the same position Scarvie is in. Local problems are not at all unimportant just because they lack national scope.

If you do choose a problem that affects a wider group, then concentrate on one with which you have direct experience and for which you can suggest a detailed plan of action.

Analyzing the Problem and Identifying a Solution

You can profitably analyze the problem by exploring it in writing. Jot down what you now know about the problem, how you know it is a problem, and why you think it is serious. Compare this problem with others you know about. Consider how it came about and what ill effects it produces by remaining unsolved.

This analysis of the problem will probably lead you to possible solutions. If no solution is apparent, one of the following creative problem-solving procedures may help:

Solve one small aspect of the problem.

Find out how a comparable problem has been solved.

Develop a solution that eliminates one or more of the problem's causes.

Think of another way to categorize the problem.

Envision the problem in another medium or context.

Consider how another person you respect (someone you know personally or a historical or fictional figure) might solve the problem.

If you cannot think of an original solution, investigate solutions that others have proposed. At some point, you will need to consider alternative solutions anyway and how they compare with your own. Remember that your solution does not have to be original, but it should be one about which you feel strongly.

To test the feasibility of your solution, try listing the steps that would be necessary to implement it. Such an outline of steps might be used later to convince readers that the solution will indeed work.

Considering Your Readers

Because your proposal must be persuasive, you first need to have some idea of who your readers will be and what they will find convincing. Will you be writing to other members of your group, to an outside committee, to an individual in a position of authority?

After you have particular readers in mind, write for a few minutes about how much they already know about the problem and what solutions they might prefer. Comment on what values and attitudes you share with your readers and how they have responded in the past to similar problems.

LEARNING MORE ABOUT YOUR READERS:
A COLLABORATIVE ACTIVITY

Your instructor may ask you to get together with two or three other students at this point in your invention process. Take turns telling one another briefly about your group, its problem, and the solution you propose. Then your partners will tell you what they know about the problem or a similar problem, what resistance they think you may encounter from your group, and what alternative solutions they think group members may be aware of.

You can benefit greatly from hearing what others know about the problem you want to solve. Listen to what they have to say. They may have encountered a problem like yours. They will very likely think of alternative solutions or objections to your proposed solution. Their responses will enable you to develop a more thoughtful, convincing proposal.

Developing an Argument

For your proposal to succeed, readers must be convinced to take the solution seriously. Try to imagine how your prospective readers will respond. Write for a few minutes defending your solution against each of these objections: I do not see that there is a problem, your solution will not really solve the problem, we cannot afford it, there is not enough time, no one will cooperate, it has already been tried, I do not see how to even get started, you are making this proposal because it will benefit you personally.

Next, try out one small part of your counterargument. Identify *one* alternative solution your readers are likely to favor. Write a few sentences comparing your solution to the alternative solution by weighing the strengths and weaknesses of each. Then explain how you might demonstrate to readers that your solution has more advantages and fewer disadvantages.

Researching Your Proposal

If you are writing about a problem in a group to which you belong, talk to other members of the group to learn more about their understanding of the problem. Try out your solution on one or two people; their objections and questions will help you sharpen your own ideas.

If you are writing about a larger social or political problem, you should do research to confirm what you remember and to learn more about the problem. You can probably locate all the information you need in a good research library; you could also interview an expert on the problem. Readers will not take you seriously unless you seem well informed.

DRAFTING

After you have completed the invention activities, you can use your exploratory writing and the notes you have compiled as the basis for a rough draft. Before you begin writing, however, you should set goals and decide on a tentative plan for your draft.

Setting Goals

Before writing, set some goals for your essay that reflect your readers' concerns and your purpose for writing. Consider, for example, how your readers are likely to view the problem. If they are unfamiliar with it, you will have to inform them. If they are vaguely aware of the problem but not inclined to take it seriously, you will have to demonstrate its seriousness, as Haynsworth and Perselay do by comparing the internationally respected German program with the ineffective American program. Consider also, in arguing for your proposed solution, how you can acknowledge your readers' legitimate concerns, as Kleiman does when he recognizes that some readers would object to missing out on college social interaction. Notice how Scarvie, recognizing that the company president will resist increased costs, makes his solution cost-free initially.

Planning Your Draft

Determining what your readers presently think and what you want them to think will help you not only formulate goals but also determine how to organize your proposal. If your readers are already familiar with the problem, for example, you may need only to refer to it in passing. If, however, they have never thought about the problem or have not perceived it in the way you want them to, you should probably spend some time at the beginning explaining the problem.

Here is a general plan you might follow if your prospective readers have already considered other solutions to the problem:

Identify the problem.

Describe your proposed solution.

Discuss the advantages of your solution compared to other solutions.

Restate the primary advantage of your proposed solution.

Scarvie, as well as Haynsworth and Perselay, follow this basic outline.

Beginning

Most proposal writers begin by presenting the problem. They may, like Loughran, assert its seriousness. They may describe the problem in vivid detail to impress readers, often presenting examples to dramatize the problem.

Avoiding Logical Fallacies

As you plan and draft your proposal, be particularly careful to avoid these logical fallacies:

- Am I committing an *either/or fallacy* by presenting my solution as the only possible solution (ignoring or dismissing alternative solutions out of hand)?
- Am I setting up alternative solutions or objections to my proposal as *straw men* (mentioning only the weak alternatives or objections that are easy to knock down)?

- Am I guilty of *oversimplifying* (suggesting that the problem is less complicated and easier to solve than it really is)?

- Am I making an *ad hominem* (Latin for "to the man") attack (criticizing or satirizing my opponents instead of addressing their ideas and arguments)?

READING A DRAFT CRITICALLY

Now that you have completed a draft of your essay, you can benefit from having one or more readers who know something about writing proposals to take a close look at what you have written and could help you see how to improve your draft. This section will help your readers give an insightful critical reading of your draft. You can use the guidelines also to give someone else useful advice. Get a written response to your draft so that later when you begin to revise, you will have specific suggestions and criticisms to follow.

While you obviously gain from receiving a critical reading, you also benefit greatly from giving one to someone else. When you complete a careful analysis of someone's draft, you learn more about the possibilities of proposal writing at just the time when you can put the learning to use in your own writing. Assuming the role of critical reader enables you to imagine more easily what your readers will be expecting from your essay.

Reading a draft critically means reading it more than once, first to get a general impression and then to analyze its basic features. Before you read, number the paragraphs so you can refer easily to specific parts of the essay.

Because you are not likely to be among the intended readers of the proposal, you must know who those readers will be so you can evaluate the draft for how successful it is likely to be in convincing them to take action on the proposed solution. This requires imaginative role playing on your part, but it is the only way you can give helpful advice on the draft.

Reading for a First Impression

Read quickly through the draft to develop an overall impression. After you have finished reading, jot down your immediate reaction. What seems likely to be most interesting or convincing to the readers of this proposal?

Reading to Analyze

Read now to focus on the basic features of a proposal to solve a problem. Read to discover what the writer has achieved, given the resources available to proposal writers, and what the writer might do to produce a more convincing argument for the proposed solution.

INTRODUCING THE PROBLEM. Look first at how well the draft introduces the problem to its intended readers. Tell the writer what you understand the problem to be. Then suggest ways the problem might be better defined and described. If you think the readers might not take the problem seriously, suggest ways the writer could demonstrate its seriousness and significance.

PRESENTING THE SOLUTION. Consider first whether the writing situation and readers require the writer to announce briefly a possible solution, as Samuelson does, or to detail the features and implementation of a solution, as Beilenson does. Advise the writer on strengthening the presentation. Perhaps the situation needs to be described more fully, or perhaps it is overloaded with unnecessary or fussy details. Point out unclear terms, hard-to-follow parts, or gaps in the information.

For readers to understand and support some solutions, they need to see a step-by-step plan for its implementation—what to do first, next, and so on to the last step—with the most demanding or complex steps detailed somewhat. Consider whether such a clear plan would strengthen this proposal in the eyes of the intended readers. If the proposal already presents a plan for implementation, advise the writer about smoothing, clarifying, and detailing the implementation.

CONVINCING READERS TO ACCEPT THE SOLUTION. Convincing requires reasoned argument, and arguing for a proposed solution requires arguing for it directly, committing yourself to specific reasons why you favor it, anticipating readers' objections and questions, and evaluating alternative solutions.

Besides asserting that a proposed solution is better than alternative solutions and claiming that readers' objections are groundless, a proposal writer must argue directly for the proposed solution, giving specific reasons why readers should support it. These reasons should be highlighted or foregrounded so readers cannot miss them. Begin by making your own list of the reasons the writer gives. If you cannot find any reasons or if they are hard to find, tell the writer. Identify reasons that might seem to the intended readers too obvious or just not convincing. Suggest reasons the writer might add to strengthen the argument.

Identify places in the draft where the writer has anticipated readers' likely objections and questions. Remembering that the writer may either acknowledge the wisdom of some objections or refute them, give advice on strengthening the handling of objections and questions. Most important, list objections or questions the writer may have overlooked.

Identify places where the writer has presented alternative solutions. The writer may borrow the best ideas in some of these or refute them. Advise the writer on strengthening this part of the argument. Perhaps the tone is too harsh or the approach unnecessarily dismissive. It may be that the writer really has not yet mounted a careful, convincing argument against each alternative. Try to think of additional alternatives about which readers may be aware.

An argument seems convincing in part because it follows a logical plan. Review the whole argument and make an outline by identifying with a brief phrase the main idea or purpose of each paragraph, numbering them as you go. (See Summarizing in Appendix 1, A Catalog of Critical Reading Strategies, for advice on outlining.) Then reflect on whether major parts of the argument are given too little or too much space and whether everything is arranged in the best possible—most logical and convincing—way. Feel free to suggest major rearrangement.

REVISING

This section provides suggestions for revising your draft, suggestions that by now will be merely reminders to you of the possibilities for developing a convincing proposal to solve a problem. Even though you have been working on this assignment for some time, you need to gather one more burst of energy for thoughtful revising. Revising means reenvisioning your draft, trying to see it in a new way, given your purpose and readers, to increase the likelihood they will support your proposed solution.

The biggest mistake you can make in revising is to focus initially on words or sentences. Instead, review your draft as a whole to assess its likely impact on your readers. Think imaginatively and boldly about cutting out unconvincing material, adding new material, and moving material around. Your computer supplies the technical wizardry that allows you to make easily the most drastic revisions, and you supply the intellectual effort to make the difficult decisions that will improve your draft.

You may have received help with this challenge from classmates who have given your draft a critical reading. If not, you can read your own draft critically, following the guidelines in Reading a Draft Critically.

As you make plans to revise, keep the following suggestions in mind.

Revising to Improve Your Introduction of the Problem

If your readers are unfamiliar with the problem or doubt that it exists, you may need to account for how it came to be, describe it in some detail, or demonstrate that it does indeed exist. You could define it carefully and compare or contrast it to other problems.

If your readers know about the problem but believe it is insignificant, you may need to argue for its seriousness, perhaps by dramatizing its current and long-term effects. You could speculate about further problems that might arise in the future if this one is not solved, create a nightmare scenario about the eventual collapse of the group or organization, or tell group members stories about ongoing bad effects of the problem.

Revising to Improve Your Presentation of the Solution

If readers could not see how to implement your proposed solution, outline the steps of its implementation. Lead them through it step by step. Demonstrate that the first step is easy to take; or, if it is unavoidably challenging, propose ways to ease the difficulty.

If a solution is beyond your expertise, detail how the expertise can be found and put to use.

If all readers can readily imagine how the solution would be implemented and how it would look once in place, reduce the amount of space you give to presenting the solution.

Revising to Convince Readers to Accept the Solution

If you have not given adequate reasons for proposing the solution, give more reasons.

If your reasons are hidden among other material, foreground them. Consider cueing them strongly by announcing them at the beginnings of paragraphs (the first reason why, second, third; the main reason why; my chief reason for; and so on). Support each reason with arguments, examples, anecdotes, statistics, quotes from authorities or members of the group, or any other appropriate strategy.

If you have not anticipated all of your readers' weighty objections and questions, do so now. Consider carefully whether you can accommodate some objections by either granting their wisdom or adapting your solution in response to them. If you refute objections or dismiss questions, do so in a spirit of continuing collaboration with members of your group; there is no need to be adversarial. You want readers to support your solution and perhaps even to join with you in implementing it.

If you neglected to mention alternative solutions some readers are likely to prefer, do so now. You may accommodate or reject these alternatives. You may be able to incorporate into your solution good points from alternatives. If you must reject all aspects of an alternative, do so through reasoned argument, without questioning the character or intelligence of those people who think they prefer the alternative. You may be able to convince some of them your solution really is better.

If readers had a problem with the overall organization of your argument, look critically at it now to see how you might reorganize. Steer readers through your argument with helpful cues that explicitly show relationships among parts.

REFLECTING ON WHAT YOU LEARNED ABOUT WRITING PROPOSALS TO SOLVE PROBLEMS

In this chapter, you have read critically several proposals and written one of your own. To remind yourself how much you have learned and to consolidate this learning so that you can use it later, pause now to reflect on your reading and writing experiences.

Write a page or so reflecting on your learning. Begin by describing what you are most pleased with in your essay and explaining what contributed to your achievement. Be very specific about this contribution. Describe it in some detail and account for its source. Was it something you observed in one of the readings? Did it come from your invention writing? Did you get good advice from someone? Try to write about your achievement in terms of the special requirements of writing that proposes solutions for problems.

Then write about anything else that accounts for your learning about this special kind of writing.

CHAPTER 9

POSITION PAPER

Chapter 8 focused on proposals, a pragmatic kind of writing used to solve problems and to get things accomplished. This chapter introduces the position paper, a related kind of writing that plays a central role in civic life. While the proposal solves problems, the position paper debates opinions on controversial issues. Proposals have a specific, practical purpose; position papers tend to be more general and philosophical. If you were concerned, for example, about the problem of drug abuse on high-school campuses, you might write a proposal recommending that students' lockers be searched. If, however, you were concerned about the issue of whether schools have the right to infringe on students' privacy by searching their lockers without permission, you would write a position paper instead. Debating such issues produces many of the laws that govern our lives and determines the kinds of schools we attend, the sort of medical care we receive, the quality of life we enjoy. Entering the debate on these issues is a sign of full, responsible citizenship.

Position papers are written on issues that are controversial, issues about which reasonable people disagree. Simply gathering information will not settle these disputes, although the more that is known about an issue, the more informed the opinions on the issue will be. What is needed is an airing of the arguments on all sides of the issue. Only when debate is open and vigorous can we fully understand what is at stake and hope to reach a consensus of opinion.

As citizens in a democracy, we have a duty to inform ourselves about the issues and to participate actively in the public debate over them. Furthermore, most professionals find many occasions to take a position in matters related to their jobs. For example, teachers debate their working conditions and argue over course requirements and standards; business executives debate marketing strategies and investment decisions; health-care providers argue over treatment options and hospital policies. As college students, you can expect to read and write position papers in many of your courses, particularly in philosophy, history, and political science. By arguing for your opinion and defending it against possible objections, you learn to think critically. You not only examine the opinions and reasoning of others but also look objectively at your own values and assumptions. Writing position papers brings you into communication with other people. It leads you to discover ways to bridge the gap between yourself and others, to recognize where you disagree and where there might be common ground for agreement.

As you read and discuss the selections in this chapter, you will discover why position papers play such an important role in college, the workplace, and civic life. You will also learn how position papers work. From the essays and from the ideas for writing that follow each selection, you will get many ideas for taking a position on an issue that you care about. As you analyze the selections and think about writing a position paper of your own, keep in mind the following assignment. The Guide to Writing Position Papers, which follows the readings, will support your writing.

THE WRITING ASSIGNMENT

Arguing a Position on an Issue

Write an essay that argues a position on a controversial issue. Take into account readers' objections, questions, and opposing viewpoints, but remember that your purpose is to state your own position clearly and to convince those who disagree with you that they must take seriously the arguments you raise.

WRITING SITUATIONS FOR ARGUING POSITIONS ON ISSUES

Writing that takes a position on a controversial issue plays a significant role in college work and professional life, as the following examples show:

- A committee made up of business and community leaders investigates the issue of regulating urban growth. Committee members prepare the arguments for and against regulation, and argue their own opinion that supply and demand will regulate development without government interference, that landowners should be permitted to sell their property to the highest bidder, and that developers are guided by the needs of the market and thus serve the people.

- For a sociology class, a student writes a term paper on surrogate mothering. She first learned about the subject from television news but feels that she needs more information to write a paper on the topic. In the library, she finds several newspaper and magazine articles that help her understand better the pros and cons of the issue. In her paper, she presents the strongest arguments on each side but concludes that, from a sociological perspective, surrogate mothering should not be allowed because it exploits poor women by creating a class of professional breeders.

- For a political science class, a student is assigned to write an essay either supporting or opposing the right of public employees to strike. Having no strong opinion on the issue herself, she discusses it with her mother, a nurse in a county hospital, and her uncle, a firefighter. Her mother feels that public employees like hospital workers and teachers should have the right to strike, but that police officers and firefighters should not because public safety would be endangered. The uncle disagrees, arguing that allowing hospital workers to strike would jeopardize public safety as much as allowing firefighters to strike. He insists that the central issue is not public safety, but individual rights. In her essay, the student supports the right of public employees to strike but argues that a system of arbitration should be used where a strike might jeopardize public safety.

PRACTICING ARGUING A POSITION
A COLLABORATIVE ACTIVITY

Work with another student to practice key strategies of arguing a position: develop an argument for one reason why you hold a position and refute objections to your argument. This brief activity will demonstrate that you already know a great deal about arguing a position.

PART 1. Get together with another student, and choose an issue that has at least two clearly opposing positions. You do not have to be authorities on the issue, but you should be familiar with some of the arguments that are usually raised on each side. Then decide which of you will argue which side. The side you take does not have to be the one you prefer; in fact, taking the opposing position can help you think through your own.

Spend five minutes alone considering the various reasons you could give to support your position. Choose the single best reason, and develop a brief argument to convince the other person why this reason should be taken seriously.

Then, with your partner, debate the issue. For each side, follow three steps: one person presents the reason for his or her position, the other person raises objections, and then the first person counterargues by qualifying the position to accommodate valid objections or refuting invalid objections.

PART 2. After the debate, spend some time discussing this argument process with your partner by considering the following questions:

On what basis did you choose the reason you gave in support of your position?

Knowing now how a person with an opposing view would object, would you still choose the same reason? Would you argue for it any differently?

How did the other person's objections alter your view of the issue or your understanding of that person?

A GUIDE TO READING POSITION PAPERS

To introduce the features and strategies of writing to take a position, we ask you to read, annotate, and write about your understanding of the essay below. Then, following guidelines we provide, you will reread the essay to examine the particular features of strong position papers.

First, though, as a reminder of the many possibilities for annotating, read this brief illustration of an annotated passage from another position paper, by Charles Krauthammer, which appears later in the chapter.

Desert Storm

Strong language

We have just come through a war fought in part over oil. Energy dependence costs Americans not just dollars but lives. It is a <u>bizarre sentimentalism</u> that would deny ourselves oil that is peacefully attainable because it risks disrupting the calving grounds of Arctic caribou.   9

I like the caribou as much as the next man. And I would be rather sorry if their mating patterns are disturbed. But you can't have everything. And if the choice is between the welfare of caribou and reducing an oil dependency that gets people killed in wars, <u>I choose man over caribou</u> every time.   10

Must we choose?

no mistaking his position

Similarly the spotted owl. I am no enemy of the owl. If it could be preserved at no or little cost, I would agree: the variety of nature is a good, a (high) aesthetic good. But it is no more than that. And sometimes [aesthetic] goods have to be sacrificed to the more [fundamental] ones. If the cost of preserving the spotted owl is the loss of livelihood for 30,000 logging families, <u>I choose family over owl.</u>   11

Isn't clean air both an aesthetic <u>and</u> a fundamental good?

The important distinction is between those environmental goods that are fundamental and those that are (merely) aesthetic. Nature is our [ward.] It is not our [master.] It is to be respected and even cultivated. But <u>it is man's world.</u> And when man has to choose between his well-being and that of nature, nature will have to accommodate.   12

Separates man from nature— doesn't make sense

Dick Teresi

THE CASE FOR NO HELMETS

This selection by Dick Teresi (b. 1945) was originally published in the June 17, 1995, *New York Times* opinion section. Teresi is the editor of *VQ,* an exclusive, semi-art magazine about customized Harley Davidson motorcycles. However, the subjects he usually writes about are particle physics, lasers, and neuroscience. He was an editor of *Omni* magazine, has written for *The Atlantic* magazine, and frequently contributes to the

New York Times Book Review. He is the author, with Leon Lederman, of *The God Particle: If the Universe Is the Answer, What's the Question?* (1993).

As the title and opening paragraphs of this essay indicate, Teresi is arguing for the repeal of laws requiring motorcycle riders to wear protective helmets. Notice, as you read and annotate the essay, that he does not make a political argument against government interference in individual rights. On what basis, then, does he argue against the helmet laws? How would you argue for or against them?

It's time for the nation's oldest bike festival. This weekend, 150,000 motorcycle enthusiasts have converged on Laconia, N.H., for the Laconia Motorcycle Rally. Ah, the joys of motorcycling! The throaty roar of your V-twin engine, the call of the open road, the wind in your hair. . . .

Wait. Forget about that last part. The riders en route to Laconia won't feel any wind in their hair. They'll just feel the rush of air over their plastic helmets—at least until they cross into New Hampshire, which doesn't require riders over 18 to wear them.

Forty-seven states have some helmet requirements. At the rally, plenty of T-shirts will deride motorcycle helmet laws. They'll sell well. In a survey of 2,500 bikers at the 1993 rally, 98 percent of the respondents said they opposed such laws. This opposition is often dismissed by nonriders as evidence of bikers' rebelliousness. But we oppose the laws for reasons other than personal freedom. Helmets are not necessarily the life-savers some people think they are. In some cases, they may be killers.

Deep in the plush recesses of any helmet approved by the Department of Transportation is a tiny warning label: "Some reasonably foreseeable impacts may exceed this helmet's capability to protect against severe injury or death." The unspecified "reasonably foreseeable impacts" are any collisions at speeds greater than 15 miles per hour. The department tests the protection provided by helmets by dropping them on an anvil from a height of six feet. This is equivalent to an impact at 14.4 miles per hour. So if you're riding to Laconia, keep your speedometer below 15 miles per hour.

But what about all those statistics purporting to prove that helmets save lives? Some studies indicate that there are fewer motorcycle deaths per one million residents in states with helmet laws than in states where helmets are not mandatory. (The study most cited was made by the Centers for Disease Control and covers 1979 to 1986.) But this is largely because there are more riders per capita in states that did not require helmets.

If you take those same statistics and count motorcycle fatality rates per 10,000 registered motorcycles rather than per general population—a more sensible approach—you find that nine states without helmet laws had a lower fatality rate (3.05 deaths per 10,000 motorcycles) than those that mandated helmets (3.38).

What about claims that helmet laws reduce deaths caused by head trauma? Jonathan Goldstein, a professor of economics at Bowdoin College, studied crash and injury statistics and found that while helmets might prevent head injuries at very low speeds, they can increase the possibility of neck injuries at high speeds.   7

This makes sense. The body, like any object under impact, breaks at its weakest point. If a biker wearing a four-pound helmet is thrown to the pavement, the head might be saved but the neck is more likely to snap.   8

Helmets, especially full-face models, suppress the normal sensations of wind and speed and thus can give riders a false sense of invulnerability and can lead to excessive risk-taking and dangerous riding habits.   9

The real problem is not uncovered heads. It's that too many bikers don't ride well and too many automobile drivers don't look out for motorcycles. To make motorcycling safer, the nation needs better driver and rider education. A 1988 study by the American Motorcyclist Association, showed that states with good motorcycle education programs and no helmet laws had an average fatality rate of 2.56 deaths per 100 motorcycle accidents while states with helmet laws but no training had a death rate of 3.09 per 100 accidents.   10

Is there a place for helmets? Sure. Anyone who rides in a car should wear one. Head injuries make up only 20 percent of serious injuries to motorcyclists but are far more common in car accidents. If the state legislators who have passed helmet laws are serious, they ought to prove it by always wearing one in the car. Meanwhile, let motorcyclists feel the wind in their hair.   11

READING FOR MEANING

Write at least a page, exploring the meaning you find in Teresi's essay. Begin by indicating what position you would take on the issue. Then write about your thoughts and reactions to Teresi's essay.

As you write, you may need to reread parts of the essay. Add to your original annotations any further thoughts you have, and do not be surprised if your views change as you reread and write.

If you have difficulty writing for at least a page, consider the following suggestions:

- In paragraph 2, when Teresi mentions the age minimum for helmet laws, he is referring to the fact that there are often two sets of laws—one for adults over 18 years old and the other for minors under 18. What is your view on this double standard?

- If, as Teresi argues in paragraph 9, helmets give "riders a false sense of invulnerability and can lead to excessive risk-taking and dangerous riding habits," would it not be as important or even more important for riders under 18, who tend to be more reckless and have more accidents, to be exempted from laws requiring helmets?

- Are you surprised that helmet laws have been passed in 47 of the 50 states even though 98 percent of bikers polled oppose such laws? How do you think such laws get passed even when the people who are most affected oppose them? Is it wrong to think that riders are more affected by motorcycle accidents than other people? How do you think motorcycle accidents might affect nonbikers?

- React to any single assertion that you find interesting or challenging, such as "helmets might prevent head injuries at very low speeds, they can increase the possibility of neck injuries at high speeds" (paragraph 7); and "Anyone who rides in a car should wear" a helmet (paragraph 11).

READING LIKE A WRITER

If you read chapter 1, you will already be familiar with some of the basic features and strategies of position papers. Here, we guide you through a systematic analysis of Teresi's argumentative strategies: *defining the issue; asserting a clear, unequivocal position; arguing directly for the position;* and *counter-arguing objections and opposing positions.* Each part of this activity briefly describes a strategy and then poses a critical reading and writing task to help you reread and annotate a part of the essay and then write about what you have observed.

Consider this section a general introduction to arguing a position. Each reading selection in the chapter has its own Reading like a Writer activity to help you analyze further one of these argumentative strategies. The Guide to Writing Position Papers at the end of the chapter suggests how you can apply what you have learned in these Reading like a Writer activities to plan and write your own position paper.

Defining the Issue

At the center of every position paper is a controversial issue, a public policy or principle over which informed, well-intentioned people disagree. In this chapter, you will read about a variety of issues, some of which you may be familiar with and have strong views about such as whether to protect the environment, whether schools should cater to students' religious beliefs, and whether affirmative-action policies should be continued.

Although position papers strive primarily to influence readers' opinions, they also inform readers about issues. In fact, the writer's initial task usually is to define the issue for readers. How writers define the issue depends on what they assume readers already know about it and what they want readers to think about it. Defining the issue often involves providing information—facts, statistics, examples, expert opinion—that enables readers to understand what is at stake and for whom. This kind of information also can give readers a sense of the issue's significance and scope.

Writers know that issues can be defined in many different ways, and that how their readers look at an issue influences their attitude toward it. For example, the issue of capital punishment could be defined in legal terms, of the constitutional protection against cruel and unusual punishment; in moral or religious terms, of the biblical injunction of an eye for an eye; in economic terms, of costs versus the benefits of life imprisonment; in sociological terms, of the likelihood of rehabilitation; and in other terms as well.

As a critical reader of position papers, you will want to consider carefully how the issue is defined.

ANALYZE. The introduction to Teresi's essay asked you to note that he does not define the issue in political terms of government infringement upon individual rights. Look for any passages that indicate terms he does use to define the issue. Also note where Teresi tries to establish for readers why the issue is important and worth their consideration.

WRITE. In a few sentences, report what you have discovered about the way Teresi defines the issue. Describe how he explains it, and speculate on why he chose to define it in these particular terms. Finally, add a sentence or two that evaluates how successfully Teresi presents the issue to his original readers, many of whom are motorcycle riders.

Asserting a Clear, Unequivocal Position

In addition to explaining the issue and indicating its significance, writers must assert a position on the issue. This assertion is the point of the essay, its thesis. Although it may be qualified carefully or may reflect sensitivity to opposing views, the essay's position must be clear and unequivocal. Writers of position papers always take sides. Their primary purpose is to assert a position of their own and to influence readers—to get them off the fence, challenge them, win their adherence.

Very often, writers assert a position in a thesis statement early in the essay. The advantage of this strategy is that it lets readers know right away where the writer stands. The thesis may also appear later in the essay, however. Postponing the thesis is particularly appropriate when a writer wants to explain the issue before asserting his or her position. To avoid confusion, writers may restate the position several times.

The position a writer takes must be arguable. Issues that can readily be resolved by fact are not arguable positions: for example, arguing over what is the world's average yearly temperature is pointless because the answer is a simple matter of fact that can be easily demonstrated. (Arguments *can* revolve around the interpretation of facts, though, so that people can legitimately argue over whether world weather records indicate, for example, ongoing global warming.) Equally pointless are arguments over matters of religious faith, because issues deeply rooted in belief are for the most part impervious to fact or reason. The best issues for position papers are matters of opinion—judgments rather than certainties. Facts and beliefs should be brought to bear on these issues but cannot easily resolve them.

ANALYZE. Find and underline the first place (apart from the title) where Teresi explicitly states his position. Speculate on why he chose to put the thesis statement at this particular place in the essay. What goes before it and what goes after? Consider also whether the thesis, as stated, is arguable. Specifically, what does the writer have to prove for readers to accept this position?

WRITE. Write a few sentences explaining what you have learned about how Teresi presents his position.

Arguing Directly for the Position

Writers of position papers give reasons and evidence—such as example, facts, authorities, statistics, and personal anecdotes—to support their position. Although their arguments may be subtle, writers of position papers usually try to make their reasoning simple and direct. They do not hint at their reasons, hoping readers will get the hint. Instead, they make explicit their reasons for holding the position. Not only do they explicitly state their reasons and provide evidence to convince readers to accept them, but also they may explain their reasoning in detail. Because writers know that some reasons will carry more weight with readers than others, they often provide several reasons, explaining why each reason is worth taking seriously.

ANALYZE. Reread the essay, looking for an explicit reason. Then note what Teresi says about this reason to explain what he means by it or why he thinks readers should pay attention to it. Note also what kind of evidence he offers to support this particular reason. Consider why you do or do not find this argument with its reason and supporting evidence convincing.

WRITE. Describe briefly how Teresi argues for his position, assessing the effectiveness of his argument.

Counterarguing Objections and Opposing Positions

In addition to arguing directly for their points of views on the issues, writers of position papers may also counterargue. If a writer anticipates readers' legitimate objections to an argument, the writer might acknowledge its limits and qualify the argument accordingly, thereby defanging the criticism. If, however, the criticism is invalid, the writer should refute it by demonstrating to readers why it is unfair or illogical. Similarly, writers try to anticipate alternative positions that readers might favor and show readers why the position being argued is better than these alternatives.

Counterarguing can enhance a writer's credibility and strengthen the argument. When readers holding an opposing position recognize that a writer understands their views on an issue, they are much more likely to listen to the entire argument. Counterargument can reassure readers that they share certain values or ideals with a writer, building a temporary bridge of common concerns between two groups that may be separated by profound differences and antagonism. Influencing people's beliefs and actions often requires thoughtful, sensitive counterargument.

As they argue for their positions, experienced writers are continually aware of the likely objections and questions of readers holding differing positions. As they write, they may *acknowledge* readers' objections by simply mentioning them, letting readers know they are aware of the objections without evaluating or refuting them. Writers may also *accommodate* readers' objections, finding at least some value and usefulness in readers' views. Finally, writers may *refute* readers' objections, that is, try to show them to be groundless or just plain wrong.

ANALYZE. Find a passage where Teresi counterargues, anticipating a possible objection to his argument or an opposing argument. Analyze the way he counterargues by considering the following questions: How does he use evidence to support his counterargument? What effect does counterarguing have on his credibility for you, as one reader? If you were a reader inclined to take a position opposed to Teresi's, how convincing would this counterargument be for you?

WRITE. Write a few sentences explaining how Teresi counterargues, and evaluating the probable success of this strategy.

READINGS

Stephen Bates

RELIGIOUS DIVERSITY AND THE SCHOOLS

Stephen Bates is a senior fellow at the Annenberg Washington Program, a conservative think tank. He is also the author of *Battleground: One Mother's Crusade, the Religious Right, and the Struggle for Control of Our Classrooms* (1993).

In this essay, which first appeared in the *American Enterprise* journal and is adapted from his book, Bates addresses the issue of religious tolerance. Many Americans probably assume that this issue was settled by the constitutional guarantee of freedom of religion. But, as Bates reminds us, the controversy continues, especially regarding the public schools. Although the separation of church and state is inscribed in the Bill of Rights, every few years heated debate flares up over whether prayer should be permitted in the schools or whether creationism should be taught as a scientific theory comparable to evolution. In his essay, Bates focuses on whether fundamentalist Christian students should be excused from "assignments that offend their beliefs."

Before reading, reflect on what you know about religious tolerance and its history. Then read and annotate the essay, noting anything that contributes to your understanding of the issue and Bates's position on it.

In countless ways, today's public schools tailor the educational experience to the individual student. Handicapped students get assignments fashioned to their abilities. Pregnant students get prenatal care, and students with infants get day care. Students who lack fluency in English spend the day in bilingual classrooms. Several states excuse conscientious objectors from dissecting animals. Some districts provide schools-within-schools for students fighting drug or alcohol addiction, for the children of alcoholics, and for chronic troublemakers or gang members. New York City and Los Angeles have special high schools for gay students. Atlanta, Philadelphia, Newark, and other districts have implemented Afrocentric curricula, some of whose advocates speak of tailoring education to black students' "special learning patterns." The National Education Association (NEA) has endorsed special programs for underachievers, for "socially promoted" students (students who don't meet advancement standards but are advanced anyway), for "displaced students of desegregated districts," and for many others with special concerns.

When it comes to the special concerns of fundamentalist Christians, however, educators often turn a cold shoulder. Excusing fundamentalists from assignments that offend their beliefs, the NEA said in a 1986 *amicus* brief, "substitutes segregation and intolerance for the democratic values that public education is designed to foster." Tolerance may indeed be the dominant theme of the modern curriculum. The authors of a recent study of American high schools concluded that "tolerating diversity is the moral glue that holds schools together." One study of American history books found toleration presented as "the only 'religious' idea worth remembering." What was being tolerated, often as not, was omitted.

Tolerance, though, can be an expansive and even elusive concept. When a Jewish girl in Yonkers, New York, asked to be excused from singing Christmas hymns in 1949, her teacher scolded her. Refusing to sing, the teacher said, would be terribly intolerant of her. A decade later, a Baltimore administrator told atheist Madalyn Murray O'Hair that her son need not pray. To be tolerant of other students, however, he would have to "stand with the rest, maintain an attitude of reverence, and just move his lips as if he were saying prayers."

Teachers today often misconstrue toleration in a different fashion, by equating it with indifferentism—the belief that all religions have equal validity. In a 1987 case, Judge Danny Boggs of the U.S. Court of Appeals for the Sixth Circuit drew a vital distinction. *Civil toleration,* he pointed out, means that adherents of all faiths deserve equal rights as citizens, whereas *religious toleration* means that all faiths are equally valid as religions. Under civil toleration, all faiths are equal in the eyes of the state; under religious toleration, all faiths are equal in the eyes of God.

5   Unfortunately, educators don't always grasp the distinction. "I hear teachers telling kids, 'It doesn't matter how you pray, just pray,' or, 'It's wonderful to have faith, and does it really matter which one?'" says Charles C. Haynes of the First Liberty Institute at George Mason University. "But that kind of well-meaning relativism . . . undermines what parents are teaching, that it *does* matter to whom one prays and how one prays. It doesn't just matter, it matters ultimately."

6   From the school's perspective, another problem arises. The curriculum often seeks to foster respect for women, gays, minorities, and other groups. What happens when parents, for religious reasons, believe that the husband must head the household, that homosexuality is a sin, and that anyone who doesn't accept Jesus as Savior is bound for hell? Educators fear that if they excuse students with such beliefs from assignments, other students will infer that the school endorses the beliefs. "It is a mission of public schools," writes school administrator Frederick W. Hill, "*not* to tolerate intolerance."

7   Tolerating everything except intolerance, however, seems self-contradictory. "If you are going to be tolerant," says Paul Vitz, a New York University psychology professor, "you are going to have to tolerate some things you don't like, including intolerance." As Tom Lehrer once quipped: "I know there are people in this world who do not love their fellow men. And I hate people like that."

8   The internal contradiction becomes more obvious in an era of multicultural education. British educators Philip H. Walkling and Chris Brannigan observe: "What makes a particular culture identifiably that culture might include essentially sexist or racist practices and principles. . . . Sexism can be, in theory, rooted in beliefs . . . which are crucial to cultural identity. That is, they can be the very sort of belief which those of us who value a multicultural society think that minorities have the right to preserve."

9   In addition, a bedrock principle of civil liberties is that the state must allow many things of which majorities disapprove: Jehovah's Witnesses distributing anti-Catholic literature in Catholic neighborhoods, Nazis marching through a predominantly Jewish suburb, and protestors setting fire to an American flag. The Constitution generally *does* tolerate intolerance. The schools ought to teach this principle and operate in accordance with it in order to prepare students for democratic citizenship.

Boundaries exist, of course. Parents can't expect the public   10
schools to teach religious dogma, and they can't expect the schools
to insulate religious objectors from other children all day long (as
New York City did by building a wall between Hasidic Jewish students and other students, until a court ruled the approach unconsti-
tutional). But parents can reasonably request secular alternatives to
religiously offensive assignments. Or they can ask to have their children sent to a study hall and take over responsibility for part of the
curriculum themselves.

Parents can't expect the school to teach their children creation-   11
ism. But they can ask the school not to teach their children evolution. Parents can't expect teachers to make religious judgments on
their behalf. But they can expect teachers to respect the parents'
judgments—unlike the teacher in the Midwest who told Jehovah's
Witnesses that their parents were wrong, God wanted them to participate in the classroom Halloween party; and unlike the kinder-
garten teacher who told an atheist's daughter that her mother was
wrong, God does exist.

Some materials, moreover, are indispensable; parents can't   12
expect to have their children excused from reading them. But as
former Massachusetts education official Charles Glenn writes, "The
number of specific texts that are truly essential to carrying out the
mission of public education is surely very limited: the Declaration of
Independence, the Bill of Rights, the Gettysburg Address, a handful
of others."

We can differ over how far schools ought to go to accommodate   13
religious objections to the curriculum—whether schools ought to
release students only from supplementary books or from single or
multiple textbooks and courses. But the presumption ought to be in
favor of accommodation.

Without such a presumption, fundamentalists will increasingly   14
wind up in religious schools and home schooling. Unable to avoid
part of the public school curriculum, they will avoid all of it—an
option that has long dismayed supporters of public education. "The
greater the proportion of our youth who fail to attend our public
schools and who receive their education elsewhere, the greater the
threat to our democratic unity," Harvard president James Bryant
Conant wrote in 1952. "Letting subcultural groups split off and form
their own private schools," writes educator James Moffett, "will
seriously deepen community and national divisions." In Moffett's
view, "America needs to accommodate plurality *within* unity, so that
various parties can pursue, on the same sites, the ramifications of
their goals and values and discover where these lead."

If we believe that pluralistic public education is an essential bul-   15
wark of a peaceful multicultural society, then we should do what
we can to keep fundamentalists (and other religious dissidents) in
the public schools. Even skipping the occasional book or class, they

benefit from and contribute to the democratic mission of public education. They acquire socially beneficial information and attitudes that they might not otherwise get. By their presence, they also give other students an object lesson in diversity.

We shouldn't panic when the difference manifests itself, as when some students leave the room or read a different book. Embracing religious diversity but forbidding its public expression is a crabbed form of pluralism, one that our public schools should forsake. | 16 |

READING FOR MEANING

Write at least a page about the meaning of this essay. Begin by briefly restating Bates's position. Then comment about anything else that interests you in this essay.

If you have trouble writing at least a page, here are some suggestions to get you started:

- Bates opens the essay by asserting that "today's public schools tailor the educational experience to the individual student" (paragraph 1). He cites several examples to support this claim. If you can, add another example from your own experience to support or to contradict Bates's point. Or, if you have experience with any of the situations Bates lists, tell about your experience and how it influences your thinking on the issue.

- Bates uses various words that have strong connotations for some readers—"relativism" (paragraph 5), "sexism" (paragraph 8), and "pluralism" (paragraph 16), to name just a few. A word's *connotations* are the attitudes and feelings people associate with it. For example, while some people think of "relativism" negatively, as lacking in values, others may think of the word positively, as being the opposite of rigid, absolutist thinking. Choose a word from the essay with strong connotations and explore its different meanings. Look specifically at the context in which Bates uses the word, and speculate on why he chose to use that particular word in his essay. What attitudes and feelings do you think he is trying to arouse in readers by using that particular word?

- Reflecting on the relation between your own religious beliefs and your schooling can help deepen your understanding of the issue. For example, has your education tended to reinforce or to undermine your beliefs? Have your interactions in school with people who have different religious beliefs or cultural attitudes been generally constructive or destructive? If anything has been "religiously offensive" to you in school, explain why you thought so and what you did (or wanted to do) about it. Relate your experience directly to the issue presented in this essay.

- Explain the possible meaning or significance of "tolerating diversity is the moral glue that holds schools together" (paragraph 2); "Teachers today often misconstrue toleration . . . by equating it with indifferentism—the belief that all religions have equal validity" (paragraph 4); "The internal contradiction becomes more obvious in an era of multicultural education" (paragraph 8), or any other statement that intrigues or puzzles you.

EXTENDING MEANING THROUGH CONVERSATION. After reading for meaning on your own, you can extend your understanding by talking with classmates who have also read and written about this selection. Before getting together with two or three other students, reread what you wrote about Bates's argument and, if you have not already done so, consider what position you would take on this issue.

Begin the conversation by telling each other what you think about the issue. Keep the focus of the conversation on the issue and on your responses to Bates's argument. Remember that it is not necessary that you agree, only that you help each other think about Bates's argument and your own arguments.

READING LIKE A WRITER
DEFINING THE ISSUE

For position papers published in the midst of a lively public debate, writers may need only to mention the issue. In most cases, however, writers need not only to identify the issue but also to explain or define it for readers. To define the issue, writers may provide several kinds of information. They may, for example, place the issue in its historical or cultural context, cite specific instances to make the issue seem less abstract, establish or redefine the terms of the debate.

Defining the issue, then, is seldom simply a matter of disinterestedly informing readers about the issue; it actually can be an important part of the argument. At the very least, how a writer defines the issue sets the stage for the argument. In a position paper like "Religious Diversity and the Schools," Bates's definition of the issue plays a key role in his argument.

ANALYZE. To see how Bates defines the issue, reread paragraphs 1 through 9 and make a scratch outline by writing a sentence describing the point of each paragraph. We have written sentences for the first two paragraphs to get you started:

Paragraph 1 provides examples of how public schools cater to the needs of individual students.

Paragraph 2 sets up a contrast, asserting that educators eager to instill tolerance in their students actually ignore the needs of fundamentalist Christian students.

Notice, as you complete the scratch outline, how Bates uses the concept of *tolerance,* specifically how he defines this key term and shows that people differ in their understanding of it. Examine the distinction he draws between civil and religious tolerance, as well as the contradiction he identifies in paragraphs 7 and 8. Consider how these efforts to define the issue help to support his own position.

WRITE. Report in a few sentences what you have learned about how Bates defines the issue and the role that his definition plays in advancing his argument.

CONSIDERING IDEAS FOR YOUR OWN WRITING

The first paragraph of this essay presents several educational policy issues you could learn more about and use as the basis for a position paper. For example, should students with infants be provided with free child care? Should students who have not yet mastered the English language be taught in their native language? There are many other school-related issues about which you might consider writing. Should college athletes whose teams help raise money for the school be paid for their labor? Should college education in public institutions be subsidized, or should students have to pay the actual costs? Should colleges prepare students for specific kinds of jobs or should they provide a more general, basic education and let students get on-the-job training after they are hired by a firm?

Donella Meadows

RUSH AND LARRY, COAST TO COAST: THIS IS NOT DEMOCRACY IN ACTION

Donella Meadows is a professor of environmental studies at Dartmouth College. She has written several books, including *The Global Citizen* (1991) and *Beyond the Limits: Confronting Global Collapse, Envisioning a Sustainable Future* (1993). Meadows also often writes opinion essays on contemporary issues, as is the case with this selection, which originally appeared in the *Los Angeles Times* in February 1993, a few months after the 1992 presidential election.

The issue of whether television and radio talk shows actually help foster democratic debate came to the fore after Ross Perot declared his candidacy on the talk show "Larry King Live." Perot promised to continue to hold the "electronic town meetings" he held during his campaign to debate solutions to the nation's problems. The town meeting is a New England institution dating from colonial times that is often cited as a model of direct democracy.

Before reading the essay, reflect on talk shows you have seen on television or heard on radio. In your experience, what do such shows contribute to the national debate on important issues? How democratic do you think they are? As you read and annotate Meadows's essay, notice how she defines democracy.

I'm a talk-show junkie. I'd rather listen to real folks stumbling to express their own thoughts than to polished puppets reading what others have written. I tune into Larry, Rush and the folks who call in, to keep myself awake, chuckling, thinking and every now and then yelling in outrage.

One item of talk I hear is about the power of talk shows. They are restoring democracy, it is said, to a nation that has concentrated too much power within one narrow East Coast Beltway. Just by venting our opinions into a national satellite feed, you and I can scuttle a congressional pay raise, elevate a wise-cracking Texan to a presidential candidacy or bring down a potential attorney general because she hired an illegal alien.[1]

We don't need Ross Perot to create an electronic town meeting, they say. It's already going on, coast-to-coast, on multiple channels, 24 hours a day.

Now, much as I like the talk shows, I'm also from New England, and I can say that there's a big difference between the Rush Limbaugh show and a town meeting. And much as I like town meetings, they are not as effectively democratic as they could be.

One problem with both call-in shows and town meetings is that they're not representative. Only those who take the trouble, and don't have to go to work, and aren't busy with the kids can participate. Even within that set, the loudest mouths and most made-up minds dominate the air time. At town meetings, you can see the shy folks, the ones who have trouble sounding off in public, leaning against the back wall or bending over their knitting. On talk radio, those people are invisible, but they're there. It's a mistake to think that the blowhards who call in speak for the nation.

A second problem is that, as we know well from town meetings, the power isn't with the people, it's with the moderator. He or she establishes the rules, decides who to call on, changes the subject, cuts people off. In talk radio, there is only one rule: Break for the commercial on time.

Some call-in moderators are neutral and courteous. Then there's Rush Limbaugh, who is funny and pompous and a scapegoater and hatemonger. His popularity could cause you to draw some terrible conclusions about the state of mind of the American people. It helps to remember that Bill Cosby is popular, too. I heard an interview the other day with a psychologist who was hired by Cosby to go over each script to be sure it contained no "put-down" humor—no joke made at the expense of any person or group. Limbaugh's show is pure put-down humor.

The purpose of the commercial media is not to foster democracy, of course; it's to entertain in order to attract attention in order to sell. Therefore, talk shows have a fast pace. They flip from topic to topic. There is time to spout off, but no time for serious debate. Talk shows can only transmit knee-jerk responses to hot-

[1]Washington, D.C., is the area within the "East Coast Beltway," Ross Perot is the "wise-cracking Texan," and Zoë Baird is the "potential attorney general" whose candidacy was withdrawn when it was discovered that she had hired an illegal alien to care for her children.

button items. They can deal with Zoë Baird's child-care arrangements, but they seem uninterested in Ron Brown's links to corporations and foreign governments. They have plenty to say about gays
in the military, but they can't fathom Yugoslavia. They get exercised
about Congress bouncing checks worth a few thousand dollars,
while billions of dollars slide away into the S&L disaster.[2]

The talk shows not only miss the biggest, most profound issues;   9
they can be a breeding grounds for careening falsehoods. One man
tells Larry King that a cellular phone gave his wife brain cancer, causing a national panic before there's a shred of evidence. Rush Limbaugh
pronounces the greenhouse effect a fiction made up by commie-pinko
environmentalists, and decades of good science are swept away.

Even if everyone could participate, even if the moderators were   10
fair and responsible, even if the pace were deliberate enough to
have a real conversation, there would be a final problem with
democracy by talk radio. We are not very good at talking to one
another. We are better at coming back with one-liners than at listening with open minds. We have few public role models showing us
how to demand and judge evidence, how to weigh conflicting opinions, how to deal with uncertainty and complication.

What I hear every day on talk radio is America's lack of educa-   11
tion—and I don't mean lack of college degrees. I mean lack of the
basic art of democracy, the ability to seek the great truths that can
come only by synthesizing the small truths possessed by each of us.

The world is richly varied and wildly complicated. Each person   12
experiences only a piece of it. To make any sense of the world, to
make the right decisions as a nation, we need many points of view—
east and west, rich and poor, male and female, liberal and conservative, urban and rural, black and white, yes, even straight and gay.
Democracy wins out over any government dominated by just one
point of view, because only democracy has at least the potential of
seeing the world complete and whole.

That's why talk shows and town meetings are good things. They   13
will be even better when they let all voices be heard with respect,
with inquiry, and with dedication to finding the truth, rather than
ridiculing the opposition.

[2]Zoë Baird is the candidate for attorney general referred to earlier, while Ron Brown
is former head of the Democratic party and secretary of commerce. Gays in the military, the war in Yugoslavia, Congress bouncing checks, and the S&L (savings and loan)
problem were all newsworthy events at the time the article was written.

READING FOR MEANING

Write at least a page developing your thoughts and responses to this essay.
Begin by briefly explaining, in your own words, what the issue is and why it is
important. Then examine any aspect of the essay that interests you.

Reread parts of the essay and add to your earlier annotations your new insights even if they appear to contradict what you wrote before. The following suggestions may help you see something new in the essay that you did not see when you first read it.

- Notice how Meadows represents herself in the opening paragraph as "a talk-show junkie." What adjectives would you use to describe the image of Meadows you get from reading this essay? How does this image affect your willingness to be convinced by her argument?

- Reread paragraphs 4 through 7 where Meadows compares talk shows with town meetings. Underline the points of difference. Then reflect on each point, indicating whether you agree or disagree with Meadows's judgment. If you can, add your own points of difference or similarity.

- In paragraph 10, Meadows asserts that Americans are not very good critical thinkers, perhaps because "We have few public role models showing us how to demand and judge evidence, how to weigh conflicting opinions, how to deal with uncertainty and complication." How well do you think you judge evidence, weigh conflicting opinions, deal with uncertainty and complication? If you think you are good at it, reflect on how you learned to think critically. If you think you are not good at thinking critically, what could you do to become better at it?

- Explain the possible meaning or significance of "One problem with both call-in shows and town meetings is that they're not representative" (paragraph 5); "there is only one rule: Break for the commercial on time" (paragraph 6); "To make any sense of the world, to make the right decisions as a nation, we need many points of view" (paragraph 12); or any other statement that catches your eye.

EXTENDING MEANING THROUGH CONVERSATION. The meaning you make on your own can be enhanced by discussing the reading with other students who have also read it carefully and explored their understanding in writing. Before getting together with two or three classmates, reread what you have written, and reflect on your current understanding of the issue and Meadows's argument.

Start the conversation by telling each other what you think is most surprising about the essay. As you share your insights, you will probably find that you have different views about the issue. You may even interpret Meadows's argument in very different ways. Probe these differences by rereading problematic passages aloud together and discussing them.

READING LIKE A WRITER

MAKING A POSITION CLEAR AND UNEQUIVOCAL

Because the purpose of writing a position paper is to argue for a particular position on an issue, it is crucially important that the position be stated clearly and unambiguously. That does not mean that the position must be simplistic or lacking in subtlety, only that it must be unequivocal, allowing no confusion or doubt about where the writer stands on the issue.

Essays that argue a position usually state and restate the position in various ways throughout the essay. To orient readers, writers often begin with a "thesis statement" that announces the writer's position and forecasts the reasons to be presented. Sometimes, however, writers postpone announcing the position until they have defined the issue and given readers an understanding of the different points of view people adopt on the issue.

ANALYZE. Reread the essay, looking for and underlining the single sentence or combination of sentences that you would identify as Meadows's thesis statement. If you find more than one statement in different parts of the essay, indicate which you would consider the clearest and most comprehensive statement of Meadows's thesis. As you read, also note any places in the essay where Meadows positions herself in relation to other points of view.

WRITE. Write a few sentences identifying the thesis statement and evaluating it in terms of clarity and placement. Is the thesis clearly stated or is it ambiguous? What advantages or disadvantages do you see in the placement of the thesis?

COMPARE. Choose any other position paper in this chapter and locate its thesis statement. Then evaluate it in terms of clarity and placement. Add another sentence or two, comparing the way the two essays present their theses.

CONSIDERING IDEAS FOR YOUR OWN WRITING

Consider any other controversial issues you can think of that involve the media—television, radio, film, performance art, music video, recording, or the Internet. For example, should sexually explicit material on the Internet be censored in some way? Should films or television programs that represent different nationalities or ethnic groups be monitored to prevent stereotyping? Should compact discs have an industry-designed rating system like the G, PG, R, and X ratings used for films?

Charles Krauthammer

SAVING NATURE, BUT ONLY FOR MAN

Charles Krauthammer (b. 1950), a respected conservative political commentator, has had a varied career as a political scientist, psychiatrist, journalist, speech writer, and television talk-show panelist. Since 1983, he has written essays for *Time* magazine. He is a contributing editor to the *New Republic,* and, since 1985, he has contributed a weekly syndicated column to the *Washington Post.* In 1981, he won a Pulitzer Prize for commentary on politics and society. He has published one book, *Cutting Edges: Making Sense of the Eighties* (1985).

In this essay, which appeared in *Time* magazine in 1991, Krauthammer attacks what he calls "sentimental environmentalism." Knowing from national polls that many adults who read magazines like *Time* support environmental causes, Krauthammer takes the risk of telling these readers either that they are wrong or that they do not understand the issue very well. You may be among these readers. As you read, pay attention to your personal responses to Krauthammer's argument. How does it feel to be challenged? What do you think of the approach he takes, of his tone, and of his attitude toward you?

1. Environmental sensitivity is now as required an attitude in polite society as is, say, belief in democracy or aversion to polyester. But now that everyone from Ted Turner to George Bush, Dow to Exxon has professed love for Mother Earth, how are we to choose among the dozens of conflicting proposals, restrictions, projects, regulations and laws advanced in the name of the environment? Clearly not everything with an environmental claim is worth doing. How to choose?

2. There is a simple way. First, distinguish between environmental luxuries and environmental necessities. Luxuries are those things it would be nice to have if costless. Necessities are those things we must have regardless. Then apply a rule. Call it the fundamental axiom of sane environmentalism: Combatting ecological change that directly threatens the health and safety of people is an environmental necessity. All else is luxury.

3. For example: preserving the atmosphere—stopping ozone depletion and the greenhouse effect—is an environmental necessity. In April scientists reported that ozone damage is far worse than previously thought. Ozone depletion not only causes skin cancer and eye cataracts, it also destroys plankton, the beginning of the food chain atop which we humans sit.

4. The reality of the greenhouse effect is more speculative, though its possible consequences are far deadlier: melting ice caps, flooded coastlines, disrupted climate, parched plains and, ultimately, empty breadbaskets. The American Midwest feeds the world. Are we prepared to see Iowa acquire Albuquerque's climate? And Siberia acquire Iowa's?

5. Ozone depletion and the greenhouse effect are human disasters. They happen to occur in the environment. But they are urgent because they directly threaten man. A sane environmentalism, the only kind of environmentalism that will win universal public support, begins by unashamedly declaring that nature is here to serve man. A sane environmentalism is entirely anthropocentric: it enjoins man to preserve nature, but on the grounds of self-preservation.

6. A sane environmentalism does not sentimentalize the earth. It does not ask people to sacrifice in the name of other creatures. After all, it is hard enough to ask people to sacrifice in the name of

other humans. (Think of the chronic public resistance to foreign aid and welfare.) Ask hardworking voters to sacrifice in the name of the snail darter, and, if they are feeling polite, they will give you a shrug.

Of course, this anthropocentrism runs against the grain of a contemporary environmentalism that indulges in earth worship to the point of idolatry. One scientific theory—Gaia theory—actually claims that Earth is a living organism. This kind of environmentalism likes to consider itself spiritual. It is nothing more than sentimental. It takes, for example, a highly selective view of the benignity of nature. My nature worship stops with the April twister that came through Andover, Kans., or the May cyclone that killed more than 125,000 Bengalis and left 10 million (!) homeless.

A nonsentimental environmentalism is one founded on Protagoras' maxim that "Man is the measure of all things." Such a principle helps us through the thicket of environmental argument. Take the current debate raging over oil drilling in a corner of the Alaska National Wildlife Refuge. Environmentalists, mobilizing against a bill working its way through Congress to permit such exploration, argue that we should be conserving energy instead of drilling for it. This is a false either/or proposition. The country does need a sizable energy tax to reduce consumption. But it needs more production too. Government estimates indicate a nearly fifty-fifty chance that under the ANWR lies one of the five largest oil fields ever discovered in America.

We have just come through a war fought in part over oil: Energy dependence costs Americans not just dollars but lives. It is a bizarre sentimentalism that would deny ourselves oil that is peacefully attainable because it risks disrupting the calving grounds of Arctic caribou.

I like the caribou as much as the next man. And I would be rather sorry if their mating patterns are disturbed. But you can't have everything. And if the choice is between the welfare of caribou and reducing an oil dependency that gets people killed in wars, I choose man over caribou every time.

Similarly the spotted owl. I am no enemy of the owl. If it could be preserved at no or little cost, I would agree: the variety of nature is a good, a high aesthetic good. But it is no more than that. And sometimes aesthetic goods have to be sacrificed to the more fundamental ones. If the cost of preserving the spotted owl is the loss of livelihood for 30,000 logging families, I choose family over owl.

The important distinction is between those environmental goods that are fundamental and those that are merely aesthetic. Nature is our ward. It is not our master. It is to be respected and even cultivated. But it is man's world. And when man has to choose between his well-being and that of nature, nature will have to accommodate.

Man should accommodate only when his fate and that of nature are inextricably bound up. The most urgent accommodation must be made when the very integrity of man's habitat—e.g., atmospheric ozone—is threatened. When the threat to man is of a lesser order (say, the pollutants from coal- and oil-fired generators that cause death from disease but not fatal damage to the ecosystem), a more modulated accommodation that balances economic against health concerns is in order. But in either case the principle is the same: protect the environment—because it is man's environment.

The sentimental environmentalists will call this saving nature with   14
a totally wrong frame of mind. Exactly. A sane—a humanistic—environmentalism does it not for nature's sake but for our own.

READING FOR MEANING

Write at least a page about the meaning of this essay. Begin by briefly restating Krauthammer's position and his primary reason for taking this position. Then write about anything else in the essay that helps you understand the issue, Krauthammer's position, and your reaction.

As you write about your understanding of this selection, you may need to reread all or part of it. Annotate material that may be useful in your writing, and quote some of this material if it helps you develop your ideas. You may find your understanding changing and growing as you write.

If you have difficulty continuing for at least a page, consider the following ideas:

- Explain in your own words what Krauthammer means by "sane environmentalism."

- List the examples Krauthammer gives of environmental necessities. List still others you can think of, and explain briefly why Krauthammer might also accept them as necessities. Then list examples Krauthammer gives of environmental luxuries. Do you agree that these are all luxuries? Explain briefly.

- Whether you agree or disagree with Krauthammer, assess what his argument contributes to the debate over the environment. What is to be gained by reading such arguments? Do you think informed people on both sides who follow the debate closely would value his argument? Explain briefly.

- Krauthammer seems to assume that all adults of voting age who hold jobs ("hardworking voters" [paragraph 6]) are indifferent to the demise of endangered species if to protect them means depriving ordinary citizens of needed benefits. Try to think of one or two other assumptions he makes.

EXTENDING MEANING THROUGH CONVERSATION. If you have not already done so, consider what position you would take on this issue. Then get together with two or three classmates and begin the conversation by telling each other what you think about the issue. Keep the focus of the conversation on the issue and on your responses to Krauthammer's argument. Remember that you do not have to agree; all you have to do is help each other think about Krauthammer's argument and your own arguments.

Looking for Patterns of Opposition

A further strategy for reading for meaning is looking for patterns of opposition. In addition to presenting their own point of view on the issue, writers of position papers also need to represent opposing views. Looking for oppositions is a critical reading strategy that can help you analyze writers' assumptions about their own views as well as their assumptions about opposing views. For example, note that in paragraph 2, Krauthammer introduces two pairs of oppositions. He names the first pair "environmental luxuries and environmental necessities" and the second pair "sane environmentalism."

For guidelines and an illustration of this strategy, turn to the section on Looking for Patterns of Opposition in Appendix 1, A Catalog of Critical Reading Strategies.

READING LIKE A WRITER
COUNTERARGUING

Although counterarguing occasionally involves modifying your position to accommodate objections you consider valid, most often it simply means refuting opposing arguments. Refutation can be a small part of an argument or it can dominate the argument. Experienced writers know that a refutation's effectiveness depends largely on how staunch readers are in defending their opinions. If readers' positions are based on fundamental values and beliefs, then even the most compelling reasons and evidence are unlikely to shake their ideological foundations. But if readers are at all tentative about their views, then refuting their arguments with good counterarguments could influence their thinking.

Because refutation risks antagonizing readers, experienced writers give a lot of consideration to who their readers will be and to the tone they should adopt. A tone that readers perceive as hostile or sarcastic could be alienating, while a tone perceived as witty or cajoling could have the opposite effect of disarming readers and making them less defensive. The more satiric a position paper, though, the more likely it really is addressed to readers who already share the writer's point of view.

ANALYZE. Reread Krauthammer's essay, paying special attention to the tone in the opening paragraph and in paragraphs 5 through 9. Underline words and phrases that strike you as good examples of the tone you perceive. Also, note in the margin where you find evidence of refutation such as renaming or redefining the opposing position or countering an argument with examples. Check to see if Krauthammer acknowledges the validity of any opposing arguments or objections, or if he ever modifies his own position to accommodate the views of others.

WRITE. In a few sentences, report what you have learned about the way Krauthammer counterargues.

COMPARE. Compare Krauthammer's method of counterarguing with that of any of the writers of other selections in this chapter, such as Jill Kuhn, whose essay on sex education in the schools concludes the readings in this chapter.

CONSIDERING IDEAS FOR YOUR OWN WRITING

Krauthammer's essay opens up the possibility for you to write a position paper on some ecological issue, such as: Should we continue to open up off-shore oil fields? Should we keep off-road vehicles out of the desert? Should we require a deposit on canned and bottled goods? Should all households be required to recycle glass, newspapers, plastic, and lawn or garden clippings?

Consider also writing a position paper on some local community issue about quality of life. Following are some possibilities: Should communities provide homeless people with free food and shelter? Should community growth be limited? Should height and design restrictions be placed on new commercial buildings? Should there be a police review board to handle complaints against the police? Should skateboarding be banned from all sidewalks? You and your classmates will think of other possibilities. One major advantage of writing a position paper on local quality-of-life issues is that you could gather information by reading what your community newspaper has reported on the issue and talking to people with different views.

Shelby Steele

AFFIRMATIVE ACTION

The son of a black truck driver and a white social worker, Shelby Steele (b. 1947) grew up in Phoenix, Illinois. He attended Coe College in Cedar Rapids, Iowa. In 1974, he earned a Ph.D. in English from the University of Utah, then joined the faculty of San Jose State University in California, where he is now a professor of English.

A collection of his essays, *The Content of Our Character: A New Vision of Race in America,* won the 1990 National Book Critics Circle Award and was a nationwide best-seller.

Steele's work has appeared in *Harper's,* the *American Scholar,* the *Washington Post,* the *New Republic,* the *Los Angeles Times,* and the *New York Times Book Review.* He won a National Magazine Award in 1989, and one of his essays on race was chosen for "The Best American Essays 1989." He has appeared on many national television shows, including *Nightline, The MacNeil/Lehrer Newshour,* and *Good Morning America.*

In this essay, from *The Content of Our Character,* Steele argues for his position on affirmative action. Affirmative action became national policy in the 1960s as part of an effort to ensure equal opportunity for African Americans and others who have been discriminated against on the basis of race or gender. Publicly supported institutions such as universities and fire departments, for example, must prove that they provide equal opportunity to people who belong to groups historically discriminated against. Opponents argue that affirmative action really gives unfair preferences to individuals even though they personally have never experienced discrimination. Affirmative action was controversial from the beginning, and, in recent years, the Supreme Court has modified the policy.

"Most ordinary Americans," writes William Raspberry, a respected African American columnist, "are torn":

> We understand, on the one hand, the importance of racial (and sexual) fairness and, on the other, the occasional necessity to give justice a boost. . . . What's fair? The answer is likely to change from one place or set of circumstances to another, and, for that reason, it may be impossible for the courts to enunciate any reliable principle. It is, finally, more a political than a judicial question. That's why I think it's important that the rest of us talk about it.

Another reason for us to talk about affirmative action is that, although the issue may seem abstract, it actually impacts the lives of most Americans whatever their race or gender. Before reading Shelby Steele's essay, reflect on your own understanding of affirmative action. What kinds of affirmative action are you aware of—in college admissions, scholarships, job opportunities? Have you ever personally benefited or suffered because of affirmative action? What is your current thinking on the issue?

As you read the essay, notice how Steele represents the spectrum of opinion on this complex, emotion-charged issue. Look for and annotate places where he acknowledges opposing points of view, and consider how he treats people with whom he disagrees.

In a few short years, when my two children will be applying to college, the affirmative action policies by which most universities offer black students some form of preferential treatment will present me with a dilemma. I am a middle-class black, a college professor, far from wealthy, but also well-removed from the kind of deprivation that would qualify my children for the label "disadvantaged." Both of them have endured racial insensitivity from whites. They have been called names, have suffered slights, and have experienced firsthand the peculiar malevolence that racism brings out in people. Yet, they have never experienced racial discrimination, have never been stopped by their race on any path they have chosen to follow. Still, their society now tells them that if they will only designate themselves as black on their college applications, they will likely do better in the college lottery than if they conceal this fact. I think there is something of a Faustian bargain* in this.

Of course, many blacks and a considerable number of whites would say that I was sanctimoniously making affirmative action into a test of character. They would say that this small preference is the meagerest recompense for centuries of unrelieved oppression. And to these arguments other very obvious facts must be added. In America, many marginally competent or flatly incompetent whites are hired everyday—some because their white skin suits the conscious or unconscious racial preference of their employer. The white children of alumni are often grandfathered into elite universities in what can only be seen as a residual benefit of historic white privilege. Worse, white incompetence is always an individual matter, while for blacks it is often confirmation of ugly stereotypes. The Peter Principle** was not conceived with only blacks in mind. Given that unfairness cuts both ways, doesn't it only balance the scales of history that my children now receive a slight preference over whites? Doesn't this repay, in a small way, the systematic denial under which their grandfather lived out his days?

So, in theory, affirmative action certainly has all the moral symmetry that fairness requires—the injustice of historical and even contemporary white advantage is offset with black advantage; preference replaces prejudice, inclusion answers exclusion. It is reformist and corrective, even repentant and redemptive. And I would never sneer at these good intentions. Born in the late forties in Chicago, I started my education (a charitable term in this case) in a segregated school and suffered all the indignities that come to blacks in a segregated society. My father, born in the South, only made it to the third grade before the white man's fields took permanent priority over his formal education. And though he educated himself into an advanced reader with an almost professional authority, he could only drive a truck for a living and never earned more than ninety dollars a week in his entire life. So yes, it is crucial to my sense of citizenship, to my ability to identify with the spirit and the interests of America, to know that this country, however imperfectly, recognizes its past sins and wishes to correct them.

Yet good intentions, because of the opportunity for innocence they offer us, are very seductive and can blind us to the effects they generate when implemented. In our society, affirmative action is, among other things, a testament to white goodwill and to black power, and in the midst of these heavy investments, its effects can be hard to see. But after twenty years of implementation, I think affirmative action has shown itself to be more bad than good and

*Faustian bargain: from the medieval legend of Faust, a pact with the devil (Ed.)

**The Peter Principle: a popular business principle asserting that employees are promoted to the level of their incompetence (Ed.)

that blacks—whom I will focus on in this essay—now stand to lose
more from it than they gain.

In talking with affirmative action administrators and with blacks   5
and whites in general, it is clear that supporters of affirmative action
focus on its good intentions while detractors emphasize its negative
effects. Proponents talk about "diversity" and "pluralism"; opponents speak of "reverse discrimination," the unfairness of quotas
and set-asides. It was virtually impossible to find people outside
either camp. The closest I came was a white male manager at a large
computer company who said, "I think it amounts to reverse discrimination, but I'll put up with a little of that for a little more diversity."
I'll live with a little of the effect to gain a little of the intention,
he seemed to be saying. But this only makes him a halfhearted supporter of affirmative action. I think many people who don't really
like affirmative action support it to one degree or another anyway.

I believe they do this because of what happened to white and   6
black Americans in the crucible of the sixties when whites were
confronted with their racial guilt and blacks tasted their first real
power. In this stormy time white absolution and black power coa-
lesced into virtual mandates for society. Affirmative action became a
meeting ground for these mandates in the law, and in the late sixties
and early seventies it underwent a remarkable escalation of its mission from simple anti-discrimination enforcement to social engineering by means of quotas, goals, timetables, set-asides and other forms
of preferential treatment.

Legally, this was achieved through a series of executive orders   7
and EEOC* guidelines that allowed racial imbalances in the workplace to stand as proof of racial discrimination. Once it could be
assumed that discrimination explained racial imbalances, it became
easy to justify group remedies to presumed discrimination, rather
than the normal case-by-case redress for proven discrimination.
Preferential treatment through quotas, goals, and so on is designed
to correct imbalances based on the assumption that they always
indicate discrimination. This expansion of what constitutes discrimination allowed affirmative action to escalate into the business of
social engineering in the name of anti-discrimination, to push society
toward statistically proportionate racial representation, without any
obligation of proving actual discrimination.

What accounted for this shift, I believe, was the white mandate   8
to achieve a new racial innocence and the black mandate to gain
power. Even though blacks had made great advances during the sixties without quotas, these mandates, which came to a head in the
very late sixties, could no longer be satisfied by anything less than
racial preferences. I don't think these mandates in themselves were
wrong, since whites clearly needed to do better by blacks and blacks

*EEOC: the Equal Employment Opportunity Commission, a federal agency charged
with abolishing discrimination in hiring based on race, gender, and religion (Ed.)

needed more real power in society. But, as they came together in affirmative action, their effect was to distort our understanding of racial discrimination in a way that allowed us to offer the remediation of preference on the basis of mere color rather than actual injury. By making black the color of preference, these mandates have reburdened society with the very marriage of color and preference (in reverse) that we set out to eradicate. The old sin is reaffirmed in a new guise.

But the essential problem with this form of affirmative action is   9
the way it leaps over the hard business of developing a formerly oppressed people to the point where they can achieve proportionate representation on their own (given equal opportunity) and goes straight for the proportionate representation. This may satisfy some whites of their innocence and some blacks of their power, but it does very little to truly uplift blacks.

A white female affirmative action officer at an Ivy League univer-   10
sity told me what many supporters of affirmative action now say: "We're after diversity. We ideally want a student body where racial and ethnic groups are represented according to their proportion in society." When affirmative action escalated into social engineering, diversity became a golden word. It grants whites an egalitarian fairness (innocence) and blacks an entitlement to proportionate representation (power). *Diversity* is a term that applies democratic principles to races and cultures rather than to citizens, despite the fact that there is nothing to indicate that real diversity is the same thing as proportionate representation. Too often the result of this on campuses (for example) has been a democracy of colors rather than of people, an artificial diversity that gives the appearance of an educational parity between black and white students that has not yet been achieved in reality. Here again, racial preferences allow society to leapfrog over the difficult problem of developing blacks to parity with whites and into a cosmetic diversity that covers the blemish of disparity—a full six years after admission, only about 26 percent of black students graduate from college.

Racial representation is not the same thing as racial development,   11
yet affirmative action fosters a confusion of these very different needs. Representation can be manufactured; development is always hard-earned. However, it is the music of innocence and power that we hear in affirmative action that causes us to cling to it and to its distracting emphasis on representation. The fact is that after twenty years of racial preferences, the gap between white and black median income is greater than it was in the seventies. None of this is to say that blacks don't need policies that ensure our right to equal opportunity, but what we need more is the development that will let us take advantage of society's efforts to include us.

I think that one of the most troubling effects of racial preferences   12
for blacks is a kind of demoralization, or put another way, an

enlargement of self-doubt. Under affirmative action the quality that earns us preferential treatment is an implied inferiority. However this inferiority is explained—and it is easily enough explained by the myriad deprivations that grew out of our oppression—it is still inferiority. There are explanations, and then there is the fact. And the fact must be borne by the individual as a condition apart from the explanation, apart even from the fact that others like himself also bear this condition. In integrated situations where blacks must compete with whites who may be better prepared, these explanations may quickly wear thin and expose the individual to racial as well as personal self-doubt.

All of this is compounded by the cultural myth of black inferiority [13] that blacks have always lived with. What this means in practical terms is that when blacks deliver themselves into integrated situations, they encounter a nasty little reflex in whites, a mindless, atavistic reflex that responds to the color black with alarm. Attributions may follow this alarm if the white cares to indulge them, and, if they do, they will most likely be negative—one such attribution is intellectual ineptness. I think this reflex and the attributions that may follow it embarrass most whites today, therefore, it is usually quickly repressed. Nevertheless, on an equally atavistic level, the black will be aware of the reflex his color triggers and will feel a stab of horror at seeing himself reflected in this way. He, too, will do a quick repression, but a lifetime of such stabbings is what constitutes his inner realm of racial doubt.

The effects of this may be a subject for another essay. The point [14] here is that the implication of inferiority that racial preferences engender in both the white and black mind expands rather than contracts this doubt. Even when the black sees no implication of inferiority in racial preferences, he knows that whites do, so that—consciously or unconsciously—the result is virtually the same. The effect of preferential treatment—the lowering of normal standards to increase black representation—puts blacks at war with an expanded realm of debilitating doubt, so that the doubt itself becomes an unrecognized preoccupation that undermines their ability to perform, especially in integrated situations. On largely white campuses, blacks are five times more likely to drop out than whites. Preferential treatment, no matter how it is justified in the light of day, subjects blacks to a midnight of self-doubt, and so often transforms their advantage into a revolving door.

Another liability of affirmative action comes from the fact that it [15] indirectly encourages blacks to exploit their own past victimization as a source of power and privilege. Victimization, like implied inferiority, is what justifies preference, so that to receive the benefits of preferential treatment one must, to some extent, become invested in the view of one's self as a victim. In this way, affirmative action nurtures a victim-focused identity in blacks. The obvious irony here is that we become inadvertently invested in the very condition we are trying to overcome. Racial preferences send us the message that there is more power in our past suffering than our present achievements—none of which could bring us a *preference* over others.

When power itself grows out of suffering, then blacks are encouraged to expand the boundaries of what qualifies as racial oppression, a situation that can lead us to paint our victimization in vivid colors, even as we receive the benefits of preference. The same corporations and institutions that give us preference are also seen as our oppressors. At Stanford University minority students—some of whom enjoy as much as $15,000 a year in financial aid—recently took over the president's office demanding, among other things, more financial aid. The power to be found in victimization, like any power, is intoxicating and can lend itself to the creation of a new class of super-victims who can feel the pea of victimization under twenty mattresses. Preferential treatment rewards us for being underdogs rather than for moving beyond that status—a misplacement of incentives that, along with its deepening of our doubt, is more a yoke than a spur.

But, I think, one of the worst prices that blacks pay for preference has to do with an illusion. I saw this illusion at work recently in the mother of a middle-class black student who was going off to his first semester of college. "They owe us this, so don't think for a minute that you don't belong there." This is the logic by which many blacks, and some whites, justify affirmative action—it is something "owed," a form of reparation. But this logic overlooks a much harder and less digestible reality, that it is impossible to repay blacks living today for the historic suffering of the race. If all blacks were given a million dollars tomorrow morning it would not amount to a dime on the dollar of three centuries of oppression, nor would it obviate the residues of that oppression that we still carry today. The concept of historic reparation grows out of man's need to impose a degree of justice on the world that simply does not exist. Suffering can be endured and overcome, it cannot be repaid. Blacks cannot be repaid for the injustice done to the race, but we can be corrupted by society's guilty gestures of repayment.

Affirmative action is such a gesture. It tells us that racial preferences can do for us what we cannot do for ourselves. The corruption here is in the hidden incentive *not* to do what we believe preferences will do. This is an incentive to be reliant on others just as we are struggling for self-reliance. And it keeps alive the illusion that we can find some deliverance in repayment. The hardest thing for any sufferer to accept is that his suffering excuses him from very little and never has enough currency to restore him. To think otherwise is to prolong the suffering.

Several blacks I spoke with said they were still in favor of affirmative action because of the "subtle" discrimination blacks were subject to once on the job. One photojournalist said, "They have ways of ignoring you." A black female television producer said, "You can't file a lawsuit when your boss doesn't invite you to the insider meetings without ruining your career. So we still need affirmative action." Others mentioned the infamous "glass ceiling" through which blacks can see the top positions of authority but never reach them. But I don't think racial preferences are a protection against this subtle discrimination; I think they contribute to it.

In any workplace, racial preferences will always create two-tiered [20] populations composed of preferreds and unpreferreds. This division makes automatic a perception of enhanced competence for the unpreferreds and of questionable competence for the preferreds— the former earned his way, even though others were given prefer- ence, while the latter made it by color as much as by competence. Racial preferences implicitly mark whites with an exaggerated supe- riority just as they mark blacks with an exaggerated inferiority. They not only reinforce America's oldest racial myth but, for blacks, they have the effect of stigmatizing the already stigmatized.

I think that much of the "subtle" discrimination that blacks talk [21] about is often (not always) discrimination against the stigma of ques- tionable competence that affirmative action delivers to blacks. In this sense, preferences scapegoat the very people they seek to help. And it may be that at a certain level employers impose a glass ceiling, but this may not be against the race so much as against the race's repu- tation for having advanced by color as much as by competence. Affirmative action makes a glass ceiling virtually necessary as a pro- tection against the corruptions of preferential treatment. This ceil- ing is the point at which corporations shift the emphasis from color to competency and stop playing the affirmative action game. Here preference backfires for blacks and becomes a taint that holds them back. Of course, one could argue that this taint, which is, after all, in the minds of whites, becomes nothing more than an excuse to dis- criminate against blacks. And certainly the result is the same in either case—blacks don't get past the glass ceiling. But this argu- ment does not get around the fact that racial preferences now taint this color with a new theme of suspicion that makes it even more vulnerable to the impulse in others to discriminate. In this crucial yet gray area of perceived competence, preferences make whites look better than they are and blacks worse, while doing nothing whatever to stop the very real discrimination that blacks may encounter. I don't wish to justify the glass ceiling here, but only to suggest the very subtle ways that affirmative action revives rather than extinguishes the old rationalizations for racial discrimination.

In education, a revolving door; in employment, a glass ceiling. [22]

I believe affirmative action is problematic in our society because [23] it tries to function like a social program. Rather than ask it to ensure equal opportunity we have demanded that it create parity between

the races. But preferential treatment does not teach skills, or educate, or instill motivation. It only passes out entitlement by color, a
situation that in my profession has created an unrealistically high
demand for black professors. The social engineer's assumption is
that this high demand will inspire more blacks to earn Ph.D.'s and
join the profession. In fact, the number of blacks earning Ph.D.'s has
declined in recent years. A Ph.D. must be developed from preschool
on. He requires family and community support. He must acquire an
entire system of values that enables him to work hard while delaying
gratification. There are social programs, I believe, that can (and
should) help blacks *develop* in all these areas, but entitlement by
color is not a social program; it is a dubious reward for being black.

  It now seems clear that the Supreme Court, in a series of re-   24
cent decisions, is moving away from racial preferences. It has disal-
lowed preferences except in instances of "identified discrimination,"
eroded the precedent that statistical racial imbalances are *prima
facie* evidence of discrimination, and in effect granted white males
the right to challenge consent degrees that use preference to
achieve racial balances in the workplace. One civil rights leader said,
"Night has fallen on civil rights." But I am not sure. The effect of
these decisions is to protect the constitutional rights of everyone
rather than take rights away from blacks. What they do take away
from blacks is the special entitlement to more rights than others
that preferences always grant. Night has fallen on racial preferences,
not on the fundamental rights of black Americans. The reason for
this shift, I believe, is that the white mandate for absolution from
past racial sins has weakened considerably during the eighties.
Whites are now less willing to endure unfairness to themselves in
order to grant special entitlements to blacks, even when these entitlements are justified in the name of past suffering. Yet the black
mandate for more power in society has remained unchanged. And I
think part of the anxiety that many blacks feel over these decisions
has to do with the loss of black power they may signal. We had won
a certain specialness and now we are losing it.

  But the power we've lost by these decisions is really only the   25
power that grows out of our victimization—the power to claim special entitlements under the law because of past oppression. This is
not a very substantial or reliable power, and it is important that we
know this so we can focus more exclusively on the kind of development that will bring enduring power. There is talk now that
Congress will pass new legislation to compensate for these new limits on affirmative action. If this happens, I hope that their focus will
be on development and anti-discrimination rather than entitlement,
on achieving racial parity rather than jerry-building racial diversity.

  I would also like to see affirmative action go back to its original   26
purpose of enforcing equal opportunity—a purpose that in itself
disallows racial preferences. We cannot be sure that the discrim-

inatory impulse in America has yet been shamed into extinction, and I believe affirmative action can make its greatest contribution by providing a rigorous vigilance in this area. It can guard constitutional rather than racial rights, and help institutions evolve standards of merit and selection that are appropriate to the institution's needs yet as free of racial bias as possible (again, with the understanding that racial imbalances are not always an indication of racial bias). One of the most important things affirmative action can do is to define exactly what racial discrimination is and how it might manifest itself within a specific institution. The impulse to discriminate *is* subtle and cannot be ferreted out unless its many guises are made clear to people. Along with this there should be monitoring of institutions and heavy sanctions brought to bear when actual discrimination is found. This is the sort of affirmative action that America owes to blacks and to itself. It goes after the evil of discrimination itself, while preferences only sidestep the evil and grant entitlement to its *presumed* victims.

But if not preferences, then what? I think we need social policies   27
that are committed to two goals: the educational and economic development of disadvantaged people, regardless of race, and the eradication from our society—through close monitoring and severe sanctions—of racial, ethnic, or gender discrimination. Preferences will not deliver us to either of these goals, since they tend to benefit those who are not disadvantaged—middle-class white women and middle-class blacks—and attack one form of discrimination with another. Preferences are inexpensive and carry the glamour of good intentions—change the numbers and the good deed is done. To be against them is to be unkind. But I think the unkindest cut is to bestow on children like my own an undeserved advantage while neglecting the development of those disadvantaged children on the East Side of my city who will likely never be in a position to benefit from a preference. Give my children fairness; give disadvantaged children a better shot at development—better elementary and secondary schools, job training, safer neighborhoods, better financial assistance for college, and so on. Fewer blacks go to college today than ten years ago; more black males of college age are in prison or under the control of the criminal justice system than in college. This despite racial preferences.

The mandates of black power and white absolution out of which   28
preferences emerged were not wrong in themselves. What was wrong was that both races focused more on the goals of these mandates than on the means to the goals. Blacks can have no real power without taking responsibility for their own educational and economic development. Whites can have no racial innocence without earning it by eradicating discrimination and helping the disadvantaged to develop. Because we ignored the means, the goals have not been reached, and the real work remains to be done.

READING FOR MEANING

Write at least a page about your understanding of Steele's essay and your response to it. Begin by stating what you think Steele hopes to accomplish with this essay. Also, speculate about whether he writes for whites or blacks or both, and explain briefly how you decided. Then write about anything else that interests you in Steele's argument.

As you write about your understanding of this selection, you may need to reread all or part of it. Annotate material that may be useful in your writing, and quote some of this material if it helps you develop your ideas. You may find your understanding changing and growing as you write.

If you have difficulty continuing for at least a page, consider the following ideas:

- In paragraphs 12 through 22, Steele argues that affirmative-action programs produce certain unintended and unfortunate effects. Reread these paragraphs, and list the effects. Which effects seem to you most likely and which least likely? Explain briefly.

- Throughout the essay, Steele sets up several contrasts, such as the following: innocence vs. power, group remedies vs. case-by-case redress, preference (or affirmative action) vs. development, representation vs. development, diversity vs. disparity, preference vs. opportunity, diversity vs. parity, constitutional rights vs. racial rights, assumed discrimination vs. actual discrimination. Choose a contrast that you found especially informative or surprising, and explain what it adds to Steele's argument.

- Speculate about how being a member of a particular racial or ethnic group influenced your reading of this essay.

- Explain the possible meaning or significance of any statement that caught your attention. You might want to consider one of the following: "affirmative action . . . does very little to truly uplift blacks" (paragraph 9); "blacks . . . need . . . the development that will let us take advantage of society's efforts to include us" (paragraph 11); "On largely white campuses, blacks are five times more likely to drop out than whites" (paragraph 14); "affirmative action nurtures a victim-focused identity in blacks" (paragraph 15); "Suffering can be endured and overcome, it cannot be repaid" (paragraph 17); "In education, a revolving door; in employment, a glass ceiling" (paragraph 22); or "The impulse to discriminate *is* subtle and cannot be ferreted out unless its many guises are made clear to people" (paragraph 26).

- Write about one question you would like to ask Steele or an objection you have to his argument.

EXTENDING MEANING THROUGH CONVERSATION. To help you develop further your own understanding of the issue as well as your critical perspective on Steele's argument, discuss with two or three classmates this rather long and complex essay. Begin the conversation by taking turns telling each other what you think is the strongest or the weakest part of Steele's argument.

As you exchange your ideas, you will quickly discover where you agree and disagree with Steele and where you are having difficulty understanding his argument. Remember that your goal is not to agree, but rather to use your different ways of understanding the essay to help each other understand it a little better.

READING LIKE A WRITER

ARGUING FOR A POSITION DIRECTLY BY USING
CAUSE-EFFECT REASONING

As suggested throughout this chapter, writers have much to do to create a successful position paper. Central to their efforts, however, must be the argument they make for a position. They may present opposing positions and counterargue, but that does not complete the argument. Readers want to know why the writer holds a position. Readers want reasons and justifications, not only indirectly through counterargument, but directly from the writer.

ANALYZE. Reread paragraphs 12 through 18, where Steele argues directly against affirmative action by exploring its effects. Underline a phrase or sentence that identifies each effect he mentions, and then make notes in the margin that define in your own words the specifics of each effect. Finally, add notes in the margin that identify Steele's strategies of argument. Does he define, illustrate, compare or contrast, give examples, mention a personal experience, or offer statistics?

WRITE. Write several sentences, explaining Steele's argumentative strategies in paragraphs 12 through 18. Illustrate your explanation by referring to specific examples in the text. Then add a few sentences that evaluate Steele's argument. What do you find most and least convincing?

CONSIDERING IDEAS FOR YOUR OWN WRITING

If your position on affirmative action differs from Steele's, consider writing an essay arguing for your position. You could also take a position on other issues currently of national importance, including the following: Should 18-year-olds be allowed to purchase alcoholic drinks or to be served drinks in bars and restaurants? Should parent groups or school boards ban certain books from high-school reading lists? Should AIDS education be required in all schools? Should condoms be distributed free in high schools? Should community service be required for high-school graduation? Should federal loans be available to any high-school graduate who wants to go to college? Should women 18 years old and younger be required to obtain permission from their parents to get an abortion? Because all of these issues are currently being debated—and some have been debated for years—you would need to research any one of them to write an authoritative position paper.

Jill Kuhn

SEX EDUCATION IN OUR SCHOOLS

Jill Kuhn wrote this essay in 1987 for a freshman composition course at California State University, San Bernardino. Her intended readers were parents of junior-high and high-school students.

The issue of sex education is not a new one, and it is likely that you are already familiar with some of the arguments advanced by both sides. You may even have a strong opinion on this issue yourself, possibly influenced by experience with sex-education courses. Before reading Kuhn's essay, take a few minutes to record your thoughts on this issue. Try to recall the various arguments you have heard over the years and what you have felt and thought about it. As you read, you will notice that Kuhn makes effective use of statements by C. Everett Koop, the respected and influential surgeon general in the second Reagan administration.

Even though sex education courses have been taught in many 1
public schools since 1967, the debate still rages over whether it is appropriate to teach sex in the schools. Now that the AIDS epidemic is upon us, we have no choice. As Surgeon General C. Everett Koop said in a report on AIDS: "we have to be as explicit as necessary to get the message across. You can't talk of the dangers of snake poisoning and not mention snakes" (Qtd. in Leo 138).

Everyone agrees that ideally sex education ought to be taught at 2
home by parents. But apparently it is either not taught at all or taught ineffectively. The Sorenson report found, for example, that over 70 percent of the adolescents studied do not talk freely about sex with their parents (Gordon 5). They complain that while their parents tend to lecture them on morality and speak in abstractions, what they need is to learn specific facts about sex and contraception. A study done on 1,873 youths found that 67 percent of the boys and 29 percent of the girls had never been given any advice on sex by their parents and, moreover, "of those who were 'advised' more than two-thirds of the boys and one-fourth of the girls felt that neither of their parents had helped them to deal effectively with the problem of sex" (Gordon 8).

Many people oppose sex education courses because they assume 3
that students are more likely to have sex after taking a course in it. Phyllis Schlafly, for example, claims that "the way sex education is taught in the schools encourages experimentation" (Leo 138). A study by Laurie Schwab Zabin comparing sexually inexperienced female high-school students with access to sex education and those without access found, however, that those with sex education

tended to postpone their first sexual experience until they were an average of seven months older than those without sex education (Leo 140).

According to the statistics, teenagers have sex, and nothing their parents or anyone else says is going to stop them. "Of the 29 million teenagers between the ages of thirteen and nineteen," according to Madelon Lubin Finkel and Steven Finkel, "12 million (41.1%) are estimated to have had sexual intercourse" (49). Moreover, they estimate that "more than one-fifth of first premarital pregnancies among teenagers occurred within the first month of initiating sex."

Surely it is preferable for sexually active adolescents to have accurate information about sex and contraception than to live in ignorance. And they are amazingly ignorant. Takey Crist administered a questionnaire on sexual anatomy to six hundred female students at the University of North Carolina at Chapel Hill, and found that among sexually active women, over one-fourth could not answer any of the questions (Gordon 19). In a nationwide study, 41 percent of the pregnant unmarried teenagers polled said that they had thought they could not get pregnant because, as they put it, "it was the wrong time of the month" (Finkel and Finkel 49). A study of unwed pregnant teenagers in Baltimore found that less than half could name three kinds of birth control and that one-third of those who did not use contraceptives were unaware that they could have used them (Gordon 19). An astonishing 91 percent of those questioned felt that they lacked adequate knowledge about how to use birth control.

Sex education courses dispel myths and misconceptions about sexual behavior in general and birth control in particular. A course taught in twenty-three Atlanta public schools entitled "Postponing Sexual Involvement" was developed specifically in answer to students' requests for help in learning how to say no without hurting anyone's feelings (Leo 142). Adrienne Davis, a health educator at UCLA, makes self-esteem the central issue in her sex education teaching (Leo 141). Although as Marilyn Hurwitz explains, adolescent sex tends to be "spontaneous, based on passion and the moment, not thought and reason," a Johns Hopkins University study of sexually active teenagers concluded that teaching about birth control "significantly increases the likelihood" that they will use contraceptives (Leo 140).

The advent of AIDS makes sex education a necessity rather than a luxury. Surgeon General Koop's report on AIDS calls for sex education to begin "at an early age, so that children can grow up knowing the behaviors to avoid to protect themselves from exposure to the AIDS virus" (Qtd. in Lewis 348). But he also emphasizes the need to focus sex education on teenagers because even though they may consider themselves invulnerable, they are actually at great risk: "adolescents and preadolescents are those whose behavior we wish especially to influence because of their vulnerability when they are exploring their own sexuality (heterosexual and homosexual) and perhaps experimenting with drugs." At least 2.5 million teenagers, according to the American Social Health Association, contract a sexually transmitted disease every year, including AIDS (Lewis 348). In fact, comparisons between Army recruits in the New York City area and the general population show that a much higher proportion of young people test positive for HIV, the virus believed to cause AIDS, and that the incidence of positive tests is "stunningly high" among minority recruits.

Parents can no longer afford to be overprotective. If they truly   8
want to protect their children, they must give up the fantasy that what their sons and daughters don't know, won't hurt them. Sex kills, and we must teach our children how to defend themselves. It is not enough to preach, "Just say no!" Adolescents always have and will continue to explore their own sexuality. What they need from us is information and openness. Parents certainly have a key role to play, but they cannot do it alone. Sex education must be taught in the schools and, as the surgeon general urges, it should begin in the early grades.

Works Cited

Finkel, Madelon Lubin, and Steven Finkel. "Sex Education in High School." *Society* (Nov./Dec. 1985): 48–51.

Gordon, Sol. *The Sexual Adolescent.* North Scituate, MA: Duxbury, 1973.

Leo, John. "Should Schools Offer Sex Education?" *Reader's Digest* Mar. 1987: 138–42.

Lewis, Ann C. "A Dangerous Silence." *Phi Delta Kappan* (June 1987): 348–49.

READING FOR MEANING

Write at least a page about your understanding of Kuhn's essay. Begin by writing a few sentences about Kuhn's attitude toward her readers, the parents of teenagers. What does she hope to accomplish with them? How does she approach them? How can you tell? Then write about anything else in the essay that interests you.

As you write about your understanding of this selection, you may need to reread all or parts of it. Annotate material that may be useful in your writing; quote some of this material if it helps you develop your ideas. Your understanding may change and grow as you write.

Consider the following suggestions if you need help continuing for at least a page:

- Describe sex-education courses or lessons that you remember from your school days. Connect your experience to Kuhn's argument by explaining how it might support or challenge her argument.

- Write about what seems to you to be missing from Kuhn's argument.
- Explain how your personal belief that sex education should or should not be offered by schools influences your response to Kuhn's argument. Point to specific parts of her argument.
- No one challenges school programs in nutrition and health, yet many parents question or oppose sex-education programs. Speculate about why this is so, connecting your speculations to Kuhn's argument.

EXTENDING MEANING THROUGH CONVERSATION. You can learn more about the essay by discussing it with two or three other students who have also read and analyzed it. Before your meeting, reread what you have written, and reflect on your current understanding of the issue and Kuhn's argument. Start the conversation by telling each other what you think is the best part of Kuhn's essay.

As you share your ideas and responses to the essay, you will likely find that you have different views. Explore these differences by rereading problematic passages together and discussing how you understand and respond to them.

Evaluating the Logic of an Argument

To be convincing, a position paper's argument must seem logical to readers; that is, it must make sense to them. You can systematically analyze and assess the logic of an argument by looking at whether the reasons and evidence support the writer's position.

To learn more about the logic of Kuhn's argument and to evaluate it thoroughly, follow the guidelines for Evaluating the Logic of an Argument in Appendix 1, A Catalog of Critical Reading Strategies.

READING LIKE A WRITER
MAKING AN ESSAY READABLE

Writers strive to present a clear, convincing argument. They understand that readers who disagree may be eager for an excuse to reject their argument or to stop reading; for example, if the writing is unclear or the organization is hard to follow. Writers of position papers, therefore, usually go to some effort to make their writing clear and coherent, easy for readers to follow from point to point even when the argument is fairly complicated.

ANALYZE. Reread Kuhn's essay, writing phrases in the margin that identify both the topic of each paragraph and its apparent role or purpose in the argument. Although connections between paragraphs can remain implicit, usually they are made explicit. Annotate how Kuhn makes them explicit, and when she does. Consider how you would divide her essay into two or three main parts. Notice particularly how she frames her argument by relating the end to the beginning (paragraphs 1–2 and 8).

WRITE. Write several sentences, explaining and evaluating how Kuhn sequences, connects, and frames her argument.

COMPARE. Choose any other position paper in this chapter to analyze. Use the same procedure you followed in analyzing the readability of Kuhn's essay. Note any similarities and differences between Kuhn's essay and the essay that you choose in relation to the strategies used to make the essay readable; for example, the explicitness of transitions connecting paragraphs, forecasting and sequencing the main points, the use of framing. Then write a few more sentences, explaining what you have learned from comparing how writers of position papers make their essays readable.

CONSIDERING IDEAS FOR YOUR OWN WRITING

What other controversial issues that relate to adolescence can you think of? List issues you think you might want to know more about. Here are a few possibilities to get you started: bilingual education, censorship of popular recordings, competency testing. Choose an issue from your list to explore as a possible topic for an essay. How would you go about researching both sides of the issue and developing an argument to support your position?

THINKING ABOUT WHAT MAKES POSITION PAPERS EFFECTIVE

You have been learning in this chapter how to read position papers—reading for meaning and reading like a writer. Before writing a position paper of your own, pause now to review what you have learned about effective position-paper writing.

ANALYZE. Choose one reading from this chapter that seems to you to be especially effective. Before rereading the selection, write down one or two things that lead you to remember it as a good position paper.

Reread your chosen selection, adding to your annotations further annotations about what makes it particularly successful as an argument. Begin by considering the essay's purpose and how well it achieves that purpose for its readers. Then focus on how well the selection

- defines the issue
- asserts the position
- argues directly for the position
- counterargues readers' objections and questions
- makes the essay readable

You can complete this activity on your own, or your instructor may ask you to work collaboratively with two or three other students who have chosen the same reading. If you work with others, take time initially for everyone to reread the selection thoughtfully, adding to their annotations as suggested above. Then discuss what makes this particular position paper so effective. Take notes. Someone in your group can later report to the class what you have learned about the effectiveness of position-paper writing, or you can individually write up what you have learned.

WRITE. Write at least a page, explaining and justifying your choice of this reading as a good position paper. Assume that your readers—your instructor and classmates—have read the selection but will not remember many details about it. They also may not remember it as an especially successful position paper. Therefore, you will want to use details and refer to specific parts of the essay as you explain how it works and justify your evaluation of its effectiveness. You need not argue that it is the best reading in the chapter or that it is flawless, only that it is, in your view, an excellent example of the genre.

A GUIDE TO WRITING POSITION PAPERS

As the selections in this chapter indicate, the position paper can be an intricate piece of writing, or it can be simple and direct. The complexity of a particular essay will depend on how complicated the issue is and how the argument is constructed. Writers of position papers must be very much aware of their readers. Because they may be writing to people with whom they disagree on the issue, they must make a special effort to gain their readers' confidence and respect. Probably the best way of doing this is by presenting a coherent, well-reasoned argument. The following guide suggests activities to help you invent, draft, read critically, and revise a position paper of your own.

INVENTION

Invention is especially important in writing a position paper because there is so much to consider as you write: how you might present the issue and indicate its significance; what opposing positions you should discuss and how you should represent them; what reasons and evidence you could offer to support your position and in what order; and what tone would be most appropriate for the particular subject and audience. The following invention activities will help you focus your thinking on these writing issues.

Choosing an Arguable Issue

Most authors of position papers choose issues about which they feel strongly and about which they already know a good deal. If you do not have a specific issue in mind, consider the issues listed in the Considering Ideas for Your Own

Writing sections that follow each selection in this chapter. You can discover other possibilities by reading newspapers or newsmagazines.

Make a list of the possibilities you are considering, indicating what you think each issue involves and what position you are presently inclined to take on it. The ideal issue will be one about which you have already formed an opinion; in writing about this issue you will have an opportunity to examine your own point of view critically. Also, your writing task will be easier if you can choose an issue on which there is a clear division of opinion. Keep in mind that the issue should be truly arguable on reasonable grounds; matters of personal morality based on religious belief or other deeply held convictions may be difficult to support or refute with fact and reasoning.

After you have selected an issue, you may need to do some background research on it, particularly if the issue is one that you have not thought very much about until now. If you need more information at this point, go to the library or interview some people. You should not get too caught up in the process of doing research, however, until you are fairly sure of your audience, because knowledge of your readers will influence the kind of information you decide to use in your paper. Remember too that you are planning to write a persuasive essay, not a report of what others think about the issue. You can certainly cite authorities, but the essay should represent your best thinking on the subject, not someone else's.

Analyzing Your Readers

Most position papers are set up as a debate in which the writer addresses readers who hold an opposing position. You may, however, choose to address your essay to readers who are undecided about the issue. At this stage in your planning, you should try to identify your prospective audience. Write a few sentences, profiling your readers. What are their views on the issue? What reasons do they most often give for their opinions? What kinds of evidence do they use to support their opinions? What basic assumptions or values underlie their claims? What are the historical, political, or ideological dimensions to their views? What kinds of personal experiences and beliefs are you likely to have in common with these readers? On what basis might you build a bridge of shared concerns with them? What kinds of arguments might carry weight with them?

LEARNING MORE ABOUT YOUR READERS:
A COLLABORATIVE ACTIVITY

Your instructor may make it possible for you to get together with two or three other students at this point in your invention process. In turn, tell each other the issue you plan to write about and the position for which you want to argue. Then your partners will tell you what they think about the issue and why. Do not try to defend your position or argue with them. Simply ask them questions that will help you understand how your prospective readers may think about the issue. Try to get them to reveal the assumptions and values that lead them to see the issue as they do.

Because you have only just begun thinking about your argument and how best to convey it to readers, you can benefit greatly from seeing how your partners react to your way of defining the issue and the statement of your position. Listen to what they have to say. They may have insights you can use to deepen your own understanding of the issue. Their responses will also enable you to better anticipate what readers will be thinking when they read your argument and, therefore, can help you make it more convincing.

Tentatively Stating Your Thesis

Having identified the issue and audience, try stating what you now think will be the position, or thesis, of your position paper. You will undoubtedly need to refine this statement as you clarify your position and develop your argument, but stating it tentatively here will help focus the rest of your invention.

Exploring Your Reasons

Now that you have chosen a promising issue and analyzed your prospective readers, you should devote your energies to exploring your own reasons for holding your position. Do this with your readers in mind, setting up a debate between yourself and your readers.

Divide a page in half vertically, and list your reasons in the left-hand column and your readers' possible responses to each reason in the right-hand column. You may not know how your readers will respond to every point you make, of course, but you should try to put yourself in their place and decide whether there are any objections they could make or on what grounds they might accept the point. Leave a space of about five lines between each of your reasons. Then use that space to develop the reason and to indicate what kinds of evidence you might use to support it. Planning an argument this way is likely to be messy, particularly if you move frequently from one column to the other. Although it may seem chaotic, this can be a very productive invention activity. These notes may serve as a rough outline after you have decided which are your best arguments and in what order you should arrange them.

Restating Your Thesis

Look back at your earlier tentative thesis statement, and revise it to conform to what you have discovered in exploring your argument. You may need only to make minor revisions to signal how you have modified or qualified your position. Or you may need to rewrite the entire statement to account for your new understanding of the issue.

DRAFTING

After a thoughtful and thorough invention process, you are ready to set goals for drafting, plan your draft, and consider how to begin the essay and avoid logical fallacies.

Setting Goals

Before writing, reorient yourself by setting goals that reflect your purpose and audience. Ask yourself specifically what you want to accomplish by writing to these readers about this issue. Are you chiefly interested in presenting your opinion to readers who will tend to agree with you? Do you want to convince readers who are basically uncommitted? Do you want to draw in readers who oppose your view and change their minds? Consider whether you are being realistic. Remember that some issues—capital punishment, for example—are so deeply rooted in values and beliefs that it is very hard to get people to change their minds. The most you can hope to do is either present your own best argument or get readers to reexamine the issue from a more objective point of view.

Consider how familiar your readers already are with the issue. If you think it is new to them, you will need to help them understand why it is important, as Meadows does when she argues that the kind of debate practiced on talk shows is anti-democratic—dedicated "to ridiculing the opposition" rather than "to finding the truth." However, if you assume readers are familiar with the issue, you might try to get them to see it in a new light. For example, because Teresi assumes that his readers will dismiss bikers' objections to helmet laws as trivial, a sign of their rebellion against authority, he tries to demonstrate that helmets cause more harm than good. It is usually safe to assume that your readers have not explored the issue as thoroughly as you, and you will therefore need to identify the main issues at stake and define the key terms.

Consider also which of your readers' values and assumptions correspond to your own. If, for example, you are writing about something your readers are likely to fear or detest, acknowledge their feelings as legitimate, and show that you share their concerns.

Finally, think of the kinds of arguments that would be most likely to convince your particular readers on this issue. Will they respect the judgment of authorities with their research studies and statistics, as Kuhn apparently assumes? Will they be especially responsive to arguments based on principle, as Bates believes?

Planning Your Draft

With these goals in mind, reread the invention writing you did under the exploring your reasons section. You should now be able to order your reasons and outline your argument. Writers often begin and end with the strongest reasons, putting weaker ones in the middle. This organization gives the best reasons the greatest emphasis. Meadows more or less follows this pattern. Another common plan is to begin with a definition like Bates does, letting the definition carry most of the argument's weight. Krauthammer organizes his essay around a refutation of opponents' arguments, while Teresi and Steele use both counter-argument and direct argument.

Beginning

The opening of a position paper sets the tone, identifies the issue, and usually establishes the writer's position. In deciding how to begin, think again about your readers and their attitudes toward the issue. Teresi, for example, begins by invoking the stereotypical image of motorcycle riders with the wind in their hair to show that helmet laws have destroyed this idyllic experience. Bates cites several examples to show that schools tailor the educational experience for many students, as they can for fundamentalist Christians as well. Krauthammer sets up an ironic view of the position he will argue against.

Avoiding Logical Fallacies

Arguing about controversial issues demands probably the most difficult kind of reasoning because emotions run high and issues tend to be extremely complex. To avoid making errors in your argument, ask yourself the following questions as you plan and draft your essay:

- Am I making *sweeping generalizations* (for instance, assuming that if killing is morally wrong, then state-licensed murder must also be wrong)?
- Am I committing an *ad hominem attack* on my opponents (criticizing their intelligence or motives rather than their arguments)?
- Am I *oversimplifying* the issue (making a complex issue seem simple)?
- Am I guilty of *either/or reasoning* (assuming that there are only two positions on an issue: yours and theirs)?
- Am I building a *straw man* (representing the opposition's argument unfairly so that I can knock it down easily)?

READING A DRAFT CRITICALLY

Now that you have written a draft, you need someone to take a close look at what you have written and to advise you on how to improve your draft. The suggestions in this section will ensure that you get helpful advice. Ask your reader to provide a written record of all comments so later, when you sit down to revise, you will have specific suggestions to follow.

Remember that reading a draft critically means reading it more than once, first to get a general impression and then to analyze its basic features and strategies. Before you begin reading, number the paragraphs for easy reference to specific parts of the draft.

Reading for a First Impression

Read quickly through the draft to get a sense of the argument. Then write a few sentences describing your general impression: How clear is the issue? How clear is the writer's position? What in the argument seems most and least convincing?

Reading to Analyze

Read the essay a second time to focus on the basic features and strategies of the position paper.

DEFINING THE ISSUE. Locate where the issue is defined. Point to any places where you do not understand what is being said about the issue or why. Ask questions. If you are surprised by the way the writer has presented the issue, possibly by the terms used to define it, briefly explain how you usually think of the issue.

ASSERTING THE POSITION CLEARLY AND UNEQUIVOCALLY. Find the clearest statement of the position and underline it. If you cannot find a clear thesis, let the writer know. If you find several restatements of the thesis, examine them closely for consistency. If the position seems extreme or overstated, suggest how it might be qualified to be more reasonable.

ARGUING DIRECTLY FOR THE POSITION. Number the reasons. Consider each reason in turn, looking at how it is explained and supported. Apply the ABC test for Evaluating the Logic of an Argument (see Appendix 1, A Catalog of Critical Reading Strategies). Indicate any reasons that need to be explained more clearly or supported more convincingly. Suggest what could be added or cut.

Look for faulty reasoning. Note any sweeping generalizations (broad statements asserted without support). Indicate whether the issue has been oversimplified or whether either/or reasoning (unfairly limiting the argument to only two alternatives) is being used. Let the writer know whether you think the essay unfairly manipulates readers' feelings; point to an example of manipulation and explain what bothers you about it.

COUNTERARGUING. Look for places where other positions on the issue are mentioned and where readers' possible objections or questions are anticipated. Pay special attention to the writer's tone in discussing opposing views or responding to objections. If you think the tone is inappropriate, point to an example and suggest how you would change it. Note any areas of potential agreement that could be emphasized more. Suggest how the writer could strengthen the refutation.

Again look for faulty reasoning. Point out any personal attacks on opponents rather than on their reasons and evidence. Notice whether only the weakest objections or opposing arguments have been acknowledged, thus misrepresenting the strength of the opposition.

READABILITY. Look at how the essay is organized. Consider whether the beginning adequately sets the stage for the argument, perhaps by establishing the tone or forecasting the points of the argument. If the organization does not seem to follow a logical plan, suggest how it might be rearranged or where transitions could be inserted to strengthen the logical connections. Note whether the ending gives the argument a satisfactory sense of closure.

REVISING

No amount of invention and planning can ensure that a draft will be complete and perfectly organized. In fact, as you draft you are likely to discover new and important points to make. You may also encounter unanticipated problems that require radical rethinking or restructuring of your essay.

Keeping in mind any advice you may have received from your instructor or other students about improving your draft, reread it carefully making a list of the two or three major problems you now think you will need to solve as well as any new dimensions you may want to add when you revise your draft. To solve these problems, you may need to make minor alterations or major changes in your draft, substitute or cut particular words, write new sentences, or rearrange the parts of your essay. At this point, focus only on the basic features of arguing a position, not on editing punctuation or other sentence-level problems.

In this section, we offer many suggestions for revising.

Revising to Define the Issue

If the issue seems too abstract or unimportant, consider adding anecdotes, examples, or graphic details to give the issue relevance and importance for readers.

If the way you define the issue polarizes opinion unnecessarily, change your language to be less extreme or make concessions to demonstrate your goodwill.

If the terms with which you define the issue seem odd to readers, try redefining the issue in more familiar terms or explaining more systematically why you see the issue as you do.

Revising to Assert the Position More Clearly

If the position seems unclear to readers, try reformulating it or spelling it out in more detail.

If your position is implied but not explicitly expressed, try to state it more directly to avoid misunderstanding.

If your thesis is not appropriately qualified to account for valid arguments or objections, modify it by limiting its scope.

Revising to Strengthen the Direct Argument

If readers have difficulty finding or separating your reasons, announce them explicitly.

If any of your reasons seem vague or weak, delete or explain those reasons more fully. Consider classifying your reasons or using comparison or contrast to show how one reason relates to another.

If your evidence seems weak or scanty, review your invention notes or do more research to find facts, statistics, quotations, or examples to bolster your evidence.

If you use any sweeping generalizations, try to be more specific and to support your assertions with specific evidence and examples.

If you have oversimplified the argument—for example, by using either/or reasoning—add some qualifying language that shows you are aware of the issue's true complexity.

Revising to Strengthen the Counterargument

If you can make any concessions without doing injustice to your own views consider doing so. Try to find common ground with readers by acknowledging the legitimacy of their concerns. Show readers where you share their values, interests, and assumptions.

If your refutation seems unconvincing, provide more or better evidence, such as facts and statistics from reputable sources, to convince readers that your argument is not idiosyncratic or personal. Avoid attacking your opponents; refute only their ideas.

If you have ignored strong, opposing arguments or reasonable objections, take account of them. If you cannot refute them, acknowledge their validity— and, if necessary, modify your position to accommodate them.

Revising to Improve Readability

If the beginning seems dull or unfocused, rewrite it perhaps by adding a surprising or vivid anecdote.

If readers have trouble following your argument, consider adding a brief forecast of your main points at the beginning of your essay.

If the reasons and counterarguments are not logically arranged, reorder them. Consider announcing each reason more explicitly or adding transitions to make the connections clearer.

If the ending seems weak or vague, search your invention notes or your draft for a memorable quotation or a vivid example to add.

REFLECTING ON WHAT YOU HAVE LEARNED ABOUT WRITING POSITION PAPERS

In this chapter, you have read critically several position papers and have written one of your own. To remind yourself how much you have learned and to help you remember it, pause now to reflect on your reading and writing experiences while working on the activities in this chapter.

Write a page or so reflecting on your learning. Describe what you are most pleased with in your essay and explain what contributed to your achievement. Be very specific about this contribution. If what you learned was from the readings, indicate which readings and specifically what you learned from them. If it came from your invention writing, point out the section or sections that helped you most. If you got good advice from a critical reader, explain exactly how the person helped you—perhaps to understand a particular problem in your draft or to add a new dimension to your writing. Try to write about your achievement in terms of what you have learned about the genre.

———

A CATALOG OF CRITICAL READING STRATEGIES

———

Serious study of a text requires a pencil in hand—how much pride that pencil carries.

IRVING HOWE

Here we present fourteen specific strategies for reading critically, strategies that you can learn readily and then apply not only to the selections in this text but also to your other college reading. Mastering these strategies may not make the critical reading process any easier, but it can make reading much more satisfying and productive and thus help you handle difficult material with confidence. These strategies are

- *Annotating:* recording your reactions to and questions about a text directly on the page
- *Previewing:* learning about a text before reading it closely
- *Outlining:* listing the main idea of each paragraph in your own words
- *Summarizing:* relying on your own words to present the main ideas
- *Paraphrasing:* relying on your own words to restate and clarify the meaning
- *Questioning to understand and remember:* asking questions about the content
- *Contextualizing:* placing a text in its historical and cultural contexts
- *Reflecting on challenges to your beliefs and values:* examining your responses to reveal your own unexamined assumptions and attitudes
- *Exploring the significance of figurative language:* seeing how metaphors, similes, and symbols enhance meaning
- *Looking for patterns of opposition:* discovering what a text values by analyzing its system of oppositions
- *Evaluating the logic of an argument:* testing the logic of a text to see if it makes sense

- *Recognizing emotional manipulation:* looking for false or exaggerated appeals
- *Judging the writer's credibility:* determining whether what a writer says can be trusted
- *Comparing and contrasting related readings:* exploring likenesses and differences between texts to understand them better

ANNOTATING

For each of these strategies, annotating directly on the page—underlining key words, phrases, or sentences; writing comments or questions in the margins; bracketing important sections of the text; connecting ideas with lines or arrows; numbering related points in sequence; making note of anything that strikes you as interesting, important, or questionable—is fundamental. (If writing on the text itself is impossible or undesirable, you can annotate on a photocopy.)

Most readers annotate in layers, adding further annotations on second and third readings. Annotations can be light or heavy, depending on the reader's purpose and the difficulty of the material. You will annotate some of the essays in this book heavily to analyze the rhetorical features each writer uses as well as to explore the writer's ideas and your reactions to them. (Chapter 1 discusses annotating in greater detail.)

For several of the strategies, you will need to build on and extend annotating by *taking inventory:* analyzing and classifying your annotations, searching systematically for patterns in the text, and interpreting their significance. An inventory is basically a list. When you take inventory, you make various kinds of lists in order to find meaning in a text.

As you review your annotations on a particular reading, you may discover that the language and ideas cluster in various ways.

Inventorying annotations is a three-step process:

1. Examine your annotations for patterns or repetitions of any kind, such as recurring images or stylistic features, related words and phrases, similar examples, or reliance on authorities.
2. Try out different ways of grouping the items.
3. Consider what the patterns you have found suggest about the meaning or writer's rhetorical choices.

The patterns you discover will depend on the kind of reading you are analyzing and on the purpose of your analysis. (See Exploring the Significance of Figurative Language and Looking for Patterns of Oppositions in this appendix for examples of inventorying annotations.)

The following selection has been annotated to demonstrate the kinds of thinking and annotating required by the critical reading strategies we describe in the rest of this catalog. As you read about each strategy, you will be referred back to this annotated example.

Martin Luther King, Jr.

AN ANNOTATED SAMPLE
FROM "LETTER FROM BIRMINGHAM JAIL"

Martin Luther King, Jr. (1929–1968) first came to national notice in 1955, when he led a successful boycott against back-of-the-bus seating of African Americans in Montgomery, Alabama, where he was minister of a Baptist church. He subsequently formed a national organization, the Southern Christian Leadership Conference, that brought people of all races from all over the country to the South to fight nonviolently for racial integration. In 1963, King led demonstrations in Birmingham that were met with violence: a black church was bombed, killing four little girls. King was arrested and, while in prison, wrote the famous "Letter from Birmingham Jail" to answer local clergy's criticism. (The complete text of King's "Letter from Birmingham Jail" followed by the clergymen's published criticism appears at the end of this appendix.)

The following brief reading selection is excerpted from the letter and annotated to illustrate some of the ways you can annotate as you read. Since annotating is the first step for all critical reading strategies in this catalog, these annotations are referred to throughout this appendix. Add you own annotations in the right-hand margin. King begins by discussing his disappointment with the lack of support he received from white moderates, such as the group of clergy who published their criticism in the local newspaper.

¶1 White moderates block progress

order vs. justice

negative vs. positive

ends vs. means

treating others like children

. . . I must confess that over the past few years I have been gravely disappointed with the white moderate. I have almost reached the regrettable conclusion that the Negro's [great stumbling block in his stride toward freedom] is not the White Citizen's Counciler or the Ku Klux Klanner, but the white moderate, who is more devoted to "order" than to justice; who prefers a negative peace which is the absence of tension to a positive peace which is the presence of justice; who constantly says: "I agree with you in the goal you seek, but I cannot agree with your methods of direct action"; who paternalistically believes he can set the timetable for another man's freedom; who lives by a mythical concept of time and who constantly advises the Negro to wait for a "more convenient season." Shallow understanding from people of good will is more frustrating than absolute misunderstanding from people of ill will. [Lukewarm acceptance is much more bewildering than outright rejection.]

¶2 Tension necessary for progress

I had hoped that the white moderate would understand that law and order exist for the purpose of establishing justice and that when they fail in this purpose they become the [dangerously structured

1

2

dams that block the flow of social progress.] I had hoped that the white moderate would understand that the present tension in the South is a necessary phase of the transition from an [obnoxious negative peace,] in which the Negro passively accepted his unjust plight, to a [substantive and positive peace,] in which all men will respect the dignity and worth of human personality. Actually, we who engage in nonviolent direct action are not the creators of tension. We merely bring to the surface the hidden tension that is already alive. We bring it out in the open, where it can be seen and dealt with. [Like a boil that can never be cured so long as it is covered up but must be opened with all its ugliness to the natural medicines of air and light, injustice must be exposed, with all the tension its exposure creates, to the light of human conscience and the air of national opinion before it can be cured.]

In your statement you assert that our actions, even though peaceful, must be condemned because they precipitate violence. But is this a logical assertion? Isn't this like condemning [a robbed man] because his possession of money precipitated the evil act of robbery? Isn't this like condemning [Socrates] because his unswerving commitment to truth and his philosophical inquiries precipitated the act by the misguided populace in which they made him drink hemlock? Isn't this like condemning [Jesus] because his unique God-consciousness and never-ceasing devotion to God's will precipitated the evil act of crucifixion? We must come to see that, as the federal courts have consistently affirmed, it is wrong to urge an individual to cease his efforts to gain his basic constitutional rights because the question may precipitate violence. [Society must protect the robbed and punish the robber.]

I had also hoped that the white moderate would reject the myth concerning time in relation to the struggle for freedom. I have just received a letter from a white brother in Texas. He writes: "All Christians know that the colored people will receive equal rights eventually, but it is possible that you are in too great a religious hurry. It has taken Christianity almost two thousand years to accomplish what it has. The teachings of Christ take time to come to earth." Such an attitude stems from a tragic misconception of time, from the strangely irrational notion that there is something in the very flow of time that will inevitably cure all ills. [Actually, time itself is neutral; it can be used either destructively or constructively.] More and more I feel that the people of ill will have used time much more effectively than have the people of good will. We will have to repent in this generation not merely for the [hateful words and actions of the bad people] but for the [appalling silence of the good people.] Human progress never rolls in on [wheels of inevitability;] it comes through the tireless efforts of men willing to be co-workers with God, and without this hard work, time itself becomes an ally of the forces of social stagnation. [We must use time creatively,

elegy=death, psalm= celebration

metaphors: quicksand, rock

¶5 *Refutes criticism*
King not an extremist

Complacency vs. hatred

Malcolm X?

¶6 *Claims to offer better choice*

¶7 *Claims his movement pre- vents racial violence.*

If...Then... Veiled threat?

¶8 *Change inevitable: evo- lution or rovo lution?*

spirit of the times

Worldwide uprising against injustice

in the knowledge that the time is always ripe to do right.] Now is the time to make real the promise of democracy and transform our pending [national elegy] into a creative [psalm of brotherhood.] Now is the time to lift our national policy from the [quicksand of racial injustice] to the [solid rock of human dignity.]

You speak of our activity in Birmingham as extreme. At first I was rather disappointed that fellow clergymen would see my nonviolent efforts as those of an extremist. I began thinking about the fact that I stand in the middle of two opposing forces in the Negro community. One is a [force of complacency,] made up in part of Negroes who, as a result of long years of oppression, are so drained of self-respect and a sense of "somebodiness" that they have adjusted to segrega-tion; and in part of a few middle-class Negroes, who because of a degree of academic and economic security and because in some ways they profit by segregation, have become insensitive to the problems of the masses. The other [force is one of bitterness and hatred,] and it comes perilously close to advocating violence. It is expressed in the various black nationalist [groups that are springing up] across the nation, the largest and best-known being Elijah Muhammad's Muslim movement. Nourished by the Negro's frustra-tion over the continued existence of racial discrimination, this movement is made up of people who have lost faith in America, who have absolutely repudiated Christianity, and who have concluded that the white man is an incorrigible "devil."

I have tried to stand between these two forces, saying that we need emulate neither the "do-nothingism" of the complacent nor the hatred and despair of the black nationalist. For there is the more excellent way of love and nonviolent protest. I am grateful to God that, through the influence of the Negro church, the way of nonvio-lence became an integral part of our struggle.

If this philosophy had not emerged, by now many streets of the South would, I am convinced, be flowing with blood. And I am fur-ther convinced that if our white brothers dismiss as "rabble-rousers" and "outside agitators" those of us who employ nonviolent direct action, and if they refuse to support our nonviolent efforts, millions of Negroes will, out of frustration and despair, seek solace and security in black-nationalist ideologies—a development that would inevitably lead to a frightening racial nightmare.

[Oppressed people cannot remain oppressed forever.] The yearning for freedom eventually manifests itself, and that is what has happened to the American Negro. Something within has reminded him of his birthright of freedom, and something without has remind-ed him that it can be gained. Consciously or unconsciously, he has been caught up by the Zeitgeist and with his black brothers of Africa and his brown and yellow brothers of Asia, South America and the Caribbean, the United States Negro is moving with a sense of great urgency toward the [promised land of racial justice.] If one recog-

5

6

7

8

nizes this [vital urge that has engulfed the Negro community,] one should readily understand why public demonstrations are taking place. The Negro has many [pent-up resentments] and latent frustrations, and he must release them. So let him march; let him make prayer pilgrimages to the city hall; let him go on freedom rides—and try to understand why he must do so. If his repressed emotions are not released in nonviolent ways, they will seek expression through violence; this is not a threat but a fact of history. So I have not said to my people: "Get rid of your discontent." Rather, I have tried to say that this normal and healthy discontent can be [channeled into the creative outlet of nonviolent direct action.] And now this approach is being termed extremist.

Why "he," not "I"?
Repeats "let him"

Not a threat?
"I" channel discontent

But though I was initially disappointed at being categorized as an extremist, as I continued to think about the matter I gradually gained a measure of satisfaction from the label. Was not Jesus an extremist for love: "Love your enemies, bless them that curse you, do good to them that hate you, and pray for them which despitefully use you, and persecute you." Was not Amos an extremist for justice: "Let justice roll down like waters and righteousness like an everflowing stream." Was not Paul an extremist for the Christian gospel: "I bear in my body the marks of the Lord Jesus." Was not Martin Luther an extremist: "Here I stand; I cannot do otherwise, so help me God." And John Bunyan: "I will stay in jail to the end of my days before I make a butchery of my conscience." And Abraham Lincoln: "This nation cannot survive half slave and half free." And Thomas Jefferson: "We hold these truths to be self-evident, that all men are created equal . . . " [So the question is not whether we will be extremists, but what kind of extremists we will be.] Will we be extremists for hate or for love? Will we be extremists for the preservation of injustice or for the extension of justice? In that dramatic scene on Calvary's hill three men were crucified. We must never forget that all three were crucified for the same crime—the crime of extremism. Two were extremists for immorality, and thus fell below their environment. The other, Jesus Christ, was an extremist for love, truth and goodness, and thereby rose above his environment. Perhaps the South, [the nation and the world are in dire need of creative extremists.]

¶9 Justifies extremism for righteous ends

Hebrew prophet

disciple founded Protestantism

preacher

freed slaves

wrote Declaration of Independence

Redeemer— all extremists for good

I had hoped that the white moderate would see this need. Perhaps I was too optimistic; perhaps I expected too much. I suppose I should have realized that few members of the oppressor race can understand the deep groans and passionate yearnings of the oppressed race, and still fewer have the vision to see that [injustice must be rooted out] by strong, persistent and determined action. I am thankful, however, that some of our white brothers in the South have grasped the meaning of this social revolution and committed themselves to it. They are still all too few in quantity, but they are big in quality. Some—such as Ralph McGill, Lillian Smith, Harry Golden,

¶10 Disappointed in white moderate critics; thanks supporters

9

10

Who are they?   James McBride Dabbs, Ann Braden and Sarah Patton Boyle—have written about our struggle in eloquent and prophetic terms. Others have marched with us down nameless streets of the South. They

left unaided   have (anguished) in filthy, roach-infested jails, suffering the abuse and brutality of policemen who view them as "dirty nigger-lovers." Unlike so many of their moderate brothers and sisters, they have recog-

framing—   nized the urgency of the movement and sensed the need for power-
recalls boil   ful ["action" antidotes] to combat the [disease of segregation.]
simile

CHECKLIST

Annotating

To annotate:

1. Mark the text using notations like these:
   - circle words to be defined in the margin
   - underline key words and phrases
   - bracket importance sentences and passages
   - use lines or arrows to connect ideas or words

2. Write marginal comments like these:
   - number and summarize each paragraph
   - define unfamiliar words
   - note responses and questions
   - identify interesting writing strategies
   - point out patterns

3. Layer additional markings on the text and comments in the margins as you reread for different purposes.

PREVIEWING

Previewing enables readers to get a sense of what the text is about and how it is organized before reading it closely. This simple critical reading strategy includes seeing what you can learn from headnotes or other introductory material, skimming to get an overview of the content and organization, and identifying the genre and rhetorical situation.

Learning from Headnotes

Many texts provide some introductory material to orient readers. Books often have brief blurbs on the cover describing the content and author, as well as a preface, an introduction, and a table of contents. Articles in professional and academic journals usually provide some background information. Scientific articles, for example, typically begin with an abstract summarizing the main points. In this book, as in many textbooks, headnotes introducing the author and identifying the circumstances under which the selection was originally published precede the reading selections.

You might want to annotate the headnotes in this book, highlighting whatever seems important and adding your own information, observations, or questions. For example, as you read the headnote to the excerpt from "Letter from Birmingham Jail" (p. 417), you might want to underscore the fact that the selection is an excerpt from a longer essay. You might also note that it was written in response to published criticism.

Because Martin Luther King, Jr., is a well-known figure, the headnote may not tell you anything you did not already know. If you know something else about the author that could help you better understand the selection, you might want to make a note of it. As a critical reader, you should think about whether the writer has authority and credibility on the subject. Information about the writer's education, professional experience, and other publications can help. If you need to know more about a particular author, you could consult a biographical dictionary or encyclopedia in the library, such as *Who's Who, Biographical Index, Current Biography, Dictionary of American Biography,* or *Contemporary Authors.*

Skimming for an Overview

When you *skim* a text, you give it a quick, selective, superficial reading. For most explanations and arguments, a good strategy is to read the opening and closing paragraphs because the first usually introduces the subject and may forecast the main points, while the last typically summarizes what is most important in the essay. You should also glance at the first sentence of every internal paragraph because it may serve as a topic sentence, introducing the point discussed in the paragraph. Because narrative writing is usually organized by time rather than by points, often you can get a sense of the progression by skimming for time markers such as *then, after,* and *later.* Heads and subheads, figures and charts, also provide clues for skimming.

To illustrate, turn again to the King excerpt, and skim it. Notice that the opening paragraph establishes the subject: the white moderate's criticism of Dr. King's efforts. It also forecasts many of the main points that are taken up in subsequent paragraphs: the moderate's greater devotion to order than to justice (paragraph 2); the moderate's criticism that King's methods, though nonviolent, precipitate violence (paragraph 3); and the moderate's "paternalistic" timetable (paragraph 4), and so on.

Identifying the Genre and Rhetorical Situation

Reading an unfamiliar text is like traveling in unknown territory. Wise travelers use a map, checking what they see against what they expect to find. In much the same way, previewing for genre equips you with a set of expectations to guide your reading. *Genre* means "kind" or "type," and is generally used to classify pieces of writing according to their particular style, form, and content. Nonfiction prose genres include autobiography, reflection, observation, explanations of concepts, and various forms of argument, such as evaluation, analysis of causes or effects, proposal to solve a problem, and position on a controversial issue. These genres are illustrated in chapters 2 through 9 with guidelines to help you analyze and evaluate their effectiveness. After working through these chapters, you will be able to identify the genre of most unfamiliar pieces of writing you encounter.

You can make a tentative decision about the genre of a text by first looking at why the piece was written and to whom it was addressed. These two elements—purpose and audience—constitute the rhetorical or writing situation. Paying attention to the genre of a particular text leads you to consider how the writing situation affected the particular way the text was written. The title "Letter from Birmingham Jail" explicitly identifies this particular selection as a letter. We know that letters are usually written with a particular reader in mind, although they may be addressed to the public in general; that they may be part of an ongoing correspondence; and that they may be personal or public, informal or formal.

If you read the clergymen's statement (pp. 465–466) and the opening of King's letter (p. 452), you will gain some insight into the situation in which he wrote the letter and some understanding of his specific purpose for writing. As a public letter written in response to a public statement, "Letter from Birmingham Jail" may be classified as a position paper, one that argues for a particular position on a controversial issue.

Even without reading the clergymen's statement and the complete letter, you can get a sense of the rhetorical situation from the opening paragraph of the excerpt. You would not be able to identify the "white moderate" with the clergymen who criticized King, but you would see clearly that he is referring to people he had hoped would support his cause but who, instead, have become an obstacle. King's feelings about the white moderate's lack of support are evident in the first paragraph based on his use of words like *gravely disappointed, regrettable conclusion, frustrating,* and *bewildering.* The opening paragraph, as we indi-cated under Skimming for an Overview, also identifies the white moderate's specific objections to King's methods. Therefore, you not only learn very quickly that this is a position paper, but you also learn the points of disagreement between the two sides and the attitude of the writer toward those with whom he disagrees.

Knowing that this is an excerpt from a position paper allows you to appreciate the controversiality of the subject King is writing about and the sensitivity of the rhetorical situation. You can see how he presents his own position at the same time that he tries to bridge the gap separating him from his critics. You can then evaluate the kinds of points King makes and the persuasiveness of his argument.

Previewing

To orient yourself before reading closely,

1. See what you can learn from headnotes or other introductory material.
2. Skim the text to get an overview of the content and organization.
3. Identify the genre and rhetorical situation.

OUTLINING

Outlining is an especially helpful critical reading strategy for understanding the content and structure of a reading. *Outlining,* which identifies the text's main ideas, may be part of the annotating process, or it may be done separately. Writing an outline in the margins of the text as you read and annotate makes it easier to find information later. Writing an outline on a separate piece of paper gives you more space to work with and therefore usually includes more detail.

The key to outlining is distinguishing between the main ideas and the supporting material such as reasons, examples, factual evidence, and explanations. The main ideas form the backbone, which holds the various parts and pieces of the text together. Outlining the main ideas helps you uncover this structure.

Making an outline, however, is not simple. The reader must exercise judgment in deciding which are the most important ideas. Because importance is relative, different readers can make different—and equally reasonable—decisions based on what interests them in the reading. Outlining may be further complicated when readers use their own words rather than select words from the text. Rephrasing can create a slight or significant shift in meaning or emphasis. Reading is never a passive or neutral act; the process of outlining shows how constructive reading can be.

You may make either a formal, multileveled outline with Roman (I, II) and Arabic (1, 2) numerals together with capital and lowercase letters or an informal, scratch outline that lists the main idea of each paragraph. A formal outline is harder to make and much more time consuming than a scratch outline. You might choose to make a formal outline of a reading about which you are writing an in-depth analysis or evaluation. For example, here is a formal outline a student wrote for a paper evaluating the logic of the King excerpt. Notice that the student uses Roman numerals for the main ideas or claims, capital letters for the reasons, and Arabic numerals for supporting evidence and explanation.

I. The Negro's great stumbling block in his stride toward freedom is . . . the white moderate
   A. *Because* the white moderate is more devoted to "order" than to justice (paragraph 2)

       1. Law and order should exist to establish justice

       2. Likens law and order to dangerously structured dams that block the flow of social progress

  B. *Because* the white moderate prefers a negative peace (absence of tension) to a positive peace (justice) (paragraph 2)

       1. The tension already exists

       2. It is not created by nonviolent direct action

       3. Boil simile: Compares society that does not eliminate injustice to a boil that hides its infections. Both can be cured only by exposure.

  C. *Because* even though the white moderate agrees with the goals, he does not support the means to achieve them (paragraph 3)

       1. Rebuts the argument that the means—nonviolent direct action—are wrong because they precipitate violence

       2. Analogy of the robbed man condemned because he had money

       3. Comparison with Socrates and Jesus

  D. *Because* the white moderate paternalistically believes he can set a timetable for another man's freedom (paragraph 4)

       1. Rebuts the white moderate's argument that Christianity will cure man's ills and man must wait patiently for that to happen

       2. Argues that time is neutral and that man must use time creatively for constructive rather than destructive ends

II. Creative extremism is preferable to moderation

  A. Classifies himself as a moderate (paragraphs 5–8)

       1. I stand between two forces: the white moderate's complacency and the Black Muslim's rage

       2. If nonviolent direct action were stopped, more violence, not less, would result

       3. "Millions of Negroes will, out of frustration and despair, seek solace and security in black-nationalist ideologies" (paragraph 7)

       4. Repressed emotions will be expressed—if not in nonviolent ways, then through violence (paragraph 8)

  B. Redefines himself as a "creative extremist" (paragraph 9)

       1. Extremism for love, truth, and goodness is creative extremism

       2. Identifies himself with creative extremists like Jesus, Amos, Paul, Martin Luther, John Bunyan, Abraham Lincoln, and Thomas Jefferson

  C. Not all white people are moderates, many are creative extremists (paragraph 10)

       1. Lists names of white writers

       2. Refers to white activists

Making a scratch outline, in contrast to a formal outline, takes less time but still requires careful reading. A scratch outline will not record as much information as a formal outline, but it is sufficient for most critical reading purposes. To make a scratch outline, you need to locate the topic of each paragraph. The topic is usually stated in a word or phrase, and it may be repeated or referred to throughout the paragraph. For example, the opening paragraph of the King excerpt (p. 417) makes clear that its topic is the white moderate.

After you have found the topic of the paragraph, figure out what is being said about it. To return to our example: If the white moderate is the topic of the opening paragraph, then what King says about the topic can be found in the second sentence, where he announces the conclusion he has come to—namely, that the white moderate is "the Negro's great stumbling block in his stride toward freedom." The rest of the paragraph specifies the ways the white moderate blocks progress.

When you make an outline, you can use the writer's words, your own words, or a combination of the two. An outline appears in the margins of the selection, with numbers for each paragraph (see pp. 417–421). Here is the same outline on a separate piece of paper, slightly expanded and reworded:

¶1   White moderates block progress in the struggle for racial justice
¶2   Tension is necessary for progress
¶3   The clergymen's criticism is not logical
¶4   King justifies urgent use of time
¶5   Clergymen accuse King of being extreme, but he claims to stand between two extreme forces in the black community
¶6   King offers a better choice
¶7   King's movement has prevented racial violence by blacks
¶8   Discontent is normal and healthy but must be channeled creatively rather than destructively
¶9   Creative extremists are needed
¶10 Some whites have supported King

CHECKLIST

Outlining

To make a scratch outline of a text,

1. Reread each paragraph systematically, identifying the topic and what is being said about it. Do not include examples, specific details, quotations, or other explanatory and supporting material.

2. List the main ideas in the margin of the text or on a separate piece of paper.

SUMMARIZING

Summarizing is one of the most widely used strategies for critical reading because it helps the reader understand and remember what is most important in the reading. Another advantage of summarizing is that it creates a condensed version of the reading's ideas and information, which can be referred to later or inserted into the reader's own written text. Along with quoting and paraphrasing, summarizing enables us to refer to and integrate other writers' ideas into our own writing.

A summary is a relatively brief restatement, in the reader's own words, of the reading's main ideas. Summaries vary in length, depending on the reader's purpose. Some summaries are very brief—a sentence or even a subordinate clause. For example, if you were referring to the excerpt from "Letter from Birmingham Jail" and simply needed to indicate how it relates to your other sources, your summary might focus on only one aspect of the reading. It might look something like this: "There have always been advocates of extremism in politics. Martin Luther King, Jr., in 'Letter from Birmingham Jail,' for instance, defends nonviolent civil disobedience as an extreme but necessary means of bringing about racial justice." If, on the other hand, you were surveying the important texts of the civil rights movement, you might write a longer, more detailed summary that not only identifies the reading's main ideas but also shows how the ideas relate to one another.

Many writers find it useful to outline the reading as a preliminary to writing a summary. A paragraph-by-paragraph scratch outline (like that illustrated on p. 426) lists the reading's main ideas following the sequence in which they appear in the original. But writing a summary requires more than merely stringing together the entries in an outline. A summary has to make explicit the logical connections between the ideas. To write a summary, you do more than translate the author's meaning into your own words, as you would when writing a paraphrase (see pp. 428–429). Writing a summary shows how reading critically is a truly constructive process of interpretation involving both close analysis and creative synthesis.

To summarize, you need to segregate the main ideas from the supporting material, usually by making an outline of the reading. You will want to use your own words for the most part, but you may use key words or quote selected key words and phrases. You may also want to cite the title and refer to the author by name, indicating with verbs like *expresses, acknowledges,* and *explains* the writer's purpose and strategy at each point in the argument.

Following is a sample summary of the King excerpt. It is based on the outline on p. 426, but is much more detailed. Most important, it fills in connections between the ideas that King left for readers to make.

> King expresses his disappointment with white moderates who, by opposing his program of nonviolent direct action, have become a barrier to progress toward racial justice. He acknowledges that his

program has raised tension in the South, but he explains that tension is necessary to bring about change. Furthermore, he argues that tension already exists. But because it has been unexpressed, it is unhealthy and potentially dangerous.

He defends his actions against the clergymen's criticisms, particularly their argument that he is in too much of a hurry. Responding to charges of extremism, King claims that he has actually prevented racial violence by channeling the natural frustrations of oppressed blacks into nonviolent protest. He asserts that extremism is precisely what is needed now—but it must be creative, rather than destructive, extremism. He concludes by again expressing disappointment with white moderates for not joining his effort as many other whites have.

CHECKLIST

Summarizing

To restate briefly the main ideas in a text,

1. Make an outline.
2. Write a paragraph or more that presents the main ideas largely in your own words. Use the outline as a guide, but reread parts of the original text as necessary.
3. To make the summary coherent, fill in connections between ideas.

PARAPHRASING

Paraphrasing, like summarizing, involves putting what you have read into your own words. But unlike a summary, which is much briefer than the original text, a paraphrase is at least as long as the original and often longer. Whereas summarizing seeks to present the gist or essence of the reading and leave out everything else, paraphrasing tries to be comprehensive and leave out nothing that contributes to the meaning. (For more on summarizing, see pp. 427–428.)

Paraphrasing works as a critical reading strategy for especially complex and obscure passages. Because it requires a word-for-word or phrase-by-phrase rewording of the original text, paraphrasing is too time consuming and labor intensive to use on long texts. But it is perfect for making sure you understand the important passages of a difficult reading. To paraphrase, you need to work systematically through the text, looking up in a good college dictionary many of the key words, even those you are somewhat familiar with. You can quote the author's words, but if you do, put quotation marks around them and be sure to define them. You may also refer, as you do when you summarize, to the author by name and use verbs like *writes, expresses,* and *argues* to indicate your understanding of the author's purpose.

Following are two passages. The first is excerpted from paragraph two of the excerpt from "Letter from Birmingham Jail." The second passage paraphrases the first.

ORIGINAL

I had hoped that the white moderate would understand that law and order exist for the purpose of establishing justice and that when they fail in this purpose they become the dangerously structured dams that block the flow of social progress. I had hoped that the white moderate would understand that the present tension in the South is a necessary phase of the transition from an obnoxious negative peace, in which the Negro passively accepted his unjust plight, to a substantive and positive peace, in which all men will respect the dignity and worth of human personality.

PARAPHRASE

King writes that he had hoped for more understanding from the white moderate—specifically that he would recognize that law and order is not an end in itself but a means to the greater end of establishing justice. When law and order do not serve this greater end, they stand in the way of progress. King expected the white moderate to recognize that the current tense situation in the South is part of a transition process that is necessary for progress. The current situation is bad because although there is peace, it is an "obnoxious" and "negative" kind of peace based on black people passively accepting the injustice of the status quo. A better kind of peace, one that is "substantive," real and not imaginary, as well as "positive" requires that all people, regardless of race, be valued.

If you compare the paraphrase to the original, you will see that the paraphrase tries to remain true to the original by including *all* the important information and ideas. It also tries to be neutral, to avoid inserting the reader's opinions or distorting the original writer's ideas. But because paraphrasing requires the use of different words and putting those words together into different sentences, the resulting paraphrase will be different from the original. The paraphrase expresses the reader's interpretation of the original text's meaning.

QUESTIONING TO UNDERSTAND AND REMEMBER

As students, we are accustomed to teachers asking us questions about our reading. These questions are designed to help us understand a reading and respond to it more fully, and often they work. When you need to understand and use new information, however, it may be more beneficial if *you* write the questions. Using this strategy, you can write questions as you read a text the first time. In difficult academic reading, you will understand the material better and remember it longer if you write a question for every paragraph or brief section.

Paraphrasing

To paraphrase information in a text,

1. Reread the passage to be paraphrased, looking up unknown words in a college dictionary.
2. Translate the passage into your own words, putting quotation marks around any words or phrases quoted from the original.
3. Revise to ensure coherence.

We will demonstrate how this strategy works by returning to the excerpt from "Letter from Birmingham Jail" (pp. 417–421) and examining, paragraph by paragraph, some questions that might be written about it.

Reread the selection. When you come to the end of each paragraph, look at the question for that paragraph in the following list. (The paragraph numbers and questions correspond.) Assume for this rereading that the goal is to comprehend the information and ideas.

Notice that each question asks about the content of a paragraph and that you can answer the question with information from that paragraph.

Paragraph	Question
I	How can white moderates be more of a barrier to racial equality than the Ku Klux Klan?
2	How can community tension resulting from nonviolent direct action benefit the civil rights movement?
3	How can peaceful actions be justified even if they cause violence?
4	Why should civil rights activists take action now instead of waiting for white moderates to support them?
5	How are complacent members of the community different from black nationalist groups?
6	What is King's position in relation to these two forces of complacency and anger?
7	What would have happened if King's nonviolent direct action movement had not started?
8	What is the focus of the protest, and what do King and others who are protesting hope to achieve?

9	What other creative extremists does King associate himself with?
10	Who are the whites who have supported King, and what has happened to some of them?

Each question focuses on the main idea in the paragraph, not on illustrations or details. Each question is expressed in the reader's own words, not just copied from parts of the paragraph.

How can writing questions during reading help you understand and remember the content—the ideas and information—of the reading? Researchers studying the ways people learn from their reading have found that writing questions during reading enables readers to remember more than they would by reading the selection twice. Researchers also compared readers who wrote brief summary sentences for a paragraph with readers who wrote questions and discovered that readers who wrote questions learned more and remembered the information longer. These researchers conjecture that writing a question involves reviewing or rehearsing information in a way that allows it to enter long-term memory, where it is more easily recalled. The result is that you clarify and "file" the information as you go along. You can then read more confidently because nothing important gets by you and meaning develops more fully, enabling you to predict what is coming next and add it readily to what you have already learned.

This way of reading informational material is very slow, and at first it may seem inefficient. In those reading situations where you must use the information in an exam or class discussion, it can be very efficient, however. Because this reading strategy is relatively time consuming, you would, of course, want to use it selectively.

CHECKLIST

Questioning to Understand and Remember

When you must remember and use your reading, especially if it is unfamiliar or difficult,

1. Pause at the end of each paragraph to review the information.
2. Try to identify the most important information—the main ideas or gist.
3. Write a question that can be answered by the main idea or ideas in the paragraph.
4. Move on to the next paragraph, and repeat the process.

CONTEXTUALIZING

The texts you read were all written sometime in the past and often embody historical and cultural assumptions, values, and attitudes different from your own. To read critically, you need to become aware of these differences.

Contextualizing is a critical reading strategy that enables you to make inferences about a reading selection's historical and cultural context and to examine the differences between its context and your own.

We can divide the process of contextualizing into two steps:

1. Reread the text to see how it represents the historical and cultural situation. Compare the way the text presents the situation with what you know about the situation from other sources—such as what you've read in other books and articles, what you have learned in school, what you have seen on television and in the movies, what you have learned from talking to people who might have been involved directly.

   Write a few sentences, describing your understanding of what it was like at that particular time and place. Note how the representation of the time and place in the text differs in significant ways from the other representations with which you are familiar.

2. Consider how much and in what ways the situation has changed. Write another sentence or two, exploring the historical and cultural differences.

The excerpt from "Letter from Birmingham Jail" is a good example of a text that benefits from being read contextually. If you knew nothing about the history of slavery and segregation in the United States, if you had not heard of Martin Luther King, Jr., or the civil rights movement, it would be very difficult to understand the passion for justice and impatience with delay expressed in this selection. Most Americans, however, have read about Martin Luther King, Jr., and the civil rights movement or have seen television histories like "Eyes on the Prize" or films like *Malcolm X*.

Here is how one reader contextualized the excerpt from "Letter from Birmingham Jail":

> 1. I am not old enough to remember what it was like in the early 1960s when Dr. King was leading marches and sit-ins, but I have seen television documentaries of newsclips showing demonstrators being attacked by dogs, doused by fire hoses, beaten and dragged by helmeted police. Such images give me a sense of the violence, fear, and hatred that King was responding to.
>
> The tension King writes about comes across in his writing. He uses his anger and frustration creatively to inspire his critics. He also threatens them, although he denies it. I saw a film on Malcolm X, so I could see that King was giving white people a choice between his nonviolent way and Malcolm's more confrontational way.
>
> 2. Things have certainly changed since the sixties. Legal segregation has ended. The term *Negro* is no longer used, but there still are racists like the detective in the O. J. case. African Americans like General Colin Powell are highly respected and powerful. The civil rights movement is over. So when I read King, I'm reading history.

But then again, police officers still beat black men like Rodney King and extremists like Ice T still threaten violence. I don't know who's playing Dr. King's role today (Jesse Jackson?).

CHECKLIST

Contextualizing

To contextualize,

1. Describe the historical and cultural situation as it is represented in the reading selection and in other sources with which you are familiar.
2. Write about differences and the similarities you see.

REFLECTING ON CHALLENGES TO YOUR BELIEFS AND VALUES

The reading we do often challenges our attitudes, our unconsciously held beliefs, or our positions on current issues. We may feel anxious, irritable, or disturbed; threatened or vulnerable; ashamed or combative. We may feel suddenly wary or alert. When we experience these feelings as we read, we are reacting in terms of our personal or family values, religious beliefs, race or ethnic group, gender, sexual orientation, social class, or regional experience.

You can grow intellectually, emotionally, and in social understanding if you are willing (at least occasionally) to reflect on these challenges instead of simply resisting them. Learning to question your own unexamined assumptions and attitudes is an important part of becoming a critical thinker.

This reading strategy involves marking the text where you feel challenged, and then reflecting on why you feel challenged. As you read a text for the first time, simply mark an X in the margin at each point where you feel a challenge to your attitudes, beliefs, or values. Make a brief note in the margin about what you feel at that point or about what in the text seems to have created the challenge. The challenge you feel may be mild or strong. It may come frequently or only occasionally. You may feel challenged by any of the following:

- an offensive word used by the writer or quoted from a source
- an example, description, action, or asserted fact that distorts or stereotypes
- an unsubstantiated, oversimplified, or self-serving idea in the text

Review the places you marked in the text where you felt challenged and consider what connections you can make among these places or among the feelings you experienced at each place. For example, you might notice that you object to only a limited part of a writer's argument, resist nearly all of an authority's quoted statements, or react to implied judgments about your own gender or social class.

Write about what you learn. Begin by describing briefly the part or parts of the text that make you feel challenged. Then write several sentences, reflecting on your responses. Keep the focus on your feelings. You need not defend or justify your feelings. Instead, try to account for them. Where do they come from? Why are they important to you? Although the purpose is to explore why you feel as you do, you may find that you can return to the text toward the end of your writing to think about how your values, attitudes, and beliefs influenced the way you understood as well as responded to the text.

Here, for example, is how one writer responded to "Letter from Birmingham Jail" (pp. 417–421).

> I'm troubled and confused by the way King uses the labels *moderate* and *extremist*. He says he doesn't like being labeled an extremist but he labels the clergymen moderate. How could it be OK for King to be moderate and not OK for the clergymen? What does *moderate* mean anyway? My dictionary defines *moderate* as "keeping within reasonable or proper limits; not extreme, excessive, or intense." Being a moderate sounds a lot better than being an extremist. I was taught not to act rashly or to go off the deep end. I'm also troubled that King makes a threat (although he says he does not).

CHECKLIST

Reflecting on Challenges to Your Beliefs and Values

1. Identify challenges by annotating the text, marking each point where you feel your beliefs and values are being opposed, criticized, or unfairly characterized.

2. Select one or two of the most troubling challenges you've identified and write a few sentences trying to understand why you feel as you do. Don't defend your feelings; but instead analyze them to see where they come from.

EXPLORING THE SIGNIFICANCE OF FIGURATIVE LANGUAGE

Figurative language (metaphor, simile, and symbol), which takes words literally associated with one object or idea and transforms them to another object or idea, communicates more than direct statement can convey. Such language enhances meaning because it embodies abstract ideas in vivid images. Figurative language also enriches meaning by drawing on a complex of feeling and association, indicating relations of resemblance and likeness. Here are definitions and examples of the most common figures of speech.

Metaphor implicitly compares two different things by identifying them with each other. For instance, when King in the selection on pp. 417–421 calls the white moderate "the Negro's great stumbling block in his stride toward freedom" (paragraph 1), he does not mean that the white moderate literally trips the Negro who is attempting to walk toward freedom. The sentence makes sense only if understood figuratively: the white moderate trips up the Negro by frustrating every effort to eliminate injustice. Similarly, King uses the image of a dam to express the abstract idea of the blockage of justice (paragraph 2).

Simile, a more explicit form of comparison, uses *like* or *as* to signal the relation of two seemingly unrelated things. King uses simile when he says that injustice is "like a boil that can never be cured so long as it is covered up" (paragraph 2). This simile makes several points of comparison between injustice and a boil. It suggests that injustice is a disease of society as a boil is a disease of the body and that injustice, like a boil, must be exposed or it will fester and worsen.

Symbolism compares two things by making one stand for the other. King uses the white moderate as a symbol for supposed liberals and would-be supporters of civil rights who are actually frustrating the cause.

How these figures of speech are used in a text reveals something of the writer's feelings about the subject and attitude toward prospective readers. It may even suggest the writer's feelings about the act of writing. Annotating and taking inventory of patterns of figurative language can provide insight into the tone of the writing and emotional effect of the text on its readers.

Exploring the patterns of figurative language involves annotating and then listing all the figures of speech you find in the reading—metaphor, simile, and symbol; grouping the figures of speech that appear to express similar feelings and attitudes, and labeling each group; and writing to explore the meaning of the patterns you have found.

The following inventory and analysis of the King excerpt (pp. 417–421) demonstrates the process of exploring the significance of figurative language.

Listing Figures of Speech

Step 1 produced the following inventory:

> order is a dangerously structured dam that blocks the flow
>
> social progress should flow
>
> stumbling block in the stride toward freedom
>
> injustice is like a boil that can never be cured
>
> the light of human conscience and air of national opinion
>
> time is something to be used, neutral, an ally, ripe
>
> > quicksand of racial injustice
>
> the solid rock of human dignity
>
> human progress never rolls in on wheels of inevitability
>
> men are co-workers with God
>
> groups springing up

promised land of racial justice

vital urge engulfed

pent-up resentments

normal and healthy discontent can be channeled into the creative
outlet of nonviolent direct action

root out injustice

powerful action is an antidote

disease of segregation

Grouping Figures of Speech

Step 2 yielded three groups:

Sickness: segregation is a disease; action is healthy, the only
antidote; injustice is like a boil

Underground: tension is hidden; resentments are pent-up,
repressed; injustice must be rooted out; extremist groups are
springing up; discontent can be channeled into a creative outlet

Blockage: forward movement is impeded by obstacles—the dam,
stumbling block; human progress never rolls in on wheels of
inevitability; social progress should flow

Exploring Patterns

Step 3 entailed about ten minutes of writing to explore the meaning of the
groups listed in step 2:

The patterns of blockage and underground suggest a feeling
of frustration. Inertia is a problem; movement forward toward progress or upward toward the promised land is stalled.
There seems to be a strong need to break through the resistance,
the passivity, the discontent and to be creative, active, vital. These
are probably King's feelings both about his attempt to lead purpose-
ful, effective demonstrations and his effort to write a convincing
letter.

The simile of injustice being like a boil links the two patterns of
underground and sickness, suggesting something bad, a disease, is
inside the people or the society. The cure is to expose, to root out,
the blocked hatred and injustice and release the tension or emotion
that has so long been repressed. This implies that repression itself is
the evil, not simply what is repressed.

Exploring the Significance of Figurative Language

To understand how figurative language—metaphor, simile, and symbol—contributes to the reading's meaning,

1. Annotate and then list all the figures of speech you find.
2. Group them and label each group.
3. Write to explore the meaning of the patterns you have found.

LOOKING FOR PATTERNS OF OPPOSITION

All texts contain voices of opposition. These voices may echo the views and values of critical readers the writer anticipates or predecessors to which the writer is responding; they may even reflect the writer's own conflicting values. You may need to look closely for such a dialogue of opposing voices within the text.

When we think of oppositions, we ordinarily think of polarities such as *yes* and *no, up* and *down, black* and *white, new* and *old.* Some oppositions, however, may be more subtle. The excerpt from "Letter from Birmingham Jail" (pp. 417–421) is rich in such oppositions: *moderate* versus *extremist, order* versus *justice, direct action* versus *passive acceptance, expression* versus *repression.* These oppositions are not accidental; and they form a significant pattern that gives a critical reader important information about the essay.

A careful reading will show that one of the two terms in an opposition is nearly always valued over the other. In the King passage, for example, *extremist* is valued over *moderate* (paragraph 9). This preference for extremism is surprising. The critical reader should ask why, when white extremists like the Ku Klux Klan have committed so many outrages against black southerners, King would prefer extremism. If King is trying to convince his readers to accept his point of view, why would he represent himself as an extremist? Moreover, why would a clergyman advocate extremism instead of moderation?

By studying the pattern of oppositions you can answer these questions more fully. You will see that King sets up this opposition to force his readers to examine their own values and realize that they are in fact misplaced. Instead of working toward justice, he says, those who support law and order maintain the unjust status quo. Getting his readers to think of the white moderate as blocking rather than facilitating peaceful change brings them to align themselves with King and perhaps even embrace his strategy of nonviolent resistance.

Looking for patterns of oppositions is a four-step method of analysis:

1. Divide a piece of paper in half lengthwise by drawing a line down the middle. In the left-hand column, list those words and phrases from the

text that you annotated because they seem to indicate oppositions. Enter in the right-hand column the word or phrase that is the opposite of each word or phrase in the left-hand column. You may have to paraphrase or even supply this opposite word or phrase if it is not stated directly in the text.

2. For each pair of words or phrases, put an asterisk next to the one that seems to be preferred by the writer.

3. Study the list of preferred words or phrases, and identify what you think is the predominant system of values put forth by the text. Do the same for the other list, identifying the alternative system or systems of values implied in the text. Take about ten minutes to describe the oppositions in writing.

4. To explore these conflicting points of view, write a few sentences presenting one side, and then write a few more sentences presenting the other side. Use as many of the words or phrases from the list as you can—explaining, extending, and justifying the values they imply. You may also, if you wish, quarrel with the choice of words or phrases on the grounds that they are slanted or oversimplify the issue.

The following inventory and analysis of the King excerpt demonstrates the method for analyzing oppositions in a text.

Listing Oppositions

This list of oppositions with asterisks next to King's preferred word or phrase in each pair demonstrates steps 1 and 2:

white moderate	*extremist
order	*justice
negative peace	*positive peace
absence of justice	*presence of justice
goals	*methods
*direct action	passive acceptance
*exposed tension	hidden tension
*robbed	robber
*individual	society
*words	silence
*expression	repression
*extension of justice	preservation of injustice
*extremist for love, truth, and justice	extremist for immorality

Analyzing Oppositions

Step 3 produced the following description of the conflicting points of view:

In this reading, King addresses as "white moderates" the clergymen who criticized him. He sees the moderate position in essentially negative terms, whereas extremism can be either negative or positive. Moderation is equated with passivity, acceptance of the status quo, fear of disorder, perhaps even fear of any change. The moderates believe justice can wait, whereas law and order cannot. Yet, as King points out, there is no law and order for blacks who are victimized and denied their constitutional rights.

The argument King has with the white moderates is basically over means and ends. Both agree on the ends but disagree on the means that should be taken to secure those ends. What means are justified to achieve one's goals? How does one decide? King is willing to risk a certain amount of tension and disorder to bring about justice; he suggests that if progress is not made, more disorder, not less, is bound to result. In a sense, King represents himself as a moderate caught between the two extremes—the white moderates' "do-nothingism" and the black extremists' radicalism.

At the same time, King substitutes the opposition between moderation and extremism with an opposition between two kinds of extremism, one for love and the other for hate. In fact, he represents himself as an extremist willing to make whatever sacrifices— and pehaps even to take whatever means—are necessary to reach his goal of justice.

Considering Alternative Points of View

Step 4 entailed a few minutes of writing exploring the point of view opposed to the author's and several more minutes of writing presenting King's possible response to this point of view:

> *The moderates' side:* I can sympathize with the moderates' fear of further disorder and violence. Even though King advocates nonviolence, violence does result. He may not cause it, but it does occur because of him. Moderates do not really advocate passive acceptance of injustice, but want to pursue justice through legal means. These methods may be slow, but since ours is a system of law, the only way to make change is through that system. King wants to shake up the system, to force it to move quickly for fear of violence. That strikes me as blackmail, as bad as if he were committing violence himself. Couldn't public opinion be brought to bear on the legal system to move more quickly? Can't we elect officials who will change unjust laws and see that the just ones are obeyed? The *vote* should be the weapon in a democracy, shouldn't it?
>
> *King's possible response:* He would probably argue that this viewpoint is naive. One of the major injustices at that time was that blacks were prevented from voting, and no elected official would risk going against those who voted for him or her. King

would probably agree that public opinion needs to be changed, that
people need to be educated, but he would also argue that education
is not enough when people are being systematically deprived of
their legal rights. The very system of law that should protect people was being used as a weapon against blacks in the South. The
only way to get something done is to shake people up, make
them aware of the injustice they are allowing to continue. Seeing
their own police officers committing violence should make people
question their own values and begin to take action to right the
wrongs.

CHECKLIST

Looking for Patterns of Opposition

To look for and analyze the patterns of opposition in a reading,

1. Annotate the selection for oppositions, and list the pairs on a separate page.
2. Put an asterisk next to the word in each pair that is preferred in the selection.
3. Examine the pattern of preferred terms to discover the system of values the
   pattern implies, and do the same for the unpreferred terms.
4. Write to analyze and evaluate these alternative systems of value.

EVALUATING THE LOGIC OF AN ARGUMENT

An argument has two essential parts: a claim and support. The *claim* asserts a
conclusion—an idea, an opinion, a judgment, or a point of view—that the writer
wants readers to accept. The *support* includes *reasons* (shared beliefs, assumptions, and values) and *evidence* (facts, examples, statistics, and authorities) that
give readers the basis for accepting the conclusion.

When you assess the logic of an argument, you are concerned about the process of reasoning as well as the argument's truthfulness. Three conditions must
be met for an argument to be considered logically acceptable—what we call the
ABC test:

A. The support must be *appropriate* to the claim.
B. All of the statements must be *believable*.
C. The argument must be *consistent* and complete.

A. Testing for Appropriateness

If readers believe a writer's reasoning to be appropriate, they see that all of
the evidence is relevant to the claim it supports. For example, if a writer claims
that children must be allowed certain legal rights, readers could readily accept as

appropriate support quotations from Supreme Court justices' decisions but might question quotations from a writer of popular children's books. Readers could probably accept a writer's reasoning that if women have certain legal rights then so should children but would almost certainly reject comparing children's needs for legal protection to the need for drivers to observe traffic laws.

As these examples illustrate, appropriateness of support comes most often into question when the writer is invoking authority or arguing by analogy. For example, in paragraph 3 of the excerpt, King argues by analogy and, at the same time, invokes authority: "Isn't this like condemning Socrates because his unswerving commitment to truth and his philosophical inquiries precipitated the act by the misguided populace in which they made him drink hemlock?" Readers not only must judge the appropriateness of comparing the Greek populace's condemnation of Socrates to the white moderates' condemnation of King's action, but also must judge whether it is appropriate to accept Socrates as an authority on this subject. Because Socrates is generally respected for his teaching on justice, his words and actions are likely to be considered appropriate to King's situation in Birmingham.

In paragraph 2, King argues that if law and order fail to establish justice, "they become the dangerously structured dams that block the flow of social progress." The analogy asserts the following logical relationship: Law and order is to progress toward justice what a dam is to water. If readers do not accept this analogy, then the argument fails the test of appropriateness. Arguing by analogy is usually considered a weak kind of argument because most analogies are only partially parallel.

There are several common flaws or fallacies in reasoning that cause an argument to fail the test of appropriateness:

- *False analogy* occurs when two cases are not sufficiently parallel to lead readers to accept the claim.

- *False use of authority* occurs when writers invoke as expert in the field being discussed a person whose expertise or authority lies not in the given field but in another.

- *Non sequitur* (Latin, meaning "it does not follow") occurs when one statement is not logically connected to another.

- *Red herring* occurs when a writer raises an irrelevant issue to draw attention away from the central issue.

- *Post hoc, ergo propter hoc* (Latin, meaning "after this, therefore because of this") occurs when the writer implies that because one event follows another, the first caused the second. Chronology is not the same as causality.

B. Testing for Believability

Believability is a measure of the degree to which readers are willing to accept the assertions supporting the claim. Whereas some assertions are obviously true, most depend on the readers' sharing certain values, beliefs, and assumptions with the writer. Readers who agree with the white moderate that maintaining law and order is more important than establishing justice are not going to accept King's claim that the white moderate is blocking progress.

Other statements such as those asserting facts, statistics, examples, and authorities present evidence to support a claim. Readers must put all of these kinds of evidence to the test of believability.

Facts are statements that can be proven objectively to be true. The believability of facts depends on their *accuracy* (they should not distort or misrepresent reality), *completeness* (they should not omit important details), and the *trustworthiness* of their sources (sources should be qualified and unbiased). In the excerpt from "Letter from Birmingham Jail," for instance, King asserts as fact that the African American will not wait much longer for racial justice (paragraph 8). His critics might question the factuality of this assertion by asking: Is it true of all African Americans? How much longer will they wait? How does King know what the African American will and will not do?

Statistics are often assumed to be factual, but they are really only interpretations of numerical data. The believability of statistics depends on the *comparability* of the data (are apples being compared to oranges?), the *accuracy* of the methods of gathering and analyzing data (representative samples should be used and variables accounted for), and the *trustworthiness* of the sources (sources should be qualified and unbiased).

Examples and *anecdotes* are particular instances that if accepted as believable lead readers to accept the general claim. The believability of examples depends on their *representativeness* (whether they are truly typical and thus generalizable) and their *specificity* (whether particular details make them seem true to life). Even if a vivid example or gripping anecdote does not convince readers, it strengthens argumentative writing by clarifying the meaning the bringing home the point dramatically. In paragraph 5, for example, King supports his generalization that there are black nationalist extremists motivated by bitterness and hatred by citing the specific example of Elijah Muhammad's Muslim movement. Conversely, in paragraph 9, he refers to Jesus, Paul, Luther, and others as examples of extremists motivated by love. These examples support his assertion that extremism is not in itself wrong, that any judgment must depend on the cause for which one is an extremist.

Authorities are people to whom the writer attributes expertise on a given subject. Such authorities not only must be appropriate, as mentioned earlier, but must be believable. The believability of authorities depends on their *credibility*, on whether the reader accepts them as experts on the topic. King cites authorities repeatedly throughout the essay; for instance, he refers not only to religious leaders like Jesus and Luther but also to American political leaders like Lincoln and Jefferson. These figures are certain to have a high degree of credibility among King's readers.

In addition, you should be aware of the following fallacies in reasoning that undermine the believability of an argument:

- *Begging the question* occurs when the believability of the support itself depends on the believability of the claim. Another name for this kind of fallacy is *circular reasoning*.

- *Failing to accept the burden of proof* occurs when the writer asserts a claim but provides no support for it.

- *Hasty generalization* occurs when the writer asserts a claim on the basis of an isolated example.

- *Sweeping generalization* occurs when the writer fails to qualify the applicability of the claim and asserts that it applies to "all" instances instead of to "some" instances.

- *Overgeneralization* occurs when the writer fails to qualify the claim and asserts that it is "certainly true" rather than that it "may be true."

C. Testing for Consistency and Completeness

Be sure that all the support works together, that none of the supporting statements contradicts any of the other statements, and that no important objection or opposing argument is unacknowledged. To test for consistency and completeness, ask: Are any of the supporting statements contradictory? Are there any objections or opposing arguments that are not refuted?

A critical reader might regard as contradictory King's characterizing himself first as a moderate between the forces of complacency and violence, and later as an extremist opposed to the forces of violence. King attempts to reconcile this apparent contradiction by explicitly redefining extremism in paragraph 9.

Similarly, the fact that King fails to examine and refute every legal recourse available to his cause might allow a critical reader to question the sufficiency of his supporting arguments.

In evaluating the consistency of an argument, you should also be aware of the following fallacies:

- *Slippery slope* occurs when the writer argues that taking one step will lead inevitably to a next step, one that is undesirable.

- *Equivocation* occurs when a writer uses the same term in two different senses in an argument.

- *Oversimplification* occurs when an argument obscures or denies the complexity of the issue.

- *Either/or reasoning* occurs when the writer reduces the issue to only two alternatives that are polar opposites.

- *Double standard* occurs when two or more comparable things are judged according to different standards; it often involves holding the opposing argument to a higher standard than the one to which the writer holds his or her own argument.

Following is one student's written evaluation of the logic of King's argument in the excerpt. The student wrote these paragraphs after applying the ABC test, evaluating the appropriateness, believability, consistency and completeness of King's supporting reasons and evidence.

King writes both to the ministers who published the letter in the Birmingham newspaper and also to the people of Birmingham. He seems to want to justify his group's actions. He challenges white moderates, but he also tries to avoid antagonizing them. Given this purpose and his readers, his supporting statements are generally appropriate. He relies mainly on assertions of shared belief with his readers and on memorable analogies. For example, he knows his readers will accept assertions like "law and order exist for the purpose of establishing justice"; it is good to be an extremist for "love, truth, and goodness"; and progress is not inevitable, but results from tireless work and creativity. His analogies seem appropriate for his readers. For example, he compares injustice to a boil that nonviolent action must expose to the air if it is to be healed. Several times, King invokes authorities (Socrates, Jesus, Amos, Paul, Luther, Bunyan, Lincoln, Jefferson) his readers revere. Throughout his argument, King avoids fallacies of inappropriateness.

Likewise, his support is believable in terms of the well-known authorities he cites; the facts he asserts (for example, that racial tension results from injustice, not from nonviolent action); and the examples he offers (such as his assertion that extremism is not in itself wrong—as exemplified by Jesus, Paul, and Luther). If there is an inconsistency in the argument, it is the contradiction between King's portraits of himself both as a moderating force and as an "extremist for love"; but his redefinition of extremism as a positive value for any social change is central to the overall persuasiveness of his logical appeal to white moderates.

CHECKLIST

Evaluating the Logic of an Argument

To determine whether an argument makes sense, apply the ABC test:

1. **Test for Appropriateness** by checking to be sure that each piece of evidence is clearly and directly related to the claim it is supposed to support.

2. **Test for Believability** by deciding whether you can accept as true facts, statistics, and the testimony of experts, and also whether you can accept generalizations based on the examples given.

3. **Test for Consistency and Completeness** by ascertaining whether there are any contradictions in the argument and also whether any important objections or opposing arguments have been ignored.

4. Write a few sentences, exploring the appropriateness, believability, consistency, and completeness of the argument.

RECOGNIZING EMOTIONAL MANIPULATION

Writers often try to arouse emotions in readers—to excite their interest, make them care, move them to action. Although nothing is wrong with appealing to readers' emotions, it is wrong to manipulate readers with false or exaggerated emotional appeals.

Many words have connotations, associations that enrich their meaning and give words much of their emotional power. For example, we used the word *manipulation* in naming this particular critical reading strategy to arouse an emotional response in readers like you. No one wants to be manipulated. Everyone wants to feel in control of his or her attitudes and opinions. This is especially true in reading arguments: we want to be convinced, not tricked.

Emotional manipulation often works by distracting readers from relevant reasons and evidence. To keep from being distracted, you will want to pay close attention as you read and try to distinguish between emotional appeals that are acceptable and those that you consider manipulative or excessive.

As you read, look for and annotate evidence of the following kinds of emotional appeals:

- *Appeal to pity:* attempting to arouse sympathy by telling hard-luck stories or by excessive or inappropriate sentimentality

- *Scare tactics:* attempting to induce fear in readers through veiled or explicit threats, alarming statistics, or frightening stories

- *Demonizing opponents:* making opponents look like devils by exaggerating their faults

- *Name calling:* using loaded words like *fascist* or *racist* to discredit opponents

- *Guilt by association:* lumping together everyone who might disagree with the writer, no matter how extreme or moderate their views

- *Ad hominen arguments:* personal attacks on opponents, perhaps criticizing their motives or ethics rather than refuting their arguments

- *Ridicule:* using humor or contempt to downplay or discredit an opponent's argument

- *False flattery:* praising readers to get them to accept the writer's views

If you find appeals that you think might be manipulative, writing about them can help you explore your response. Here is an example of one student's reaction to the emotional appeal of "Letter from Birmingham Jail":

> As someone King would probably identify as a white moderate, I can't help reacting negatively to some of the language he uses in this reading. For example, in the first paragraph, he equates white moderates with members of the Ku Klux Klan even though he admits that white moderates were in favor of racial equality and justice. I guess this would fall under the category of guilt by associa-

tion. He also uses name calling when he puts down white moderates for being *paternalistic.* Finally, he uses scare tactics when he threatens "a frightening racial nightmare." This is probably also an example of demonizing—with the demons being black nationalists like Malcolm X.

Recognizing Emotional Manipulation

To assess whether emotional appeals are unfairly manipulative,

1. Annotate places in the text where you sense emotional appeals being used.
2. Write a few sentences exploring your responses and identifying the kinds of appeals you found.

JUDGING THE WRITER'S CREDIBILITY

Writers often try to persuade readers to respect and believe them. Because readers may not know them personally or even by reputation, writers must present an image of themselves in their writing that will gain their readers' confidence. This image cannot be made directly but must be made indirectly, through the arguments, language, and the system of values and beliefs implied in the writing. Writers establish credibility in their writing in three ways:

- By showing their knowledge of the subject
- By building common ground with readers
- By responding fairly to objections and opposing arguments

Testing for Knowledge

Writers demonstrate their knowledge through the facts and statistics they marshal, the sources they rely on for information, and the scope and depth of their understanding. As a critical reader, you may not be sufficiently expert on the subject yourself to know whether the facts are accurate, the sources reliable, and the understanding sufficient. You may need to do some research to see what others are saying about the subject. You can also check credentials—the writer's educational and professional qualifications, the respectability of the publication in which the selection first appeared, any reviews of the writer's work—to determine whether the writer is a respected authority in the field. King brings with him the authority that comes from being a member of the clergy and a respected leader of the Southern Christian Leadership Conference.

Testing for Common Ground

One way writers can establish common ground with their readers is by basing their reasoning on shared values, beliefs, and attitudes. They use language that includes their readers (*we*) rather than excludes them (*they*). They qualify their assertions to keep them from being too extreme. Above all, they acknowledge differences of opinion and try to make room in their argument to accommodate reasonable differences. As a reader, you will be affected by such appeals.

King creates common ground with readers by using the inclusive pronoun *we,* suggesting shared concerns between himself and his audience. Notice, however, his use of masculine pronouns and other references ("the Negro . . . he," "our brothers"). Although King addressed this letter to male clergy, he intended it to be published in the local newspaper, where it would be read by an audience of both men and women. By using language that excludes women, King misses the opportunity to build common ground with half his readers.

Testing for Fairness

Writers display their character by how they handle objections to their argument and opposing arguments. As a critical reader, you want to pay particular attention to how writers treat possible differences of opinion. Be suspicious of those who ignore differences and pretend everyone agrees with their viewpoint. When objections or opposing views are represented, you should consider whether they have been distorted in any way; if they are refuted, you want to be sure they are challenged fairly—with sound reasoning and solid evidence.

One way to gauge the author's credibility is to identify the tone of the argument. Tone is concerned not so much with what is said as with how it is said. It conveys the writer's attitude toward the subject and toward the reader. By reading sensitively, you should be able to evaluate the writer's stance and attitude through the tone of the writing. To identify the tone, list whatever descriptive adjectives come to mind in response to either of these questions: How would you characterize the tone of this selection? Judging from this piece of writing, what kind of person does the author seem to be? Here is an answer to the second question, based on the excerpt from "Letter from Birmingham Jail" (pp. 417–421).

> I know something about King from television programs on the civil rights movement. But if I were to talk about my impression of him from this passage, I'd use words like *patient, thoughtful, well educated, moral, confident.* He doesn't lose his temper but tries to convince his readers by making a case that is reasoned carefully and painstakingly. He's trying to change people's attitudes; no matter how annoyed he might be with them, he treats them with respect. It's as if he believes that their hearts are right, but they're just confused. If he can just set them straight, everything will be fine. Of course, he also sounds a little pompous when he compares himself to Jesus and Socrates, and the threat he appears to make in

paragraph 8 seems out of character. Maybe he's losing control of his self-image at those moments.

Judging the Writer's Credibility

To decide whether you can trust the writer,

1. As you read and annotate, consider the writer's knowledge of the subject, how well common ground is established, and whether the writer deals fairly with objections and opposing arguments.
2. Write a few sentences exploring what you discover.

COMPARING AND CONTRASTING RELATED READINGS

When you *compare* two reading selections, you look for similarities. When you *contrast* them, you look for differences. As a critical reading strategy, comparing and contrasting enables you to see both texts more clearly.

Comparing and contrasting depends on what you are looking at or for. We often hear that it is fruitless to compare apples and oranges (pun intended). It is true that you cannot add or multiply them, but you can put one against the other and come up with some interesting similarities and differences. It all depends on how imaginative you are in preparing the grounds or basis for comparison. Comparing apples and oranges, for example, in terms of their role as symbols in Western culture from Adam and Eve to the Apple computer could be quite productive. The grounds or basis for comparison, like a camera lens, brings some things into focus while blurring others.

To demonstrate how this strategy works, we compare and contrast the excerpt from "Letter from Birmingham Jail" (pp. 417–421) with the following selection by Lewis H. Van Dusen, Jr.

Lewis H. Van Dusen, Jr.

LEGITIMATE PRESSURES AND ILLEGITIMATE RESULTS

A respected attorney and legal scholar, Lewis H. Van Dusen served as chair of the American Bar Association Committee on Ethics and Professional Responsibility. This selection comes from an essay, "Civil Disobedience: Destroyer of Democracy," that first appeared in the *American Bar Association Journal.* As you read it, notice the annotations we made as we developed our comparison with the essay by King.

There are many civil rights leaders who show impatience with the process of democracy. They rely on the sit-in, boycott, or mass picketing to gain speedier solutions to the problems that face every citizen. But we must realize that the legitimate pressures that [won concessions in the past] can easily escalate into the illegitimate power plays that might (extort) demands in the future.] The victories of these civil rights leaders must not shake our confidence in the democratic procedures, as the pressures of demonstration are desirable only if they take place within the limits allowed by law. Civil rights gains should continue to be won by the persuasion of Congress and other legislative bodies and by the decision of courts. Any illegal entreaty for the [rights of some] can be an injury to the [rights of others,] for mass demonstrations often trigger violence.

to get something by force or intimidation

Those who advocate [taking the law into their own hands] should reflect that when they are disobeying what they consider to be an immoral law, they are deciding on a possibly immoral course. Their answer is that the process for democratic relief is too slow, that only mass confrontation can bring immediate action, and that any injuries are the inevitable cost of the pursuit of justice. Their answer is, simply put, that the end justifies the means. It is this justification of any form of demonstration as a form of dissent that threatens to destroy a society built on the rule of law.

King's concern with time

ends/means debate

any form?

Our Bill of Rights guarantees wide opportunities to use mass meetings, public parades and organized demonstrations to stimulate sentiment, to dramatize issues and to cause change. The Washington freedom march of 1963 was such a call for action. But the rights of free expression cannot be mere force cloaked in the garb of free speech. As the courts have decreed in labor cases, free assembly does not mean mass picketing or sit-down strikes. These rights are subject to limitations of time and place so as to secure the rights of others. When militant students storm a college president's office to achieve demands, when certain groups plan rush-hour car stalling to protest discrimination in employment, these are not dissent, but a denial of rights to others. Neither is it the lawful use of mass protest, but rather the unlawful use of mob power.

these are legal

right to demonstrate is limited

can't deny others' rights

Justice Black, one of the foremost advocates and defenders of the right of protest and dissent, has said:

> . . . Experience demonstrates that it is not a far step from what to many seems to be the earnest, honest, patriotic, kind-spirited multitude of today, to the fanatical, threatening, lawless mob of tomorrow. And the crowds that press in the streets for noble goals today can be supplanted tomorrow by street mobs pressuring the courts for precisely opposite ends.

Society must censure those demonstrators who would trespass on the public peace, as it must condemn those rioters whose pillage would destroy the public peace. But more ambivalent is society's posture toward the civil disobedient. Unlike the rioter, <u>the true civil disobedient commits no violence.</u> Unlike the mob demonstrator, he <u>commits no trespass on others' rights.</u> The civil disobedient, while deliberately violating a law, <u>shows an oblique respect for the law</u> by voluntarily submitting to its sanctions. He neither resists arrest nor evades punishment. Thus, <u>he breaches the law but not the peace.</u>

Isn't he contradicting himself?

But civil disobedience, whatever the ethical rationalization, is still an <u>assault</u> on our democratic society, an <u>affront</u> to our legal order and an <u>attack</u> on our constitutional government. To indulge civil disobedience is to invite <u>anarchy</u>, and the permissive arbitrariness of anarchy is hardly less tolerable than the repressive arbitrariness of tyranny. Too often the license of liberty is followed by the loss of liberty, because into the dessert of anarchy comes the man on horseback, a Mussolini or a Hitler.

Threatens repression as retaliation

6

We had already read and annotated the King excerpt, so we read the Van Dusen selection looking for a basis for comparison. We decided to base our contrast on the writer's different views of nonviolent direct action. We carefully reread the Van Dusen selection, annotating aspects of his argument against the use of nonviolent direct action. These annotations led directly to the first paragraph of our contrast, which summarizes Van Dusen's argument. Then we reread the King selection, looking for how he justifies nonviolent direct action. The second paragraph presents King's defense, plus some of our own ideas on how he could have responded to Van Dusen.

King and Van Dusen present radically different views of legal, nonviolent direct action, such as parades, demonstrations, boycotts, sit-ins, or pickets. Although Van Dusen acknowledges that direct action is legal, he nevertheless fears it; and he challenges it energetically in these paragraphs. He seems most concerned about the ways direct action disturbs the peace, infringes on others' rights, and threatens violence. He worries that even though some groups make gains through direct action, the end result is that everyone else begins to doubt the validity of the usual democratic procedures of relying on legislation and the courts. He condemns advocates of direct action like King for believing that the end (in this case, racial justice) justifies the means (direct action). Van Dusen argues that demonstrations often end violently and that an organized movement like King's can in the beginning win concessions through direct action but then end up extorting demands through threats and illegal uses of power.

In contrast, King argues that nonviolent direct action preserves the peace by bringing hidden tensions and prejudices to the surface where they can be acknowledged and addressed. Direct action enhances democracy by changing its unjust laws and thereby strengthening it. Since direct action is entirely legal, to forgo it as a strategy for change would be to turn one's back on a basic democratic principle. Although it may inconvenience people, its end (a more just social order) is entirely justified by its means (direct action). King would no doubt insist that the occasional violence that follows direct action results always from aggressive, unlawful interference with demonstrations, interference sometimes led by police officers. He might also argue that neither anarchy nor extortion followed from his group's actions.

Notice that these paragraphs address each writer's argument separately. An alternative plan would have been to identify Van Dusen's main points and then compare and contrast the two writers' arguments point by point.

Comparing and Contrasting Related Readings

To compare and contrast two reading selections,

1. Read them both to decide on a basis or ground for comparison or contrast.
2. Reread and annotate one selection to identify points of comparison or contrast.
3. Write up your analysis of the first selection, or reread the second selection, annotating for the points you have already identified.
4. Write up your analysis of the second selection, revising your analysis of the first selection to correspond to any new insights you have gained. Or write a point-by-point comparison or contrast of the two selections.

Martin Luther King, Jr.

LETTER FROM BIRMINGHAM JAIL

Here is the complete text of the "Letter from Birmingham Jail," followed by the published statement that precipitated the letter. You can find the excerpt, used as an example throughout this catalog, in paragraphs 23 through 32.

MY DEAR FELLOW CLERGYMEN:

While confined here in the Birmingham city jail, I came across your recent statement calling my present activities "unwise and untimely." 1

Seldom do I pause to answer criticism of my work and ideas. If I sought to answer all the criticisms that cross my desk, my secretaries would have little time for anything other than such correspondence in the course of the day, and I would have no time for constructive work. But since I feel that you are men of genuine good will and that your criticisms are sincerely set forth, I want to try to answer your statement in what I hope will be patient and reasonable terms.

I think I should indicate why I am here in Birmingham, since you   2
have been influenced by the view which argues against "outsiders coming in." I have the honor of serving as president of the Southern Christian Leadership Conference, an organization operating in every southern state, with headquarters in Atlanta, Georgia. We have some eighty-five affiliated organizations across the South, and one of them is the Alabama Christian Movement for Human Rights. Frequently we share staff, educational, and financial resources with our affiliates. Several months ago the affiliate here in Birmingham asked us to be on call to engage in a nonviolent direct-action program if such were deemed necessary. We readily consented, and when the hour came we lived up to our promise. So I, along with several members of my staff, am here because I was invited here. I am here because I have organizational ties here.

But more basically, I am in Birmingham because injustice is here.   3
Just as the prophets of the eighth century B.C. left their villages and carried their "thus saith the Lord" far beyond the boundaries of their home towns, and just as the Apostle Paul left his village of Tarsus and carried the gospel of Jesus Christ to the far corners of the Greco-Roman world, so am I compelled to carry the gospel of freedom beyond my own home town. Like Paul, I must constantly respond to the Macedonian call for aid.

Moreover, I am cognizant of the interrelatedness of all communi-   4
ties and states. I cannot sit idly by in Atlanta and not be concerned about what happens in Birmingham. Injustice anywhere is a threat to justice everywhere. We are caught in an inescapable network of mutuality, tied in a single garment of destiny. Whatever affects one directly, affects all indirectly. Never again can we afford to live with the narrow, provincial "outside agitator" idea. Anyone who lives inside the United States can never be considered an outsider anywhere within its bounds.

You deplore the demonstrations taking place in Birmingham. But   5
your statement, I am sorry to say, fails to express a similar concern for the conditions that brought about the demonstrations. I am sure that none of you would want to rest content with the superficial kind of social analysis that deals merely with effects and does not grapple with underlying causes. It is unfortunate that demonstrations are taking place in Birmingham, but it is even more unfortunate that the city's white power structure left the Negro community with no alternative.

In any nonviolent campaign there are four basic steps: collection   6
of the facts to determine whether injustices exist; negotiation; self-
purification; and direct action. We have gone through all these steps
in Birmingham. There can be no gainsaying the fact that racial injustice engulfs this community. Birmingham is probably the most thoroughly segregated city in the United States. Its ugly record of
brutality is widely known. Negroes have experienced grossly unjust
treatment in the courts. There have been more unsolved bombings
of Negro homes and churches in Birmingham than in any other city
in the nation. These are the hard, brutal facts of the case. On the
basis of these conditions, Negro leaders sought to negotiate with
the city fathers. But the latter consistently refused to engage in
good-faith negotiation.

Then, last September, came the opportunity to talk with leaders   7
of Birmingham's economic community. In the course of the negotia-
tions, certain promises were made by the merchants—for example,
to remove the stores' humiliating racial signs. On the basis of these
promises, the Reverend Fred Shuttlesworth and the leaders of the
Alabama Christian Movement for Human Rights agreed to a mora-
torium on all demonstrations. As the weeks and months went by,
we realized that we were the victims of a broken promise. A few
signs, briefly removed, returned; the others remained.

As in so many past experiences, our hopes had been blasted, and   8
the shadow of deep disappointment settled upon us. We had no
alternative except to prepare for direct action, whereby we would
present our very bodies as a means of laying our case before the
conscience of the local and the national community. Mindful of the
difficulties involved, we decided to undertake a process of self-purifi-
cation. We began a series of workshops on nonviolence, and we
repeatedly asked ourselves: "Are you able to accept blows without
retaliating?" "Are you able to endure the ordeal of jail?" We decided
to schedule our direct-action program for the Easter season, realizing that except for Christmas, this is the main shopping period of
the year. Knowing that a strong economic-withdrawal program
would be the by-product of direct action, we felt that this would be
the best time to bring pressure to bear on the merchants for the
needed change.

Then it occurred to us that Birmingham's mayoral election was   9
coming up in March, and we speedily decided to postpone action
until after election day. When we discovered that the Commissioner of Public Safety, Eugene "Bill" Connor, had piled up enough votes
to be in the run-off, we decided again to postpone action until the
day after the run-off so that the demonstrations could not be used
to cloud the issues. Like many others, we wanted to see Mr. Connor defeated, and to this end we endured postponement after postponement. Having aided in this community need, we felt our
direct-action program could be delayed no longer.

You may well ask, "Why direct action? Why sit-ins, marches, and   10
so forth? Isn't negotiation a better path?" You are quite right in calling for negotiation. Indeed, this is the very purpose of direct action.
Nonviolent direct action seeks to create such a crisis and foster
such a tension that a community which has constantly refused to
negotiate is forced to confront the issue. It seeks so to dramatize
the issue that it can no longer be ignored. My citing the creation of
tension as part of the work of the nonviolent-resister may sound
rather shocking. But I must confess that I am not afraid of the word
"tension." I have earnestly opposed violent tension, but there is a
type of constructive, nonviolent tension which is necessary for
growth. Just as Socrates felt that it was necessary to create a tension in the mind so that individuals could rise from the bondage of
myths and half-truths to the unfettered realm of creative analysis
and objective appraisal, so must we see the need for nonviolent gad-
flies to create the kind of tension in society that will help men rise
from the dark depths of prejudice and racism to the majestic heights
of understanding and brotherhood.

The purpose of our direct-action program is to create a situation   11
so crisis-packed that it will inevitably open the door to negotiation. I
therefore concur with you in your call for negotiation. Too long has
our beloved Southland been bogged down in a tragic effort to live in
monologue rather than dialogue.

One of the basic points in your statement is that the action that I   12
and my associates have taken in Birmingham is untimely. Some have
asked: "Why didn't you give the new city administration time to
act?" The only answer that I can give to this query is that the new
Birmingham administration must be prodded about as much as the
outgoing one, before it will act. We are sadly mistaken if we feel that
the election of Albert Boutwell as mayor will bring the millennium
to Birmingham. While Mr. Boutwell is a much more gentle person
than Mr. Connor, they are both segregationists, dedicated to main-
tenance of the status quo. I have hoped that Mr. Boutwell will be
reasonable enough to see the futility of massive resistance to desegregation. But he will not see this without pressure from devotees of
civil rights. My friends, I must say to you that we have not made a
single gain in civil rights without determined legal and nonviolent
pressure. Lamentably, it is an historical fact that privileged groups
seldom give up their privileges voluntarily. Individuals may see the
moral light and voluntarily give up their unjust posture; but, as Rein-
hold Niebuhr has reminded us, groups tend to be more immoral
than individuals.

We know through painful experience that freedom is never vol-   13
untarily given by the oppressor; it must be demanded by the
oppressed. Frankly, I have yet to engage in a direct-action campaign
that was "well timed" in the view of those who have not suffered
unduly from the disease of segregation. For years now I have heard

the word "Wait!" It rings in the ear of every Negro with piercing familiarity. This "Wait" has almost always meant "Never." We must come to see, with one of our distinguished jurists, that "justice too long delayed is justice denied."

We have waited for more than 340 years for our constitutional and God-given rights. The nations of Asia and Africa are moving with jetlike speed toward gaining political independence, but we still creep at horse-and-buggy pace toward gaining a cup of coffee at a lunch counter. Perhaps it is easy for those who have never felt the stinging darts of segregation to say, "Wait." But when you have seen vicious mobs lynch your mothers and fathers at will and drown your sisters and brothers at whim; when you have seen hate-filled police-men curse, kick, and even kill your black brothers and sisters; when you see the vast majority of your twenty million Negro brothers smothering in an airtight cage of poverty in the midst of an affluent society; when you suddenly find your tongue twisted and your speech stammering as you seek to explain to your six-year-old daughter why she can't go to the public amusement park that has just been advertised on television, and see tears welling up in her eyes when she is told that Funtown is closed to colored children, and see ominous clouds of inferiority beginning to form in her little mental sky, and see her beginning to distort her personality by developing an unconscious bitterness toward white people; when you have to concoct an answer for a five-year-old son who is asking, "Daddy, why do white people treat colored people so mean?"; when you take a cross-country drive and find it necessary to sleep night after night in the uncomfortable corners of your automobile because no motel will accept you; when you are humiliated day in and day out by nagging signs reading "white" and "colored"; when your first name becomes "nigger," your middle name becomes "boy" (however old you are) and your last name becomes "John," and your wife and mother are never given the respected title "Mrs."; when you are harried by day and haunted by night by the fact that you are a Negro, living constantly at tiptoe stance, never quite knowing what to expect next, and are plagued with inner fears and other resentments; when you are forever fighting a degenerat-ing sense of "nobodiness"—then you will understand why we find it difficult to wait. There comes a time when the cup of endurance runs over, and men are no longer willing to be plunged into the abyss of despair. I hope, sirs, you can understand our legitimate and unavoidable impatience.

You express a great deal of anxiety over our willingness to break laws. This is certainly a legitimate concern. Since we so diligently urge people to obey the Supreme Court's decision of 1954 outlaw-ing segregation in the public schools, at first glance it may seem rather paradoxical for us consciously to break laws. One may well ask: "How can you advocate breaking some laws and obeying others?" The answer lies in the fact that there are two types of laws: just and unjust. I would be the first to advocate obeying just laws. One has not only a legal but a moral responsibility to obey just laws. Conversely, one has a moral responsibility to disobey unjust laws. I would agree with St. Augustine that "an unjust law is no law at all."

Now, what is the difference between the two? How does one [16] determine whether a law is just or unjust? A just law is a man-made code that squares with the moral law or the law of God. An unjust law is a code that is out of harmony with the moral law. To put it in the terms of St. Thomas Aquinas: An unjust law is a human law that is not rooted in eternal law and natural law. Any law that uplifts human personality is just. Any law that degrades human personality is unjust. All segregation statutes are unjust because segregation distorts the soul and damages the personality. It gives the segregator a false sense of superiority and the segregated a false sense of inferiority. Segregation, to use the terminology of the Jewish philosopher Martin Buber, substitutes an "I-it" relationship for an "I-thou" relationship and ends up relegating persons to the status of things. Hence segregation is not only politically, economically, and sociologically unsound, it is morally wrong and sinful. Paul Tillich has said that sin is separation. Is not segregation an existential expression of man's tragic separation, his awful estrangement, his terrible sinfulness? Thus it is that I can urge men to obey the 1954 decision of the Supreme Court, for it is morally right; and I can urge them to disobey segregation ordinances, for they are morally wrong.

Let us consider a more concrete example of just and unjust laws. [17] An unjust law is a code that a numerical or power majority group compels a minority group to obey but does not make binding on itself. This is *difference* made legal. By the same token, a just law is a code that a majority compels a minority to follow and that it is willing to follow itself. This is *sameness* made legal.

Let me give another explanation. A law is unjust if it is inflicted on [18] a minority that, as a result of being denied the right to vote, had no part in enacting or devising the law. Who can say that the legislature of Alabama which set up that state's segregation laws was democratically elected? Throughout Alabama all sorts of devious methods are used to prevent Negroes from becoming registered voters, and there are some counties in which, even though Negroes constitute a majority of the population, not a single Negro is registered. Can any law enacted under such circumstances be considered democratically structured?

Sometimes a law is just on its face and unjust in its application. [19] For instance, I have been arrested on a charge of parading without a permit. Now, there is nothing wrong in having an ordinance which requires a permit for a parade. But such an ordinance becomes unjust when it is used to maintain segregation and to deny citizens the First-Amendment privilege of peaceful assembly and protest.

I hope you are able to see the distinction I am trying to point out. 20
In no sense do I advocate evading or defying the law, as would the
rabid segregationist. That would lead to anarchy. One who breaks
an unjust law must do so openly, lovingly, and with a willingness to
accept the penalty. I submit that an individual who breaks a law that
conscience tells him is unjust, and who willingly accepts the penalty
of imprisonment in order to arouse the conscience of the community over its injustice, is in reality expressing the highest respect for
law.

Of course, there is nothing new about this kind of civil disobedi- 21
ence. It was evidenced sublimely in the refusal of Shadrach, Meshach,
and Abednego to obey the laws of Nebuchadnezzar, on the ground
that a higher moral law was at stake. It was practiced superbly by
the early Christians, who were willing to face hungry lions and the
excruciating pain of chopping blocks rather than submit to certain
unjust laws of the Roman Empire. To a degree, academic freedom is
a reality today because Socrates practiced civil disobedience. In our
own nation, the Boston Tea Party represented a massive act of civil
disobedience.

We should never forget that everything Adolf Hitler did in Ger- 22
many was "legal" and everything the Hungarian freedom fighters did
in Hungary was "illegal." It was "illegal" to aid and comfort a Jew in
Hitler's Germany. Even so, I am sure that, had I lived in Germany at
the time, I would have aided and comforted my Jewish brothers. If
today I lived in a Communist country where certain principles dear
to the Christian faith are suppressed, I would openly advocate disobeying that country's antireligious laws.

I must make two honest confessions to you, my Christian and 23
Jewish brothers. First, I must confess that over the past few years I
have been gravely disappointed with the white moderate. I have
almost reached the regrettable conclusion that the Negro's great
stumbling block in his stride toward freedom is not the White Citizen's Counciler or the Ku Klux Klanner, but the white moderate,
who is more devoted to "order" than to justice; who prefers a negative peace which is the absence of tension to a positive peace
which is the presence of justice; who constantly says, "I agree with
you in the goal you seek, but I cannot agree with your methods of
direct action"; who paternalistically believes he can set the timetable
for another man's freedom; who lives by a mythical concept of time
and who constantly advises the Negro to wait for a "more convenient season." Shallow understanding from people of good will is
more frustrating than absolute misunderstanding from people of ill
will. Lukewarm acceptance is much more bewildering than outright
rejection.

I had hoped that the white moderate would understand that law 24
and order exist for the purpose of establishing justice and that when
they fail in this purpose they become the dangerously structured

dams that block the flow of social progress. I had hoped that the white moderate would understand that the present tension in the South is a necessary phase of the transition from an obnoxious negative peace, in which the Negro passively accepted his unjust plight, to a substantive and positive peace, in which all men will respect the dignity and worth of human personality. Actually, we who engage in nonviolent direct action are not the creators of tension. We merely bring to the surface the hidden tension that is already alive. We bring it out in the open, where it can be seen and dealt with. Like a boil that can never be cured so long as it is covered up but must be opened with all its ugliness to the natural medicines of air and light, injustice must be exposed, with all the tension its exposure creates, to the light of human conscience and the air of national opinion, before it can be cured.

In your statement you assert that our actions, even though   25
peaceful, must be condemned because they precipitate violence. But is this a logical assertion? Isn't this like condemning a robbed man because his possession of money precipitated the evil act of robbery? Isn't this like condemning Socrates because his unswerving commitment to truth and his philosophical inquiries precipitated the act by the misguided populace in which they made him drink hemlock? Isn't this like condemning Jesus because his unique God-consciousness and never-ceasing devotion to God's will precipitated the evil act of crucifixion? We must come to see that, as the federal courts have consistently affirmed, it is wrong to urge an individual to cease his efforts to gain his basic constitutional rights because the quest may precipitate violence. Society must protect the robbed and punish the robber.

I had also hoped that the white moderate would reject the myth   26
concerning time in relation to the struggle for freedom. I have just received a letter from a white brother in Texas. He writes: "All Christians know that the colored people will receive equal rights eventually, but it is possible that you are in too great a religious hurry. It has taken Christianity almost two thousand years to accomplish what it has. The teachings of Christ take time to come to earth." Such an attitude stems from a tragic misconception of time, from the strangely irrational notion that there is something in the very flow of time that will inevitably cure all ills. Actually, time itself is neutral; it can be used either destructively or constructively. More and more I feel that the people of ill will have used time much more effectively than have the people of good will. We will have to repent in this generation not merely for the hateful words and actions of the bad people but for the appalling silence of the good people. Human progress never rolls in on wheels of inevitability; it comes through the tireless efforts of men willing to be co-workers with God, and without this hard work, time itself becomes an ally of the forces of social stagnation. We must use time creatively, in the

knowledge that the time is always ripe to do right. Now is the time to make real the promise of democracy and transform our pending national elegy into a creative psalm of brotherhood. Now is the time to lift our national policy from the quicksand of racial injustice to the solid rock of human dignity.

You speak of our activity in Birmingham as extreme. At first I was   27
rather disappointed that fellow clergymen would see my nonviolent efforts as those of an extremist. I began thinking about the fact that I stand in the middle of two opposing forces in the Negro community. One is a force of complacency, made up in part of Negroes who, as a result of long years of oppression, are so drained of self-respect and a sense of "somebodiness" that they have adjusted to segregation; and in part of a few middle-class Negroes, who because of a degree of academic and economic security and because in some ways they profit by segregation, have become insensitive to the problems of the masses. The other force is one of bitterness and hatred, and it comes perilously close to advocating violence. It is expressed in the various black nationalist groups that are springing up across the nation, the largest and best-known being Elijah Muhammad's Muslim movement. Nourished by the Negro's frustration over the continued existence of racial discrimination, this movement is made up of people who have lost faith in America, who have absolutely repudiated Christianity, and who have concluded that the white man is an incorrigible "devil."

I have tried to stand between these two forces, saying that we   28
need emulate neither the "do-nothingism" of the complacent nor the hatred and despair of the black nationalist. For there is the more excellent way of love and nonviolent protest. I am grateful to God that, through the influence of the Negro church, the way of nonviolence became an integral part of our struggle.

If this philosophy had not emerged, by now many streets of the   29
South would, I am convinced, be flowing with blood. And I am further convinced that if our white brothers dismiss as "rabble-rousers" and "outside agitators" those of us who employ nonviolent direction action, and if they refuse to support our nonviolent efforts, millions of Negroes will, out of frustration and despair, seek solace and security in black-nationalist ideologies—a development that would inevitably lead to a frightening racial nightmare.

Oppressed people cannot remain oppressed forever. The yearn-   30
ing for freedom eventually manifests itself, and that is what has happened to the American Negro. Something within has reminded him of his birthright of freedom, and something without has reminded him that it can be gained. Consciously or unconsciously, he has been caught up by the *Zeitgeist,* and with his black brothers of Africa and his brown and yellow brothers of Asia, South America and the Caribbean, the United States Negro is moving with a sense of great urgency toward the promised land of racial justice. If one recognizes

this vital urge that has engulfed the Negro community, one should readily understand why public demonstrations are taking place. The Negro has many pent-up resentments and latent frustrations, and he must release them. So let him march; let him make prayer pilgrimages to the city hall; let him go on freedom rides—and try to understand why he must do so. If his repressed emotions are not released in nonviolent ways, they will seek expression through violence; this is not a threat but a fact of history. So I have not said to my people: "Get rid of your discontent." Rather, I have tried to say that this normal and healthy discontent can be channeled into the creative outlet of nonviolent direct action. And now this approach is being termed extremist.

But though I was initially disappointed at being categorized as an [31] extremist, as I continued to think about the matter I gradually gained a measure of satisfaction from the label. Was not Jesus an extremist for love: "Love your enemies, bless them that curse you, do good to them that hate you, and pray for them which despitefully use you, and persecute you." Was not Amos an extremist for justice: "Let justice roll down like waters and righteousness like an everflowing stream." Was not Paul an extremist for the Christian gospel: "I bear in my body the marks of the Lord Jesus." Was not Martin Luther an extremist: "Here I stand; I cannot do otherwise, so help me God." And John Bunyan: "I will stay in jail to the end of my days before I make a butchery of my conscience." And Abraham Lincoln: "This nation cannot survive half slave and half free." And Thomas Jefferson: "We hold these truths to be self-evident, that all men are created equal . . . " So the question is not whether we will be extremists, but what kind of extremists we will be. Will we be extremists for hate or for love? Will we be extremists for the preservation of injustice or for the extension of justice? In that dramatic scene on Calvary's hill three men were crucified. We must never forget that all three were crucified for the same crime—the crime of extremism. Two were extremists for immorality, and thus fell below their environment. The other, Jesus Christ, was an extremist for love, truth and goodness, and thereby rose above his environment. Perhaps the South, the nation and the world are in dire need of creative extremists.

I had hoped that the white moderate would see this need. Per- [32] haps I was too optimistic; perhaps I expected too much. I suppose I should have realized that few members of the oppressor race can understand the deep groans and passionate yearnings of the oppressed race, and still fewer have the vision to see that injustice must be rooted out by strong, persistent and determined action. I am thankful, however, that some of our white brothers in the South have grasped the meaning of this social revolution and committed themselves to it. They are still all too few in quantity, but they are big in quality. Some—such as Ralph McGill, Lillian Smith, Harry

Golden, James McBride Dabbs, Ann Braden, and Sarah Patton Boyle—have written about our struggle in eloquent and prophetic terms. Others have marched with us down nameless streets of the South. They have languished in filthy, roach-infested jails, suffering the abuse and brutality of policemen who view them as "dirty nigger-lovers." Unlike so many of their moderate brothers and sisters, they have recognized the urgency of the movement and sensed the need for powerful "action" antidotes to combat the disease of segregation.

Let me take note of my other major disappointment. I have been 33 so greatly disappointed with the white church and its leadership. Of course, there are some notable exceptions. I am not unmindful of the fact that each of you has taken some significant stands on this issue. I commend you, Reverend Stallings, for your Christian stand on this past Sunday, in welcoming Negroes to your worship service on a nonsegregated basis. I commend the Catholic leaders of this state for integrating Spring Hill College several years ago.

But despite these notable exceptions, I must honestly reiterate 34 that I have been disappointed with the church. I do not say this as one of those negative critics who can always find something wrong with the church. I say this as a minister of the gospel, who loves the church; who was nurtured in its bosom; who has been sustained by its spiritual blessings and who will remain true to it as long as the cord of life shall lengthen.

When I was suddenly catapulted into the leadership of the bus 35 protest in Montgomery, Alabama, a few years ago, I felt we would be supported by the white church. I felt that the white ministers, priests, and rabbis of the South would be among our strongest allies. Instead, some have been outright opponents, refusing to understand the freedom movement and misrepresenting its leaders; all too many others have been more cautious than courageous and have remained silent behind the anesthetizing security of stained glass windows.

In spite of my shattered dreams, I came to Birmingham with the 36 hope that the white religious leadership of this community would see the justice of our cause and, with deep moral concern, would serve as the channel through which our just grievances could reach the power structure. I had hoped that each of you would understand. But again I have been disappointed.

I have heard numerous southern religious leaders admonish their 37 worshipers to comply with a desegregation decision because it is the law, but I have longed to hear white ministers declare: "Follow this decree because integration is morally right and because the Negro is your brother." In the midst of blatant injustices inflicted upon the Negro, I have watched white churchmen stand on the sideline and mouth pious irrelevancies and sanctimonious trivialities. In the midst of a mighty struggle to rid our nation of racial and economic injustice, I have heard many ministers say: "Those are social issues, with which the gospel has no real concern." And I have watched many churches commit themselves to a completely other-worldly religion which makes a strange, un-Biblical distinction between body and soul, between the sacred and the secular.

I have traveled the length and breadth of Alabama, Mississippi, and all the other southern states. On sweltering summer days and crisp autumn mornings I have looked at the South's beautiful churches with their lofty spires pointing heavenward. I have beheld the impressive outlines of her massive religious-education buildings. Over and over I have found myself asking: "What kind of people worship here? Who is their God? Where were their voices when the lips of Governor Barnett dripped with words of interposition and nullification? Where were they when Governor Wallace gave a clarion call for defiance and hatred? Where were their voices of support when bruised and weary Negro men and women decided to rise from the dark dungeons of complacency to the bright hills of creative protest?"   38

Yes, these questions are still in my mind. In deep disappointment I have wept over the laxity of the church. But be assured that my tears have been tears of love. There can be no deep disappointment where there is not deep love. Yes, I love the church. How could I do otherwise? I am in the rather unique position of being the son, the grandson, and the great-grandson of preachers. Yes, I see the church as the body of Christ. But, oh! How we have blemished and scarred that body through social neglect and through fear of being nonconformists.   39

There was a time when the church was very powerful—in the time when the early Christians rejoiced at being deemed worthy to suffer for what they believed. In those days the church was not merely a thermometer that recorded the ideas and principles of popular opinion; it was a thermostat that transformed the mores of society. Whenever the early Christians entered a town, the people in power became disturbed and immediately sought to convict the Christians for being "disturbers of the peace" and "outside agitators." But the Christians pressed on, in the conviction that they were "a colony of heaven," called to obey God rather than man. Small in number, they were big in commitment. They were too God-intoxicated to be "astronomically intimidated." By their effort and example they brought an end to such ancient evils as infanticide and gladiatorial contests.   40

Things are different now. So often the contemporary church is a weak, ineffectual voice with an uncertain sound. So often it is an archdefender of the status quo. Far from being disturbed by the presence of the church, the power structure of the average community is consoled by the church's silent—and often even vocal—sanction of things as they are.   41

But the judgment of God is upon the church as never before. If 42 today's church does not recapture the sacrificial spirit of the early church, it will lose its authenticity, forfeit the loyalty of millions, and be dismissed as an irrelevant social club with no meaning for the twentieth century. Every day I meet young people whose disappointment with the church has turned into outright disgust.

Perhaps I have once again been too optimistic. Is organized reli- 43 gion too inextricably bound to the status quo to save our nation and the world? Perhaps I must turn my faith to the inner spiritual church, the church within the church, as the true *ekklesia* and the hope of the world. But again I am thankful to God that some noble souls from the ranks of organized religion have broken loose from the paralyzing chains of conformity and joined us as active partners in the struggle for freedom. They have left their secure congregations and walked the streets of Albany, Georgia, with us. They have gone down the highways of the South on tortuous rides for freedom. Yes, they have gone to jail with us. Some have been dismissed from their churches, have lost the support of their bishops and fellow ministers. But they have acted in the faith that right defeated is stronger than evil triumphant. Their witness has been the spiritual salt that has preserved the true meaning of the gospel in these troubled times. They have carved a tunnel of hope through the dark mountain of disappointment.

I hope the church as a whole will meet the challenge of this deci- 44 sive hour. But even if the church does not come to the aid of justice, I have no despair about the future. I have no fear about the outcome of our struggle in Birmingham, even if our motives are at present misunderstood. We will reach the goal of freedom in Birmingham and all over the nation, because the goal of America is freedom. Abused and scorned though we may be, our destiny is tied up with America's destiny. Before the pilgrims landed at Plymouth, we were here. Before the pen of Jefferson etched the majestic words of the Declaration of Independence across the pages of history, we were here. For more than two centuries our forebears labored in this country without wages; they made cotton king; they built the homes of their masters while suffering gross injustice and shameful humiliation—and yet out of a bottomless vitality they continued to thrive and develop. If the inexpressible cruelties of slavery could not stop us, the opposition we now face will surely fail. We will win our freedom because the sacred heritage of our nation and the eternal will of God are embodied in our echoing demands.

Before closing I feel impelled to mention one other point in your 45 statement that has troubled me profoundly. You warmly commended the Birmingham police force for keeping "order" and "preventing violence." I doubt that you would have so warmly commended the police force if you had seen its dogs sinking their teeth into unarmed, nonviolent Negroes. I doubt that you would so quickly commend the policemen if you were to observe their ugly and inhumane treatment of Negroes here in the city jail; if you were to watch them push and curse old Negro women and young Negro girls; if you were to see them slap and kick old Negro men and young boys; if you were to observe them, as they did on two occasions, refuse to give us food because we wanted to sing our grace together. I cannot join you in your praise of the Birmingham police department.

It is true that the police have exercised a degree of discipline in handling the demonstrators. In this sense they have conducted themselves rather "nonviolently" in public. But for what purpose? To preserve the evil system of segregation. Over the past few years I have consistently preached that nonviolence demands that the means we use must be as pure as the ends we seek. I have tried to make clear that it is wrong to use immoral means to attain moral ends. But now I must affirm that it is just as wrong, or perhaps even more so, to use moral means to preserve immoral ends. Perhaps Mr. Connor and his policemen have been rather nonviolent in public, as was Chief Pritchett in Albany, Georgia, but they have used the moral means of nonviolence to maintain the immoral end of racial injustice. As T. S. Eliot has said, "The last temptation is the greatest treason: To do the right deed for the wrong reason." 46

I wish you had commended the Negro sit-inners and demonstrators of Birmingham for their sublime courage, their willingness to suffer, and their amazing discipline in the midst of great provocation. One day the South will recognize its real heroes. They will be the James Merediths, with the noble sense of purpose that enables them to face jeering and hostile mobs, and with the agonizing loneliness that characterizes the life of the pioneer. They will be old, oppressed, battered Negro women, symbolized in a seventy-two-year-old woman in Montgomery, Alabama, who rose up with a sense of dignity and with her people decided not to ride segregated buses, and who responded with ungrammatical profundity to one who inquired about her weariness: "My feets is tired, but my soul is at rest." They will be the young high school and college students, the young ministers of the gospel and a host of their elders, courageously and nonviolently sitting in at lunch counters and willingly going to jail for conscience' sake. One day the South will know that when these disinherited children of God sat down at lunch counters, they were in reality standing up for what is best in the American dream and for the most sacred values in our Judaeo-Christian heritage, thereby bringing our nation back to those great wells of democracy which were dug deep by the founding fathers in their formulation of the Constitution and the Declaration of Independence. 47

Never before have I written so long a letter. I'm afraid it is much too long to take your precious time. I can assure you that it would have been much shorter if I had been writing from a comfortable desk, but what else can one do when he is alone in a narrow jail cell, 48 other than write long letters, think long thoughts, and pray long prayers?

If I have said anything in this letter that overstates the truth and   49
indicates an unreasonable impatience, I beg you to forgive me. If I have said anything that understates the truth and indicates my having a patience that allows me to settle for anything less than brotherhood, I beg God to forgive me.

I hope this letter finds you strong in the faith. I also hope that cir-   50
cumstances will soon make it possible for me to meet each of you, not as an integrationist or a civil-rights leader but as a fellow clergyman and a Christian brother. Let us all hope that the dark clouds of racial prejudice will soon pass away and the deep fog of misunderstanding will be lifted from our fear-drenched communities, and in some not too distant tomorrow the radiant stars of love and brotherhood will shine over our great nation with all their scintillating beauty.

Yours for the cause of Peace and Brotherhood,
MARTIN LUTHER KING, JR.

Public Statement by Eight Alabama Clergymen

April 12, 1963

We the undersigned clergymen are among those who, in January,   1
issued "An Appeal for Law and Order and Common Sense," in dealing with racial problems in Alabama. We expressed understanding that honest convictions in racial matters could properly be pursued in the courts, but urged that decisions of those courts should in the meantime be peacefully obeyed.

Since that time there has been some evidence of increased fore-   2
bearance and a willingness to face facts. Responsible citizens have undertaken to work on various problems which cause racial friction and unrest. In Birmingham, recent public events have given indication that we all have opportunity for a new constructive and realistic approach to racial problems.

However, we are now confronted by a series of demonstrations   3
by some of our Negro citizens, directed and led in part by outsiders. We recognize the natural impatience of people who feel that their hopes are slow in being realized. But we are convinced that these demonstrations are unwise and untimely.

We agree rather with certain local Negro leadership which has   4
called for honest and open negotiation of racial issues in our area. And we believe this kind of facing of issues can best be accomplished by citizens of our own metropolitan area, white and Negro, meeting with their knowledge and experience of the local situation. All of us need to face that responsibility and find proper channels for its accomplishment.

Just as we formerly pointed out that "hatred and violence have   5
no sanction in our religious and political traditions," we also point
out that such actions as incite to hatred and violence, however technically peaceful those actions may be, have not contributed to the
resolution of our local problems. We do not believe that these days
of new hope are days when extreme measures are justified in Birmingham.

We commend the community as a whole, and the local news   6
media and law enforcement officials in particular, on the calm manner in which these demonstrations have been handled. We urge the
public to continue to show restraint should the demonstrations
continue, and the law enforcement officials to remain calm and continue to protect our city from violence.

We further strongly urge our own Negro community to with-   7
draw support from these demonstrations, and to unite locally in
working peacefully for a better Birmingham. When rights are consistently denied, a cause should be pressed in the courts and in negoti-
ations among local leaders, and not in the streets. We appeal to
both our white and Negro citizenry to observe the principles of law
and order and common sense.

Signed by:

C. C. J. CARPENTER, D. D., LL.D., *Bishop of Alabama*

JOSEPH A. DURICK, D.D., *Auxiliary Bishop, Diocese of Mobile-Birm-ingham*

Rabbi MILTON L. GRAFMAN, *Temple Emanu-El, Birmingham, Alabama*

Bishop PAUL HARDIN, *Bishop of the Alabama-West Florida Confer-ence of the Methodist Church*

Bishop NOLAN B. HARMON, *Bishop of the North Alabama Confer-ence of the Methodist Church*

GEORGE M. MURRAY, D.D., LL.D., *Bishop Coadjutor, Episcopal Dio-cese of Alabama*

EDWARD V. RAMAGE, *Moderator, Synod of the Alabama Presbyteri-an Church in the United States*

EARL STALLINGS, *Pastor, First Baptist Church, Birmingham, Alabama*

A P P E N D I X   2

STRATEGIES FOR RESEARCH AND DOCUMENTATION

Many of the selections in this text are based on field and library research: Writers have visited places and interviewed people, and have gone to the library to gather necessary information. Critical readers are often called on to do research, following up on ideas or claims, looking firsthand at a source mentioned by the writer, or finding more information about a writer they admire. Writers also have occasion to do research: Unless they write solely from memory, writers will rely in part on research for their essays, reports, and books.

Many of the Considering Ideas for Your Own Writing sections in this text invite field or library research. As a writer at work using this text—and for writing you do for many of your college courses—you have to do research. You will often need to document your sources, indicating precisely where you found certain information. This appendix offers some strategies and guidelines for field and library research, along with instructions for documenting your sources.

FIELD RESEARCH

In universities, government agencies, and the business world, field research can be as important as library research or experimental research. In specialties such as sociology, political science, anthropology, polling, advertising, and news reporting, field research is the basic means of gathering information.

This section is a brief introduction to two of the major kinds of field research: observations and interviews. The writing activities involved are central to several academic specialties. If you major in education, journalism, or one of the social sciences, you probably will be asked to do writing based on observations and interviews. You will also read large amounts of information based on these ways of learning about people, groups, and institutions.

OBSERVATION

Getting Access

If the place you propose to visit is public, you probably will have easy access to it. If everything you need to see is within view of anyone passing by or using the place, you can make your observations without any special arrangements. Indeed, you may not even be noticed. However, if you require special access, you will need to arrange your visit, calling ahead or making a get-acquainted visit, to introduce yourself and state your purpose. Find out the times you may visit, and be certain you can get to the place easily.

Announcing Your Intentions

State your intentions directly and fully. Say who you are, where you are from, and what you hope to do. You may be surprised at how receptive people can be to a student on assignment from a college course. Not every place you wish to visit will welcome you, however. A variety of constraints on outside visitors exist in private businesses as well as public institutions. But generally, if people know your intentions, they may be able to tell you about aspects of a place or an activity you would not have thought to observe.

Taking Your Tools

Take a notebook with a firm back so that you will have a steady writing surface, perhaps a small stenographer's notebook with a spiral binding across the top. Take a writing instrument. Some observers dictate their notes into portable tape recorders, a method you may wish to try.

Observing

Some activities invite multiple vantage points, whereas others seem to limit the observer to a single perspective. Take advantage of every perspective available to you. Come in close, take a middle position, and stand back. Study the scene from a stationary position and also try to move around it. The more varied your perspectives, the more you are likely to observe.

Your purpose in observing is both to describe the activity and to analyze it. You will want to look closely at the activity itself, but you will also want to think about what makes this activity special, what seems to be the point of it.

Try to be an innocent observer: Pretend you have never seen anything like this activity before. Look for typical features of the activity as well as unusual features. Look at it from the perspective of your readers. Ask what details of the activity would surprise and inform and interest them.

Taking Notes

You undoubtedly will find your own style of note taking, but here are a few pointers: (1) Write only on one side of the page. Later, when you organize your notes, you may want to cut up the pages and file notes under different headings. (2) Take notes in words, phrases, or sentences. Draw diagrams or sketches, if they help you see and understand the place. (3) Note any ideas or questions that occur to you. (4) Use quotation marks around any overheard conversation you take down.

Because you can later reorganize your notes quite easily, you do not need to take notes in any planned or systematic way. Your notes should include information about the setting, the people, and your personal reactions.

THE SETTING. The easiest way to begin is to name objects you see. Start by listing objects. Then record details of some of these objects—color, shape, size, texture, function, relation to similar or dissimilar objects. Although your notes probably will contain mainly visual details, you might also want to record sounds and smells. Be sure to include some notes about the shape, dimensions, and layout of the place. How big is it? How is it organized?

THE PEOPLE. Record the number of people, their activities, their movements and behavior. Describe their appearance or dress. Record parts of overheard conversations. Note whether you see more men than women, more of one racial group than of another, more older than younger people. Most important, note anything surprising and unusual about people in the scene.

YOUR PERSONAL REACTIONS. Include in your notes any feelings you have about what you observe. Also record, as they occur to you, any hunches or ideas or insights you have.

Reflecting on What You Saw

Immediately after your visit (within a few minutes, if possible), find a quiet place to reflect on what you saw, review your notes, and add to them. Give yourself at least a half hour for quiet thought.

What you have in your notes and what you recall on reflection will suggest many more images and details from your observations. Add these to your notes.

Finally, review all your notes, and write a few sentences about your main impressions of the place. What did you learn? How did this visit change your preconceptions about the place? What surprised you most? What is the dominant impression you get from your notes?

Interviews

Interviewing tends to involve four basic steps: (1) planning and setting up the interview, (2) note taking, (3) reflecting on the interview, and (4) writing up your notes.

Choosing an Interview Subject

The first step is to decide whom to interview. If you are writing about something in which several people are involved, choose subjects representing a variety of perspectives—a range of different roles, for example. If you are profiling a single person, most, if not all, of your interviews will be with that person.

You should be flexible because you may be unable to speak to the person you targeted and may wind up with someone else—the person's assistant, perhaps. You might even learn more from an assistant than you would from the person in charge.

Arranging an Interview

You may be nervous about calling up a busy person and asking for some of his or her time. Indeed, you may get turned down. If so, do ask if someone else might talk to you.

Do not feel that just because you are a student you do not have the right to ask for people's time. People are often delighted to be asked about themselves. And, because you are a student on assignment, some people may feel that they are doing a form of public service to talk with you.

When introducing yourself to arrange the interview, give a short and simple description of your project. If you say too much, you could prejudice or limit the person's response. It is a good idea to exhibit some enthusiasm for your project, of course.

Keep in mind that the person you are interviewing is donating time to you. Be certain that you call ahead to arrange a specific time for the interview. Be on time. Bring all the materials you need, and express your thanks when the interview is over.

Planning for the Interview

Make any necessary observational visits and do any essential background reading before the interview. Consider your objectives. Do you want an orientation to the place (the "big picture") from this interview? Do you want this interview to lead you to other key people? Do you want mainly facts or information? Do you need clarification of something you have heard in another interview or observed or read? Do you want to learn more about the person, or learn about the place through the person, or both? Should you trust or distrust this person?

The key to good interviewing is flexibility. You may be looking for facts, but your interview subject may not have any to offer. In that case, you should be able to shift gears and go after whatever your subject has to discuss.

PREPARE SOME QUESTIONS IN ADVANCE. Take care in composing questions; they can be the key to a successful interview. Bad questions rarely yield useful answers. A bad question places unfair limits on respondents. Two specific types to avoid are forced-choice questions and leading questions.

Forced-choice questions are bad because they impose your terms on your respondents. Consider this example: "Do you think rape is an expression of sexual passion or of aggression?" A person may think that neither sexual passion nor aggression satisfactorily explains rape. A better way to phrase the question would be to ask, "People often fall into two camps on the issue of rape. Some think it is an expression of sexual passion, while others argue it is really not sexual but aggressive. Do you think it is either of these? If not, what is your opinion?" This form of questioning allows you to get a reaction to what others have said and at the same time it gives the person freedom to set the terms.

Leading questions are bad because they assume too much. An example of this kind of question is the following: "Do you think the increase in the occurrence of rape is due to the fact that women are perceived as competitors in a severely depressed economy?" This question assumes that there is an increase in the occurrence of rape, that women are perceived (apparently by rapists) as competitors, and that the economy is severely depressed. A better way of asking the question might be to make the assumptions more explicit by dividing the question into its parts: "Do you think there is an increase in the occurrence of rape? What could have caused it? I've heard some people argue that the economy has something to do with it. Do you think so? Do you think rapists perceive women as competitors for jobs? Could the current economic situation have made this competition more severe?

Good questions come in many different forms. One way of considering them is to divide them into two types: open and closed. *Open questions* give the respondent range and flexibility. They also generate anecdotes, personal revelations, and expressions of attitudes. The following are examples of open questions:

- I wonder if you would take a few minutes to tell me something about your early days in the business. I'd be interested to hear about how it got started, what your hopes and aspirations were, what problems you faced and how you dealt with them.
- Tell me about a time you were (name an emotion).
- What did you think of (name a person or event)?
- What did you do when (name an event) happened?

The best questions are those that allow the subject to talk freely but to the point. If the answer strays too far from the point, a follow-up question may be necessary to refocus the talk. Another tack you may want to try is to rephrase the subject's answer, to say something like: "Let me see if I have this right," or "Am I correct in saying that you feel . . . " Often, a person will take the opportunity to amplify the original response by adding just the anecdote or quotation for which you have been looking.

Closed questions usually request specific information. For example,

- How do you do (name a process)?

- What does (name a word) mean?
- What does (a person, object, or place) look like?
- How was it made?

Taking Your Tools

You will need a notebook with a firm back so you can write on it easily without the benefit of a table or desk. We recommend a full-size ($8\frac{1}{2} \times 11$) spiral or ring notebook.

In this notebook, divide several pages into two columns with a line drawn vertically from a distance of about one third of the width of the page from the left margin. Use the left-hand column to record details about the scene, the person, the mood of the interview, other impressions. Head this column Details and Impressions. At the top of the right-hand column, write several questions. You may not use them, but they will jog your memory. This column should be titled Information. In this column, record what you learn from answers to your questions.

Taking Notes during the Interview

Because you are not taking a verbatim transcript of the interview (if you wanted a literal account, you would use a tape recorder or shorthand), your goals are to gather information and to record a few good quotations and anecdotes. In addition, because the people you interview may be unused to giving interviews and so will need to know you are listening, it is probably a good idea to do more listening than note taking. You may not have much confidence in your memory, but, if you pay close attention, you are likely to recall a good deal of the conversation afterward. During the interview, you should take some notes: a few quotations; key words and phrases to jog your memory; observational jottings about the scene, the person, and the mood of the interview. Remember that *how* something is said is as important as *what* is said. Pick up material that will give the interview write-up texture—gesture, physical appearance, verbal inflection, facial expression, dress, hairstyle, body language, anything that makes the person an individual.

Reflecting on the Interview

As soon as you finish the interview, find a quiet place to reflect on it, and review your notes. This reflection is essential because so much happens in an interview that you cannot record at the time. You need to spend at least a half hour, maybe longer, adding to your notes and thinking about what you learned.

At the end of this time, write a few sentences about your main impressions from the interview. What did you learn? What surprised you most? How did the interview change your attitude or understanding about the person or place? How would you summarize your main impressions of the person? How did this interview influence your plans to interview others or to reinterview this person? What do you want to learn from these next interviews?

LIBRARY RESEARCH

Library research involves a variety of diverse activities: checking the card or online catalog, browsing in the stacks, possibly consulting the *Readers' Guide to Periodical Literature,* asking the reference librarian for help. Although librarians are there to help, all college students should learn basic library research skills. Here we present a search strategy, a systematic and efficient way of doing library research (see Figure A1, Overview of a Search Strategy).

The search strategy was developed by librarians to make library research manageable and productive. Although specific search strategies will vary to fit the needs of individual research tastes, the general process will be demonstrated here: how to get started; where to find sources; what types of sources are

FIGURE A1.   Overview of a Search Strategy

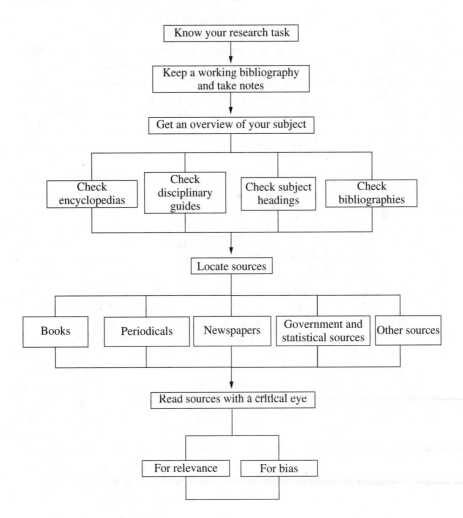

available and what sorts of information they provide; how to evaluate these sources; and, most important, how to go about this process of finding and evaluating sources *systematically.*

Library research can be useful at various stages of the writing process. How you use the library depends on the kind of essay you are writing and the special needs of your subject. You may, for example, need to do research immediately to choose a subject. Or you may choose a topic without the benefit of research but then use the library to find specific information to support your thesis. But no matter when you do library research, you will need to have a search strategy. This search strategy will guide you in setting up a working bibliography and a documentation style, in searching for key words or subject headings, in seeking background information, in finding bibliographies, and in using the card catalog and specialty indexes. Finally, it will help you evaluate the sources that you will use with a critical eye.

A WORKING BIBLIOGRAPHY

A working bibliography is a preliminary, ongoing record of books, articles, pamphlets—all the sources of information you discover as you research your subject. (A final bibliography lists only sources actually used in your paper.) Some of the sources in your working bibliography may turn out to be irrelevant, while others simply will be unavailable. In addition, you can use your working bibliography as a means of keeping track of any encyclopedias, bibliographies, and indexes you consult, even though you may not list these resources in your final bibliography.

Practiced researchers keep their working bibliography on index cards, in a notebook, or in a computer file. They may keep bibliographical information separate from notes they take on the sources. Many researchers find index cards most convenient because they are so easily alphabetized. Others find them too easy to lose and prefer instead to keep everything—working bibliography, notes, and drafts—in one notebook. Researchers who use computers set up working bibliographies in word-processing programs or bibliographic management programs, such as Endnote Plus, that work in conjunction with word-processing programs. Whether you use cards, a notebook, or a computer, the important thing is to make your entries accurate and complete. If the call number for a book is incomplete or inaccurate, for example, you will not be able to find the book in the stacks.

Because you must eventually choose a documentation style for your essay, you may want to select it now, at the beginning of your research, so that all sources listed in your working bibliography will conform to the documentation style of your essay. The Acknowledging Sources section of this appendix presents two different documentation styles, one adopted by the Modern Language Association (MLA) and widely used in the humanities, and the other advocated by the American Psychological Association (APA) and used in the social sciences. Individual disciplines often have their own preferred styles of documentation, which your instructor may wish you to use.

CONSULTING ENCYCLOPEDIAS

You first need an overview of your topic. If you are researching a concept or an issue in a course you are taking, then your textbook or other course materials provide the obvious starting point. Your instructor can advise you about other sources that provide overviews of your topic. If your topic is just breaking in the news, then current newspapers and magazines might be sufficient. For all other topics—and for background information—encyclopedias and disciplinary guides are often the place to start.

Specialized encyclopedias can be a good place to start your research. General encyclopedias, such as *Encyclopaedia Britannica* and *Encyclopedia Americana,* cover many topics superficially, whereas specialized encyclopedias cover topics in the depth appropriate for college writing. In addition to providing an overview of a topic, a specialized encyclopedia often includes an explanation of issues related to the topic, definitions of specialized terminology, and selective bibliographies of additional sources.

As starting points, specialized encyclopedias have two further advantages: (1) they provide a comprehensive introduction to key terms related to your topic, terms that are especially useful in identifying the subject headings used to locate material in catalogs and indexes; and (2) they provide a comprehensive presentation of a subject, enabling you to see many possibilities for focusing your research on one aspect of it. Specialized encyclopedias can be found in the catalog under the subject heading for the discipline, such as "psychology," and the subheading "dictionaries and encyclopedias."

Two particular reference sources can help you identify specialized encyclopedias covering your topic:

ARBA Guide to Subject Encyclopedias and Dictionaries (1986). Lists specialized encyclopedias by broad subject category, with descriptions of coverage, focus, and any special features.

First Stop: The Master Index to Subject Encyclopedias (1989). Lists specialized encyclopedias by broad subject category and provides access to individual articles within them. By looking under the key terms that describe a topic, you can find references to specific articles in any of over four hundred specialized encyclopedias.

CONSULTING DISCIPLINARY GUIDES

Once you have a general overview of your topic, you will want to consult one of the research guides in that discipline. The following guides can help you identify the major handbooks, encyclopedias, bibliographies, journals, periodical indexes, and computer databases in the various disciplines. You need not read any of these extensive works straight through, but you will find them to be valuable references.

Guide to Reference Books, 10th ed. (1986). Edited by Eugene P. Sheehy.

The Humanities: A Selective Guide to Information Sources, 4th ed. (1994). By Ron Blazek and Elizabeth S. Aversa.

Scientific and Technical Information Sources, 2nd ed. (1987). By Ching-chih Chen.

Sources of Information in the Social Sciences: A Guide to the Literature, 3rd ed. (1986). Edited by William H. Webb.

Introduction to Library Research in Anthropology (1991). By John M. Weeks.

Visual Arts Research: A Handbook (1986). By Elizabeth B. Pollard.

Education: A Guide to Reference and Information Sources (1989). By Lois Buttlar.

On the Screen: A Film, Television, and Video Research Guide (1986). By Kim N. Fisher.

A Student's Guide to History, 6th ed. (1994). By Jules R. Benjamin.

Reference Works in British and American Literature (1990). By James K. Bracken.

Literary Research Guide: A Guide to Reference Sources for the Study of Literatures in English and Related Topics, 2nd ed. (1993). By James L. Harner.

Music: A Guide to the Reference Literature (1987). By William S. Brockman.

Philosophy: A Guide to the Reference Literature (1986). By Hans E. Bynagle.

Information Sources of Political Science, 4th ed. (1986). By Frederick L. Holler.

Library Research Guide to Psychology: Illustrated Search Strategy and Sources (1984). By Nancy E. Douglas.

A Guide to Reference and Information Sources (1987). By Stephen H. Aby.

Introduction to Library Research in Women's Studies (1985). By Susan E. Searing.

CHECKING SUBJECT HEADINGS

To carry your research beyond encyclopedias, you need to find appropriate subject headings. Subject headings are specific words and phrases used in libraries to categorize the contents of books and periodicals. As you read about your subject in an encyclopedia or other reference book, you should look for possible subject headings.

To begin your search for subject headings, consult the *Library of Congress Subject Headings (LCSH),* which usually can be found near the library catalog. This reference book lists the standard subject headings used in catalogs and indexes and in many encyclopedias and bibliographies. Figure A2 is an example from the *LCSH.*

Home schooling *(May Subd Geog)*   ◄—   **Place names may follow heading**
    Here are entered works on the provision of compulsory educa-
tion in the home by parents as an alternative to traditional public or
private schooling. General works on the provision of education in
the home by educational personnel are entered under Domestic
Education.

Used for —► UF Education, Home
               Home-based education
               Home education   **NT = Narrower term**
               Home instruction   **SA = See also**
               Home teaching by parents
               Homeschooling
               Instruction, Home
               Schooling, Home
Broader Term—► BT Education
Related Term —► RT Education—United States
               Education—Parent participation

FIGURE A2.   **Library of Congress Subject Heading Entry for "Home Schooling"**

Subject headings provide you with various key words and phrases to use as you
look through catalogs and indexes. For example, the preceding entry proved
particularly useful because when the student found nothing listed in the library
catalog under "home schooling," she tried the other headings until "Education—
Parent participation" and "Education—United States" yielded information on
three books. Note, too, that this entry explains the *type* of articles that would be
found under these headings—and those that would be found elsewhere. Keep in
mind that the terms listed in the *LCSH* might not be the *only* ones used for your
subject; don't be reluctant to try terms that you think might be relevant.

CONSULTING BIBLIOGRAPHIES

A bibliography is simply a list of publications on a given subject. Whereas an
encyclopedia may give you only background information on your subject, a bibliography gives you an overview of what has been published on the subject.
Its scope may be broad or narrow. Some bibliographers try to be exhaustive,
including every title they can find, but most are selective. To discover how
selections were made, check the bibliography's preface or introduction.

The best way to locate a comprehensive, up-to-date bibliography on your
subject is to look in the *Bibliographic Index.* A master list of bibliographies that
contain fifty or more titles, the *Bibliographic Index* includes bibliographies from
articles, books, and government publications. A new volume is published every
year. (Note that because this index is not cumulative, you should check back
over several years, beginning with the most current volume.)

Even if you attend a large research university, your library is unlikely to hold
every book or journal article a bibliography might direct you to. The library

catalog and serial record (a list of the periodicals the library holds) can tell you whether the book or journal is available.

FINDING BOOKS

When you begin your research project, find out how best to gain access to the various resources you will need. Many libraries now offer access to their online card catalog, periodical holdings, periodical and newspaper indexes, government documents, some specialized CD-ROM products, or even the holdings of other libraries through public access terminals. Check the menu screen of one of the terminals; it usually indicates the resources that are available through the system.

The primary source for books is the library catalog. Now nearly every college library offers a computerized catalog, sometimes called an online catalog. The library may also maintain a card catalog consisting of cards filed in drawers. The online catalog provides more flexibility in searching subject headings and may even tell you whether the book has already been checked out. Another distinct advantage is its ability to print out source information, making it unnecessary for you to copy it by hand. Since an online catalog often contains material received and catalogued only after a certain date, however, you should check both catalogs.

Library catalogs organize sources by author, subject, and title. For each book there is a card or computer entry under the name of each author, under the title, and under each subject heading to which the book is related. Author, title, and subject cards or entries all give the same basic information. Each card includes a *call number* in the upper left-hand corner. You will want to copy this number carefully, for it guides you to the location in your library of the source you seek.

FINDING PERIODICAL ARTICLES

The most up-to-date information on a subject usually is found not in books but in articles in magazines and journals, or periodicals. Articles in periodicals usually are not listed in the library catalog; to find them, you must instead use periodical indexes and abstracts. Indexes list articles, whereas abstracts summarize as well as list them. Library catalogs list the indexes and abstracts held in the library and note whether they are available in printed form, as microforms, or as computer databases. Those indexes listed in this section that are available as computer databases are labeled online and/or *CD-ROM* (for compact disc–read only memory). Names for these databases, if different from the print index, are also given. Check with a librarian to see what databases are available at your library.

Periodical indexes and abstracts are of two types: general and specialized.

General Indexes

General periodical indexes list articles in nontechnical, general-interest publications and cover a broad range of subjects. Most have separate author and subject listings as well as a list of book reviews. Following are some general indexes:

Readers' Guide to Periodical Literature (1900–; online and CD-ROM, 1983–); updated quarterly. Covers about two hundred popular periodicals and may help you start your search for sources on general and current topics. Even for general topics, however, you should not rely on it exclusively. Nearly all college libraries house far more than two hundred periodicals, and university research libraries house twenty thousand or more. The *Readers' Guide* does not attempt to cover the research journals that play such an important role in college writing.

Magazine Index. On microfilm (1988–), online (1973–), and on CD-ROM as part of InfoTrac (1973–); see below. Indexes over four hundred magazines.

InfoTrac. On CD-ROM. Includes three indexes: (1) the *General Periodicals Index* (current year and past four), which covers over 1,100 general-interest publications, incorporating the *Magazine Index* and including the *New York Times* and *Wall Street Journal*; (2) the *Academic Index* (current year and past four), which covers four hundred scholarly and general-interest publications, including the *New York Times*; and (3) the *National Newspaper Index* (current year and past three), which covers the *Christian Science Monitor, Los Angeles Times, New York Times, Wall Street Journal,* and *Washington Post.* Some entries also include abstracts of articles.

Humanities Index (1974–; also online and on CD-ROM). Covers archaeology, history, classics, literature, performing arts, philosophy, and religion.

Social Sciences Index (1974–; also online and on CD-ROM). Covers economics, geography, law, political science, psychology, public administration, and sociology.

Public Affairs Information Service Bulletin (PAIS) (1915–; also online and on CD-ROM). Covers articles and other publications by public and private agencies on economic and social conditions, international relations, and public administration. Subject listing only.

Specialized Indexes and Abstracts

Specialized periodical indexes list or abstract articles devoted to technical or scholarly research. Here is a list of specialized periodical indexes that cover various disciplines:

Accountant's Index (1944–).

American Statistics Index (1973–).

Applied Science and Technology Index (1958–). Online, CD-ROM.

Art Index (1929–).

Biological and Agricultural Index (1964–). CD-ROM.

Education Index (1929–). Online, CD-ROM.

Engineering Index (1920–).

Historical Abstracts (1955–).

Index Medicus (1961–). Online, CD-ROM (called MEDLINE).

MLA International Bibliography of Books and Articles in the Modern Languages and Literature (1921–). Online, CD-ROM.

Music Index (1949–).

Philosopher's Index (1957–). Online.

Psychological Abstracts (1927–). Online (called PsycINFO), CD-ROM (Psyc-LIT).

Physics Abstracts (1898–). Online (called INSPEC).

Science Abstracts (1898–).

Sociological Abstracts (1952–). Online, CD-ROM (called Sociofile).

Many periodical indexes and abstracts use the Library of Congress subject headings, but some have their own systems. *Sociological Abstracts,* for example, has a separate volume for subject headings. Check the opening pages of the index or abstract you are using, or refer to the system documentation, to see how it classifies its subjects. Then look for periodicals under your chosen Library of Congress subject heading or the heading that seems most similar to it.

Computer Databases

Your library may subscribe to *online* database networks and may own *CD-ROM* machines that are accessed through the library's computer terminals. Most research databases—like those noted in the preceding lists—are electronic indexes listing thousands of books and articles.

You may be able to use a CD-ROM database yourself, but you will probably need a librarian to conduct an online search. Because you may be charged for access time and printing for an online search, or given a limit on time at the terminal and number of entries you can print from a CD-ROM database, you may want to talk with a librarian before consulting a database. Also keep in mind that because most electronic indexes cover only the most recent years of an index, you may need to consult older printed versions as well.

In addition to the database versions of the indexes listed earlier, many libraries subscribe to computer services that provide abstracts and/or the full text of articles, either in the database (so you can see them on screen) or by mail or fax for a fee, and that list books in particular subject areas. The use of computers for scholarly research is becoming more widespread, with new technology being developed all the time, so be sure to check with a librarian about what's available in your library. Some common computer services include the following:

ERIC (Educational Resources Information Center) (1969–). Indexes, abstracts, and gives some full texts of articles from 750 education journals.

Business Periodicals Ondisc (1988–) and ABI/INFORM (1988–). Provides the full text of articles from business periodicals. If your library has a laser printer attached to a terminal, you can print out articles, including illustrations.

PsycBooks (1987–). A CD-ROM database that indexes books and book chapters in psychology.

Carl/Uncover (1988–). An online document delivery service that lists over three million articles from twelve thousand journals. For a fee, you can receive the full text of the article by fax, usually within a few hours.

Interlibrary networks. Known by different names in different regions, these networks allow you to search in the catalogs of colleges and universities in your area and across the country. In many cases, you can request a book, periodical article, or newspaper article by interlibrary loan. It may take several weeks for you to receive your material.

FINDING NEWSPAPER ARTICLES

Newspapers provide useful information for many research topics in such areas as foreign affairs, economic issues, public opinion, and social trends. Libraries usually miniaturize newspapers and store them on microfilm (reels) or microfiche (cards) that must be placed in viewing machines to be read.

Newspaper indexes, such as the *Los Angeles Times, New York Times Index,* and the London *Times Index,* help you locate specific articles on your topic. College libraries usually have indexes to local newspapers as well.

Your library may also subscribe to newspaper article and digest services, such as the following:

National Newspaper Index. On microfilm (1989–), online (1979–), and on CD-ROM, as part of InfoTrac. Indexes the *Christian Science Monitor, Los Angeles Times, New York Times, Wall Street Journal,* and *Washington Post.*

NewsBank (1970–). On microfiche and CD-ROM. Full-text articles from five hundred U.S. newspapers. A good source of information on local and regional issues and trends.

Newspaper Abstracts (1988–). An index and brief abstracts of articles from nineteen major regional, national, and international newspapers.

Facts on File (weekly). A digest of U.S. and international news events arranged by subject, such as foreign affairs, arts, education, religion, and sports.

Editorials on File (twice monthly). Editorials from 150 U.S. and Canadian newspapers. Each entry includes a brief description of an editorial subject followed by fifteen to twenty editorials on the subject, reprinted from different newspapers.

Editorial Research Reports (1924–). Reports on current and controversial topics, including brief histories, statistics, editorials, journal articles, endnotes, and supplementary reading lists.

Foreign Broadcast Information Service (FBIS) (1980–). Foreign broadcast scripts, newspaper articles, and government statements from Asia, Europe, Latin America, Africa, Russia, and the Middle East.

FINDING GOVERNMENT AND STATISTICAL INFORMATION

Following is a list of government publications and sources of statistical information that report developments in the federal government. The types of material they cover include congressional hearings and debates, presidential proclamations and speeches, Supreme Court decisions and dissenting opinions, as well as compilations of statistics. Frequently, government documents are not listed in the library catalog. Ask a reference librarian for assistance if you have trouble finding them.

Congressional Quarterly Almanac (annual). A summary of legislation, election results, roll-call votes, and significant speeches and debates.

Congressional Quarterly Weekly Report. Up-to-date summaries of committee actions, votes, and executive branch activities.

Statistical Abstract of the United States (annual). Generated by the Bureau of the Census, includes social, economic, and political statistics.

American Statistics Index (1974–; annual with monthly supplements). Federal government publications containing statistical information.

Statistical Reference Index (1980–). American statistical publications from sources other than the U.S. government.

The Gallup Poll: Public Opinion (1935–). Results of public opinion polls.

USING THE INTERNET FOR RESEARCH

The *Internet* is a global network that connects computers and that enables computer users to share information and resources quickly and easily. Using the Internet, people can send and receive electronic mail (e-mail), read documents or post them for others to read, communicate with other people who share similar interests, and store, send, and receive documents, graphic images, videos, and computer applications. Your school may provide its students with access to the Internet, possibly at little or no cost. Using a computer and a modem or a direct network connection, students can gather information about a research subject from sources all over the world. To find out whether you can access the Internet on campus, check with the reference librarian or computer services office.

If you cannot gain access to the Internet through your university or college, you may use your own computer and modem to access a commercial Internet service provider. Using these large services can become expensive, however. In most areas of the country, less expensive local Internet service providers now exist. Check the local computer stores or computer-user groups to compare pricing among the services available in your area.

Research on the Internet is very different from library research. Information is stored on many different computers, each with its own system of organization. There is no central catalogue, reference librarian, or standard classification system for the vast resources on the Internet. As a result, it can be difficult to determine the sources of information and to evaluate their reliability. Depending on your topic, purpose, and audience, the sources you find on the Internet may not be as credible or authoritative as library sources (see pp. 489–491 for information on determining the credibility of sources). When in doubt about the reliability or acceptability of online sources for a particular assignment, be sure to check with your instructor. In most cases, you will probably need to balance or supplement online sources with library sources. As with sources you locate in the library, you need to include proper documentation for all online sources that you cite (see Acknowledging Sources, pp. 491–493).

Since the Internet is so large and relatively unorganized, you may wonder how to find information relevant to your topic. Various resources have been developed to make it easier to find information on the Internet. One popular resource is the WorldWide Web; others include Telnet, File Transfer Protocol, Archie, and Gopher.

SEARCHING THE WORLDWIDE WEB

The *WorldWide Web* was initially developed to allow scientists to link related information wherever that information might be located. Using the Web, for example, a physicist in California who published a paper on the Internet could create a link to a related paper by a colleague in Sweden. Anyone reading the first paper could simply click on the link for instant access to the second paper.

Since its inception, the WorldWide Web has grown and developed rapidly to include many other uses. People may now include not only text but also graphic images, sound, animation, and even video in documents, all of which can be shared with others. New programs make it much easier to search, view, and create Web documents. Presently, more than 2.6 million sources of information exist on the WorldWide Web, and its explosive growth continues as businesses, educational institutions, government agencies, libraries, museums, and private individuals have rushed to set up their own Web sites.

Becoming Familiar with Web Sites

A particular *Web site* usually consists of a home page and the pages connected with it on a specific computer. A *home page* is the page you most often find first when you access a Web site; it typically provides a title heading, a brief introduction, and a table of contents consisting of *links* to the information available at that site. At the bottom of the home page you will usually find the name of the person or group responsible for the site and an e-mail address. However, you should note that home pages and Web sites vary in content, design, and organization.

On a WorldWide Web home page, links to other information are often indicated by underlined text (sometimes the words may be in bold type or highlighted in another way). Note also that the boxes on the home page are buttons that, when clicked, link readers to further information. On a color monitor, links to additional information are indicated by a different color. After a color-coded link has been clicked on and the reader returns to the original page, the link changes color (usually to red) to show that it has been visited. In addition to providing connections to other documents, the links on a home page can perform many other functions: for example, they may open a form to be filled out by the reader, start a video, play music or sound, or provide a form for sending an e-mail message to the author, among other uses.

There are Web sites for people interested in finding the text of a recently passed law, browsing a college catalogue, listening to a jazz performance, or viewing prehistoric cave art from France. You can find Web pages that serve as indexes to information about particular topics and Web pages that allow browsers to search the Web using keywords for topics or names. Increasingly, many Web pages are interactive, allowing browsers to send comments or questions to the Web page author, respond to a survey, contribute to a collaborative work of fiction, or make purchases via the network.

Each Web has its own address or *Uniform Resource Locator (URL),* which functions much like a traditional telephone number. The URL allows people anywhere in the world to locate a particular Web page. When you find a Web page that you think you may want to visit again, it's a good idea to create a "bookmark" for that page by choosing the "Add bookmark" function from the Web program menu. The address of the Web page will be added to a list in the bookmark menu.

Using Web Browsers

A *Web browser,* also called a *Web client program,* is software that allows you to display a Web page, including any graphic images, video, or sound that is included on that page. A Web browser also allows you to navigate among Web pages. In addition, a browser helps you find, read, download, and save the text of documents, graphic images, video, or sounds.

The first graphic Web browser, MOSAIC, was created at the University of Illinois. Currently, the most widely used graphic browsers are Netscape and MacWeb, while other programs are under development. A plain-text browser, Lynx, does not display graphics or video and is used for computer or modem connections that lack the processing speed needed for graphic browsers such as MOSAIC and Netscape. Web browsers differ slightly in their format and features, though they share similarities that make them easy to use. Web browsers exist for virtually every computer platform, including IBM, Macintosh, and UNIX, and they are widely available at no cost to students and others at academic institutions.

Searching the Web for Information on Your Topic

A Web page often provides links to additional information about a subject at other Web sites. You may also use one of the special search engines on the Web itself. *Search engines* are resources available for searching the WorldWide

Web. They are found on pages especially set up to allow you to enter a keyword or phrase. The search engine scans the Web for your keyword and produces a list of direct links to pages containing the keyword. Usually, the list includes a brief description of each page. The program searches both the titles of Web pages and the actual text of those pages for the keyword. By clicking on one of the links returned by the search, you can directly access a specific Web page.

The success of a Web search depends on the keywords you choose; if a search yields few sources or irrelevant ones, try rephrasing your keywords or choosing more specific ones to locate the most useful information. If your topic is *ecology,* for example, you may find information under the terms *ecosystem, environment, pollution,* and *endangered species,* as well as a number of other related key-words, depending on the focus of your research. As with library searches, how-ever, you may need to narrow your topic in order to keep the number of sources manageable. When you find a source that seems promising, be sure to create a bookmark for the Web page so you can return to it easily later on.

Finally, while the Web cannot provide the helpful advice and expertise of a reference librarian, you can contact authors of Web pages by e-mail to find addi-tional resources.

USING OTHER TOOLS TO ACCESS THE INTERNET

In addition to the WorldWide Web, other resources for accessing information on the Internet include Telnet, File Transfer Protocol (FTP), Archie, and Gopher. Helpful in research, these resources are available on the Internet, through computer-user groups, and from Internet service providers.

Telnet

Telnet is a software networking tool that allows you to log on to another com-puter—called the *host computer*—through your modem or a direct network con-nection. The host computer may be in the same room or on the other side of the world. Once connected, you can access any services or information that the host computer makes available. For example, you might browse the card catalogues of various college libraries or read newspaper articles, government documents, and reports of recent scientific research. Many different kinds of information can be located through Telnet. Telnet makes it possible for you to use FTP, Archie, and Gopher to find and download information stored in thousands of host computers all over the world.

File Transfer Protocol (FTP)

File Transfer Protocol (FTP) is a standard communication format that allows files to be transferred across computer networks, even across networks com-posed of different kinds of computers. For example, documents created on a Macintosh computer may be downloaded and read on an IBM-compatible computer through FTP. Although similar in function to Telnet in that it allows you to log on to and read information stored in host computers, FTP can also transfer that information to your computer, provided you are granted access. FTP also allows you to create, delete, and rename files on a remote system when you have been granted these privileges.

Generally, when people refer to FTP as a research tool, they are referring to *anonymous FTP*—a special "public" space provided by many host computers for storing documents that may be accessed freely by anyone. To retrieve a file using anonymous FTP, you log on to the host computer using the login name *anonymous* and any password (usually your e-mail address). You then search the directories and files of the public archives on that host computer and download the file you wish to retrieve. FTP works best when you know the location of the information you are seeking.

Archie

Because the Internet is such a large collection of networks, it can be difficult for you to find and keep track of the locations of all the information you seek. *Archie* is a system that indexes files on host computers that allow the general public to gain access to them, and thereby provides a way of searching for specific kinds of information. Under this system, host computers register as Archie servers; once a month, each Archie server is asked to update its list of files on the system's master index.

You can conduct an online search of the Archie index by file name (or part of it) using an Archie client program, such as Anarchie, which is available online as well as from service providers and computer-user groups. Following the Archie search, you would use FTP to access the host computer where the file is located.

Gopher

The *Gopher* system functions like the subject cards in a library's card catalogue, allowing you to browse by topic, rather than by file name or location, and to find information on the same subject grouped together. In addition, you can browse the Internet by choosing resources from menus. When you find a source that interests you, Gopher can retrieve it for you to read or save without using FTP. Most Gopher client programs, like WorldWide Web browsers, also include the bookmark feature, which makes it easy to return to sources.

Gopher indexing services vary, particularly in the way subjects are organized and classified. Therefore, you need to be resourceful, trying out different approaches to locate information on a particular topic.

USING SPECIAL INTEREST GROUPS ON THE INTERNET

Joining Discussion Groups

To conduct research on a particular topic on the Internet, you may also find it helpful to join a *computer discussion group* on your topic. Discussion groups operate like large mailing lists. Members of a group communicate with each other through e-mail. A message sent by any group member to the list is automatically distributed to everyone who subscribes to that list.

Various discussion groups and their e-mail addresses can be found in computer publications, special interest magazines, print directories in the library, and by word of mouth. You may also conduct online searches to find discussion groups on particular topics. Many discussion groups are managed by special software such as listserv, which automatically takes care of the details of operating the list: adding new subscribers, distributing messages, and deleting the addresses of members who leave the group (unsubscribing). You can subscribe to most discussion groups at no cost. To subscribe to a particular group, you simply send an e-mail request to the group's listserv e-mail address. Once you are a member, any messages sent to the group are automatically sent to you, and any messages you send are automatically distributed to the other members of the group.

Participating in Newsgroups

Newsgroups are similar to discussion groups except that membership is not required. You can read and post messages to a newsgroup even if you do not subscribe to it. Messages sent to the newsgroup are posted for anyone to read and respond to, much like a public bulletin board. Readers can browse the messages, dropping in and following a discussion that interests them and ignoring the rest.

Thousands of newsgroups currently exist on the Internet. As with discussion groups, they are organized primarily by topic. Software programs such as Nuntius and Newswatcher are widely available and make it easy to browse, read, and save newsgroup messages.

Using Discussion Groups and Newsgroups

Although discussion groups and newsgroups are not authoritative sources of factual information in the same way that published library sources are, they can serve many useful functions in research and writing. A computer group can help you conduct preliminary research on a topic or seek some general background information on a controversy—how it developed and whether it has been resolved.

- For a paper proposing changes in public schools, a group focusing on child development may alert you to some interesting new research on how play supports language development, suggesting new models for learning environments.
- For a paper explaining the concept of ecology, you may find that there are various interpretations of the concept among scholars in the field. Reading messages posted to a group on ecology can give you a good sense of the major questions, issues, and trends related to your topic.

Discussion groups and newsgroups can provide a means of conducting field research on a topic. For example, you might conduct an informal public opinion poll, sample the current thinking about a topic, or post a question you'd like answered. Groups can also help you find and evaluate useful sources on a topic.

- For a paper arguing the position that there ought to be import quotas on Japanese cars, you might send a message to a discussion group or newsgroup on trade issues, asking for recent sources of information on trade practices.

- For a paper proposing a solution to the problem of endangered species, you might post a request for help in evaluating sources: "What are the three most important books or articles to read on the preservation of critical habitats?"

- For an essay arguing the position that the government should be more flexible in seeking to preserve wetlands, you may have found two important sources that contradict each other. You might describe the contradiction, and ask the group members whether recent opinion has favored one point of view over the other.

Discussion groups vary from lively to nearly inactive; members may be extremely polite or openly combative; and the level of discussion may range from technical and scholarly to casual. Read enough messages from a particular group to get a sense of the tone and level of the discussion before subscribing or posting a message to the group yourself. Be polite when asking for help, and gracious in thanking those who respond.

Establishing E-mail Contact with Experts

Another advantage of using the Internet for research is that you can contact other researchers—authors, scholars, scientists, government officials, and so on—directly by sending e-mail. Of course, you may also contact these experts by letter or telephone, but you are most likely to receive a response if you send an e-mail message. Many people are willing to respond to specific requests for information. For instance, if you have additional questions after reading an article on your topic, you might send your questions to the author. To locate a person's e-mail address, try looking at published papers, books, or online documents, many of which now include the writer's e-mail address.

You may also find e-mail useful for requesting an interview with an expert. In your e-mail message, introduce yourself, briefly describe the purpose and general topic of the interview, and request a time and place convenient for the person you wish to interview. You might even conduct the interview by e-mail if the interviewee cannot meet with you personally. After the interview, be sure to send a note of thanks via e-mail or regular mail.

The following sources of information about the Internet can help you learn more about this valuable research tool.

Hahn, Harley, and Rick Stout, *The Internet Complete Reference.* Berkeley: Osborne McGraw-Hill, 1994.

Krol, Ed. *The Whole Internet User's Guide and Catalogue.* Sebastopol, CA: O'Reilly & Associates, 1994.

LaQuey, Tracy. *The Internet Companion: A Beginner's Guide to Global Networking.* 2nd ed. Reading, MA: Addison-Wesley, 1994.

READING SOURCES WITH A CRITICAL EYE

From the very beginning of your search, you should evaluate potential sources to determine which ones to use in your essay. Obviously, you must decide which sources provide information relevant to the topic. But you also must read sources with a critical eye to decide how credible or trustworthy they are. Just because a book or essay appears in print does not necessarily mean the information or opinions within it are reliable.

SELECTING RELEVANT SOURCES

Begin your evaluation of sources by narrowing your working bibliography to the most relevant works. Consider them in terms of scope, date of publication, and viewpoint.

Scope and Approach

To decide how relevant a particular source is to your topic, you need to examine the source in depth. Do not depend on title alone, for it may be misleading. If the source is a book, check its table of contents and index to see how many pages are devoted to the precise subject you are exploring. In most cases you will want an in-depth, not a superficial, treatment of the subject. Read the preface or introduction to a book or the abstract or opening paragraphs of an article and any biographical information given about the author to determine the author's basic approach to the subject or special way of looking at it. As you look at these elements, consider the following questions:

- Does the source provide a general or specialized view? General sources are helpful early in your research, but you then need the authority or up-to-date coverage of specialized sources. Extremely specialized works, however, may be too technical.

- Is the source long enough to provide adequate detail?

- Was the source written for general readers? Specialists? Advocates? Critics?

- Is the author an expert on the topic? Does the author's way of looking at the topic support or challenge your own views?

Date of Publication

Although you should always consult the most up-to-date sources available on your subject, older sources often establish the principles, theories, and data upon which later work rests and may provide a useful perspective for evaluating it. Since many older works are considered authoritative, you may want to become familiar with them. To determine which sources are authoritative, note the ones that are cited most often in encyclopedia articles, bibliographies, and recent works on the subject.

Viewpoint

Your sources should represent a variety of viewpoints on the subject. Just as you would not depend on a single author for all of your information, so you do not want to use authors who all belong to the same school of thought. For suggestions on determining authors' viewpoints, see the next section, Identifying Bias.

Using sources that represent different viewpoints is especially important when developing an argument for one of the essay assignments in chapters 6–9. During your invention work in those chapters, you may want to research what others have said about your subject to see what positions have been staked out and what arguments have been made. You will then be able to define the issue more carefully, collect arguments supporting your position, and anticipate arguments opposing it.

IDENTIFYING BIAS

One of the most important aspects of evaluating a source is identifying any bias in its treatment of the subject. Although the word *bias* may sound like a criticism or drawback, it simply refers to the fact that most writing is not neutral or objective and does not try or claim to be. Authors come to their subjects with particular viewpoints. In using sources, you must consider carefully how these viewpoints are reflected in the writing and how they affect the way authors present their arguments.

Although the text of the source gives you the most precise indication of the author's viewpoint, you can often get a good idea by looking at the preface or introduction or at the sources the author cites. When you examine a reference, you can often determine the general point of view it represents by considering the following elements:

- *Title.* Does the title or subtitle indicate the text's bias? Watch for "loaded" words or confrontational phrasing.

- *Author.* What is the author's professional title and/or affiliation? What is the author's perspective? Is he or she in favor of something or at odds with it? What has persuaded the author to take this viewpoint? How might the author's professional affiliation affect his or her perspective? What is the author's tone? Information on the author may also be available in the book or article itself or in biographical sources available in the library.

- *Presentation of argument.* Almost every written work asserts a point of view or makes an argument for something the author considers important. To determine this position and the reason behind it, look for the main point. What evidence does the author provide as support for this point? Is the evidence from authoritative sources? Is the evidence persuasive? Does the author accommodate or refute opposing arguments?

- *Publication information.* Was the book published by a commercial publisher, a corporation, a government agency, or an interest group? What is that organization's position on the topic? Is the author funded by or affiliated with the organization?

- *Editorial slant.* What kind of periodical published the article—popular, academic, or alternative? Knowing some background about the publisher or periodical can help determine bias, because all periodicals have definite editorial slants. In cases where the publication title does not indicate bias, there are reference sources that may help you determine this information. Two of the most common are the *Gale Directory of Publications and Broadcast Media* (1990) and *Magazines for Libraries* (1992).

ACKNOWLEDGING SOURCES

Much of the writing you will do in college requires you to use outside sources in combination with your own firsthand observation and reflection. When you get information and ideas from reading, lectures, and interviews, you are using sources. In college, using sources is not only acceptable, it is expected. Educated people nearly always base their original thought on the work of others. In fact, most of your college education is devoted to teaching you two things: (1) what Matthew Arnold called "the best that has been thought and said," and (2) the way to analyze the thoughts of others, integrate them into your own thinking, and effectively convey what you think to others.

Although there is no universally agreed-on system for acknowledging sources, there is agreement on both the need for documentation and the items that should be included. Writers should acknowledge sources for two reasons— to give credit to those sources and to enable readers to consult the sources for further information. When documenting sources, include (1) name of author; (2) title of publication; and (3) publication source, date, and page.

Most documentation styles combine some kind of citation in the text with a separate list of references keyed to the textual citations. There are basically two ways of acknowledging sources: (1) citing sources within the essay, enclosing the citation in parentheses, and (2) footnotes (or endnotes) plus a bibliography. The MLA, a professional organization of English instructors, had until 1984 endorsed the footnote style of documentation. Since then, the *MLA Handbook* has prescribed the simpler parenthetical citation method similar to the style endorsed by the APA—the style used by many social and natural science instructors.

If you find that you need more information, consult the *MLA Handbook for Writers of Research Papers,* Fourth Edition (1995), or the *Publication Manual of the American Psychological Association,* Fourth Edition (1995).

CITING SOURCES WITHIN YOUR ESSAY

The MLA and APA styles both advocate parenthetical citations within an essay keyed to a works-cited or references list at the end. However, they differ on what should be included in the parenthetical citation. The MLA author-page system requires that in-text citations include the author's last name and the page number of the original passage being cited. The APA author-year system calls for the last name of the author and the year of publication of the original work in the citation. If the cited material is a quotation, you also need to include the page number of the original. If the cited material is not a quotation, the page number is optional.

MLA   Dr. James is described as a "not-too-skeletal Ichabod
        Crane" (Simon 68).

APA   Dr. James is described as a "not-too-skeletal Ichabod
        Crane" (Simon, 1982, p. 68).

Notice that the APA style uses a comma between author, year, and page as well as "p." for page (Simon, 1982, p. 68), whereas the MLA style puts only one space between author and page (Simon 68). Note also that both citations come before the final period. With block quotations, however, put the citation two spaces after the final period.

For the MLA style, if the author's name is mentioned in the essay, put the page reference in parentheses as close as possible to the borrowed material, but without disrupting the flow of the sentence. For the APA style, cite the year in parentheses directly following the author's name, and place the page reference in parentheses before the period ending the sentence. In the case of block quotations for both MLA and APA, put the page reference in parentheses two spaces after the period ending the sentence.

MLA   Simon describes Dr. James as a "not-too-skeletal Ichabod
        Crane" (68).

APA   Simon (1982) describes Dr. James as a "not-too-skeletal
        Ichabod Crane" (p. 68).

To cite a source by two or three authors, the MLA uses all the authors' last names; for works with more than three authors, it uses all the authors' names or just the first author's name followed by *et al.* To cite works with three to five authors in the APA style, use all the authors' last names the first time the reference occurs and the last name of the first author followed by *et al.* subsequently. If a source has more than six authors, the APA uses only the last name of the first author and *et al.* at first and subsequent references.

MLA   Dyal, Corning, and Willows identify several types of
        students, including the "Authority-Rebel" (4).

APA   Dyal, Corning, and Willows (1975) identify several types of
        students, including the "Authority-Rebel" (p. 4).

MLA   The Authority-Rebel "tends to see himself as superior to
        other students in the class" (Dyal, Corning, and
        Willows 4).

APA   The Authority-Rebel "tends to see himself as superior to
        other students in the class" (Dyal et al., 1975, p. 4).

To cite one of two or more works by the same author(s), the MLA includes the author's last name, a shortened version of the title, and the page. The APA uses the author's last name plus the year (and the page, if you are citing a quotation). When more than one work being cited was published by an author in the same year, the APA style uses lowercase letters with the date (*1973a, 1973b*).

MLA   When old paint becomes transparent, it sometimes shows the
        artist's original plans: "a tree will show through a
        woman's dress" (Hellman, Pentimento 1).

APA   When old paint becomes transparent, it sometimes shows the
        artist's original plans: "a tree will show through a
        woman's dress" (Hellman, 1973, p. 1).

To cite a work listed only by its title, both the MLA and APA use a shortened version of the title.

MLA   An international pollution treaty still to be ratified
        would prohibit all plastic garbage from being dumped at sea
        ("Awash" 26).

APA   An international pollution treaty still to be ratified
        would prohibit all plastic garbage from being dumped at sea
        ("Awash," 1987).

To quote material taken not from the original source but from a secondary source that quotes the original, both the MLA and the APA give the secondary source in the list of works cited, and acknowledge that the original was quoted in a secondary source in the text.

MLA   E. M. Forster says "the collapse of all civilization, so
        realistic for us, sounded in Matthew Arnold's ears like a
        distant and harmonious cataract" (qtd. in Trilling 11).

APA   E. M. Forster says "the collapse of all civilization, so
        realistic for us, sounded in Matthew Arnold's ears like a
        distant and harmonious cataract" (as cited in Trilling,
        1955, p. 11).

CITING SOURCES AT THE END OF YOUR ESSAY

Keyed to the parenthetical citations in the text, the list of works cited or references identifies all the sources you used in the essay. Every source cited in the text must refer to an entry in the works-cited or references list. Conversely, every entry in the works-cited or references list must correspond to at least one parenthetical citation in the text.

Whereas the MLA style uses the title "Works Cited," the APA prefers "References." Both alphabetize the entries according to the first author's last name. However, when several works by an author are listed, the APA recommends the following rules for arranging the list:

- Same-name single-author entries precede multiple-author entries:

```
Aaron, P. (1990).
Aaron, P., & Zorn, C. R. (1985).
```

- Entries with the same first author and different second author should be alphabetized according to the second author's last name:

```
Aaron, P., & Charleston, W. (1987).
Aaron, P., & Zorn, C. R. (1991).
```

- Entries by the same authors should be arranged by year of publication, in chronological order:

```
Aaron, P., & Charleston, W. (1987).
Aaron, P., & Charleston, W. (1993).
```

- Entries by the same author(s) with the same publication year should be arranged alphabetically by title (according to the first word after *A, An, The*), and lowercase letters (*a, b, c,* and so on) should follow the year within the parentheses:

```
Aaron, P. (1985a). Basic . . .
Aaron, P. (1985b). Elements . . .
```

In the MLA style, multiple works by the same author (or same group of authors) are alphabetized by title. The author's name is given for the first entry only; in subsequent entries, three hyphens and a period are used.

```
Vidal, Gore. Empire. New York: Random, 1987.
---. Lincoln. New York: Random. 1984.
```

The essential difference between the MLA and APA styles of listing sources is the order in which the information is presented. The MLA follows this order: author's name; title; publication source, year, and page. The APA puts the year after the author's name. In the examples that follow, note also the differences in capitalization and arrangement between the two documentation styles.

The MLA style requires a "hanging indent," which means that the first line of a works-cited entry is not indented but subsequent lines of the entry are indented. The MLA specifies an indent of half an inch, or five spaces.

The APA recommends that only the *first* line of each entry be indented five to seven spaces for papers intended for publication; for student papers, however, it notes that a hanging indent of five to seven spaces may be preferred. The following examples demonstrate a hanging indent of five to seven spaces for both documentation styles.

Books

A BOOK BY A SINGLE AUTHOR

MLA   Guterson, David, <u>Family Matters: Why Homeschooling Makes Sense</u>. San Diego: Harcourt, 1992.

APA   Guterson, D. (1992). <u>Family matters: Why homeschooling makes sense</u>. San Diego: Harcourt Brace.

A BOOK BY AN AGENCY OR CORPORATION

MLA   Association for Research in Nervous and Mental Disease. <u>The Circulation of the Brain and Spinal Cord: A Symposium on Blood Supply</u>. New York: Hafner, 1966.

APA   Association for Research in Nervous and Mental Disease. (1966). <u>The circulation of the brain and spinal cord: A symposium on blood supply</u>. New York: Hafner.

A BOOK BY MORE THAN ONE AUTHOR

MLA   Gottfredson, Stephen G., and Sean McConville. <u>America's Correctional Crisis</u>. Westport: Greenwood, 1987.

APA   Gottfredson, S. G., & McConville, S. (1987). <u>America's correctional crisis</u>. Westport, CT: Greenwood.

MLA   Dyal, James A., William C. Corning, and Dale M. Willows. <u>Readings in Psychology: The Search for Alternatives</u>. 3rd ed. New York: McGraw. 1975.

APA   Dyal, J. A., Corning, W. C., & Willows, D. M. (1975). <u>Readings in psychology: The search for alternatives</u> (3rd ed.). New York: McGraw-Hill.

For works by more than three authors, the MLA lists all the authors' names or the name of the first author followed by *et al.* The APA cites all authors' names regardless of the number.

MLA   Nielsen, Niels C., Jr., et al. <u>Religions of the World</u>. 3rd ed. New York: St. Martin's, 1992.

A BOOK BY AN UNKNOWN AUTHOR. Use title in place of author.

MLA   Rand McNally Commercial Atlas. Skokie: Rand, 1993.

APA   Rand McNally commercial atlas. (1993). Skokie, IL: Rand McNally.

A BOOK WITH AN AUTHOR AND EDITOR

APA   Arnold, M. (1966). Culture and anarchy (J. Dover Wilson,
           Ed.). Cambridge: Cambridge University Press. (Original
           work published 1869)

If you refer to the text itself, begin the entry with the author:

MLA   Arnold, Matthew. Culture and Anarchy. Ed. J. Dover Wilson.
           Cambridge: Cambridge UP, 1966.

If you cite the editor in your paper, begin the entry with the editor:

MLA   Wilson, J. Dover, ed. Culture and Anarchy. By Matthew
           Arnold. 1869. Cambridge: Cambridge UP, 1966.

AN EDITED COLLECTION

MLA   Carter, Kathryn, and Carole Spitzack, eds. Doing Research
           on Women's Communication. Norwood: Ablex, 1989.

APA   Carter, K., & Spitzack, C. (Eds.). (1989). Doing research
           on women's communication. Norwood, NJ: Ablex.

A WORK IN AN ANTHOLOGY OR COLLECTION

MLA   Fairbairn-Dunlop, Peggy. "Women and Agriculture in Western
           Samoa." Different Places, Different Voices. Ed. Janet
           H. Momsen and Vivian Kinnaird. London: Routledge,
           1993. 211-26.

APA   Fairbairn-Dunlop, P. (1993). Women and agriculture in
           western Samoa. In J. H. Momsen & V. Kinnaird (Eds.).
           Different places, different voices (pp. 211-226).
           London: Routledge.

A TRANSLATION

APA   Tolstoy, L. (1972). War and peace. (C. Garnett, Trans.).
           London: Pan Books. (Original work published 1868-1869)

If you refer to the work itself, begin the entry with the author:

MLA   Tolstoy, Leo. War and Peace. Trans. Constance Garnett.
           London: Pan, 1972.

If you cite the translator in your text, begin the entry with the translator's name:

MLA   Garnett, Constance, trans. War and Peace. By Leo Tolstoy.
           London: Pan, 1972.

AN ARTICLE IN A REFERENCE BOOK

MLA   Suber, Howard. "Motion Picture." Encyclopedia Americana.
1991 ed.

APA   Suber, H. (1991). Motion picture. In Encyclopedia
Americana (Vol. 19, pp. 505-539). Danbury, CT: Grolier.

AN INTRODUCTION, PREFACE, FOREWORD, OR AFTERWORD

MLA   Holt, John. Introduction. Better Than School. By Nancy
Wallace. Burnett: Larson, 1983. 9-14.

APA   Holt, J. (1983). Introduction. In N. Wallace, Better than
school (pp. 9-14). Burnett, NY: Larson.

A GOVERNMENT DOCUMENT

MLA   United States. Cong. Senate. Subcommittee on Constitutional
Amendments of the Committee on the Judiciary.
Hearings on the "Equal Rights" Amendment. 91st Cong.,
2nd sess. S. Res. 61. Washington: GPO, 1970.

APA   U.S. Department of Health, Education and Welfare. (1979).
Healthy people: The surgeon general's report on health
promotion (DHEW Publication No. 79-55071). Washington,
DC: U.S. Government Printing Office.

AN UNPUBLISHED DOCTORAL DISSERTATION

MLA   Bullock, Barbara. "Basic Needs Fulfillment among Less
Developed Countries: Social Progress over Two Decades
of Growth." Diss. Vanderbilt U. 1986.

APA   Bullock, B. (1986). Basic needs fulfillment among less
developed countries: Social progress over two decades
of growth. Unpublished doctoral dissertation.
Vanderbilt University, Nashville, TN.

Articles

AN ARTICLE FROM A DAILY NEWSPAPER

MLA   Wilford, John Noble. "Corn in the New World: A Relative
Latecomer." New York Times 7 Mar. 1995, late ed.: C1+.

APA   Wilford, J. N. (1995, March 7). Corn in the New World: A
relative latecomer. The New York Times, pp. C1, C5.

AN ARTICLE FROM A WEEKLY OR BIWEEKLY MAGAZINE

MLA   Glastris, Paul. "The New Way to Get Rich." U.S. News & World Report 7 May 1990: 26-36.

APA   Glastris, P. (1990, May 7). The new way to get rich. U.S. News & World Report, 108, 26-36.

AN ARTICLE FROM A MONTHLY OR BIMONTHLY MAGAZINE

MLA   Rohn, Alfie. "Home Schooling." Atlantic Monthly Apr. 1988: 20-25.

APA   Rohn, A. (1988, April). Home schooling. Atlantic Monthly, 261, 20-25.

AN ARTICLE IN A SCHOLARLY JOURNAL WITH CONTINUOUS ANNUAL PAGINATION. The volume number follows the title of the journal.

MLA   Natale, Jo Anna. "Understanding Home Schooling." Education Digest 9 (1993): 58-61.

APA   Natale, J. A. (1993). Understanding home schooling. Education Digest, 9, 58-61.

AN ARTICLE IN A SCHOLARLY JOURNAL THAT PAGINATES EACH ISSUE SEPARATELY. The issue number appears after the volume number. For the MLA, a period separates the two numbers; for the APA, the issue number is in parentheses.

MLA   Epstein, Alexandra. "Teen Parents: What They Need to Know." High/Scope Resource 1.2 (1982): 6.

APA   Epstein, A. (1982). Teen parents: What they need to know. High/Scope Resource, 1(2), 6.

AN ANONYMOUS ARTICLE

MLA   "Awash in Garbage." New York Times 15 Aug. 1987, sec. 1: 26.

APA   Awash in garbage. (1987, August 15). The New York Times, p. A26.

AN EDITORIAL

MLA   "Stepping Backward." Editorial. Los Angeles Times 4 July 1989: B6.

APA   Stepping backward. (1989, July 4). [Editorial]. The Los Angeles Times, p. B6.

A LETTER TO THE EDITOR

MLA   Rissman, Edward M. Letter. Los Angeles Times 29 June 1989: B5.

APA   Rissman, E. M. (1989, June 29). [Letter to the editor]. The Los Angeles Times, p. B5.

A REVIEW

MLA   Anders, Jaroslaw. "Dogma and Democracy." Rev. of The
           Church and the Left, by Adam Minchik. New Republic 17
           May 1993: 42-48.

If you don't know the author, start with the title. If the review is untitled, begin with the words *Rev. of* and alphabetize under the title of the work being reviewed.

APA   Anders, J. (1993, May 17). Dogma and democracy [Review of
           the book The church and the left]. The New Republic,
           208, 42-48.

Other Sources

COMPUTER SOFTWARE

MLA   SPSS/PC+ Studentware Plus. Diskette. Chicago: SPSS, 1991.

APA   SPSS/PC+ Studentware Plus [Computer software]. (1991).
           Chicago: SPSS.

MATERIAL FROM NEWSBANK

MLA   Sharpe, Lora. "A Quilter's Tribute." Boston Globe 25 Mar.
           1989. NewsBank: Social Relations (1989): fiche 6, grids
           B4-6.

MATERIAL FROM A DATABASE ON CD-ROM. If publication data is available for the work, it should be included. For MLA, the electronic publication date appears at the end of the reference.

MLA   Braus, Patricia. "Sex and the Single Spender." American
           Demographics 15.11 (1993): 28-34. ABI/INFORM. CD-ROM.
           UMI-ProQuest. 1993.

APA   Braus, P. (1993). Sex and the single spender [CD-ROM].
           American Demographics, 15(11), 28-34. Available:
           ABI/INFORM.

When print and electronic versions of the material are identical, APA prefers a reference to the print version.

MATERIAL FROM AN ONLINE COMPUTER SERVICE. Both the MLA and the APA include publication information (if available), the medium, and the name of the service. Because information available through a computer service may not be the same as the original print version, the MLA includes the date the information was accessed. So that readers can locate the article, APA provides the path number at the end of the reference. Notice that the MLA uses a nonhyphenated spelling of the word *online,* while the APA uses a hyphenated spelling, *on-line.*

MLA   Reece, Jerry S. "Measuring Investment Center Performance."

Harvard Business Review 56.3 (1978): 28-40. Online.

Dialog. 7 Mar. 1995.

APA   Reece, J. S. (1978). Measuring investment center

performance. Harvard Business Review [On-line] 56(3).

28-40. Available: Dialog file 107, item 673280 047658

Notice that final periods are omitted from entries that end with electronic addresses or with path, file, or item numbers.

ARTICLE FROM AN ONLINE JOURNAL. The MLA includes the volume number and issue number, if given, after the title of the journal. The number of pages or paragraphs appears after the colon, if the source gives them; otherwise, *n. pag.* (for "no pagination") appears. The date of access appears at the end. In the MLA style, the electronic address for the document is optional. If given, it appears after the date of access, preceded by the word *Available* and a colon. The APA requires an availability statement that includes the specific information (such as path, directory, file name, and so on) needed to access the source.

MLA   Moulthrop, Stuart. "You Say You Want a Revolution?

Hypertext and the Laws of Media." Postmodern Culture

1.3 (1991): 53 pars. Online. BITNET. 10 Jan. 1993.

APA   Nielsen, R. (1995, March). Radon risks [16 paragraphs].

Carcinogens [On-line serial], 4(12). Available FTP:

Hostname: princeton.edu Directory: pub/carcinogens/

1995 File: radon.95.3.12.radonrisks

A WORLDWIDE WEB SITE. The following MLA format is from an adaptation of MLA style guidelines prepared by Janice W. Walker and approved by the Alliance for Computers and Writing ("ACW Style Sheet," jwalker@chuma.cas.usf.edu). The author's name appears first, if known. Otherwise, begin with the title. If the file is part of a larger work, the title of the complete work follows the title of the work you are citing. The http address and date of access complete the reference. The APA format is derived from the APA's general guidelines for citing online sources.

MLA   Burka, Lauren P. "A Hypertext History of Multi-User

Dimensions." MUD HISTORY. http://www.ccs.neu.edu/home/

lpb/mud-history.html (5 Dec. 1994)

APA   Burka, L. (1994). "A hypertext history of multi-user

dimensions." MUD HISTORY [On-line]. Available:

http://www.ccs.neu.edu/home/lpb/mud-history.html

A POSTING ON A DISCUSSION GROUP OR NEWSGROUP. The following MLA format is from an adaptation of MLA style guidelines prepared by Janice W. Walker and approved by the Alliance for Computers and Writing ("ACS Style Sheet," jwalker@chuma.cas.usf.edu). The name of the author appears first, followed by the subject line and the address of the listserv or newslist. The date appears last. If the author's name is not known, begin with the subject. The APA format is derived from the APA's general guidelines for citing online sources.

MLA   Seabrook, Richard H. C. "Community and Progress."

        cybermind@jefferson.village.virginia.edu (22 Jan.

        1994).

APA   Seabrook, R. H. C. Community and progress [On-line].

        Available: cybermind@jefferson.village.virginia.edu

The APA requires that electronic conversations carried out via an electronic discussion group be cited within the text.

PERFORMANCES

MLA   Hamlet. By William Shakespeare. Dir. Jonathan Kent. Perf.

        Ralph Fiennes. Belasco Theatre, New York. 20 June

        1995.

A TELEVISION PROGRAM

MLA   "The Universe Within." Nova. Narr. Stacy Keach. Writ. Beth

        Hoppe and Bill Lattanzi. Dir. Goro Koide. PBS. WNET.

        New York. 7 Mar. 1995.

APA   Hoppe, B., & Lattanzi, B. (1995). The universe within (G.

        Koide, Director). In P. Apsell (Producer), Nova.

        Boston: WGBH.

A FILM

MLA   Boyz N the Hood. Writ. and Dir. John Singleton. Perf. Ice

        Cube, Cuba Gooding, Jr., and Larry Fishburne.

        Columbia. 1991.

APA   Singleton, J. (Writer and Director). (1991). Boyz n the

        hood [Film]. New York: Columbia.

A MUSIC RECORDING. Unless the medium is a compact disc, the MLA indicates the medium ahead of the name of the manufacturer for an audiocassette, audiotape, or LP.

MLA   Beethoven, Ludwig van. Violin Concerto in D Major, op. 61.

        U.S.S.R. State Orchestra. Cond. Alexander Gauk. David

        Oistrikh, violinist. Audiocassette. Allegro, 1980.

        Springsteen, Bruce. "Dancing in the Dark." Born in the

        U.S.A. Columbia, 1984.

APA   Beethoven, L. van. (1806). Violin concerto in D major, op.

        61 [Recorded by USSR State Orchestra]. (Cassette

        Recording No. ACS 8044).

      Springsteen, B. (1984). Dancing in the dark. On <u>Born in the</u>

        <u>U.S.A.</u> [CD]. New York: Columbia.

If the recording date differs from the copyright date, APA requires that it appear in parentheses after the name of the label. If it is necessary to include a number for the recording, use parentheses for the medium; otherwise, use brackets.

AN INTERVIEW

MLA   Lowell, Robert. "Robert Lowell." Interview with Frederick

        Seidel. <u>Paris Review</u> 25 (1975): 56-95.

      Franklin, Ann. Personal interview. 3 Sept. 1983.

When using the APA style, do not list personal interviews in your references list. Simply cite the person's name in your text, and in parentheses give the notation *personal communication* and the date of the interview. For published interviews, use the appropriate format for an article.

C R E D I T S

Waldman, Steven, "The Tyranny of Choice." From *The New Republic*, January 27, 1992. Reprinted by permission of The New Republic. Copyright © 1992, The New Republic, Inc.

Figure 1: The West German Education System. Source: Adapted from Max Planck, "Institute for Human Development and Education," in *Between Elite and Mass Education*. Published in 1983 by State University of New York Press and reprinted with permission.

T O P I C A L I N D E X

This index classifies readings by topic in order to facilitate topic-centered discussions and special writing assignments.

INDEX OF AUTHORS, TITLES, AND TERMS

Instructor's Manual to Accompany

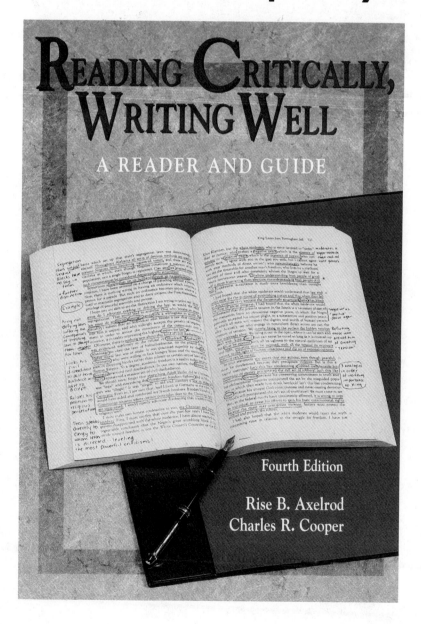

READING **C**RITICALLY,
WRITING **W**ELL

A READER AND GUIDE

Fourth Edition

Rise B. Axelrod
Charles R. Cooper

INSTRUCTOR'S MANUAL to accompany

READING CRITICALLY, WRITING WELL

A Reader and Guide

FOURTH EDITION

Rise B. Axelrod

*California State University,
San Bernardino*

Charles R. Cooper

*University of California,
San Diego*

Kristin Hawkinson

*University of California,
San Diego*

ST. MARTIN'S PRESS
NEW YORK

For information, write:

St. Martin's Press, Inc.
175 Fifth Avenue
New York, NY 10010

ISBN: 0-312-11526-1

CONTENTS

EVALUATING STUDENT WRITING, HANDLING THE PAPER
LOAD, AND KEEPING RECORDS

Part 5 SUGGESTED STRATEGIES FOR TEACHING CHAPTER 1: INTRODUCTION

Part 6 TEACHING THE ASSIGNMENT CHAPTERS (2–9)

Part 7 BIBLIOGRAPHIES

This *Instructor's Manual* supports teaching with *Reading Critically, Writing Well*, Fourth Edition. Beginning teachers will find comprehensive support for planning a course, presenting and discussing the readings, and giving and evaluating writing assignments. Experienced instructors will find varied resources to complement their teaching styles and to orient them quickly to the readings.

Part 2 of the manual offers a rationale for the basic features of the text, and Part 3 outlines alternative course plans. Part 4 presents basic teaching activities to support your work with this text, strategies like presenting and discussing readings, assigning journals, organizing students to work collaboratively, organizing workshops, conferencing, evaluating students' work, and managing the workload. Instead of giving general advice, we share specific strategies and activities we have developed in our own programs. If you are a beginning instructor, you will find Part 4 particularly helpful. It will enable you to approach your course confidently and to get good work from your students right away. Part 5 discusses ways to introduce the critical reading strategies presented in Chapter 1 of the text.

Part 6, the longest part, takes up each genre chapter (2–9) in turn, providing an orientation to the writing assignment at the core of the chapter, the sample essay that opens each chapter and the exercises based on it, an overview of readings, resources for teaching each reading, and comments on the guide to writing that closes each chapter.

To conclude the *Instructor's Manual*, Part 7 presents two bibliographies, one on composition studies, the other on learning from text.

Part 2   RATIONALE FOR THE BASIC FEATURES OF THE TEXT

This section explains briefly why we wrote *Reading Critically, Writing Well* the way we did. Our discussion of the ideas behind the text takes up the following topics:

- the relation between reading and writing in a writing course
- why critical reading strategies must be taught and how their practice contributes to writing development
- why students need a comprehensive framework of support as they draft and revise, with a focus on systematic invention
- the text's chapter sequence and relations among the chapters
- the possibilities for library and field research in a course using this text

RELATING READING AND WRITING BY GENRE

Schemas—memory for text—guide our reading and writing. Novice writers must develop schemas for the genres they will read and write in college and on the job. These schemas are learned through reading many essays in a genre, by analyzing selected essays rhetorically and stylistically, and by writing and revising essays with genre criteria in mind. Genre schema permit more confident, efficient reading and foster productive global planning during composing and revising.

We understand a genre to be a social construct that has evolved over time to meet writers' needs in recurring and now familiar writing situations. We consider genres to be heuristics that enable composing. While there can be a wide variation of form and strategy within a genre—as readings in each of this text's chapters illustrate—experienced readers and writers in a culture recognize paradigmatic instances. Genres are not fixed but change over time in response to a culture's changing rhetorical demands.

Current discourse theory and professional writers' experience confirm that each of the genres in Chapters 2–9—autobiography, observation, reflection, explanation of concepts, evaluation, speculation about causes or effects, proposal to solve a problem, and position paper—requires of students a special way of thinking and composing. In each genre, students must solve unique rhetorical problems and use information, memories, or arguments in particular ways.

We believe that, on their own, few students will discover the constraints and possibilities of our culture's key nonfiction genres. Unless they read widely and critically on their own or come from high schools with comprehensive writing programs where teachers understand the instructional implications of genre theory, students will need careful, focused instruction in the reading and writing of key genres. This text provides the materials, exercises, and assignments for such instruction.

This text relates reading and writing by genre. Students write autobiography as they are reading it, or they write proposals to solve problems as they are reading problem-solution essays. The readings collected in each of the readings chapters (2–9) illustrate a wide range of generic forms and strategies for development. Students observe many ways to begin, end, pattern, and develop a genre. They see writers solving predictable generic problems in different ways. This close matching of reading and writing by genre is the best way to realize fully the contribution reading can make to writing development in a composition course.

The text does more than simply match reading and writing by genre, however. An activity we call *Reading like a Writer,* which follows each reading, helps students understand the constraints and possibilities of a genre. They learn to read a genre—and they learn to read it as a writer does.

CRITICAL READING

The proven critical reading strategies we offer enable students to read more confidently and to get more out of their reading. Reading critically, we believe, is an approach—a stance—students can learn. Essentially, we teach students specific ways to act on a text and knowledge about how texts work.

We don't promise to make critical reading easy. In fact, we make reading harder and slower—but more productive. For every selection in the text, we invite students to read for meaning first and then to read like writers. And we ask them to read with pencil in hand, annotating the text from these two perspectives. Most important, we ask them to write about what they discover, using writing itself to explore ideas and to consolidate what they have learned. Writing becomes part of critical reading—an essential activity of critical reading that provides a tentative record of meanings and insights stuents can then share with others and thereby further enlarge what they can learn from a text.

Briefly, we offer two stances of critical reading (reading for meaning and reading like a writer); three actions of reading critically (annotating, inventorying annotations, and extending writing); and several specific strategies of critical reading:

- previewing
- contextualizing
- questioning to understand and remember
- reflecting on challenges to your beliefs and values
- outlining and summarizing
- paraphrasing
- reflecting on challenges to your beliefs and values
- exploring the significance of figurative language
- looking for patterns of opposition
- evaluating the logic of an argument
- recognizing emotional manipulation
- judging the writer's credibility
- comparing and contrasting related readings

These critical reading strategies are collected in Appendix 1, A Catalog of Critical Reading Strategies. Annotating and inventorying are illustrated there, as well as in Chapter 1, which introduces students to our basic stances and actions.

The appendix strategies are gradually introduced to students following appropriate readings as they make their way through the book. They practice each strategy at least once and most strategies more than once. You may, of course, decide to have students use an appendix strategy with other appropriate readings.

This comprehensive, approachable, theory-based and research-supported program of critical reading provides no panacea, however. What students get from a reading depends in part on what they bring to it. (At the same time, students sometimes bring more to a reading than they imagine: that's where previewing and contextualizing come in.) We know that reading for meaning can be considerably enriched by discussion: textual meaning-making at its best is in part a social activity. While recognizing that reading depends on prior knowledge and is enhanced by sharing tentative meanings with others, we don't want to claim too much for what a text like this can do. At the same time, we have made it easy for you to help students preview and contextualize readings as you assign them and then to share their writing in response to the Reading for Meaning and Reading like a Writer activities following every reading.

There are three primary reasons for teaching strategies of critical reading in a college writing course: (1) a writing course in which readings play a major role should be a course in reading critically, (2) insightful critical reading is essential to writing development, and (3) research indicates that carefully taught and well-practiced critical reading strategies enable students to understand better and remember longer their reading and to use it more effectively in other situations, like writing.

WRITING INSTRUCTION

The pencil-in-hand critical reading strategies discussed in the preceding section contribute directly to students' writing development. Critical reading is necessary for writing development in that genre, but it is not sufficient. Students also need comprehensive support for invention, composing, and revising of a genre. This text provides such support through various activities and guides.

PRACTICING [THE NAME OF THE GENRE]: A COLLABORATIVE ACTIVITY. This activity, coming early in each chapter, enables students to practice the genre orally in a collaborative exercise that gives them confidence that they already know something about "writing it."

READING LIKE A WRITER ACTIVITIES. Students complete a full rhetorical analysis of each chapter's opening sample essay. In addition, they analyze a key rhetorical strategy of each reading in a chapter. If they complete these for every reading, they learn about all the basic writing strategies of a genre. What they learn greatly improves the chances for successful peer critique and workshop discussions. (Part 4 discusses methods of peer critique.)

CONSIDERING IDEAS FOR YOUR OWN WRITING. Following each reading in Chapters 2–9 is a section titled Considering Ideas for Your Own Writing, which offers many specific ways students can write in the genre they are learning to read critically. The ideas for writing present possible subjects within which students choose their own topics and find a focus for them. Attempting to write about the subject in a particular genre immediately engages students in analyzing the rhetorical situation. They must decide what their purpose is given their expected readers and determine what these readers are likely to know, think, and feel about a possible subject.

THINKING ABOUT WHAT MAKES [NAME OF GENRE] EFFECTIVE. In this activity, coming at the end of the readings and just before they begin working on the writing assignment, students review and consolidate everything they have learned about the rhetorical features of a genre.

GUIDES TO WRITING. Each assignment chapter (2–9) concludes with a concise but comprehensive guide to writing. This guide leads (and encourages) students through the process of invention, drafting, and revising. There now is solid evidence that guided, systematic invention enables school and college students to write better. Therefore, each chapter provides genre-specific invention activities that are based on established heuristics like freewriting, answering questions, list-making, outlining, and analyzing readers. Each activity requires only a few minutes (as few as one or two and rarely more than thirty). (See Part 4 of this manual for a discussion about assigning and encouraging invention.)

The invention activities, all of which involve some writing, enable students to find a topic, generate ideas about it, explore their writing situation fully, and even carry out any necessary research. These writings may record several days of a potentially rich invention process; students' first drafts are then longer, more thoughtful, more interesting, and closer to their best work on a topic. New to invention is a collaborative activity, Learning More About Your Readers, that helps students think more deeply about what their readers know and believe.

The guides also help students give and get critical readings of their drafts, set goals before and during drafting, and organize invention materials prior to drafting. Each guide concludes with advice about revising to strengthen the essay and improve its readability and with an invitation to reflect on what has been learned. The guides to critical reading and reflection are new to this edition.

These guides to writing complement the critical reading strategies. Together, they provide a comprehensive program in reading and writing. They bring reading and writing together in a way that gives every student a chance to become more literate.

CHAPTER SEQUENCE

Although the chapters in the text can be presented in different sequences (see the discussion of various course plans in Part 3), we offer here a brief rationale for the text sequence. These are the chapters:

Chapter 2: Autobiography
Chapter 3: Observation
Chapter 4: Reflection
Chapter 5: Explaining Concepts
Chapter 6: Evaluation
Chapter 7: Speculation about Causes or Effects
Chapter 8: Proposal to Solve a Problem
Chapter 9: Position Paper

In chapter clusters, the sequence moves from expressive, observational, and explanatory (2–5) to persuasive or argumentative (6–9) writing. While an autobiographical essay is not necessarily easier to write than a position paper, there are certain advantages to our sequence. Beginning with autobiography, firsthand observation, and reflection delays the need for finding and using secondary sources and for struggling with library research. Students work with familiar or immediate—though not necessarily very manageable—material. Strategies of description and narration practiced in autobiography are central to observation. The anecdotes important to autobiography and reflection can emerge again very usefully in certain arguments.

Both observation and explanation engage students in solving problems of presenting information that are central to all types of academic writing and to all forms of argument. These two genres may very well encompass the majority of writing situations in some academic and professional specialties.

Chapter 6 begins an argument sequence that comprises half the assignment chapters in the text. This sequence begins with evaluation and speculation about causes or effects because theorists of argument say that these genres are basic to all other forms of argument. For example, when students write a proposal to solve a problem in Chapter 8, they may argue the causes or effects of the problem and evaluate alternative solutions. Cause and evaluation can also be central to position papers on controversial issues.

The argument chapters emphasize strategies for devising plausible arguments for particular readers. The students' writing situation in each chapter can be viewed this way:

Chapter 6. demonstrating the validity of a judgment
Chapter 7. conjecturing about possible causes or effects
Chapter 8. arguing the feasibility of a solution to a problem
Chapter 9. defending a position on an issue

This sequence provides a challenging introduction to the critical reading and writing of arguments.

EMPHASIS ON LIBRARY AND FIELD RESEARCH

Since research can strengthen student writing in Chapters 3 and 5–9, the text regularly invites library or field research. In addition, Appendix 2 provides guidance with both kinds of research. Although research can be emphasized toward the end of a course, students have so much to learn about finding and evaluating sources, integrating sources into their essays, and citing sources properly that we believe they should be doing some research early in the course. Hence, the text features field research in Chapter 3, Observation, and library research in Chapter 5, Explaining Concepts. All subsequent chapters regularly invite students to do research. Such an emphasis on research provides a realistic introduction to writing in academic and professional specialties. Many of the readings, including student readings, use and cite sources.

Part 3   SUGGESTED COURSE PLANS

Composition instructors typically organize their courses around writing assignments. Since *Reading Critically, Writing Well* covers eight different genres and includes many ideas for writing in each genre chapter, it offers different possibilities for designing a course. This section describes a variety of course plans you can use as the basis of your own syllabus, beginning with a six-assignment plan. Then come plans for a two-semester program, a one-semester argument course, and a two-quarter program. Finally, we discuss the opportunities for research with the text, including the extended library-research paper.

ONE-SEMESTER PLAN: SIX ASSIGNMENTS

This plan permits six essay assignments from Chapters 2–9. Though this plan does not include a formal, extended research paper, many assignments invite or require limited research. For example, Chapter 4, Observation, requires field research (observing and interviewing), and Chapter 5, Explaining Concepts, invites students to research the concepts they write about.

From this plan, you could readily devise a syllabus for your course. A syllabus specifies for each class meeting the assignments, readings, and activities, with exact page references to the text.

All of the suggested course plans in this section assume that you might be requiring frequent writing in a journal, giving collaborative learning assignments, arranging in-class writing workshops for peer critiques of drafts, holding tutorial conferences over drafts, or assigning further reading. Part 4 offers advice on all such activities.

Here are the essay assignments, by chapter title, in this plan:

> Autobiography
> Observation
> Reflection
> Explaining Concepts
> Evaluation
> Proposal to Solve a Problem

This plan gives balanced attention to personal writing (Chapters 2, 4), explanatory writing (Chapters 3, 5), and argument (Chapters 6, 8). It uses all chapters except Chapter 7, Speculation about Causes or Effects, and Chapter 9, Position Paper. Chapters 7 or 9 could be substituted for Chapters 6 or 8.

Our impression is that most writing programs on the semester plan give five to seven major writing assignments. Along with work on the critical reading strategies and a revision of each essay, the six-assignment plan we propose here is quite full. This full plan can be reduced by dropping an assignment or expanded by adding one. Whatever the details of your own syllabus, our proposed plan suggests a manageable pace and a way to sequence and integrate activities.

Keeping in mind that each of our assignment chapters offers many critical readings and writing activities, you might want to allow as much as three weeks for each assignment, especially if you ask students to revise their essays. In that case, you would want to assign only five chapters, or perhaps even as few as four during a typical fourteen- or fifteen-week semester. Here's how one assignment sequence might play out over a three-week period in a class meeting three times weekly:

Week 1

M: Discuss chapter opening and writing situation
   Do group-inquiry activity
   Assign introductory reading, Exercise 1, and half of Exercise 2
W: Discuss Exercises 1 and 2
   Assign remainder of Exercise 2
F: Discuss Exercise 2
   Do first reading and reading activities in class
   Assign second and third readings and reading activities

Week 2

M: Discuss second and third readings
   Assign fourth and fifth readings and reading activities

W: Discuss fourth and fifth readings
   Discuss possible essay topics in Ideas for Your Own Writing following each reading
   Assign first half of invention in guide to writing
F: Evaluate essay topics
   Review invention work
   Assign remainder of invention work and first draft of essay

Week 3
M: Workshop on drafts
W: Workshop on drafts
   Assign revision
F: Revision due
   Introduce next assignment

TWO-SEMESTER PLAN: TEN ASSIGNMENTS

Several colleges use *Reading Critically, Writing Well* as the basic text, usually along with a handbook or one or more tradebooks, for a two-semester writing program. A capacious two-semester plan like the following allows multiple resources in certain chapters to be used to the fullest. Here we list a possible essay sequence, assuming a pattern of course activities and assignments like that of the one-semester plan detailed above.

Assignment	*Chapters*
1	2, Autobiography: Narrating an Event
2	2, Autobiography: Characterizing a Person
3	3, Observation
4	4, Reflection
5	5, Explaining Concepts
6	6, Evaluation
7	7, Speculation about Causes or Effects (speculating about causes)
8	7, Speculation about Causes or Effects (speculating about effects)
9	8, Proposal to Solve a Problem
10	9, Position Paper

SEMESTER PLAN FOR AN ARGUMENT COURSE

The text includes enough material on argument to fill out a one-semester course concerned solely with argument or persuasion:

Assignment	*Chapters*
1	6, Evaluation
2	7, Speculation about Causes or Effects (speculating about causes)
3	7, Speculation about Causes or Effects (speculating about effects)

4	8, Proposal to Solve a Problem
5	9, Position Paper (without research)
6	9, Position Paper (with research)

This plan could make good use of the critical reading strategy Evaluating an Argument in Appendix 1.

QUARTER PLAN: FOUR ASSIGNMENTS

One-quarter courses can accommodate four of our assignments, though we know of courses using our text that give three to five assignments. Many programs at quarter-system campuses require students to complete two quarters of composition.

A one-quarter program faces hard choices. A sampling of personal, explanatory, and persuasive writing might look like this:

Assignment	Chapters
1	2, Autobiography
2	3, Observation
3	8, Proposal to Solve a Problem
4	9, Position Paper

TWO-QUARTER PLAN: EIGHT ASSIGNMENTS

A two-quarter program, with four assignments each quarter, might be organized as follows:

Assignment	Chapters
1	2, Autobiography
2	3, Observation
3	4, Reflection
4	5, Explaining Concepts
5	6, Evaluation
6	7, Speculation about Causes or Effects
7	8, Proposal to Solve a Problem
8	9, Position Paper

WHAT ABOUT THE RESEARCH PAPER?

Except for the Chapter 3 observational essay, every essay arising from Chapters 2–9 can be completed without research. In fact, the ideas for writing following each reading and the finding a topic section at the beginning of the invention sequence of each writing guide are designed to suggest many possibilities for writing that allow students to rely on their own present knowledge, experience, and resources. At the same time, every chapter except

9

Autobiography and Reflection can engage students in research, if the instructor wishes. We expect at least limited research with nearly all of the assignments in our own programs. Here we briefly outline the possibilities.

Chapter 3, Observation: Visiting a place, observing, interviewing, taking notes

Chapter 5, Explaining Concepts: Library research on the concept students explain

Chapter 6, Evaluation: Reseeing, revising, or rereading the subject being evaluated and taking notes

Chapter 7, Speculation about Causes or Effects: Library research on the event, trend, or phenomena speculated about in order to describe it fully and to survey others' proposed causes or effects

Chapter 8, Proposal to Solve a Problem: Interviewing people to understand more fully a problem affecting them and to anticipate their preferred solutions; library research on methods of implementing a proposed solution

Chapter 9, Position Paper: Library research on an issue in order to define and describe it adequately and to assess others' positions

Appendix 2 of the text provides comprehensive support for both field (observing and interviewing) and library research.

If your program requires an extended library-research paper, the most likely candidates in the text are Chapters 5 or 9, the one explanatory, the other argumentative. These chapters, along with Library Research and Acknowledging Sources in Appendix 2, provide full support for an extended, documented essay. Any of our proposed plans above could be adjusted to allow time during the final three or four weeks of a course for a library-research paper.

Part 4   TEACHING ACTIVITIES FOR A COURSE USING THIS TEXT

This section outlines basic teaching activities to support your work with this text. These activities, we believe, are important to the success of any composition course, whatever the textbook or other materials.

If you are a beginning instructor, you will find this section particularly helpful. Along with a syllabus based on one of our course plans in Part 3, the activities outlined in this section permit you to organize a complete course from start to finish: schedule, assignments, classroom and homework activities, evaluation of student writing, and record-keeping.

Instead of offering general advice in this section, we share specific activities, assignments, and materials we presently use in our own programs. Between the two of us authors, we have accumulated (to our amazement) fifty-four years of teaching writing and administering writing programs at six colleges in California, Colorado, and New York. What follows presents the best we know about organizing and teaching a writing course.

Note: This section presents general teaching activities; the next sections (Part 5 and 6) provide specific support for teaching the introductory chapter and each genre chapter.

PRESENTING AND DISCUSSING READINGS

If students are to succeed with an essay assignment in one of our genre chapters, they should read—and critically reread—the readings in that chapter. They should compare and contrast readings in order to see the full range of possibilities for their own essay in a genre. Class discussions of readings should be focused, efficient, productive, and encouraging to students as writers. How might you ensure such critical reading and discussions? This section provides an answer.

GIVING CLEAR AND COMPLETE ASSIGNMENTS. Even in a casual, slow-moving course using *Reading Critically, Writing Well,* assignments will be frequent: both the writing and the reading must be moved along by almost daily student work. If you find our other recommendations in this section persuasive, there will be several complementary strands of work to be moved along simultaneously in your course, engaging students in a variety of out-of-class assignments each week.

We believe the most effective way to give assignments is to prepare carefully a once-a-week handout. Even though we give students a rather detailed course syllabus, we further detail assignments for each week. We put assignments in writing because students do not all hear the same thing, it seems, when we give assignments orally, and also because class time is not lost in dictating assignments or writing them on the board. The weekly handout precludes hasty last-minute assignments as students gather up books and head for the door. Most important, we think, preparing the weekly assignment handout gives us an opportunity to think through carefully what we want to accomplish in a given week.

Except for drafting and revising full essays, assignments in a course using this text are relatively brief. For example, a single reading and its reading activities might take an hour. Exploring in the journal an idea for writing following a reading might take ten or fifteen minutes. The introduction to each chapter might require two hours, time best divided into two or more working periods during one or two days. In the guide to writing in any genre chapter, invention work entails brief writings spread over two or three days. Such frequent writing—our goal for students is *daily* writing—lets the mind work on the readings, consolidate new rhetorical learning, and produce ideas for writing. Consequently, *frequency* and *variety* of writing are essential. Pacing of work during the week and from week to week is crucial. Your weekly assignment handout paces, sequences, and clarifies this work. Students' limited time is used efficiently, and they are prepared for class.

We give weekly assignments at the beginning of the first class meeting of each week and take a few minutes to go over the assignments and answer any questions. Because there is a handout, students who come late rarely take our time after class to discuss assignments. A student who must be absent can later pick up the assignment handout at the writing program office, or a friend in the class can take one for the absent student.

If you file your assignments in a personal computer, there is a substantial time savings the next time you teach the course. You can easily revise or move certain assignments.

Some of our instructors append brief comments to the assignment handout—reiterating course goals, previewing an especially challenging assignment, forecasting a change of pace, praising or exhorting, summarizing progress and anticipating next developments, relating concepts and assignments in order to give students a larger view of the course, and so on.

PREVIEWING READINGS. Most of the genre-chapter readings are preceded by previewing questions. These questions are designed to help students activate prior knowledge of the subject, discover the genre of the text, speculate about its historical or cultural context, or sample its content. These questions enrich readings, and they may also entice or invite students to read a reading. As you assign a reading, you can do still more, however, to entice students to read it:

> Tell them some things you may know about the historical or cultural context of the reading.

> Tell them something about the author, or read a brief excerpt from one of the author's books (for example, when you assign "A Chase" by Annie Dillard in Chapter 2, read a few of Dillard's arresting, memorable aphorisms and analogies about writing from her best-selling book *The Writing Life)*.

> Show them the book or an issue of the magazine from which the reading was selected and talk about the impact of the book or about what you learned from it, or explain the purpose and readership of the magazine.

> Preview what they will learn as a writer from the reading.

> Relate the reading to other readings in the chapter.

These enticements take only a few minutes, but they can increase students' willingness to begin a reading in the odd moments and places where homework gets done.

SETTING UP A READING JOURNAL. A reading journal and collaborative reading/learning assignments (described later in this section) are essential features of our courses. A reading journal differs from a personal journal, a writer's journal, or an exploratory "dialogic" (or "double-entry") journal in that it is concerned mainly or exclusively with using writing to learn about reading, with goal-focused journal tasks assigned by the instructor. For students keeping a reading journal in a course using this text, the frequent journal writings assist them in learning from their reading what a *writer* needs to know. This is a special kind of rhetorical learning. It is based on critical reading (and especially on critical rereading). Its mode is analytic and its outcome is conceptual. One of us has completed research (with Susan MacDonald) suggesting that in an assigned-readings course where a particular type of writing is to be the outcome, the reading journal we are proposing teaches students far more than an exploratory journal in which students initiate all the writing. (A dialogic or personal journal could be just the right choice in other learning situations.)

How do you set up a reading journal? After much trial and error over several years, here is what works best for us and our instructors. Students buy a special loose-leaf three-ring binder and label it *Reading Journal.* (We recommend an inexpensive version about a half-inch thick at the binder with a flexible cover—much more portable than heavy-duty binders.) Each journal assignment begins on a separate piece of paper labeled with the student's name, the date, and the source of the entry (Chapter 2, Dillard, Reading like a Writer), and any other information that will facilitate your record-keeping.

Give reading journal assignments once a week as part of your weekly assignment handout. Going week-by-week, rather than planning journal assignments for a longer period, gives you flexibility to speed or slow the pace; to insert assignments that arise from special problems or opportunities; and, most important, to match the assignments precisely to the week's sequence of reading and writing activities.

We collect loose-leaf journal entries every week or two and return them to students to insert in their binders at the next class meeting. The first time or two we spend more time reading and commenting than we will later: we want to be sure students know what we expect of their reading journals. If the entries are brief and thin, we insist on more writing in future journal entries. If the writing seems too serious, cautious, or planned, we encourage exploration, risk-taking, digressions, even playfulness.

If you number your journal assignments sequentially from beginning to end of your course and ask students to do the same in their journals, then you always know where each student is in the sequence and whether at the midpoint or end of the course students have completed all assignments.

Our instructors weight the reading journal 20 percent or 25 percent of the course grade. We tell students that they must complete all journal assignments in a timely fashion in order to receive a C in the course. We do not actually grade the journal. Instead, we skim it quickly at the end of the course and decide whether it is exemplary, very good, acceptable, or complete but thin and perfunctory, and inform students of our judgment in a brief final note. Some instructors record a plus, check, or minus in the response to each set of journal entries they examine during the course.

The goal is to spend as little time as possible reading journals and still encourage students to sustain their work in the journal.

How should students approach reading journal assignments? We outline various types of journal assignments below, each requiring a different approach. We can say in general, however, that journal writing is relatively informal. It is first-draft writing, not painstakingly planned, not tight or cautious. It is exploratory, discursive, digressive, associational. A student may begin a journal entry with one idea and end it with quite a different one. In the reading journal, a student *writes to learn,* not merely to report what has been learned.

Journal entries may (probably *should*) exhibit lined-out (less time-consuming than erasing) phrases or sentences, marginal or interlinear additions, one or more parts added later to the end. They should not strike the reader as perfunctory. Instead, there should be evidence of commitment to learning through writing, of insight, discovery, confusion, questioning.

What kinds of reading journal assignments might you give? We recommend three basic kinds:

1. Critical reading activities from Chapter 1 and the assignment chapters. Keep in mind that our critical reading activities—Reading for Meaning and Reading like a Writer—require writing. The reading journal collects and organizes *all* critical reading activities—no small convenience for you when, in a semester plan like the one we propose in Part 3 of this manual, students may complete thirty to forty critical reading activities during the course. The loose-leaf format enables students to exchange single entries and you to evaluate one or more activities at a time.

2. Copy and comment, as in the Commonplace Book, a staple of liberal arts education since the Middle Ages. Students occasionally copy a particularly striking sentence or brief passage from one of the readings and then comment/react/analyze for a page or so. You could assign copy/comment once with each genre chapter. In this way, our reading journal poses an activity prized by advocates of the dialogic journal.

3. Reflections on learning and on the course. Recent research demonstrates that when students step back and review what they are learning, they remember it longer and put it to better use. In a course using this text, students learn how to read and write certain genres; or, to put it another way, they acquire rhetorical or textual knowledge. As students complete each genre chapter and its essay, they could write a journal entry reflecting on what they have learned. Here is a journal task we use:

> Now that you have completed the work in Chapter 2, Autobiography, take twenty or thirty minutes to review all the materials you've produced for this assignment. Begin by reviewing Reading Autobiographical Essays: A Summary at the end of the chapter. Skim your invention work and essay draft, and then reread your revision. Finally, skim the writing you completed for the critical reading strategies following readings. Then write one and a half to two pages summing up what you've learned about reading and writing autobiography. Develop your explanation not in general terms *(interesting, coherent, organized, lively style)* but in terms specific to autobiography *(narration, pacing, tension or suspense, dialogue, specific narrative action, scene, point of view, concrete sensory details, dominant impression, autobiographical significance)*. Use these terms in your discussion. Refer to particular readings and to your own writing (journal entries, invention, the essay). Your explanation can be more exploratory than decisive: write to figure out just what it is you learned. There's no need to plan carefully. Don't waste time worrying about what to write. Just identify one thing you've learned and start writing. Other things will occur to you as you write.

You can easily revise this example for a reflecting-on-learning journal task at the end of each genre chapter you assign. For later chapters in the text, you could add to this task the request that students bring along rhetorical knowledge from previous chapters. For example, students reflecting on what they have learned in Chapter 3, Observation, could be asked which rhetorical concepts from Chapter 2 informed their reading and writing of observational discourse, or students moving through the argument chapters (6–9) could be asked to compare and contrast the different types of argument.

Students might also be asked to comment on the course. With these tasks, you want to deflect personal evaluations of other students and of you and invite frank assessments of progress problems with assignments or materials, misunderstandings, special insights, frustrations. Questions like these, in various combinations, have worked very well for us:

> What has most surprised you so far about this course? Account for your surprise. (We ask this question and the next two early in a course.)
>
> What has most pleased you so far about this course? Most disappointed you? Account for your pleasure and disappointment.
>
> How is this course different from your high-school English courses, and how is it similar to them?
>
> How is this course influencing your reading and writing in your other courses? Give specific examples.

How are your reading and writing changing as a result of this course? Give specific
   examples.
We are now at the halfway point in the course. What are you most pleased with about
   your development as a reader and writer? What are your goals for the second half
   of the course?
What one thing could I do to make the course more satisfying for you? What one thing
   could you do? Explain why these changes could be important for you.

We like to pose a journal task like this every two weeks or so. From students' writing we
learn a lot about the students and the course. You will readily think of other questions to ask
as you get to know your students.

GIVING QUIZZES. For many years, we resisted quizzing students to discover whether they
had completed our assignments, assuming they had developed a mature understanding of the
consequences of neglecting reading assignments. Now we give a quiz at the beginning of most
class meetings for which readings have been assigned. The reasons we changed our position
are that (1) we came to recognize the competing demands on students' time, and (2) we
gradually came to understand how important thoughtful critical reading is to students'
development as writers. Therefore, we now provide every possible encouragement for students
to complete reading assignments. Giving clear reading assignments, previewing readings
enticingly, and giving reading journal assignments on the reading provide much of the
encouragement. Quizzes provide the rest. Students rarely come to our reading-day discussions
unprepared. And as a consequence, their essays are stronger because they are informed by
rhetorical strategies from the assigned readings.
   We rely on three basic quiz questions, which we give orally (we give only *one* for the
quiz).

   1. Tell me what you know about reading X.
   2. Tell me what a writer can learn from reading Y. (For these two questions we choose
   one of the two or three assigned readings.)
   3. Tell me how readings X and Y are alike and different. (For this question we choose two
   of the assigned readings.)

   Students write quickly for no more than ten minutes. Students who are tardy or absent may
not make up a missed quiz. We take up the quizzes and file them with other quizzes in a folder
for each student. We do not grade or return them. Instead, we may periodically review these
folders and write a note to (or chat with) a student whose quizzes are unsatisfactory. Most
students write satisfactory quizzes. In one or two minutes, you can skim a quiz folder in order
to tell any anxious student how well he or she is doing on the quizzes.
   At the end of the course, you can just as quickly tell which students have consistently
performed well on the quizzes. You can overlook one or two missing quizzes. We usually
weight quizzes 10 percent of the final grade.
   Early in the course you can read aloud a few outstanding quizzes to give students an idea
of what you expect. Be firm about the quizzes. Tell students why you give them. And then
treat them lightly within the context of the whole course: quizzes are only one small means
toward a consequential end—better essays.

GIVING COLLABORATIVE LEARNING ASSIGNMENTS. There is a growing interest—and an expanding literature—in collaborative writing and learning. For twenty years or more in the schools there has been serious experimentation with collaborative learning. Most projects have been concerned with concept-learning in science or history. Studies and reviews of studies indicate that students learn more through carefully planned small-group activities.

Collaborative learning has always been central, of course, to writing workshop courses or to any composition course where students meet in or out of class to discuss work in progress. For quite a while now, experienced, informed writing instructors have seen themselves as collaborators with students to improve their composing.

And there is new interest within composition studies in collaborative *writing*—those occasions in academia, bureaucracies, and the professions when two or more writers collaborate to produce a single piece of writing. For the last two years a few of our instructors have occasionally given a collaborative writing assignment—usually in Chapter 7, Speculation about Causes or Effects, or Chapter 8, Proposal to Solve a Problem. One of them (M. A. Syverson) has researched the problems collaborative writing groups encounter and convinced us that we need to know much more about how to arrange collaborative writing assignments in order for freshmen to succeed with them.

We have few reservations, however, about the contribution collaborative *learning* can make to our program. We ask students to meet in small groups *outside of class* to discuss *readings* and elaborate and consolidate their learning of rhetorical and textual concepts. Each student reads assigned readings and then meets with his or her collaborative learning group to complete tasks we pose. These meetings are occasions primarily for rereading and talking, though some writing usually results as well. We sometimes talk about these groups as collaborative *reading* groups.

Here are our two basic activities. We try to assign one or the other in each genre chapter.

Group Report on a Reading

Carefully read the essay assigned to your group, complete the Reading for Meaning and Reading like a Writer activities, and then meet with your group to prepare a presentation for the rest of the class.

You will present what you have learned by sharing your Reading like a Writer responses, rereading the essay, and discussing what you've learned about the genre. What strategies did the writer use? What did you learn that will help when you are writing your essay?

In preparing your presentation with your group, you should review the summary at the end of the chapter. You may use these strategies as the focus of your discussion.

You should expect other members of the class to be familiar with the essay you will present. Needless to say, be sure that you are familiar with the essays assigned to the other groups. You must be prepared to participate in the discussion about the essays that the other groups present.

Group Evaluation of Two Readings

Your group has been assigned two readings. Carefully read the two assigned essays before you meet with your group. Before you read, though, review the summary at the end of each chapter where you find the readings. Then, as you read both readings, take notes on how they fulfill the basic features of the genre. Also complete the Reading Like a Writer activity at the end of each reading. Decide on your own which reading you think is the better example of the genre.

Then meet with your group and discuss each person's choice of the better example. Arrive at some consensus and prepare an oral report about your evaluation for the rest of the class.

In your report, you should explain your group's judgment and the reasons for making it. Be sure that you refer to the basic features of the genre. If one or two of you cannot agree with the other members of your group, feel free to file minority and majority reports.

You should expect other members of the class to be familiar with these essays. Likewise, be sure that you are familiar with the essays assigned to the other groups. You must be able to participate in the other groups' presentations of their evaluations.

You will see many possible variations on these basic activities. For example, for the evaluation of two-readings activity, you could ask groups to report on similarities and differences between the two readings rather than to argue that one is better.

How do you arrange collaborative reading groups? As soon as possible, assign each student to a group of four. You may have one group of three or five; but five have greater difficulty in finding a common meeting time than four, and three are sometimes reduced to two and then are not really a "group." If students drop out during the term, you may need to combine reduced groups. On what basis do you form these groups? Try to avoid homogeneous groupings. We recommend a mix of different genders, cultural backgrounds, age, or other factors that will ensure a heterogeneous group. You may also want to ensure a range of writing abilities in each group.

Give students a moment to meet in class to schedule a regular time to meet. They will need a two-hour time block when they can all meet outside of class.

Explain to them that the collaborative discussion of readings will contribute to their success in your course, and offer them general guidelines for collaboration. Their goal—at least in these two basic activities—is to prepare a brief report (five to eight minutes, depending on how many groups you have and how long your class meets) on what they learn about the readings. Tell them they must report as a *panel*, with each person contributing. Since the reports tend to sprawl, you will have to enforce time limits so that all groups may report and you will have time for other activities.

FACILITATING CLASSROOM DISCUSSION OF READINGS. The day arrives when students come to class to discuss the readings—a crucial moment in a course hoping to help students read critically and write well. This is potentially the *worst* moment in a writing course. Students look at the floor. No one volunteers to take your first question. The first person you call on wasn't able to do the reading. The second person you call on thought the readings were assigned for the next class meeting. The third person you call on seems to have misread or partially read the reading. The mood changes. You feel grim. The students feel embarrassed. What to do? Probably the only thing to do is to allow time for everyone to read a reading before you attempt to discuss it. As a result, only one of the three readings you assigned receives any attention.

This nightmare scenario will likely never be realized in your course if you include in your course planning and assignments the activities we have described in earlier sections:

Reading assignments given by you on a weekly handout

Motivation to read from your enticing previews

Reading journal assignments to complete the critical reading activities following assigned
readings

A collaborative reading-group assignment on the readings

A quiz on the readings

Here's the plan we follow for a class meeting to learn as much as possible about assigned readings:

Quiz

Reading aloud of journal entries (two to four students), followed by discussion and/or

Collaborative learning group reports, followed by discussion and/or

Your own close reading of a text or a monologue from you on the context of a text, its
author, its major ideas, and so on

Your own (or a student's) summary of readings/discussion in terms of rhetorical features
of the type of writing and the students' writing task

Notice that even though students have prepared carefully and must contribute to the presentation and discussion of readings, there is still a major role for you to play. Experienced teachers can arrange for students to say most of what needs to be said about readings, but they can rarely get them to say *all* that needs to be said. And so you say what they are not yet prepared to say. You make connections that will not be apparent to them as they are beginning to study a genre. They especially need your help in looking closely at features of a particular essay. As they observe you reading critically—reading rhetorically, reading like a writer—they learn to do it themselves.

It is important to begin each discussion by reminding students of the purpose for discussing the readings: to examine the basic features of and writers' strategies in a particular genre and to improve students' own writing as a result of this examination. As the discussion progresses, keep reminding students of the connections between the various readings and their own writing.

As the discussion proceeds, keep summarizing the main points of your exploration of the reading, perhaps using the chalkboard. Remind students often of the relation between the reading and their own writing.

To complete the discussion of each reading, ask students to summarize the main things they have learned. This could be a quick, focused summary by one or two students. Some instructors go around the room, asking each student to make a brief summarizing comment on the essay. You can then reiterate the main points of the discussion, and help students to see the connections between each reading and the other readings.

End the discussion session by once again reiterating the basic features of the type of writing and the rhetorical strategies used in the essays you have discussed. An in-class journal question can help students focus and reflect on what they have learned during the discussion.

Give up on discussions that don't seem to be going anywhere or that aren't engaging most of the students. Do not stay on a single point (or a single essay) for too long. Instead, keep the pace of the discussion fairly quick so that students remain attentive.

Try to involve every student in every discussion so that a few students are not doing all the talking. Many students are somewhat shy about speaking in class, so this may take some special effort on your part. One way to elicit a spoken response from even the shyest of students is to ask a simple, low-key question such as, What do you remember best about this selection? Most students should be able to answer this question on the spot, and they can then be encouraged to speculate about why a certain feature makes the selection memorable.

ORGANIZING WORKSHOPS

The workshop brings class members together to read and respond to work in progress—usually first or second drafts of a piece of writing. In this section, we describe two workshop formats: (1) two students exchange drafts and write an analysis of each other's drafts, and (2) two or three students bring copies of their drafts for the whole class and then read their drafts aloud, followed by a whole-class discussion. In one of our programs, classes meet for two hours twice a week; consequently, we are able to use both formats on a workshop day, devoting about an hour to each one. Very likely your classes meet for an hour. In that case, you could use one or the other of our formats or use one at one class meeting and the other at the next.

WRITTEN ANALYSIS. In a two-hour workshop class, we typically begin by asking students to exchange drafts with another class member. Each student then spends the first forty-five or fifty minutes reading the partner's draft silently and writing a critical response to it. Questions to guide this process can be found under Reading [the genre of a chapter]: A Summary at the end of each genre chapter. As students first exchange drafts, they brief their partners on particular points they would like the partners to critique. They write their responses on separate sheets of paper, labeled at the top to look like this:

Autobiographical Essay Draft
Workshop Response for John Smith by Yolanda Jenkins

During the first part of the workshop, while students are working silently on each others' drafts, you may choose to move among them to offer advice. Alternatively, you can arrange in advance for students to bring copies of their drafts for you to review during this time. When students have finished their written responses, each partner returns the draft and response to the other, taking a minute to look over the response and ask the partner about anything confusing.

To facilitate this critical exchange, you may want to pair students according to their writing abilities, changing the pairs so that each student receives responses from several others during the course.

Student writers tend to write their first workshop responses with some anxiety. A few will launch into devastatingly honest evaluations of a partner's draft, but most err on the side of conciliation. Influenced perhaps by the knowledge that their own drafts are undergoing similar scrutiny, they are usually eager to praise and offer little substantial criticism. At the beginning of the course, they also lack the experience to make recommendations to the writer.

19

One way to address this problem in the first workshop is to take students through the summary questions at the end of each chapter, modeling for them the kind of critique that would let the writer know what works, what needs work, and what might be done about weaknesses. A good response points to specific things in the draft, describing their effect on the reader tactfully but honestly, and suggests options the writer might consider. Questions to the writer beginning with How about . . . ? are often useful. To model such a critique, you can use copies of a class member's draft or copies of an anonymous draft written for a similar assignment in a previous course.

Student pairs could arrange to meet outside of class, exchange drafts, and complete a written analysis. Arriving in class with analyses in hand, they could review and discuss them and then move on to analyzing still another student's draft in class or to discussion of a draft with the whole class. As attractive as this alternative may seem—it can save class time for other matters—it has not worked well for us. Student pairs do not seem to finish their drafts very far in advance of the workshop class itself, or one student in a pair finishes in time for the scheduled exchange of drafts and the other does not. All students seem to benefit from the same specific deadline: a draft must be completed by the time of the workshop class. In class, you can review with all of them the criteria for an analysis and coach them in making a useful analysis.

DISCUSSION. During the second hour of a workshop, we change the pace by moving to oral readings and responses. One format is to arrange in advance for one or two students to bring enough copies of their drafts for the other class members to share a copy between every two students. The writer tells the class about any particular problems he or she has had in the draft and then reads it aloud while the rest of the class follows along on the copies, making marginal notes where appropriate. The class will respond better if they hear and see the draft simultaneously. At the end of the oral reading, the instructor chairs a discussion of the draft, appointing a scribe to record specific suggestions for revisions on behalf of the writer. The questions in the end-of-chapter summary can form the basis of this discussion. At the end of the discussion, the scribe gives the writer the discussion notes and other students pass along their copies with marginal notes.

This whole-class discussion of one draft at a time simulates the traditional writers' workshop widely used in MFA programs. Many instructors using this workshop format ask that the writer not participate in the discussion. There are good reasons for this rule. At the draft stage, writers need to listen to the discussion, reflect thoughtfully on what readers say, why they misunderstand, what they have questions about. From listening to this sort of discussion of one's draft, a writer can know whether it struck readers as honest, engaging, authentic, informative, or convincing, especially if the readers also add further reactions in writing to copies of the draft as the discussion moves along and then return all of those copies to the writer at the end of the workshop.

You may choose to reverse our plan and begin a workshop class with whole-class discussion rather than with written analysis so that you can review the basic issues and requirements of the assignment. Even with the help of the guide to writing, there will still be students who have not quite brought the assignment into focus yet. By concentrating initially on one or two papers with the whole class, you can remind students of the basic issues of that kind of writing. At the end of the discussion, you can summarize these basic issues on the chalkboard and relate them to points in the end-of-chapter summary. This should give students more confidence in helping each other and keep them focused on the central rhetorical issues of the assignment rather than the peripheral ones.

Working with the whole class on one draft allows you to guide the discussion and make observations that are relevant to the assignment and not just to the draft in hand. An alternative is to divide the class into small groups of four or five, with one member of each group bringing copies of his or her draft for the others in the group and reading it aloud to them. In a large class, this allows more students to receive group responses to their drafts and encourages the more reticent students to participate in the discussion. You can join one group or move among the groups. This format works best when students know what is expected and can work productively without your guidance.

PRACTICAL CONSIDERATIONS. When a student comes to class late or without a draft, you have several options, depending on which workshop format the class is using:

Have the student work on his or her own draft
Have the student join a pair and read a draft page by page as one partner finishes
Have the student wait for another late student to show up
Have the student respond to a copy of a draft that has been duplicated for the whole class

In all these cases, the student must be reminded that he or she is responsible for obtaining another student's response to his or her own draft.

When the first and second draft of the same assignment are read in subsequent workshops, some instructors ask students to choose a different partner to respond to the second draft. Other instructors allow students to choose the same partner to read the second draft so that the partner can comment on the progress the writer has made since the first draft.

Some instructors find it useful to have students put their phone numbers on their workshop responses, so that writers can call their workshop partners if they find they have questions as they revise their drafts.

Some instructors ask all students to bring an extra copy of their drafts. During the pair-workshop, while pairs are quietly writing their critiques of each other's drafts, the instructor quickly reviews all drafts, looking for the obvious general problems.

HOLDING TUTORIAL CONFERENCES

Conferences with students are time-consuming and difficult to schedule when classes are large, but we recommend them highly as a teaching practice, even if you can see students individually only once or twice during the course. Conferences allow you to develop a rapport with students, thus building the trust and self-confidence that many students need before they will take the risks in their writing that lead to real progress. For many students, these conferences are their only opportunities to work individually with a college instructor.

A conference may be scheduled at any time during the composing process. We find it most useful after the first or second draft of an essay has been written, at a point when the student has spent some time thinking about the assignment, generating invention notes, and making at least one attempt to put the ideas into draft form but before the student has finished work on the essay. Ideally, the first draft is discussed in a conference and the second draft in a workshop with other students, or vice versa, before the student writes the final revision of the essay.

In the one-quarter courses we teach, we like to see students in conference three times. The second of these, the midterm conference, allows us to review the student's progress and discuss the goals for the remainder of the course.

INDIVIDUAL CONFERENCES. We find that the best length for individual conferences is half an hour, although it is possible to make some progress in twenty minutes if the time is spent carefully.

The student comes to the conference with a draft in hand and may at first expect you to play the role of mechanic, making the necessary repairs on it while he or she waits in anxious silence. It is often tempting to take the draft from the student and go to work on it, but this defeats the objective of conferencing, which is to help students learn to work on their own drafts. To this end, we leave the draft in the student's hands for most of the conference and usually begin by asking the student either to read it aloud or talk about it. In the most successful conferences, the students do at least half the talking; our comments merely draw them out and let them make discoveries for themselves.

Because our questions at the beginning of the conference, or after the student has read the draft aloud, tend to be the same, we give them to students in advance on a handout, leaving space between questions for their notes. This means that students come to the conference prepared with a list of things to say and questions to ask, and we can begin work immediately. Following are general questions we might ask students about their drafts:

1. What pleases you most about this draft? Which part seems most successful?
2. Which areas of the draft do you feel need work, and why? What would your toughest reader be likely to say about the draft?
3. Which were the hardest and easiest parts to write?
4. What did you notice when you read this draft aloud to a friend?
5. What have you learned from this assignment so far?
6. What changes are you considering for the next draft?
7. What new writing strategy were you trying to use in this draft?
8. What questions would you like to ask me about this draft?

Following are questions we ask students about a draft of an essay analyzing the causes of a trend. We tend to assign a trend, rather than an event or a phenomenon, options in Chapter 7. You could readily write such questions for any genre assignment.

1. What trend are you analyzing?
2. Why is it a trend, as opposed to a fad or a phenomenon?
3. What causes are you presenting to explain this trend? Which causes seem to you to be the strongest? Weakest?
4. Do you have a strongest or most convincing cause? Why have you selected this one particular cause as likely to be most convincing for your readers?
5. What have you done thus far in this assignment that you feel confident about? It can be anything from your research to the ideas you've developed to explain the trend you're writing about.

6. What problems are you having with this essay? Do they have to do with library research, listing possible causes, or evaluating causes? Are you unsure as to whether you are talking about a trend or a fad? In what specific ways can I help you?

Questions like these provide a good starting point for discussion, and they encourage students to take responsibility for their writing and assume an active role in improving it.

SMALL-GROUP CONFERENCES. An alternative to the individual conference is the small-group conference. Instead of meeting with each student for half an hour, the instructor meets with three students for an hour, spending twenty minutes on each student's draft. In a typical group conference, each student brings copies of the draft for the other two students and the instructor. They each read their drafts aloud while the listeners make notes on their copies. At the end of each reading, the instructor and the student talk about the draft. The other two students may quietly audit the discussion or contribute their views and suggestions. After twenty minutes, the writer collects the annotated copies and attention turns to the next student's draft.

The group conference lacks the privacy of an individual conference, an important consideration for shy students. On the other hand, the group may generate ideas that would not emerge in a one-on-one conference. Some of the comments we make about the first student's draft usually apply to the other two as well, and students often decide to change their own drafts after the discussion of another student's draft. Neither conference format is inherently better than the other; we recommend that you try both to decide which you prefer.

SCHEDULING CONFERENCES. One way of scheduling conferences is to have students sign up for time slots in the class meeting before conference week, writing down their names and phone numbers on a sheet that you can then post on the door of your office. If students find that they cannot keep the conference appointment, they go to the posted sheet and get the names and numbers of classmates who might change appointments with them. In this way, students are able to take care of rescheduling largely on their own, without having to call you.

One instructor finds it helpful to have students sign up for conference times *two* class meetings in advance—in pencil. She brings the list to the last meeting before the conference and circulates it once more so that students can double-check times and location and reschedule if necessary.

Students should be reminded to be on time for conference meetings, as even a few minutes can throw off your carefully planned schedule.

EVALUATING STUDENT WRITING, HANDLING THE PAPER LOAD, AND KEEPING RECORDS

Students completing an essay assignment will have generated a good deal of writing. We find it very important to have a system of accounting for all the writing turned in and a method of reading and responding to it that allows us to give students helpful feedback while processing the pile of student work in a reasonable amount of time.

At the beginning of the course, we give students a handout that specifies what they are to turn in for each writing assignment. Here is an example:

When you finish each assignment, you will turn in not only the final revision but *all* the writing you did for the assignment. Put this work in a file folder with your name, your section, and the assignment written clearly on the outside. Each folder you turn in should contain the following five parts:

1. *Invention:* Numerous pages of rough, unpolished invention from the Guide to Writing for the assignment in *Reading Critically, Writing Well.*
2. *Drafts:* Either one or two rough exploratory drafts, depending on the length of the assignment. They should be legible and labeled with your name, the assignment title, and the draft number. Number the pages.
3. *Workshop Response:* The response written on one of your drafts by a classmate during the workshop. The classmate's name should be on the response.
4. *Revision:* The final, revised version of the essay. This should be typed and proofread with any errors neatly corrected. Double-space, type on one side of the page only, and number each page. The title page should be labeled in the top right-hand corner like this:

    [Your name]
    [Chapter title for the assignment]
    Revision
    [Date]
5. *Reflecting on What You Have Learned:* Follow the guidelines in the activity of this name at the end of each assignment chapter.

This handout gives students a checklist of all the work they are to turn in. We find it reduces confusion, eases our management of the large amounts of writing, and speeds the reading and response process.

When we pull the handful of work from the student's folder, we skim to see that all the assigned writing is there and to see what the student has accomplished in the invention and drafts. The invention tends to be a good indicator of the depth and thoroughness of the revised essay, and problems in the revision can often be traced to deficiencies in the invention. We try to make this connection clear to students early in the course.

To keep track of the student's performance in the various stages of the composing process for each assignment, we keep a record sheet for the student. (An example of such a record sheet is at the end of this section.) This sheet is for our own records, and students do not see it. As we read the student's writing for each assignment, we make notes in the appropriate boxes on the record sheet. We find this helpful in reviewing each student's progress during the course.

The student's self-evaluation (Reflecting on What You Have Learned) asks them to reflect critically on their composing process, to think about what they have written, and to take responsibility for the decisions they have made. At its worst, a self-evaluation will say no more than "here it is—I like it—hope you do too," as the student declines the invitation to take responsibility. At its best, however, it provides the student with an account of his or her composing process, and it provides you with a critical introduction to the essay. It can also clearly indicate the student's level of involvement with the assignment. We usually read the self-evaluation carefully, after we skim the whole package.

We then spend several minutes on the revision. We make a few comments in the margins, noting both strong and weak points in the writing, and add a few sentences or a paragraph of comments at the end, on a separate sheet of paper. You may want to keep a copy of these comments for your own records. We try to find something in the essay to praise, and we find that critical comments work best when phrased in terms of what the student might have done in the essay or should try to do in the next one. Questions are useful, too, when they lead students to think about ways they might have addressed the problems in the paper. This approach casts the instructor in the role of expert adviser rather than hanging judge.

Our response to a student's essay is influenced by its location in the sequence of assignments. Our comments will be different in each of the following situations:

1. The student is to revise the essay one more time.
2. We plan to repeat the assignment.
3. The assignment will not be made again in the course, and we want to summarize the student's achievement.
4. The assignment is the first or last in a series of related writing assignments (for example, Chapters 6–9 on argument).

When time is limited, we respond to features in the essay in order of priority. In an autobiographical essay, we would begin by considering the larger rhetorical issues: what the writer has tried to accomplish in telling the story, its structure, the beginning and ending, and the pacing of the narrative. Next, we would look at some particular feature of the genre: the quantity and vividness of descriptive details, the writer's recollection of feelings at the time of the event or toward the person, the use of dialogue, and the proportion of narration, description, and commentary in the story. Finally, we would comment on the writer's style, diction, and sentence structure.

We do not comment on everything that could be improved in a paper. An inexperienced writer can be easily overwhelmed by too much criticism and become too discouraged to work on any of the problems. Rather, we try to focus on a few of the most important things that need attention, thereby giving the student achievable goals. We follow the same policy with mechanical errors and stylistic infelicities, assuming that if we mark every transgression in a weak writer's paper, the student will most likely attend to none of the problems. Instead, we mark every error in a particular section—a whole page or one or two paragraphs on a page—by placing a check mark in the margin next to the line where the error occurs. We put parentheses around long phrases or whole sentences that need to be revised. This conveys the message that the mechanics and style need serious attention, draws the student's attention to some particular examples, and saves us the bother of marking every mistake in the entire essay.

Then, most important, we ask students to identify and correct their mistakes. If you include the correction symbol from your handbook with each marginal check mark or set of parentheses, then students can go to the handbook for assistance in identifying the mistake and correcting it. We ask them to rewrite on the revision any sentence containing an error. If the error rate is high, a whole section may need to be rewritten. We check these rewrites as soon as possible, asking students to rewrite still again any errors that remain uncorrected. After two or three revisions have been marked and corrected in this way, we ask students to identify and analyze their own error patterns. They list and classify their errors, again using the handbook for assistance, and then write up briefly what they have learned. The result is that students begin to take responsibility for reducing error, syntactic garbles and awkwardness, and stylistic infelicities in their own writing—and they learn to use a handbook.

Finally, we do not hesitate to ask a student to revise still again an essay which fails to meet minimal requirements established by the readings and guide to writing in each chapter. This request sets standards more effectively than a low grade.

We do not grade individual essays. A letter grade is at best a cryptic indication of performance, and grades on individual essays can involve instructor and students in unproductive appeals and justifications. Furthermore, the risk of a low grade can discourage an inexperienced writer from taking creative chances. We recognize, however, that students need some indication of their progress before the obligatory letter grades at the end of the course, so we fill out for all students midterm progress reports with grades that indicate what they can expect at the end of the course if they continue at their present levels of performance. This form shows students where they need to focus their attention in the remainder of the course.

At the end of the course, we use a final course report form to write a response to the final essay submitted and an evaluative summary of the student's performance in the whole course. (Examples of these forms are included at the end of this section.) This summary, and the course grade, is based on a quick review of a student's revised essays—we ask that they be turned in along with the revision of the final essay. We also review our records of a student's attendance, reading journal entries, quizzes, workshop responses, and any other work we might have assigned. Then we give a final grade based on three criteria:

1. Whether all the assigned work has been completed in a timely fashion.
2. Whether the work has improved during the course.
3. Whether revised essays are fully realized rhetorically; that is, whether the student's revisions reveal substantial learning about the rhetorical and composing possibilities of the various genres assigned in the course.

Keep in mind that standards of success on the assignments in *Reading Critically, Writing Well* are comprehensively established by the readings in each chapter, the activities at the beginning of each chapter and following each reading, the guide to writing at the end of each chapter, and Reading a Draft Critically.

While we look at all of a student's revisions again at the end of the course, we might go still further and put in place a formal "portfolio" requirement. There is considerable interest now in portfolio assessment—in both high schools and colleges. Portfolios might serve two evaluation goals in a college writing program: (1) giving individual grades, and (2) establishing program-wide standards.

Here is a possible portfolio scheme that could work well in a writing course like the one we have described in this manual:

1. Students arrange a portfolio of their work to give you at the end of the course.

A number of types of collections are possible:
All revisions
All revisions and one of them revised still further

A small selection of the best work, to include at least one revision, one workshop response, one complete writing process (invention, drafts, revision), and some small number of reading journal entries. (You will no doubt think of other variations.)

2. Students write you a thoughtful letter commenting on their portfolio work. You would want to provide careful guidelines for the letter. The purpose of the letter would be to engage students in thoughtful reflection on the whole course.

3. You review the portfolio and respond in writing.

The portfolio, especially if it includes further revised work, might be the culminating assignment in your course, replacing an essay assignment. Students could confer with each other and with you about portfolio selections and about further revision of one essay.

You could exchange and discuss portfolios with other instructors in your program. With coordination from your program director, these exchanges could serve the purpose of greater uniformity in final course grades.

Course _____ Student _____

Section _____ Midterm Grade _____ Final Grade _____

Assignment	Topic	Invention	Drafts	Workshop Response	Self-Evaluation	Revision
Autobiography						
Observation						
Reflection						
Explanation						
Evaluation						
Proposal						

MIDTERM PROGRESS REPORT

Student_____   Instructor_____

Course_____   Date_____

Semester_____   Section_____

Quantity of Work. Has the student completed all the assignments?

Invention_____

Drafts & Revisions_____

Quizzes _____

Workshop Responses_____

Critical Reading Activities_____

Self-Evaluations_____

Attendance_____

Quality of Work. Has the student:

Used the guides to writing creatively?_____

Revised drafts substantially?_____

Given helpful workshop responses?_____

Written perceptive self-evaluations?_____

Edited and proofread carefully?_____

Completed thoughtfully the critical reading activities?_____

Participated in class discussions?_____

These areas need special attention in the remainder of the course:

Midterm Grade _____

FINAL COURSE REPORT

Student_____   Instructor_____

Course_____   Date_____

Semester_____   Section_____

Remarks on Final Essay

_____

_____

_____

_____

_____

_____

_____

Remarks on Whole Course

_____

_____

_____

_____

_____

_____

_____

Final Grade_____

We believe our introductory chapter to be approachable and not a sentence longer than it needs to be to introduce students to what we mean by "reading critically" and "writing well." Because this chapter introduces so many concepts and activities that will be essential to students' success in the course, we recommend spending a substantial amount of time in and outside of class working with the material presented in the chapter. Many of our instructors spend at least the first week of a ten-week term on Chapter 1, and refer students back to it whenever appropriate throughout the course.

The chapter offers six activities:

1. Reflecting on Your Own Past Reading Experience
2. Practice in Reading Critically
    2a. Reading for Meaning
    2b. Reading like a Writer
3. Reflecting on Your Own Writing Experience
4. Previewing the Writing Assignments
5. Previewing a Guide to Writing

Activities 1 and 3 through 6 ask students to either preview the text or write about their own reading and writing experiences. Activities 2a and 2b introduce students to the two critical reading activities that follow every reading in *Reading Critically, Writing Well*: Reading for Meaning and Reading like a Writer.

DEMONSTRATING READING CRITICALLY

Using an essay, "The Dirty Secret in Fraternity Drinking Songs," that takes a position on a controversial issue, we demonstrate annotating, first as it might appear when reading for meaning and then as it might appear when reading like a writer. For each of these ways of reading, we show how exploratory writing can develop ideas. It looks simple enough in our demonstration, but it's actually harder to do well than it first appears. Consequently, you will want to help students attend carefully as you talk them through the demonstration. Following our demonstration of annotation and exploratory writing for both reading for meaning and reading like a writer, we provide students with a second sample essay, "There Is No Safe Sex." Here, in Activities 2a and 2b, students will have a chance to practice on their own the strategies we've demonstrated for them.

READING FOR MEANING: DEMONSTRATION OF ANNOTATION. Here, we introduce students to annotating, a strategy central to the making of meaning from texts. While many students are accustomed to highlighting as they read, we find this method is rarely adequate. Instead, students need to be guided to read more closely and mark their texts more discriminately. The annotated sample essay following the introductory discussion of annotation demonstrates one student's annotations for meaning; students should note that the student is

31

responding here to the *content* of the selection, defining unfamiliar terms, keeping a running summary, and responding on a personal basis to the essay.

READING FOR MEANING: DEMONSTRATION OF EXPLORATORY WRITING. In this section, we show students how, using annotation as a starting point, a reader continues to clarify and extend his or her understanding of a text by writing about it. It's important for students to notice two things about our sample of exploratory writing: First, like the annotations on which it is based, it is a response to the content of the essay; second, in the same way that there are no "right" or "wrong" ways to annotate, there is no preexisting standard for exploratory writing. While the reader's exploratory paragraphs show the development of her understanding since she made the earlier annotations on the text, she has not attempted to come to any distinct conclusion about the essay. At this stage, the reader is still responding on a personal basis, asking questions, speculating about the authors' purpose, and registering surprise (and occasionally confusion).

READING LIKE A WRITER: DEMONSTRATION OF ANNOTATION. Students may need a considerable amount of guidance in making the crucial transition from reading for meaning to reading like writers. By walking them very carefully through this demonstration, you can help them understand the difference between these two ways of reading. The same sample essay appears following the introduction to this section, this time with the addition of annotations from a writer's point of view. Be sure students notice that, rather than responding to the content of the essay, the reader's annotations address the rhetorical strategies used by the authors and the basic features of this type of writing.

READING LIKE A WRITER: DEMONSTRATION OF EXPLORATORY WRITING. Students may already have noted that the student reader's second set of annotations not only identify the basic features of writing to take a position but also begin to comment on how well the writers' strategies achieve the goals of this type of writing. The exploratory writing demonstrates the student reader's developing analysis of each of the basic features of the essay, as well as her evaluative comments on how well the essay achieves its purpose. You can point out to students that even a very brief examination of each basic feature of the essay helps the reader to extend her understanding of the essay.

PRACTICING READING CRITICALLY

Once you have guided students carefully through the demonstrations of annotating and exploratory writing for both reading for meaning and reading like a writer, students should be ready to practice these strategies on their own. For this purpose, we provide a second position essay, "There Is No Safe Sex," by Robert C. Noble. Following the pattern of activities established in the previous demonstration, students will annotate and do exploratory writing based on their reading for meaning; then they will annotate and complete the exploratory writing task based on their reading like writers. Let students know that these exercises are prototypes of the exercises that will follow each reading selection throughout the text. You will want to have students at least start these exercises in class so that you can be readily available to provide guidance and encouragement. With patient coaching from you, students will persist

32

with these exercises, and they will be prepared for extraordinary engagement with the readings in Chapters 2–9.

READING FOR MEANING. Here, we ask students to annotate Noble's essay for meaning and to explore in writing their understanding of the essay based on their annotations. We expect students to be able to write at least a page in response to the essay; you might remind students that the more thorough their annotations, the more readily they'll be able to generate substantial exploratory writing. Even with the specific suggestions we offer to help students sustain their exploration, you may find that some students need to be steered away from mere summary. We find that students do tend to have fairly strong personal responses to Noble's argument; they may need to be reassured that these types of responses are appropriate at this stage of the reading process.

New to this edition is an optional Reading for Meaning activity, Extending Meaning through Conversation. Should you decide to use it later, you will want to have students practice it now. Follow up by discussing with students what meanings seemed to emerge during conversation, what consensus was reached, what differences remain, and how in general conversation complements making meaning on your own.

READING LIKE A WRITER. Making the transition from reading for meaning to reading like writers may prove to be a hurdle even for your best students. Because this transition is so critical, be prepared to provide extra guidance in the form of class discussions and individual coaching at this stage to help students get the most out of the specific guidance provided by the text.

Once again, we ask students to annotate Noble's essay, this time focusing not on the content but on the basic features of the essay and the strategies the writer uses to achieve his purpose. We name the three most basic features of this type of writing and provide specific guidelines for analyzing each feature as it appears in the essay. While this exercise by no means provides the basis for a truly comprehensive analysis of a position paper, it offers students an accessible introduction to the kinds of thinking involved in reading like a writer.

Defining the Issue. This task asks students to look for two things: the writer's definition of the issue, and the writer's indication of the issue's significance. Because Noble tends to present the issue in black-and-white, all-or-nothing terms, students should have little difficulty responding to this task.

Asserting a Position. Noble makes his position abundantly clear, avoiding qualifying or limiting it in any way. Some students will appreciate his rather surprising identification with the "prude" in his first paragraph. Noble's references to the "perky, fresh-faced teenage girl," the "young, attractive woman," and the "sweet and gentle" gay AIDS victims who represent the "opposing position" may strike some students as being somewhat condescending.

Arguing Directly for the Position. Once again, this is a two-part task, asking students both to identify and to evaluate the evidence Noble presents. Students should readily note that Noble draws on a range of types of evidence, including statistics, anecdotes, and quotations from authorities. Even students who disagree with Noble's position will be likely to accept the authority of his evidence.

We recommend that you collect students' written responses to these exercises, reading them quickly and making occasional comments. Although you will want to record some form of credit for students as they complete the exercises, there is no need to evaluate closely or grade their responses. Collecting student responses to these exercises in Chapter 1 and checking them quickly sets a precedent near the beginning of the course, letting students know that you take their work seriously.

PREVIEWING WRITING WELL

Most of the material in this section serves as a preview for students of the guides to writing in each of the upcoming assignment chapters. Besides inviting students to scrutinize their own experience as writers, this section encourages students to begin to familiarize themselves with the textbook.

Part 6   TEACHING THE ASSIGNMENT CHAPTERS (2–9)

This section provides suggestions for teaching Chapters 2–9, the text chapters with readings and the major writing assignments. Each of these chapters opens with a guide to reading and closes with a guide to writing.

USING THE CHAPTER INTRODUCTIONS AND GUIDES TO READING

Each assignment-chapter introduction includes the following features:

- description of the type of writing, including comparisons or contrasts with related types
- the writing assignment
- academic and professional writing situations
- a collaborative activity that actively engages students with the rhetorical situation of the essay they will write
- a guide to reading the type of writing, which offers a reading selection and two critical reading activities: Reading for Meaning and Reading like a Writer

These activities provide students with a full introduction to the genre they will be reading and writing. Most important, the reading selection and critical reading activities together illustrate for students the work they will do with each reading selection in the chapter. There is one small but significant difference, however: here the Reading like a Writer activity surveys all of the major features of the genre, while the same activity following each chapter reading singles out only one salient genre feature of that reading.

ILLUSTRATIVE ACADEMIC AND PROFESSIONAL WRITING SITUATIONS. Each chapter opens with typical writing assignments from college courses across the disciplines and from professional life. We made up very few of the academic assignments: nearly all came from current academic texts or instructor's manuals. We did revise several of them to foreground aspects of the rhetorical situation, making explicit what the student is expected to know and do. Unfortunately, not all academics consistently make clear to students what is required in essay-exam questions or paper topics.

There is much you can do to involve students in analyzing these academic assignments. Here are two examples:

You can analyze one for them, emphasizing all of its thinking/writing demands and then they can analyze another (either in small groups or as a class)

You can ask each student to find another assignment in a textbook in another course or to construct a likely one based on information in the textbook

COLLABORATIVE ACTIVITY. Practicing [name of the genre]: A Collaborative Activity engages students immediately in an interactive, oral rehearsal of the situation they will encounter when they write the chapter's essay assignment.

You'll notice that each collaborative activity divides distinctly into two parts: first, the rehearsal of the writing situation, and second, a reflection on what happened and what students learned. You may have to help students make this shift. The whole activity need not take more than twenty minutes or so. Because students *experience* the writing situation early in the chapter, we have found they are much more interested in the readings and questions. It starts them into a chapter in a surprisingly productive way. Don't skip this activity!

THE CRITICAL READING ACTIVITIES. As we recommend in Part 3 of this manual, you can easily devote two one-hour class meetings to these exercises. Don't rush these. First-year students have very little experience with close textual analysis, and what they have to learn about each of our genres will be a revelation to them.

While the activities presented in Reading for Meaning are quite flexible, those suggested in Reading like a Writer go after specific textual information. You might do one or two parts together in class when you assign Reading like a Writer, just to get everyone started. Or you could give students time in groups of two or three to help each other make notes toward an answer they will later write up individually.

Students will need encouragement. They may not go deep enough at first in their rhetorical analysis, but if you select and read aloud two or three strong answers to certain parts of Reading like a Writer, they will get the idea.

ASSISTING STUDENTS IN USING EACH CHAPTER'S GUIDE TO WRITING

Every assignment chapter concludes with a guide to writing that leads students through a systematic composing process. Each guide is divided into four parts: Invention, Drafting, Reading a Draft Critically, and Revising. Here are some suggestions for integrating instruction on the writing process into a course on critical reading.

ENCOURAGING INVENTION. Many of your students may never have met the term *invention* before, and they may not immediately see the benefits of prewriting. To the inexperienced writer, writing prior to drafting can look like needless busywork. Consequently, students may be tempted to skip this stage of the composing process; if you stress the need to complete it, they may even be tempted to do the invention procedures *after* they have drafted their essays. While doing invention activities after drafting and before revising can be of use, it obviously defeats the objective of invention.

Each guide includes a sequence of invention activities designed specifically to help students ask themselves questions and generate ideas and information useful for their essays. Since so few students have ever participated in systematic invention, we are especially careful to introduce them to the invention activities. We ask the students to open their books to the invention section and then briefly explain the purpose of each activity. By having students turn the pages and skim the invention exercises while you preview them orally for the students, you will be able to reduce their apprehension about these unfamiliar activities and greatly increase the probability that they will successfully complete the invention section before beginning their draft.

This is also the time to remind students of the time-frame for invention: suggest that they begin work right away, but spread the work out over several sessions; tell them what day the invention will be due, and that you will be checking it on that day to ensure that their invention base is adequate to begin planning and drafting.

You could do the first part of the invention, Finding a Subject, in class as whole-class brainstorming or in small groups, beginning with suggestions in the book (including those in Ideas for Your Own Writing following each reading) and then move to choosing a subject and exploring it. Students will progress through the invention sequence at different rates, but you can help them stay on track by requiring that they reach a certain point by a certain class meeting. If you ask them to bring their invention-in-progress to every class meeting, you can ask them to share certain sections with their peers in pairs or small groups, while you circulate and examine each student's work-to-date.

Research is comfortably included in our broad definition of invention—everything that happens before and during writing to produce ideas and evaluate them. Except for the writing assignments in Chapters 2 and 4, all the other writing assignments can include formal research. Where research is appropriate, the guide to writing invites it. You can decide how much research students should do or leave it to them to decide. We provide additional guidance in Appendix 2.

MAKING DRAFTING PRODUCTIVE. Invention may produce a number of complete paragraphs, several lists, freewriting, an interview, or notes on library research—a plethora of material that must be organized before the student can write a draft. This much material poses for many students a new problem: what to do with all of it

36

The guide to writing in each chapter urges students to consider several alternative plans before settling on one. Often students are unaware of alternatives; we find it helpful to illustrate several, sometimes from the reading selections and sometimes from topics suggested by students.

Each planning section reminds students, as they go on to draft, that what they have developed is only a plan. In other words, it is expendable. The final test for the paper is not whether it follows the outline, but whether it works. Like many other parts of the guide to writing, this may demand from inexperienced writers a new approach, a new order of priorities.

Up to the drafting stage, the student has been dealing with pieces or facets; now for the first time the student will attempt to see the material as a whole. We suggest that students write their first rough drafts in a single sitting lasting about two to three hours. The drafting session resembles extended freewriting: it lasts longer, it allows the student to pause much more, and of course the writer is trying for a more ordered product; but as in freewriting, the writer should work as fast as possible and not worry too much about grammatical details or spelling.

The objective of this approach is to keep the student focused on the larger shape of the essay, not on distracting details. Research shows that most competent writers occasionally write garbled sentences in their first drafts and that writers who struggle to perfect each sentence as it is written are inefficient. Of course, there are exceptions, and students should remember that the guide to writing is just that—a guide, not a set of inflexible orders.

GIVING AND GETTING CRITICAL COMMENTS. New to this edition is a comprehensive guide to advising another writer about how to improve a draft. It is titled Reading a Draft Critically, and it poses a truly valuable critical reading task for students, especially those who have experience only with simplified all-purpose peer-critique guidelines, often in checklist form.

The goal is to get students to read a draft closely in light of what they have learned about the genre and to write a couple of pages that describe the text, evaluating it using criteria appropriate to the genre, and advise on possible revisions. Framing the student's work in this chapter, the analysis is organized around the genre features introduced at the very beginning. See Organizing Workshops in Part 4 of this manual for ways to use Reading a Draft Critically.

We would stress here that without coaching and modeling, students will not be able to realize the benefits of giving and getting a critical reading with our guidelines. Therefore we recommend that you talk them through at least one step of the analysis the first time you assign a critical reading. When they complete their first critical reading of each others' drafts, you can then select some expansive, helpful sections of analysis to share with them as examples of what you expect from all of them.

PLANNING TO REVISE. Research has shown that successful revising depends on what the writer knows about the type of discourse. The more examples novice writers have seen, the larger the repertoire of strategies they can draw upon to achieve their particular purpose for their readers. When revising, writers must also keep their focus on global issues rather than sentence-level errors and infelicities. In teaching students to revise, peer critique and student-teacher conferences are invaluable.

For information on class activities to support students' revising, see Organizing Workshops and Holding Tutorial Conferences in Part 4 of this manual.

REFLECTING ON THE LEARNING PROCESS. Each guide to writing concludes with an activity that asks students to reflect on what they have learned about reading and writing in a particular genre. It is titled Reflecting on What You Have Learned. You may need to encourage students to write full, demanding, detailed reflections on their reading and writing experiences. After you assign this activity as homework, you might give them five minutes of class time, the day the assignment is due, to develop and expand on their reflections. Some additional coaching can also be very useful. Sometimes you need to help students see that every aspect of the process, from reading through invention, drafting, and revising, can be revealing. If students reflect in thoughtful detail on their own reading and writing processes, they can learn much about how they read and write. Students' responses to this activity can also help guide your own comments on their papers. The student who has written a miserable paper, and is miserable about it, might get very different treatment from one who has done poorly but is uncritical. We believe that there is pedagogical value in responding directly to the student's reflections so that the teacher's comments are not self-contained, but are part of a dialogue about the paper.

Chapter 2 AUTOBIOGRAPHY

Students should find the readings in this chapter accessible and engaging, but the point emphasized in the introduction to the chapter is that autobiography is more than just entertaining storytelling: it is an attempt to find meaning in experience. The selections in this chapter and the questions that follow them aim to show students that autobiography requires writers not merely to present people, places, and events, but also to interpret these subjects—to reveal their causes and implications and draw conclusions about them.

In learning about autobiographical writing, students are engaged in a fundamental process of discourse—making meaning from experience. In autobiography, the experience and its significance may be personal to the writer, but readers can recognize, believe, and understand this significance by virtue of common human ties. In drawing conclusions from their experience and supporting these conclusions with illustrative examples, students will be engaged in the kinds of composing they will encounter repeatedly in *Reading Critically, Writing Well*. In Chapter 3, for instance, students will see writers sharing their observations of life around them and drawing or implying conclusions about these observations. Chapters 2 and 3, therefore, represent a movement from writing that focuses on the self and relies on memory to writing that focuses on the world and relies on fresh observations and on-the-spot notes.

WRITING ASSIGNMENT: Autobiography

Here is the writing assignment that appears near the beginning of Chapter 2:

Write an autobiographical essay about a significant event, phase, or person in your life. Choose a topic with your readers in mind, one that you feel comfortable disclosing to others and that could lead them to reflect on their own lives.

Present your experience dramatically and vividly so readers can imagine what it was like for you. Through your choice of words and details, convey the meaning and importance—what we call the *autobiographical significance*—of this event, phase, or person in your life.

Possible topic ideas (Considering Ideas for Your Own Writing) follow each reading. A general list of topics is also included as part of the Invention section in the Guide to Autobiographical Writing.

Autobiographical Writing Situations

The three brief descriptions of writing situations for remembered events, phases, and people show students a range of possible occasions for this sort of writing. The three examples illustrate the role of autobiographical writing in both academic and nonacademic settings and also suggest a range of different purposes for autobiographical writing. You might want to use the situations in a discussion of possible topics by pointing out how the writers have chosen personally significant topics, how they have enough emotional distance from these topics to be able to discuss their significance, and how they achieve the self-disclosure and depth of insight for which students writing this assignment should aim.

Practicing Autobiography: A Collaborative Activity

If you are beginning the course with this chapter, this group activity provides a particularly good starting point. It has students tell each other stories—something everyone enjoys—and it gives students a chance to get to know one another and to begin forming good working relationships. But wherever this chapter falls in your course, this activity is a very effective way of introducing the assignment. It will increase students' interest in the chapter and their confidence that they will be able to write effective essays about remembered events, phases, or people. This activity guides students through a rehearsal for the essays they will later write and prepares them to think seriously about autobiography. Because students *experience* the writing situation early in the chapter, we have found that they are much more interested in the readings and activities. It starts them into a chapter in a surprisingly productive way, and is well worth the time it takes.

This activity divides distinctly into two parts: first, the rehearsal of the writing situation and, second, a reflection on what happened and what students learned. You may have to help students make that shift. The whole activity need not take more than twenty minutes or so.

In this chapter, the activity gives students direct, hands-on practice with the issues of purpose and audience they will encounter throughout their reading and writing for this assignment. Specifically, it will ask them to experiment with making topic choices, with telling a vivid story and presenting scenes and people, and with disclosing the autobiographical significance of their topics. As they reflect (as a group, but perhaps also individually) on their experience of telling their own stories and listening to those of others, students will begin to anticipate both the challenges and the rewards facing them as both readers and writers of autobiography.

A GUIDE TO READING AUTOBIOGRAPHY

This section introduces students to the critical reading and writing strategies they will use throughout the chapter and throughout the course: reading for meaning and reading like a writer. It is worth spending quite a bit of time on this section, as many of the issues it raises will be new to most students. The section begins with a brief illustration of annotation, the activity which enables the reading strategies students will be using. The section then walks students through a critical reading of a complete sample essay. For class activities to be used in conjunction with this section, see Part 5 of this instructor's manual.

The sample essay provided for these exercises, a piece by Audre Lorde, clearly demonstrates the basic strategies used by autobiographical writers: telling the story, presenting scenes and people, and creating an autobiographical impression. The Reading like a Writer section following the essay will break these down into more specific strategies.

Reading for Meaning

The first set of questions and suggestions following the sample essay are designed to help students focus closely on the text, speculating about the significance of the event and clarifying their understanding of Audre Lorde's essay. A similar section follows each of the readings in the chapter. As students use these suggestions to make their own meaning, you can expect that students will find somewhat different meanings in the essay because their own experience and interests lead them to focus on different parts of it.

Reading like a Writer

This section helps students shift their focus from what happens in the story to how the writer tells the story—from reading exclusively as readers to reading as prospective writers. Students are introduced to four major strategies of autobiographical writing—*telling the story, describing the scene, describing a person,* and *conveying the autobiographical significance.* Through a series of brief critical reading and writing tasks, students focus on how Lorde uses each of these strategies. *Telling the story* is presented specifically in terms of shaping the story and pacing the story; sections on use of detail and point of view contribute to *describing the scene.* Strategies for *describing a person* include physical description, revealing personality and motive, and suggesting relationships, while *conveying the autobiographical significance* is discussed in terms of presenting the authorial persona and disclosing the autobiographical significance.

While the Reading like a Writer section following this sample essay presents a full range of strategies for autobiographical writing, corresponding sections following each of the subsequent readings in the chapter will focus more narrowly on one or two strategies particularly appropriate to the analysis of each essay.

Telling the Story: Shaping and Pacing. Students may note that Lorde's narrative does not reach the specific afternoon of the event until paragraph 13—more than halfway through the essay—and that the story does not reach its climax until paragraph 18, just two paragraphs before the end. Students should also note that the simple chronological narrative leading up to the event is interrupted in several places by Lorde's reflections—from both her adolescent and her later adult perspectives—on American racism and her parents' response to it. The "action" of the story is also briefly slowed by the richly detailed list of foods in paragraph 4. When you discuss students' responses to this task, you might encourage them to speculate about how Lorde's essay would have been different if her narrative had led quickly and directly to the central event, leaving the more reflective material until after the climax of the action.

This task should help students recognize the function of Lorde's deliberate interruptions of her narrative in building tension or suspense. You may find that while some students find these interruptions contribute to the sense of mounting tension, other students may find these passages—particularly a lengthy reflective passage such as paragraph 7—distracting.

Describing the Scene: Detail and Point of View. This task asks students to look closely at the descriptive passages of Lorde's essay. They may be surprised by the distribution of details in Lorde's descriptions: she focuses very little on the sights and sounds of Washington, D.C., which might have been expected to loom larger in a young visitor's memory. Instead, she uses the most detail in her descriptions of the two food-related scenes, "bracketing" the central event with contrasting descriptions of atmosphere, from the warmth and comfort of the train scene to the atmosphere in the ice cream parlor which shifts from pleasantly cool to icy and hostile.

Students might also note that Lorde uses a variety of points of view—fixed and moving, close up and distant. In the train, the scene is observed close up; some students may suggest that, while the point of view is essentially fixed, the scene also suggests movement, a sense of excitement. This excitement is dimmed and the point of view becomes more distant on the streets of Washington, D.C.—a distance imposed by the writer's vision problem but also by her increasing discomfort and sense of alienation. Finally, her excitement is extinguished altogether in the ice cream parlor, and the point of view is fixed almost to paralysis until indignation takes over.

Describing People: Providing Physical Description, Revealing Personality, and Suggesting Relationships. This activity has several functions. By helping students focus on the very specific *purpose* of Lorde's physical description, this task should help students anticipate a common pitfall for inexperienced writers of autobiography: the tendency to include too much physical description, creating a police-blotter effect without contributing to the story.

In addition, this task should help students see that most autobiographical writers rely on a combination of strategies to reveal the personalities of characters in their stories, both telling the reader directly about people and "showing" the reader the people through their own words and actions. Students should also consider Lorde's purpose in this essay, and how the essay might have been different if her purpose had been to create a fully developed portrait of either or both of her parents.

As Lorde's parents play a central role in her first encounters with racism, students should note that Lorde's attitude toward her parents is neither wholly positive nor wholly negative; instead, her portrayal reflects an ambivalence appropriate to the complexity of her family relationships and the situation they are in. This concept of ambivalence may help students avoid the tendency in their own writing to either condemn or idealize their subjects.

Conveying the Autobiographical Significance. This task helps students compare the writer's past perspective at the time of the event with her later perspective at the time of writing. Students may note that, while both the young and the later Lorde are critical not only

41

of racism but of her parents' attitude toward it, the somewhat naive indignation of the earlier perspective becomes a deeper, more informed bitterness in the writer's later perspective.

Students should have little trouble discerning that the significance of this event is that the trip to Washington, D.C., serves not as a "reward" for Lorde but as an abrupt introduction to the realities of racism. Students might refer to their responses to the previous task to examine how this significance has deepened as the writer has matured. Some students may note Lorde's use of her vision problem as a kind of metaphor for the pain of having one's eyes rudely opened.

RESOURCES FOR TEACHING THE READINGS

The reading selections in this chapter, beginning with the sample essay described above, represent the major types of autobiographical subjects: remembered incidents, phases, people, and places. Like Audre Lorde, Annie Dillard and Russell Baker focus on single incidents in their child- or young adulthoods. The next selection, by Itabari Njeri, treats an extended and significant phase of the author's life. The fourth selection, Laurie Abraham's portrait of her father after her parents' divorce, focuses on a person. The final selection is by a student, Brad Benioff, recounting how he and his water polo coach won each other's respect.

These selections cover a variety of subjects and reveal a range of strategies and approaches to these subjects. Students can learn from these diverse essays that autobiographical writing addresses many topics—some humorous, some painful—tells about them in an engaging way, describes them vividly so that readers can imagine them, and explains their significance in the writers' lives. Students can also see that autobiographical writing contains self-disclosure, and that readers are attracted by writers' willingness to share personal information.

The material that follows introduces each reading selection and offers some suggestions for engaging students with the sections on reading for meaning and reading like a writer and the ideas for writing following each reading.

Annie Dillard, **A Chase**

This selection is an example of the narration of a single incident from the autobiographer's childhood. Although the incident is brief and seemingly mundane, Dillard clearly considers it important; this selection should help students see how real autobiographical significance can be located in the most ordinary of events.

Reading for Meaning

This section encourages students to read and reread the essay closely, beginning with some speculations about what Dillard wants her readers to undertand. Starting with the author's reasons for writing about a specific incident ensures that as students explore meaning, they will stay closer to the text. Speculating about purpose requires thinking about the fundamental "why" of a text. Then students can go on to explore any meanings that interest them. For the first reading in each chapter, we suggest that you lead your class through this activity, helping students understand how the activity works and reminding them of the important roles of rereading and annotating in making meaning from a text before inviting them to write on their own in response to the activity. Also, especially after this first reading selection in the chapter, you might want to collect students' writing in response to this activity, going over it quickly to see how thoroughly students are exploring the meaning of the text. You could also read a few of the more interesting responses aloud in class.

Extending Meaning through Conversation. This section also introduces a new feature in the fourth edition of *Reading Critically, Writing Well*: a group activity called Extending Meaning through Conversation in which students discuss, with one or two other students, their possibly differing impressions of the meaning of Dillard's story. Through corresponding activities following each reading selection, as well as the more general collaborative activities that open each assignment chapter, students should become increasingly conscious of important issues of purpose and audience. If you are beginning your course with this chapter, you might set aside some class time following this activity to discuss how it went and what meanings seemed to emerge in conversation.

Reading like a Writer: Telling a Story Dramatically

This section highlights word choice, and particularly the choice of verbs—an element often overlooked by inexperienced readers but very useful to the writer of autobiography. In the crucial "chase" scene, students are asked to focus on the verbs Dillard chooses.

Students should note that Dillard chooses verbs that are interesting and appropriately dramatic—*choking, pounding, fling, aim, dive*—and should note the role these "action verbs" play in heightening the drama of the narrative. Astute students may also notice that the variety of Dillard's sentence length and structure serves not only to vary the rhythm of her writing, but also to enhance the drama: the sense of tension generated in the short, choppy sentences of paragraph 11 is released in the long, complex sentences of paragraphs 12, 13, and 14, for instance.

Considering Ideas for Your Own Writing

This section helps students begin to consider possible topics for their own autobiographical essays, and to anticipate some of the challenges specific to particular types of topics. A corresponding section follows each reading selection in the chapter. If students write out their ideas for writing, then they can try them out in class and you can begin to help them think through the issues involved in choosing an autobiographical topic.

Russell Baker, **Smooth and Easy**

Baker tells a fast-paced amusing narrative about failure and success. In our introduction to this selection, we ask students to notice how Baker uses humor in writing about an experience that probably didn't seem funny at the time. Baker has so much emotional and temporal distance from this event that he can emphasize the humorous aspects of what must have been an ordeal for him. The autobiographical significance is located in the paradox that he had to lose control of himself before he could gain control of the aircraft; he had to accept failure in order to succeed. In this selection, students see a writer telling a funny, revealing story about himself. They see that autobiographical writing need not be solemn or earnest to be successful.

Reading for Meaning

We invite students to reread Baker's essay as more than merely an amusing story by focusing on complex underlying issues and attitudes. Again, though, here they choose what to write about, what meanings to explore. If one of our suggestions for making meaning seems especially important to you, however, you could lead a class discussion about it or ask students to discuss it in small groups.

Extending Meaning through Conversation. Students are also invited to develop their understanding of Baker's story by discussing it with one or two classmates. Students may find that their reactions to this essay vary broadly; some will see it as a charming and lighthearted "coming of age" story, while others may perceive disturbing undertones in the attitudes Baker's essay represents toward war, women, and drinking. You could follow up briefly on this activity by talking in class about how these differences among the meanings made by different readers are natural and even useful.

Contextualizing (A Further Strategy for Reading for Meaning). Before students attempt this exercise, have them see the section on contextualizing in Appendix 1, A Catalog of Critical Reading Strategies. There students will find a demonstration of this strategy in use. Periodically throughout assignment Chapters 2–9, we refer students to this catalog. Following selected readings in each chapter, students are asked to complete a critical reading task in addition to Reading for Meaning and Reading like a Writer, thus ensuring that they gain extensive practice with a broad range of strategies.

In this case, we introduce students to the important strategy of contextualizing. This task guides students through a reading of Baker's essay in its social and historical context. Students are asked to identify the values and attitudes underlying the text, and to compare and contrast these with their own sensibilities. This particular strategy is especially appropriate to the reading of Baker's essay. As students learn in the Reading like a Writer section following the piece, the suspense of the narrative depends in part on the extent to which the reader is able to empathize with the writer. Students whose immediate reaction to Baker's story was strongly negative will find themselves more likely to empathize with Baker when they understand that he is writing out of a particular social and historical situation.

Reading like a Writer: Describing People

This task serves two functions. It should help students to see that physical description need not be lengthy to be effective, and that, in fact, the carefully chosen small detail, such as Total Loss Smith's "movie killer" lips, may be more dramatically revealing of character than the most thorough physical portrait. In addition, this exercise should help students begin to recognize the importance of dialogue in presenting people.

Compare. This feature, new to the fourth edition of *Reading Critically, Writing Well*, appears after one or two reading selections in each chapter. By encouraging students to complete this activity, you can help them not only to make basic connections between and among the readings, identifying both similarities and differences, but also to become increasingly aware of the full range of strategies available to writers in each genre. In this case, students should note that both Baker and Dillard are quite selective in their choice of details in describing people. As novice writers of autobiography may tend to over-describe the people in their stories, presenting large chunks of description which interrupt the narrative of their essays, this is an important activity.

Considering Ideas for Your Own Writing

This section invites students to consider writing about an event similar to the one in the selection they have just read. The questions highlight the issue of past versus present perspective, asking students to consider whether they have enough emotional distance from the events about which they may write.

Itabari Njeri, **Land of the Doo-Wops**

Unlike the previous reading selections in this chapter which focus on specific incidents or events, Njeri's piece treats an entire phase of her life during which she was led to reevaluate her abilities and aspirations, and to make a major change in her career and life goals. In the introduction to this selection, students are asked to consider not only what they learn about Njeri from reading her story, but also what Njeri might have learned about herself in writing it—an important reminder of the effects of autobiographical writing not only on the reader but on the writer.

Reading for Meaning

Students are invited to focus on the autobiographical significance of this phase in Njeri's life, examining the differences between Njeri's past and present perspectives as well as the differences between her musical training and the "real world" of music as a business.

Extending Meaning through Conversation. Once again, we invite students to explore their understanding of the selection by discussing it with one or two other students. Because Njeri's essay at least implicitly points to provocative issues of race and gender, you may find that students will bring a wide range of meanings to their discussion; in order to ensure that their conversations remain focused on the text itself, you might find it useful to circulate among pairs or groups.

Reading like a Writer: Presenting a Phase through Anecdotes

Students will need to recognize the differences between writing about an event and writing about a longer phase. This section should help them focus on the decisions Njeri makes regarding precisely which incidents to select for her narrative. Students' attention is also drawn to the transitions Njeri uses between incidents.

Considering Ideas for Your Own Writing

This section asks students to consider writing about phases in their own lives during which they were involved in new or challenging activities. Students are invited to reflect on the people and incidents involved in these phases of their lives.

Laurie Abraham, **Divorced Father**

While the writers of the previous selections focus on specific events or phases, Abraham's piece illustrates a third option for writers of autobiography: a significant person in the writer's life, in this case, her father.

45

Reading for Meaning

Once again, this section offers students suggestions for enriching their understanding of the meaning of Abraham's story, beginning with general guidelines for reflection on the selection, and concluding with specific ideas for developing an understanding of Abraham's relationship with her father. Although we do not invite students here to relate the essay to their personal experiences, you may find that many students have strong feelings about parent-child relationships and about divorce. If students are using their personal experience to make meaning from the text, you might invite them to do so orally in class, being sure that they do not move entriely away from the text itself. You can help them make explicit connections between their experience and the text.

Extending Meaning through Conversation. Students are also invited to discuss the meanings they have constructed on their own with one or two of their classmates. Once again, because students may be bringing their own experience to bear heavily on their undertandings of this selection, you might want to help them stay on track by moving from group to group.

Reading like a Writer: Describing a Person through Anecdotes and Recurring Activities

This section alerts students to the fact that autobiographical writers often choose both one-time and recurring incidents to create revealing portraits of people they have known over a long period of time. Students should note how the balance of specific anecdotes and recurring events helps Abraham convey not only a portrait of her father, but also a sense of the autobiographical significance of their relationship.

Considering Ideas for Your Own Writing

This section reminds students that, especially in writing about people they have known over long periods of time, they will need to consider carefully their selection of both anecdotes and recurring activities in presenting their subjects.

Brad Benioff, **Rick**

Benioff shows how his relationship with Rick developed over a short period of time, and what he learned about himself as a result of it. Like the preceding selection by Laurie Abraham, his essay is therefore about a phase in his life, as well as about a person.

Reading for Meaning

Here we remind students that autobiographical essays about remembered people are primarily essays about *relationships*. Students are invited to focus on what we learn not only about the subject of the essay but about the writer himself in this selection.

Extending Meaning through Conversation. Their impressions of the autobiographical significance of Benioff's story should provide interesting material for discussion with other students in this activity. While some students will find Benioff's essay a successful example of writing in this genre, others may find it somewhat predictable and heavy-handed.

Reading like a Writer: Describing a Person through Visual Details and Dialogue

This section asks students to focus specifically on the strategies writers use in presenting people: through physical description and through actions and words. If you have time to preview this activity, you might refer students back to the strategies for presenting people discussed in the Reading like a Writer section following the sample essay by Audre Lorde, and also to the corresponding section following Russell Baker's piece.

Writing up the results of their analysis, students should note that Benioff uses physical description fairly sparingly, concentrating it primarily at his own first sight of his subject in paragraph 6. (Students may differ over whether Benioff's repetitive sentence structure in this paragraph is deliberate or merely clumsy.) He later echoes specific details of his coach's appearance, using the coach's trademark dark glasses, which he removes only at the end of the essay, to signify the change in his relationship to his subject. Students will have no problem seeing that Benioff moves from using details that create a negative, almost sinister impression in his initial description to using details in the conclusion (the smile, the handshake) to create a positive, friendly impression. More sophisticated readers may find the abrupt about-face in the coach's attitude at once predictable and unconvincing. Students should also note Benioff's use of dialogue (or, before the coach's change in attitude, monologue) and how this contributes to his characterization of his subject.

Compare. This activity helps students focus on two important strategies writers of autobiography use in presenting people: visual description and dialogue. Comparing Benioff's essay with the previous selection by Laurie Abraham should help students gain a sense of the options open to them as they plan their own autobiographical essays.

Reading like a Writer: A Follow-up Activity

Once students have completed the Reading like a Writer activities in each chapter, they will have produced a substantial amount of writing about what they have learned about each genre. You might encourage them at this point to review all the writing they have done, and to select one piece to revise and expand through further analysis. They would turn this in with their essay packages, or with their end-of-course portfolios.

Considering Ideas for Your Own Writing

Many students have had experiences similar to Benioff's, in which a particular adult has won their respect, perhaps after some initial conflict. The strength of Benioff's essay lies in the suspense generated by the tension between him and Rick. If your students have not had such difficulties with the person they want to write about, they will need to find something else in the relationship that they did not expect, or that made it memorable. Remind students that even though this kind of writing focuses on another person, it is still autobiographical and should therefore reveal something about the writer as well as the subject. It is best not to let students write about people they have met only recently, or with whom they are still in disagreement. Students can seldom achieve the necessary emotional distance from such subjects to recognize their autobiographical significance.

THINKING ABOUT WHAT MAKES AUTOBIOGRAPHY EFFECTIVE

This section, new in the fourth edition of *Reading Critically, Writing Well*, helps students focus on important strategies of autobiographical writing by rereading one selection from the chapter, either alone or with a small group, and by writing briefly about how the writer in question fulfills the basic features of successful autobiographical writing. This important new activity enables students to review and consolidate what they have learned about the genre of autobiography before they attempt to write in this genre themselves.

A GUIDE TO AUTOBIOGRAPHICAL WRITING

The guide leads students through a composing process that follows these stages:

Invention
    Finding an Autobiographical Topic
    Probing Your Topic
        Recalling First Impressions
        Exploring Your Present Perspective
        Discovering Autobiographical Significance
            Learning More about Your Readers: A Collaborative Activity
        Detailing the Scene
        Reconstructing Dialogue
        Restating Autobiographical Significance

Drafting
        Setting Goals
        Planning Your Draft
        Beginning
        Choosing Relevant Details
Reading a Draft Critically
        Reading for a First Impression
        Reading to Analyze
            Telling the Story
            Describing the Scene
            Describing People
            Conveying the Autobiographical Significance
Revising
        Revising to Tell the Story
        Describing the Scene
        Describing a Person
        Conveying the Autobiographical Significance
    Reflecting on What You Have Learned about Writing Autobiography

In order to represent an incident or person vividly, students will need to generate many concrete details. You may need to encourage students to complete this invention activity fully and thoughtfully, pointing out that, although they are unlikely to use all of the details they generate during the invention sequence in their actual essays, it will be to their benefit to have a rich wealth of details from which to choose as they draft their own essays.

Whether they are writing about an event, phase, or person, many students tend to opt for the simplest structure—a chronological sequence—without stopping to consider alternatives. A chronological structure is quite acceptable (and most of the selections in this chapter follow this order) but students should realize that they need not begin their stories at the beginning and follow them all the way through to the end. A simple variation, for instance, is to begin the essay by engaging readers with some dialogue or action, or with a patch of vivid description, before filling in the context. And even if they do choose to follow a strict chronological sequence, students should remember that they can control the pace of the narrative, slowing down to present the important parts in detail and summarizing the less important parts. In their first drafts, students often spend too much time on less significant, preliminary incidents, and not enough time on the most important moments.

SPECIAL PROBLEMS OF THIS WRITING ASSIGNMENT. We have noticed that students facing this assignment for the first time may have problems developing a well-paced, dramatic narrative and achieving the self-disclosure necessary to reveal the significance of the event, person, or phase.

In their first drafts of autobiographical essays, student writers tend to draw on what they know of storytelling conventions. Typically, this involves beginning with a general introduction, setting the scene or declaring the significance of the subject in broad terms. The succession of events is then played out in the body of the paper without much alteration in pace to include descriptive details, the writer's feelings at the time, and reflections with hindsight. A writer often forgets to show rather than to tell, to bring an experience alive with sensory detail rather than merely to record the sequence of events.

Many writers have initial difficulties managing the pace of a narrative, not realizing that the climax of an event can easily be undercut if pages of incidental events have misdirected readers' expectations. We find it useful to spend some time explaining ways to adjust the flow of time and control suspense. The readings offer good examples of how writers can do this.

For many writers, the companion to the convention of beginning a story with a general introduction is the convention of ending it with a moral. Unused to probing the personal significance of events, people, or phases they write about, inexperienced writers tend to translate this convention into a moralistic conclusion. Again we use the readings to point out ways in which reflection on the significance of an event, a person, or a phase can be woven into the narrative.

Self-disclosure does not come naturally to many students, and we find they need a good deal of encouragement and reassurance, particularly if the topic is a sensitive one. Often they go no further than to say that an event was very frightening or great fun, or that a person was wonderful or terrible. We encourage them to go deeper, to look at reasons for their actions and reactions. We find that few students explore the humorous or absurd possibilities of their topics and the personal insights that these can provide.

PROMISING AND UNPROMISING TOPICS. The writing assignment in this chapter gives students a wide choice of topics. This choice, as students soon discover, presents problems as well as opportunities. The chief problem comes when students choose subjects from which they do not have enough emotional distance.

When asked to choose a significant event, person, or phase, students frequently want to write about the first topic that comes to mind, often a recent experience or a traumatic one. An event that happened very recently may only appear to be important because it is on the writer's mind. While writing about such an event will help the writer understand it, the event may turn out not to have much meaning after all.

Traumatic events may also be problematic as topics, not because they lack significance but because they are too meaningful. Writing about a traumatic event may involve more self-disclosure than seems appropriate given the writing situation. On the other hand, the student may decide that writing about a traumatic event such as the death of a loved one can be therapeutic.

Looking back over the events and phases of their lives, as well as people they have known, for possible topics, writers understandably tend to think big. Major emotional landmarks readily suggest themselves: graduation, making the team, having an accident, failing the big test.

Some of these peak experiences represent initiations or rites of passage. They are prominent in the minds of many students and can make excellent autobiographical topics. A problem with these topics, however, is that many of them are common experiences, familiar to almost everyone. The challenge in writing about such a subject is to avoid the cliché, to find something unusual in the experience, or to give readers a new perspective on it. We encourage students to think twice before writing about their first experience on the ski slopes, the prom that was not all it promised to be, the event that would have embarrassed anyone. Experiences that exactly match expectations contain nothing surprising for readers, no new insights about themselves or discoveries about human nature. Students would do better to look beyond the obvious and consider some of the subtler experiences they may have had—moments of intense awareness, realizations, important changes that took place within themselves.

Chapter 3 OBSERVATION

The selections in this chapter are closely related to those in the preceding and following chapters. The discussion of Chapter 5 in this manual will cover some differences between observational, reflective, and explanatory writing. Here we would like to point out a few of the key differences between observational and autobiographical writing.

Whereas autobiographical writing attempts to find personal meaning in experience, and to transmit this meaning to readers through vivid storytelling, observational writing aims to present what writers have discovered about a subject outside of themselves by investigating it personally. Informing readers in a vivid, engaging way is the main purpose of observational writing.

WRITING ASSIGNMENT: Observation

Here is the writing assignment that appears near the beginning of Chapter 3:

Write an observational essay about an intriguing person, place, or activity in your community. Your essay may be a brief profile of an individual based on one or two interviews; a description of a place or activity observed once or twice; or a longer, more fully developed profile of a person, place, or activity observed once or twice; or a longer, more fully developed profile of a person, place, or activity based on several observational visits and interviews conducted over several weeks.

Observe your subject closely, and then present what you have learned in a way that both informs and engages readers.

Possible topic ideas follow each reading selection in a special section called Considering Ideas for Your Own Writing. A general list of topics is also included as part of the Invention section in the Guide to Observational Writing.

Observational Writing Situations

The situations that open this chapter suggest some of the possibilities for this kind of writing. Students can see right away that a profile may focus on a place (radio station), a person (scientist, artist), or an activity (urban renewal project). But they also see that these categories overlap: writing about a place involves presenting personalities and their activities; writing about a person involves describing his or her activities and the places in which they occur. Finally, these situations show that observational writing generally emphasizes the incongruous or unexpected, centering on the contrast between expectation and reality (the personal discovery about a radio station, for instance). Sometimes a controversy is uncovered (as in the case of the urban renewal project), while sometimes what is revealed is simply a fascinating observation, such as mural painting.

Practicing Observation: A Collaborative Activity

This group activity enables students to explore the rhetorical situation of the profile and prepares them to reflect on what they have learned. In Part 1, as they try out an idea with two or three fellow students, they become aware of what may interest readers. Then they step back in Part 2 to reflect on what they have learned. Because students find this activity so engaging, you will need to remind them to shift from telling about their subjects in Part 1 to discussing the rhetorical situation in Part 2.

A GUIDE TO READING OBSERVATIONAL WRITING

In this section, students are asked to read on two different levels: as readers and as writers. For class activities to use in conjunction with this section, see Part 5 of this manual.

Here, following a brief illustration of annotation, students are introduced to a sample essay—a selection from *Among School Children*, by Tracy Kidder. Students will want to note that, while Kidder's project is clearly to profile one person, teacher Chris Zajac, he relies on observations of activities, a place, and—especially—other people in presenting his profile.

Reading for Meaning

This section helps students develop meaning from the text by rereading it and by considering it in light of their personal knowledge and experience. You might want to have a few students share their responses in class as a way of encouraging a broader discussion of the meaning of the piece.

Reading like a Writer

Here, students are asked to shift their focus from the meaning of the essay to the specific strategies the writer uses to make meaning. These strategies fall into the broad categories of *detailing the scene and people, organizing the observations, engaging and informing readers,* and *conveying an impression of the subject.* In the critical reading and writing tasks that follow, each of these strategies is focused on more narrowly: *detailing the scene and people* focuses on ways in which writers of observation offer vivid presentations of their subjects, while *organizing the observations* draws students' attention toward methods of providing tension and drama through narrative or other methods of organization. (Both of these strategies should be familiar to students from the previous assignment in autobiographical writing.) *Engaging and informing readers* helps students see how writers engage and sustain readers' interest by presenting information in entertaining ways. *Conveying an impression of the subject* is discussed in terms of expressing an attitude toward the subject and conveying an interpretation or theme.

Detailing the Scene and People. Especially if they've just completed the autobiographical assignment presented in Chapter 2, students are likely to notice immediately that Kidder goes well beyond the visual in describing Zajac's classroom, incorporating a range of sounds, smells, and tactile sensations. Most students will find Kidder's characterizations of students and of Zajac herself both economical and effective; likewise, students will probably find that Kidder's presentation of the elementary classroom scene evokes a universal experience. In their written responses to this task, students should probably be able to comment on the importance of careful selection of detail in Kidder's presentation of scene and people.

Organizing the Observations. Students will learn in this chapter that writers of observation often use a narrative framework, as Kidder does, to organize their observations. If your students have worked with the previous chapter, Chapter 2: Autobiography, they should be familiar with the strategies by which writers shape and pace their narratives. If you have not used Chapter 2, or if you feel students need a review of these strategies, you might find it useful to walk students through the essay, helping them to notice that Kidder manipulates his narration to replicate the transition from drowsiness to excitement experienced by Zajac's students. You might point out, for instance, that the pace of the narrative picks up dramatically at the end of paragraph 4, where Zajac decides to surprise her students by reversing her role with theirs.

Engaging and Informing Readers. Students will immediately notice the specificity with which Kidder's selection begins, drawing readers into a particular and very likely familiar scene. Through careful use of narrative strategies, students should note, Kidder is able to capture the interest of his readers. Students should also see that Kidder inserts diverse information—gathered over a long period of prior observation of and interviews with his subject—into his narrative.

Conveying an Impression of the Subject. Students may need to be reminded that observational writing rarely involves a simple, neutral presentation of a subject: in most cases, writers exhibit a distinct attitude toward their subjects. While Kidder, like most observational writers, comes across as being somewhat detached, he clearly admires Chris Zajac as a teacher and is, at least occasionally, amused by her interactions with her students.

In addition to expressing their attitudes toward their subjects, observational writers generally attempt to present an interpretation or evaluation of their topics. In this sense, this assignment provides an opportunity to preview assignments in which students will be asked to defend a point of view, detailed in later chapters in the text.

Although this task may seem simple, it helps students bring together the strategies for successful observational writing discussed so far: keeping in mind the attitude and interpretation they've discussed in the two previous sections, and their examinations of the way Kidder details scenes and people from the first task, students will note that all of these elements are interrelated. Each detail is carefully selected to contribute to Kidder's implicit interpretation of his subject.

RESOURCES FOR TEACHING THE READINGS

This chapter presents a variety of examples of observational writing. The first essay, by an unidentified staff writer of the *New Yorker*, describes the extraordinary soup kitchen of Mr. Albert Yeganeh. The second reading, Lisa Jones's *Girls on the Strip*, profiles African-American comic-strip artist Barbara Brandon. *Bull Riding School*, by Jane and Michael Stern, offers an account of the unusual and colorful curriculum of the school named in the title. John McPhee's *The New York Pickpocket Academy* gives a sharply focused profile of pickpockets who frequent a farmer's market in Brooklyn. The rich details of people and activities and the immediacy of the profile is in part a consequence of McPhee's decision to present his observations from his point of view as a worker in the market. The final essay, *Dead Air*, by college student Craig Elsten, profiles a college radio station.

The readings in this chapter illustrate various kinds of observational writing: profiles of people, places, and events. By reading and analyzing these selections, students will discover that good observational writing is generally characterized by a specific subject and a main point or interpretation, a vivid description of the subject so that readers can imagine what the writer observed, and a clear organization so that readers can follow the essay easily.

The following material introduces each reading and explores the possibilities of the sections on reading for meaning and reading like a writer and the ideas for writing that follow each reading.

The New Yorker, Soup

Two things are quickly noticeable in this portrait of Albert Yeganeh and his soup kitchen. The first is that the writer introduces the essay with a long monologue by Mr. Yeganeh. Most observational essays, especially short ones, would summarize or break up such a long speech. The second thing most readers notice is the writer's decision to organize the essay by presenting a strong character portrait of Mr. Yeganeh and then by shifting to a point of view that makes readers feel as if they are approaching Mr. Yeganeh's soup kitchen for the first time.

Reading for Meaning

This section asks students to consider the writer's purpose in writing about Mr. Yeganeh's soup kitchen, and about the writer's attitude toward his or her subject. Students are encouraged to annotate as they read and reread the essay; you might remind them of the importance of this critical reading strategy by referring them back to the sample of annotation that opens A Guide to Reading Observational Writing. The section also encourages students to connect their own experiences and attitudes directly to the text of the essay. Especially as this is the first reading in the chapter, you might collect and quickly skim students' writing for this activity, making sure students are on track and perhaps reading aloud a few of the more thoughtful responses.

Extending Meaning through Conversation. This section, a corresponding version of which follows each of the readings in the text, invites students to develop their understanding of the meaning of this selection by discussing it in pairs or small groups, with particular attention to differences among student perceptions of the piece. While many students will find Mr. Yeganeh a colorful and somewhat charming character, for instance, others may find his approach a bit abrasive. You may find it helpful to move among pairs or groups of students as they discuss the essay, offering suggestions and helping groups stay focused on the reading. As usual, especially with the first reading in each chapter, you may want to set aside some class time so that students can share the results of this activity with you and the class as a whole.

Reading like a Writer: Detailing the Scene and People

This section asks students to analyze several paragraphs of the essay closely, looking for the details the writer has selected in presenting Mr. Yeganeh and his soup kitchen. As they write briefly based on their analyses, students should be able to report that the physical details do more than simply describe the scene and people: they also contribute to the writer's portrait of Mr. Yeganeh by revealing his attitudes toward his customers (paragraph 4) and his interactions with his employees (paragraph 5) and customers (paragraphs 7–10). Once again, for the first reading in the chapter, you might lead your students through the analysis as a group, guiding them in a thorough analysis of the paragraphs. This is a useful opportunity to remind students of the importance of rereading, annotating, and note-taking in reading critically. Once students have completed the writing activity, you could ask a few of them to share their responses in class.

Considering Ideas for Your Own Writing

With our students, unusual places on campus or in the community are favorite subjects for the observational essay assignment. Help your students consider the implications of their choices: how they would go about observing the place, when they would observe, whom they would interview, from what vantage point would they observe, and so on. Help them imagine themselves carrying through with the entire assignment; encourage them to think like writers at work.

Lisa Jones, **Girls on the Strip**

As the introductory material to this selection points out, Jones's essay differs from the previous selection in two important ways: it focuses less on a particular person than on that person's work, and it more distinctly foregrounds the role of the observational writer herself. As students begin to plan their own observational writing, they will want to consider the options suggested by these differences. The introduction to the piece also reminds students that writing in this genre need not be formal, but that, in fact, observational writers often achieve their effects through direct, lively language, and, sometimes, through references to their own experiences.

Reading for Meaning

Like the introductory material, this section begins by drawing students' attention to the author's personal connection with her subject, providing a useful starting point from which students can expand on their impressions of the meaning of the selection.

Extending Meaning through Conversation. In this activity, students are once again invited to share their perceptions of the essay in small groups. As Jones's piece goes beyond a simple portrait of an artist to touch on deeper issues of race and gender, this activity should elicit some interesting discussion; you might provide some class time following this activity for students to share their responses with you and the larger group.

Reading like a Writer: Engaging and Informing Readers

One challenge that students will face as they proceed with their own observational writing projects is how to present background information while keeping readers' interest engaged. While the information presented in Jones's profile of Barbara Brandon is by no means dry or technical, the writer has nevertheless carefully considered its placement within the essay. Students should already have noticed that, as in the sample essay by Tracy Kidder, Jones's firsthand observation of Brandon and her work—much of it presented through lively quotations—is interspersed with background information about Brandon's career and about "black comic strip history." Once students have analyzed and written briefly about this aspect of Brandon's essay, you might give them time to compare their responses in pairs or small groups, and then allow them a few minutes to add to their own writing what insights they have gained.

Considering Ideas for Your Own Writing

This section invites students to consider writing about an entrepreneur of any variety, examining the challenges and rewards of such work. Because this type of profile, like Jones's, is likely to be largely interview-based, we offer some specific suggestions for gathering material from profile subjects.

Jane and Michael Stern, Bull Riding School

As students compare this selection to previous readings in the chapter, they will probably notice that it contains more narrative action (especially in paragraphs 12-16) than the previous selection by Lisa Jones; they may also note that, while each of the previous essays, by Kidder, the anonymous *New Yorker* writer, and Jones, focus on single people, the Sterns also include brief but telling profiles of secondary characters: the students at Gary Leffew's bull-riding school. If your students have worked with Chapter 2: Autobiography, this selection provides a good opportunity to review strategies of both narration of action and description of people; if you have not used Chapter 2, this is a fine opportunity to introduce and reinforce students' understanding of these strategies.

Reading for Meaning

This activity encourages students to explore their impressions of the Sterns's essay, directing their attention to the authors' treatment of the school itself, the teacher, and the students. As students reread and annotate the essay, they should find their impressions of the Sterns's attitude toward their subject becoming clearer.

Extending Meaning through Conversation. Students may find that their views of this piece differ widely: while many will read this as a straightforward and colorful essay about an interesting topic, some students may perceive a certain amount of condescension on the part of the writers toward both Gary Leffew and his pupils, while others may be disturbed by the intimations of cruelty represented by the "electric prod" mentioned in paragraph 13. You might ask each pair or group of students to report to the class briefly on differences that remain after discussion, and you could talk to the class about the acceptability of differences among readers.

<u>Exploring the Significance of Figurative Writing (A Further Strategy for Reading for Meaning)</u>. This supplemental activity calls students' attention to the role of figurative language, not only in creating a colorful profile but in in conveying the writers' attitudes toward their subject. Students are referred to Appendix 1, where this critical reading strategy is presented in more detail. Once students have completed this activity, you might ask them to share their findings briefly in class.

Reading like a Writer

The preceding exercise in exploring the figurative language in the essay should help students move smoothly into this activity, as the authors rely heavily on figurative language in detailing Gary Leffew, and, to a somewhat lesser extent, his students. In addition, students who have worked with Chapter 2: Autobiography will be familiar with many of the resources highlighted in this section, which are based on strategies of narration and description. We draw students' attention to specific paragraphs in which the writers draw upon a full range of resources in detailing their subject. Students are then asked to comment on how successful the writers have been in selecting details to provide a full and engaging profile.

   <u>Compare</u>. In this activity, which follows one or two readings in each chapter, students are asked to go beyond their analysis and writing about a specific essay to compare and contrast the ways different writers in the chapter use the same strategies. This type of comparison helps students gain a broader sense of possible use of strategies within each genre, and it is such an important activity that you might want to lead the class through it, giving them time afterwards to reflect briefly in writing on the class discussion.

Considering Ideas for Your Own Writing

This section invites students to consider writing about a specialized class or training program, such as the bull riding school featured in the reading selection, and to refer to their own experience as they select such a topic. You might remind students that a topic of this type will probably demand quite a bit of planning, as observations may need to be arranged in advance.

John McPhee, **The New York Pickpocket Academy**

   In this selection, McPhee describes scenes from a day in the Brooklyn farmers' market, where he observes the interactions between petty thieves and their victims. The accumulation of observed details is characteristic of McPhee's style. The selection offers little commentary, but readers can infer McPhee's purpose from the way he has selected and arranged his details and examples. The scenes and anecdotes speak for themselves. Another feature of the selection is McPhee's use of the present tense to convey the unfolding drama of a day in the market.

Reading for Meaning

   In observational writing, where it can often seem to students that the writer is merely telling what he or she experienced, the main point may not be immediately apparent. However, students should realize that writers like McPhee make points about their subjects as they describe and narrate them, even though they rarely announce their points in thesis statements. Clearly, one of McPhee's purposes in this selection is to describe the extent of crime in the market. "Possibly Fifty-ninth Street is the New York Pickpocket Academy," he remarks, and he provides plenty of supporting evidence for this observation. However, he also seems to be making the point that altruism and honesty occasionally appear even amid so much crime and are appreciated by those who benefit from them. McPhee's purpose seems to be to present a complex view of the market and the different impulses demonstrated by people who work, shop, and steal there every day.

Extending Meaning through Conversation. Once again, students are invited to develop their understanding of the essay by discussing it with one or two other students. You could give students a few minutes following this activity to extend their own notes on the reading, adding any insights they have gleaned from their discussion.

Reading like a Writer: Organizing the Observations

As they plan and write their own observational essays, one of the most important decisions students will make is whether to organize their material narratively or topically. Drawing students' attention to the fact that, unlike the earlier selections in this chapter, McPhee's profile is organized around a narrative framework, we ask students to outline his essay carefully, using strategies which are further detailed in Appendix 1. Students are then asked to explore their findings briefly in writing.

Compare. This activity, which follows one or two readings in each chapter, should help students gain a sense of the possibilities open to writers in each genre. By examining the decisions made by two or more writers in each chapter, students will be better prepared to begin making the same types of decisions as they begin their own essays. In this case, students will find it especially interesting to speculate about how McPhee's essay would have been different if he had presented his material topically, and how "Soup" or "Bull Riding School" might have been different if their writers had relied more heavily on narrative in presenting their observations.

Considering Ideas for Your Own Writing

We ask students to consider writing their own observational essays about large public places, filled with people and action. While these types of topics offer rich material for writers of observation, you might remind students that they will face the challenge of limiting and focusing their observations, as McPhee does. As usual, part of the point of this activity is to connect students' task as writers immediately to what they have learned as readers.

Craig Elsten, **Dead Air**

Elsten's essay about a radio station on the campus where he is a student helps students see that good topics for observational essays can be found close to home, at their own schools or in their own communities.

Reading for Meaning

Students are asked to explore their understanding of Elsten's essay, commenting on the impression he seems to convey of KSDT. Students should also consider the extent to which Elsten's essay is successful in combining information and entertainment. As students reread and annotate the essay, they will be able to see how these basic features of observational writing function in Elsten's essay. Students are also invited to relate their own experiences to Elsten's observations. As many students may use their own job experiences to make meaning from this text, you might make sure that they aren't moving too far away from the text itself by inviting to share their stories in class, so that you can lead them back to the essay to make explicit connections between their experiences and the text.

Extending Meaning through Conversation. As students continue to explore and develop their understanding of the meaning of this piece by discussing it with one or two classmates, you might circulate from group to group, helping students stay focused on the text itself. Remind students that they can reread and annotate the text together as part of this activity.

Reading like a Writer: Conveying an Impression

While there will probably be some variety in the possible interpretations students impute to Elsten's essay, most will agree that his interpretation of his subject revolves around the curious phenomenon of a radio station to which almost no one is able to listen. Students should note that, in addition to his own commentary, Elsten allows the employees of KSDT to speak for themselves in support of his interpretation. Once students have completed these analyzing and writing activities, you might ask them to share their responses briefly in small groups or with the class.

Reading like a Writer: A Follow-up Activity

To help students continue to develop their understanding of observational writing, you might have them go back over the writing they have generated in response to the Reading like a Writer activities throughout the chapter. After reviewing their own writing, students could choose one piece to expand through further analysis and writing. You could have students turn this piece in with the essay package or in an end-of-course portfolio.

Considering Ideas for Your Own Writing

We find that this writing idea has special appeal for our students. There turn out to be many "scenes" on campus worth looking behind. How *does* the soccer team prepare for a game? How *is* the student newspaper or an academic journal produced? How *are* materials processed in a library archive? There are many possibilities. Help students imagine how they would go about developing a behind-the-scenes profile.

THINKING ABOUT WHAT YOU HAVE LEARNED ABOUT OBSERVATIONAL ESSAYS

As students prepare to begin their own essays, we find it especially important that they pause to consider and articulate what they have learned from the readings about the features of each genre. Students are asked to focus closely on the strategies used by writers of observation by choosing one essay from the chapter to analyze in more detail. After examining the author's (or authors') purpose and audience, we ask students to comment on how—and how well—the essay fulfills what we have identified following each reading as the basic features of successful observational writing. Concentrating on one essay at this point should help students to review, remember, and eventually use the observational writing strategies to which they've been exposed throughout the chapter. Whether you have students complete this activity individually or work in small groups with other students who have selected the same essay, you might give them the opportunity to share their ideas in class as a way of stimulating a productive discussion of the features of successful writing of this type. One way of doing this would be to outline the features of observational writing on the board, and then have students comment on how successfully each writer meets the challenges of each feature.

A GUIDE TO OBSERVATIONAL WRITING

The guide leads students through a composing process that follows these steps:

Invention
    Choosing a Subject
    Probing Your Subject
    Investigating Your Subject
        Visiting a Place
        Interviewing a Person
        Gathering Published Information
    Deciding on the Impression You Mean to Convey
    Analyzing Your Readers
        Learning More about Your Readers: A Collaborative Activity
Drafting
    Setting Goals
    Planning Your Draft
    Beginning
Reading a Draft Critically
    Reading for a First Impression
    Reading to Analyze
        Detailing the Scene and People
        Organizing the Observations
        Engaging and Informing Readers
        Conveying an Impression
Revising
    Revising to Detail the Scene and People
    Revising to Organize the Observations
    Revising to Engage and Inform Readers
    Revising to Convey an Impression of the Subject
Reflecting on What You Have Learned about Observational Writing

Choosing a suitable topic is particularly important for this assignment because students will need to invest a good deal of their time visiting the place or person, conducting interviews, and/or doing firsthand research. If students are unable to think of a topic by sitting alone in their rooms with a blank sheet of paper or brainstorming with family and friends, you might be able to help them by suggesting some sources of topics: the business index at the back of the phone book is a ready-made list of potential profile topics ranging from jewelry designers to printing companies; a map of the area can reveal some potentially interesting places to investigate; local newspapers can be another source of inspiration. The main criteria for an observational writing topic are that it be personally interesting to the student, potentially interesting to readers, and accessible or researchable within the time available for the assignment.

    Students may wonder why they need to do the exercises under Probing Your Subject with their topics. While not all the questions may be relevant for every student's topic, probing the subject helps students establish their preconceptions about the subject (which may contrast with what they later discover) and decide whether the topic seems interesting enough to pursue. This step in the invention sequence is a small investment of time that could save them the trouble of investigating less interesting topics.

As students do begin to investigate their topics, you will want to stress the importance of field research in observational writing: it is an essential part of the work students will do for this assignment. Depending on their subjects, students are likely to use both observation and interviews; most students will not have much experience with either. In Appendix 2: Strategies for Research and Documentation, we give students a detailed overview of strategies for these types of research. We lead students step by step through the observation and interview process, and, while some of this advice may seem like common sense (take a writing implement, prepare some interview questions in advance), students will find it useful. You might emphasize in particular the importance of reflecting on their observations and interviews immediately after the fact, reviewing and adding to their notes rather than relying on memory.

Students often have difficulty deciding on what impression they want to convey in their observational essays, so you may want to devote some class time to discussing the questions under this heading in the invention sequence. At this stage, the impression need only be a provisional one; reassure students that they can change it as they learn more about their subjects.

The next invention step is analyzing readers, and this is another stage at which students often need guidance, simply because few students are used to writing with any particular audience in mind aside from their instructor. You might want to specify a local newspaper or periodical that publishes observational articles, or you might let students identify the publication they would like to write for. The publication might be hypothetical, or you might insist that students write for an actual publication and encourage the most successful to submit their final typescripts to it. When analyzing their readers, then, students should describe the editors and readers of the publication, and perhaps the style of article that appears in it. We also invite students to analyze their readers further by briefly presenting potential subjects for their own observational essays in small groups; we find that hands-on, collaborative activities of this sort are especially useful in preparing students for the challenges they will face as they embark on their own essays.

When planning the organization of their essays, students often choose the easiest plan and merely organize information in the order in which they discovered it. Remind them that writers often organize their material according to a topical plan rather than a narrative. If students opt for a chronological sequence as their organizational principle, they should do so because that is a better plan than the alternatives, not because it is the only one they have considered. Likewise, remind students of the variety of beginnings demonstrated by the selections in this chapter, and tell them that they need not wait for the ideal beginning before they start drafting. Revision allows the beginning to be added later.

SPECIAL PROBLEMS OF THIS WRITING ASSIGNMENT. There are essentially two problems students have with this assignment. The first has to do with scheduling and the other with focusing. One of the best ways to focus an observational essay is to organize it around a dominant impression of the subject. By this we mean a unique or fresh perspective on a given subject, something that reveals a new or unexpected insight into that subject.

The scheduling problem arises from the difficulty many freshmen have in sustaining a long research project. In the guide to writing, we recommend that students establish their own research schedules. But we also suggest that you set up deadlines for various stages of the project—such as writing up notes on observational visits and interviews, preparing an outline, or writing the first draft—to help students keep on schedule. You could easily have students write up their observations and interviews and then use class time for peer workshops on these notes and write-ups.

Writing up their notes from observations and interviews and exchanging these write-ups with others in the class can also help students focus their observations. The focusing problem results from the overwhelming quantity of information students usually gather. The more they work with their material—analyzing it, writing about it, finding connections and patterns in it—the more cohesive their essays ultimately will be. As their drafts become more organized and cohesive, students will also be able to develop or discover the impressions they wish to convey in their essays.

PROMISING AND UNPROMISING TOPICS. Because the scope of this assignment is so broad, the opportunities for topics may seem so rich as to be inexhaustible. For many novice writers who have just arrived at a university (or a new city), the observational essay offers an ideal chance for exploration. Students should be encouraged to seek out unusual activities, people, or places. When you make the assignment, urge them to avoid topics with which they are overly familiar (for example, the summer job they have had for the last four years, their college dorm, etc.). If your students are writing a longer profile, they will need to pick a topic with plenty of activity, enough people for several interviews, and a circumscribed place that can be described specifically (profiles about "the beach" or "downtown" generally don't work, for instance).

Two other problems with selecting a topic are those of accessibility and security. Subjects that may sound exciting in theory may not be possible or appropriate in practice. A doctor or scientist may not be available for interviews; legal considerations might prevent a student from profiling an emergency room; a military installation or a nuclear power plant may be off-limits to the general public.

Similarly, you may want to discourage students from exploring topics that are potentially dangerous. It is natural, even commendable, for some people to want to do something a little daring, but it is not always a good idea. Students should think twice about profiling something like the county jail (which may be off-limits anyway), a place in a neighborhood with a high incidence of crime, or some activity that presents a health or safety hazard. On the one hand, you don't want your students to select mundane or drab topics, but on the other hand, you should urge them to use discretion when picking a subject to observe. All you really need to do is to encourage them to explore unfamiliar places or activities—the experience of discovery should be enough to yield a fresh and insightful angle. Part of the task, of course, is for students to get beneath the surface of whatever it is they are observing.

One way to involve all students in evaluating each other's topic choices is to circulate topic sheets. At the top of a sheet of paper students write a tentative title for their essays. Then they describe in two or three sentences the person, location, or activity that will be the subject of their profile. In one sentence, they identify possible readers (class members, readers of a particular newspaper or magazine, or perhaps a special group of readers with a need to know what the writer will discover). These sheets then circulate around the class, with students writing questions or comments, and even commenting on other students' comments.

We evaluate—approving, questioning, rejecting—students' topic choices for all our assignments. We evaluate the observational essay assignment most carefully of all because students are unlikely to have undertaken such a writing project and consequently cannot foresee the possibilities and problems of a topic.

Chapter 4 REFLECTION

What distinguishes the reflective essay, to borrow Virginia Woolf's words, is its "fierce attachment to an idea." In introducing this assignment, you might help students make connections between this assignment and the two previous assignments in the text: while autobiographers spin tales about significant events and people in their lives, and writers of observation present what they have discovered about a subject by investigating it personally, writers of reflection spin webs of ideas.

Reflective writing is a natural outgrowth of both autobiographical and observational writing. All three have their roots in personal experience, and all are concerned with the meaning or significance of that experience. But whereas autobiographers and most observational writers need only present their experience vividly to convey its significance, reflective writers must explore the meaning they find.

While autobiographers bring out personal significance, reflective writers, like writers of observation, look for general implications. Reflection stems from an observation or experience that raises a question or leads to an insight about the human situation. Reflective essayists write about the ways in which we live and interact with one another, the goals toward which we strive, and the shortcomings that hobble us. The reflective essay is typically a public meditation on what makes us human. The readings in this chapter, and the accompanying commentary and activities, should help students appreciate the value of this genre.

WRITING ASSIGNMENT: Reflection
Here is the writing assignment that appears near the beginning of Chapter 4:

> Write a reflective essay based on something you experienced or observed. Describe it vividly so that readers can understand what happened and will care about what you have to say. In reflecting on what the particular occasion suggests, explore your own and society's attitudes and values. Reflective writing is like a conversation—you are writing not just for yourself but to share your thoughts with others, to stimulate their thinking as well as your own.

Possible topic ideas (Considering Ideas for Your Own Writing) follow each reading selection. A general list of topics is also included as part of the Invention section in the Guide to Reflective Writing.

Reflective Writing Situations
The three brief writing situations suggest a few of the possibilities for reflective writing. You could help your students notice that reflective writing takes place in both academic and

non-academic settings, that it is written by both professional and nonprofessional writers, and that it has room alike for humor and for serious social commentary.

Practicing Reflection: A Collaborative Activity

This group activity enables students to imagine themselves as reflective writers, preparing them to approach the upcoming reading selections from a writer's perspective. As they try out ideas with two or three fellow students, they are reminded of the important dimensions of purpose and audience; then they step back to examine the rhetorical situation of writing a reflective essay. Because students are likely to get deeply involved in this activity, you may need to remind them to shift from their conversation about the occasion their group has chosen in part one to reflect more broadly on other considerations of the genre in part two.

A GUIDE TO READING REFLECTIVE WRITING

This section calls students' attention to the fact that they will be asked to read the upcoming selections from two different perspectives: that of readers, and that of writers of reflective essays. For class activities to use in conjunction with this section, see Part 5 of this manual.

Following a brief illustration of annotation, students are presented with a sample essay by Nicollette Toussaint entitled "Hearing the Sweetest Songs"—a reflection on her experiences with being "differently abled." Toussaint's essay is a good example of a short reflective essay, a meditation that explores and illustrates general ideas with concrete details.

Reading for Meaning

In this section, as in corresponding sections throughout the text, students are encouraged to focus closely on the content of the reading selection. Here, students are asked to respond to "Hearing the Sweetest Songs," beginning by considering the insights Toussaint provides into being disabled. Students are also invited to respond to Toussaint's reflections in light of their own experiences or observations, in addition to being offered several other suggestions for exploring the meaning of the essay.

Reading like a Writer

In this series of tasks, the focus shifts from the content and purpose of the essay to the specific strategies the reflective writer uses in achieving that purpose: *presenting the particular occasion, developing the reflections, maintaining topical coherence,* and *engaging readers*. In the following critical reading and writing tasks, each of these strategies is broken down more specifically. *Presenting the particular occasion* entails both narrating and describing, while *developing the reflections* takes place through asserting ideas, giving examples, posing questions, and comparing and contrasting. *Maintaining topical coherence* is discussed in terms of establishing a theme that connects all parts of a reflective essay. Students also learn that *engaging readers* involves the writer in presenting reflection vividly, perhaps in ways which surprise the reader. While the Reading like a Writer section following the sample essay provides a comprehensive catalog of these strategies, corresponding sections following each of the subsequent reading selections focus more narrowly on strategies particularly appropriate to the analysis of each essay. In each case, students will be asked to engage in a two-part activity including both analyzing and writing; following two of the readings in the chapter, they will also be invited to compare the ways in which two or more authors use specific strategies.

Presenting the Particular Occasion. We point out to students that Toussaint's essay begins not with a single particular occasion but with a pair of significantly related incidents. While Toussaint's narrative of these incidents is not as sustained, nor her description, perhaps, as detailed, as that of many of the writers in Chapter 2: Autobiography, and Chapter 3: Observation, students should nonetheless recognize many of these familiar strategies at work in this essay.

Developing the Reflections. This section helps students to understand that a successful reflective essay is generally a balance of general ideas or statements on the one hand, and specific examples on the other, and that the relationship between the general and the specific in a reflective essay is likely to be highly symbiotic, as each strategy is used successfully mainly in relation to the other. This activity asks students to identify and analyze both general and specific material in Toussaint's essay, directing them toward specific paragraphs as they analyze and write.

Maintaining Topical Coherence. One of the greatest challenges facing writers of reflective essays, as students are bound to discover as they begin their own drafts, is to maintain a sense of coherence, a controlling idea which underlies and makes relevant seemingly disparate material. As students analyze and write about whether and how Toussaint sustains this coherence, we direct their attention toward her use of cues for the reader, including transitions between paragraphs and repetition of thematic material.

Engaging Readers. This section helps students see that, particularly in reflective writing, personal engagement on the part of the writer invites the same on the part of the reader. However, as they reread and analyze Toussaint's essay, students are encouraged to consider not only the personal but the social significance of her reflections. As part of the point of the reflective essay is its commentary on larger human experience, this will be an important consideration for students beginning their own reflective writing.

RESOURCES FOR TEACHING THE READINGS

This chapter offers six readings of varying length and difficulty, including the sample essay by Nicollette Toussaint described in the preceding section. The next essay, by Brent Staples, takes on another serious subject: our cultural attitudes toward gender and racial difference. Barbara Ehrenreich reflects on the disturbing issue of family violence. Ishmael Reed's essay is a meditation on multiculturalism. Diana Trilling's essay once again picks up the theme of gender difference, while the final essay, by student Katherine Haines, continues this theme, this time in the context of self-perception.

The following material introduces each reading and explores the possibilities for classroom use of the sections on reading for meaning and reading like a writer and the ideas for writing that follow each essay.

Brent Staples, **Black Men and Public Space**

The introductory note to this essay reminds students that reflective essays are based on a combination of particular occasion and general reflection; you might also encourage students very directly to read it in the context of what they have learned from their examination of the sample essay by Nicollette Toussaint.

Reading for Meaning

This section directs students back to the text to explore their own understanding of and response to Staples's essay. Students are also invited to read Staples's essay in light of their own experience, and to identify with Staples himself as well as his "victim."

Extending Meaning through Conversation. In this activity, students are encouraged to develop their understanding of the meaning of Staples's essay by discussing it with one or two other students. As this piece touches on issues of race and gender, you may find that students have particularly strong feelings about it; once students have explored the meaning of the essay in small groups, you might facilitate a class discussion revolving around these issues. Another option would be to ask each pair or group to report briefly in class on any notable differences that remain after discussion; you might then lead a class discussion about the acceptability—and even usefulness—of such differences among readers.

Looking for Patterns of Opposition (A Further Strategy for Reading for Meaning). This task calls students' attention to the oppositions within the essay, perhaps beginning with the discrepancies between how Staples views himself and how others view him. Students are referred to Appendix 1, A Catalog of Critical Reading Strategies. Expect students to need some guidance in getting started with this exercise, as well as in exploring the implications of these oppositions.

As usual following the first reading in each chapter, you might want to collect students' writing based on these activities, partly in order to monitor how well they are grasping the material and partly so that you can share aloud a sample of student responses.

Reading like a Writer: Presenting the Particular Occasion

This section calls attention to the particular occasion out of which Staples's reflection develops. Students who have completed the autobiographical assignment in Chapter 2 should be prepared to analyze the building of tension in this brief narrative; if you have not yet discussed narrative with your students, this question offers a good opportunity to do so. Whether or not your students have worked with Chapter 2, we once again suggest that you lead your class as a group in the analysis portion of this activity for the first reading of the chapter, showing them explicitly how to annotate and take useful notes on the reading. Students should be able to note the specificity of Staples's nouns and verbs—the economical but vivid narration of the specific action of the "characters" in the occasion. We also draw students' attention to the relationship between the particular occasion and the more general subject of Staples's reflection.

Compare. It is important at this stage that students recognize the variety of particular occasions open to them as prospective writers of reflective essays. This activity, whether students complete it individually or in groups, should also help them focus on how occasions are used by different writers.

Considering Ideas for Your Own Writing

Staples's essay calls attention to the way Americans, as a society, conceive of public and private space. To write on this subject, students would have to do some observational or field research. You might suggest that they study spatial relationships among people in different places and situations—a shopping mall, a football game, a large party, waiting for a movie, on a bus or train. They also might look at spatial relationships among different groups—men and women, the elderly and the young, people at work and people at play.

Barbara Ehrenreich, **Are Families Dangerous?**

Students may find this essay, like several of the selections in the chapter, not merely thought provoking, but disturbing. These readings should help students see that, while the purpose of reflective writing is not to take a stand or to exhort its readers to action, it can nonetheless evoke powerful responses in its readers.

Reading for Meaning

In this section, students are asked to consider Ehrenreich's purpose and audience, beginning by considering the precise nature of the dangers she locates within the family. Students are also invited to recall their own experiences in the context of Ehrenreich's reflections. Because this essay may elicit highly personal responses from some students, you may find that you need to help students stay focused on the essay itself, making explicit connections between their experiences and the text.

Extending Meaning through Conversation. Here, we encourage students to enhance their understanding of Ehrenreich's essay by discussing it with one or two other students. While many students will recognize, either intuitively or from experience, the dangers Ehrenreich identifies, others may be put off by what they perceive to be an attack on "family values." As students explore these tensions in conversation, they also gain a fuller understanding of Ehrenreich's reflections.

Reading like a Writer: Maintaining Topical Coherence

Students should recall from their work with the sample essay in this chapter that although reflective essays tend to appear casual on the surface, their writers actually work hard to maintain topical coherence. Here, we draw students' attention to the cues Ehrenreich uses to help readers follow her reflections, including transitions, topic sentences, and repeated words and phrases. If students have a hard time getting started on this activity, you could point out the repetition in the first few paragraphs of "nest" and "cradle" (paragraph 2) and "lie down" (paragraphs 3 and 5) as a possible starting point.

Considering Ideas for Your Own Writing

Like the preceding essays in this chapter focusing on racism and disability, Ehrenreich's selection deals with a difficult topic. Here, we ask students to consider taking on a similar challenge, writing their own reflective essays about subjects that are not often openly discussed. Especially if students are basing their essays on personal experience, you may find that emotional distance becomes an issue; if your students have already worked with Chapter 2: Autobiography, you might refer them back to pertinent sections of that chapter.

Ishmael Reed, **What's American about America?**

This essay takes up the fascinating and timely concept of multiculturalism. In the headnote, students are encouraged to consider what they already know about this subject.

Reading for Meaning

Here, students are asked to respond in some depth to Reed's reflections on the cultural diversity of American society. As with many of the readings in this text, students are invited to relate Reed's reflections to their own observations and experiences. Depending on the demographics of your particular student population, this exercise is likely to elicit a rich range of interesting responses. If students do rely on their personal experiences to make meaning from the selection, you will want to be sure that they do not move too far from the essay itself; one way of making sure you can encourage them to make explicit connections between the text and their own experience is to invite them to share their responses orally in class.

Extending Meaning through Conversation. Once again, students are invited to explore the meaning of a reading by discussing it with one or two other students. Because students are likely to have strong personal responses to this particular essay, you might find it useful to circulate among pairs or groups, making sure students are making connections between their experience and Reed's essay.

Reading like a Writer: Developing the Reflections by Piling Up Examples

Students will notice immediately that, unlike the other selections in the chapter, Reed's essay opens with a series of occasions. Most students will note that the diversity of this series is appropriate to the subject on which Reed proceeds to reflect. Students are also asked to scrutinize Reed's use of examples throughout the essay, and to comment in detail on their function in Reed's reflections. Careful readers will see that some of Reed's examples, such as that of the Puritans (paragraphs 10–12) support a distinctly critical perspective; as with the preceding selection by Barbara Ehrenreich, students may be divided as to whether or not this is appropriate in reflective writing. In order to facilitate fruitful discussion here, you might ask a few students to read their responses aloud to the class.

Considering Ideas for Your Own Writing

This section invites students to consider their own experiences with or observations of cultural diversity as a basis for their reflective writing. Again, this is likely to be a valuable source of possible topics for many of your students.

Diana Trilling, **On Sexual Separatism**

The introductory material to this piece highlights the main ideas of Trilling's essay, and notes that students may find these ideas somewhat surprising. As with other selections in this chapter, we aim to help students see that reflective essays may take on difficult and even disturbing topics, and may do so in ways that may challenge readers to question their own assumptions.

Reading for Meaning

Students are encouraged to reread the text closely, beginning by speculating about Trilling's purpose in writing this essay. We provide some further suggestions to help students develop their understanding of the meaning of the piece.

Extending Meaning through Conversation. Here we invite students to enhance their understanding by discussing the essay with one or two other students. Trilling's reflections are likely to elicit lively discussion; you might allow some time in class for students to share their ideas once they have explored them in small groups. You may find that, as in the case of Ehrenreich's essay, the responses of male and female students differ here.

Reading like a Writer: Developing the Reflections through Comparison and Contrast

Strategies of comparison and contrast may be familiar to students from their high school experiences with writing; this section should help them to see how useful these strategies can be to writers of reflective essays. We ask students to examine Trilling's use of comparison and contrast closely, and to write briefly about her use of these strategies.

Considering Ideas for Your Own Writing

Students are invited to consider writing their own reflective essays on either same- or opposite-gender relations, beginning by identifying a specific occasion which might elicit such reflections.

Katherine Haines, **Whose Body Is This?**

Like the essays by Brent Staples, Barbara Ehrenreich, and Diana Trilling, this essay reflects, in part, on gender distinctions and self-concepts. Although the topic may be serious, most students will find this essay accessible and easy to read.

Reading for Meaning

Because Haines is so open about her own feelings and experiences (and perhaps because, unlike the other writers represented in this chapter, she is a fellow student and not a professional author), students are likely to have a fairly distinct impression of Haines as a person. When it comes to identifying their own experiences and observations with Haines's, though, you may once again see a certain discrepancy between the responses of male and female students.

Extending Meaning through Conversation. We try to encourage students to acknowledge and comment on this discrepancy in this activity, in which they will discuss their understanding of the meaning of the essay with one or two other students. As always, if you find students are relying perhaps too heavily on personal experience in interpreting the reading, you could check this tendency by moving among pairs or groups, helping students make explicit connections between their experiences and the text.

Reading like a Writer: Engaging Readers

This section helps students to see the ways in which writers of reflective essays are aware of their readers. We ask students to reread, analyze, and write briefly about Haines's attention to her audience, focusing on the techniques she uses to engage and sustain the interest of her readers. Students are likely to differ somewhat on how successful Haines is at engaging her readers' interest; asking a few students to share their responses to this activity in class may elicit a useful discussion of this important aspect of the genre.

Compare. As they embark on their own reflective essays, students will find it useful to compare the variety of ways, ranging from cajoling to challenging in tone, in which different writers attempt to engage their readers.

Reading like a Writer: A Follow-up Activity

As students complete the Reading like a Writer activities throughout the chapter, they will generate a substantial amount of writing on the reading selections. In order to enhance further their understanding of the genre, you might ask students to review their writing, selecting one piece to revise and extend by doing more analysis. This expanded piece of writing would be turned in along with the essay package or in students' end-of-course portfolios.

Considering Ideas for Your Own Writing

Issues related to cultural ideals of "beauty" and "success" tend to lurk just below the surface of most of our students' awareness, providing a rich source of topic possibilities for reflective essays. You might encourage students to consider this type of subject from different perspectives; while students may naturally approach these issues on a very personal basis, they can also examine them on broader cultural and historical levels.

THINKING ABOUT WHAT MAKES REFLECTIVE WRITING EFFECTIVE

Once again, we give students a chance to review and consolidate what they have learned by reading a number of writing selections in a particular genre. Referring students back to the Guide to Reading Reflective Writing following the sample essay by Nicollette Toussaint at the beginning of the chapter, we ask students to select an essay they feel to be especially effective in fulfilling the basic features of successful reflective writing, and to write briefly about their reasons for selecting this piece. Whether students complete this activity individually or in small groups, you might plan some time in class for them to share their responses.

A GUIDE TO REFLECTIVE WRITING

The guide leads students through a composing process that follows these stages:

Invention
> Finding a Particular Occasion and General Subject
> Choosing a Subject
> Developing the Particular Occasion
>> Learning More about Your Readers: A Collaborative Activity
> Developing Your Reflections on the Subject
>> Generalize about It
>> Give Examples of It
>> Compare and Contrast It
>> Extend It
>> Analyze It
>> Apply It

Drafting
    Setting Goals
    Planning Your Draft
    Beginning
Reading a Draft Critically
    Reading for a First Impression
    Reading to Analyze
        Presenting the Particular Occasion
        Developing the Reflections
        Maintaining Topical Coherence
        Engaging Readers
Revising
    Revising to Enliven the Particular Occasion
    Revising to Develop Your Reflections
    Revising to Ensure Coherence
    Revising to Engage and Hold Your Readers' Interest
Reflecting on What You Have Learned about Writing Reflection

As they search for topics for their own essays, encourage students to think in terms of both general subjects and particular occasions. The most important point is that there must be corresponding entries in the two columns of their invention chart. For every general subject there must be at least one particular example to illustrate it; for each particular occasion students must think of at least one general idea it embodies. This correspondence between the abstract and the particular is the most crucial element in reflective writing.

Notice the final comment on the topic chart in the text. Students may complete much of it at one sitting, but they should spread their topic selection process over several days, returning to review and add to their charts every day. This will allow them to reconsider their ideas and discover others they did not think of earlier.

After students have made a tentative selection, the exploratory writing exercise labeled Choosing a Subject is a valuable investment of time. If the topic proves promising, they can use the ideas they have written; if the exercise reveals that they have less to say than they had thought, the fifteen minutes spent exploring the topic will have saved them from wasting even more time trying to write a draft on that topic.

Students accustomed to writing only for teachers may not immediately see the purpose of analyzing their readers. If they found some of the selections in this chapter easier to read and understand than the others, you might refer to this experience to demonstrate that writers make different assumptions about their readers and modify their writing accordingly. The guide offers further advice on writing for particular readers in the Setting Goals section.

SPECIAL PROBLEMS OF THIS WRITING ASSIGNMENT. In our experience, problems student writers have with this assignment fall into two fairly predictable categories: choosing workable subjects (see Promising and Unpromising Topics below) and developing their reflections on these subjects. In the latter area, students' difficulties mainly have to do with achieving some balance between particular material—in the form of occasions, examples, and illustrations—and general statements. Exploratory drafts tend toward one extreme or the other. As our students begin writing, we often see first drafts that either look very much like essays about events (especially if students have recently completed the autobiographical assignment in Chapter 2) based completely on particular occasions, or that consist almost entirely of vague, abstract statements. A third type of problem draft comes to us from students who believe they need to reach some kind of conclusion about their subject, perhaps anticipating upcoming argument assignments. All of these types of problems can be minimized if you help students pay careful attention to both the general and the particular components of each reading selection as well as of their own developing essays.

PROMISING AND UNPROMISING TOPICS. Although students will have had quite a bit of practice selecting and working with various topic possibilities during the collaborative activity early in the chapter and as they read the Considering Ideas for Your Own Writing sections following each reading, you may be surprised at how much difficulty they encounter in actually settling on subjects for their own essays. Once again, these problems are generally reflected in three distinct ways: on the one hand is the student who confuses the subject of the essay with the particular occasion that triggers the reflection; on the other hand is the student who takes on a very abstract concept (love, truth, justice, etc.) and then is paralyzed by his or her inability to ground the subject in concrete occasions, examples, and illustrations. A third type of student will want to "reflect" on a controversial issue such as abortion or capital punishment, and is very likely to wind up writing a position paper rather than a reflective essay. As instructors, it is easy for us to see that each of these types of topics might in fact be perfectly appropriate for a reflective essay; our task is to help students see that their problems may not be with topic choice itself, but with how they plan to handle these topics in the context of the reflection essay. You may find that you need to coach students individually through these early stages of the writing process.

Chapter 5 EXPLAINING CONCEPTS

If your students are going from Chapter 4: Reflection, to Chapter 5, you might take time to discuss the similarities and differences between reflective and explanatory writing. Like reflective writing, writing to explain a concept often begins with particular firsthand observations and then "moves beyond description of specific objects and scenes to general concepts and ideas," as the introductory note to the chapter indicates. However, whereas the purpose of reflective writing is to try out the writer's ideas and help the reader see even the familiar in a new light, the main purpose of explanatory writing is just that—to explain something to the reader. While explanatory writing may be every bit as entertaining and thought-provoking as a reflective essay, it never loses sight of its primary goal: to inform the reader.

Likewise, if your students are going directly from Chapter 3 to Chapter 5, you might want to point out some of the similarities and differences between observational and explanatory writing. Both aim to present information in a way that readers will find intelligible and interesting. Observational writing derives mainly from the writer's firsthand experiences and observation, and it often relies on narrative and vivid description to communicate what the writer has seen or learned about the subject. Explanatory writing, on the other hand, typically derives from a variety of sources that may include the writer's personal experience and observation but usually depends heavily on what the writer has learned from others through reading and listening. Writers of explanation synthesize, review, or summarize the work of others. They present information, draw connections, and discuss implications. They may also translate technical or specialized information to the language and contexts of readers outside the discipline.

In this chapter, we focus on a particular aim of explanatory writing—writing to explain concepts. This focus enables students to work on the kind of explanation they are reading and writing in most of their courses. Throughout the disciplines, particularly in introductory courses, students are learning basic concepts. They learn by reading and by writing. Understanding the rhetoric of explanatory discourse can help them become better learners as well as more effective explainers.

WRITING ASSIGNMENT: Explaining Concepts

This is the writing assignment that appears near the beginning of Chapter 5:

> Write an essay that explains a concept. Choose a concept that interests you and that you want to study further. Consider carefully what your readers already know about the concept and how your essay might add to what they know.

Possible essay topics (Considering Ideas for Your Own Writing) follow each reading, and additional suggested concepts appear in the Invention section of the Guide to Writing Explanations of Concepts.

Writing Situations for Explaining Concepts

The writing situations that open this chapter demonstrate a wide range of academic and non-academic occasions for explaining concepts and educating readers about a subject. The situations involve a wide variety of sources of information, as well as a variety of writing strategies. Students can readily see why readers will need or want to know the information explained by each writer. They can also see how these writers purposefully seek to increase their readers' knowledge of and appreciation for a concept.

Practicing Explaining Concepts: A Collaborative Activity

This activity gives students their first classroom opportunity to explain a concept, in this case orally, briefly, and informally, to a small group of their peers. This activity should not take more than twenty minutes or so. The list of possible concepts is diverse enough to allow sufficient choice. Before they begin the activity, you could review with students the interactive nature of the exercise: following each mini-presentation, listeners share with the presenter something they learned about the concept. Part 2 requires students to distance themselves from explaining concepts in order to reflect on what they have learned about the genre. You may have to encourage them to move to part 2. Whole-class follow-up can refocus on the questions at the end of the activity; this discussion should be productive as students will already have examined these questions in their small groups.

A GUIDE TO READING ESSAYS EXPLAINING CONCEPTS

This section once again guides students through the reading of an essay on two levels: as readers and as prospective writers of explanatory pieces. For class activities to use in conjunction with this section, see Part 5 of this manual.

After a brief illustration of annotation, we provide students with a sample essay by David Quammen. Most students will find this essay to be thoroughly entertaining and informative. It shows that explanatory writing need not be dry or dull, and that scientific concepts can be truly fascinating. Although he is not a scientist, Quammen comes across as an expert on the subject: his expertise, like that of most students themselves, comes from research into secondary sources.

Reading for Meaning

From the headnote to the selection, students know that Quammen's readers are interested in, but not necessarily highly informed about, topics relating to nature and the environment. Here we invite students to comment briefly on what Quammen's essay has taught them about parthenogenesis; we then provide a number of suggestions to help them develop their responses. If time permits, you might give students a few minutes of class time to discuss their responses, either in small groups or as a class. Perhaps especially if you have students from a variety of academic backgrounds, discussion will help students to consider the writer's awareness of his readers and how much they are likely to know about his topic.

Reading like a Writer

In this section, we help students shift their focus from the content and purpose of the essay to the strategies the writer uses in achieving that purpose. These strategies include *devising a readable plan, using appropriate explanatory strategies, using sources responsibly,* and *engaging readers' interest.* In the critical reading and writing tasks that follow, each general strategy is broken down more specifically: *devising a readable plan* calls students' attention to the cueing strategies Quammen and other writers use to make their essays "reader-friendly," while *using appropriate explanatory strategies* offers students a brief catalog of the types of rhetorical strategies writers in this genre find most useful. The section called *using sources responsibly* helps students to understand that writers must select sources purposefully and integrate them smoothly into the explanation. Finally, *engaging readers' interest* invites students to consider the strategies writers of potentially dry explanations of abstract concepts use to attract and sustain reader interest. In each of these sections, we ask students to analyze Quammen's use of the strategy in question, and then to write briefly based on their analyses.

The Reading like a Writer section following the sample essay offers a comprehensive catalog of these strategies. Corresponding sections following each of the subsequent readings in the chapter focus closely on individual strategies; in each case, students are asked to analyze the writer's use of a particular strategy and to report the results of their analyses.

Devising a Readable Plan. This section encourages students to examine the organization of Quammen's essay, focusing in particular on the cueing devices he and other successful writers use in explaining concepts which are likely to be unfamiliar to their readers. To illustrate these cueing devices, we call attention to Quammen's use of a forecasting statement, topic sentences, transitions, and summaries; students will want to keep these in mind as they begin to plan their own essays. While these devices will be familiar to many of your students, you might find it useful to walk the class through part or all of Quammen's essay, making sure students can identify where and how Quammen uses each. In addition to focusing on transitions between paragraphs, students should be able to identify readily Quammen's brief use of forecasting (in paragraph 2, for instance) and summary.

Using Appropriate Writing Strategies. This exercise will be central in its importance to students both as readers and as writers of essays explaining concepts; the strategies discussed here will also figure prominently in upcoming chapters in this textbook. While this section introduces students to six specific strategies, it asks them to focus on any one in particular; thus, you can expect a range of responses to this task. Once again, although your students may be familiar with these strategies (many, for instance, will have written "comparison and contrast" essays in high school), they may need extra help in identifying precisely how each functions in Quammen's essay; the text provides paragraph references to help them get started. You might ask students who have focused on different strategies to share their written responses to this exercise briefly in class.

Using Sources Responsibly. One important decision students will need to make as they write their own essays is which source material to summarize, which to paraphrase and which to quote directly. This task asks students to consider Quammen's decision in paragraphs 11 and 16 to quote directly, and to note the smooth integration of the quotations into his own text. This exercise is particularly important, as many students fail to realize how vital the responsible use of sources will be to their success in writing at the college level.

Engaging Readers' Interest. Most students are likely to note that the first paragraph engages readers' curiosity even before Quammen names and defines the concept in the penultimate sentence. Paragraph 4, like paragraph 2, uses direct address to get readers' attention. Paragraphs 10 and 12 present the presumed advantages of parthenogenesis—both aphids and humans—in a witty way, which most students will appreciate but which some may find heavy-handed.

If your students have completed the assignment presented in Chapter 3: Observation, they will be quite familiar with the goal of at once entertaining and informing readers, and with the challenge of meting out potentially dry information carefully so that it does not lessen the more entertaining aspect of the essay. Students should be able to report in some detail on Quammen's handling of these challenges.

RESOURCES FOR TEACHING THE READINGS

This chapter has five readings, including the sample essay by David Quammen described in the preceding section. All of the selections explain a concept in a particular discipline or field. Perry Nodelman discusses "reading against texts," a concept from contemporary literary theory, while Deborah Tannen introduces a concept from linguistics: "markedness." Philip Elmer-DeWitt explains the concept of cyberspace; Mihaly Csikszentmilhalyi presents the psychological concept of the autotelic self. Our last selection is written by student Melissa McCool, who explains the concept of reincarnation.

The following material discusses each reading and offers advice on using the sections on reading for meaning and reading like a writer and the ideas for writing that follow each selection.

Perry Nodelman, **Reading against Texts**

As is the case with many essays explaining concepts, the concept introduced by Perry Nodelman calls into question previously held assumptions, in this case about the reading process.

Reading for Meaning

This section helps students extend and clarify their understanding of Nodelman's essay by explaining in their own words the concept of reading against the text, as well as the rather abstract subconcepts Nodelman uses in his own explanation. As usual, this section also invites students to explore their understanding of the concept by applying it to their own experience. If students do use their personal experience to make meaning from the text, you might invite them to do so orally in class; in this way, you can be sure that students who do use personal experience aren't moving too far away from the text itself, but that they return to the essay to make the connections between their experiences and the text explicit. Also, as usual with the first reading selection in each chapter, you might consider collecting students' writing for this activity, looking over it quickly, and reading some responses out loud to your class. This not only helps you monitor how well students are understanding the reading, but also allows you to provide examples of more or less successful responses to the activity.

Extending Meaning through Conversation. This activity, which follows each of the readings in the textbook, invites students to develop their understanding of each text more fully by discussing it with one or two other students. Especially after the first reading in each chapter, you might set aside some class time to discuss with the class as a group how the activity went and what meanings seemed to emerge from conversations.

Questioning to Understand and Remember (A Further Strategy for Reading for Meaning). Here, we refer students to Appendix 1, A Catalog of Critical Reading Strategies, where they will find this strategy demonstrated on a sample text. Students may be surprised at how useful this fairly simple strategy can be in helping them identify, understand, and remember the main points of difficult texts. You might point out that, in addition to helping students understand Nodelman's essay, this strategy will stand them in good stead throughout their academic careers.

By completing at least the first set of Reading for Meaning activities—those following the first reading in each chapter—together in class, with you leading and taking notes on the board, you can help students understand how these activities work, and remind them of the need to continue to reread and annotate each selection.

Reading like a Writer: Devising a Readable Plan

Students are likely to have noticed Nodelman's use of headings to indicate the division of information; here, we call their attention to his use of forecasting and of topic sentences as well. These strategies should be familiar to students from their reading of the essay by David

Quammen earlier in the chapter, but analyzing and writing briefly about Nodelman's use of these cueing devices will help students further appreciate their importance in this type of writing. As usual with the first reading in each chapter, you might lead students through the analysis section, showing them how to do a thorough analysis by annotating and taking notes. Once students have completed both the analysis and writing portions of this activity, you might either collect their responses and skim them briefly or have students share them orally in class, keeping a list on the board in either case of the cueing devices students locate in the essay.

Considering Ideas for Your Own Writing

This section steers students toward literary studies or composition theory and rhetoric as a possible source of topics for their own essays. Encourage students not only to choose a potential topic, but to consider the specific writing strategies they might use in explaining the concept they've chosen.

Deborah Tannen, **Marked Women**

Some of your students may already be familiar with Tannen's work through her best-selling books; nearly all students will find her essay on linguistic markedness and its implications for gender relations interesting and provocative.

Reading for Meaning

As usual, this section directs students back to the text, asking them to explore and clarify their understanding of the essay by paraphrasing Tannen's explanation of the concept of linguistic markedness. We give students several suggestions for developing their understanding of the concept; you may find that they are also interested in relating it to their own experiences as either men or women. Because students are likely to find Tannen's topic particularly provocative, you may find that you need to monitor their responses, either by collecting and skimming their writing or by having them share their thoughts in class, in order to make sure they are not straying too far from the text itself as they bring to bear their personal experiences.

Extending Meaning through Conversation. As we do following each reading selection, we encourage students here to explore the meaning of the essay in more detail by talking about it with one or two other students. Once again, because this particular essay raises some sensitive issues, you may find that you need to help students keep on track, perhaps by circulating among pairs or groups of students.

Reading like a Writer: Explaining through Illustration

This section calls students' attention to the importance of the use of concrete illustration in explaining abstract concepts. While students should be able to readily identify Tannen's use of illustration throughout the essay, we ask them to scrutinize two sections in particular, looking for ways in which the illustrations Tannen chooses allow her to draw larger generalizations about her topic. We also ask students to comment on whether they feel Tannen's explicit connection between the illustrations and the concept of markedness is helpful to them as readers. Some students are likely to find Tannen's interpretations somewhat off-putting; you might help students to speculate about what other options Tannen might have had in explaining her subject.

Considering Ideas for Your Own Writing

The fields of linguistics, gender studies, and sociology offer a wealth of topics for this essay. You might want to remind students that they needn't already be experts in any of these areas in order to write successful explanations of concepts, and that, in fact, writing on a topic about which they are just learning themselves may offer certain advantages, as students may be more likely to anticipate what their audience does or does not already know about the concept.

Philip Elmer-DeWitt, **Welcome to Cyberspace**

Students should find Elmer-DeWitt's essay interesting and accessible. Like David Quammen in his essay explaining the concept of parthenogenesis, which appears as the sample essay earlier in the chapter, Elmer-DeWitt presents potentially complex scientific information in—for the most part—layperson's terms.

Reading for Meaning

Where students were asked to explore their understanding of the previous essay by paraphrasing its main concept, here, we ask students to develop their understanding of the essay by summarizing. You may find this a useful opportunity to review for students the difference between these two reading (and writing) strategies, as well as to foreground once again the value of rereading and annotating. We also provide a number of other suggestions for further exploring the meaning of the essay as students write briefly about it.

Extending Meaning through Conversation. In this section, we once again invite students to explore their understanding of the piece in more depth by discussing it with other students. While Elmer-DeWitt's essay is perhaps less likely than the previous selection to raise sensitive social issues, students should still have much to say on the timely subject of cyberspace.

Reading like a Writer: Explaining through Comparison and Contrast

This section once again refers students to the list of writing strategies following the sample essay by David Quammen. Many students will find the use of comparison and contrast a valuable strategy as they embark on their own explanations of concepts; encourage them to complete this activity thoroughly and thoughtfully.

Compare. This activity, which follows one or two readings in each chapter, helps students focus on how different writers make use of the same set of strategies—in this case, comparison and contrast. We draw students' attention to two other readings in the chapter. You might want to encourage students to comment on why, where both Tannen and Csikszentmilhalyi rely primarily on contrast in explaining their topics, Elmer-DeWitt finds comparison a more useful strategy, as it helps his readers relate the abstract concept of cyberspace to their everyday experience with such objects as telephones.

Considering Ideas for Your Own Writing

You and your students may have already discovered, through previous activities following this reading selection, that students are likely to bring a wide variety of computer experience into the classroom. Once again, you might point out that, while the topics suggested here may seem ideal for computer science majors, students need not be experts in a particular field to write a successful essay explaining a topic. We also invite students to consider using strategies of comparison or contrast in explaining this type of topic.

Mihaly Csikszentmilhalyi, **The Autotelic Self**

Where previous selections in this chapter have explained concepts from linguistics, sociology, and the sciences, this selection deals with a concept from the field of psychology. As they read, students may find it useful to keep in mind that, like Tannen and (to some extent) Nodelman, Csikszentmilhalyi is a specialist writing for non-specialists, whereas Quammen, for instance, writes as a nonscientist about a scientific topic. Students might want to consider how this difference affects each writer's choice of strategies.

Reading for Meaning
As always in this section, students are asked to explore their understanding of the selection by responding to the content of the text; we give them a number of fairly specific suggestions for writing briefly about the selection. If your students have worked with Chapter 2: Autobiography in this text, they may find it particularly interesting to apply the author's concept of the autotelic self to one (or more) of the essays in that chapter.

Extending Meaning through Conversation. Especially in the case of a complex and unfamiliar topic such as the one dealt with in this essay, students are likely to find it useful to explore their understanding of the essay further by discussing it with one or two other students. Because students may have trouble getting started on this activity, we draw their attention to possible starting points; you might also allow them to relate the concept to their own experiences, as long as this does not lead them too far from the text itself.

Summarizing (A Further Strategy for Reading for Meaning). Students will already be familiar with summarizing from their work earlier in the chapter. Here, referring students to Appendix 1, A Catalog of Critical Reading Strategies, we give students the opportunity to practice the strategy, a critical reading technique they will find useful throughout their reading for this and other courses, in more detail. You might collect and quickly skim students' responses to this task to make sure they are on the right track.

Reading like a Writer: Explaining through Narrating a Process
In this section, as we do following each reading, we ask students to analyze and write briefly about a specific strategy used by the writer. If your students have worked with Chapter 2: Autobiography, they will already be familiar with narrative as a writing strategy; here, we aim to show them that this strategy can be as useful for writers of explanation as it is for autobiographers. You might introduce this activity by discussing in class the differences students are likely to see between the use of narrative in the two chapters. If your students have not read Chapter 2, you can still help them see that concepts often involve processes, and to pinpoint how two writers from the present chapter use narrative to describe these processes.

Considering Ideas for Your Own Writing
This section asks students to imagine writing about a concept from the field of psychology. Students are directed to basic references in their college libraries to get ideas for possible topics; as students will almost certainly be using the library regardless of the topics they ultimately choose, this activity is a good way of introducing them to reference sources.

Students are also invited to begin thinking about the specific writing strategies they will use in writing their own essays.

Melissa McCool, **Reincarnation**

As they read this essay by student Melissa McCool, students will notice her extensive and careful use of source material. You might encourage students to keep track of the proportion of the essay McCool devotes to sources in relation to her own commentary and analysis.

Reading for Meaning
As always, this section directs students back to the text of the essay, asking them to further their understanding of the concept of reincarnation by briefly summarizing McCool's explanation. In addition to once again highlighting the importance of rereading and annotating, this section invites students to develop their understanding of the concept by putting it in the context of their own prior knowledge and/or religious or spiritual beliefs.

Extending Meaning through Conversation. As students discuss their understanding of McCool's explanation of reincarnation in pairs or small groups, they will find that they gain a better sense of the meaning of the essay; we give them a number of suggestions for getting their discussions started. Especially if your students come from a variety of religious backgrounds and/or feel strongly about religious beliefs, you might find it useful to move from group to group, getting an idea how discussions are going and helping them stay focused on the meaning of McCool's essay.

Reading like a Writer: Using Sources
The careful use of sources is likely to be crucial to the success of each student's essay explaining a concept. This section helps students focus closely on McCool's use of sources. While some students may feel that McCool relies too heavily on published sources, they should be able to report that the source material she uses is generally integrated smoothly into her own text, and that her sources are carefully documented. Once again, you might remind students how important the skillful use of sources will be as they write at the college level.

Reading like a Writer: A Follow-up Activity
Once students have completed all of the Reading like a Writer activities in the chapter, they will have accumulated a substantial amount of written commentary about the reading selections. Don't overlook the usefulness of having them review their writings, selecting one to revise and extend by doing further analysis. Students would turn this expanded piece in with their essay packages, or include it in their end-of-course portfolios.

Considering Ideas for Your Own Writing
Religion and philosophy provide a wealth of topic possibilities for student writers. Students with strong religious beliefs, however, may need to be reminded that the purpose of this type of essay is *explanatory*, not persuasive or judgmental. We invite students to begin thinking not only about possible topics for their own essays, but also about their own use of sources.

THINKING ABOUT WHAT MAKES ESSAYS EXPLAINING CONCEPTS EFFECTIVE

As we do following the readings in each chapter, we ask students here to review and consolidate what they have learned about writing in a genre. Referring students back to the list of features—originally presented following the sample essay in the chapter introduction—of successful essays of this type, we invite students to choose the one essay from the chapter they feel to be most successful in achieving its purpose and fulfilling these features. Asking students to justify their choices helps them focus even more closely on the features of the genre.

A GUIDE TO WRITING ESSAYS EXPLAINING CONCEPTS

The guide leads students through the following steps:

Invention
> Listing Possible Concepts
> Choosing a Concept
> Analyzing Your Readers
> Finding Out More about Your Concept
>> Finding Information at the Library or on the Internet
>> Consulting an Expert
>> Focusing Your Research
>> An Example: Melissa McCool's Research Process
> Deciding Which Explanatory Strategies to Use
> Beginning
>> Learning More about Your Readers: A Collaborative Activity

Drafting
> Setting Goals
> Planning Your Draft

Reading a Draft Critically
> Reading for a First Impression
> Reading to Analyze
>> Using Appropriate Explanatory Strategies
>> Making the Draft Readable
>> Using Sources Responsibly
>> Engaging Readers

Revising
> Revising to Improve the Plan
> Revising the Explanatory Strategies
> Revising the Use of Sources
> Revising to Engage Readers

Reflecting on What You Have Learned about Writing Concept Explanations

A number of points in this composing process need special emphasis. The first is topic choice. Students may not already be experts on their topics, but their writing improves when they have a genuine curiosity about the subject. If a student neither knows nor cares much about a topic, good writing is unlikely to result.

When they first choose topics, students often think in broad terms, so you may need to help them narrow their topics to the point where they can produce explanatory essays of suitable depth.

The biggest challenge for writers of explanatory discourse is selecting and arranging the material in a way that will be clear and interesting to readers. Three steps in the composing process address this problem, and students should give them special attention: analyzing readers' knowledge, needs, and interest in the subject; deciding which explanatory strategies to use; and working out an organizational plan for the essay. Thinking carefully about these three steps—and then following through with a rich, exploratory period of invention writing—can help prevent students' essays from being dry, dull lists of information.

SPECIAL PROBLEMS OF THIS WRITING ASSIGNMENT. In our experience, the main problems that student writers have in this assignment fall into two categories: choosing an appropriate concept and then analyzing and synthesizing the available information on it. One solution to the problem of topic choice is to encourage students to write about subjects introduced in their other courses. In the invention section, some academic subjects are suggested. This assignment lends itself to cross-disciplinary writing.

If students lack confidence in writing about academic subjects, you might allow them to write about concepts drawn from extracurricular interests.

Students may ask you "What *is* a concept?" We propose an answer that paraphrases the dictionary definition: "a general idea derived from specific instances." Each reading in this chapter enables students to understand that many specific observations or instances lead to a concept and eventually to its particular name. It is interesting to consider that certain concepts can be intuited or fully recognized long before they are named.

Students will need your help in finding a focus for their essays. Many concepts are too big—too much is known about them—for a college essay, even one of substantial length. Consequently, you will likely want them to write about one *aspect* of the concept. Notice how the invention activities are set up to lead students first to a broad overview of the concept and then to a focus on one interesting aspect of it. Only with a focus in mind do they begin collecting research information.

For this assignment we approve both the concept-choice and the concept-focus. At both stages, we hear from each student and involve the whole class in evaluating topic choices and foci.

Presenting a technical concept in a way that is clear and interesting to a general audience challenges student writers. Students may become very concerned with the specificity and accuracy of the information they report, and, in the process, forget about engaging readers' interest. The purpose of the essay is to give readers interesting new knowledge. The greatest challenge of this assignment may not be the gathering and reporting of information, but the presenting of information in a way that allows readers to understand key terms, follow the organization of the essay, and remain interested in the topic. To succeed with this challenge, students will need to pay particular attention to the tone they use, the cues they provide for readers, and the defining and classifying strategies they use.

The assignment can also be a good way to introduce students to library research. The student who knows little about a concept but is curious about it can gather information from the library or by talking with experts. You may want to require some library research from all students. Both firsthand and secondary research strategies are covered in some detail in Appendix 2; you might want to refer students to this section of the text fairly early in the assignment.

Still another problem with this writing task is that student writers may allow themselves to be eclipsed by their sources. Their essays then become dumping grounds for unprocessed information, leaving readers to guess at its significance. Remind students that they must use sources judiciously, providing enough of their own commentary to help readers interpret the significance of source material. Referring students back to the reading selections in the chapter will help them to see how other writers have handled this challenge.

A related challenge is the problem of selecting and arranging the information, using the range of available strategies to achieve the purpose. Student writers often have difficulty designing a plan that will organize the information in a way readers will find interesting and comprehensible. A common problem is the essay that grasps at a simple, ready-made structure, often following the writer's process of discovering the information and ignoring what readers know or need to know about the subject. Again, analyzing the structure of the readings can show students how to avoid this problem.

PROMISING AND UNPROMISING TOPICS. The least problematic topics are those which are inherently concepts, such as existentialism or bilingualism. Students who choose such topics will probably have little difficulty finding and maintaining a conceptual focus. Other kinds of topics are no less promising, but they can be problematic in different ways:

- Concepts undergoing change: Some concepts may be treated from a static and historical perspective. For example, the concept of musical harmony can be considered to be stable and fixed. It might appear this way if one researched it only through reference sources and books. On the other hand, if one researched extensively in specialized periodicals, one could discover challenges by avant-garde musicians to traditional concepts of harmony. In this case, either treatment seems justified, depending on the purpose and audience. For other concepts, however, acknowledgment of recent developments and rapidly evolving trends seems vital to an accurate portrayal of the concept; notions of mental illness and democracy, for example, have undergone major transformations in recent years.

- Concepts about controversial issues: If your course will cover both explanatory writing (Chapter 5) and persuasive writing (Chapters 6–9), now is the time to begin discussing with your students the differences between the two genres. For this essay, we emphasize that their opinion should not be foregrounded or obviously stated, though it will certainly guide their selection and presentation of material. Students who have chosen a concept they have strong feelings about, for example, racism or recycling, will need your guidance to help them shape a balance, informative treatment of the topic, rather than a partisan, argumentative one.

- Concepts about personal life: Some students may be attracted to concepts for which personal experience will be their sole resource. Topics in this category from the Practicing Explaining Concepts: A Collaborative Activity section early in the chapter include romantic love, body image, and role model. Students may be more likely to choose these topics if the class has already done personal experience writing (Chapters 2 and 4). While this focus is certainly valid, you may choose to discourage it if other students will be developing concepts in ways that move beyond personal experience to involve published sources. Your guidance here can be supportive and enlightening: many students will be surprised to discover that library sources are available on such concepts as romance and body image, and that material from these sources may be interwoven with personal experience anecdotes to create an effective essay.

We recommend reviewing students' topic choices. They can't succeed at this assignment unless they've made appropriate topic choices.

Chapter 6 EVALUATION

This is a pivotal chapter in the book, the first that deals with argument. The preceding chapters introduced types of personal and explanatory discourse. In this chapter, students encounter discourse that makes and defends value judgments. Evaluation is one of the basic elements of argument, and students will need to recognize evaluative arguments in the remaining chapters of the book. In essays conjecturing about causes or speculating about effects, for example, writers judge the relative value of alternative explanations or predictions. Similarly, writers of proposals evaluate alternative solutions, and any piece of writing that advances an opinion is built on value judgments. Evaluation, then, is at the heart of any argument. In this chapter, students learn to recognize value judgments and to examine the standards on which they are based.

This chapter begins with a discussion of evaluations students make every day and suggests academic and other occasions for evaluative writing. The purpose here is to remind students that they already know something about evaluative discourse—when and why evaluations are written as well as by and to whom. This chapter builds on and refines what they already know.

The introduction also draws a distinction between expressions of taste and evaluations. Students could explore this distinction by defining terms such as *taste, preference,* and *judgment,* and by conjecturing about the different purposes of expressing, explaining, justifying, and convincing. The main point here is to help students classify evaluation as argumentative discourse.

WRITING ASSIGNMENT: Evaluation
This is the writing assignment that appears near the beginning of Chapter 6:

Write an essay, evaluating a particular subject. State your judgment clearly, and back it up with reasons and evidence. Describe the subject for readers unfamiliar with it, and give them a context for understanding it. Your principal aim is to convince readers that your judgment is informed and your reasons are based on generally accepted standards for judging this kind of subject.

For this general assignment, many specific topics are possible. Suggested topics (Considering Ideas for Your Own Writing) follow each reading, and there is a list of topic possibilities as part of the Invention section in the Guide to Writing an Evaluation.

Evaluative Writing Situations

The three writing situations early in the chapter illustrate a wide range of evaluations, academic and otherwise. The first two are clear negative evaluations, one academic and one on the job. Each demonstrates the characteristics mentioned in the writing assignment, presenting a definitive judgment, backing it up with sound reasons, and supporting these with specific evidence. The third situation, in which a college student evaluates colleges for his younger brother, does not highlight judgment quite as prominently; the writer narrows his choice to two colleges and then provides criteria by which his brother might make his own judgment. This example might be useful in introducing the role of comparison in evaluative writing.

Practicing Evaluation: A Collaborative Activity

This group activity is designed to engage students in the most basic and yet most difficult aspect of evaluative writing: choosing appropriate standards. Notice that the activity has two parts. First, students discuss the standards they would use for evaluating the kind of entertainment they have chosen and select the three they agree are most important. Then, they reflect on the process of choosing standards. The second part of the task will likely be new for them because few students—indeed few people other than experts in a field—think about the standards by which they judge things. Normally we just make judgments without thinking seriously about the values underlying our judgments. Through this group activity, you can lead students to recognize the importance of self-reflection and critical analysis. They will find the activity valuable in itself as well as for its rhetorical effectiveness.

If students have difficulty coming up with standards, you might advise them to think of a particular instance with which they are all familiar and to consider how they would judge that. The group activity asks them to arrive ultimately at a consensus about the two or three most important standards they might apply to a particular form of entertainment. But the process of consensus building often involves argument. They should also expect to disagree, and this activity will help them see how such disagreement can help them anticipate and handle the rhetorical situation in which they will be writing.

A GUIDE TO READING EVALUATIVE WRITING

This section once again leads students through the critical reading and writing strategies they will use throughout the chapter. For class activities to be used in conjunction with this section, see Part 5 of this manual.

Following a brief illustration of annotation, a sample essay by Amitai Etzioni clearly demonstrates the central features of evaluative writing: presenting the subject, asserting an overall judgment, giving reasons and supporting evidence, and establishing credibility. The Reading like a Writer section following the essay will break these down into specific strategies.

Reading for Meaning

As in each chapter, the first set of questions and suggestions following the sample essay are designed to help students focus closely on the text, exploring in writing their understanding of Etzioni's essay. We begin by asking students to summarize Etzioni's argument and identify his judgment of his topic. Students are also invited to reflect on their own work experience in relation to Etzioni's argument. This section, like the corresponding sections following each of the readings in the chapter, is likely to generate a wide range of responses as students find their own meanings in the text; students may need to be reminded that there is no "right" or "wrong" meaning.

Reading like a Writer

This section helps students shift their focus from the content of the essay to how the writer presents his evaluation—from reading exclusively as readers to reading as prospective writers. Students are introduced here to the major elements of evaluative writing: *presenting the subject, asserting an overall judgment, giving reasons and supporting evidence,* and *establishing credibility.* Through a series of brief critical reading and writing tasks, students focus on the strategies Etzioni, like other evaluative writers, uses to achieve each of these elements. Strategies for presenting the subject are discussed specifically, as are strategies for asserting a judgment. We then call attention to the important role of reasons and supporting evidence in presenting an evaluative argument; finally, we help students see that Etzioni establishes credibility both by projecting authority and by implying a bond of shared standards or values with his readers.

While the Reading like a Writer section following the sample essay presents a full range of strategies for evaluative writing, corresponding sections following each of the subsequent readings in the chapter will focus more narrowly on one or two strategies particularly appropriate to the analysis of each essay.

Presenting the Subject. Students will notice that Etzioni derives his information about his subject from a combination of sources, citing "studies" in his second paragraph, but also clearly relying largely on first- and secondhand observation of his subject. Students may point out that Etzioni's portrayal of the typical fast-food restaurant is rather extreme, conjuring up images of Orwellian automatons—hardly the image students are likely to have of themselves or their former selves and peers. Many students may be bothered by his tone; some will pinpoint the source of their discomfort in the fact that, regardless of his final exhortation to "go back to school," Etzioni is primarily writing not to the teenage "victims" of McDonald's but to their parents—and that, in fact, he seems undecided as to whether teenagers *are* in fact victims, or whether they're at best lazy and irresponsible, at worst criminals.

Asserting an Overall Judgment. Students should note that, while Etzioni's judgment is stated emphatically at the very beginning of the essay, it is restated in slightly different forms throughout the selection. For instance, at the end of paragraph 11, he aims his thesis specifically toward "minority youngsters." Students are also asked to consider whether Etzioni modifies his judgment at any point. You might guide students to see how acknowledging both good and bad qualities about a subject serves to make an evaluative argument more powerful.

Giving Reasons and Supporting Evidence. This task asks students to analyze and evaluate one of Etzioni's reasons for his judgment, along with the evidence he offers in support of that reason. Students are asked to consider the reason's appropriateness to Etzioni's overall argument, and then to judge the reliability of the supporting evidence. Once again, students may find that the three reasons from which the task asks them to choose—that fast-food jobs are too "routinized," that these jobs interfere with education, and that on-the-job supervision is inadequate or inappropriate—seem calculated to appeal not to teenagers or students, but to their parents. Students may also be critical of the evidence on which Etzioni draws to support these reasons. While the evidence of long hours and late closing times seem plausible in support of the second reason, the evidence in support of Etzioni's claims about routinization and supervision may strike students as being exaggerated, condescending, or both.

Establishing Credibility. This task asks students to examine the ways in which Etzioni invites readers' confidence in his judgment, and to evaluate the extent to which he is successful in maintaining his credibility. Students may note that Etzioni's authority derives from three areas: his own educational and professional background as a sociologist and researcher, the firsthand experience of his teenage sons, and his reference to various studies of the issue. Once again, students should note that, although Etzioni draws statistical material in support of his argument from these studies (two-thirds of American high schoolers work part time; minorities represent 21 percent of fast-food workers), he rejects the conclusions suggested in each study. Students may find that Etzioni's confidence in refuting these conclusions—presumably reached by experts—enhances their sense of his own authority. Also, as establishing credibility depends in large part on referring to standards or values with which readers will be able to identify, we encourage students to consider the values underlying Etzioni's judgment; most will recognize his invocation of the work ethic and self-reliance.

RESOURCES FOR TEACHING THE READINGS

The selections in this chapter offer evaluations in a range of fields including cinema, sports, literature, computer science, and the environment, offering students a sense of the broad scope of this genre. David Ansen's review of the movie *Quiz Show* is followed by Roger Angell's evaluation of the 1993 World Series; then comes Martha C. Nussbaum's essay on William Bennett's *Book of Virtues*. The pseudonymous Scorpia offers her evaluation of the computer game Menzoberranzan, followed by student Ilene Wolf's evaluation of an environmental magazine.

These essays demonstrate the essential characteristics of good evaluative writing. From them, students learn that writers of evaluations define their subjects clearly and provide readers with information about them; make value judgments about the subjects, base these judgments on appropriate standards, and support them with reasons and evidence. Students can also see that writers of reviews and other kinds of evaluative discourse must know a good deal about their subjects, but they often write for audiences who lack this knowledge. Writers therefore must find ways to inform their readers sufficiently so that they will be able to follow the argument.

The material that follows introduces each reading and offers advice for using the sections on reading for meaning and reading like a writer and the ideas for writing that follow each reading selection.

David Ansen, **When America Lost Its Innocence—Maybe**

This piece introduces a type of evaluation—the review—important within and outside the university. The film, released in 1994, is a powerful movie on an important subject that will be sure to elicit stimulating class discussion. Many of your students may have seen the movie; if not, you might consider showing it in class. Reading Ansen's evaluation after seeing and discussing the film will help students grasp the rhetorical situation in which the review was written; understanding the rhetorical situation will help them understand how evaluative writing, like all writing, is bound by its social context.

Reading for Meaning

This section helps students focus closely on the text, rereading and adding annotations as they develop their understanding. We ask students to write briefly as part of this activity; especially as this is the first reading selection in the chapter, you might want to collect their written responses and skim them quickly, not only to get a sense of how well they are understanding the reading, but also to read aloud a few of the more thoughtful responses.

Extending Meaning through Conversation. Once students have explored the meaning of each piece on their own, we ask them to share their insights with one or two other students in order to expand their understanding of the reading. Particularly following the first reading in each chapter, you might ask one student from each group to report briefly on a meaning, idea, or insight at which the group arrived during their discussion, a facet of the reading that extended the meanings each had come up with on his or her own. You could then lead a brief class discussion of how this group activity functions in the critical reading of the selections.

Reading like a Writer: Presenting the Subject

Before they begin this section, you might refer students back to the corresponding section on Presenting the Subject following the sample esay by Amitai Etzioni earlier in this chapter, where we point out that, in the act of naming and describing their subjects, writers often also indicate at least implicit value judgments. Here, students are asked to focus on the ways in which Ansen's very description of his subject suggests a certain judgment: the task of an evaluative writer is to both inform and convince, and the two are often combined.

Especially in the case of this first selection in the chapter, you could lead students through the Analyze section of this activity as a class, perhaps beginning by steering their attention toward the passage at the end of paragraph 5 beginning "It's about . . ." Students should be able to see how, in his description of the movie, Ansen incorporates what he feels to be its larger political messages. In leading students through the Analyze section, you can show them how to do a thorough analysis of a text, continuing to reread and annotate; once students have written their responses to this activity, you might invite them to share their writing in class.

Considering Ideas for Your Own Writing

This section asks students to consider writing movie reviews of their own. It invites them to rehearse the composing process by making the kinds of decisions they will need to make when they actually write their evaluative essays: choosing and presenting their topics and determining reasons for their judgments,

This is a challenging activity, one that you might want to support by taking class time to discuss their tentative decisions in small groups or with the whole class. You might consider grouping students according to current films they've seen and allow them to debate their evaluations.

Roger Angell, **Oh, What a Lovely War**

This selection moves away from the movie review to a type of evaluation perhaps equally familiar to many students: the sports review. Angell's evaluation of the 1993 World Series helps students to see that sportswriting need not be simply a play-by-play, statistics-filled report, but can actually make for lively and informative reading.

Reading for Meaning

Students are learning that perhaps the most important challenge facing the writer of an evaluation is to provide reasons for his or her judgment. We begin this activity by asking students to identify the reasons supporting Angell's positive judgment of the 1993 Series; in order to help students accomplish this part of the activity, you might need to remind them once again of the importance of rereading and annotating each text.

Extending Meaning through Conversation. Once again, we ask students to develop their understanding of the selection by discussing it with one or two other students. In this case, you may find that your students have a wide range of responses to sports-related topics, ranging from the completely uninterested to the fanatical. You can help them begin on common ground by calling their attention to our suggestion that they begin by focusing on Angell's seemingly oxymoronic title; you might further ensure that conversation continues to be fruitful by circulating among groups, offering suggestions and facilitating discussion.

Reading like a Writer: Asserting an Overall Judgment

This section should help students to see that although many writers of evaluation present their judgments clearly toward the beginning of their essays, others embed their judgments throughout the text, as Angell does. You may need to help students see that Angell's judgment of the 1993 Series is suggested at both the beginning and the the end of the first paragraph, and then developed at the beginnings of the third and fifth paragraphs. We call students' attention to the use of value terms; you might point out that these often appear in the form of adjectives, as in the case of Angell's characterization of the Series as "excessive and astounding."

Compare. This important activity, which follows one or two of the readings in each chapter, helps students see how different writers use the same strategies. In this case, we ask students to compare Angell's use of value terms to Etzioni's or Ansen's use of such terms. Students may note that Angell's terms, like those of many sportswriters, tend to be highly colorful (as in "grisly or glorious" in paragraph 1) if not hyperbolic. Once students have completed this activity, you might invite them to share their responses briefly in class.

Considering Ideas for Your Own Writing

Here, we invite students to consider evaluating a sports-related topic. Whether students think about evaluating an event, team, or sports figure, you may need to remind them that, in addition to establishing standards by which their potential readers are likely to judge such subjects, they will need to present concrete evidence of how their subject does or does not measure up to such standards.

Martha C. Nussbaum, **Divided We Stand**

Here we move from movie reviews and sportswriting to a third, and probably equally familiar, type of evaluation: the book review. Students are likely to find Nussbaum's essay particularly challenging, rich with references and sophisticated vocabulary, so you might plan on spending some extra class time to guide them through it.

Reading for Meaning

We ask students to begin by paraphrasing Nussbaum's judgment of Bennett's book; you might take a moment to remind students of the value of paraphrasing in making meaning from a text. Once students have completed the Reading for Meaning section, you could ask a few of them to share their responses in class, both as a way of encouraging discussion of the piece and as a way for you to monitor how well they are understanding this somewhat difficult reading.

Extending Meaning through Conversation. As students develop their understanding of this selection in conversation with one or two of their classmates, you may find that you need to supervise the pairs or groups fairly closely, answering questions about the text and helping students stay focused on Nussbaum's judgment. Once students have completed this activity, you could have one member of each group report briefly to the class on a meaning arrived at by the group that extended the meanings students had found separately.

Contextualizing (A Further Strategy for Reading for Meaning). Periodically throughout the text, at least once in each chapter, we refer students to the supplemental critical reading strategies presented in Appendix 1 of the text. In this case, we are inviting students to develop their understanding of the meaning of the reading selection in a very specific historical and political context. You might help them to get started with this activity by referring them to the headnote introducing the piece.

Reading like a Writer: Establishing Credibility

Students should have little trouble noting that Nussbaum is obviously well read; they should also appreciate that she brings not only her academic background but also her personal experience to bear on her evaluation of Bennett's book. This activity also draws students' attention to the crucial issue of *balance* in evaluations. You might take a few minutes of class time to preview this idea for students by asking them to consider whether, as readers, they would be more likely to be convinced, on the one hand, by a review that was either completely positive, acknowledging none of the weaknesses in its subject, or completely negative, acknowledging none of its subject's strong points, or, on the other hand, by a review that presented both the strengths and the weaknesses of its subject, and then made a thoughtful case for either a positive or a negative judgment.

Compare. As students continue to analyze and write about Nussbaum's piece, they will find it useful to compare it to other selections in the chapter. If students have trouble getting started on this activity, you might suggest that they compare Nussbaum's evaluation to the sample essay by Amitai Etzioni, perhaps approaching their comparison by commenting on

89

how much balance each writer achieves in what is basically a negative evaluation of his or her topic.

Considering Ideas for Your Own Writing

We do not personally wish to encourage moral evaluation, but students might learn how it differs from other standards of judgment by doing a brief moral evaluation of a poem or short short story you have copied for them and then doing another brief evaluation based on other standards.

Scorpia, **Beware of the Under Drow**

The inclusion of this selection in the textbook helps to remind students that evaluations are often highly specialized. While some of your students are very likely to be familiar with computer role-playing games, many are not; you might open a discussion of this piece by taking an informal survey of your class to see which students are familiar or unfamiliar with the subject, and then by asking them to be particularly aware of how this affects their understanding as they read the essay.

Reading for Meaning

As usual, we ask students to begin this activity by putting the writer's judgment in their own words. Most students will have no trouble recognizing that, although Scorpia acknowledges both strong and weak points in her subject, her overall judgment is negative, as expressed at the beginnings of paragraphs 7 and 19. As students proceed through this activity, remind them of the importance of rereading and annotating in making meaning from a text.

Extending Meaning through Conversation. If you have introduced this selection by asking which students are familiar with this type of computer game and which are not, you might try to arrange pairs or groups so that each includes at least one student who has some experience with the subject. Keep students focused on the essay itself by moving from group to group, calling students' attention to the selection as an example of evaluative writing.

Reading like a Writer: Giving Reasons

By now, students should understand that writers of evaluation need to offer specific reasons in support of their judgments. Once students identify what Scorpia sees as the one strength (the auto-mapping system) and the two major weaknesses of this game (that its setup is too linear and that it has programming problems), they should be able to analyze the reasons Scorpia offers in support of these assertions. Once students have completed this activity, you might invite a few of them to share their responses in class.

Considering Ideas for Your Own Writing

Computer-related topics offer a wealth of possibilities for students planning their own evaluative essays. You could remind students here that they will need to consider their audience carefully, deciding whether they are writing for readers who are novices, computer experts, or merely moderately computer-literate.

Ilene Wolf, Buzzworm: **The Superior Magazine**

As they read this final selection in this chapter, written by student Ilene Wolf, students should note her use of comparison and contrast, as well as her standards for judgment.

Reading for Meaning

This section asks students to focus closely on the text, clarifying their impressions of the magazine *Buzzworm*, as well as their understanding of Wolf's evaluation of her subject. Students should find this essay accessible and interesting, and should have little trouble commenting on its meaning.

<u>Extending Meaning through Conversation</u>. Here, as usual, we invite students to develop their understanding of the selection by discussing it with one or two other students. You may find that students are somewhat uncritically accepting of Wolf's views; our suggestions that they examine some of the assumptions underlying her evaluation should help students broaden their own and each others' perspectives.

Reading like a Writer: Supporting Reasons with Examples

This section highlights the role of specific examples in supporting evaluative arguments. Students will have little difficulty identifying Wolf's use of examples in support of her judgment. Students should also note that Wolf's essay revolves around her comparison and contrast of two magazines, *Buzzworm* and *Sierra*, and that her extensive use of specific examples from each help make her evaluation more convincing. Some students may point out that the element of contrast is missing in paragraph 4, perhaps weakening the effect of the specific examples cited in that paragraph.

Reading like a Writer: A Follow-up Activity

As students complete the Reading like a Writer activities in each chapter, they should review the considerable amount of writing they have generated in response to the reading selections. They may be surprised at how much they have learned about the genre. You might ask students to choose one piece of their own writing to revise and expand; they would turn this piece in with their final essay packages or with their end-of-course portfolios.

Considering Ideas for Your Own Writing

This section invites students to consider writing their own evaluations of written works, and to begin to consider the standards by which they would judge a magazine, newspaper, essay, story, poem, or book. Depending on your own assessment of the Wolf essay, you might wish to point out to students using it as a model that, though it is undeniably a good essay, it does not necessarily represent a pinnacle of achievement in student writing.

THINKING ABOUT WHAT MAKES EVALUATION EFFECTIVE

As in each chapter in the text, we ask students to reflect on the reading and writing they have done, reviewing and consolidating what they have learned about each genre. You can ensure that students get the most out of this activity by making sure they look back at the four basic features of evaluative writing (presenting the subject, asserting a judgment, giving reasons and supporting evidence, and establishing credibility) as they are presented in A Guide to Reading Evaluative Writing early in the chapter.

A GUIDE TO WRITING AN EVALUATION

The guide leads students through a composing process that follows these steps:

Invention
    Choosing a Subject
    Exploring Your Subject
    Analyzing Your Readers
        Learning More About Your Readers: A Collaborative Activity
    Considering Your Judgment
    Listing Reasons
    Finding Evidence to Support Your Reasons
    Drawing Comparisons
Drafting
    Setting Goals
    Planning Your Draft
    Beginning
    Avoiding Logical Fallacies
Reading a Draft Critically
    Reading for a First Impression
    Reading to Analyze
        Presentation of the Subject
        Statement of the Overall Judgment
        Supporting Reasons and Evidence
        Credibility
Revising
    Revising to Present the Subject
    Revising to Clarify the Overall Judgment
    Revising to Strengthen the Reasons and Evidence
Reflecting on What You Have Learned about Writing Evaluation

Topic choice is a crucial step for all students, and a difficult step for many. You might ask students to bring to class a list of possible subjects they might evaluate, and devote some class time to discussing these topics in small groups. Or you might ask the whole class to brainstorm a list of potential topics. By sharing potential topics with their classmates, students will discover which are of immediate interest to others. They will also get a sense of which subjects require extended description and what standards are generally applied to them. Other students' ideas will probably also inspire those who are having difficulty choosing a subject.

From studying the readings, students should grasp the importance of providing enough information about a subject to enable readers to follow an evaluative argument about it. Students also need to anticipate any prejudices in their readers they may have to overcome. Pairs of students might rehearse their arguments and refutations to counterarguments with each other. These dialogues should help students imagine how other readers might respond to their argument.

In setting goals, students should reconsider the larger rhetorical issues of purpose and audience before planning their organization. Often, inexperienced writers get stuck because they feel there is one right way to begin or to organize an essay. It is important for writers to view drafting more flexibly and to consider their decisions in terms appropriate to their particular aims and the needs of their readers.

SPECIAL PROBLEMS OF THIS WRITING ASSIGNMENT. This seems like a straightforward assignment: say whether you like or dislike something, and then say why. It can, nevertheless, go wrong in many ways the first time student writers try it. Students may not be willing to assert firm judgments, or they may not understand—even after the readings and Reading like a Writer activities in the text—that they are to make and defend by reasoned argument their own judgments. In addition, because they are unaccustomed to being held to the rhetorical requirements of a specific writing situation, student writers may overlook the requirement to describe the subject for readers who are unfamiliar with it. They may also unwittingly merge or blur their reasons because they lack confidence in them. Likewise, they may underestimate how well they grasp the standards for evaluating a particular subject or assume standards are generally shared when they are not.

These problems suggest that before you ask students to analyze each other's drafts, you may want to lead a class discussion of two or three drafts. During this discussion, you can insist firmly that the writers meet the rhetorical requirements of the assignment. Furthermore, the problems of the assignment make the evaluation a good choice for a double assignment in which you ask students immediately to do a second essay on a different subject. For the first essay, you could give them two or three choices of subjects, such as the same story or movie, and then they could choose their own subjects for the second essay.

Perhaps the biggest problem of all arises when students risk doing this assignment from memory. A subject to be evaluated needs to be studied and restudied before and during invention and drafting. Students should not evaluate a movie unless they can see it two or three times, nor should they evaluate a novel unless they have time to reread it. Likewise, they should not evaluate a consumer product unless they are currently using it.

Evaluation essays are so well understood, their features so well established, that we can hold students to a standard of performance that may startle them in its fullness and precision.

PROMISING AND UNPROMISING TOPICS. The first step in the Invention section for this chapter asks students to list possible subjects for their evaluation essays. We provide a list of general topic areas to get students started, a list drawn from our own experience with successful and unsuccessful topics. As you can see, we suggest a range of possible topic areas—including media, arts, literature, education, government, campus, and leisure—that extends far beyond the few examples we have provided through the chapter readings. Though each item on this list is a potentially fruitful source of ideas for evaluation topics, each item nevertheless poses its own peculiar problems and dangers. You may wish to narrow down this list for your own students and preclude certain topics.

Our experience has shown us that the most successful essays are those that draw heavily on an individual student's interest or expertise. Students who express an avid interest in skateboarding often write fine essays on skateboard magazines, skateboard parks, or skateboard models. Not only are they familiar with the standards that are usually applied to that field of interest, but they have also been able to make comparisons and contrasts to related subjects (for example, other skateboard magazines, parks, or models) with some ease. The topics themselves can be quite ambitious—we have had some remarkable essays evaluating such things as strategic nuclear arms treaties and UAW contracts—but they are successful only when the student has either a fair amount of expertise or a deep interest in the topic itself. You should, by all means, encourage your students to draw on their own strengths, knowledge base, and interests when choosing topics.

By and large, students have the least amount of difficulty evaluating consumer products. Standards are fairly easy to establish, the essays themselves are not difficult to structure and control, and comparisons can often be found in personal experience or a recent issue of *Consumer Reports*. Still, there are some significant dangers in permitting students to write essays of this type. Students all too often have a tendency to slip into a kind of Madison Avenue prose, uncritically touting the virtues of their chosen product and making claims of "comfort" or "style" that are unsupported by any kind of evidence. Trivial criteria and matters of personal taste can run rampant in evaluations of consumer products, and students should be warned about such flaws in advance. We discourage essays about consumer products, and some instructors forbid them.

Evaluations of people are also likely to be successful as long as students are careful to establish clear and reasonable standards and show some awareness that no one is perfect (or perfectly bad). Generally speaking, the worst topic choices are people with whom the writer is too emotionally involved. Teachers are a popular topic for evaluation, but watch out for essays that lapse into simple narratives or make claims ("He was a friend to his students as well as a teacher . . .") without any kind of support.

We are also wary of topics that try to evaluate abstract concepts such as "friendship" or "greed." Though it is theoretically possible to write such evaluations, it is extremely difficult to decide upon appropriate standards. Even more difficult is determining the kind of evidence that might be brought to bear on such a topic. Our students have occasionally written credible essays evaluating "capitalism" or "democracy," but the key to their success seems to lie in the fact that these concepts can be illustrated by referring to specific examples (for example, the United States, Great Britain). Evaluations of philosophical abstractions almost always lead to more problems than rewards.

Easily the most promising topics are discrete, tangible objects or events that can be revisited and analyzed—a story or novel, movie, musical recording, concert, play performance, essay in this book, magazine, restaurant, college program or service. Before drafting, students can revisit the subject, taking careful notes. They can revisit once again before revising, keeping the subject *present* throughout the writing process. Such immediate presence of the subjects makes it easier for students to amass the evidence or examples required in a strong evaluation essay.

Chapter 7 SPECULATION ABOUT CAUSES OR EFFECTS

This is the second in a series of three closely related chapters dealing with important types of argument or persuasion. In Chapter 6, students learned about the basic building block of argument—value judgment. This chapter introduces them to causal argument—argument about the influence of one thing on another when the nature of this influence is not clear. Since this kind of argumentation concerns explanation and prediction, it is a crucial mode of inquiry and writing in the sciences and social sciences.

Arguments about causes or effects in turn become important elements in proposals, the topic of Chapter 8, as writers use these arguments to explain what has caused a problem, what its effects will be if no solution is found, and what effects each possible solution is likely to have.

In discussing the introduction to this chapter, you should help students see that the focus is on analysis and argument—on conjecture and speculation about possible causes or effects of events, trends, or phenomena. The selections do not simply summarize uncritically others' proposed causes or effects but argue inventively for the writers' own proposed causes or effects for a subject that cannot presently (or perhaps ever) be explained definitively or scientifically. The students' essays will also present such speculative arguments. Students may very well research other proposed causes or effects for their topic, but not in order to collect and summarize these causes or effects in the essay. Instead, they will weigh and evaluate each cause or effect, analyzing it in light of their understanding of the topic and the argument they want to make. Students must argue for their preferred causes or effects, whether they discovered them on their own or turned them up in their research.

WRITING ASSIGNMENT: Speculating about Causes or Effects

Here is the writing assignment that appears near the beginning of Chapter 7:

Choose a subject that invites you to speculate about its causes or effects—why it might have happened or what its effects may be. Write an essay, arguing for your proposed causes or effects. Essays about causes look to the past to ponder why something happened, whereas essays about effects guess what is likely to happen in the future. Whether you are writing an essay about causes or effects, you need to do two things: (1) establish the existence and significance of the subject (an event, a phenomenon, or a trend) and (2) convince readers that the causes or effects you propose are plausible.

This writing assignment is both challenging and satisfying for students. It helps them develop their powers of creativity as they speculate about possible causes or effects, their powers of judgment as they weigh the possibilities and choose the most plausible ones, and their powers of reasoning as they devise an argumentative strategy to present their conclusions to readers. The assignment is presented in generic terms, and possible topics are listed following each reading (Considering Ideas for Your Own Writing) and in the Invention section of the Guide to Writing. You may wish to limit the range of possible topics (see Special Problems of this Writing Assignment, below).

Cause or Effect Writing Situations

The three writing situations presented early in the chapter demonstrate that writers analyze and explain the causes and effects of events, phenomena, and trends in both academic and non-academic settings. The three situations also illustrate two important decisions students will make as they begin to consider writing their own essays: first, whether to write about causes or effects, and second, whether to write about events, phenomena, or trends. The first writing situation examines the causes of a phenomenon (which students may note might also have been treated as a trend); the second speculates about causes of a trend, and the third analyzes the effects of a subject that could be treated as either phenomenon or trend. These situations will inform students about the essay they will be writing, especially if you discuss the situations with them, emphasizing both the particular decisions the writers had to make and the unique features of this kind of writing.

Practicing Speculation about Causes or Effects: A Collaborative Activity

This activity is designed to engage students in making the kinds of decisions they will make as writers about causes or effects. In the first part of the activity, students are asked to decide as a group on an event, a phenomenon, or a trend, and then to speculate briefly about its causes or effects. In the second part of the activity, students are asked to reflect on and discuss the process of cause-and-effect speculation. Students may need help making the shift between the first and second parts of the activity.

A GUIDE TO READING SPECULATION ABOUT CAUSES OR EFFECTS

This section leads students through the critical reading and writing strategies they will use throughout the chapter. For class activities to be used in conjunction with this section, see Part 5 of this manual.

The sample essay provided in this section, following a brief illustration of annotation, clearly demonstrates the central features of writing about causes or effects: presenting the subject, making a cause or effect argument, handling objections and alternative causes or effects, and establishing credibility. The Reading like a Writer section following the essay will break these down into more specific strategies.

Stephen King's essay on the phenomenon of the appeal of horror movies has the advantages of a quick pace and a familiar topic—nearly everyone has squirmed through at least one horror film. Because students' attitudes toward horror movies are likely to vary from repulsion to indifference to the "craving" noted by King, this essay can introduce a discussion of how different readers may react to the same argument. King's essay also illustrates how moving from obvious causes to deeper or "hidden" causes is a convincing argumentative strategy, and how an expressive personal voice is appropriate in some argumentative writing situations.

Reading for Meaning

As usual, this section asks for students' general reactions to the content of the selection, inviting them to explore their understanding of and response to Stephen King's essay. Students are invited to speculate about King's assumptions regarding his audience, and to delve further into some of the issues raised in King's argument. You might use students' responses to this section as the basis for class discussion; the section is designed to stimulate students' interest in the reading and to increase the likelihood that they will want to analyze it closely.

Reading like a Writer

Here, students move from examining the content or ideas in the essay to analyzing the features of this type of writing and the specific strategies used by the writer. This work directly anticipates the thinking they will do as they read the other selections in the chapter and as they plan and draft their own essays. This section introduces students to the major elements of writing about causes and effects: *presenting the subject, making a cause or effect argument, handling objections and alternative causes or effects,* and *establishing credibility.* Students will examine how King establishes the existence and significance of his subject; they will also focus on King's causal argument: the ways in which he proposes possible causes, constructs a plausible argument, and handles objections and alternative explanations. Finally, students will examine how—or whether—King establishes credibility by gaining the confidence and respect of his readers.

The Reading like a Writer section following the sample essay presents a full range of strategies for writing about causes or effects. Corresponding sections following each of the subsequent reading selections in the chapter will focus more closely on one or two strategies particularly appropriate to the analysis of each essay. You may want to remind students that, while there are technically no "right" or "wrong" responses to this section, students are accountable for the depth and precision of their engagement with specific aspects of the text.

Presenting the Subject. Students will notice that King presents his subject as a phenomenon, rather than as an event or a trend. This is a good opportunity to discuss how presenting the subject may be weighted somewhat differently depending on whether the subject is an event, a phenomenon, or a trend: in general, establishing the existence of an event or a phenomenon is relatively simple, while suggesting its significance may be somewhat more difficult; in the case of a trend, students will be challenged both to establish the existence of a trend and its significance. Students should note that King seems to assume that the existence of his phenomenon is a foregone conclusion, and that he suggests its significance in part through his claim that all humans share a kind of generic insanity, and that horror movies provide a safety release valve that is relatively harmless compared with the alternatives King implies in his mention of serial murderers and psychopaths.

Making a Cause or Effect Argument. Students will note first of all that King focuses on the causes rather than the effects of the phenomenon in question; they should also note that he proposes three main causes for the popularity of horror movies, ranging from (1) the "simple and obvious" fact that such movies allow viewers to prove to others—and to themselves—that they "are not afraid," to (2) the idea that horror movies help maintain our sense of the normal, to (3) the claim that these movies provide a specific type of "fun." While some students may find King's second proposed cause—that even the most extreme horror films are perversely reassuring—the most sophisticated and intriguing, they will note that King's discussion glosses over this cause in favor of his third and final proposed cause. His rather provocative thesis that the "fun" of horror movies functions as a necessary antidote to our shared insanity is foreshadowed in his first paragraph. In expanding on a seemingly obvious cause, "having fun," King develops his proposed cause, a hidden cause with deeper implications: We go to horror movies, he argues, to at once exercise and control emotions that might be harmful to society if released. It is worth noting that, although King's essay focuses primarily on *causes*, his proposed *cause* for the popularity of horror movies is based on the psychological *effect* of the movies themselves.

As students continue to analyze and write briefly about King's argument, we invite them to examine its plausibility, focusing on his use of analogy. In particular, students are asked to analyze very closely and write briefly about his analogy between viewing horror movies and riding roller coasters. Students are then encouraged to extend this analysis to King's analogies of horror films to football games and "sick jokes."

97

Handling Objections and Alternative Causes or Effects. In a sense, King's entire essay is planned to refute objections: its argumentative stance is clear from the first sentence. But it is not easy to pick out specific points at which King refutes a specific objection or counterargument. The objection most likely to occur to a student reader is this: "I enjoy horror movies, but I don't think I'm sick or insane." King anticipates this objection by asserting that "sanity" is, in fact, "a matter of degree." Students should also note that the "alternative explanations" King presents are not seen in opposition to his proposed main cause, and that King acknowledges and accommodates these alternatives.

Students are asked to comment in writing on King's handling of the objection implied in the rhetorical question "why bother?" (paragraph 13); they are also invited to pose other objections or questions. For instance, some students may note that King's somewhat glib treatment avoids the issue of the psychological and emotional effects of exposure to violence, whether real or cinematic.

Establishing Credibility. Students should recall from the evaluation assignment in Chapter 6 that writers of evaluations establish credibility by projecting authority and by establishing, or at least suggesting, a sense of shared values with their readers; and they should note that King's essay follows the same basic pattern. Since King is a well-known writer of horror novels, several of which have been made into movies, the reader is clearly expected to consider him an authoritative source. Students may or may not find this authority convincing on its own. They may ask why King's argument makes no reference to the large body of psychological or social science research on this subject; some may suggest that, given King's audience, such reference is neither necessary nor appropriate.

King attempts to build a bond with readers by linking his observations about human behavior to common actions most people have experienced or witnessed: "We've all known people who talk to themselves," we've all heard "sick jokes," most of us have experienced emotions that might be called "uncivilized. Recognition of these shared experiences, reflected in King's use of the first-person plural pronouns *we* and *us*, helps readers to accept King's credibility in presenting his argument.

Although King's conversational tone and familiar style seem engaging and believable for many readers, students may challenge King's authority on a number of points: He is not an expert in psychology or social science, nor does he quote any such expert; he does not unequivocally refute objections and alternative causes; his own proposed cause is highly speculative. Astute readers may also want to examine the possible connections between the fact that King's audience is the readers of *Playboy* and the fact that both the victims and the much-tried "survivors" of most horror movies tend to be young women.

RESOURCES FOR TEACHING THE READINGS

The readings in this chapter cover a range of events, phenomena, and trends. The sample essay by Stephen King critically examines the causes of the phenomenal popularity of horror movies. The four following essays also deal with social issues in the form of either phenomena or trends: Natalie Angier speculates about the causes of a trend of increased intolerance toward "boyish" behavior, while Andrew Greeley examines the causes of the phenomenon of Catholics remaining faithful to the Catholic church. Jonathan Kozol writes about the effects of the phenomenon of illiteracy in America, and Steven Waldman explores the effects of the trend toward a proliferation of choice. Student writer Reese Mason speculates about the causes of an "event": the decision by college basketball star Hank Gathers to risk his life by continuing to compete after a diagnosis of heart trouble.

These readings represent a range of different approaches to speculating about the causes or effects of things that have happened, are happening now, or may happen in the future. Across this range, students can identify the basic features of argumentative discourse in each of the essays: a clear definition and demonstration of the event, trend, or phenomenon; speculation about its causes or effects; and a consideration of alternative causes or effects—all presented to readers reasonably and authoritatively.

The material that follows introduces each reading and explores the possibilities in the sections on reading for meaning and reading like a writer and the ideas for writing that follow each reading.

Natalie Angier, **Intolerance of Boyish Behavior**

With this essay, we move from speculation about the causes of a phenomenon, as in Stephen King's piece, to an examination of the causes of a trend. You will need to make sure that students understand that a trend, unlike a phenomenon, is something that changes over time.

Reading for Meaning

This section asks students to reread the text closely, beginning by concentrating on Angier's presentation of the trend. For this first reading in the chapter, we suggest that you lead students through this activity as a class, making notes on the board as students explore the meaning of the text.

Extending Meaning through Conversation. Once you have explored the meaning of the text as a class, students can further develop their understanding of the piece by discussing it with one or two classmates. You may find that male and female students respond to this selection differently; be sure to invite them to explore these differences as a valuable way of making meaning from the text. Once students have completed this activity, you could set aside some class time to discuss how it went and what meanings were developed through group conversation.

Reading like a Writer: Handling Objections

Anticipating the concerns and objections of readers is a fundamental component of all argumentative writing; here, we help students to focus on this important aspect of writing about causes and effects. We draw students' attention to specific paragraphs in which Angier seems to respond to possible questions on the part of her readers. As students analyze and write about the ways in which Angier handles potential objections, they should begin considering how they will respond to readers' concerns in their own essays. Once again, for this first reading selection in the chapter, you could guide students through the analysis portion of the activity as a class, and then allow them to write briefly on their own before asking them to share their observations with the class.

Considering Ideas for Your Own Writing

Here, we ask students to consider speculating about trends in group behavior, a rich source of topic ideas for this assignment. This section invites students to practice the two main strategies they'll need to use if they decide to write about the causes of a trend: First, they will need to establish the existence of the trend (a crucial step that poses a real challenge for beginning writers); then they will propose a possible cause (or causes) of the trend. You might ask students to discuss their own experiences or observations in groups of three or four, and then open up the discussion to include the entire class, perhaps listing proposed possible causes on the board.

Andrew M. Greeley, **Why Do Catholics Stay in the Church? Because of the Stories**

Whatever your students' religious orientations, they are likely to enjoy Greeley's somewhat surprising explanation of the phenomenon of the faithfulness of Catholics to their church.

Reading for Meaning

We ask students to begin exploring the meaning of Greeley's essay by examining his audience and purpose, rereading and annotating in order to develop their understanding of the piece. We also ask students to refer to their own experience in making meaning from this piece; as religion is often a challenging topic for students to discuss objectively, you may want to handle this part of the activity as a class discussion, inviting students to share their opinions orally. In this way, you can help students make explicit connections between their experiences and the text, ensuring that students who are using their own experience to make meaning from the reading are not moving entirely away from the essay itself.

Extending Meaning through Conversation. As in each assignment in this textbook, we ask students to extend the meanings they develop on their own by discussing the reading selection with one or two classmates. To help students keep on track, you might want to move from group to group, offering suggestions and drawing their attention back to the text itself.

Recognizing the Emotional Appeal of an Argument (A Further Strategy for Reading for Meaning). Periodically throughout the text, we refer students to one of the supplemental critical reading strategies outlined in the first appendix. In this case, we ask students to examine the emotional appeal of Greeley's essay, commenting on whether they feel manipulated by his argument. Once they have written a few sentences, you could ask them to share their responses to this activity either in small groups or as a class; because some students are likely to feel strongly about religious topics, you may find that you need to guide their discussion.

Reading like a Writer: Making a Causal Argument through Examples

In this section, we guide students through a careful analysis of Greeley's argument. Before students start this activity, take the opportunity to remind them of the importance of close rereading and annotating in learning about the strategies different writers use. Once students have completed their analyses and written briefly in response to this activity, you could have them share their responses orally in class, keeping a list on the board of the examples students have identified in Greeley's essay.

Considering Ideas for Your Own Writing

Where we invited students to consider analyzing a trend in group behavior following the previous selection, here we ask them to think about examining the causes of a phenomenon in group behavior. If some of your students do choose to write about religious phenomena (or trends, for that matter), you may need to stress the importance of maintaining an appearance of objectivity, avoiding proselytizing.

Jonathan Kozol, **The Human Cost of an Illiterate Society**

The essays by King, Angier, and Greeley all examine causes. This essay by Kozol is the first of the readings that looks at effects—in this case, of a phenomenon. Kozol demonstrates the problem of illiteracy in the United States and explains the significance of illiteracy for individuals and for the nation, arguing that it is a moral problem that challenges the notion of democracy in America.

Reading for Meaning

This section directs the students back to the text, asking them to explore their understanding of Kozol's argument. Students are asked to focus specifically on Kozol's use of examples, and invited to comment on the persuasiveness of his argument. Once students have written briefly in response to our suggestions, you might ask a few students to share their writing orally in class as a way of generating discussion of the meaning of the piece.

Extending Meaning through Conversation. As students discuss the meanings they have found in Kozol's essay with one or two classmates, they may find that they have different understandings of the text. Students who have had difficulty with reading themselves, for instance, may find Kozol's argument especially compelling, as they are more easily able to empathize with Kozol's subject.

Reading like a Writer: Making an Effects Argument by Organizing and Sequencing Effects

Kozol mentions at least twenty results of illiteracy, but students will probably come up with varying numbers, because some of the results are clustered together. The point is not for students to determine the exact number of results, but to see that there are many, and that they may be interrelated and interdependent. Students may describe the effect of the enumeration as impressive—even overwhelming. Some may feel that Kozol gives more results than necessary to make his point; others may argue that readers need this comprehensive survey of everyday information most people take for granted, but which is beyond the reach of the illiterate, before they can appreciate the magnitude and seriousness of the problem. Once students have written brief evaluations of Kozol's presentation of possible effects, you might have them share their responses in small groups or with the class as a whole.

Considering Ideas for Your Own Writing

These writing ideas ask students to speculate on the effects of a social problem or a controversial decision made by community or college leaders. A key element in each assignment is students' personal involvement in the problem or decision. You might remind students of the effect of Kozol's involvement in the illiteracy problem on the tone of his essay;

you might also remind them that the writing suggestions call for argument, not just guesswork. Students will probably be able to point to present effects of the problem or decision as well as future ones.

Steven Waldman, **The Tyranny of Choice**

Waldman's humor and irony stand in strong contrast to the serious appeals of Kozol in the preceding selection in this chapter. Waldman catalogs the less than positive effects of the trend toward more and more choices. The introductory note to the selection asks students to consider briefly their own experience with making choices before reading Waldman's essay.

Reading for Meaning

This section asks students once again to connect their ideas directly to the essay, beginning by identifying and commenting on the effects they feel to be most convincing in Waldman's essay. Further suggestions invite students to focus closely on specific aspects of the text; once students have completed this activity, you could have them share their responses in class as a way of facilitating discussion of the piece.

Extending Meaning through Conversation. You might help students get started in their small-group discussions of this essay by suggesting that each student offer an example from his or her own experience of facing many choices. Be sure, however, that their conversations return to the essay itself, making explicit connections between the text and students' own experience.

Reading like a Writer: Presenting the Subject by Establishing the Trend

Like all writers speculating about the causes or effects of a trend, Waldman must first convince his readers that such a trend actually exists, and is not an ongoing phenomenon, an isolated event, or a superficial fad. This task asks students to analyze and write briefly about Waldman's presentation of the trend. Students should note that Waldman employs an effective combination of statistical material, citation of an authority, and personal anecdote in establishing the existence of the trend. You might ask students to consider the effect on Waldman's argument if he had relied solely either on statistics and authorities or on personal anecdotes.

Considering Ideas for Your Own Writing

Although Waldman's essay is somewhat humorous in tone, this section invites students to think seriously about such issues as commitment and political alienation. This is another good opportunity to discuss the differences between trends and phenomena, for instance, you might point out that political alienation could be treated either as an ongoing phenomenon or as a trend on the increase in our century. Students could also focus on either the causes or the effects of either the phenomenon or the trend. They need to see that these decisions, usually made early in the writing process, will have a significant effect on the overall approach they take to their own essays.

Reese Mason, **Basketball and the Urban Poor**

While Mason's title suggests that he might be writing about either a phenomenon or a trend, his essay actually addresses what might be called an event: the decision by basketball star Hank Gathers to continue to play after a medical diagnosis of heart problems, and Gathers's subsequent on-court death.

If your students have done or will do the reflection essay assignment presented in Chapter 4, you might point out that Mason's essay resembles a reflective essay in that it uses a particular "occasion" as a starting point.

Reading for Meaning

This section directs students back to the text, asking them to begin by identifying the causes the writer proposes. Students are also invited to examine their own reasons for attending college, as well as their own conceptions of the American Dream; these suggestions should provide a useful basis for class discussion, as well as for the following activity.

Extending Meaning through Conversation. As usual, we ask students to expand on the meanings they have made from the text on their own by discussing the essay with one or two other students. As the Reading for Meaning suggestions imply, students will very likely find their personal experience useful in making meaning from this particular text; you might circulate among groups to make sure conversations do not move entirely away from the essay itself.

Reading like a Writer: Establishing Credibility

Students will have little trouble understanding the importance of credibility in an argument essay. We ask the students to reread and annotate Mason's essay, identifying the methods by which Mason attempts to establish his own credibility and commenting on the success of these methods. Some students will find Mason's argument more or less credible than others; some, for instance, may be put off by Mason's use of generalizations and his evocation of the familiar—almost cliché—scenario of young African-American men pulling themselves up out of the inner cities by their Nike laces. Other students will not have even recognized this aspect of Mason's essay, or may not see it as a weakness.

Compare. As we do following one or two reading selections in each chapter, we ask students to develop their analyses of a piece by comparing it with another essay in the same chapter. In this case, we ask students to reread and annotate for Mason's and one other writer's attempts to establish credibility. You might help students get started by asking them whether Mason's use of the first person adds to or detracts from their sense of his credibility, and then asking them to consider the use of the first person by one of the other writers in the chapter (King, Greeley, or Waldman).

Reading like a Writer: A Follow-up Activity

As students complete this last Reading like a Writer activity in the chapter, they will have generated a substantial amount of writing in response to the selections in the text. To help them review and consolidate what they have learned about writing in this genre, we suggest that you have them choose one of their Reading like a Writer responses to revise and extend by doing further analysis. Students would turn this piece in with their final essay packages or in their end-of-course portfolios.

Considering Ideas for Your Own Writing

This section invites students to consider writing about phenomena, trends, or events in sports. You might need to remind students that, if they choose to examine a *trend* in sports, their first task will be to establish that the trend exists.

THINKING ABOUT WHAT MAKES SPECULATION ABOUT CAUSES OR EFFECTS EFFECTIVE

In this section, which follows the reading selections in each chapter, we remind students of the basic features—originally listed following the sample essay—of successful writing in each genre. By selecting the one essay from the chapter they feel to be the most effective, rereading and annotating it, and finally justifying their choices of essay, students develop and consolidate what they have learned about each type of writing. This activity helps students focus closely on the features of the genre as they embark on their own essays.

A GUIDE TO WRITING SPECULATION ABOUT CAUSES OR EFFECTS

The guide leads students through a composing process that follows these steps:

Invention
> Choosing a Subject
> Exploring Your Subject
> Considering Causes or Effects
> Researching Your Subject
> Analyzing Your Readers
>> Learning More about Your Readers: A Collaborative Activity
> Rehearsing Your Argument

Drafting
> Setting Goals
> Planning Your Draft
> Avoiding Logical Fallacies

Reading a Draft Critically
> Reading for a First Impression
> Reading to Analyze
>> Presenting the Subject
>> Making a Cause or Effect Argument
>> Handling Objections and Alternative Causes or Effects
>> Establishing Credibility

Revising
> Revising to Improve the Presentation of Your Subject
> Revising to Strengthen Your Cause or Effect Argument
> Revising to Improve Your Handling of Objections and Alternative Causes or Effects
> Revising to Enhance Your Credibility

Reflecting on What You Have Learned about Writing Essays Speculating about Causes or Effects

Students often complain of difficulty finding a topic, so the text lists some areas where they can look. You might help them by adding some local examples to the list of possibilities.

Some students have trouble understanding the terms *trend* and *phenomenon*. Perhaps the simplest way to define and distinguish these terms would be to say that a trend is a changing pattern of human behavior, while a phenomenon is a pattern that remains constant. Perennial traditions and persistent problems are phenomena; shifts in the pattern of human behavior, and problems that are improving or deteriorating, are trends. If your students find this distinction too subtle, illustrate it by discussing with them the difference between the causes of a longstanding local problem and the causes of a sudden worsening of this problem. Different reasons are needed to explain the changing situation.

Some students also have difficulty distinguishing between a trend and a fad. A trend has some momentum and staying power, and reflects significant changes in behavior or circumstances. Fads may be widespread, but they tend to be short-lived and whimsical—changes in fashion, for instance, caused simply by the human desire for novelty.

When students reach the stage of considering causes or effects, they may need some guidance to distinguish causes from effects, and to distinguish various kinds of causes and effects from each other. Background causes precede and prepare indirectly for an event or a trend; immediate causes trigger it; and perpetuating causes sustain a trend or phenomenon. If they are writing an analysis of effects, students should consider immediate, long-term, and indirect effects of their event, trend, or phenomenon. If it has been around for some time, they may also be able to consider past effects. Ask students to work out the relationships among their causes or effects. For instance, are any of the causes connected? Are there chains of causes to be traced? Which are the most influential causes?

It might be a good idea to assign the invention process up to this point as homework. Then have students discuss their notes in class with you and other students before proceeding with their topics.

Students used to writing only for teachers often have difficulty understanding the importance of analyzing their readers. To help them imagine an audience for their essay, ask them to choose a place where their speculation about causes or effects might be published, and then to describe the readers of this publication. It will also help if they keep a particular reader of this publication—especially a skeptical reader—in mind as they write.

The suggestions given at the goal-setting and planning stages of the composing process make numerous references to the selections in this chapter, reminding students that there are many possible approaches to a speculation about causes or effects. The list of questions points out the kinds of decisions writers often make at this stage in the composing process, just before they begin drafting.

SPECIAL PROBLEMS OF THIS WRITING ASSIGNMENT. One problem with this assignment is that some students who choose to write about a trend are reluctant to demonstrate that a trend is actually a trend, that it is *increasing* or *decreasing* over a specific time period. This task really requires a double argument: the writer must first argue that a trend exists and then argue for some possible causes of it. You will need to give those students who have chosen to write about trends special encouragement and help with this first argument—demonstrating the existence of the trend.

Other problems students may encounter with this task include:

- Choosing a widely recognized trend or phenomenon and presenting only predictable or obvious causes for it so that the reader thinks "So what?"
- Choosing a trend that has very recently changed directions or lost momentum (such as the divorce rate) and thus may be difficult to interpret or project
- Devoting considerable attention to establishing the existence of the phenomenon or trend and neglecting to mention any causes for it
- Failing to consider alternative causes
- Mentioning alternative causes but not refuting or accepting them
- Failing to consider readers' possible objections to proposed causes

Though this writing task is problematic, with your help nearly all students can succeed at it and experience the very great satisfaction of accomplishing an intellectual challenge. The guide to writing has been devised to forestall the problems we mention in this section. Students who use it with care can succeed at this task—if they have your guidance and encouragement.

Responding to the challenge of this assignment, instructors of UCSD's Third College Writing Program some years ago devised a "communal" assignment to orient students to the research and writing possibilities of causal analysis. In the communal assignment, which prepares students for their individual causal essays, small groups (three to five students) work together to research and draft quickly one causal argument, each group developing a different topic.

PROMISING AND UNPROMISING TOPICS. Limit students to topics that must be argued. Steer them away from events with a single, obvious explanation, for which presenting the causes would involve only reporting, not arguing.

Students need careful guidance in choosing topics for this assignment. If they write about phenomena or trends, they should be able to demonstrate that their subjects are phenomena, involving patterns of behavior rather than one-time events, or that they are trends, involving long-term changes in patterns of behavior rather than short-term, faddish shifts.

Some types of topics pose particular challenges for students:

- Historical phenomena or historically completed trends (for instance, an explanation of the increase in brain size during early human evolution). These subjects involve students in a different kind of research than that required by more current topics. These essays tend to read like research reports of others' observations on the subject.
- Phenomena observed in personal life (competitiveness, procrastination, popularity, laziness). Students writing about these topics may tend to rely exclusively on anecdotal information drawn from their own experience, rather than generalizing from their own experience to much larger conclusions about the phenomenon.
- Trends relating to technology (increased use of videocassette recorders, declining cost of handheld calculators, increasing use of personal stereos). Students often choose to write about these subjects because it is easy to document the existence of the trend itself; however, students have difficulty in going beyond the obvious explanation of technological advances in analyzing the causes of the trends.

- Subjects that could be approached as either phenomena or trends (teenage suicide, popular activities like windsurfing or snowboarding). Students will need to decide whether to treat the topic as a trend or as a phenomenon.

Since topic choice is a special problem, you might try this activity. After discussing the readings, list several possible events, phenomena, or trend topics on the board. Ask students in groups of two or three to choose a topic and prepare a defense of it for the class. They must argue that the topic is actually an event, a phenomenon, or a trend (and not a fad), that it is a researchable essay topic, that its causes are not already settled and therefore still require speculation, and that the topic will interest some particular readers they identify.

You will no doubt think of additional ways to enable students to propose and evaluate topics.

Chapter 8 PROPOSAL TO SOLVE A PROBLEM

Although simple in structure, proposals are one of the most complex kinds of argument because they can incorporate so many other kinds of writing—most, in fact, of the kinds presented in the preceding chapters of this book. Writers often begin a proposal with personal experience of a problem, for example, or by reflecting on a problem they have observed but not experienced. If readers are unfamiliar with the problem, it must be explained in enough detail to convince them that it exists. Writers also need to evaluate the problem, to demonstrate that it is a problem; the most common way to do this is by describing its negative effects, present and future. Since the best solutions treat a problem at its root, analyzing the causes of the problem can provide the criteria necessary to evaluate possible solutions. Writers can also evaluate solutions by conjecturing regarding their likely effects. Proposals, then, usually involve a combination of other kinds of writing, some of it argumentative, some of it merely informative, and they draw on a wide range of writing skills. They are an important and common kind of writing in most fields, and many students can expect to write proposals at some point during their post-college careers.

You might survey the many contexts in which proposals are typically written. Although students do not ordinarily read such proposal writing in school, public policy and business could not function without proposals. Studying proposal writing helps students learn to reconceive situations in terms of problems and solutions. The educational system teaches students to think in terms of good and bad (appropriate to writing evaluations), cause and effect (appropriate to speculation about causes and effects), and right and wrong (appropriate to position papers), but not in terms of problem and solution (appropriate to proposals). Nevertheless, problem-solving is basic to creativity and an invaluable way of looking at the world.

WRITING ASSIGNMENT: Proposal to Solve a Problem
This is the writing assignment that appears near the beginning of Chapter 8:

> Write an essay, proposing a solution to a clearly defined problem affecting a group or community to which you belong. Your task is to establish that the problem exists, to offer a solution that can reasonably be implemented, to lay out the particulars by which

your proposal would be put into effect, and to consider objections and alternative solutions.

Possible subjects students might write about (Considering Ideas for Your Own Writing) follow each reading, and additional suggestions appear in the Invention section of the Guide to Writing Proposals to Solve a Problem.

Writing Situations for Proposing Solutions to Problems

The chapter opens with four writing situations that suggest a range of occasions when proposals might be written. One of the situations involves writing for a college political science course, while another is written for an economics course. There is one business writing situation, certainly one of the most common areas for proposal writing. The situation on AIDS tracing deals with a menacing social problem.

You could give a brief presentation to your students on the rhetorical features of one of the situations. Using your presentation as a model, students could then work in small groups to develop their own presentations on the rhetorical features of the remaining situations, each small group taking one situation. After all the groups have given their presentations to the class, discussion could center on the similarities and differences among the rhetorical features of the situations. Here is our rhetorical analysis of the third situation, the proposal written in a political science class:

Topic: the four-year presidency

Writer: college student

Audience: the professor, hypothetical policymakers

Problem: presidents are only productive for half of their four-year terms

Reason: they spend too much time getting organized, running for reelection, or being lame ducks

Evidence: examples from recent history

Solution: a six-year nonrenewable presidential term

Reason: it would give presidents four or five years of good time

Objections: it could make presidents less responsive to the public will

Refutation: the system of legislative checks and balances would prevent this problem

Alternative solution: none

Practicing Proposing Solutions to Problems: A Collaborative Activity

Conducting this group activity so early in the process, long before they begin to consider their own topics and even before they discuss the chapter readings, students will nevertheless be drawn surprisingly quickly into the complexities and possibilities of proposing solutions to problems. This activity has the benefits of preparing the students for the readings and anticipating the entire chapter. After about fifteen minutes, shift the students to Part 2 of the activity, which asks them to step back and reflect together on the experience. After a few more minutes, shift the focus to whole-class discussion to share reflections on and reactions to the process of proposing solutions.

A GUIDE TO READING A PROPOSAL TO SOLVE A PROBLEM

This section reminds students that they will be reading the selections in this chapter both as readers and as writers of proposals to solve problems. For class activities to use in conjunction with this section, see Part 5 of this manual.

Here, following a brief illustration of annotation, we present a sample essay by Robert Samuelson. As you preview the essay for your students, you might ask them to consider how Samuelson's audience—*Newsweek* readers—affects his presentation of both the problem he introduces and the solution he proposes.

Reading for Meaning

This section, like corresponding sections following each reading selection in the chapter, encourages students to explore their understanding of Samuelson's proposal. The section gives students a range of specific suggestions for initiating and sustaining their explorations of Samuelson's argument; students are also asked to consider his purpose and audience, and to relate their own observations and experiences to Samuelson's assertions.

Reading like a Writer

In this section, students are encouraged to shift their focus from the content of the essay to the specific strategies used by the writer to achieve his purpose. Strategies employed by writers of proposals to solve problems include *introducing the problem, presenting the solution,* and *convincing readers to accept the solution.* In the critical reading and writing tasks that follow, each of these strategies is broken down more specifically: *introducing the problem* requires that writers both describe the problem and declare its significance, while *presenting the solution* requires writers to describe the solution and to show readers how the solution could be implemented. *Convincing readers to accept the solution* is discussed in terms of arguing directly for the solution and counterarguing readers' objections and questions, and evaluating alternative solutions.

The Reading like a Writer section following the sample essay presents a full range of strategies for writing proposals. Corresponding sections following each of the subsequent reading selections in the chapter will focus more closely on one or two strategies particularly appropriate to the analysis of each essay.

Introducing the Problem. Because Samuelson's proposed solution rests, in part, on his belief that the problem has not been recognized or adequately identified, this strategy is especially central to the success of his argument. Where other observers attribute the weakness of our educational system to schools or to teachers, Samuelson locates the problem in the students themselves. Students—many of them recently out of high school—will readily see that, in so doing, Samuelson runs the risk of alienating a substantial part of his audience. Students will probably suggest that Samuelson might have strengthened this aspect of his argument by providing more and different types of information in support of his interpretation of the problem.

Writers of proposals must also convince their readers of the significance of the problems they present. Especially if your students have completed the speculation about causes or effects presented in Chapter 7 of the text, they should have no problem recognizing that the analysis of both the causes and, especially, the effects of lack of motivation among students plays a

109

major role in Samuelson's argument for the significance and pervasiveness of the problem. Again, you can expect students to remain somewhat critical of Samuelson's seeming inability or unwillingness to defend his redefinition of what he clearly considers a serious problem.

Presenting the Solution. Many students will find Samuelson's actual presentation of his proposed solution rather sketchy. Although this section mentions the tentative and speculative nature of Samuelson's solution, you might want to remind students of this before they respond to the task.

Likewise, this might be a good opportunity to remind students of the centrality of purpose and audience in our consideration of each essay, and of the roles these play in this particular essay. As they evaluate Samuelson's decision not to detail the implementation of his proposed solution, students will want to consider how Samuelson expects his readers to react to his argument. Most students are likely to agree with the evaluation implied in the writing task in this section: that Samuelson might easily have done more to suggest how his solution might be implemented.

Convincing Readers to Accept the Solution. Here we draw students' attention to the strategies of direct argument for a solution, counterargument, and evaluating alternative solutions. Students should have little trouble recognizing Samuelson's direct argument for his solution, but they may need some help in identifying and analyzing his use of the other two strategies.

This section reminds students of three ways in which writers counterargue readers' objections or questions: by acknowledging, accommodating, or refuting them. Students will encounter these again in the upcoming chapter on writing position papers. In Samuelson's case, students will probably observe that, rather than accommodating possible objections to his position, he refutes them quite bluntly ("Forget it," paragraph 7; "let's be candid," paragraph 14).

In the same way—and much the same tone—in which he refutes possible objections to his position, Samuelson unequivocally rejects the alternate solutions suggested in paragraphs 10 and 11, dismissing them as "fictitious," "irrelevant," and failures. Students will probably note that Samuelson's use of this strategy fits in with the overall pattern and tone of his argument.

In the paragraphs specified at the end of this task, Samuelson argues for his solution primarily by presenting his personal opinions, backed up in several places by statistical evidence. Students may suggest that a wider range of types of evidence might have helped Samuelson argue for his solution more convincingly. Some students may be especially troubled by the elusiveness of Samuelson's argument for his solution, pointing out that the evidence in the paragraphs in question tends to relate more to the *need* for a solution than to the solution itself.

RESOURCES FOR TEACHING THE READINGS

The readings in this chapter address a range of education, social, political, and work-related problems. The first essay, by Mark Kleiman, proposes an alternative way of getting a B.A. degree. Next comes Edward J. Loughran's proposal for preventing juvenile delinquency.

John Beilenson proposes giving young volunteers a larger voice in national service programs, while Toby Haynsworth and Gerald Perselay propose an ambitious apprenticeship program for American high school students. The final essay, written by Will Scarvie, a student, illustrates proposal writing in the workplace.

Students can learn from these essays that proposals are written in a variety of different tones and styles, and that they share common features: they must define the problem clearly, demonstrate that it exists and that it has harmful consequences, and support the solution by arguing that it would be effective, feasible, and better than the alternatives. Students can also learn from the readings that proposal writers must gauge how much readers know about the problem and what difficulty they might have accepting the proposed solution, and that they must find ways of overcoming readers' resistance.

The following material introduces each reading and explores the possibilities offered by the sections on reading for meaning and reading like a writer and the ideas for writing that follow each reading.

Mark Kleiman, Confer College Degrees by Examination

To college students, this article should be a provocative introduction to proposals. There should be no difficulty in generating discussion, but you might help students preview the article by asking what they think the purpose of a college education is and what they think a degree is presently worth in the marketplace. The headnote gives a brief overview of the essay and asks students to consider why getting a college degree might be viewed as problematic. Because Kleiman's proposal is controversial, students should be encouraged to respond to his argument, pointing out shortcomings he has failed to mention or alternatives he has overlooked.

Reading for Meaning

This section asks students to consider how Kleiman's purpose and audience affect his approach to his argument. Students are also invited to explore their understanding of the problem Kleiman locates, and of the solution he proposes. In addition, they are encouraged to consider Kleiman's argument in light of their own educational experience. As usual after the first reading selection in each chapter, we suggest that you collect students' writing for this activity, reading over it quickly to see how they're doing and perhaps reading a few responses out loud in class.

Extending Meaning through Conversation. Students can continue to develop their understanding of the meaning of Kleiman's essay by talking about it with one or two classmates. You might help students get started on this activity by once again reminding them of Kleiman's projected audience—business managers. Invite students to imagine themselves in this position, and ask each to comment on how he or she would receive Kleiman's proposal. If students find they respond differently, which they undoubtedly will, this will be a useful basis for further discussion of the proposal, both in their small groups and in the class as a whole.

Reading like a Writer: Convincing Readers to Accept the Solution by Counterarguing Objections

Kleiman considers two objections to his proposed solution. He acknowledges the possible truth of the first—that people who get degrees by exam "might miss out on the opportunities college provides for social interaction and other forms of personal and intellectual development"—but suggests that it is "not conclusive." Some students may feel that, as Kleiman's audience is less likely to be concerned with "social interaction" than with the financial bottom line, it is perhaps natural for Kleiman to brush this objection aside. Kleiman responds to the second objection—that "B.A.'s by exam" would be denied the breadth and depth of a standard college education—in somewhat more detail, by modifying and expanding on his solution. Students are also encouraged to suggest objections in addition to the two mentioned by Kleiman; most will have no trouble coming up with one or more fairly serious objections to his argument.

We suggest that you approach the Analyze section of this activity as a group before students write up their individual responses. You would lead students through the text, showing them how to do a thorough analysis by rereading, annotating, and taking notes. Once students have completed the Write portion of the activity, be sure to have some students share their responses in class, both so that you can monitor how well they are understanding the material and as a starting point for further class discussion.

Considering Ideas for Your Own Writing

While we often discourage students from taking on problems at the state or national level unless we are sure they will have adequate time to do research, we find that many students are successful at writing proposals to solve problems they have observed or experienced on their own campuses. These topics are accessible to students, and they enjoy writing about issues that relate to their everyday lives.

Edward J. Loughran, **Prevention of Delinquency**

Loughran's essay offers an expert's point of view on a disturbing trend: the increasing number of young people who are put in jail each year. In the introductory note to the section, students are encouraged to consider the trend itself before reading the essay, and to note the way Loughran presents the problem.

Reading for Meaning

To explore and clarify their understanding of Loughran's arguments, students are asked to paraphrase Loughran's solution and then to examine his argument. As usual, we offer a number of further suggestions for making meaning from the text, ending with the suggestion that students can make meaning from the essay by analyzing their own experiences and observations in light of Loughran's presentation of both the problem and the solution.

Extending Meaning through Conversation. As students develop their understanding of the meaning of the essay by discussing it with one or two classmates, you might want to circulate among pairs or groups, helping students keep personal experience or opinion tied explicitly to the text. If you find that students have strong feelings about this topic, you could ask one member of each pair or group to share the results of this activity in class as a way of generating useful discussion of Loughran's argument.

112

<u>Judging the Writer's Credibility (A Further Strategy for Reading for Meaning)</u>. Before students begin this activity, have them see the section on judging a writer's credibility in Appendix 1, A Catalog of Critical Reading Strategies, where they will find a demonstration of the strategy in use. Periodically throughout this textbook, we refer students to supplemental activities outlined in the appendices to the text, each of which is designed to help students further develop their understanding of the particular genre. Once students have completed this activity, you might have them share their written responses, either in small groups or as part of a larger class discussion. While most students will find Loughran's argument credible, it is important that they also understand *why* it is credible.

Reading like a Writer: Introducing the Problem

Alerted by the introductory material preceding the selection, students will probably have noticed that Loughran goes into considerably more detail in presenting the problem than do the writers of the two previous essays. If your students have recently completed the assignment in writing about causes or effects in Chapter 7, they will probably recognize Loughran's strategy in presenting the problem: as is the case for many writers analyzing the causes of a trend, if Loughran can show that the trend in question exists, most readers will accept without question the significance of the trend. Thus, Loughran relies on statistics to demonstrate the existence of the problem, and on a brief causal analysis (paragraphs 8–11) to lead from his discussion of the problem to his presentation of a solution.

Considering Ideas for Your Own Writing

This section gives students a range of fairly specific suggestions for writing about social problems. Once again, we steer students away from overly broad topics, encouraging them to focus on "immediate, local, troublesome social problems." Since the best proposals tend to be ones in which the writer has some personal involvement or to be based on problems the writer can observe closely, it is advisable to restrict students' choices to some degree.

John Beilenson, **Giving the Young a Voice in National Service Programs**

Beilenson identifies a problem in what he otherwise sees as a good program: the absence or paucity of "youth voice" in President Clinton's National Service Corporation. Students should note that Beilenson's proposed solution is broken down into several components, and that, in addition to his proposal, he outlines its effects and benefits in some detail.

Reading for Meaning

Here, as we often do in this section, we ask students to begin exploring the meaning of the text by summarizing a key passage. You might take this opportunity to remind students of the importance of summarizing and paraphrasing as critical reading strategies. We give students a number of other suggestions for making meaning from the text individually before they proceed to the following activity.

<u>Extending Meaning through Conversation</u>. As students continue to develop their understanding of Beilenson's argument by discussing it with one or two classmates, we ask them to begin by considering Beilenson's audience. Remind students that proposal essays are usually meant to elicit action on the parts of their audience; ask them to speculate about how successful Beilenson's proposal is likely to be, given what they know about his readers. As students proceed with their conversation about this piece, they may find that some of them

113

detect a slight "us-them" tone—a rather artificial distinction between "young people" and "adults"—while others may find Beilenson's presentation of this distinction perfectly acceptable. We encourage students to explore these differences in understanding as they discuss the essay.

Reading like a Writer: Presenting the Solution

The introductory material for this task reminds students once again that the writer's awareness of his audience helps to determine the overall shape of his argument—in Beilenson's case, leading him to present his solution, as does Loughran, in more detail than do Kleiman and Samuelson. We steer students back to the six paragraphs where Beilenson presents his solution; as students reread and annotate this section of the essay, they should see that, in addition to breaking his solution down into five clear components, Beilenson also anticipates readers' questions or objections, stating, for instance, that "the over-30 crowd . . . need not worry" in paragraph 5. Once students have completed the writing portion of this activity, you might ask a few of them to share their responses in class, both as a way of monitoring how well they are understanding the material and of encouraging discussion of the essay.

Considering Ideas for Your Own Writing

These ideas offer specific guidelines and suggestions for thinking about problems related to organizations or institutions. Most students will readily be able to come up with one or two examples of such problems. If you wanted to use this as a class activity, you could have the whole class brainstorm to generate a list of problems, help them narrow it down to the two or three most interesting issues, and ask them to speculate as a group on how they might research and present solutions to these problems.

Toby Haynsworth and Gerald Perselay, A U.S. Youth Apprenticeship Program

Students will by now have noticed that each of the proposals in the chapter so far, including the sample essay by Robert J. Samuelson, deals with a topic affecting young people; in the case of this essay, the authors propose the adoption of a broad-based youth apprenticeship program in order to mitigate what they see to be weaknesses in the U.S. educational system. Students will want to pay specific attention to the authors' handling of alternate solutions; this may be an important consideration in their own proposal essays.

Reading for Meaning

As always, this section asks students to scrutinize the content of the essay closely, relating it to their own experience where appropriate. If you find that students are using their personal experience to make meaning from the text, you might invite them to do so orally in class, making sure that they do not move entirely away from the essay itself, but that they continue to make explicit connections between their experiences and the text.

Extending Meaning through Conversation. We ask students to begin their small-group discussion by considering Haynsworth and Perselay's audience. Remind students that they will need to continue rereading and annotating the essay as they develop their understanding of its meaning through conversation. Once again, especially if you find that students are relying heavily on their own experience to make meaning from the text, you might want to circulate among groups, making sure conversations are remaining anchored in the text itself.

Reading like a Writer: Convincing Readers to Accept the Solution by Evaluating Alternate Solutions

Here, we help students begin to appreciate the important role of alternate solutions in proposal essays. Students who have not been exposed to this type of writing before may assume that introducing alternate—often competing—solutions might weaken an argument; with this essay, we help them see that alternate solutions must be taken into account, and that, as writers either dismiss them or incorporate them into their own proposed solutions, alternate solutions actually strengthen this type of argument. Once students have completed the writing portion of this activity, you might have them share their responses, either in small groups or as a class as a way of facilitating discussion of the essay.

Considering Ideas for Your Own Writing

In this section, we continue the theme of alternate or competing solutions, asking students to imagine themselves in the position of proposing a solution that is different from the favored or obvious solution. As students begin to consider topics for their own essays, we generally encourage them to address subjects with which they have had experience or which they've been able to observe; in this case, we invite them to consider writing a proposal essay about a school- or campus-wide program. You might have each student come up with one or two ideas, and then share them in class.

Will Scarvie, **Proposal to Increase Efficiency in the Computer Section**

While many students may not find the content of Scarvie's proposal engaging, how he responds to the situation in which he is writing should interest them. This selection may encourage some of your students to write proposals that they could submit in their workplaces, communities, or schools.

Reading for Meaning

Because Scarvie's proposal is presented as a memo to his superior, considerations of audience and purpose may seem especially immediate to students. Most students will recognize that, because Scarvie's audience is defined as it is, he must be especially diplomatic, taking extreme care to avoid appearing either ill-informed about or overly critical of the existing situation. Since students know from the introductory note to the selection that Scarvie's proposal was in fact implemented, students will want to focus on *why* it was taken seriously.

Extending Meaning through Conversation. As students develop their understanding of the meaning of Scarvie's essay through conversation, they will need to continue to reread and annotate, keeping the basic features of proposal writing in mind as they comment on the strengths and weaknesses of the essay.

Reading like a Writer: Convincing Readers to Accept the Solution

If students make a scratch outline of Scarvie's proposal as they annotate, they will see that it follows a logical order: Scarvie begins by introducing the problem—the backlog of projects in the computer section—and then proceeds to identify the cause of the problem. As in Loughran's essay earlier in the chapter, Scarvie uses a brief causal analysis to lead from his discussion of the problem into his proposed solution. The solution is presented in two parts: a comprehensive planning chart and a coordinator for the computer section. Scarvie goes on to introduce and dismiss an alternate solution, and then to anticipate three objections his reader might raise. He refutes the charge that his solution would be "cumbersome," although he acknowledges that some time and expense would be involved in hiring a coordinator. He also acknowledges that it will be difficult to estimate how much time projects will take, but suggests that this difficulty will lessen once the plan is implemented.

Most students will find Scarvie's organization solid and effective. A few may suggest that, in addition to identifying the *cause* of the problem, Scarvie might have gone into the *effects* of the problem as well, thus strengthening the reader's impression of its significance.

Reading like a Writer: A Follow-up Activity
Once students have completed the last Reading like a Writer activity, they will have generated quite a bit of written commentary about the readings in the chapter. You can help them review what they have learned by having them look back over the writing they have done, choosing one piece to revise and expand through further analysis. They would then turn in this revised writing with their final essay packages or in their end-of-course portfolios.

Considering Ideas for Your Own Writing
This section urges students to think of problems related to their own jobs. We find that students do best writing proposals for work sites or organizations with which they are familiar. Students are invited to practice describing the problem, proposing a solution, and searching for alternate solutions.

THINKING ABOUT WHAT MAKES PROPOSALS EFFECTIVE
As we do following the reading selections in each chapter of this text, we ask students to review and consolidate what they have learned about writing in each genre. Referring students back to the list of features of successful proposals—originally presented following the sample essay by Robert J. Samuelson early in the chapter—we invite students to choose the one essay from the chapter they believe to be the most successful in achieving its purpose and fulfilling these features. Asking students to justify their choices helps them focus even more closely on the features of the genre.

A GUIDE TO WRITING PROPOSALS TO SOLVE PROBLEMS

The guide leads students through a composing process that follows these steps:

Invention
    Choosing a Problem
    Analyzing the Problem and Identifying a Solution
    Considering Your Readers
        Learning More about Your Readers: A Collaborative Activity
    Developing an Argument
    Researching Your Proposal
Drafting
    Setting Goals
    Planning Your Draft
    Beginning
    Avoiding Logical Fallacies

Proposal writing is ideal for helping students develop audience awareness—necessary for all writing, but essential for persuasion. You might have students work in small groups and take turns playing the role of their classmates' intended readers. After describing his or her intended reader, the writer could summarize the problem and then briefly argue for the proposed solution. The group would then respond as the intended reader might. Since each group member would be likely to respond somewhat differently, a discussion about audience is likely to ensue.

In setting goals, students should reconsider their purpose and readers and adopt a tone suitable to both. Although the text describes a general organization they might follow and suggests ways they might begin their essays, remind students that writers have many options and that their decisions must be made in the context of their particular purpose and audience.

To alert students to common pitfalls in reasoning, the text lists some logical fallacies typical of proposal writing. Students should keep those fallacies in mind as they draft and certainly refer to them when they revise. The either/or and the "straw man" fallacies are generally the most troubling to students.

Again, remind students to keep their purpose and audience in focus as they revise. In particular, stress the importance of building their argument upon a solid foundation of shared values and beliefs. You might invite them to explore these underlying assumptions in writing before revising their essays.

SPECIAL PROBLEMS OF THIS WRITING ASSIGNMENT. Special difficulties students sometimes encounter as they write proposals involve topic choice and the need to establish the problem's existence and seriousness. Even though students are asked to write about a problem faced by a group to which they belong, they sometimes take on problems that are too abstract or complicated for them to handle effectively in a short time. It is understandable that students should want to solve some of the major problems we as a society face—such as the threat of nuclear annihilation, the lack of shelter for the homeless, or the deterioration of our industrial urban centers. As much as we do not want to discourage students from trying to understand these problems and even possibly contributing to their solutions, we also do not want them to fail in their attempts to write successful proposals because their writing is too general. This chapter is designed to teach students how to gather the information they need to make their writing more specific.

A good proposal does two things: it defines a problem and then argues for a particular solution. We have found that even the student who argues effectively for a solution may sometimes fail to establish the problem's existence and seriousness. Defining the problem actually requires careful assessment of the rhetorical situation. The student must decide just how aware of the problem the readers are and how best to convince them that it is worthy of their attention and possibly their time and money as well.

PROMISING AND UNPROMISING TOPICS. Choosing an appropriate topic is probably the hardest part of proposal writing. Some students know immediately what they want to write about, while others are at a loss. Perhaps the greatest stumbling block is abstractness. The more distant the problem is from the writer's personal experience the harder it is to write about. That is why we urge students to choose a problem plaguing a community or group to which they belong. Even the most abstract problems can be treated in the context of a local group. Those concerned with broad educational problems, for example, might find evidence of the problem in their own high school or college. Those concerned with social and economic problems like homelessness and unemployment might look in their communities.

Writing about a problem in a group to which they belong will also help students with the crucial task of analyzing their readers. They can more easily anticipate possible objections to their solution and alternative solutions others might offer. They can also draw on common values and experience to establish the seriousness of the problem and argue for the feasibility of the proposed solution.

Chapter 9 POSITION PAPER

The introduction to this chapter contrasts the position paper with the proposal, pointing out that proposals have a specific, practical purpose, whereas position papers tend to be more general and philosophical. The position paper relates to the proposal in rather the same way that the reflective essay relates to the autobiographical essay. Just as reflective writing differs from autobiographical writing in its "fierce attachment to an idea," so the position paper differs from the proposal in its central concern for principles. The crux of a proposal is often a pragmatic issue—whether a particular solution will solve the problem at hand; at the heart of a position paper there are nearly always ethical questions, values, and assumptions—questions of right and wrong that can seldom be resolved by facts alone.

When students take a position on a controversial issue, they discover not only that people differ but also that they have good reasons for their different views. They learn to respect the complexity of these issues and the subtlety of others' reasoning. Because these chapters emphasize the rhetorical aspects of argumentation, they help students avoid polemics. Students learn to develop an argument that is responsive to their readers' concerns, that builds a bridge of shared values.

The writing assignment requires that students examine the issue critically. Instead of framing an argument to support an already-formed opinion, we encourage students to analyze and evaluate the pros and cons of the issue before reaching their own conclusions. We urge them to examine their own underlying assumptions as critically as they would those of their opponents. We want them to recognize the value of thinking through the issue and of basing their position on solid reasoning and evidence, not merely to convince others but for their own sake as well.

WRITING ASSIGNMENT: Arguing a Position on an Issue
Here is the writing assignment that appears near the beginning of Chapter 9:

> Write an essay that argues a position on a controversial issue. Take into account readers' objections, questions, and opposing viewpoints, but remember that your purpose is to state your own position clearly and to convince those who disagree with you that they must take seriously the arguments you raise.

Possible issues students might write about (Considering Ideas for Your Own Writing) follow each reading selection. In addition, suggestions appear in the Invention section of the Guide to Writing Position Papers.

Writing Situations for Arguing Positions on Issues
The three brief writing situations presented early in the chapter demonstrate that writers argue for positions on controversial issues in both academic and nonacademic settings. The situations also suggest some of the many issues debated in position papers: the regulation of urban development, surrogate motherhood, and the right of public employees to strike. You might ask your students to brainstorm a list of other issues even before reading further in the chapter, or you might refer back to these writing situations just before asking students to list topics on which they might consider writing.

Practicing Arguing a Position: A Collaborative Activity
As the introductory paragraph suggests, this activity will reassure students that they already know a great deal about arguing a position; it will also alert them to certain challenges of this type of writing that they may not have anticipated. As usual, this is a two-part activity; students are asked first to debate an issue with a partner, and then to reflect on the argument process itself. Although this activity may seem time-consuming, it is a very effective method of orienting students to the upcoming writing task.

A GUIDE TO READING POSITION PAPERS

This section leads students through the critical reading and writing strategies they will use throughout the chapter. For class activities to be used in conjunction with this section, see Part 5 of this manual.

The sample essay provided in this section, following a brief illustration of annotation, clearly demonstrates the central features of writing to take a position: defining the issue, asserting a clear and unequivocal position, arguing directly for a position, and counterarguing objections and opposing positions. The Reading like a Writer section following the essay will break these down into more specific strategies.

Dick Teresi's essay, which argues that helmet laws should be repealed, provides a useful bridge from the proposal assignment in the previous chapter to the position paper assignment; students will have little problem seeing the connections between these two types of argument.

Erdrich's example is also useful in that it clearly refers to personal experience as well as drawing on factual information.

Reading for Meaning

This section invites students to respond to the content of the selection, exploring their understanding of and response to Teresi's essay. The section begins by asking students to articulate their own positions on the issue of helmet laws; it then encourages them to respond to his argument, which students will find more or less convincing depending on their own experience and observations. You might give students five or ten minutes of class time to write about their responses to the suggestions in this section, and then use those responses as the starting point for class discussion of the essay.

Reading like a Writer

This section helps students move from examining the content and purpose of the essay to analyzing the features of this type of writing and the specific strategies used by the writer to accomplish her purpose. The tasks in this section directly anticipate the thinking students will do as they read the other selections in this chapter and as they begin to work on their own essays. The section introduces students to the major elements of writing to take a position: *defining the issue, asserting a clear and unequivocal position, arguing directly for a position, and counterarguing objections and opposing positions.* Students will probably recognize that defining the issue and indicating its significance are strategies parallel to ones in earlier assignment chapters; this section will also remind them that the writer must assert a clear, unequivocal position and also acknowledge the opposing position. Students will see that convincing readers to take the position seriously requires that the writer argue directly for the position and counterargue against readers' objections and questions.

The Reading like a Writer section following the sample essay presents a full range of strategies for writing to take a position. Corresponding sections following each of the reading selections in the chapter will focus more narrowly on strategies particularly appropriate to the analysis of each essay. You may want to remind students once again that they are responsible for responding thoughtfully and specifically to the activities in these sections.

Defining the Issue. This exercise directs students' attention to the fact that writers of position papers must inform their readers about the issue as well as convincing them of its significance. Because Teresi can assume that most readers are familiar with helmet laws, he needn't spend much time presenting the issue itself; instead, he can proceed to define the issue in his own terms. Where many opponents of helmet laws see such laws as a threat to individual liberty, Teresi clearly frames the issue as one of safety, arguing that these laws, in fact, do not protect motorcycle riders from injury.

Asserting a Clear, Unequivocal Position. This section reminds students that, while informing readers about the issue is certainly part of a writer's task in taking a position, writers must go beyond the mere reporting of information and assert a definitive position on the issue. In pointing out that writers may choose to assert their positions at different points in their essays, this section foreshadows the upcoming discussion of devising a logical plan.

In the case of Teresi's essay, students are asked to pinpoint his assertion wherever this assertion appears in his essay. Possibly drawing on their responses to previous exercises, students should be able to report that Teresi's position, or "thesis," is stated relatively late in his essay, toward the end of the third paragraph ("we oppose the laws . . ."). They should also note that his thesis is arguable: in stating a position that flies in the face of what many readers believe about motorcycle safety, he seems openly to invite opposing viewpoints.

Arguing Directly for the Position. The introduction to this section directs students' attention to the kind of reasoning writers of position papers use; we also invite them to consider how the awareness of their audiences affects writers' approaches to position papers. Students are asked to comment specifically in writing on Teresi's reasons for his position. Students will note that he relies on a combination of different types of information, ranging from what is undoubtedly personal experience to the use of statistics, in support of his position. You could use this as a class activity, asking students to identify specific reasons and keeping a list of these on the board, as a way of helping students understand this feature.

Counterarguing Objections and Opposing Positions. This section reminds students that writers of position papers must anticipate readers' objections and opposing positions; most students will have little trouble noting that Teresi confronts objections head-on, using rhetorical questions, for instance, at the beginnings of paragraphs 5 and 7 to introduce—and quickly refute—possible opposing arguments. Students will probably vary in how convincing they find Teresi's counterarguments: while some will be satisfied that he has proved his point, others may find his attitude somewhat cavalier.

RESOURCES FOR TEACHING THE READINGS

The readings in this chapter take up a variety of controversial issues. The sample essay by Dick Teresi concerns the safety issues surrounding motorcycle helmet laws. The second selection, by Stephen Bates, focuses on important issues of religious tolerance, while Donella Meadows takes a position against media talk shows. Next comes Charles Krauthammer's argument against "sentimental environmentalism," and Shelby Steele's argument regarding the role of affirmative action programs. The final selection on sex education in schools was written by Jill Kuhn, a student.

The following material discusses each reading and offers advice on using the sections on reading for meaning and reading like a writer and the ideas for writing that follow each reading.

Stephen Bates, **Religious Diversity and the Schools**

Bates's essay addresses the timely and controversial issue of separation of church and state, in the form of religious tolerance in schools. The introductory note asks students to consider what they know about the history of the issue before reading Bates's argument.

Reading for Meaning

Here, students are asked to go back to the text to explore their understanding of the meaning of Bates's argument. As usual, we ask them to begin by paraphrasing the argument, putting Bates's position in their own words in order to clarify their own understanding. Because any topic dealing with religion is likely to elicit highly personal reactions in some readers, you might monitor students' responses to this piece by inviting them to share their writing in class;

in this way, you can not only see how well they are understanding the material, but also make sure that they do not stray too far away from the text itself in making meaning.

Extending Meaning through Conversation. Likewise, you might find it helpful to circulate among groups during this part of the activity, listening for indications that personal experience or beliefs may be drawing conversations too far off track, and offering suggestions to help students make explicit connections between their experience and the text.

Reading like a Writer: Defining the Issue

Students should recall from their work with the sample essay by Dick Teresi that writers of position papers often have some options in defining the issue in question: where Teresi defines the issue of helmet laws as one of safety rather than of individual rights, Bates offers a surprising twist on the issue of religion in the schools by pointing out that a system that purports to promote tolerance is actually *in*tolerant in some ways. We direct students' attention specifically to the paragraphs in which he presents the issue, asking them to make a scratch outline as they reread and annotate; you might take this opportunity to remind students of the value of keeping an informal outline as a critical reading strategy.

For this first reading selection in the chapter, we suggest that you lead the class in the Analyze portion of the activity, perhaps constructing a scratch outline as a group on the board, before having students complete the Write section of the activity on their own.

Considering Ideas for Your Own Writing

Here, we ask students to consider writing their own position papers about issues based on educational policies. Most students will readily come up with one or two possible ideas; you might make this a group activity by having each student come up with a possible topic, listing these on the board, and then discussing them in class.

Donella Meadows, **Rush and Larry, Coast to Coast: This Is Not Democracy in Action**

This essay considers the role of media talk shows in a democracy; as the title suggests, Meadows argues that these shows are not the democratic forums that they are often assumed to be. Most students will be familiar with one or more of the programs Meadows mentions, and we ask them to reflect on their own opinions about these shows before reading Meadows's essay.

Reading for Meaning

In this section, as usual, we encourage students to continue to reread and annotate as they develop their understanding of the text, paraphrasing Meadows's presentation of the issue and going on to explore other specific aspects of the essay before discussing their insights with one or two other students in the following activity.

Extending Meaning through Conversation. Because this essay touches on politics (the right-wing talk-show host Rush Limbaugh, for instancee, is one of Meadows's prime examples), student discussions of the meaning of the essay are likely to be lively and interesting. To ensure that students do not stray too far from the text itself in their conversations, you might circulate among pairs or groups, offering comments that help students make connections between their experience and the essay. You could also allow some class time following this activity so that students can share the meanings resulting from their conversations.

Reading like a Writer: Making a Position Clear and Unequivocal
As students analyze and write briefly about Meadows's argument, they should have little trouble seeing that her position is stated quite clearly at several points in the essay, including paragraphs 4–5, 9, and 10. This exercise will be particularly useful for students who, perhaps based on high school writing experience, are looking for a single, clearly discernible "thesis statement." You might suggest that students once again use the critical reading strategy of making a scratch outline as they read and reread Meadows' essay, noting the passages where her position is stated most strongly.

Compare. Once or twice in each chapter, we ask students to develop their understanding of a writer's use of a particular strategy more fully by comparing it to another writer's use of the same strategy. Here, we ask students to focus on various writers' presentation of their theses; students will probably note that many of the writers in this chapter avoid opening bluntly with a cut-and-dried thesis statement, as many students have been taught to do.

Considering Ideas for Your Own Writing
This section asks students to consider writing an essay about a controversial issue involving the media. Options suggested here revolve around regulation of various media—a rich source of topic possibilities for many students.

Charles Krauthammer, **Saving Nature, but Only for Man**

While Meadows writes for readers who may very likely sympathize with her position, Krauthammer takes a position that is likely to be unpopular with his audience, including many students. The introductory note asks students to monitor their initial responses to Krauthammer's argument.

Reading for Meaning
Because Krauthammer's position on this issue is somewhat unpopular, students may have quite a lot to say in response to this section. Students should take the time to consider carefully Krauthammer's assumptions regarding his audience; this should help students, as the text suggests, to understand not only the issue itself but Krauthammer's position and their own reactions to his argument.

Extending Meaning through Conversation. As students continue to make meaning from the essay by discussing Krauthammer's argument in pairs or small groups, we remind them to stay focused on the issue as Krauthammer presents it. To help students avoid straying into highly personal reactions to Krauthammer's position, you might remind students to reread and annotate at least parts of the essay together.

Looking for Patterns of Opposition (A Further Strategy for Reading for Meaning). Krauthammer presents some of the terms in which he defines the issue as sets of oppositions—a strategy inexperienced readers may not have noticed. Here, as we do periodically throughout the text, we refer students to Appendix 1: A Catalog of Critical Reading Strategies. You may find that you need to help students see how sets of oppositions such as "sane" vs. "sentimental" or "necessities" vs. "luxuries" help Krauthammer present his position.

Reading like a Writer: Counterarguing

Here, we direct students' attention to the specific paragraphs in which Krauthammer argues against what he labels "sentimental environmentalism," asking them to examine his refutation of this position and to write briefly about it. You might have students share their responses to this activity, either in small groups or in class, as a way of generating discussion of the important strategy of counterarguing.

Compare. As students compare Krauthammer's use of counterargument to that of another author in the chapter, you will want to remind students that writers of position papers have some options in dealing with possible objections or opposing positions: they can refute them, as Krauthammer does here, or they can modify their own positions to accommodate valid objections; in addition, writers have the option of choosing the tone they feel will be the most effective with their particular audiences. Most students will already have noticed the distinctive tone of Krauthammer's argument, which some students are bound to find somewhat abrasive. Encourage them to compare this tone carefully with that of one of the other writers in the chapter.

Considering Ideas for Your Own Writing

This section suggests three different general types of topics students might consider for their own essays. You might help them anticipate the particular challenges and rewards of each type of subject. First, students are asked to consider writing about fairly broad ecological issues such as oil drilling and recycling. While students are likely to have strong feelings on these issues, they will also need to do research to present their subjects and substantiate their positions. Students might also choose to write about environmental issues that are closer to home, perhaps in evidence on campus or in the local community. Students will have learned from the previous proposal assignment that personal interest or even involvement in an issue will very likely strengthen their arguments, but that they will also need to maintain a certain amount of emotional distance from the controversy in question. Last, students are challenged to choose an *unpopular* position, as Krauthammer does.

Shelby Steele, **Affirmative Action**

Like the selection by Charles Krauthammer, Steele's essay seems to take an unpopular, or at least surprising, position in objecting to affirmative action programs as they currently exist or have existed in the past. As with the Krauthammer essay, you might ask students to consider how Steele's argument might have been presented in terms of an evaluation, a speculation about causes or effects, or a proposal to solve a problem.

Reading for Meaning

Because this essay is long and complex, students will find it especially necessary to annotate carefully as they read and reread. Students are, as always, asked to consider Steele's purpose and audience, and to relate their own observations and experiences directly to his position. They are also invited to examine Steele's analysis of the effects of affirmative action, as well as the contrasting terms (innocence vs. power, intentions vs. effects) in which he presents his position.

Extending Meaning through Conversation. Because the issue of affirmative action is likely to be one about which students feel strongly, you might move among pairs or groups, making sure that conversations are not moving too far away from the text itself. Once students have further explored their understanding of the meaning of the essay by discussing amongst themselves, you could have one member of each group report to the class on the results of this activity.

Reading like a Writer: Arguing Directly for a Position Using Cause-Effect Reasoning

Once again, students will note that the analysis of effects figures prominently in Steele's argument against affirmative action. Many students will find Steele's specific examples of African Americans affected by affirmative action policies especially effective in supporting his position.

Considering Ideas for Your Own Writing

Students are invited to take on the challenge of writing about affirmative action or other issues of current or ongoing national importance. Reminders following a list of possible topics reiterate that students are responsible both for justifying their own positions on an issue and for anticipating the objections of those who may oppose those positions.

Jill Kuhn, **Sex Education in Our Schools**

The issue addressed in this position paper should be familiar to your students. It deals with the perennial question of whether schools should offer sex education courses. As many of your students will discover when they write their own position papers, Kuhn found that she needed to do some library research to understand others' arguments better and to substantiate her own position.

Reading for Meaning

Students are asked to consider Kuhn's purpose and audience, mentioned in the headnote to the essay. This section also invites students to connect their own experiences and beliefs to Kuhn's argument, examining how their responses to Kuhn's essay are influenced by their own backgrounds.

Extending Meaning through Conversation. As students continue to explore and develop their understanding of Kuhn's argument by discussing it with one or two other students, they will undoubtedly be referring to their own experiences with sex education. This will be a useful starting point for their discussions of the essay, but you may need to remind them of the purpose of the activity, drawing them back to the text itself.

Evaluating the Logic of an Argument (A Further Strategy for Reading for Meaning). Once again, we refer students to Appendix 1: A Catalog of Critical Reading Strategies. Encourage students to devote their full attention to this activity, as it draws attention to crucial elements of the genre. This section of the appendix points out that the support for a writer's claim must be appropriate, believable, consistent, and complete; here, we ask students to evaluate Kuhn's argument to see whether it meets these criteria.

Reading like a Writer: Making an Essay Readable

Most students will note that Kuhn's argument is divided into three sections—three reasons that support her claim. Each reason (that parents are providing sex education ineffectively or not at all, that sexually active adolescents are often ignorant, and that AIDS makes sex education a necessity, especially for adolescents) is supported with references to authorities on the subject. Two references to then-Surgeon General C. Everett Koop—a prominent supporter of Kuhn's position—form an effective frame for her argument.

Compare. Once again, we ask students to focus on a particular feature of a genre by comparing different writers' use of similar strategies. You might help students get started with this activity by suggesting that they make a scratch outline of Kuhn's essay, identifying the features mentioned in the exercise, and that they then make a similar outline of a second essay from the chapter.

Reading like a Writer: A Follow-up Activity

By the time students complete this last section in the chapter of Reading like a Writer activities, they will have produced a rich amount of writing about this type of essay. Don't overlook the usefulness of having them select one of their responses to revise and extend through further analysis, thus reviewing and reinforcing what they have learned about the genre. They would then turn in this expanded piece as part of their final essay folders or end-of-course portfolios.

Considering Ideas for Your Own Writing

Students should be able to think of many issues relating to teenagers or young adults. They may also have had direct experience that relates to such issues. You might want to devote some class time to discussing these possibilities because students will be able to help each other and generate and consider topics.

THINKING ABOUT WHAT MAKES POSITION PAPERS EFFECTIVE

We ask students to focus on the central features of effective position papers, introduced following the sample essay at the beginning of the chapter, and to select the essay in the chapter that they feel best illustrates these features. You might have students who identify the same essay as most successful complete this activity as a group, perhaps sharing their responses in class as a way of facilitating a discussion of the genre.

A GUIDE TO WRITING POSITION PAPERS

The guide leads students through a composing process for position papers that follows these steps:

Invention
    Choosing an Arguable Issue
    Analyzing Your Readers
        Learning More about Your Readers: A Collaborative Activity
    Tentatively Stating Your Thesis
    Exploring Your Reasons
    Restating Your Thesis

Students should choose an issue on which they have already formed an opinion. If they are unsure of their position on an issue, students may substitute for their own thinking the position and arguments of someone who has already written on the issue, or their essays may merely summarize the two opposed points of view without siding with either. Students must establish and support a position, and that position should not be on the fence.

Other chapters have mentioned the importance of the invention step of analyzing readers, particularly because many readers are unaccustomed to the idea of writing to anyone besides their teachers. Even if they do grasp the need to address readers other than their instructors, their initial formulations of audience may be vague, general, and ill-defined. Since their position papers may be addressed to readers who hold an opposite position, and since the success of the paper depends on its ability to convince readers of the sense in the writer's position, understanding who these readers are and how they are likely to react is exceedingly important in a position paper.

The guide reminds students to think about their readers throughout the composing process, but you might give this initial step of analyzing readers some special attention, perhaps using student topics as examples to demonstrate the importance of accurately assessing an audience's knowledge, values, and positions on the issue. You might even play the role of a skeptical or opinionated audience to give students a sense of how their arguments might run into difficulties if they do not consider their readers carefully.

It is sometimes helpful to point to the painstaking market research routinely conducted in the business world as a practical example of "analyzing readers." Students should realize that considering an audience is an essential skill in the workplace and in all situations where they want to communicate their ideas to others. The invention process for the position paper stresses the need to identify the assumptions or values on which readers' opinions are based, and to look for assumptions and values the writer shares with readers as a means of opening communication between the opposed positions.

As they develop support for their best reasons, remind students to analyze their reasoning. Advise them to reread Evaluating the Logic of an Argument in Appendix 1: A Catalog of Critical Reading Strategies. Students should be aware of whether their appeals are mainly logical or emotional, and on what kind of evidence they are relying. Urge them to try to anticipate readers' objections and look for ways to refute or, possibly, accommodate them. From the essays in this chapter, they should have learned that the pattern of concession plus rebuttal is an essential one in argument.

When advising students on setting goals for their position papers, remind them that for some issues it is unrealistic to seek to change readers' minds. This is an important point, because students often believe that the objective of a position paper is to prove the opposition wrong. In fact, many position papers have much more modest goals, setting out merely to convince an entrenched opposition that the writer's position is reasonable and deserves more serious consideration and respect. Readers may finally disagree with the writer, but a position paper will have served a valuable purpose if they gain a better understanding of the writer's position and a more tolerant attitude toward it.

SPECIAL PROBLEMS OF THIS WRITING ASSIGNMENT. Probably the greatest problem students encounter when they begin writing position papers is mistaking assertion for argumentation. This problem manifests itself in sweeping generalizations unsupported by reasons and evidence. Students with little experience developing an argument usually assume that all they need do is state what they think. They don't realize that they have to give the reasons for their position and offer various kinds of evidence to support it. Nor do they recognize how important it is to anticipate readers' objections and questions and then either to modify their own position by acknowledging reasonable objections or to defend it by refuting unreasonable ones.

For some students, the essential problem is lack of experience in reasoning. Some students simply may be unused to setting out their reasons in a way that others can follow. For them, reading a diversity of arguments will provide instructive models. If, however, the problem stems from a lack of thoughtfulness, from the habit of relying on unexamined assumptions and biases, then the solution becomes more difficult. These students need first to accept the value of introspection and logical reasoning. They must recognize that the aim of argumentation is not merely to voice your own opinion but to examine it critically.

The root of the problem might be cognitive as well as emotional immaturity. Students who have not yet overcome their own egotism may have little experience with other points of view; therefore, they have few strategies for self-analysis, let alone for audience analysis. They may be able to assert their own opinions forcefully, but tend to have difficulty looking critically at their own assumptions or describing carefully their own train of thought. In our experience, students with this kind of problem respond well when argumentative writing is presented as an act of communication rather than as an act of aggression. When the emphasis is on creating common ground instead of squashing your opponents into the ground, students feel less defensive and more open to alternative ways of seeing.

PROMISING AND UNPROMISING TOPICS. We have found that there is no simple rule for prejudging the promise of topics for position papers. Many experienced instructors feel differently; for example, they often eliminate from consideration issues having to do with matters of faith like abortion and creationism. We find, however, that students can handle issues such as these reasonably if they take seriously other points of view. What we find most limiting is lack of information. If students are not well informed about a topic and do not have time or inclination to inform themselves, then their argument is likely to be fatuous—full of generalization and lacking in reasons and evidence.

Without making the assignment a full-blown research project, you might encourage students to discuss the issue with others and to do some reading about it. Exploring opposing views should be a natural part of the invention process. Sometimes, however, students make their research one-sided. It is good to seek reasons and evidence to support a position, but students also need to learn about the other side. They need to be able to anticipate objections and to appeal to values and concerns they share with others.

In the guide to writing, we offer a list of possibilities to get students thinking about issues they could write about. Many of the topics we suggest are ones we think students will know and also care about. Caring about the topic is essential for good writing, particularly for argumentative writing. This requirement comes as a surprise to some students and may even be threatening to them.

We have been amazed at the number of students who are reluctant to express an opinion. Many have been taught that it is inappropriate for them to do so. Some have been made to feel that they know too little to have an opinion worth sharing. Others believe that they are in college to consume ideas and opinions, not to produce them. For these students, we emphasize the process over the product. We explain that taking a position teaches them to analyze issues critically and to evaluate arguments pro and con. With experience, students gain confidence in their reasoning abilities and come to enjoy developing a thoughtful, well-supported argument.

Part 7 BIBLIOGRAPHIES

The following selected bibliographies, brief as they are, will remind experienced colleagues of the published resources in the field. They will also provide newcomers with a starting point for serious reading in composition studies and on learning from text.

COMPOSITION STUDIES JOURNALS. To follow new theory and pedagogy, writing instructors read these journals:

College English
College Composition and Communication
Journal of Advanced Composition
Rhetoric Review
Rhetoric Society Quarterly

Journal of Basic Writing
The Writing Instructor
Journal of Teaching Writing
Writing Program Administration
Journal of English Teaching Techniques
Teaching English in the Two-Year College

HISTORICAL SOURCES. Composition studies have a rich historical tradition reaching back to Greece in the fifth century B.C.E. The selections in this category highlight the major works from classical times, the English Renaissance, and the nineteenth century. All are currently available in reprints, most as paperbacks.

Plato, *Gorgias* (387 B.C.E.); *Phaedrus* (370 B.C.E.)
Aristotle, *Rhetoric* (335 B.C.E.)
Cicero, *De Inventione* (87 B.C.E.); *De Oratore* (55 B.C.E.)
Quintilian, *Institutio Oratoria* (95)
Erasmus, *On Copia of Words* (1512)
Wilson, *The Arte of Rhetorique* (1553)
Ramus, *The Logic* (1574)
Bacon, *The Advancement of Learning* (1605)
Campbell, *The Philosophy of Rhetoric* (1776)
Blair, *Lectures on Rhetoric and Belles Lettres* (1783)
Day, *Elements of the Art of Rhetoric* (1850)

RECENT HISTORICAL STUDIES. There has been a resurgence of interest in the history of writing instruction in American schools and colleges.

Berlin, J. A. (1984). *Writing instruction in nineteenth-century American colleges*. Carbondale: Southern Illinois University Press.

Berlin, J. A. (1987). *Rhetoric and reality: Writing instruction in American colleges, 1900–1985*. Carbondale: Southern Illinois University Press.

Connors, R. J., Ede, L. S., and Lunsford, A. A. (Eds.). (1984). *Essays on classical rhetoric and modern discourse*. Carbondale: Southern Illinois University Press.

Crowley, S. (1990). *The methodical memory: Invention in current-traditional rhetoric*. Carbondale: Southern Illinois University Press.

Horner, W. B. (1983). *The present state of scholarship in historical and contemporary rhetoric*. Columbia: University of Missouri Press.

Johnson, N. (1991). *Nineteenth-century rhetoric in North America*. Carbondale: Southern Illinois University Press.

Murphy, J. J. (Ed.). (1983). *Renaissance eloquence: Studies in the theory and practice of Renaissance rhetoric*. Berkeley: University of California Press.

Murphy, J. J. (Ed.). (1982). *The rhetorical tradition and modern writing*. New York: Modern Language Association.

Murphy, J. J. (1983). *A synoptic history of classical rhetoric*. Davis, CA: Hermagoras Press.

MODERN DISCOURSE THEORY. Modern theorists study the nature of written discourse, seeking to classify its many forms and to understand particular forms better.

Beale, W. H. (1987). *A pragmatic theory of rhetoric.* Carbondale: Southern Illinois University Press.

Britton, J., Burgess, T., Martin, N., McLeod, A., and Rosen, H. (1975). *The development of writing abilities (11–18).* London: Macmillan.

Burke, K. (1950, 1969). *A rhetoric of motives.* Berkeley: University of California Press.

Crusius, T. W. (1989). *Discourse: A critique and synthesis of major theories.* New York: Modern Language Association.

Kinneavy, J. L. (1971). *A theory of discourse.* New York: W. W. Norton.

Moffett, J. (1981). *Active voice.* Montclair: Boynton/Cook.

Perelman, C., and Ulbrechts-Tyteca, L. (First published in French in 1958. Translated and published in English in 1969.) *The new rhetoric: A treatise on argumentation.* Notre Dame: University of Notre Dame Press.

Toulmin, S. (1958). *The uses of argument.* Cambridge: Cambridge University Press.

RESEARCH. To follow research developments in composition studies, you would want to read two journals:

Research in the Teaching of English
Written Communication: A Quarterly Journal of Research Theory and Applications

Here we mention just a few recent book-length research reports, reviews of research, or collections of research studies:

Applebee, A. N. (Ed.). (1984). *Contexts for learning to write: Studies of secondary school instruction.* Norwood, NJ: Ablex.

Barton, D., and Ivanic, R. (Eds.). (1991). *Writing in the community.* Thousand Oaks, CA: Sage.

Beach, R., and Bridwell, L. S. (1984). *New directions in composition research.* New York: Guilford Press.

Beaugrande, R. de. (1984). *Text production: Toward a science of composition.* Norwood, NJ: Ablex.

Britton, B. K., and Black, J. B. (Eds.). (1985). *Understanding expository text.* Hillsdale, NJ: Lawrence Erlbaum.

Chafe, W. L. (Ed.). (1980). *The pear stories: Cognitive, cultural, and linguistic aspects of narrative production.* Norwood, NJ: Ablex.

Christensen, F. (1967). *Notes toward a new rhetoric.* New York: Harper & Row.

Cooper, C. R., and Greenbaum, S. (Eds.). (1986). *Studying writing: Linguistic approaches.* Newbury Park, CA: Sage.

Cooper, C. R., and Odell, L. (Eds.). (1978). *Research on composing: Points of departure.* Urbana, IL: National Council of Teachers of English.

Couture, B. (Ed.) (1986). *Functional approaches to writing.* Norwood, NJ: Ablex.

Dijk, T. A. van. (1980). *Macrostructure: An interdisciplinary study of global structures in discourse, interaction, and cognition.* Hillsdale, NJ: Lawrence Erlbaum.

Dillon, G. (1981). *Constructing texts*. Bloomington: Indiana University Press.

Freedman, S. W. (1985). *The acquisition of written language: Response and revision*. New York: Academic Press.

Halliday, M. A. K., and Hasan, R. (1976). *Cohesion in English*. New York: Longman.

Heath, S. B. (1983). *Ways with words*. New York: Cambridge University Press.

Hillocks, G., Jr. (1986). *Research on written composition*. Urbana, IL: National Council of Teachers of English.

Kirsch, G., and Sullivan, P. (1992). *Methods and methodology in composition studies*. Carbondale: Southern Illinois University Press.

Martlew, M. (Ed.). (1983). *The psychology of written language*. New York: John Wiley.

McClelland, B. W., and Donovan, T. R. (Eds.). (1985). *Perspectives on research and scholarship in composition*. New York: Modern Language Association.

McDonald, S. P. (1994). *Professional academic writing in the humanities and social sciences*. Carbondale: Southern Illinois University Press.

Nystrand, M. (Ed.). (1982). *What writers know: The language, process, and structure of written discourse*. New York: Academic Press.

Odell, L., and Goswami, D. (Eds.). (1985). *Writing in nonacademic settings*. New York: Guilford.

Purves, A. C. (Ed.). (1988). *Writing across languages and culture: Issues in contrastive rhetoric*. Newbury Park, CA: Sage.

Rose, M. (Ed.). (1985). *When a writer can't write: Studies in writer's block and composing-process problems*. New York: Guilford.

Scinto, L. F. M. (1986). *Written language and psychological development*. New York: Academic Press.

Smagorinsky, P. (Ed.). (1994). *Speaking about writing: Reflections on research methodology*. Thousand Oaks, CA: Sage.

Walvord, B. E., and McCarthy, L. (1990). *Thinking and writing in college: A naturalistic study in four disciplines*. Urbana, IL: National Council of Teachers of English.

Important research studies have appeared in two continuing-research monograph series:

Urbana, IL: National Council of Teachers of English for the Committee on Research:

Applebee, A. (1981). *Writing in the secondary school*.

Emig, J. (1971). *Composing processes of twelfth graders*.

Langer, J. A., and Applebee, A. N. (1987). *How writing shapes thinking*.

Mellon, J. C. (1969). *Transformational sentence-combining*.

Carbondale: Southern Illinois University Press for the Conference on College Composition and Communication:

Gere, A. R. (1987). *Writing groups: History, theory, and implications*.

Halpern, J. W., and Liffett, S. (1984). *Computers and composing*.

Kirsch, G. (1993). *Women writing the academy: Audience, authority, and transformation*.

LeFevre, K. B. (1987). *Invention as a social act.*

Markels, R. B. (1984). *A new rhetoric on cohesion in expository paragraphs.*

Rose, M. (1984). *Writer's block: The cognitive dimension.*

TEACHING PRACTICES. We have learned so much about teaching writing from so many different people that we would like to acknowledge them all here with references. But we must limit ourselves to just a few books that would be good starting points for beginning instructors. We are exceedingly rich in reported practice in composition studies:

Anson, C. M. (Ed.). (1989). *Writing and response.* Urbana, IL: National Council of Teachers of English.

Cope, B., and Kalantzis, M. (Eds.). (1993). *The powers of literacy: A genre approach to teaching writing.* Pittsburgh: University of Pittsburgh Press.

Elbow, P. (1981). *Writing with power.* New York: Oxford University Press.

Freedman, A., and Medway, P. (Ed.). *Learning and teaching genre.* Portsmouth, NH: Heinemann.

Graves, D. H. (1983). *Writing: Teachers and students at work.* Portsmouth, NH: Heinemann.

Hillocks, G., Jr. (1995). *Teaching writing as reflective practice.* New York: Teachers CollegePress.

Moffett, J. (1969, 1983). *Teaching the universe of discourse.* Boston: Houghton Mifflin.

Moran, C., and Herrington, A. (Eds.). (1992). *Writing, teaching, and learning in the disciplines.* New York: Modern Language Association.

Murray, D. M. (1985). *A writer teaches writing.* (2nd ed.). Boston: Houghton Mifflin.

Olson, G. A. (Ed.). (1984). *Writing centers: Theory and administration.* Urbana, IL: National Council of Teachers of English.

Secor, M., and Charney, D. (Eds.). (1992). *Constructing rhetorical education.* Carbondale: Southern Illinois University Press.

EVALUATION. These are good starting points:

Black, L., Daiker, D., Sommers, J., and Stygall, G. (Eds.). (1994). *New directions in portfolio assessment.* Portsmouth, NH: Heinemann.

Cooper, C. R., and Odell, L. (Eds.). (1977). *Evaluating writing.* Urbana, IL: National Council of Teachers of English.

Davis, B. G., Scriven, M., and Thomas, S. (1987). *The evaluation of composition instruction.* New York: Teachers College Press.

Gorman, T. P., Purves, A. C., and Degenhart, R. E. (Eds.). (1988). *The IEA study of written composition I: The international writing tasks and scoring scales.* New York: Pergamon Press.

Greenberg, K. L., Wiener, H. S., and Donovan, R. A. (Eds.). (1986). *Writing assessment. Issues and strategies.* New York: Longman.

White, Edward M. (1994). *Teaching and assessing writing.* (2nd ed.) San Francisco: Jossey-Bass.

Witte, S. P., and Faigley, L. (1983). *Evaluating college writing programs.* Carbondale: Southern Illinois University Press.

LEARNING FROM TEXT

Applebee, A. N. (1984). Writing and reasoning. *Review of Educational Research*, 54, 577–596. This important review, while insisting on how little we know for certain about the role of writing in learning, argues that we may confidently infer from recent research and theory that writing fosters understanding and recall of reading, as well as the use of reading in new situations. Reviewed studies examine the influence on reading of writing answers to questions, notetaking, summarizing, paraphrasing, and analogizing.

Anderson, T. H., and Armbruster, B. B. (1984). Studying. In P. D. Pearson (Ed.), *Handbook on reading research* (pp. 657–679). New York: Longman. This comprehensive review examines the research support for several common studying techniques: underlining, notetaking, summarizing, questioning, outlining, and schematizing. The authors conclude that all of these techniques can enhance students' understanding and use of reading materials, but only if students are trained in their use and encouraged to use them purposefully. The most demanding uses for reading are best used through outlining and schematizing, the most time-consuming study techniques.

Baker, L., and Brown, A. L. (1984). Metacognitive skills and reading. In P. D. Pearson (Ed.), *Handbook on reading research* (pp. 353–394). New York: Longman. This review argues that self-monitoring during reading ("checking one's own cognitive activities") is essential for confident, productive reading. Comprehension monitoring, the research indicates, improves when readers can ask themselves questions (as in annotating a text), bring any relevant current knowledge to bear on the reading (as in previewing), recognize the main ideas (learned from summarizing texts), and follow the structure (learned from outlining texts).

Dole, J. A., Duffy, G. G., Roehler, L. R., and Pearson, P. D. (1991). Reading comprehension instruction. *Review of Educational Research*, 61, 239-264. After a wide-ranging theory review, effective reading comprehension instruction is conceptualized as depending on a set of five proven comprehension strategies: determining important information, summarizing information, drawing inferences, generating questions, and monitoring comprehension.

Glover, J. A., Plake, B. S., Robert, B., Aimmer, J. W., and Palmere, J. (1981). Distinctiveness of encoding: The effects of paraphrasing and drawing inferences on memory from prose. *Journal of Educational Psychology*, 73, 736–744. Two studies of college students support the conclusion that "what readers remember from reading passages is determined by the activities they engage in during reading." The researchers found that two activities were especially productive: paraphrasing and making inferences after paragraphs or brief sections.

134

Haller, E. P., Child, D. A., and Walberg, H. J. (1988). Can comprehension be taught? A quantitative synthesis of "metacognitive" studies. *Educational Researcher*, 17, 5–8. This review of twenty studies found that certain question-asking and writing activities (self-questioning, paraphrasing, summarizing, making predictions, integrating prior knowledge, awareness of text organization, comparing or contrasting main ideas) increase comprehension. Students in the studies were in elementary and secondary schools.

Kennedy, M. L. (1985). The composing process of college students writing from sources. *Written Communication*, 2, 434–456. This study of writing from sources analyzed the reading and writing strategies of six college students who were asked to write an essay about three articles on communication. The writing sessions were recorded in thinking-aloud protocols. Contrasting strategies of the three students with high-scoring essays to the three students with low-scoring essays, the researcher noticed that the successful writers were much more likely to paraphrase, summarize, evaluate, and annotate as they worked with the readings.

King, A. (1992). Comparison of self-questioning, summarizing, and notetaking-review as strategies of learning from lectures. *American Educational Research Journal*, 29, 303–323. Self-questioning and summarizing enabled underprepared college students to recall more from lectures and to remember it longer. Self-questioning was the most successful for long-term retention. Students were carefully trained to use these two productive strategies.

Langer, J. A., and Applebee, A. N. (1987). *How writing shapes thinking*. Urbana, IL: National Council of Teachers of English. In an ambitious, comprehensive study of writing in secondary schools, the authors learned that many kinds of writing activities (short-answer, summaries, notetaking, extended essays) enable students to learn more from their reading than if they had merely read or studied it. They also learned that different kinds of writing lead to different kinds of learning; summary, for example, to a comprehensive but superficial focus on reading material and extended essays to "deeper meaning about less information."

Marshall, J. D. (1987). The effects of writing on students' understanding of literary texts. *Research in the Teaching of English*, 21, 30–63. Eleventh-grade students wrote study-question answers, personal essays, and analytic essays about short stories. Students learned more about the stories when they wrote extended personal or analytic essays about the stories. In extended writing, students "construct an intellectual representation of the story—a representation that may stay with them and become for them, finally, the basis for what is remembered and understood about the story over time."

Newell, G. E. (1984). Learning from writing in two content areas: A case study/protocol analysis. *Research in the Teaching of English*, 18, 265–287. Eleventh-grade students read science and social science materials and then either took notes, answered study questions, or wrote extended essays. Students learned more concepts from the materials when they wrote essays. Essay writing "produced more writing and learning operations" and "required more extensive thought and consideration of content."

Simpson, M. L., and Nist, S. L. (1990). Textbook annotation: An effective and efficient study strategy for college students. *Journal of Reading*, 34, 122–129. One group of college students was given careful training in annotating, another group in previewing and then devising questions to guide reading. Both groups then were tested on knowledge of three 3,000 word passages they were given in advance to either annotate or devise questions about. Students who annotated performed better on the tests even though they reported spending less time studying.

Vacca, R. T. (1981). *Content area reading*. Boston: Little, Brown. Current texts on reading and study skills instruction provide useful catalogs of research-supported methods, many of them involving writing. Chapter 7 in this typical text presents strategies for previewing and analyzing reading through questions and discussions. Chapter 8 reviews several types of outlining and notetaking.

Wong, B. Y. L. (1985). Self-questioning instructional research: A review. *Review of Educational Research*, 55, 227–268. This theory-based review of twenty-seven studies (seventeen of them involving secondary-school or college students) concludes that when students ask themselves questions as they read, they process prose more confidently and comprehend it more fully. These studies examine the usefulness of three types of self-questions: to reflect on relevant prior knowledge, to understand the content, and to monitor understanding while reading.

St. Martin's